Responding Supportively (continued)

SKILL BUILDERS ⊘ Advice-Giving

SKILL

Presenting suggestions and proposals a partner could use to satisfactorily resolve a situation

USE

To comfort our partners after a supportive climate has been established and our partners are unable to find their own solutions

PROCEDURE

1. Ask for permission to give advice.
2. Word the message as one of many suggestions in a way that the recipient can understand.
3. Present any potential risks or costs associated with following the advice.
4. Indicate that you will not be offended should your partner choose to ignore your recommendation or look for another choice.

EXAMPLE

After a friend has explained a difficult situation she faces, Felicia might say something like the following:

"I have a suggestion if you'd like to hear it. As I see it, one way you could handle this is to talk to your co-worker about this issue. This is just one idea—you may come up with a different solution that's just as good. So think this one over, and do what you believe is best for you."

SKILL BUILDERS ⊘ Clarifying Supportive Intentions

SKILL

Openly stating that your goal in the conversation is to help your partner

USE

To let people in need of support know that your motive is simply and solely to help them, to let them know that someone is "on their side," and to provide a context for their understanding of your comments

PROCEDURE

1. Directly state your intentions, emphasizing your desire to help.
2. Remind your partner about your ongoing relationship.
3. Indicate that helping is your only motive.
4. Phrase your clarification in a way that reflects helpfulness.

EXAMPLE

After listening to Sonja complain about flunking her geology midterm, her friend Deepak replies:

"Sonja, you're a dear friend, and I'd like to help if you want me to. I did well enough on the midterm that I think I could be of help; maybe we could meet once a week to go over the readings and class notes together."

SKILL BUILDERS ⊘ Positive Facework

SKILL

Providing messages that affirm a person or a person's actions in a difficult situation

USE

To protect the other person's respectability and approval

PROCEDURE

1. Convey positive feelings about what your partner has said or done in the situation.
2. Express your admiration for your partner's courage or effort in the situation.
3. Acknowledge how difficult the situation is.
4. Express your belief that your partner has the qualities and skills to endure or succeed.

EXAMPLE

Anja has learned that Ken has suffered his brother's anger because of an intervention Ken initiated to help his brother. Anja says: "I really respect you for the way you have acted during this. It takes a lot of guts to hang in there like you've been doing, especially when you've been attacked for doing so. I know that you've got the skills to help you get through this."

Message Formation (continued)

SKILL	USE	PROCEDURE	EXAMPLE
Mentally or verbally accounting for individual differences when generalizing	To avoid "allness" in speaking	1. Before you make a statement, consider whether it pertains to a specific object, person, or place. 2. If you use a generalization, inform the listener that it does not necessarily apply in the situation being discussed.	"He's a politician and I don't trust him, although he may be different from most politicians I know."

Listening for Understanding

SKILL BUILDERS ▽ **Perception Checking**

SKILL	USE	PROCEDURE	EXAMPLE
A statement that expresses the meaning you get from the behavior of another	To clarify the accuracy of our perceptions of another person's behavior	1. Watch the behavior of another. 2. Ask yourself: What does that behavior mean to me? 3. Describe the behavior (to yourself or aloud) and put your interpretation of the nonverbal behavior into words to verify your perception.	As Dale frowns while reading Paul's first draft of a memo, Paul says, "From the way you're frowning, I take it that you're not too pleased with the way I phrased the memo."

SKILL BUILDERS ▽ **Turn-Taking**

SKILL	USE	PROCEDURE	EXAMPLE
Engaging in appropriate turn-taking	Determining when a speaker is at a place where another person may talk if he or she wants	1. Take your share of turns. 2. Gear turn length to the behavior of partners. 3. Give and watch for turn-taking and turn-exchanging cues. Avoid giving inadvertent turn-taking cues. 4. Observe and use conversation-directing behavior. 5. Limit interruptions.	When John lowers his voice as he says, "I really thought they were going to go ahead during those last few seconds," Melissa, noticing that he appears to be finished, says, "I did, too. But did you notice . . . "

Disclosure (continued)

SKILL BUILDERS ○ Praise

SKILL
Sincerely describing the specific positive behaviors or accomplishments of another and the positive effects those behaviors/accomplishments have on others

USE
To help people see themselves positively

PROCEDURE
1. Make note of the specific behavior or accomplishment that you want to reinforce.
2. Describe the specific behavior and/or accomplishment.
3. Describe the positive feelings or outcomes that you or others experience as a result of the behavior or accomplishment.
4. Phrase the response so that the level of praise appropriately reflects the significance of the behavior or accomplishment.

EXAMPLE
"Marge, that was an excellent writing job on the Miller story. Your descriptions were particularly vivid."

SKILL BUILDERS ○ Assertiveness

SKILL
Behaving in a way in which you declare your personal preferences and defend your personal rights while at the same time respecting the preferences and rights of others

USE
To show clearly what you think or feel

PROCEDURE
1. Identify what you are thinking or feeling.
2. Analyze the cause of these feelings.
3. Choose the appropriate skills necessary to communicate these feelings, as well as predict the outcome you desire.
4. Communicate these feelings to the appropriate person. Remember to own your feelings.

EXAMPLE
When Gavin believes that he is being unjustly charged for his drink, he says, "I have never been charged for a refill on iced tea before—has there been a change in policy?"

SKILL BUILDERS ○ Behavior, Consequences, and Feelings (b-c-f) Sequence

SKILL
Describing a conflict in terms of behavior, consequences, and feelings (b-c-f)

USE
To help the other person understand the problem completely

PROCEDURE
1. Own the message, using "I"-centered statements.
2. Describe the behavior that you see or hear.
3. Describe the consequences that result from the behavior.
4. Describe your feelings that result from the behavior.

EXAMPLE
Jason says, "I have a problem that I need your help with. When I tell you what I'm thinking and you don't respond (b), I start to think you don't care about me or what I think (c), and this causes me to get very angry with you (f)."

Disclosure (continued)

SKILL BUILDERS ▽ Providing Constructive Criticism

SKILL

Diplomatically describing the specific negative behaviors or actions of another and the effects those behaviors/actions have on others

USE

To help people see themselves as others see them

PROCEDURE

1. Begin by describing the person's behavior or action.
2. Whenever possible, preface negative statements with positive ones.
3. Be as specific as possible.
4. When appropriate, suggest how the person can change the behavior or action.

EXAMPLE

Carol says, "Bob, I've noticed something about your behavior with Jenny. Would you like to hear it?"

After Bob assures her that he would, Carol continues, "Although you seem really supportive of Jenny, there are times when Jenny starts to relate an experience and you interrupt her and finish telling the story. You did this a few times while Jenny was trying to talk about her trip to Colorado and she looked a little hurt. She's pretty sensitive about being interrupted, so you might want to try to let her finish her stories the rest of this evening or she might get upset."

SKILL BUILDERS ▽ Asking for Feedback

SKILL

Asking others for their reaction to you or to your behavior

USE

To get information that will help you understand yourself and your effect on others

PROCEDURE

1. Think of personal feedback as being in your best interest.
2. Before you ask, make sure that you are ready for an honest response.
3. Take the initiative to ask for personal feedback.
4. Specify the kind of personal feedback you are seeking.
5. Avoid loaded questions.
6. Try to avoid negative verbal or nonverbal reactions to the feedback.
7. Paraphrase what you hear.
8. Show gratitude for the feedback you receive.

EXAMPLE

Lucy asks, "Tim, when I talk with the boss, do I sound defensive?"

Tim replies, "I think so—your voice gets sharp and you lose eye contact, which makes you look nervous."

"So you think that the tone of my voice and my eye contact lead the boss to perceive me as defensive?"

"Yes."

"Thanks, Tim. I've really got to work on this."

Listening for Understanding (continued)

SKILL BUILDERS ▽ Questioning

SKILL

Phrasing a response designed to get further information or to remove uncertainty from information already received

USE

To help get a more complete picture before making other comments; to help a shy person open up; to clarify meaning

PROCEDURE

1. Be specific about the kind of information you need to increase your understanding of the message.
2. Deliver questions in a sincere tone of voice.
3. Limit questions or explain that you need to ask multiple questions.
4. Put the burden of ignorance on your own shoulders.

EXAMPLE

When Connie says, "Well, it would be better if she weren't so sedentary," Jeff replies, "I'm not sure I understand what you mean by 'sedentary'—would you explain?"

SKILL BUILDERS ▽ Paraphrasing

SKILL

Verifying one's understanding of a message by putting it in one's own words and sharing it with the speaker

USE

To increase listening efficiency; to avoid message confusion; to discover the speaker's motivation

PROCEDURE

1. Listen carefully to the message.
2. Notice what ideas and feelings seem to be contained in the message.
3. Determine what the message means to you.
4. Create a message in your own words that conveys these ideas and/or feelings.

EXAMPLE

Grace says, "At two minutes to five, the boss gave me three letters that had to be in the mail that evening!" Bonita replies, "I understand; you were really resentful that your boss dumped important work on you right before quitting time, when she knows that you have to pick up the baby at daycare."

Disclosure

SKILL BUILDERS ▽ Describing Feelings

SKILL

Explaining emotions one feels in a precise and unemotional manner

USE

To self-disclose either positively or negatively to someone honestly and without resorting to strong emotion

PROCEDURE

1. Indicate what has triggered the feeling.
2. Identify what you are feeling—think specifically. Am I feeling amused? Pleased? Happy? Ecstatic?
3. Own the feeling by using an "I" statement.

EXAMPLE

"As a result of not getting the job, I feel depressed and discouraged."

"Because of the way you stood up for me when I was being put down by Leah, I'm feeling very warm and loving toward you."

Responding Supportively

SKILL

The cognitive process of identifying with or the vicarious experiencing of the feelings, thoughts, or attitudes of others

USE

To prepare yourself for providing an appropriate supporting response

PROCEDURE

1. Show respect for the person by actively attending to what the person says.
2. Concentrate on understanding both the verbal and nonverbal messages conveyed to you, using paraphrasing and perception checking.
3. Experience an emotional response by employing one of the three types of empathy: empathic responsiveness, perspective taking, or sympathetic responsiveness.

EXAMPLE

When Daryl says, "I was really hurt when Sarah returned the ring I had given her," Mary listens closely to what Daryl says, observes his verbal and nonverbal behaviors, and experiences an emotional response to Daryl's message by either sharing Daryl's feelings directly, imagining herself in Daryl's situation, or feeling concern, compassion, or sorrow for Daryl in a more generalized manner.

SKILL

Offering information, observations, and opinions that enable the receiver to better understand or see his or her situation in a different light

USE

To support others when you believe they have made interpretations based on incomplete information or have not considered other viable explanations

PROCEDURE

1. Listen to how your partner is interpreting events.
2. Notice information that your partner may be overlooking or overemphasizing in the interpretation.
3. Clearly present relevant, truthful information, observations, and opinions that enable your partner to develop a less ego-threatening explanation of what has happened.

EXAMPLE

Pam: "Katie must be really angry with me. Yesterday she walked right by me at the market and didn't even say 'Hi.'"
Paula: "Are you sure she's angry? She hasn't said anything to me. And you know, when she's mad I usually hear about it. Maybe she just didn't see you."

Responding Supportively (continued)

SKILL BUILDERS ⊘ Negative Facework

SKILL

Providing messages that offer information, opinions, or advice

USE

To protect the other person's freedom and privacy

PROCEDURE

1. Ask for permission before making suggestions or giving advice.
2. Verbally defer to the opinions and preferences of your partner.
3. Use tentative language to hedge and qualify opinions and advice.
4. Offer suggestions indirectly by describing similar situations or hypothetical options.

EXAMPLE

Judy has learned that Gloriana has been badly hurt by rejection from a best friend. Judy says: "Would you like any advice on this?" Gloria says that she would, and Judy then offers suggestions: "These are just a few suggestions, and I think you should go with what you think is best. Now, I'm not sure that these are the only way to go, but I think . . ." After stating her opinions, Judy says, "Depending on what you want to accomplish, I can see a couple ways that you might proceed . . ."

SKILL BUILDERS ⊘ Other-Centered Messages

SKILL

Focusing on the needs of the person in need of support through active listening, expressions of compassion and understanding, and talk encouragement

USE

To help partners in their efforts to reevaluate an emotionally distressing event

PROCEDURE

1. Ask questions that prompt your partner to elaborate on what happened.
2. Emphasize your willingness to listen to an extended story.
3. Use vocalized encouragement and nonverbal encouragement to communicate your continued interest without interrupting your partner as the account unfolds.
4. Affirm, legitimize, and encourage exploration of the feelings expressed by your partner.
5. Demonstrate that you understand and connect with what has happened but avoid changing the focus to you.

EXAMPLE

Angie begins to express what has happened to her. Allison says: "Really, what happened then?" As Angie utters one more sentence and then stops, Allison says: "Tell me *all* about it, and don't worry about how long it takes. I want to hear the whole thing from start to finish." During Angie's discussion, Allison shows her encouragement: "Go on . . . ," "And then . . . ?," and she nods her head, leans forward, and so on. To affirm, Allison says: "Yes, I can see that you're disappointed. Most people would be disappointed in this situation. Is this as difficult as when . . . ?" Allison then continues: "I know that I felt angry when my sister did that to me. So what happened then?"

Message Formation

SKILL BUILDERS ▽ Adapt Language to Listeners

SKILL

Using vocabulary, jargon, and slang that listeners understand

USE

To avoid words that listeners do not understand

PROCEDURE

1. Use simpler synonyms or familiar terms for words.
2. Explain jargon terms to listeners who may not understand them.
3. Use slang words only with listeners who understand it.

EXAMPLE

Instead of saying, "Jose is in his penultimate year of work," Larry can say, "Jose is in his next to last year of work." Sally can say, "Your asset-to-liability ratio, which is a calculation of how much money you have compared to how much money you owe, is really quite good."

Judy can say a rock star is "hot" when talking with a friend but describe the star as "cute" when talking with her aunt.

SKILL BUILDERS ▽ Dating Information

SKILL

Including a specific time referent to clarify a message

USE

To avoid the pitfalls of language that allow you to speak of a dynamic world in static terms

PROCEDURE

1. Before you make a statement, consider or find out when the information was true.
2. If not based on present information, verbally acknowledge when the statement was true.

EXAMPLE

When Jake says, "How good a hitter is Steve?" Mark replies by dating his evaluation: "When I worked with him two years ago, he couldn't hit the curve."

SKILL BUILDERS ▽ Owning Feelings and Opinions

SKILL

Making an "I" statement rather than a generalization to identify yourself as the source of an idea or feeling

USE

To help others understand that the feeling or opinion is yours

PROCEDURE

When an idea, opinion, or feeling is yours, say so.

EXAMPLE

Instead of saying, "Maury's is the best restaurant in town," say, "I believe Maury's is the best restaurant in town."

TWELFTH EDITION

Inter-Act

New York   Oxford

OXFORD UNIVERSITY PRESS

2010

Inter-Act

Interpersonal Communication Concepts, Skills, and Contexts

Kathleen S. Verderber
NORTHERN KENTUCKY UNIVERSITY

Rudolph F. Verderber
UNIVERSITY OF CINCINNATI

Cynthia Berryman-Fink
UNIVERSITY OF CINCINNATI

Oxford University Press, Inc., publishes works that further Oxford University's
objective of excellence in research, scholarship, and education.

Oxford   New York
Auckland   Cape Town   Dar es Salaam   Hong Kong   Karachi
Kuala Lumpur   Madrid   Melbourne   Mexico City   Nairobi
New Delhi   Shanghai   Taipei   Toronto

With offices in
Argentina   Austria   Brazil   Chile   Czech Republic   France   Greece
Guatemala   Hungary   Italy   Japan   Poland   Portugal   Singapore
South Korea   Switzerland   Thailand   Turkey   Ukraine   Vietnam

Published by Oxford University Press, Inc.
198 Madison Avenue, New York, New York 10016
http://www.oup.com

Library of Congress Cataloging-in-Publication Data
Verderber, Kathleen S., 1949–
    Inter-act: interpersonal communication concepts, skills, and contexts/Kathleen S. Verderber,
    Rudolph F. Verderber, Cynthia Berryman-Fink.—12th ed.
        p. cm.
    ISBN 978-0-19-537891-7
    1. Interpersonal communication. 2. Interpersonal relations. I. Verderber, Rudolph F.
    II. Berryman-Fink, Cynthia, 1952–   III. Title
        BF637.C45V47   2010
        158.2—dc22

                                                                    2009004572

Printing number: 9 8 7 6 5 4 3

Printed in the United States of America on acid-free paper

Brief Contents

Contents

CHAPTER 6 ▶ Communication across Cultures • 148

CHAPTER 9 ▷ Empathizing with and Supporting Others • 232

CHAPTER 10 ▷ Managing Personal Information:
Disclosure and Privacy • 264

CHAPTER 11 ▸ Using Interpersonal Influence Ethically • 296

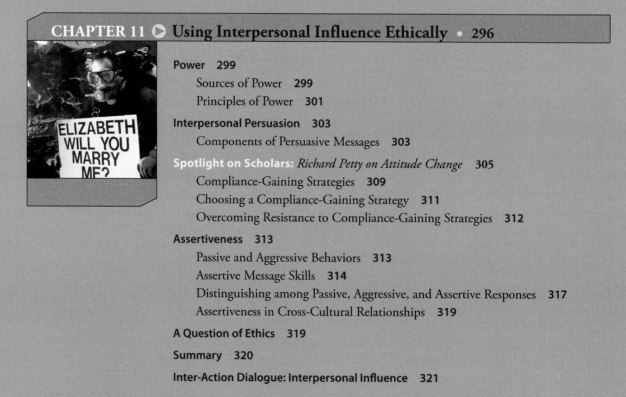

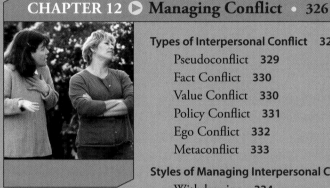

CHAPTER 14 ▶ Communicating in the Workplace • 390

Preface

You are so lucky. This term you are going to study something that will help you with one of the most important things in your life—your relationships with others. Do you wonder why some people are just easier to talk with than others? Have you ever drifted apart from a close friend but couldn't put your finger on why? Are you wondering why it's so difficult to keep the "spark" alive in a romantic relationship? Do you wonder what went wrong in someone else's relationship? Over this term you will learn theories and concepts that will help you answer these questions and many others. Interpersonal communication is at the heart of all of our relationships, and this book explains how interpersonal communication skills can help you to form and maintain satisfying relationships, as well as repair relationships when they become damaged.

◗ Brief Overview of the Twelfth Edition

When we wrote the first edition of *Inter-Act,* the scholarly study of interpersonal communication was in its infancy. As the years have gone on, the field has grown immensely, and we now have well-developed theories at our disposal that serve as "road maps" to the "territories" of this area of study. This twelfth edition of *Inter-Act* is naturally the most up-to-date version of the book yet. We have updated the text in a wide number of areas to reflect the changes in our knowledge of interpersonal communication, along with changes in the field's practice.

For example, this edition reflects technological advances that have and will continue to change the modes by which we manage our relationships with others. Today, you might meet your soul mate through a social networking site online instead of at a party. You may keep up to date with family and friends through e-mails, IMs, posts on your personal blog, or updates to your MySpace or Facebook page rather than writing letters. Or you may telecommute to your job rather than go to an office every day. When we wrote the last edition of *Inter-Act,* research and theorizing about these changes had only just begun to be published. Today, while research and theory building continues, we know much more than we did just a few years ago. Likewise, scholarship has continued to identify how cultural, ethnic, racial, sexual, and age diversity affects communication patterns in relationships. So in this edition we present a contemporary understanding of the diverse ways in which people communicate and how these practices affect relationships between diverse people.

In addition to adding the latest scholarship and to keep the text at a reasonable length, we have also pruned from the text material that instructors have told us is less central to their courses or less useful to their students than it used to be.

In the process of adding and subtracting, however, we have been careful to retain the signature elements that have made *Inter-Act* a favorite teaching and learning tool. As always, you will find a logical and cumulative sequence of topics both across the book and within chapters, clear explanations of sometimes complex topics backed up with illustrative examples, and a wide variety of special features to help you understand the concepts and master interpersonal communication skills. We are very excited about this new edition, and we hope that by the end of this course you will agree that the text has made learning about interpersonal communication interesting, easy, and enjoyable.

⊙ Philosophy and Goals of the Text

If you are like most students in an interpersonal communication class, while you may enjoy learning about how communication works within relationships, what you really want is to know how to be more skilled at handling your own relationships with others. So the philosophy of the text is to both describe and prescribe. We describe current interpersonal communication concepts, frameworks, and theories to help you understand how your communication behaviors and those of your partners (acquaintances, friends, family members, and others) create, develop, maintain, or end your relationships. But we also prescribe specific interpersonal communication skills that you can learn to use to help you make interactions and relationships more effective and satisfying. And because there are cultural, gender, and other variations regarding how communication behaviors affect relationships, the text also describes these variations and encourages you to develop and practice interpersonal communication flexibility.

As with previous editions, the twelfth edition of *Inter-Act* is founded not only on the overall "describe and prescribe" philosophy but also on six specific goals that we hope will enhance your learning process: (1) to explain important communication concepts, frameworks, and theories that have been consistently supported by careful research so that you can understand the conceptual foundations of interpersonal communication; (2) to teach you specific communication skills that research has shown facilitate effective relationships; (3) to present you with ethical frameworks that can guide competent communication; (4) to encourage you to consider how communication needs, rules, and processes differ among diverse people; (5) to challenge you to think critically and creatively about the concepts and skills you learn; and (6) to provide you with features and activities that significantly enhance your learning.

⊙ New to the Twelfth Edition

For the convenience of those who are familiar with the previous edition of *Inter-Act*, the chapters in this twelfth edition follow the same logical flow. To enhance what already works, the following key features are new or enhanced in this edition.

- **New chapter on diversity.** While we continue to discuss diversity throughout the book, in response to feedback from those of you who have used this text, we have added a new Chapter 6, "Communication across Cultures," to Part I, "Understanding Interpersonal Communication." This chapter brings together the foundational concepts and theories for understanding the central role that culture plays in what is considered appropriate and effective communication.

- **Expanded learning tools.** The learning tools that have made *Inter-Act* a leading text in this field (Observe and Analyze, Inter-Act with Technology, Learn about Yourself, A Question of Ethics, Skill Builders, Diverse Voices, and Spotlight on Scholars) have been updated and expanded to accommodate new material. Nearly every chapter now includes at least one of each type of learning tool.

- **Enhanced focus on technology.** Throughout the text we have integrated a completely up-to-date discussion of new technology and its affect on interpersonal communication, for example, social networking sites as vehicles for identity formation and relational maintenance, mobile technology as nonverbal communication, uses of the Internet for therapy and grieving, disclosure and privacy issues in cyberspace, online verbal abuse and violence, and technology tools for virtual teamwork.

⊙ Chapters Strengthened in the Twelfth Edition

In addition to the new and enhanced features just described, each and every chapter of this twelfth edition has been streamlined to make the understanding of concepts as easy as possible. In addition, many of the chapters have been updated to meet the learning needs of contemporary students of interpersonal communication.

- Chapter 1, "An Orientation to Interpersonal Communication," presents new information on emotional intelligence and its effects on communication.

- Chapter 3, "Communicating in Relationships: Basic Concepts," now discusses seven characteristics that define relationship stages and life cycles.

- Chapter 4, "Verbal Communication," features a new Spotlight on Scholars feature about Ronald L. Jackson II, whose work has helped us understand communication accommodation and codeswitching in relation to cultural identity. New emphasis is also given to the effects of technology on verbal communication.

- Chapter 7, "Holding Effective Conversations," includes new information on the effects of technology on issues of mobility, initiation, multiplicity, privacy, characteristics, and rules of conversations.
- Chapter 8, "Listening Effectively," includes a new Spotlight on Scholars piece about Judi Brownell and the six factors of listening effectiveness: hearing, understanding, remembering, interpreting, evaluating, and responding.
- Chapter 10, "Managing Personal Information: Disclosure and Privacy," has been reorganized to examine the disclosure-privacy dialectic, including communication privacy management theory and the development of disclosure-privacy rules. This chapter also now includes a new Spotlight on Scholars feature about Sandra Petronio and the development and application of communication privacy management theory.
- Chapter 14, "Communicating in the Workplace," expands coverage of electronic job searching and introduces communication tools for teamwork that include electronic newsletters, e-calendars, podcasts, e-surveys, and wikis.

◕ Supplementary Materials

As a user of this text, you also have access to supplementary materials developed at Oxford University Press. Materials prepared by Oxford are divided into those that are relevant for students and those that are relevant for faculty.

▷ Student Materials
The *Student Success Manual* features study tips, chapter outlines and summaries, review questions, key terms, and critical thinking exercises.

The companion website www.oup.com/us/interact12 offers a wealth of resources for both students and instructors, including online self-testing and other study aids, links to a variety of communication-related websites, and "Now Playing" reviews of recent films.

▷ Faculty Materials
The *Instructor's Manual* (available in paperback and CD-ROM) includes an extensive test bank and suggested class activities.

The companion website www.oup.com/us/interact12 offers a wealth of resources for both students and instructors, including online self-testing and other study aids, links to a variety of communication-related websites, and "Now Playing" reviews of recent films.

◒ Acknowledgments

Although the writing team is ultimately responsible for what appears in print, we would be unable to do our jobs without the help of many people who generously gave of their time and talents to help us birth this new edition.

We acknowledge the following colleagues who reviewed the eleventh edition and provided us with useful suggestions about what to keep, what to change, and what to trim: Len Assante, Volunteer State Community College; Tanya Boone, California State University, Bakersfield; Ceilidh Charleson-Jenning, Collin County Community College; Derek Clapp, McLennan Community College; Todd Lee Goen, University of Georgia; Anneliese Harper, Maricopa Community College; Krista Hoffmann-Longtin, Indiana University–Purdue University, Indianapolis; Beverly Kelley, California Lutheran University; Rebecca Ann Lind, University of Illinois, Chicago; Stan McKinney, Campbellsville University; Randall R. Mueller, Gateway Technical College; and Michael Wittig, Waukesha County Technical College.

We would like to thank the members of the Oxford University Press team who helped make this revision process a smooth and enjoyable one, including Peter Labella, Executive Editor; Josh Hawkins, Associate Editor; Courtney Roy, Editorial Assistant; Barbara Mathieu, Senior Production Editor; and Bruce Cantley, Development Editor.

In addition, we'd like to thank others who helped shape this edition, including Ellen Bremen, Highline Community College, for assistance and creativity in updating the companion website and the Inter-Act with Media feature in each chapter; Jennifer Pitts, Volunteer State Community College, who revised the *Instructor's Manual*; and Leah Bryant, DePaul University, who created the new *Student Success Manual.*

We are grateful to the Department of Communication at the University of Cincinnati for the tangible assistance provided to two of us during our many years as faculty and for the classroom support that enabled us to develop and test much of the material through the numerous editions of *Inter-Act*.

Finally, we thank our families for their love and patience during this process.

Kathleen S. Verderber

Rudolph F. Verderber

Cynthia Berryman-Fink

Inter-Act

1

An Orientation to Interpersonal Communication

After you have read this chapter, you should be able to answer these questions:

▶ What is interpersonal communication?

▶ Why is interpersonal communication important?

▶ What are the components of interpersonal communication?

▶ How does the interpersonal communication process work?

▶ What principles provide the foundation for interpersonal communication?

▶ What are ethical principles communicators must follow?

▶ Why should a communicator be concerned about diversity?

▶ What is communication competence?

▶ Why are knowledge, skills, and motivation important in interpersonal communication?

"Hey, Nicole, where are you? You sent me a text over an hour ago to say that you'd be home from work soon."

"Sorry, Katie. I'm about to finish up. I'll be there shortly."

"Well, actually it's too late now. Ethan stopped by and we're out getting coffee."

"That's fine. I just have a couple more e-mails to send and I'm on my way."

"OK, but I waited in our room for you thinking you'd be there in a few minutes, but it was more than ½ hour, so when Ethan stopped by and asked if I wanted to go for coffee, I thought, 'Might as well.' I was getting pretty bored hanging around there and waiting."

"Why are you making such a big deal out of it? I said I'd be there 'soon' and I will."

"Well to me, 'soon' is 10–15 minutes, not an hour."

"OK, sorry about that. You know I'm really swamped here at work, so I assumed you'd know that 'soon' meant at least an hour. But anyway you're out having coffee with Ethan now, so it's all good."

"Yeah, well it would have been nice to know. Look, I'll be home about 4:00. Will you be home then?"

Have you ever had an experience like the one described here, in which it is obvious that you and the person you are speaking with are having a misunderstanding? Both the simple and the not-so-simple misunderstandings that occur in everyday communication can damage relationships. Although misunderstandings have always been a part of the communication process, they may be even more common today. Now that we are increasingly able to "stay close" to others using personal communication technologies like cell phones, text messaging, e-mail, and instant messaging, we also have more opportunities to miscommunicate. As a result, taking the time to learn more about the communication process and improving your communication skills can help you to develop better and more satisfying interpersonal relationships.

Most of us don't remember when we learned to talk and listen. As infants, we learn basic and vital human interaction skills by observing and imitating the communication behaviors of those around us. Through these observations we form our own "theories of communication" and draw on these "implicit theories" as we grow older to help us communicate with others. When our personal theories are correct, we interact effectively with others, but when our theories are incorrect or incomplete, we may create misunderstanding and harm our relationships.

This book and the course in which you use it will help you to become a more effective interpersonal communicator. During this term you will begin a formal study of the theories of interpersonal communication—theories that are more valid, reliable, and complete than the personal theories you developed as an infant because they are based not on intuition but on the research of communication scholars. By understanding the concepts, relationships, and predictions of these theories, you will become better equipped to behave in ways that result in improved relationships rather than damaged ones. Moreover, you will learn and practice a variety of communication skills in a "safe" classroom setting before you try them out in your relationships with your family, friends, partners, co-workers, acquaintances, and others.

In this first chapter, we present introductory information for this study. We (1) define interpersonal communication, (2) discuss the functions that it serves, (3) present interpersonal communication components, (4) identify the basic principles that are fundamental to understanding interpersonal communication, (5) discuss the ethical principles that underlie interpersonal communication, (6) explain how human diversity complicates the interpersonal communication process, and (7) describe what it means to be competent in interpersonal communication.

◐ Definition of Interpersonal Communication

We define **interpersonal communication** as the process through which people create and manage their relationships, exercising mutual responsibility in creating meaning. Let's examine the parts of this definition more closely to help clarify the definition as a whole.

First, *interpersonal communication is a process*. A process is a systematic series of behaviors that occur over time and lead to a purpose. For instance, during a twenty-minute phone call with your mother to catch up on family news or during a five-minute impromptu meeting with a co-worker to solve a customer problem, a series of purposeful behaviors occurs. You catch up with your mom to show your affection, find out about events in the lives of other family members, and perhaps gather information, such as your brother's new cell phone number. You meet with your co-worker about the customer complaint so that she can help you arrive at a solution that is both fair to the customer and in keeping with company policy.

Second, *in interpersonal communication the people involved exercise mutual responsibility in creating meaning*. For example, imagine Tonika says to her roommate while standing in the kitchen, "How about if we keep it a little cleaner around here?" While Tonika may be referring to the entire apartment, her roommate may think that Tonika means just keeping the kitchen clean. So the interpersonal communication that has taken place between the roommates does not depend on what one of them says or does, but rather on the meaning that is created between them. In this case, the meaning has not been mutually understood. Tonika might have said, "How about if we keep this apartment a little cleaner?" to ensure that she and her roommate mutually understood the communication, or her partner might have followed up with the question, "Do you mean the kitchen or the whole apartment?"

Third, *through interpersonal communication, we create and manage our relationships*. Without communication, relationships cannot exist. A relationship

Interpersonal communication—the process through which people create and manage their relationships, exercising mutual responsibility in creating meaning.

begins when one person first communicates with another. Over time, continued interactions define the nature of the relationship and what it will become. Is the relationship more personal or impersonal, closer or more distant, romantic or platonic, healthy or unhealthy, dependent or interdependent? The answers to these questions depend on how the people in the relationship talk to and behave toward each other.

◑ Functions of Interpersonal Communication

You may have registered for this course because you were curious, because a friend or a teacher recommended it, because it fit your schedule, or because it is a requirement for your major. Whatever may have brought you to this class, we believe that before the term is over you'll be thankful that you have studied interpersonal communication. Why? Because interpersonal communication serves at least five functions that are important to your social and psychological health.

1. Through interpersonal communication we attempt to meet our social needs. Because human beings are by nature social animals, our interactions with other people are just as essential as food, water, and shelter. Often what we talk about when we interact with other people is unimportant. We may just converse happily for hours online or in person about relatively inconsequential matters, exchanging little information that impacts our lives on any deep level. On the other hand, we may have "heart-to-heart" conversations in which we probe deep feelings central to our well-being. But regardless of how inconsequential or important a conversation may be, we often carry away from any successful communication a pleasant, satisfied feeling that comes from having met the social need to interact.

2. Through interpersonal communication we attempt to achieve goals. Though we may not be consciously aware of the goals we attempt to meet when communicating, we are always trying to achieve some purpose. The goal may be as simple as trying to be friendly or as complex as trying to influence a boss to give us a raise. But in any communication situation, our interactions with others help us to move some aspect of our lives forward, preventing us from getting "stuck."

3. Through interpersonal communication we develop a sense of self. Communicating and developing relationships with others is the only way we are able to learn who we are as human beings, what we are good at, and how others react to us. Without interpersonal communication we become detached from ourselves and become unable to interact socially.

4. Through interpersonal communication we acquire information. While we get some of the information upon which we base our decisions through direct observation, reading, and the media, we receive a great deal of that information through conversations with others. For example, Jeff runs out to get a bagel and coffee. When he returns, Tom asks, "What's it like out there this morning?" Jeff replies, "Wow, it's cold—it couldn't be more than twenty degrees." Tom reacts to this news by sighing and says, "I was just going to wear my hoodie, but I guess I'd better break out the old winter coat." To make decisions as mundane as this one or as important—even life-saving—as determining whether to enter a dangerous situation, we need to gather much of our information through interpersonal communication.

5. Through interpersonal communication we influence and are influenced by others. In a typical day you engage in countless exchanges in which your purpose is to influence others or to respond to the influence of others. From convincing your roommate to loan you a sweater or persuading your instructor to change your course grade to listening to a political candidate trying to get your vote or responding to a co-worker whose point you disagree with, interpersonal communication is essential to maintaining a sense of order in both small and large situations.

◆ Components of Interpersonal Communication

Because adult individuals have been communicating with others for as long as they can remember, they don't consciously think about what takes place during a conversation or other interaction. The thoughts and behaviors involved in the communication process have become subconscious, or automatic. In reality, however, any interpersonal communication episode is the result of a complex series of both cognitions (thinking) and behaviors (doing). To illuminate what really goes on during interpersonal communication, let's take a look at the components that make up the communication process: participants, context, messages, channels, noise, and feedback. As you read, refer to Figure 1.1, which illustrates the process in a communication between two individuals.

How does it feel when you know that someone is really understanding what you are saying?

▷ Participants

The **participants** are the people who communicate, assuming the roles of senders and receivers during the communication. The **sender** is the participant in an interaction who assumes the role of forming messages and attempting to communicate them to others. The **receiver** is the participant in an interaction who assumes the role of listening, interpreting, and reacting to the messages

Participants—the people who communicate, assuming the roles of senders and receivers during the communication.

Sender—the participant in an interaction who assumes the role of forming messages and attempting to communicate them to others.

Receiver—the participant in an interaction who assumes the role of listening, interpreting, and reacting to the messages of others.

Functions of Interpersonal Communication

Think of an important conversation that you had recently with one other person. Analyze the functions met by that conversation. Specifically, was your social need to interact met? What was your goal for that conversation, and was it fulfilled? What did you learn about yourself from that conversation? What information did you acquire? How did you influence the other person, and how did the other person influence you?

Context—the setting in which a communication encounter occurs, including what precedes and follows what is said.

Physical context—the place where the participants exchange messages.

of others. In most interpersonal situations participants enact the two roles simultaneously.

In general, it is easier for participants to communicate effectively when they are similar and have a common base for understanding meaning. According to Berger (2002), when people share similar knowledge, assumptions, or beliefs, they are said to have common ground, which makes communication more accurate and more efficient (p. 182). It would be easier, for instance, for two people who have both worked in retail sales jobs to understand each other quickly and accurately during a conversation about the stress of working on the day after Thanksgiving than it would be for one participant to convey that experience to someone who has never held a retail sales job.

▷ Context

Context is the setting in which a communication encounter occurs, including what precedes and follows what is said. The context affects the expectations of the participants, the meaning these participants derive, and their subsequent behavior. Context includes the physical, social, historical, psychological, and cultural circumstances that surround a communication episode.

The **physical context** of a communication episode is the place where the participants exchange messages. In many communication situations, the participants are located in the same physical space. In these cases, the environmental conditions (temperature, lighting, noise level) and the physical proximity of participants to each other can affect the messages that are exchanged and the meaning that is shared. Increasingly, however, interpersonal exchanges do not occur face-to-face. Rather, space is mediated by technology, resulting in communications that are influenced by the quality and type of technology used. For instance,

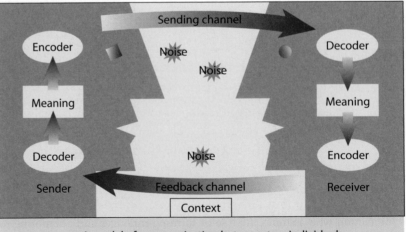

FIGURE 1.1 A model of communication between two individuals

when you call someone on your cell phone and each of you is in a different place, your conversation will be influenced by the spaces both of you occupy as well as by the quality of the phone connection between you. Likewise, conversations that occur in cyberspace may be affected by whether the technology used is synchronous or asynchronous.

Synchronous communication is real-time communication that occurs through an electronically mediated system, such as a live conversation on a telephone/cell phone or via instant messaging, while **asynchronous communication** is delayed communication that occurs through an electronically mediated system, such as voice mail, e-mail, or blogging.

The **social context** is the type of relationship that may already exist between the participants. Whether communication takes place among family members, friends, acquaintances, work associates, or strangers influences what and how messages are formed, shared, and understood. For instance, most people change how they interact when communicating with their family members as compared to how they interact when talking with their friends. When interacting with strangers, participants may find themselves assuming or searching for a shared social context to make a connection. For example, have you ever been introduced to someone at a party without the person who introduced you providing any clue as to what you might have in common? Did you find yourself and your new acquaintance searching for something to talk about?

The **historical context** is the background provided by previous communication episodes between the participants that influences understandings in the current encounter. For instance, suppose one morning Eduardo tells Anna that he will pick up the draft of the report they had left for their boss to read in the afternoon. As Anna enters the office that afternoon, she sees Eduardo and says, "Did you get it?" Another person listening to the conversation would have no idea what the "it" is to which Anna is referring. Yet Eduardo may well reply, "It's on my desk." Anna and Eduardo understand one another because of the earlier exchange.

The **psychological context** includes the moods and feelings each person brings to the interpersonal encounter. For instance, suppose Corinne is under a great deal of stress. While she is studying for an exam, a friend stops by and pleads with her to take a break and go to the gym with her. Corinne, who is normally good-natured, may respond in an irritated tone of voice. Why? Because her stress level provides the psychological context within which she hears this message, affecting how she responds.

The **cultural context** is the set of beliefs, values, and attitudes that belong to a specific culture and are used by each participant in an interpersonal encounter. Everyone is a part of one or more cultural groups (e.g., racial, ethnic, and religious cultures or cultures defined by other characteristics, such as region or country of birth, gender, sexual orientation, physical ability, etc.), though we may differ in how much we identify with our cultures. Even so, culture penetrates into every aspect of our lives, affecting how we think, behave, and communicate. When two people from different cultures interact, misunderstandings may occur because of

Synchronous communication—real-time communication that occurs through an electronically mediated system.

Asynchronous communication—delayed communication that occurs through an electronically mediated system.

Social context—the type of relationship that may already exist between the participants.

Historical context—the background provided by previous communication episodes between the participants that influences understandings in the current encounter.

Psychological context—the moods and feelings each person brings to the interpersonal encounter.

Cultural context—the set of beliefs, values, and attitudes that belong to a specific culture and are used by each participant in an interpersonal encounter.

the cultural variation between them, so it is important to be aware and respectful of cultural differences and how they affect communication.

▷ Messages

Interpersonal communication takes place through the exchange of **messages,** which are a person's verbal statements and nonverbal behaviors that transmit meaning during communications. To appreciate the complex way in which messages work, you need to understand the components of messages (meaning and symbols) and the processes that occur during messages (encoding and decoding).

Meaning is the significance of what is said and how what is said is interpreted. It is important to realize that meaning is not only what the sender intends but also what the person receiving the message understands. In other words, meaning is determined by both people in the exchange. For instance, if Sarah describes her old and fat cat to Tiffany through an exchange of messages, both Sarah and Tiffany must together come to some mutual understanding of what "old" and "fat" mean. When there is agreement, meaning has been shared; when there is disagreement, there is misunderstanding.

Symbols are words, sounds, and actions that represent specific ideas and feelings and are used to convey meaning. Messages are comprised of symbols that are arranged according to the syntactical and cultural rules of the language community to which the speaker belongs. When you communicate, you not only choose word symbols arranged to express your meaning but you also use commonly understood facial expressions, eye contact, bodily gestures, and tone of voice—all symbolic nonverbal cues—to accompany your words and augment the meaning of your message. For instance, if Zach says to Mollie, "I'm really tired," while simultaneously yawning, covering his mouth, and placing emphasis on the word "really," he conveys the extent of his exhaustion through multiple symbols.

In any communication encoding and decoding of messages occurs. **Encoding** is the process of forming messages by putting our thoughts and feelings into words and nonverbal cues. **Decoding** is the process of interpreting messages that we receive from others. Ordinarily, you do not consciously think about either the encoding or the decoding process. Only when there is a difficulty, such as when you are speaking in a language in which you are not fluent or using simplified vocabulary with children or nonfluent speakers of your language, do you become aware of encoding. The same is true of decoding, which you become aware of only when you have difficulty following what someone else is saying, such as when their message is presented in a confusing order, they are using words you don't know, or they are having difficulty communicating in your language.

▷ Channels

Channels are the sensory routes by which messages travel. In face-to-face spoken communications, verbal symbols are transmitted and received orally/aurally, while nonverbal cues are transmitted and received orally/aurally, visually, and in some cases by touch. When the encounter is mediated through technology,

---

Messages—a person's verbal statements and nonverbal behaviors that transmit meaning during communications.

Meaning—the significance of what is said and how what is said is interpreted.

Symbols—words, sounds, and actions that represent specific ideas and feelings and are used to convey meaning.

Encoding—the process of forming messages by putting our thoughts and feelings into words and nonverbal cues.

Decoding—the process of interpreting messages that we receive from others.

Channels—the sensory routes by which messages travel.

however, the sensory channels that are used differ and are more limited. For example, in written communications like letters, e-mails, or text messages the information is transmitted through a written visual channel only, so the meanings of the messages that are usually conveyed through the nonverbal means like facial expressions, gestures, touch, and tone of voice are lost. Similarly, when messages are mediated by phone, information is sent and received orally/aurally only. Although tone of voice cues can help with interpretation, the meaning of the message that is conveyed by other nonverbal cues is lost.

▷ Noise

Noise is any stimulus that interferes with shared meaning. Noises can be external, internal, or semantic.

External noises are sights, sounds, and other stimuli that draw people's attention away from intended meaning. For instance, a pop-up advertisement may draw your attention away from your ability to read a Web page or blog. Likewise, static or service interruptions can play havoc in cell phone conversations, the sound of a fire engine may distract you from a professor's lecture, or the smell of donuts may interfere with your train of thought during a conversation with a friend.

Internal noises are thoughts and feelings that interfere with meaning. If you tune out the message of the person with whom you are communicating and tune into a daydream or a past conversation instead, then you are experiencing internal noise. Likewise, if you have an emotional reaction to what someone is saying and are distracted by your emotions, you are experiencing internal noise.

Semantic noises are distractions aroused by a speaker's symbols that interfere with meaning. For instance, if a friend describes a forty-year-old secretary as "the girl in the office," and you think "girl" is an odd and condescending term for a forty-year-old woman, you might not even hear the rest of what your friend has to say. Whenever we react emotionally to a word or a behavior we are experiencing semantic noise. Similarly, if a speaker simply misuses vocabulary in other ways or expresses himself or herself in an unclear manner then that person is producing semantic noise.

▷ Feedback

Feedback is a receiver's response to a message that indicates to the sender whether his or her message was received effectively. Receivers can provide feedback verbally through words or nonverbally through body language. More often than not, our feedback is nonverbal. For instance, in face-to-face encounters, we continuously give nonverbal feedback when we listen, adjusting our posture, gaze,

Noise—any stimulus that interferes with shared meaning.

External noises—sights, sounds, and other stimuli that draw people's attention away from intended meaning.

Internal noises—thoughts and feelings that interfere with meaning.

Semantic noises—distractions aroused by a speaker's symbols that interfere with meaning.

Feedback—a receiver's response to a message that indicates to the sender whether his or her message was received effectively.

OBSERVE AND ANALYZE ●

The Communication Process

Describe two recent communication episodes in which you participated. One should be an episode that you thought went really well. The other should be one that you thought went poorly. Compare and contrast the episodes. Describe the participant similarities and differences, the contexts in which the communications happened, the meanings and symbols that were used to create the message, the channels used, any noise that interfered with the messages, and the feedback that was shared. Does your analysis help you to understand why one episode was successful and the other less so?

and other nonverbal behaviors to signal that we are confused, amused, interested, angered, and so on by what is being said. However, we may also wish to be very direct in our feedback by verbalizing, for example, by saying, "I don't understand the point you are making" or "That's a great comment you just made."

In technologically mediated communications, any feedback we provide to another person's text message, instant message (IM), e-mail, and so forth will be verbal, for example, when you open an e-mail and reply to it. Feedback is important to senders because it helps them to know if and how well they are being understood. Armed with this information, senders may choose to adjust their messages so that receivers are more accurately able to understand the intended meaning of the message.

● Principles of Interpersonal Communication

Now that we have described the interpersonal communication components and process, we will explain the five basic principles (or essential qualities) that describe interpersonal communication: Interpersonal communication is purposeful, continuous, transactional, relational, and irreversible.

▷ Interpersonal Communication Is Purposeful

When people communicate with one another, they have a purpose for doing so. Or, as Charles Berger (2002), a leading researcher on interpersonal contexts, puts it—social interaction is a goal-directed activity (p. 181). The purpose of a given interaction may be serious or trivial, but one way to evaluate the success of the communication is to ask whether it has achieved its purpose. When Beth calls Leah to ask if she'd like to join her for lunch to discuss a project they are working on, her purpose may be to resolve a misunderstanding, to encourage Leah to work more closely with her, or simply to establish a friendly atmosphere.

People may not always be aware of their purpose when they communicate. For instance, when Jamal passes Tony on the street and says lightly, "Tony, what's happening?" Jamal probably doesn't consciously think, "Tony's an acquaintance and I want him to understand that I see him and consider him worth recognizing." In this case Jamal's social obligation to recognize Tony is met spontaneously with the first acceptable expression that comes into Jamal's mind. Regardless of whether Jamal consciously thinks about the purpose, it still motivates his behavior. In this case, Jamal will have achieved his goal if Tony responds with an equally casual greeting.

▷ Interpersonal Communication Is Continuous

Whenever we are in the presence of other people and are aware of each other's presence, we consciously or subconsciously send and receive continuous messages. These messages may be verbal, but in many cases they are not. For instance, when you are in a room with someone else and you are silent, the other person may infer meaning from your silence or may interpret messages you give off through your facial expressions (Are you frowning? Smiling? Looking anxious?) and body movements (Are you shaking? Fidgeting? Stretching out in relaxation?). As skilled communicators, we need to be aware of the messages, whether explicit or implicit, we are constantly sending to others.

▷ Interpersonal Communication Is Transactional

In a business or consumer transaction, each person or entity involved in the transaction gives and gets something. This is also true in an interpersonal communication episode, in which each person involved in the communication gives and receives messages, gives and receives feedback, gets his or her goals met and helps others fulfill goals, and gives and receives information. It is impossible for only one of the parties to gain something from an interpersonal communication episode. Both parties get something, even if there are differences in what each person gets or how much information, feedback, or goal fulfillment each person gets. For instance, even in a seemingly one-sided communication in which Ben's boss angrily tells Ben that he must promise to be on time for work from now on and Ben merely says, "Yes, I promise," Ben and his boss nonetheless both gain from the transaction. Ben and his boss both receive messages and feedback, both give and receive information, and both fulfill goals—Ben's boss may appear to be the only one in the exchange to fulfill his goal (of achieving employee efficiency), but Ben also fulfills his unexpected goal (of reacting positively and assuaging the situation).

▷ Interpersonal Communication Is Relational

In many interpersonal communication settings the people involved not only share messages about content but they also make an emotional transaction—they negotiate their relationship. For instance, when they are getting in the car to leave for a holiday and Laura says to Darryl, "I've remembered to bring the map," she is not merely sending a simple message, reporting information, and fulfilling a basic goal. Through the way she says it and the psychological and historical context in which she says it, she is also communicating something about the relationship, whether that be, "You can always depend on me"; "I know you were busy with other things"; "I know I forgot last time, but not this time"; "If it weren't for me we'd be missing an important document for our trip"; or "You never remember to think of these things."

Although the preceding list of potential meanings may seem complicated, essentially only two aspects of a relationship can be negotiated during an interaction: (1) establishing a positive or negative affect (love or hate) in the relationship or (2) defining who is in control in the relationship (Watzlawick, Beavin, & Jackson, 1967, p. 51).

As an example of positive or negative affect, when José says, "Hal, good to see you," the nonverbal behavior and tone of voice that accompany the words

How do people communicate power differences in complementary relationships?

Complementary exchange—
a communication that reflects differences in power between the people involved.

Symmetrical exchange—
a communication that reflects similarity in power between the people involved.

may show Hal if José is genuinely happy to see him (positive affect) or not (negative affect). If José smiles, has a sincere sound to his voice, looks Hal in the eye, and perhaps pats him on the back or shakes his hands firmly, then Hal will recognize the signs of affection. If, however, José speaks quickly with no vocal inflection, makes a deadpan facial expression, or doesn't look Hal in the eye, Hal will perceive the comment as insincere, solely intended to meet some social expectation or even to be intentionally ironic.

As an example of defining control, when Tom says to Sue, "I know you're concerned about the budget, but I'll see to it that we have money to cover everything," he may, through his words, tone of voice, and nonverbal behavior, be saying that he is "in charge" of finances, that he is in control. In turn, Sue may respond by either verbally or subtly showing that she agrees with his control or by challenging him and asserting her desire to control the budget. In other words, the control aspect of the relationship is communicated in either a complementary or a symmetrical manner.

A **complementary exchange** is a communication that reflects differences in power between the people involved. In such exchanges, the communication messages of one person may assert dominance while the communication messages of the other person may accept the other's dominance. For instance, when Sue agrees with Tom's control over the budget or when Joey says to Jason, "Pick me up at work at 4 o'clock," and Jason says, "OK, I'll be there," thus agreeing to Joey's demand, complementary exchanges have occurred.

A **symmetrical exchange** is a communication that reflects similarity in power between the people involved. That power similarity may be the result of desire for shared control, or it may be a result of one person asserting control and the other person refusing to accept the assertion of control by the other. A symmetrical exchange through agreement may occur when Elka says, "How can we decide on a restaurant and a movie that we're both excited about?" to which Eileen replies, "Maybe we could make a list of restaurant choices and movie choices with you picking the restaurant and me selecting the movie," and Elka concludes, "That's a great idea, as long as we both agree on all the choices on the lists." In contrast, a symmetrical exchange achieved through disagreement would sound quite different. For example, Tom may say, "I think we need to cut back on credit card expenses for a couple of months," to which Fran may respond, "No way! I need a new suit for work, the car needs new tires, and you promised we could replace the couch." Here, both people are asserting similar levels of control.

Relational control is not negotiated in a single exchange. Rather, it is determined through many message exchanges over time. There may or may not be one type of exchange that most characterizes a relationship. For instance, two people may typically engage in complementary exchanges throughout their relationship, or they may have mostly complementary exchanges regarding social aspects of the relationship but symmetrical exchanges regarding the child-rearing aspect of their relationship.

▷ Interpersonal Communication Is Irreversible

Once an interpersonal exchange has taken place, we can never ignore it, take it back, or pretend it did not occur. In other words, we can never go back in time and reverse the communication. Although in face-to-face encounters your messages are generally not subject to widespread distribution, usually remaining private, semi-private, or circulated as gossip only to a small community of friends, they are nonetheless unchangeable. The same is true of electronic messages—in fact, they are even less likely to be forgotten because they are more public. Your computer, your Internet provider, and many of the Web sites you visit track your online activities and store your messages. When you participate in an online discussion or leave a post on a blog, you are leaving an electronic "footprint" that others can follow and read. E-mails, IMs, and text messages are not private, either. For example, if you trash-talk your manager in an e-mail to your colleague, you have no guarantee that the message you sent won't be forwarded to someone else or even forwarded on to your manager. Once you push the "send" button, you have no control at all over that message. Not only can't you take it back, but you have no control over where it goes.

INTER-ACT WITH ◗ TECHNOLOGY

How do various forms of technology impact the communication process in your relationships? List each form of technology that you use to communicate with others (such as land line telephones, cell phones, e-mail, text messaging, voice mail, IMs). Now examine how each form of technology affects your various relationships positively or negatively. For example, when you communicate via technology, do you generally send messages that are more candid, use harsher language, or make claims that you would not make in person? Do you tend to favor one form of technology over another, depending on the person with whom you are communicating? Why or why not?

◗ Ethics and Interpersonal Communication

In any encounter, we choose whether we will communicate ethically. **Ethics is a set of moral principles that may be held by a society, a group, or an individual.** Ethics are both societal and personal. On the one hand, societal entities like the government, religious groups, communities, schools, and families uphold certain ethical standards that can help us with our personal value judgments. These standards are typically generalized and are open to some interpretation. The law, religious beliefs, and community, school, and family standards are often debated and sometimes revised. This is because a societal ethical standard does not tell us exactly what to do in any given situation, only what general principles to consider when making ethical decisions. It directs our attention to the reasons behind the rightness or wrongness of any act and helps us find our own solutions.

On the other hand, each of us must also develop a personal ethic—one that guides our specific behavior. Your personal ethic is based on your belief

Ethics—a set of moral principles that may be held by a society, a group, or an individual.

in and acceptance of the societal standards you consider to be ethical. When we behave ethically, we voluntarily act in a manner that complies with expected societal standards because these standards are the glue that holds society together and because most of us regard ourselves as accountable to serve the greater good. However, we also need to interpret these societal standards in a way that not only serves the greater good but also serves our own personal beliefs. Every field of study—from psychology and biology to sociology and history—also has its own general ethical principles designed to guide the practice of that field. Interpersonal communication is no exception. Every time we communicate, we make choices with ethical implications, and those choices must fulfill both the greater good and one's own personal interpretations of them. The general ethical principles that inform interpersonal communication follow.

1. Ethical communicators are truthful and honest. Truthfulness and honesty are ethical standards that compel us to refrain from lying, misleading, or deceiving. "An honest person is widely regarded as a moral person, and honesty is a central concept to ethics as the foundation for a moral life" (Terkel & Duval, 1999, p. 122). The fundamental requirement of this standard is that we should not intentionally deceive, or try to deceive, others or even ourselves.

Truthfulness and honesty—ethical standards that compel us to refrain from lying, misleading, or deceiving.

Only when we are confronted with a **moral dilemma**—a situation in which none of the choices of action are satisfactory—should we even consider lying. Examples of moral dilemmas include whether to lie to protect the safety of others or determining if you should lie to protect someone's confidentiality. Even in such situations, the best course of action is to tell the truth if you possibly can. One way we can avoid direct lies in a moral dilemma is simply to refuse to discuss the issue at hand.

Moral dilemma—a situation in which none of the choices of action are satisfactory.

2. Ethical communicators act with integrity. Integrity is the ethical standard that necessitates maintaining consistency in belief and action (keeping promises). Terkel and Duval (1999) say, "A person who has integrity is someone who has strong moral principles and will successfully resist the temptation to compromise those principles" (p. 135). In short, integrity is the opposite of hypocrisy. A person who had promised to take a friend to the doctor would live up to this promise even if he or she had an opportunity to go out with another friend. Likewise, a person who consistently says and demonstrates that he or she believes in maintaining open communication with others would demonstrate a lack of integrity if he or she suddenly deviated from that belief in words or actions.

Integrity—the ethical standard that necessitates maintaining consistency in belief and action (keeping promises).

3. Ethical communicators behave fairly. Fairness is the ethical standard of achieving the right balance of interests without regard to one's own feelings and without showing favor to any side in a conflict. Fairness implies impartiality or lack of bias. To be fair to someone is to gather all of the relevant facts, consider only circumstances relevant to the decision at hand, and not be swayed by prejudice or irrelevancies. For example, if two of her children are fighting, a mother is exercising fairness if she allows both children to explain "their side" before she decides who is at fault.

Fairness—the ethical standard of achieving the right balance of interests without regard to one's own feelings and without showing favor to any side in a conflict.

4. Ethical communicators demonstrate respect. Respect is the ethical standard of showing regard or consideration for a person, that person's point of view,

Respect—the ethical standard of showing regard or consideration for a person, that person's point of view, and that person's rights.

and that person's rights. Often we talk of respecting another as a fellow human being, but sometimes respect is impeded by biases related to economic status, job status, gender, race, ethnic background, sexual orientation, physical ability, or other factors. These matters should not influence how we communicate with another person. We demonstrate respect through listening and understanding others' points of view, even when they are vastly different from our own, and filtering out prejudices.

5. Ethical communicators are responsible. Responsibility is the ethical standard of being accountable for one's actions. Being responsible is something that we are bound to do either through promise or obligation or because of our role in a group or community. It may involve fulfilling the societal principle of promoting the greater good or a duty to another human being. Some would argue that we merely have a passive responsibility to avoid harming or interfering with others. Others would argue that responsibility is not only passive but is also active—that we have a responsibility to help others not only in emergency situations but also by being an active participant in society through volunteering, social activism, and other such acts.

Responsibility—the ethical standard of being accountable for one's actions.

6. Ethical communicators are empathetic. Empathy is the ethical principle of understanding the feelings of others. Although similar to the ethical principle of respect, empathy is about more than respecting the point of view of others; it is also about understanding where others are coming from emotionally in order to grasp not just the facts presented but also the emotional reasons behind the facts. Often empathy means being able to cross over gender lines to understand meaning. Carol Gilligan, in her classic 1982 book *In a Different Voice: Psychological Theory and Women's Development*, introduced the concept that men and women may think in fundamentally different ways. She posited that women are more likely to base their thinking on concrete aspects of situations rather than on abstract rules and principles, as many men do. More recent theories have suggested that people from different ethnic cultures and sexual orientations also arrive at their conclusions through different paths. Therefore, interpersonal communicators must develop an ability to empathize with the thought processes of others.

Empathy—the ethical principle of understanding the feelings of others.

At various places in this text we will confront situations where the ethical standards just discussed come into play. We will discuss ethical dilemmas where we must sort out what is more or less the right or wrong ethical choice to make. In addition to discussing these dilemmas within the chapters, the end of each chapter features a box entitled "A Question of Ethics," in which you will be asked to think about and discuss various ethical dilemmas that relate to the chapter content.

○ Diversity and Interpersonal Communication

Diversity, the variations between and among people, affects nearly every aspect of the interpersonal communication process we have just discussed. Whether we understand each other depends as much on who we are as it does on the words

Diversity—the variations between and among people.

we use. We in the United States are part of one of the most multicultural nations in the world. The U.S. Census Bureau estimates from 2006 indicated that while non-Hispanic whites accounted for about two-thirds of the total U.S. population, that percentage has decreased with each census report. About one-third of the U.S. population is part of a racial or ethnic minority group, including African Americans (12.8 percent), Asian Americans (4.4 percent), Native Americans and Pacific Islanders (1.2 percent), and multiracial individuals (1.6 percent). People of Hispanic/Latino origin comprise 14.8 percent of the U.S. population and are the largest and fastest-growing minority group. The relative youth of the Hispanic population means that it will supply much of the U.S. population growth for decades to come (Population Reference Bureau, 2006). Today, English is not the primary language spoken at home for almost 20 percent of the people living in the United States.

You'll recall from our discussion of the cultural context of communication that **culture** is the system of beliefs, values, and attitudes shared by a particular

Culture—the system of beliefs, values, and attitudes shared by a particular segment of the population.

How might the differences between these people affect their conversation?

segment of the population. Culture encompasses a variety of groups living in the United States—from groups defined by a shared race to groups defined by shared ethnic background to groups defined by other factors, such as religious background, age, gender, socioeconomic class, sexual orientation, and ability status—and it is a central factor to consider when thinking about diversity. Peter Andersen, a well-respected intercultural communication scholar, goes so far as to say that "every communicator is a product of his or her culture" (Andersen, 2000, p. 260). Thus, as we become an increasingly diverse nation, the study of intercultural communication is more important than ever.

We who live in the United States hold to the ideal that ours is a country of opportunity while simultaneously knowing that it is also a country of hypocrisy, a land where people are afforded unequal treatment and unequal opportunity based on race, sex, religion, class, ability, country of origin, sexual orientation, and so on. Therefore, we need to look carefully at ourselves and at our communication behaviors when we speak with anyone, because, as we interact with others from cultural backgrounds that differ from our own, we are vulnerable to communicating unintentionally in ways that are culturally inappropriate or insensitive, thus undermining our relationships. To help facilitate an understanding of cultural diversity, within each chapter of this book we will discuss the ways people act in communication situations that are an outgrowth of diverse cultural backgrounds. In addition, the "Diverse Voices" feature provides opportunities for us to empathize with the communication experiences of a variety of individuals.

⬤ Increasing Interpersonal Communication Competence

Communication competence is the perception that communicative behavior is both effective and appropriate in a given relationship (Spitzberg, 2000, p. 375). Communication is *effective* when it achieves its goals. It is *appropriate* when it conforms to the social expectations of the situation. The definition of competent communication acknowledges that competence is a perception that one person forms about another's communication abilities. We try to project that we are competent communicators by the verbal messages we send and the nonverbal behaviors that accompany them. But determining our competence always rests with the other person.

One of your goals in this course will be to learn how to increase the likelihood of others viewing you as a competent communicator. In the "Spotlight on Scholars" in this chapter (page 23), we feature Brian Spitzberg, who believes that perceptions of interpersonal communication competence depend on three things: personal knowledge, skills, and motivation (see also Spitzberg, 2000, p. 377). In other words, to be a competent communicator we have to (1) know what to say and do (knowledge), (2) know how to say and do it (skills), and (3) have a desire to improve (motivation).

Communication competence—the perception that communicative behavior is both effective and appropriate in a given relationship.

Social Perception

by Arturo Madrid

Arturo Madrid is the Norine R. and T. Frank Murchison Distinguished Professor of Humanities at Trinity University. From 1984 to 1993 he served as the founding President of Tomas Rivera Center, the nation's first institute for policy studies on Latino issues. In 1996 he was awarded the Charles Frankel Prize in Humanities by the National Endowment for the Humanities. In this classic selection, Madrid describes the conflicting experiences of those who see themselves as different from what has stereotypically been described as "American." Experiencing oneself and being perceived as "other" and "invisible" are powerful determinants of one's self-concept and form a very special filter through which one communicates with others.

My name is Arturo Madrid. I am a citizen of the United States, as are my parents and as were my grandparents, and my great-grandparents. My ancestors' presence in what is now the United States antedates Plymouth Rock, even without taking into account any American Indian heritage I might have.

I do not, however, fit those mental sets that define America and Americans. My physical appearance, my speech patterns, my name, my profession (a professor of Spanish) create a text that confuses the reader.

I am very clearly the *other,* if only your everyday, garden-variety, domestic *other.* I've always known that I was the *other,* even before I knew the vocabulary or understood the significance of otherness.

Despite the operating myth of the day, school did not erase my *otherness.* The true test was not our speech, but rather our names and our appearance, for we would always have an accent, however perfect our pronunciation, however excellent our enunciation, however divine our diction. That accent would be heard in our pigmentation, our physiognomy, and our names. We were, in short, the *other.*

Being the *other* involves a contradictory phenomenon. On the one hand, being the *other* frequently means being invisible. On the other hand, being the *other* sometimes involves sticking out like a sore thumb. What is she/he doing here?

If one is the *other,* one will inevitably be seen stereotypically; will be defined and limited by mental sets that may not bear much relation to existing realities.

There is sometimes a darker side to otherness as well. The *other* disturbs, disquiets, discomforts. It provokes distrust and suspicion. The *other* frightens, scares.

For some of us being the *other* is only annoying; for others it is debilitating; for still others it is damning. For the majority otherness is permanently sealed by physical appearance. For the rest otherness is betrayed by ways of being, speaking, or of doing.

The first half of my life I spent downplaying the significance and consequences of otherness. The second half has seen me wrestling to understand its complex and deeply ingrained realities; striving to fathom why otherness denies us a voice or visibility or validity in American society and its institutions; struggling to make otherness familiar, reasonable, even normal to my fellow Americans.

One of the principal strengths of our society is its ability to address on a continuing and substantive basis the real economic, political, and social problems that have faced and continue to face us. What makes the United States so attractive to immigrants are the protections and opportunities it offers; what keeps our society together is tolerance for cultural, religious, social, political, and even linguistic difference; what makes us a unique, dynamic, and extraordinary nation are the power and creativity of our diversity.

The true history of the U.S. is the one of struggle against intolerance, against oppression, against xenophobia, against those forces that have prohibited persons from participating in the larger life of the society on the basis of their race, their gender, their religion, their national origin, their linguistic and cultural background. These phenomena are not only consigned to the past. They remain with us and frequently take on virulent dimensions.

If you believe, as I do, that the well-being of a society is directly related to the degree and extent to which all of its citizens participate in its institutions, then you will have to agree that we have a challenge before us. In view of the extraordinary changes that are taking place in our society we need to take up the struggle again, unpleasant as it is. As educated and educator members of this society we have a special responsibility for assuring that all American institutions, not just our elementary and secondary schools, our juvenile halls, or jails, reflect the diversity of our society. Not to do so is to risk greater alienation on the part of a growing segment of our society; is to risk increased social tension in an already conflictive world; and, ultimately, is to risk the survival of a range of institutions that, for all their defects and deficiencies, provide us the opportunity and the freedom to improve our individual and collective lot.

Let me urge you, as you return to your professional responsibilities and to your personal spaces, to reflect on these two words—*quality* and *diversity*—and on the mental sets and behaviors that flow out of them. And let me urge you further to struggle against the notion that quality is finite in quantity, limited in its manifestations, or is restricted by considerations of class, gender, race, or national origin; or that quality manifests itself only in leaders and not in followers, in managers and not in workers; or that it has to be associated with verbal agility or elegance of personal style; or that it cannot be seeded, or nurtured, or developed.

Excerpted from Madrid, A. (1994). Diversity and its discontents. In L. A. Samovar & R. E. Porter (Eds.), *Intercultural Communication: A Reader* (7th ed., pp. 127–131). Belmont, Calif.: Wadsworth. Reprinted by permission of Black Issues in Higher Education.

First, people need to have knowledge about the communication process to be competent. As communicator knowledge increases, so does communicator competence. In other words, the more people understand how to behave in a given situation, the more likely they are to be perceived as competent. We gain knowledge about how to interact by observing what others do, by asking others how we should behave, and by learning through trial and error. For instance, to be regarded as competent in talking with her boss about increasing her responsibilities, Annette must know about the various ways of presenting her request that her boss would find acceptable and persuasive. She may do so by observing her boss' behavior in similar situations, asking co-workers how best to approach the situation, and analyzing how similar communications with her boss went in the past.

Second, people need to practice communication skills to become more competent. **Skills** are goal-oriented actions or action sequences that we can master and repeat in appropriate situations. As communicator skill increases, so does communicator competence. The more communication skills you have mastered, the more likely you are to be able to structure an effective and appropriate message. For instance, Annette must not only know how to influence her boss but must also be able to do so during the actual conversation using specific skills such as message-formation skills, conversational-climate skills, listening-for-understanding skills, empathic-response skills, and disclosure skills. Mastery of the skills in each of these skill groups is at the heart of becoming a competent communicator, and you will learn about each group during this course. The more practice you have in using these specific skills, the more likely it is that you will be able to draw on these skills in a real situation.

Finally, people need to have the motivation to improve both their knowledge and skills to communicate competently. As communicator motivation increases, so does communicator competence. People are likely to be more motivated to become competent communicators if they are confident and if they see potential rewards arising from their competence. If Annette has confidence in her ability to

Skills—goal-oriented actions or action sequences that we can master and repeat in appropriate situations.

persuade her boss and/or if she thinks it's likely that the conversation will result in more challenging job responsibilities, then she will be motivated to communicate in ways that are likely to be seen as competent.

The combination of interpersonal communication knowledge, skills, and motivation leads us to perform competently in our encounters with others. The following sections will explore knowledge, skills, and motivation in more detail, and the rest of this book is aimed at helping you increase the likelihood that you will be perceived as a competent communicator.

▷ Increasing Knowledge: Factual Knowledge and Emotional Intelligence

To be competent interpersonal communicators, we must not only have theoretical and factual knowledge of the communication process and situation at hand—as illustrated in the earlier example involving Annette and her boss—but we must also have knowledge about the emotional factors involved. **Emotional intelligence** is the ability to monitor your own and others' emotions and to use this information to guide your communications (Salovey & Mayer, 1990, p. 189). People differ in the degree to which they are able to identify their own emotions and detect and interpret the emotions of others. In addition, people vary in their abilities to understand slight variations in emotion and to use these variations in communications. No one is born with emotional intelligence, but it can be learned and developed over time. Throughout this book, we will provide information to help you develop your emotional intelligence.

Emotional intelligence—the ability to monitor your own and others' emotions and to use this information to guide your communications.

▷ Developing Skills: Skills Categories and Behavioral Flexibility

As Brian Spitzberg also outlines, competent communicators additionally must develop specific communication skills. These skills are based on interpersonal communication theories and research and are critical in interpersonal settings. By understanding why certain skills are effective, you will be better equipped to improvise and creatively use the skills in unfamiliar and ambiguous situations. Although each skill can be used in a variety of settings and all skills contribute to perceptions of competence, we have grouped the skills into diagnostic categories so that you may review the skills more easily when you are seeking to improve a particular aspect of your communication repertoire. The five categories are:

1. **Message-formation skills.** These skills increase the likelihood that you will send clear and accurate messages to others.
2. **Conversational-climate skills.** These skills increase the likelihood that you will develop supportive and trusting relationships with others.
3. **Listening-for-understanding skills.** These skills increase the likelihood that you understand the meaning of what others communicate to you.
4. **Empathic-response skills.** These skills increase the likelihood that you understand and respond to the emotional experiences of others.

Brian Spitzberg
Professor of Communication at San Diego State University, on
Interpersonal Communication Competence

Although Brian Spitzberg has made many contributions to our understanding of interpersonal communication, he is best known for his work in interpersonal communication competence, which began at an interpersonal communication seminar at the University of Southern California. At that seminar, he described the research that had been done on interpersonal communication competence and found that in much of this research, conclusions went in different directions. Spitzberg believed the time was ripe for someone to synthesize these perspectives into a comprehensive theory of competence. His final paper for the seminar was his first attempt to construct a competence theory.

Today, the model of interpersonal communication competence Spitzberg formulated guides most of our thinking and research in this area. He views interpersonal communication competence neither as an innate trait nor as a set of steps to follow, as in learning to assemble a model airplane. Rather, Spitzberg says that interpersonal communication competence is a matter of perception. People are more likely to be satisfied in a communication situation when they perceive themselves as competent and when the other person involved in the communication also views the speaker as competent.

As Spitzberg was trying to organize his thinking about competence, he was taking another course in which he became acquainted with theories of dramatic acting. These theories held that an actor's performance depended on his or her motivation, knowledge of the script, and acting skills. Spitzberg found that these same variables could be applied to communication competence, and he incorporated them into his theory. How well we communicate depends, first, on how knowledgeable we are about what behaviors are appropriate in similar conversational situations; second, on how skilled we are at actually using these appropriate behaviors during the conversation; and third, on how motivated we are to ensure the conversation is a successful one. In addition, Spitzberg's theory suggests that context variables such as the ones discussed in this chapter also affect how we choose to act in a conversation and affect the perception of competence.

While Spitzberg formed most of these ideas while he was still in graduate school, he and others have spent the last twenty years refining the theory, conducting programs of research based on his theory, and measuring the effectiveness of the theory. The research has fleshed out parts of the theory and provided some evidence of the theory's accuracy. Over the years, Spitzberg has developed about a dozen specific instruments to measure parts of the theory. One of these measures, the Conversational Skills Rating Scale, has been adopted as the standard measure of interpersonal communication skills by the National Communication Association (a leading national organization of communication scholars, teachers, and practitioners). His most recent work involves translating the model and measures of competence into the computer-mediated context. To what extent are the skills we use in face-to-face communication similar to those we use in computer-based interaction? Several research projects are currently investigating this question.

Spitzberg's continuing interest in communication competency has led him to study abusive or dysfunctional relationships from a competence perspective. Recently he has studied obsessive relational intrusion (ORI) and stalking. In ORI and stalking situations, the intruder's motivation is at odds with the motivation of the victim. Specifically, the intruder is wishing to begin, escalate, or continue a relationship with the victim, who does not agree with the relationship definition under which the intruder is operating. Their interactions, then, are really "arguments" over the very definition of the relationship. The intruders may perceive themselves to be "competent" within what they consider the relationship to be, while victims may respond in ways they believe to be "competent" within their definition. Spitzberg's research with his colleagues has begun to identify the profile of ORI, which may signal the development of stalking. Such a profile could help relationship partners to see the stalking coming and remove themselves from a relationship before it becomes dangerous. Recently, Spitzberg has expanded his ORI work to examine the phenomenon of "cyber stalking."

Whether the situation is a first date or a job interview, a conflict with your roommate or an intimate discussion of your feelings, Spitzberg believes it is important that others perceive you to be competent. For some of Spitzberg's publications on competence, see Spitzberg and Duran (1995) and Spitzberg (2000).

5. Disclosure skills. These skills increase the likelihood that you share your ideas and feelings with others in an honest and sensitive manner.

Your effectiveness depends not only on your ability to master the skill sets we just described but also on your ability to adapt your behavior to the situation in which you find yourself. **Behavioral flexibility** is the ability to analyze a communication situation and adapt your use of various communication skills to fit the situation. In other words, behavioral flexibility means listening to feedback during a communication situation and adjusting the skills you are using to communicate so that your messages and behavior are effective.

Behavioral flexibility occurs in several steps: First, you make a prediction about what type of communication skills are likely to be appropriate for a particular situation; second, you enact or use those communication skills; third, you pay attention to how the other person is reacting, that is, monitor feedback; and fourth, you either change the communication skills you use based on the feedback or not. In the fourth step, you should modify or change the communication skills you use if the feedback tells you that your original method isn't working or continue using the same skills if your original method is working. It is up to you to pay attention to feedback and to use it to influence the remainder of your conversation.

Let's look at a concrete example of behavioral flexibility. Imagine that Grace finds herself in a situation in which her friend Mary Lou starts emotionally sharing a host of problems just as she is about to leave to go to the library. Grace must make many decisions and think about the various contexts in which the conversation is taking place. She should think about whether their location is the best physical context for such a sensitive interaction, whether the social context of her relationship with Mary Lou warrants her dropping her library plans to speak with Mary Lou, whether the historical context of her interactions with Mary Lou indicates that this is a serious or a routine situation, and whether the psychological context leads her to feel that she is in the best psychological state to help Mary Lou at this time. Depending on the situation, Grace may also want to examine the cultural context, for instance, if Mary Lou reveals that her problems relate to her cultural background in some way.

If Grace decides to stay and interact with Mary Lou, she has many choices about what to say and how to behave. Should she merely listen and be a sounding board (listening-for-understanding skills)? Should she offer messages of comfort (empathic-response skills)? Should she disclose her own feelings and experiences with related problems (disclosure skills)? Should she offer advice (conversational-climate skills)? As part of behavioral flexibility, Grace must decide what communication skills she thinks are best for this situation. Suppose Grace starts by merely listening but receives feedback that Mary Lou wants emotional support. In that case, Grace should be flexible about moving to a new communication skill. With each new interpersonal skill she tries, Grace must analyze whether that skill is effective while adapting to what the situation requires, within the bounds of appropriateness and her own needs.

Behavioral flexibility—the ability to analyze a communication situation and adapt your use of various communication skills to fit the situation.

Learning to use new skills is difficult. You must not only understand the skills but also become comfortable using them in real-life situations. Improving communication skills is like learning a new hobby or sport. If you are learning to play golf, for instance, you will need to learn techniques that feel uncomfortable at first. You will find it difficult to determine what skills to use when and how to use those skills smoothly and effortlessly. Because some of the communication skills may not be in your repertoire now, as you work on them you are likely to feel awkward and to see the skills as creating unrealistic or "phony"-sounding messages. Communication skills must be practiced until they feel comfortable and automatic. The more you practice, the easier it will become to use a skill smoothly and with little conscious effort. Throughout this book we will elaborate further on the basic categories of skills listed here so that you can draw upon them to help you become more competent as a communicator.

▷ Gaining Motivation: Writing Communication Improvement Plans

Becoming competent in communication is a lifelong journey, one that involves not only knowledge and skills but also motivation, as described earlier. One way we recommend to gain motivation is to commit to specific goals by writing formal communication improvement plans.

Before you can do so, you must first analyze your current communication knowledge and skills repertoire and determine where you can make improvements. Once you have identified these, you should write a communication improvement goal statement by following these four steps for each communication situation in which you feel you need improvement (Figure 1.2 provides an additional example):

1. State the problem. Start by writing down a communication problem that you have. For example: "Problem: Even though my boss consistently gives all of

---

GOAL STATEMENT

Problem: I have developed the bad habit of ending sentences with "you know." This has become noticeable and results in others perceiving me as less self-assured. I tend to use this language when the person with whom I am speaking is not providing enough verbal feedback. I need to become aware of when I am using this phrase and consciously choose to avoid saying it.

Goal: To improve my message formation skills by avoiding the overuse of "you know" by specifically requesting feedback.

Procedure: I will monitor my messages for excessive use of "you know." When I detect a problem I will use the skill of questioning to get direct feedback from the receiver.

Test of Achieving Goal: This goal will be considered achieved when I am aware of excessive "you knows" and able to reduce my usage by directly requesting feedback.

FIGURE 1.2 Communication improvement plan

the interesting tasks to co-workers, I haven't spoken up because I'm not very good at describing my feelings."

2. State the specific goal. A goal is *specific* if it is measurable and you know when you have achieved it. For example, to deal with the problem stated here, you might write, "Goal: To describe my feelings about task assignments to my boss."

3. Outline a specific procedure for reaching the goal. To develop a plan for reaching your goal, first consult the chapter in this book that covers the skill you wish to hone. Then translate the general steps recommended in the chapter to your specific situation. This step is critical because successful behavioral change requires that you follow a route to reach your goal: You can't just jump from problem to solution and skip the steps in between. For example: "Procedure: I will practice the steps of describing my feelings to others. (1) I will identify the specific feeling I am experiencing. (2) I will describe the emotion I am feeling accurately. (3) I will indicate what has triggered the feeling. (4) I will own the feeling as mine. (5) I will then put that procedure into operation when I am talking with my boss."

A QUESTION OF ETHICS ◎ What Would You Do?

Louisa and Rachelle became friends during high school and now live together in an off-campus apartment. Louisa, an only child, is a high-strung, anxious, and emotional person, while Rachelle, the oldest of six children, is easy-going and calm. Louisa depends on Rachelle to listen to her problems and to comfort and advise her; usually she is a good friend and supports Rachelle as well.

Currently, at work and at school Louisa is under a lot of stress. Because of that, she hasn't had time to talk with Rachelle about what is going on in Rachelle's life. When they talk, the conversation is always about Louisa. Even when Rachelle tries to talk about what is happening to her, Louisa is distracted and manages to redirect the conversation back to her own problems. In the last two weeks, Louisa forgot that they had made plans to have dinner together, and another time she canceled their plans at the last minute.

This morning, Louisa told Rachelle: "I don't have time to pick up my prescription at the drug store so you will have to do it, and my project group from biology is coming over to work this evening so I need you to straighten up this place. I don't have time to vacuum or dust, but I know that you have a break between classes and when you have to leave for work. Oh, and I'm really stuck in my Soc class. You know how slammed I am for time and I have a one-page position paper due

tomorrow. I know that you aced Soc last semester so it would be great if you would do a first draft for me. The assignment directions are on my desk. Well, I've got to run. See you tonight."

After Louisa left, Rachelle plopped down in the chair and tried to sort out her feelings. As she talked to herself, she realized that while she was deeply concerned for Louisa, who seemed to be spinning out of control, she also believed that Louisa was taking advantage of her. It appeared to Rachelle that the relationship had become one-sided, with Louisa in control expecting Rachelle to serve her. Rachelle felt sad and abandoned as she recognized that Louisa had quit even trying to meet Rachelle's needs. "How," she asked herself, "has this happened?"

1. How do the functions of interpersonal communication help you to understand what is happening to Rachelle and Louisa?
2. How do the social, historical, psychological, and cultural contexts help you to understand Louisa and Rachelle's behavior?
3. Is this relationship symmetrical or complementary?
4. What ethical principles are involved in this case? Which principles does each woman violate?
5. What should Rachelle do now?

4. Devise a method of determining when the goal has been reached. A good goal is measurable, and the fourth part of your goal-setting effort is to determine your minimum requirements for knowing when you have achieved a given goal. For example: "Test of Achieving Goal: This goal will be considered achieved when I have described my feelings to my boss the next time he bypasses me for an interesting assignment."

Once you have written a communication improvement goal statement, you may want to present it to another person to witness your commitment and serve as a consultant, coach, and support person. This gives you someone to talk with about your progress and is a critical part of this course. At the end of each chapter of this book you will be challenged to develop a goal statement related to the material presented. You might choose to form a partnership with a classmate, with each of you serving as witness and consultant for the other. If you have a consultant, you might meet with this person periodically to assess your progress, troubleshoot problems, and develop additional procedures for reaching your goal.

◐ Summary

We have defined interpersonal communication as the process through which people create and manage their relationships, exercising mutual responsibility in creating meaning.

Interpersonal communication is important because it helps us to meet five basic functions: to meet our social needs, achieve goals, develop our sense of self, acquire information, and influence/be influenced by others.

Interpersonal communication is based on six components: (1) participants—the people who assume the roles of senders and receivers during communication; (2) context—the physical, social, historical, psychological, or cultural setting in which the communication occurs; (3) messages—the meaning, symbols, and encoding/decoding that occur during communication; (4) channels—the routes messages take; (5) noise—the external, internal, and semantic stimuli that get in the way of meaning; and (6) feedback—responses to messages.

Five principles underlie our interpersonal communication: Interpersonal communication is (1) purposeful; (2) continuous; (3) transactional; (4) relational, occurring in complementary or symmetrical exchanges; and (5) irreversible.

Ethics is a set of moral principles that may be held by a society, a group, or an individual. When we communicate, we make choices with ethical implications involving truthfulness and honesty, integrity, fairness, respect, responsibility, and empathy. Diversity, variations between and among people, affects nearly every aspect of the communication process. Communicating with people from diverse backgrounds requires an understanding of culture, the system of beliefs, values, and attitudes shared by members of a group.

Communication competence is the impression that communicative behavior is both appropriate and effective in a given relationship. It involves increasing knowledge, skills, and motivation. Knowledge consists of factual knowledge and emotional intelligence, both contributing to one's interpersonal communication competence. The five categories of skills are message-formation, conversational-climate, listening-for-understanding, empathic-response, and disclosure skills. Behavioral flexibility is a larger skill that encompasses all of the other skills and requires communicators to adapt skills used based on feedback. Motivation is essential to improving knowledge and skills to become a competent communicator and can be enhanced by writing communication improvement plans.

○ Chapter Resources

Key Words ○

Interpersonal communication, *p. 5*	Meaning, *p. 10*	Truthfulness and honesty, *p. 16*
Participants, *p. 7*	Symbols, *p. 10*	Moral dilemma, *p. 16*
Sender, *p. 7*	Encoding, *p. 10*	Integrity, *p. 16*
Receiver, *p. 7*	Decoding, *p. 10*	Fairness, *p. 16*
Context, *p. 8*	Channels, *p. 10*	Respect, *p. 16*
Physical context, *p. 8*	Noise, *p. 11*	Responsibility, *p. 17*
Synchronous communication, *p. 9*	External noises, *p. 11*	Empathy, *p. 17*
Asynchronous communication, *p. 9*	Internal noises, *p. 11*	Diversity, *p. 17*
Social context, *p. 9*	Semantic noises, *p. 11*	Culture, *p. 18*
Historical context, *p. 9*	Feedback, *p. 11*	Communication competence, *p. 19*
Psychological context, *p. 9*	Complementary exchange, *p. 14*	Skills, *p. 21*
Cultural context, *p. 9*	Symmetrical exchange, *p. 14*	Emotional intelligence, *p. 22*
Messages, *p. 10*	Ethics, *p. 15*	Behavioral flexibility, *p. 24*

Skill Practice ○ Find more on the web @ www.oup.com/us/interact12

Skill Practice exercises challenge you to master the material you have read in this chapter. For additional Skill Practice activities, visit our website at www.oup.com/us/interact12.

Identifying Communication Elements
For the following episode identify the contextual factors, participant differences, channels, messages, noise, and feedback.

Jessica and her daughter Rita are shopping. As they walk through an elegant boutique, Rita, who is feeling particularly happy, sees a blouse she wants. With a look of great anticipation and excitement, Rita says, "Look at this, Mom—it's beautiful. Can I try it on?" Jessica, who is worried about the cost, frowns, shrugs her shoulders, and says hesitantly, "Well—yes—I guess so." Rita, noticing her mother's hesitation, continues, "And it's marked down to twenty-seven dollars!" Jessica relaxes, smiles, and says, "Yes, it is attractive—try it on. If it fits, let's buy it."

Inter-Act with Media ○ Find more on the web @ www.oup.com/us/interact12

Television

30 Rock, episode: "The Rural Juror" (2007). Tina Fey, Jane Krakowski.
Brief Summary: Writer Liz Lemon (Fey) and actress Jenna Maloney (Krakowski) both work on the variety show *TGS.* Jenna performs in a movie, *The Rural Juror,* as a side job. Liz and her

colleagues screen the movie and find it horrible. However, for years Liz has used a formula for evaluating Jenna's performances: She thinks of one nice thing to say and then hugs her. The episode flashes back over the years to Liz grappling for post-performance compliments for Jenna: "You looked so beautiful"; "The lighting was really neat"; "The programs were really easy to read." When Jenna asks Liz directly what she thought of *The Rural Juror,* Liz says she likes the soundtrack and Jenna's facial expressions. Jenna then reveals that she's caught on to Liz's approach. "You did that condescending compliment thing you always do," Jenna tells her. When Jenna presses for Liz's real opinion, Liz summarizes the movie as a "train wreck." This honesty results in a series of personal attacks between the women. The exchange highlights the difficulty in ethical, honest communication, particularly when involving personal feelings and ego.

IPC Concepts: Ethics of interpersonal communication, truthfulness and honesty, integrity, respect.

Cinema

Juno (2007). Jason Reitman (director). Ellen Page, Michael Cera, Allison Janney, J. K. Simmons, Jason Bateman, Jennifer Garner.

Brief Summary: Juno (Page) is a wise-beyond-her-years teenager who unexpectedly becomes pregnant by her friend Paulie Bleeker (Cera). Juno exhibits a consistently direct communication style—what is on her mind comes out of her mouth. She wastes no time telling Bleeker about her pregnancy and shares her intentions to end it. When Juno speaks to a clinic, she tells them the reception is bad because she is "on her hamburger phone." Once Juno decides to have the baby, she tells her father and stepmother, "I'm pregnant. I'm going to give it up for adoption and I already found the perfect couple." Juno then laments on her current symptoms. When Juno meets the potential parents of her baby, Vanessa and Mark Loring (Bateman, Garner), they ask how sure she is that she will give up the baby. Juno replies, "104% sure" and says that if she could give the baby to the couple right then, she would, but it "probably looks like a sea monkey." When Vanessa and Mark end up divorcing, Juno leaves a note on Vanessa's door: "If you're still in, I'm still in." Regardless of the communication style of those around her, Juno strives for transactional communication with quick wit, self-deprecating humor, and candor.

IPC Concepts: Functions of interpersonal communication, transactional and relational aspects of interpersonal communication, ethical communication, communication competence, behavioral flexibility.

What's on the Web
Find links and additional material, including self-quizzes, on the companion website at www.oup.com/us/interact12.

2

Forming and Using Social Perceptions

"Hey, happy birthday, Jodi" is one of many messages posted on Jodi's Facebook wall. She also finds flowers, teddy bears, and balloons from Reid, Akeelah, Torry, and Kris posted in her gift box.

Jodi sends an event invitation to everyone on her friends list: "I can't believe I'm 21 today. Meet me tonight at Woody's for a really big party."

Becky RSVPs to the event invitation and replies on Jodi's message board, "Get ready for the best night of your life."

"What's the best birthday present you've ever gotten?" Joey posts on her wall.

"My kitten Pedro," says Jodi

J odi's Facebook page describes her life and her hopes and dreams. It includes favorite poems and quotes and some 100 pictures of her at play, at work, and with her friends, family, and pets. There are over 300 people on her friends list and lots of messages on her wall. What does Jodi's Facebook page say about her? In addition to providing basic facts about her life, on a deeper level it communicates her self-concept and her identity. Everyone who visits her page develops perceptions and impressions of Jodi, and the messages they leave may reveal how they view her.

Jodi's Facebook page is an illustration of **social perception**, or **social cognition**, the set of processes by which people perceive themselves and others. Our social perceptions of ourselves and others influence how we communicate. Understanding these processes, then, provides a foundation for your study of interpersonal communication. We begin this chapter by defining the word "perception" and describing the cognitive process of perception. We then examine how the perceptions you have about yourself are formed and changed. Next we describe how your self-perceptions affect your interpersonal communication and how you present yourself to others. Then we change our focus a bit and explain how you perceive others and the problems that can develop in perceiving others. Finally, we discuss how you can increase the accuracy of your self-perceptions as well as your perceptions of others.

Social perception—the set of processes by which people perceive themselves and others.

○ The Perception Process

Perception is the process of selectively attending to information that we receive through our senses and assigning meaning to it. Perception forms our understanding of reality. In other words, what we see, hear, and interpret is what we consider to be true. Another person who may see, hear, and interpret something entirely different from the same situation will regard that different perception as true. So sometimes our perceptions of the world, other people, and ourselves agree with the perceptions of others. At other times our perceptions are significantly different from those of other people. When our perceptions are different from those with whom we interact, sharing meaning becomes more challenging.

Perception—the process of selectively attending to information that we receive through our senses and assigning meaning to it.

To get a better idea of the process of perceiving, let's explore each of the three stages. First your brain attends to and selects the information, or stimuli, that it receives from your senses; then it organizes the stimuli; and finally it interprets the stimuli.

▷ Attention to and Selection of Stimuli

Although we are subject to a constant barrage of sensory stimuli, we focus our attention on relatively little of it, and we choose, or select, what stimuli matter to us based in part on our needs, interests, and expectations.

Needs are those things we consciously or unconsciously feel we require to sustain us biologically or psychologically. We are likely to pay attention to those things that meet these biological and psychological needs and filter out those

Needs—those things we consciously or unconsciously feel we require to sustain us biologically or psychologically.

things that don't. For instance, when you go to class, how well in tune you are to what is being discussed is likely to depend on whether you believe the information is important to you—that is, does it meet a need? Will your physical or psychological health be affected by what you learn?

In contrast to needs, **interests** are things that prompt our curiosity but aren't essential to sustain us biologically or psychologically. In addition to what we need, we are likely to pay attention to information that pertains to our interests and filter out that which does not interest us. For instance, you may not even notice that music is playing in the background until you find yourself realizing that it is something you recognize and/or enjoy. Similarly, when you are really interested in a person, you are more likely to pay attention to what that person is saying.

Expectations are those things that we notice because we are habituated to noticing them. In addition to perceiving things that fulfill our needs and interests, we are likely to see what we expect to see and to ignore information that violates our expectations. As a persuasive example, take a quick look at the phrases in the triangles in Figure 2.1. OK, now that you've looked, did you notice anything unusual about the wording? If you have never seen this example before, you probably read "Paris in the springtime" in the first triangle, "Once in a lifetime" in the second triangle, and "Bird in the hand" in the third triangle. But if you reexamine the words, you will see that what you perceived was not exactly what is written. Do you now see the repeated words? It is easy to miss the repeated words because we don't *expect* to see them.

In interpersonal situations, we may not notice when people change their behavior because we expect them to behave as they always have. So if Karen doesn't usually thank Chris for walking the dog, Chris may not even notice when she does.

▷ Organization of Stimuli

Once we attend to and select the stimuli that fulfill our needs, interests, and/or expectations, our brains then go through the process of organizing the selected stimuli. Even though our attention and selection process limits the stimuli our brain must process, the amount of discrete stimuli we allow to filter through is still substantial. Our brains therefore use certain processes to arrange these

Interests—those things that prompt our curiosity but aren't essential to sustain us biologically or psychologically.

Expectations—those things that we notice because we are habituated to noticing them.

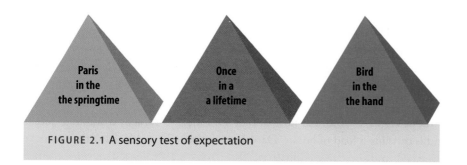

FIGURE 2.1 A sensory test of expectation

Simplification—the organization of stimuli into easily recognizable forms.

Pattern recognition—the organization of stimuli into easily recognizable patterns, or systems of interrelated parts.

stimuli to make sense out of them. Two of the most common processes we use are simplification and pattern recognition.

Simplification is the organization of stimuli into easily recognizable forms. For instance, based on a glance at what a woman is wearing, how she is standing, and the expression on her face, we may simplify the many things we perceive and choose to recognize her as "a successful businesswoman," "a flight attendant," or "a soccer mom." Similarly, we simplify the verbal messages we receive. So, for example, Tony might walk out of an hour-long performance review meeting with his boss, simplifying the many topics discussed into one sentence and plan of action: "If I don't do well on this new project, I'm going to get fired."

Pattern recognition is the organization of stimuli into easily recognizable patterns, or systems of interrelated parts. For example, when you see a crowd of people, instead of perceiving each individual human being, your brain organizes the complex set of stimuli into patterns that are easier to grasp. For instance, you may focus on the characteristic of sex and "see" men and women, or you may focus on age and "see" children, teens, adults, and seniors. Similarly, in our interactions with others, we try to find patterns that will enable us to interpret and respond to their communication behaviors. For example, if each time Jason and Bill encounter Sara, she hurries over and begins an animated conversation, yet when Jason is alone and runs into Sara, she barely says "Hi," Jason may detect a pattern to Sara's behavior. She is warm and friendly when Bill is around and not so friendly when Bill is absent.

▷ Interpretation of Stimuli

As the brain attends to, selects, and organizes the stimuli it receives from the senses, it also interprets the information by assigning meaning to it. Look at the following three sets of numbers. What do you make of them?

    A. 781 631 7348
    B. 285 37 5632
    C. 4632 7364 2596 2174

In each of these sets, your mind looked for clues to give meaning to the numbers. Because you use similar sets of numbers every day, you probably interpreted A as a telephone number. How about B? Likely you interpreted it is a Social Security number. And C? You may have interpreted this set as a credit card number.

Interpreting number patterns often leads to similar conclusions. However, because two people are unlikely to select the same stimuli, or to organize stimuli in the same way in communication situations, they may often arrive at different interpretations in these situations. For instance, suppose Sal and Daniel pass Tito on the way to eat lunch. Even though they both greet him, Tito walks past without saying a word. Sal notices that Tito looks troubled, is walking quickly, and is carrying a load of books. Daniel notices that Tito glanced at them quickly, grimaced, and then averted his eyes. "Boy," says Sal, "I guess Tito must really be worried about the history paper." "You think so?" Daniel replies. "I'd say that he's still angry at me for hitting on Carmen."

◉ Self-Perception: Self-Concept and Self-Esteem

The first component of social perception is **self-perception**, the overall view people have of themselves, of which self-concept and self-esteem are parts. **Self-concept** is our description of our competencies and personality traits (Baron & Byrne, 2003). **Self-esteem** is our evaluation of our competence and personal worthiness (based on Mruk, 2006). In this section we explain how we form our self-concept and our self-esteem, and therefore our overall self-perception. Then we describe what determines how well our self-perception matches others' perceptions of us.

▷ Forming and Maintaining a Self-Concept

When we develop a self-concept, how do we learn what our competencies and personality traits are? Our self-concept comes from the unique interpretations about ourselves that we make based on our experience and from the reactions and responses of others to us.

Experience is critical to forming self-concept. We cannot know if we are competent at certain things until we have experience trying them, and we cannot find out what our personality traits are until we uncover them through experience. This is why we place especially great emphasis on the first experiences we have with particular situations (Centi, 1981). For instance, someone who is rejected in his first try at dating may perceive himself to be unattractive to others. If additional experiences in the same situation produce results similar to the first experience, the initial perception will be strengthened. But even when the first experience is not repeated, it is likely to take more than one contradictory additional experience to change the original perception. On the other hand, when we have a positive first experience, we are likely to believe that we innately possess the competencies and personality traits that we associate with that experience. So if Sonya discovers at an early age that she is good at math and absorbs mathematical concepts easier than other children, she is likely to incorporate "competent mathematician" into her self-concept. If she continues to excel at math throughout her life, that self-concept will be reinforced and maintained.

Self-perception—the overall view people have of themselves, of which self-concept and self-esteem are parts..

Self-concept—our description of our competencies and personality traits.

Self-esteem—our evaluation of our competence and personal worthiness.

How will winning or losing this spelling bee affect these children's self-concepts?

In addition to being formed and maintained by our experiences, our self-concept is shaped by how others react and respond to us (Rayner, 2001, p. 43). We use other people's comments as a check on our descriptions of ourselves. These comments serve to validate, reinforce, or alter our perceptions of who and what we think we are. For example, if during a brainstorming session at work, one of your co-workers tells you, "You're really a creative thinker," you may decide that this comment fits your image of who you are, thus reinforcing your self-concept as someone with a competent sense of creativity. Not all reactions and responses we receive have the same effect on our self-concept, however. Reactions and responses are likely to be more powerful when you respect the person making the comment (Rayner, 2001) or when you are close to the person (Aron, Mashek, & Aron, 2004). This is especially important in families. Since your self-concept begins to form early in life, information you receive from your family deeply shapes your self-concept (Demo, 1987). One of the major responsibilities that family members have, therefore, is to talk and act in ways that will help develop accurate and strong self-concepts in other family members. For example, the mother who says, "Roberto, your room looks very neat; you are very organized," or the brother who comments, "Kisha, lending Tomika five dollars really helped her out; you are very generous," both help their family members to understand or maintain their self-concepts. Unfortunately, in some families members do not fulfill these responsibilities. Sometimes family members can negatively and inaccurately shape self-concept and therefore self-esteem, which is especially harmful to children. Communicating blame, calling names, and repeatedly pointing out another's shortcomings are particularly damaging to self-concept formation and maintenance. On the other extreme, families that provide positive but inaccurate information about the skills and abilities of children also foster inaccurate self-concept formation.

▷ Developing and Maintaining Self-Esteem

You'll recall that self-concept and self-esteem are two different but related components of self-perception. While self-concept is our description of our competencies and personality traits, self-esteem is our positive or negative evaluation of our self-concept. Our evaluation of our personal worthiness is rooted in our values and develops over time as a result of our experiences. Self-esteem is not just how well or poorly we do things (self-concept), but the importance or value we place on what we do well or poorly (Mruk, 2006). For instance, as part of Chad's self-concept, he believes he is an excellent piano player, a thoughtful person, and a faithful friend. But if Chad doesn't believe that these or other competencies and personality traits he possesses are worthwhile or valuable to have, then he will not have high self-esteem. It takes both the perception of having a competency and personality trait and a personal belief that the competency or personality trait is of positive value to produce high self-esteem (Mruk, 2006). When we successfully use our competencies and personality traits in worthwhile endeavors, we raise our self-esteem. When we are unsuccessful in doing so, and/or when we use them in unworthy endeavors, we lower our self-esteem.

It is important to notice that self-esteem depends not only on what each individual views as worthwhile but also on the ideas, morals, and values of the family, group, and society to which the individual belongs. So if Chad comes from a family where athletic success is valued but artistic talents are not, if he hangs out with friends who laugh at his piano playing, and if he lives in a society where rock guitarists, not piano players, are the superstars, then he is unlikely to be proud of his piano-playing ability.

▷ Accuracy of Self-Concept and Self-Esteem

The accuracy of our self-concept and self-esteem depends on the accuracy of our own perceptions and how we process the reactions and responses of others. All of us experience success and failure, and all of us hear praise and criticism. If we are overly attentive to successful experiences and positive responses, our self-concept may become overdeveloped and our self-esteem inflated. If, however, we perceive and dwell on failures and give little value to our successes, or if we remember only the criticism we receive, our self-concept may be underdeveloped and our self-esteem low.

In either case described here, self-concept and self-esteem may suffer from **incongruence**, a situation in which there is a gap between self-perception and reality. Incongruence is a problem because our perceptions of self are more likely to influence our behaviors than our true abilities do (Weiten, 2002). For example, Sean may actually possess all of the competencies and personality traits needed for effective leadership, but if he doesn't perceive that he has these talents and characteristics, he won't step forward in a situation where leadership is needed.

Unfortunately, individuals tend to reinforce their self-perceptions by adjusting their behaviors to conform to them rather than attempting to break free from them. That is, people with high self-esteem behave in ways that lead to more affirmation, whereas people with low self-esteem tend to act in ways that confirm their low esteem. Two important ways in which people rationalize their inaccurate behaviors are engaging in self-fulfilling prophecies and filtering messages.

Self-fulfilling prophecies are events that happen as the result of being foretold, expected, or talked about. They may be self-created or other-imposed.

When self-fulfilling prophecies are self-created, they are the result of "talking ourselves into" success or failure. Researchers have found that when people expect rejection, they are more likely to behave in ways that lead others to reject them (Downey, Freitas, Michaelis, & Khouri, 2004, p. 437). For instance, if Aaron perceives himself as unskilled in establishing new relationships he may say to himself, "I bet I'll know hardly anyone at the party—I'm going to have a miserable time." Because Aaron fears encountering strangers and sees himself as incompetent in this area, he is likely to feel awkward about introducing himself

OBSERVE AND ANALYZE ▽

Who Am I?

Write a short essay on the subject "Who am I?" To begin this task, list all of the competencies and personality traits that you believe describe you. To begin, try completing the following sentences: "I am skilled at . . ."; "I have the ability to . . ."; "I know things about . . ."; "I am competent at doing . . ."; and "One part of my personality is that I am . . ." Do this over and over again. List as many characteristics in each category as you can think of.

Then develop a second list, only this time complete the following statements: "Other people believe that I am skilled at . . ."; "Other people believe that I have the ability to . . ."; "Other people believe that I know things about . . ."; "Other people believe that I am competent at doing . . ."; and "One part of my personality is that other people believe that I am . . ." Again, complete these statements over and over, as many times as you can.

Compare your lists of self-perceptions and others' perceptions. How are they similar? Where are they different? Do you understand why they differ? Are your lists long or short? Why do you suppose that is? Reflect on how your own interpretations of your experiences and what others have told you about you have influenced your self-concept. Now organize the lists you have created, perhaps finding a way to group characteristics. Use this information to write an essay titled "Who I Am, and How I Know This."

Incongruence—situation in which there is a gap between self-perception and reality.

Self-fulfilling prophecies—events that happen as the result of being foretold, expected, or talked about.

"As near as I can understand it, they're my real Mom and Dad."

Filtering messages—perceptional distortions of messages we receive that reinforce what we already think.

to anyone at the party and, just as he predicted, is likely to spend much of his time standing around alone thinking about when he can leave. Self-esteem has an important effect on the prophecies people make. People with high self-esteem view success positively and confidently predict that they can repeat successes; people with low self-esteem attribute their successes to luck and so predict that they will not repeat their successes (Hattie, 1992, p. 253).

The prophecies or predictions others make about you also affect what you do and your self-concept. For example, if the soccer coach tells Javier, a person struggling with low self-esteem, "I don't think you have the scoring abilities to play first string this game," Javier is likely to believe this and will come to act in ways that are consistent with the prediction. Other-created prophecies have a powerful way of changing our self-concepts. For example, when a child hears, "Jump, I know you can do this," the child is likely to try to jump off the side of the pool and, because of the positive prediction, may succeed. But if a child hears, "Be careful, it's dangerous, you could drown," the child will probably not jump and may develop a fear of water that makes it difficult to learn to swim.

A second way that our self-perceptions can become distorted is through **filtering messages**, which are perceptual distortions of messages we receive that reinforce what we already think. We are prone to pay attention to messages that reinforce our current self-concept, while messages that contradict this image may not "register" or may be downplayed in our brains. When self-esteem is low, we may filter out positive messages. For example, suppose you have prepared a fund-raising plan for your service organization and someone comments that you're a good organizer. If you have low self-esteem, you may not really hear the remark, ignore it, or reply, "Anyone could have done that—it was nothing special." This behavior could lead the sender of the message to agree with you. If, however, you have high self-esteem and think you are a good organizer, you are more likely to pay attention to the compliment and may even reinforce it by responding, "Thanks, I've had a lot of experience with organizing fund-raising campaigns and really like being able to contribute."

▷ Cultural and Gender Influences on Self-Perception

It is difficult to generalize about social perception without taking into consideration the influences of culture and gender.

A person's culture has a strong influence on the perception process (Chen & Starosta, 1998). In some cultures, described as individualistic cultures, people stress the self and personal achievement. In these cultures, the individual is treated as the most important element in a social setting. In individualistic cultures, people care about self-concept and self-esteem. The United States is considered an individualistic culture. In fact, all of the information thus far in this chapter reflects an individualistic cultural perspective on perception. On the other hand, cultures that are considered collectivist tend to downplay the individual. Groups and social norms are more important in collectivist cultures. People are expected to be interdependent and to see themselves in terms of the group. Notions of self-concept and self-esteem have little meaning in collectivist cultures.

Similarly, men and women are socialized to view themselves differently and to value who they are based on whether their behavior corresponds to or challenges the behavior expected of their sex in their culture. There are norms of what it means to be feminine and what it means to be masculine in both individualist and collectivist cultures. Gender expectations in a society inevitably influence our perceptions, sense of self, social construction of self, and behavior.

▷ Changing Self-Perception

Self-concept and self-esteem are enduring characteristics of self-perception, but they can be changed. At times, comments that contradict self-fulfilling prophecies will get past the filter and a person can begin to change his or her self-perceptions. Then, the newly changed self-perceptions begin to filter other comments and are used as the basis of new self-fulfilling prophecies. So over the course of your life, your self-concept and self-esteem may change.

Certain situations seem to lend themselves to expediting this process. When people experience profound changes in their social environments they are likely to drop their filters and absorb information that in other circumstances they would have filtered out. Life transitions are times when we become more susceptible to dropping our filters. For instance, when children begin school, when teens begin the independence process, when young adults leave home, and when people start new jobs or begin college, fall in love, commit to or dissolve relationships, become parents, retire, and grieve the death of someone they love, they are more likely to attend to messages that are at odds with their current self-perception. As a result of these new experiences, people change their picture of who they are and begin to predict new things for themselves.

The use of therapy and self-help techniques can assist in the goal of changing one's self-concept and improving one's self-esteem. Numerous research studies have shown that self-esteem is increased through hard work and practice (Mruk, 2006). So why is it important to work on improving the accuracy of your self-concept and raising your self-esteem? Because an accurate self-concept allows you to really know who you are and what you have to offer others with whom you form relationships. Likewise, your self-esteem affects whom you choose to relate to. Research has reported that "people with high self-esteem are more committed to partners who perceive them very favorably, while people with low self-esteem are more committed to partners who perceive them less favorably" (Leary, 2002, p. 130). Imagine how difficult it is for two low self-esteem individuals to maintain a healthy and satisfying relationship.

❖ The Effects of Self-Perception on Communication

Your self-perception influences your communication in a variety of ways. It influences how you talk to yourself, how you talk about yourself with others, how you talk about others to yourself, and how you communicate with others.

▷ Self-Perception Influences How You Talk to Yourself

Self-talk is communicating with yourself through your thoughts. For example, when you think to yourself, "I handled that situation well," you are self-talking. If we feel good about ourselves, that is, if we have positive self-esteem, then our self-talk is likely to be more accurate. If we have negative self-esteem, then our self-talk is likely to be distorted and negative. In addition, people with positive self-esteem generally are better able to monitor accurately how they come across in a situation. They can be more realistic about what they are doing well and about what they are not doing well. People with negative self-esteem often overemphasize negative self-talk or, ironically, may inflate their sense of self. In other words, to compensate for a sense of insecurity they may tell themselves they are good at everything they do, thus showing an inability to talk to themselves accurately.

▷ Self-Perception Influences How You Talk about Yourself with Others

Just as our self-perception influences how we talk with ourselves, it also affects how we talk about ourselves with others. If we have positive self-perception, we are likely to communicate that we like ourselves and take credit for our successes. If we feel bad about ourselves, or have negative self-perception, we are likely to communicate negatively by downplaying our accomplishments. Why do some people put themselves down regardless of what they have done? People who have low self-esteem are likely to be unsure of the value of their contributions and to expect others to view them negatively. As a result, perhaps, people with a poor self-concept or low self-esteem find it less painful to put themselves down than to hear the criticism of others. Thus, to preempt the likelihood that others will comment on their unworthiness, they do it first.

Some research suggests that the Internet can influence how we communicate about ourselves with others in unique ways. Some Internet discussion groups, for example, are designed to be online journals in which the user engages in reflection and introspection. These users are actually communicating with themselves while imagining a reader. On the Internet, people can be more aware of themselves and less aware of the people to whom they are talking (Shedletsky &

Self-talk—communicating with yourself through your thoughts.

Aitken, 2004, p. 132). Such pervasive opportunities to engage in self-perception influence how we communicate with others.

▷ Self-Perception Affects How You Talk about Others with Yourself

Self-concept and self-esteem are important not only because of the way they moderate our self-talk but also because they affect how we talk about others with ourselves. First, the more accurate our self-perception, the more accurately we are likely to perceive others. Both self-perception and perception of others start with our ability to process data accurately. Second, the higher our self-esteem, the more likely we are to see others favorably. Studies have shown that people who accept themselves as they are tend to be more accepting of others; similarly, those with low self-esteem are more likely to find fault in others. Third, our own personal characteristics influence the types of characteristics we are likely to perceive in others. For example, people who are secure tend to see others as equally secure. If you recall that we respond to the world as we perceive it to be (and not necessarily as it is), you can readily see how low self-esteem can account for misunderstandings and communication breakdowns.

▷ Self-Perception Influences How You Communicate with Others

Research demonstrates that we communicate our self-concept and self-esteem when we interact with others (Campbell, 1990, p. 538). Not only will our self-perception influence what we say about ourselves, but it will also affect whether and how we offer our opinions and how vigorously we defend our positions when they conflict with the positions of others. People with rich self-concepts are more likely to share their ideas in areas in which they believe they have competence. People with high self-esteem are likely to defend their positions during conflict since they value themselves and expect others to value them as well. When people have impoverished self-concepts they are less likely to share their ideas since they can't be sure that their ideas are good ones. People with low self-esteem are less likely to engage in behaviors that will lead to successful conflict resolution.

◗ Presenting Self to Others: The Social Construction of Self

Our self-concept and self-esteem are our "true" perceptions as far as we are concerned, whether accurate or not. But when we interact with others, we often present just the parts of ourselves that we think are appropriate to the situation. In these social interactions we construct or create different "selves" to present in different situations and with different people. We also analyze how we come across to others so that we can adjust these socially constructed selves to the changing needs of the situation. And we go to great lengths to present ourselves

We present our self-image and self-esteem to others through the roles we enact.

in ways that shape the impressions that others get of us. In other words, the "self" a person presents to others is not the totality of who a person is but rather who he believes he needs to be in a particular situation. We socially construct who we are in a situation through three processes: role taking, self-monitoring, and impression management.

▷ Role Taking

One of the processes we use as we construct a social self is **role taking**, which is the process of meeting the perceived demands of the communication situation by adopting a role comprised of an expected or appropriate set of behaviors. Typically we decide what roles we want to take and what persona we want to affect in a certain situation or relationship. As a result, we present differing personas in response to different situations and relationships, and we change ourselves in the process. For instance, think of your behavior when you are enacting the role of "sibling" while talking with your sister or "sales associate" at your job. How does what you say and do differ in these contexts from what you say and do when you are interacting with your classmates during a study group meeting?

To get a better idea of what role taking is, let's look at all the different personas or selves that one person adopted over a few days. As a restaurant server, Keiko is very polite, helpful, agreeable, and attentive to others. She does not talk about herself much or use profanity. She is confident, moves quickly, and cares

Role taking—the process of meeting the perceived demands of the communication situation by adopting a role comprised of an expected or appropriate set of behaviors.

about being efficient and productive. When Keiko goes out with her friends after work, she is more casual and less concerned about time. She is louder and more boisterous, talks about herself more, curses occasionally, and gets into heated debates about issues and ideas. When Keiko visits her grandmother, she behaves in a more reserved and polite manner. She listens attentively, answers quietly, and works hard to show her grandmother the honor that is due to an older relative. Online, Keiko may present a party-girl image through a personal profile, photos, and listings of favorite activities. Or she may assume totally different identities through avatars in multiplayer games. Keiko will enact other selves at school, when she babysits her five-year-old niece, when she goes on a date, or when she meets with her tennis partner. Which is Keiko's real self? They all are, because she constructs "self" via her social interactions.

Today many people experiment with their identities online. Do you have a MySpace or Facebook page? Think of the time and effort you spent creating that "self." Does it accurately reflect all of who you are? Did you pick and choose what you would present to those who would view your page? The Internet allows you to experiment with a wide variety of roles. Some users experiment with gender and age switching or pretend to have a different job. The ethics of intentionally misrepresenting oneself in cyberspace is problematic, since the people with whom one interacts have no way to independently access the accuracy of the persona. However, it is a fact of the online environment. And in face-to-face interactions we often do the same thing. We choose what parts of ourselves we allow others to see not only through what we talk about but also through how we behave, and we alter who we are to fit the situation and the relationship.

OBSERVE AND ANALYZE ⊙

What Roles Do I Take?

List all the roles that you take in your face-to-face interactions with others during one week. Also, list all of the roles that you take in online interaction with others during one week. How are these roles similar and different from each other? Which roles positively affect your self-esteem? Which roles negatively affect your self-esteem? How do these different identities shape you as a whole person? Are the face-to-face and online roles you play seen as part of or as separate from your sense of self?

▷ Self-Monitoring

Another process we practice when we communicate with others is **self-monitoring**, the internal process of being aware of yourself and how you are coming across to others when you communicate with them. To determine whether the roles and behaviors we enact in various situations are appropriate or not, we analyze how we are presenting ourselves and how others are responding to us. Self-monitoring involves being sensitive to other people's expressions and reactions (feedback) and using this information in deciding how to adjust your behavior and the "self" you are presenting. In other words, it is a process of observing, analyzing, and regulating your own behavior in relation to the responses of others. Think of the times when you consciously monitored how you were coming across in a situation. If you have ever been in an unfamiliar situation and made a flip remark that was met with disapproval, you may have said to yourself, "Wow, that was a stupid thing to say! Let me see if I can fix it." Then, based on this self-monitoring, you are able to make a repair to your presentation of self.

People differ in when and how carefully they self-monitor. Some people are very cautious and are always vigilant in monitoring the situations and relationships

Self-monitoring—the internal process of being aware of yourself and how you are coming across to others when you communicate with them.

with which they are faced. Other people will be careful to self-monitor in what they perceive to be "risky" or new situations but will be less attentive in situations or relationships that they perceive as safer. A few people seem unable to self-monitor. As a result, they tend to frequently say and do the wrong things because they are not paying attention to how they are coming across. You may know someone who seems to always say the wrong thing or act inappropriately.

Most of us are aware of the need to self-monitor when we are in a new relationship or an unfamiliar situation. Because we are not sure of how to act in an unfamiliar situation, there is more uncertainty felt and more analysis that needs to be made regarding how to present ourselves. When we are communicating in an unfamiliar situation, we may be saying to ourselves things like, "Why did I make that silly remark?," or "I'm not coming across well here," or "I think he liked that comment I just made." Even in familiar and comfortable situations, skilled communicators do some self-monitoring. Being self-aware and attentive to others' feedback is part of the important skill of behavioral flexibility, which we described in Chapter 1 as necessary to all communication interactions.

▷ Impression Management

In addition to role taking and self-monitoring when communicating with others, we also engage in **impression management**, the process of consciously trying to influence what others are thinking about us during an interaction.

Impression management—the process of consciously trying to influence what others are thinking about us during an interaction.

Think of all the times you have carefully selected certain clothes, rehearsed in your mind what you were going to say in an upcoming encounter, and purposefully acted a certain way to make a good first impression on someone. Then think of how you continued to manage the other person's impressions while you spoke with him or her. People practice impression management in all communication situations, but the process is especially important during initial encounters such as a job interview, a first date, the first day on a new job, a court appearance, or an initial visit to a professor's office. In trying to make a good first impression and managing that impression further, we are paying close attention to the role we are taking and the image we are projecting. First impressions are based not only on how we appear and what we say but also on the perceptions others form about us. So impression management is not a one-way process. Neither party has total control over first or subsequent impressions; instead, the parties interact as sender and receiver to construct impressions jointly.

Researchers have found that first impressions are especially powerful because they often form the basis of whether two people will ever interact again (Hazen & Shaver, 2004). For example, if the first time two people meet is a brief conversation about tabloid headlines while waiting in line at the grocery store, there is no reason to think that they necessarily would have to interact again. In this case, any possible future relationship depends heavily on the first impressions they form of each other—whether the pair discovered any common ground or developed any liking for each other. As the saying goes, you never get a second chance to make a good first impression. Evaluations formed during initial conversations have been found to influence long-term impressions of close relationships (Sunnafrank & Ramirez, 2004, p. 49). This means that even if you have known someone for years, the first impressions that you had of each other still influence the current relationship.

Impressions are formed not only in face-to-face communications but also in online interactions. Creating an individual profile for a social networking site and then adding to or altering it later is an exercise in impression management. By describing yourself and your interests, uploading photos of yourself, and writing daily journal entries, you are shaping others' impressions of you. People care about creating the right impressions online through the timeliness of their responses, their use of chat room nicknames, and their use of appropriate vocabulary, grammar, and manners (sometimes called netiquette). Initial interaction online often begins with the answer to the "ASL" question: age, sex, and location. This is a getting-to-know-you question, which allows for cultural-level predictions and the forming of a first impression. Creating personal home pages also relates to self-identity and first impressions. Creating a personal home page is an opportunity to reflect upon yourself and to think about how you want to represent yourself to the world. It is an attempt to influence others' impressions (Thurlow, Lengel, & Tomic, 2004).

Michael Hecht and his colleagues believe that we develop identity through our communications with others, including role taking, self-monitoring, and impression management. Hecht's "communication theory of identity" suggests that there are four different aspects of identity that we work out in our transactions and relationships with oth-

What are the individuals in this photograph communicating through their physical appearance, dress, and behavior?

ers. See the "Spotlight on Scholars" feature on pages 46–47 to learn more about Hecht's communication theory of identity and how it adds to our understanding of how we communicate with others.

❍ Perception of Others

We now move from self-perception and how that affects communication to our perception of others. As you encounter others, you are faced with a number of questions: Do you have anything in common? Will they accept you? Will you be able to get along? A major perceptual goal in interacting with others is discovering what we have in common with others so that we can reduce uncertainty and feel more comfortable with them. Also, when perceiving others we tend to take shortcuts that lead to perceptual inaccuracies. In this section we will discuss the

Michael L. Hecht

Professor of Speech Communication, Head of the Department of Speech Communication, College of Arts and Sciences, Pennsylvania State University, on

Interethnic Communication and Ethnic Identity

Michael L. Hecht's passion is people. His native curiosity has led him to devote his life to scholarly endeavors that help us to understand how people from different ethnic backgrounds communicate with others in ways that they perceive are satisfying and effective, as well as how that information can be used to impact their lives. When he was in graduate school, many scholars were interested in studying ineffective communication. But Hecht, an optimist, was more interested in understanding what led people to feel satisfied with a conversation. For his Ph.D. dissertation at the University of Illinois, Hecht developed a theory to help us understand and to measure communication satisfaction. His theory and measures are widely used today. But Hecht's contribution to our understanding of communication satisfaction and effectiveness did not end when he received his degree. Instead, it provided the foundation from which he continues to explore what leads people to be effective and satisfied with their conversations.

As a Jewish American growing up in a tightly knit ethnic community, Hecht has always been interested in intergroup communication from an ethnic perspective. His earliest work in this area examined perceptions of conversational satisfaction in conversations between African Americans and European Americans. After graduate school, Hecht teamed up with a grad school contemporary and friend, Sidney Ribeau (who is now president of Howard University), to continue to study communication satisfaction between African Americans and European Americans. At that time, communication satisfaction had been studied only from a European American perspective. Hecht and Ribeau discovered that African Americans and European Americans abide by different communication rules. Thus, when African Americans and European Americans interact, one party is likely to violate the communication rules expected by the other. These rule violations make conversations between people from these two groups less likely to be perceived as satisfying.

Hecht is also fascinated with how people form and communicate their personal identities. Recently, he formulated the communication theory of identity. The basic premise of this theory is that identity is a communicative process. Hecht and his co-authors believe that there are four different "frames" or perspectives from which we can understand identity: the personal frame, the enactment frame, the relational frame, and the communal frame. The personal frame suggests that identity is based on self-concept derived from feelings, self-knowledge, or spiritual sense of self. The enactment frame indicates that we consciously and unconsciously communicate our identity to others when we interact with them—we act out who we are as we talk. The relational frame demonstrates that we negotiate identity within a particular relationship context. For instance, we may interact differently in a relationship in which we are the parent than in a relationship in which we are the child. The relational perspective also allows us to notice how relationships take on identities themselves. For instance, when people get married they often find that others see them as part of a couple rather than as separate individuals, and they may see themselves this way too. Finally, the communal frame indicates that people gain identity through the groups that bond them to others. These communities develop certain behaviors that they teach to new members and expect members to enact. Hecht and his colleagues suggest that if we want to understand identity, we must look at all four frames in combination. I work out who I am (personal frame) by trying out certain behaviors as I interact (enactment frame) with others (relational frame), and, in part, how I act is based on the behavior that is expected of members of those groups to which I see myself belonging (communal frame).

Recently, Hecht's research has combined his interest in understanding identity theory with a desire to use his research to help others. Hecht has worked with an interdisciplinary team to identify strategies (refuse, explain, avoid, and leave) that teens use to resist invitations to use drugs. An educational program using these strategies was developed for groups of ethnically diverse junior high students. Early results suggest that this approach is slowing the rate at which students begin using drugs. In addition, the study has provided evidence that Latino American and African American teens who are proud of their ethnic identity are less prone to drug use. This finding is in keeping with the communication theory of identity.

Although it is common for faculty to invite graduate students to work with them on projects, Hecht finds doing research with undergraduate students to be especially rewarding. Hecht has created undergraduate research apprenticeship programs. In the program, undergraduates receive classroom credit for becoming part of research teams. Some students make sub-stantial contributions to projects and are invited to co-author scholarly articles.

Michael Hecht is currently serving as the head of the Department of Speech Communication at The Pennsylvania State University. Since his drug resistance studies are financed by large grants from outside agen-cies to whom he must account and report, Hecht finds himself doing more administrative work these days. Nonetheless, Professor Hecht still finds time for his first love, teaching courses in interpersonal and non-verbal communication at the undergraduate level and courses in identity and intergroup communication at the graduate level.

ways that we reduce uncertainty when perceiving others and the ways in which we may be inaccurate in our perceptions of others.

▷ Reducing Uncertainty

Because uncertainty in social situations is uncomfortable, we naturally try to al-leviate it by finding answers to questions about other people. Charles Berger and James Bradac (1982) coined the term **uncertainty reduction theory**, a theory that explains the ways in which individuals monitor their social environments in order to know more about themselves and others (Littlejohn & Foss, 2005). In other words, people seek information to reduce uncertainty—especially during initial encounters with others—so that they can become more comfortable in their communications (Guerrero, Andersen, & Afifi, 2007).

We seek information about others because if we are uncertain about what they are like, we will have a difficult time predicting their behaviors and the outcome of our interactions with them, and this leads to discomfort. When we experience uncertainty we work to reduce it based on our knowledge. We use the cultural, sociological, and psychological information we have available to aid us in perceiving others and in reducing our uncertainty about them (Miller & Steinberg, 1975).

When we first meet someone, we don't have much available information to help us make predictions about him or her. So we tend to make so-called cultural-level predictions about the person based on what we can see. We make such predictions based on stereotypes of race, sex, age, and appearance. Because these predictions are broad generalizations based on very abstract and general informa-tion, they frequently tend to be inaccurate, so we need to interact with the person further to move to a greater level of certainty that is not based on stereotypes.

As we do so, we tend to ask questions about the groups to which the person be-longs. Getting-to-know-you conversations often involve a series of questions about occupations, education, places of residence, hobbies, and interests. This questioning allows us to make less stereotypical and more sociological-level predictions based on the other person's membership groups. Answers to these questions allow us to discover common ground, thus easing our discomfort and allowing us to make more accurate predictions about how the other is likely to act. Increasingly, people are using the Internet as a way of getting to know others at a sociological level. It's

Uncertainty reduction theory— a theory that explains the ways in which individuals monitor their social environments in order to know more about themselves and others.

not uncommon today for people to research new acquaintances by searching the web using Google or other search engines. It's even socially acceptable to admit that we've been researching our acquaintances, classmates, and potential romantic partners (Engdahl, 2007).

Sociological-level knowledge of others is still limited and based on stereotypes, however, so over time, as we come to know another person better, we refine our predictions based on the unique experiences and qualities of that person, rather than on appearance or group memberships. Eventually, we come to know with a great deal of accuracy, though never with total accuracy, how this unique person may respond in a situation. This last level of prediction is called the psychological level, and because it is based on individual differences among people rather than generalizations across large groups of people, it is the most accurate level of prediction. When we reach this level with a person, we feel closer to and more comfortable with that person.

▷ Perceptual Inaccuracies

As we work to reduce uncertainty during the communication process with others by moving from the cultural level of perception to the psychological level, we also must be careful to reduce perceptual inaccuracies. Because perception is a complex process, we use shortcuts to help us focus attention, interpret information, and make predictions about others. Implicit personality theories, halo effects, selective perceptions, faulty attributions, forced consistency, and prejudice are shortcuts that lead to perceptual inaccuracies.

Implicit personality theories are inaccurate perceptions of others based on the association of physical characteristics or other characteristics with personality traits (Michener & DeLamater, 2004). We are often guilty of making these associations. For instance, many assume that all heavy-set people are jolly, that all people with glasses are bookish, or that women are nurturing. However, none of these assumptions are accurate. There is no rule that says people who are heavy-set can't be quiet and restrained, that people who wear glasses can't be athletic and sociable, or that women can't be independent and ambitious.

In addition to inaccurately associating physical characteristics with personality traits, we may also inaccurately associate personality traits with other personality traits. The **halo effect** is inaccurately perceiving that a person has a whole set of related personality traits when only one trait has actually been observed. For instance, Heather sees Martina personally greeting and welcoming every person who arrives at a meeting. Heather views this behavior as a sign of warmth. She further associates warmth with generosity and generosity with honesty. As a result, she perceives that Martina is warm, generous, and honest. In reality, Martina has demonstrated only the trait of warmth. Martina has not demonstrated whether she is the slightest bit generous or honest. She may be both of these things, but there is no evidence of this. This example demonstrates a "positive halo" (Heather assigned Martina a string of positive traits based on witnessing

Implicit personality theories—inaccurate perceptions of others based on the association of physical or other characteristics with personality traits.

Halo effect—inaccurately perceiving that a person has a whole set of related personality traits when only one trait has actually been observed.

only one trait). We also, however, are often prone to inaccurately attributing bad traits to people based on witnessing a single trait. In fact, negative information more strongly influences our impressions of others than positive information does (Hollman, 1972). So we are more likely to give others negative halos than positive halos.

Halo effects seem to occur most frequently under one or more of three conditions: (1) when the perceiver is judging traits with which he or she has limited experience, (2) when the traits have strong moral overtones, and (3) when the perception is of a person that the perceiver knows well.

Selective perception is the perceptual distortion that arises from paying attention only to what we expect to see or hear and from ignoring what we don't expect. Recall Figure 2.1 at the beginning of this chapter. Because we do not expect to read a line like "Paris in the the springtime," we do not pay attention to the repeated word. As another example, have you ever had the experience of buying a new type of car and then seeing that brand of car quite frequently on the road? Those cars were on the road before your purchase, but you were not noticing them. This is a classic example of selective perception. Sometimes we engage in selective perceptions of other people. For instance, if Donna sees Nick as a man with whom she would like to develop a strong relationship, she will tend to see the positive side of Nick's personality and overlook or ignore the negative side that is apparent to others. Similarly, if Dean thinks that his landlord is mean and unfair, he will ignore or disregard any acts of kindness or generosity by the landlord.

Faulty attributions are inaccurate reasons we give for our own and others' behavior. We often attempt to construct, or attribute, reasons for why people behave as they do. What we attribute—rightly or wrongly—to be the causes of others' behavior has a direct impact on our perceptions of them. For instance, suppose a co-worker with whom you had a noon lunch date has not arrived by 12:20. If you like and respect your co-worker, you are likely to attribute his negative behavior (lateness) to something external: an important phone call at the last minute, the need to finish a job before lunch, or an accident that may have occurred. This is known as **situational attribution**, attributing behavior to an external situation, outside of a person's control. If you are not particularly fond of your co-worker, you are likely to attribute his lateness to something internal: forgetfulness, inconsiderateness, or malicious intent. This is known as **dispositional attribution**, attributing behavior to someone's internal disposition, or personality. In either case, your attribution affects your perception of the person. Faulty attributions may be so strong that they resist contrary evidence. If you do not particularly care for the person, when he does arrive and explains that he had an emergency long-distance phone call, you are likely to disbelieve the reason or discount the urgency of the call.

Forced consistency is the inaccurate attempt to make several of our perceptions of another person agree with each other. It arises from the need people

Selective perception—perceptual distortion that arises from paying attention only to what we expect to see or hear and ignoring what we don't expect.

Faulty attributions—inaccurate reasons we give for our own and others' behavior.

Situational attribution—attributing behavior to an external situation, outside of a person's control.

Dispositional attribution—attributing behavior to someone's internal disposition, or personality.

Forced consistency—the inaccurate attempt to make several of our perceptions of another person agree with each other.

Prejudice—a form of selective perception where the characteristics of a group to which the person belongs are ascribed to the person without regard to how the person may vary from the group characteristic.

Discrimination—acting differently toward a person based on prejudice.

have to eliminate contradictions in their perceptions of a phenomenon. In the context of a communication situation, imagine that Leah does not like Jill, the office assistant at the car dealership where they both work. If Jill supplies some missing information on a form that Leah has given her to process, Leah is likely to perceive Jill's behavior as interference, even if Jill's intention was to be helpful. If Leah likes Jill, however, she would likely perceive the very same behavior as helpful—even if Jill's intention was to interfere. In each case, the perception of "supplying missing information" is shaped by the need for consistency. It is consistent to regard someone we like as doing favors for us. It is inconsistent to regard people we don't like as doing favors for us. However, consistent perceptions of others are not necessarily accurate.

Selectively perceiving a person based on the characteristics of a group to which the person belongs without regard to how the person may vary from the group characteristic is called **prejudice** (Jones, 2002). Prejudice can lead to **discrimination**, which is acting differently toward a person based on prejudice (Jones, 2002). Prejudice deals with perception and attitudes, while discrimination involves actions. For instance, when Laura meets Wasif and learns that he is Muslim, she may use her knowledge of women's roles in Islamic countries to inform her perception of Wasif and conclude that he is a chauvinist without really talking to him. This is prejudice. If based on this prejudice she refuses to be in a class project group with him she would be discriminating. Although he is Muslim and was born in Iraq, Wasif may be a feminist, but Laura's use of the perceptual shortcut may prevent her from getting to know Wasif for the person he really is, and she may have cost herself the opportunity of working with the best student in class.

Racism, ethnocentrism, sexism, heterosexism, ageism, and **able-ism** are various form of prejudice, in which members of one group believe that the behaviors and characteristics of their group are inherently superior to those of another group. All people can be prejudiced and act on their prejudices by discriminating against others. Nevertheless, "prejudices of groups with power are farther reaching in their consequences than others" (Sampson, 1999, p. 131). Because such attitudes can be deeply ingrained and are often subtle, it is easy to overlook behaviors we engage in that in some way meet this definition. Prejudicial perceptions may be unintentional, or they may seem insignificant or innocuous, but even seemingly unimportant prejudices rob others of their humanity and severely impede accurate communication.

Have you ever discriminated against a homeless person? How?

◌ Improving the Accuracy of Your Social Perception

Improving perceptual accuracy is an important first step in becoming a competent communicator. The following guidelines can aid you in constructing a more realistic impression of others, as well as in assessing the validity of your own perceptions.

1. Question the accuracy of your perceptions. Questioning accuracy begins by saying, "I know what I think I saw, heard, tasted, smelled, or felt, but I could be wrong. What other information should I be aware of?" By accepting the possibility that you have overlooked something, you will become interested in increasing your accuracy. In situations where the accuracy of perception is important, take a few seconds to double-check. It will be worth the effort.

Racism, ethnocentrism, sexism, heterosexism, ageism, able-ism—various forms of prejudice, in which members of one group believe that the behaviors or characteristics of their group are inherently superior to those of another group.

LEARN ABOUT YOURSELF ◌

Take this short survey to learn something about yourself. Answer the questions based on your first response. There are no right or wrong answers. Just be honest in reporting your true attitudes. For each question, select one of the following numbers that best corresponds to your opinion:

1 = Strongly Agree
2 = Agree Somewhat
3 = Neutral
4 = Disagree Somewhat
5 = Strongly Disagree

_____ **1.** My country should be the role model for the world.
_____ **2.** Most other countries are backward compared to mine.
_____ **3.** People in my country have the best customs of anywhere.
_____ **4.** People in other cultures could learn a lot from my culture.
_____ **5.** Other cultures should try to be more like my culture.
_____ **6.** I respect the customs and values of other cultures.
_____ **7.** I am interested in the customs and values of other cultures.
_____ **8.** Each culture should preserve its uniqueness.
_____ **9.** People from my culture act strange when they go to other cultures.
_____ **10.** Although different, the values of other countries are as valid as ours.

Scoring the Survey:

Add scores for questions 1, 2, 3, 4, and 5   Total 1: _____
Add scores for questions 6, 7, 8, 9, and 10   Total 2: _____

This is a test of ethnocentrism, the tendency to use your own cultural standards when perceiving people from different cultures. Each score for Total 1 and Total 2 separately can range from 5 to 25. The lower (closer to 5) your score on Total 1, the more you are exhibiting ethnocentrism. The higher (closer to 25) your score on Total 2, the more you are exhibiting ethnocentrism.

Adapted from: Neuliep, J. W., & McCroskey, J. C. (1997). The development of a U.S. and generalized ethnocentrism scale. *Communication Research Reports, 14,* 385–398.

2. Seek more information to verify perceptions. If your perception has been based on only one or two pieces of information, try to collect further information so that your perceptions are better grounded. Note that your perception is tentative—that is, subject to change. The best way to get additional information about people is to talk with them. It's OK to be unsure about how to treat someone from another group. But rather than letting your uncertainty cause you to make mistakes, talk with the person and ask for the information you need to become more comfortable.

3. Try to get to the psychological level of predictions. Remember that the cultural and sociological levels of predictions lead to the least accurate perceptions. By getting to know each person as a unique individual, you will increase the accuracy of your perceptions and predictions.

4. Realize that your perceptions of a person will change over time. People often base their behavior on perceptions that are old or based on incomplete information. So when you encounter someone you haven't seen for a while, you will want to become reacquainted and let the person's current behavior rather than past actions or reputation inform your perceptions. A former classmate who was "wild" in high school may well have changed and become a mature, responsible adult.

5. Use the skill of perception checking to verify your impressions. A **perception check** is sharing your perception of another's behavior to see if your interpretation is accurate. It is a process of describing what you have seen and heard and asking for feedback from the other person. By doing a perception check, you can verify or adjust the predictions you make about others. Perception checking calls for you to watch the behavior of the other person and ask yourself, "What does that behavior mean to me?" Then you are ready to describe the behavior and put your interpretation into words to verify your perception.

The following examples illustrate the use of perception checking. In each of the examples, the final spoken sentence is a perception check. Notice that body language sometimes provides the perceptual information that needs to be checked, whereas at other times the tone of voice provides this information. Also notice that the perception-checking statements do not express approval or disapproval of what is being received—they are purely descriptive statements of the perceptions.

> Valerie walks into the room with a completely blank expression. She neither speaks to Ann nor acknowledges that Ann is even in the room. Valerie sits down on the edge of the bed and stares into space. Ann says, "Valerie, did something happen? You look like you're in a state of shock. Am I right? Is there something I can do?"
>
> While Marsha is telling Jenny about the difficulty of her midterm chemistry exam, she notices Jenny smiling. She says to Jenny, "You're smiling. I'm not sure how to interpret that. What's up?" Jenny may respond that she's smiling because the story reminded her of something funny or because she had the same chemistry teacher last year and he purposely gave an extremely difficult midterm to motivate students, but then he graded them on a favorable curve.

Perception check—sharing your perception of another's behavior to see if your interpretation is accurate.

Cesar, speaking in short, precise sentences with a sharp tone of voice, gives Bill his day's assignment. Bill says, "From the sound of your voice, Cesar, I get the impression that you're upset with me. Are you?"

When we use the skill of perception checking, we encode the meaning that we have perceived from someone's behavior and feed it back so that it can be verified or corrected. For instance, when Bill says, "I get the impression that you're upset with me. Are you?" Cesar may say: (1) "No. Whatever gave you that impression?" in which case Bill can further describe the cues that he received; (2) "Yes, I am," in which case Bill can get Cesar to specify what has caused the feelings; or (3) "No, it's not you; it's just that three of my team members didn't show up for this shift." If Cesar is not upset with him, Bill can examine what caused him to misinterpret Cesar's feelings; if Cesar is upset with him, Bill has the opportunity to change the behavior that caused Cesar to be upset.

To see what might happen when we respond without checking the accuracy of our perceptions, suppose that in place of the descriptive perception check, Bill had said to Cesar, "Why are you so upset with me?" Rather than describing his perception, Bill has made a judgment based on the perception. Replying as if his perception were "obviously" accurate would have amounted to mind reading.

You should check your perceptions whenever the accuracy of your understanding is important (1) to your current communication, (2) to the relationship you have with the other person, or (3) to the conclusions you draw about that person. Perception checking is especially important in new relationships or when you haven't talked with someone for a long time.

How might the woman in this photo use perception checking?

○ Summary

Social perception is a set of processes by which people perceive themselves and others. Perception is the process of selectively attending to information that we receive through our senses and assigning meaning to it. Our perceptions are a result of our selection, organization, and interpretation of stimuli.

Self-perception is the overall view people have of themselves and consists of self-concept and self-esteem. Self-concept is our description of our competencies and personality traits. Self-esteem is our evaluation of our competence and personal worthiness. Self-concepts are interpretations of self based on our experience and the reactions and responses of others to us. Self-esteem develops in the same way, but it is also based on the worth an individual places on self-concepts. Our self-concept and self-esteem can be impeded by self-fulfilling prophecies and filtering messages. Cultural and gender expectations influence our perceptions as well.

Self-perception influences communication in that it affects how we talk to ourselves, how we talk about ourselves to others, how we talk about others to ourselves, and how we communicate with others.

In presenting ourselves to others, we create multiple selves based on the different roles we play in various situations. We also use self-monitoring to observe others' reactions to us and to adjust our behavior to fit the situation. And we engage in impression management to influence the impressions that others have of us.

In perceiving others, we uncover information about them so we can find areas of commonality and reduce uncertainty. To reduce uncertainty, we should try to move from the cultural level of prediction through the sociological level and finally to the psychological level, the most accurate level of prediction. Sometimes the shortcuts we take in perception, such as relying on implicit personality assumptions, the halo effect, selective perception, faulty attributions, forced consistency, and prejudices, lead to distortions or inaccuracies in perceiving others.

SKILL BUILDERS ○ **Perception Checking**

SKILL	USE	PROCEDURE	EXAMPLE
A statement that expresses the meaning you get from the behavior of another	To clarify the accuracy of our perceptions of another person's behavior	1. Watch the behavior of another. 2. Ask yourself: What does that behavior mean to me? 3. Describe the behavior (to yourself or aloud) and put your interpretation of the nonverbal behavior into words to verify your perception.	As Dale frowns while reading Paul's first draft of a memo, Paul says, "From the way you're frowning, I take it that you're not too pleased with the way I phrased the memo."

You can learn to improve social perception if you question the accuracy of your perceptions, seek more information to verify perceptions, try to get to the psychological level of prediction, realize that perceptions of people need to change over time, and use the skill of perception checking to verify your impressions.

A QUESTION OF ETHICS ● What Would You Do?

Rustown is a small Midwestern factory town. Over the years the white, middle-class citizens have grown together to form a close-knit community that prides itself on its unity. Corpex, a large out-of-town corporation, which had just bought out the town's major factory, recently decided to move its headquarters there and to expand the current plant, creating hundreds of new jobs. This expansion meant that the new people coming into the town to manage and work in the factory would spend money and build homes, but also it meant that the composition of the small community would change.

Rustown inhabitants had mixed reactions to this takeover. The owners of land and shops were excited by the increased business that was expected, but many in the community recognized that since most people in town had been born and raised there, the inhabitants of Rustown were pretty much alike—and they liked it that way. They knew that many of the new factory managers as well as some of the new employees were African and Latin Americans. Rustown had never had a black or Latino family, and some of the townspeople openly worried about the effects the newcomers would have on their community.

Otis Carr was one of the Corpex managers who had agreed to move to Rustown because of the opportunities that appeared to await him and his family, even though he recognized that as a black man he might experience resentment. At work on the first day, Otis noticed that the workers seemed very leery of him. By the end of the first week, however, the plant was running smoothly and Otis was feeling the first signs of acceptance. On Monday morning of the next week, however, he accidentally overheard a group of workers talking on their break, trading stereotypes about African Americans and Latinos and using vulgarities and racist slurs in discussing specific new co-workers.

A bit shaken, Otis returned to his office. He had faced racism before, but this time it was different. This time he had power and the responsibility to make a difference. He wanted to reach his workers for the sake of the company, the town, and other minority group members who would be coming to Rustown. Although he knew he had to do something, he realized that just using his power would get him nowhere. He understood the prejudices, but not how to change them.

Devise a plan for Otis.

1. How can he reach his workers?
2. How can he use his own social perceptions of Rustown to address this problem in a way that is within ethical interpersonal communication guidelines?

● Chapter Resources

Communication Improvement Plan: Perception ● Find more on the web @ www.oup.com/us/interact12

Would you like to improve your use of the following aspects of forming and using social perception discussed in this chapter?

- Forming self-concepts
- Developing and maintaining self-esteem
- Presenting self
- Perception checking

Pick one of these categories, and write a communication improvement plan. You can find a communication improvement plan worksheet on our website at www.oup.com/us/interact12.

Key Words ▼

Skill Practice ▼ Find more on the web @ www.oup.com/us/interact12

Skill Practice exercises challenge you to master the material you have read in this chapter. For additional Skill Practice activities, visit our website at www.oup.com/us/interact12.

Perception Checking

Write well-phrased perception checks for each of the following situations:

Franco comes home from the doctor's office with a pale face and slumped shoulders. Glancing at you with a forlorn look, he shrugs his shoulders.

You say:

As you return the tennis racket you borrowed from Liam, you smile and say, "Here's your racket." Liam stiffens, grabs the racket, and starts to walk away.

You say:

Natalie dances into the room with a huge grin on her face.

You say:

In the past, your advisor has told you that almost any time would be all right for working out your next term's schedule. When you tell her you'll be in on Wednesday at 4 P.M., she pauses, frowns, sighs, says "Uh-huh," and nods.

You say:

Compare your written responses to the guidelines for effective perception checking discussed earlier. Edit your responses where necessary to improve them. Now say them aloud. Do they sound "natural"? If not, revise them until they do.

Inter-Act with Media:
Forming and Using Social Perceptions ▼ Find more on the web @ www.oup.com/us/interact12

Television

How to Look Good Naked (2008). Host: Carson Kressley.

Brief Summary: In this reality show, Host Carson Kressley encourages women of all sizes and shapes to reframe their appearance perceptions without extreme measures, such as plastic surgery or fad dieting. In one episode, Kressley works with Shannon, a mother of four, whose negative body image prevents her from swimming in the family's pool because she won't be seen in a bathing suit. Kressley strives to reframe Shannon's self-perception by having her strip to her bra and underwear and deconstructing the positive attributes of her physique. This "naked" image of Shannon is later magnified and shown to people on the street, who offer positive comments—perceptions incongruent with Shannon's certainties about her appearance. Further inconsistencies arise when Shannon compares her body size to other real women, also in their bra and underwear. Shannon perceives herself as larger than all the women, but learns that her hip size is actually the smallest. The show's conclusion finds Shannon with a more favorable and realistic self-perception as she receives a professional makeover and models swimsuits in a backyard fashion show.

IPC Concepts: Self-perception, self-concept, self-esteem, social perception, incongruence.

Cinema

Superbad (2007). Greg Mottola (director). Jonah Hill, Michael Cera, Christopher Mintz-Plasse, Martha MacIsaac, Emma Stone.

Brief Summary: Overweight, foul-mouthed Seth (Hill) and gangly, geek-smart Evan (Cera) are lifelong friends about to graduate from high school. Seth and Evan perceive themselves as underdogs who have perpetual misses with women. While the young men endure slight teasing from classmates, they do not receive the perpetual haranguing exhibited in other movies focusing on high school outsiders. In fact, two attractive young women, Jules (Stone) and Becca (MacIsaac), truly appear to like them. Seth considers the possibility that Jules is using him to get alcohol for a party she is hosting; Evan seems completely aloof when Becca speaks to him. In actuality, Becca and Jules do not share Seth and Evan's perception about their own social standing. Jules reveals that she doesn't even drink and although Becca makes physical overtures toward Evan while intoxicated, her interest remains consistent when she sees him the next day at the mall. The interactions between these characters exemplify incongruence in self-perception and uncertainty reduction theory.

IPC Concepts: Self-perception, accuracy of self-concept and self-esteem, incongruence, uncertainty reduction theory, selective perception, attributions.

What's on the Web

Find links and additional material, including self-quizzes, on the companion website at www .oup.com/us/interact12.

3

Communicating in Relationships

Basic Concepts

After you have read this chapter, you should be able to answer these questions:

- ▶ What are the major types of relationships?

- ▶ What is a "Johari window"?

- ▶ What is the role of communication in relationship stages?

- ▶ What strategies will maintain a relationship?

- ▶ What are relationship dialectics, and how do we manage them?

- ▶ What are relational turning points?

- ▶ What is interpersonal needs theory?

- ▶ What is exchange theory?

"Yvonne, wasn't that Pauli that I saw you with again? I thought you've been dating Lonnie."

"Yeah, I was with Pauli, but we're just friends."

"Just friends! Come on, girl, I see you with him a lot. Are you sure he doesn't think it's serious between the two of you?"

"I see him a lot because I am really able to talk with him. We're just comfortable with each other. But before you get too worried about his feelings, he and Leona are getting pretty close."

"And she doesn't mind you spending time with him? Are you sure you're not just kidding yourself?"

"Hey, I don't know if she minds, but Pauli and I just aren't together—there's no chemistry. Actually, he's more like a brother to me. I tell him my problems as well as what's going right with me. And he talks with me about his problems, too. It's great to have a close guy friend to confide in. If something happened between us, I'd really miss him."

Relationship—a set of expectations two people have for their behavior based on the pattern of interaction between them.

Interpersonal relationship—a series of interactions between two individuals known to each other.

Good relationship—one in which the interactions are satisfying to and healthy for those involved.

Yvonne is lucky because she has someone she can really talk with—she has a healthy relationship. The interpersonal skills you will learn in this course can help you start, build, and maintain healthy relationships with others. "A **relationship** is a set of expectations two people have for their behavior based on the pattern of interaction between them" (Littlejohn & Foss, 2008, p. 194). An **interpersonal relationship** may be defined as "a series of interactions between two individuals known to each other" (Duck & Gilmour, 1981, p. 2). A **good relationship** is one in which the interactions are satisfying to and healthy for those involved.

Good relationships do not just happen, nor do they grow and maintain themselves automatically. In fact, as Canary and Dainton (2002, p. xiii) state, "Most sane people know that relationships require work. That is, partners need to spend time and effort to maintain functional, satisfying relationships. Without such efforts, relationships tend to deteriorate." In this chapter we will describe the various types of interpersonal relationships, discuss the stages that typically comprise the life cycle of a relationship, explain relational dialectics (tensions) and how to manage them, describe the turning points in relationships, and consider two theories that help to explain relationships.

◆ Types of Relationships

Our relationships vary in their intensity from impersonal to personal (LaFollette, 1996, p. 4). An **impersonal relationship** is a relationship in which a person relates to another person merely because the other fills a role or satisfies an immediate need. In these relationships you don't care who the person is who fulfills the role and you don't care about this person; your only concern is that the person filling the role does it well. For instance, at a restaurant Elaine may prefer a particular server, but she will be satisfied if whoever waits on her does it competently. By contrast, a **personal relationship** is one in which people care about each other, share large amounts of information with each other, and meet each other's interpersonal needs. So if Carlos and Derek are teammates who enjoy talking about *The World of Warcraft*—an online role-playing game—as they work out together, they have a personal relationship.

Our personal relationships vary in how close or familiar we are with others. Therefore, we differentiate our relationships with others, thinking of them as acquaintances, friends, or close friends/intimates.

▷ Acquaintances

Acquaintances are people we know by name and talk with when the opportunity arises, but with whom our interactions are limited. Many of your acquaintance relationships grow out of a particular context. You become acquainted with those who live in your apartment building or dorm or in the house next door, who sit next to you in class, who go to your place of worship, or who belong to the same club. For example, Melinda and Paige are acquaintances. They met in biology class and talk regularly with each other about class-related topics, but they haven't shared any personal information or ideas, and they haven't made plans to meet outside of class.

▷ Friends

Over time some acquaintances become our friends. **Friends** are people with whom we have voluntarily negotiated more personal relationships (Patterson, Bettini, & Nussbaum, 1993, p. 145). As your friendships develop, less of your interactions center around exchanging role-related information and more of your interactions center around talking about personal topics. For example, over time as Melinda and Paige continue to sit next to each other in biology class, they begin to talk about non-class-related topics and find out that each of them enjoys pilates exercise, so they go to a pilates class together. As they continue to discover other things they have in common and find that they enjoy each other's company, they may eventually become friends.

Some of our friendships are context bound. For example, you may have soccer friends, work friends, or college friends. These context friendships exist within a limited situation, so your work friends may never meet your college friends—and these friendships may fade when the context changes. For instance, it is common

Impersonal relationship—a relationship in which a person relates to another person merely because the other fills a role or satisfies an immediate need.

Personal relationship—a relationship in which people care about each other, share large amounts of information with each other, and meet each other's interpersonal needs.

Acquaintances—people we know by name and talk with when the opportunity arises, but with whom our interactions are limited.

Friends—people with whom we have voluntarily negotiated more personal relationships.

Friendship competencies—the communication skills people use to make and keep friends.

for close high school friends to lose touch after graduation if they go to different schools, if they choose different careers, or if one friend leaves the area.

Your ability to make and keep friends depends on your communication skills. **Friendship competencies** are the communication skills people use to make and keep friends, and they are broken down into five areas: initiation, responsiveness, self-disclosure, emotional support, and conflict management (Samter, 2003).

- **Initiation.** Friendships begin and are maintained when you or your partner makes the first move to get in touch with the other or to start a conversation. Competent initiations are smooth, relaxed, and enjoyable. While we laugh at rehearsed "pick-up" lines, friendships are unlikely to develop if neither partner is adept at beginning enjoyable conversations.
- **Responsiveness.** Friends are sensitive and aware of their partners, so listening and responding skills help you focus on your friends' needs and react appropriately. It is difficult to form and maintain friendships with others who focus only on themselves, and for this reason responsiveness is a key friendship competency.
- **Self-disclosure.** Because friends share personal information and feelings with each other, a friendship is unlikely to form if people discuss only abstract ideas or surface issues. So the skill of self-disclosure—describing feelings and behaviors—is important to maintaining friendships.
- **Emotional support.** People expect to be comforted and supported by their friends. Therefore, knowing how to empathize and provide comfort and praise are important to providing the emotional confirmation your friends need.
- **Conflict management.** It is inevitable that friends will disagree about ideas or behaviors. Maintaining your friendships depends on how you handle these disagreements. The skills of collaboration and constructive criticism—both of which are types of conflict management—can help you to strengthen your friendships through times of disagreement.

In Part II of this book, "Developing Interpersonal Skills," you will have the opportunity to learn and practice the skills associated with these five competences so that you can become more adept at managing your friendships.

▷ Close Friends or Intimates

Public opinion polls consistently show that the number one thing that gives meaning to people's lives is their close personal relationships (Moore, 2003). **Close friends or intimates** are those few people with whom we share a high degree of commitment, trust, interdependence, disclosure, and affection. You probably have countless acquaintances and many friends, but you likely have only one, two, or a few truly intimate friends. A close friend is one you commit to by spending a lot of time. You trust this friend; that is, you believe and count on your

INTER-ACT WITH ▷ TECHNOLOGY

Watch a portion of a movie or TV program where friends are having a conversation. Analyze it in terms of the expectations you have of your friendships, including the enjoyment of talking with your friends, the feeling of trust you experience, the sharing of personal feelings you partake in, the level of commitment you have, and the enduring nature of friendships you expect. Which of these seem evident in the conversation? What other elements are shown in the conversation? Do these seem to contribute to or detract from the relationship? Explain.

friend to behave fairly and honestly and not to harm you intentionally. In a close friendship, not just one of you is dependent on the other, nor are the two of you independent. Rather, you are interdependent of each other—each of you relies on the other. You are highly likely to share personal and private information and feelings with a close friend, and your friend reciprocates by doing the same. You care deeply about your close friends, and your affection may range from fondness to love. In close relationships, there is a fusion of self and other to the point where each person's self-concept tends to become closely related to the other person. In other words, you define who you are in part through your close relationships (Aron, Aron, Tudor, & Nelson, 2004).

Research shows that women and men tend to differ regarding the factors that lead to close friendships. This may be because society teaches women and men to behave differently to follow norms of femininity and masculinity. Women tend to develop close relationships with others through talking, disclosing personal history, and sharing personal feelings. Women seem to develop their sense of "we-ness" by gaining this knowledge of the innermost being of their partner. Men tend to develop close friendships through joint activities, doing favors for each other, and successive tests of how dependable their friend is. When asked to define a "close friend," men are less likely than women to mention someone with whom they can share feelings. For men, close friends are the people they can depend on to help them out of a jam and the people with whom they regularly choose to pursue enjoyable activities (Wood & Inman, 1993). It is important to note that these differences are more pronounced in same-sex friendships. When men and women develop close friendships or intimate relationships with each other, these distinctions tend not to apply.

In Chapter 12 you will learn about communicating in intimate relationships, including with friends, spouses, and families.

◑ Characteristics of Relationship Stages and Life Cycles

Relationships are not something we "have"; rather, they are something we "make" through our communications with others. So over time, in the give and take of your conversations, you create, re-create, and sometimes destroy your relationships (Parks, 2007). Even though no two relationships develop in exactly the same manner, all relationships tend to move through identifiable stages that include beginning, developing, maintaining, and perhaps deteriorating (Baxter, 1982; Duck, 1987; Knapp & Vangelisti, 2005; Taylor & Altman, 1987). Relationships can move in a linear fashion through these stages, but it is more likely that over time a relationship will cycle back and forth through the stages. Therefore, it is useful to think about the life cycle of a relationship. How a relationship moves through these stages and what the course of its life cycle is depend on the interpersonal communication that occurs between relational partners. As

Close friends or intimates—those few people with whom we share a high degree of commitment, trust, interdependence, disclosure, and affection.

one communication scholar, Steven Duck, has said, "Talking is fundamental to relationships—whether they are starting, getting better, getting worse, or just carrying on" (2007, p. 12). In fact, as our "Spotlight on Scholars" feature by Steven Duck shows (page 65), how we talk with one another may be the most important variable in starting and building relationships.

In this section we begin our study of relationship stages and life cycles by describing a basic framework that will help you to understand the role that self-disclosure and feedback play in relationship development. Then we will discuss the characteristics or dimensions that define the stages relationships go through during their life cycles. Finally, we will discuss the hallmarks and communication patterns in each relationship stage.

▷ Self-Disclosure and Feedback in Relationship Development

As you interact in a relationship, you will begin to tell the other person things about yourself and will also begin to share what you observe about your partner. Likewise, your partner will disclose things and will share observations about you. A healthy interpersonal relationship is marked by an appropriate balance of **self-disclosure** (sharing biographical data, personal ideas, and feelings with others) and **feedback** (providing verbal and physical responses to people and/or their messages) within the relationship.

The **Johari window**, named after its two originators, Jo Luft and Harry Ingham, is a visual framework for understanding the extent of and connection between self-disclosure and feedback in a relationship (Luft, 1970). The window represents all of the information about you that there is. You and your partner each know some (but not all) of this information. The window has four "panes," or quadrants, as shown in Figure 3.1: the "open" pane, the "secret" pane, the "blind" pane, and the "unknown" pane.

The first quadrant is called the "open" pane of the window because it represents the information about you that both you and your partner know. It includes information that you have self-disclosed and the observations about you that your partner has shared with you through feedback. It might include basic information that you share with most people, such as your college major, but it also may include information that you disclose to relatively few people. Similarly, it can include simple observations that your partner has made, such as how cute you look when you wrinkle your nose, or more serious feedback you have received from your partner about your interpersonal style.

The second quadrant is called the "secret" pane because it contains all of those things that you know about yourself but have chosen to maintain as private so your partner does not know these things about you. Secret information is made known through the process of self-disclosure. When you choose to share the information with your partner, the information moves into the open pane of the window. For example, suppose that you had been engaged to be married once, but on

Self-disclosure—sharing biographical data, personal ideas, and feelings with others.

Feedback—providing verbal and physical responses to people and/or their messages.

Johari window—a visual framework for understanding the extent of and connection between self-disclosure and feedback in a relationship.

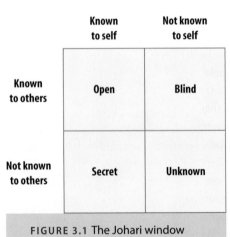

FIGURE 3.1 The Johari window

Steven Duck

Daniel and Amy Starch Research Chair at the Communication Studies Department at the University of Iowa, on

Personal Relationships

What began as a personal curiosity about the friendships he developed as a college student has turned out to be the focus of Steven Duck's lifelong work. He was curious about why some people become close friends while others remain acquaintances, so he selected this topic for a research term paper assigned in one of his classes. At that time, Duck's hypothesis was that people who have similar attitudes are likely to become attracted to each other and to become friends. Over the years his understanding of how relationships are formed, developed, and maintained has changed considerably. In fact, in Duck's work you can see how scholars develop and test theories only to replace them with more meaningful theories.

Many of Duck's breakthroughs in relationship theory came from his interdisciplinary study in psychology, sociology, family studies, and communication. Duck saw the need to integrate research findings across disciplines as so important that he founded the *Journal of Social and Personal Relationships* and the International Network on Personal Relationships, a series of international conferences on the subject to promote interdisciplinary scholarship.

While scholarship in many disciplines has contributed to how he views relationships, Duck believes that his move to the University of Iowa, where he encountered colleagues whose backgrounds were in rhetoric, caused a fundamental shift in his thinking. Based on discussions with these colleagues, who assume that people are connected to one another through language, Duck began to see that conversations and talk were more than the instrument through which relationships were developed; they were also crucial to maintaining relationships.

Duck's early theories were based on the premise that what makes a relationship work is the degree of similarity between the personalities, backgrounds, and so forth of the participants. He saw "talk" as simply the channel through which these similarities are uncovered. This model can be seen in the operation of most dating services. Clients with similar profiles are "matched" and come together to talk to each other to learn about their similarities. Then—presto!—the relationship develops. Although people with many similarities often don't develop lasting relationships, this premise dominated the thinking on personal relationships for many years.

In his 1994 book *Meaningful Relationships: Talking, Sense and Relating,* however, Duck first proposed a revision to his original premise. He argued that we "do" our relationships in everyday talk as we interact. "I just don't enjoy talking with him"; "I really feel like she listens to me and understands"; "We seem to have a lot in common, but we just can't seem to connect"; and "We've become good at talking things out so that we work through our differences and both feel good about it" are not simple statements about the communication in the relationship—they are statements about the relationship itself.

Thus, according to Duck's new model, when two people begin to date, the way their relationship develops most directly depends on how they talk to each other, not simply whether they have similar personalities. If this is so, then from a practical standpoint it is important to pay attention to how we say things and to how we respond to what others say. For example, while a dating service may be a convenient way to meet new people with similar interests, the development of relationships depends on how the two people manage the relationship as they talk.

Duck thinks that it is time for scholars to focus more of their analysis on people's everyday and ordinary conversations, rather than on what he calls the "peaks and valleys," since everyday talk is at the heart of understanding how relationships grow, stabilize, and change. For example, while communication scholars have studied how people deal with significant conflicts in great detail, Duck says that they have paid scant attention to studying how people manage minor conversational annoyances, such as unwanted swearing behavior. In addition, Professor Duck admires recent work on "the dark side of relationships" and has recently published an article on understanding "enemyship."

Duck, who received his Ph.D. from the University of Sheffield (United Kingdom) in 1971, has taught in the United States for twenty-two years. He has authored or edited over forty books and hundreds of articles and papers on personal relationships. A prolific scholar, Duck still recognizes the need to refresh his own ideas by engaging in intense study of the work of other scholars. Periodically, professors take a break from the rigors of the classroom, administrative responsibilities, and discovery research and go back into a "learning model" on what is called a sabbatical. In the spring of 2006, Professor Duck spent his sabbatical in the library, reading and thinking about the recent work of other scholars of personal relationships. Refreshed by this intense study period, Duck returned to his classes with a fresh perspective on our knowledge of personal relationships. For a list of some of Duck's major publications, see the reference list for this chapter at the end of the book.

the day of the wedding your fiance backed out. You may not want to share this part of your history with casual acquaintances, so it will be in the secret pane of your window in many of your relationships. But when you disclose this fact to a friend, it moves into the open part of your Johari window with this person. As you disclose information, the secret pane of the window becomes smaller and the open pane is enlarged.

The third quadrant is called the "blind" pane because this is the place for information that the other person knows about you but about which you are unaware. Most people have blind spots—parts or effects of their behavior about which they are unaware. Information moves from the blind area of the window to the open area through feedback from others. When someone gives you an insight about yourself and you accept the feedback, then the information will move into the open pane of the Johari window you have with this person. Thus, like disclosure, feedback enlarges the open pane of the Johari window, but in this case it is the blind pane that becomes smaller.

The fourth and final quadrant is called the "unknown" pane because it contains information about you of which neither you nor your partner are aware. Obviously, you cannot develop a list of this information. So how do we know that this information exists? Well, because periodically we "discover" it. If, for instance, you have never tried hang gliding, then neither you nor anyone else can really know how you will react at the point of takeoff. You might chicken out or follow through, do well or crash, love every minute of it or be paralyzed with fear. But until you try it, all of this information is unknown. Once you try it, you gain information about yourself that becomes part of the secret pane, which you can move to the open pane through disclosure. Also once you have tried it, others who observe your flight will have information about your performance that you may not know unless they give you feedback.

As you disclose and receive feedback, the sizes of the various windowpanes change. These changes reflect the closeness of the relationship. So the panes of the Johari window you have with different people will vary in size. Figure 3.2 shows four Johari windows, each with a different level of self-disclosure and feedback represented.

In Figure 3.2A, we see an example of a relationship where there is little self-disclosure or feedback occurring. This person has not shared much information and has received little feedback from the partner. We would expect to see this pattern in a new relationship or one between casual acquaintances.

Figure 3.2B shows a relationship in which a person is disclosing to a partner, but the partner is providing little feedback. As you can see, the secret pane is smaller, but the blind pane is unchanged. A window like this indicates that the individual is able to disclose information, but the partner is unable or unwilling to give feedback (or, perhaps, that the individual refuses to accept the feedback that is being given). Since part of the way that we learn about who we are comes from the feedback we receive from others, relationships in which one partner does not provide feedback can become very unsatisfying to the other individual.

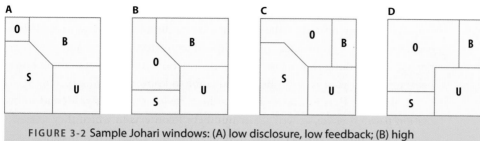

FIGURE 3-2 Sample Johari windows: (A) low disclosure, low feedback; (B) high disclosure, low feedback; (C) low disclosure, high feedback; (D) high disclosure, high feedback

Figure 3.2C shows a relationship where a partner is good at providing feedback, but the other individual is not self-disclosing. Since most of us disclose only when we trust our partners, this pattern may be an indication that the nondisclosing individual does not have confidence in the relational partner.

Figure 3.2D shows a relationship in which the individual has self-disclosed a good deal of information and received generous feedback. So the open pane of the window has enlarged as a result of both processes. Windows that look like this indicate that there is sufficient trust and interest in the relationship that both partners are willing to take risks by self-disclosing and giving feedback.

Obviously, to get a complete "picture" of a relationship, each partner's Johari window would need to be examined. A healthy interpersonal relationship is marked by a balance of self-disclosure and feedback, so that both people are participating. As you might imagine, acquaintances, friends, and intimate relationships vary on the amounts of self-disclosure and feedback that have been exchanged.

OBSERVE AND ANALYZE ▽

Johari Windows

Working with a friend, each of you should draw a window that represents his or her perception of the relationship with the other person. Then each of you should draw a window that represents what you perceive to be the other person's relationship with you. Share the windows. How do they compare? If there are differences in the representations, talk with your friend about them.

▷ Seven Characteristics That Define Relationship Stages and Life Cycles

Personal relationships are complex. Therefore, we need to understand the basic dimensions of relationships and how these dimensions vary during the different stages (beginning, middle, and end) of relationships. These dimensions are interdependence, depth, breadth, commitment, predictability, communication coding, and communication frequency (Parks, 2007)). In general, relationships develop as these dimensions increase, and relationships deteriorate as they decrease. Let's take a look at each dimension:

1. Interdependence. Relationships vary in terms of how much each partner is able to influence the other. The more interdependent partners are, the more one person's behavior will affect the other. For example, when you are just getting to know someone, you are not as likely to adapt your behavior to theirs. But when you are intimate with someone, the other person's moods, likes and dislikes, and so forth are likely to affect how you feel and what you think.

2. Depth. Relationships vary depending upon how intimate the partners are. Depth is directly related to the amount and nature of self-disclosure and feedback. Generally, as your relationship with someone develops, you and your partner are more willing to disclose private information, and this mutual disclosure helps to deepen your relationship as you come to know each other better.

3. Breadth. Relationships vary regarding the variety of activities and information partners share, as well as the number of contexts in which they interact. As your relationship with a partner develops, you and your partner share a greater range of activities and your conversations cover a wider range of topics. Likewise, you are likely to be with your partner in different contexts. If you meet someone on a blind date where you go to a movie and then for a drink, you may find your conversation centering on your opinions of that movie and others you've seen. But if a romantic relationship develops, you may also shop, do chores, study, exercise, do favors for each other, disagree, and make vacation plans. The wider range of activities and the increased time you spend together will lead you to discuss other topics and to see your partner in other contexts.

4. Commitment. Relationships vary in terms of how dedicated or loyal partners are to each other. Commitment is how much partners want to, feel that they ought to, and feel that they have to continue the relationship. In a relationship, you may feel committed to your partner because you enjoy being with them, and therefore you have a personal desire to continue the relationship. In addition, you may feel a moral commitment to the relationship and feel guilty if you think about ending it. For example, after living with someone for three years, you may feel that you should stay with them. Sometimes there may be external forces or structural reasons to be committed to the relationship. For instance, if you have a legally binding relationship such as a marriage or a shared apartment lease, you may feel committed to the relationship because of your contract.

5. Predictability. Relationships vary with regard to how well partners understand and can predict each other's behaviors. As you and your partner self-disclose and receive feedback, you grow to understand each other better. Because of this knowledge, uncertainty is reduced and you are better able to predict how your partner will feel and act in a particular situation. Over time you become experts about each other's feelings and behaviors. This is why couples married for years are able to anticipate each other's needs and finish the other's sentences.

6. Communication coding. Relationships vary depending on how the partners in the relationship use language to communicate. As a relationship develops, the partners develop a personalized language unique to them. This includes using pet names, private expressions, and inside jokes. It can also include relationship symbols like a special song, movie, or other personalized references. In addition, partners may begin to finish each other's sentences, learn to read each other's nonverbal messages, and in other ways shortcut the need for verbal conversation.

7. Communication frequency. Finally, relationships vary regarding the amount of communication that occurs between partners. As a relationship develops the frequency of communication increases. Likewise, as a relationship deteriorates the amount of interaction decreases.

To assess what stage a relationship is in, you need to look at all seven of the characteristics and determine whether the relationship is increasing or decreasing across these dimensions. These dimensions work together to indicate the stage of a relationship's life cycle. Next, let's look at how these dimensions indicate whether the relationship is beginning, developing, maintaining, or deteriorating.

When you meet someone new, how do you decide if you like the person enough to spend more time with him or her?

▷ Beginning Relationships

At the beginning of a relationship, the levels of each of these seven dimensions tend to be quite low. The parties do not have strong connections to each other and they tend to talk about surface rather than private or deep topics. They have not shared many activities, they do not know if the relationship will have a future, and they know very little about each other. Early on in relationships, people communicate very generally and do not have a long history of communication together.

Communication during the first stage of beginning a relationship is initially focused on getting information about the other person. As we have explained, all initial interactions and prospective relationships begin with uncertainty. If we don't know anything about another person, we don't know how to treat that person because we don't know how to predict his or her behavior. As we gather information, we can make decisions about how to act with the other person.

Let's look at an example of two college roommates, Whitney and Madeline, who are beginning a relationship. During their first few conversations, they will want to get to know each other so they can reduce uncertainty and better predict each other's behavior. Therefore, they may talk about where each one went to high school, what major each is pursuing, what hobbies they like, and their eating, studying, and sleeping schedules. This chitchat serves a real purpose in reducing uncertainty and helping Whitney and Madeline to gain knowledge about each other.

Today more than ever, the initial stage of relationship development may occur electronically. Online communication may present a potentially less difficult way to meet and interact with others than traditional interactions. The initial interaction can occur in the comfort of your own home and at your own pace. You need not be concerned about physical aspects of yourself or the other person, and you can more precisely select what you are going to say (Ward & Tracey, 2004). Perhaps Whitney and Madeline initially agreed to be each other's Facebook friends, e-mailed each other, or spoke on the telephone once they were

Friendships That Bridge Differences

by Brenda J. Allen

How do we come to develop relationships with people of different backgrounds? Brenda J. Allen, University of Colorado, describes her interracial friendship with a lesbian woman. As you read, try to identify the different stages of their relationship to determine how their windows of self-disclosure and feedback changed as the relationship developed.

I expected to like Anna even before I met her. . . . Since that time over six years ago, Anna and I have evolved from colleagues to best friends. From the beginning, Anna seemed to exchange cordial greetings as we passed in the halls. Students liked and respected her and I heard many comments about her excellence in teaching. Because I enjoyed a similar reputation as a teacher, I felt a sort of kinship with Anna. In addition, she dressed with a certain flair that I appreciated because in the public housing development (a.k.a. "the projects") where I grew up, we black people took a special pride in how we looked. I admired how Anna, a white woman, knew how to coordinate her clothes and jewelry.

As luck would have it, Anna and I were assigned adjacent desks. As a result of such proximity, I couldn't help but hear how she interacted with her students. I often teased her about her den-mother approach to their problems. She began to do the same with me and we would laugh at ourselves but feel good about our mutual concerns for the students' welfare. Anna and I also found that we had similar ideas about issues, activities, and improvements on our own critical thinking skills in the classroom.

We soon discovered that we had much more in common than our teaching philosophies. We were both baby boomers from the Midwest, only months apart in age. We also came from lower-class families, and religion played a strong role in our childhoods. We were both spiritually grounded and sometimes prayed together. We were both raised to be caring and nurturing. Early in our relationship I began to appreciate the strong sense of reciprocity that I felt with Anna.

About a year into our friendship, a major turning point occurred in our relationship. Anna invited me to lunch off campus, and when I met her at the restaurant, she seemed somber. "I have something that I must tell you because our friendship is important to me." She took a deep breath and told me that she was a lesbian. After my initial surprise I thanked her for sharing something so personal and assured her that it would never negatively affect our friendship.

To the contrary, we have grown closer. As a heterosexual I had never before given much thought to sexual orientation of gays, "coming out of the closet." Thanks to Anna, I have become far more sensitive and enlightened. When she first invited me to her home, she showed me the room that had become her bedroom when family members visited because only a few people knew that she and her "roommate" were partners. I was amazed by the extent of the masquerade that she felt compelled to perform to maintain a façade of being straight. Anna has since related many stories about the effort that she and gays make to maintain a heterosexual image.

I tend to be a private person with a clear demarcation between my work and my personal life. Nonetheless, after Anna opened up to me about her personal life I began to reciprocate. We now discuss every aspect of our relationships with family, friends, significant others, colleagues, and students. Whenever I find a prospective mate, Anna is usually the first and often only person I will tell. Once the relationship fizzles, she is always there to help me to get back out there in my quest for a significant other. I have often been pleasantly surprised by the similarities of issues that confront us both as we try to develop and maintain positive, intimate relationships.

I have grown comfortable enough with Anna to let her in on the "black" ways of communicating. I find myself calling her "Girl," an affectionate appellation that I normally reserve for African American sisters.

When I moved from a predominately white neighborhood to a racially mixed neighborhood, Anna understood why I felt more at home in my new surroundings. She had felt the same way in settings with a majority of gays and lesbians. We both seem to enjoy a similar sense of validation and contentment that differs from how we feel at work, where I am the only African American and she is the only lesbian on the faculty.

Anna and I laugh a great deal, often at each other, as well as cry together about personal trials and tribulations and the plight of our world.

Despite our similarities in personal style and background, Anna and I would probably not have become such good friends if she were straight. Because of her sexual orientation she can be empathetic with me in ways that my other white straight friends cannot. Thus, I believe that our marginalized positions in society and academia have been a major factor in forming the center of our friendship.

In regard to the title of this essay, Sapphire was a black female character in the old radio and television series Amos 'n' Andy. She was sassy, verbose, and intensely expressive. Sappho was a Greek poet (circa 600 B.C.) from the isle of Lesbos who wrote about romantic love between women. Each of these characters personifies one aspect of the multifaceted identifies that Anna and I rarely allow others to see. Because we trust and respect one another, we are comfortable being our authentic selves—in all their complexities—with one another.

Excerpted from Allen, B. J. (2001). Sapphire and Sappho: Allies in authenticity. In A. Gonzalez, M. Houston, & V. Chen (Eds.), *Our Voices— Essays in Cultural Ethnicity and Communication* (3rd ed., pp. 179–183). Los Angeles: Roxbury Publishing Company.

assigned as college roommates. The more they interact, the more connected they become, the more deeply they come to know each other, and the more predictable each becomes to the other.

Although the beginning stage may go quite smoothly with people who are similar to you, the process may become more difficult when you try to develop a relationship with someone different from you. In the "Diverse Voices" selection that appears on pages 70–71 of this chapter, Brenda J. Allen describes the process that resulted in her developing a deep intimate friendship with a person who differed from her in many ways. Perhaps as a result of reading this selection you will feel more comfortable in making the effort to get to know people from whom you differ.

▷ Developing Relationships

Moving from establishing a relationship to developing one involves movement along the seven dimensions discussed earlier. As relationships develop, the parties develop stronger connections to each other, and they tend to share more private or deep topics. They will interact with each other across more activities and contexts, understand each other better, expect that the relationship will continue into the future, share common languages or stories, and interact more often with each other. If a relationship is developing, then the people involved will perceive a sense of psychological closeness, noticing that the relationship is developing to encompass more interpersonally intimate levels. This also can happen via online relationships. Some people report that they achieve more closeness in online relationships than in equivalent, off-line relationships (Walther, 1996). Indeed, rapid and exaggerated intimacy can be part of the fun of online relationships (Rabby & Walther, 2003).

Let's say the relationship between Whitney and Madeline is working out well. They come to depend on each other, share more activities, get to know each other well, and consider themselves to be close friends. Many people who are developing their relationship begin to self-disclose more personal information and depend upon each other for favors and support. At this stage they are likely to seek each other out for help with a problem or to talk for hours, sharing both the joys and the sorrows of their lives. Over time, Whitney and Madeline may share their innermost feelings with each other, cry on each other's shoulders during hard times, or lend each other money. Now they may engage in many activities together, including shopping for groceries, exercising, studying, and socializing on the weekends. Because their relationship is developing, they will come to understand each other more and be less surprised by the attitudes, reactions, or behaviors of the other. They may plan for the future, including joining the same organizations or being roommates again next year. Because they share a history and common activities, they will come to develop a common language, including inside jokes, pet expressions, and references unique to their relationship. Clearly they communicate with each other more than when the relationship was just beginning. Perhaps they text or call each other during the day to check in, share a humorous tidbit, or make plans.

▷ Maintaining Relationships

Maintaining a relationship means that both parties participate in keeping the relationship at a particular level of closeness or intimacy. At this stage, the parties are trying to keep the status quo, avoiding greater closeness and, at the same time, less closeness. Relationships can go in and out of maintenance and move from less to more developed stages in almost imperceptible ways.

Researchers have cataloged many strategies used during the maintenance stage, including spending time together, merging social networks, making sacrifices, and being forgiving (Rusbult, Olsen, Davis, & Hannon, 2004). You probably unconsciously use many of these techniques. Obviously when you spend more time with someone you are likely to become closer. When face-to-face interactions are difficult, online communication may become the primary vehicle for maintaining closeness. Online communication can be the main vehicle for maintaining a long distance relationship (Shedletsky & Aitken, 2004). In general, as the parties in a relationship interact less frequently, the relationship will become less close. A second technique you may use to maintain your relationships is the merging of your social networks. When some of your partner's friends are your friends, and vice versa, the relationship becomes easier to maintain. In addition, the merging of social circles creates greater connection or interdependence. If you develop additional friendships through a friend, you are likely to want to maintain your relationship with the friend who opened you up to new relationships. Social networking sites like Facebook may make merging social networks easy. A third relationship maintenance strategy is sacrificing for your partner. Sacrifice means sometimes putting your own needs or desires on hold. Since all relationships involve give-and-take, at times, being willing to do what is best for the other person or the overall relationship can help maintain the relationship. Finally, relationships can be maintained by forgiveness. Conflict is inevitable in relationships, so we may do or say things that hurt our partners. If not handled properly, such transgressions can harm the relationship and move it to a level of less intimacy. By forgiving minor transgressions, we can keep a relationship at the desired level of closeness.

Whitney and Madeline are likely to use all of these strategies to maintain their relationship. Maybe they decide to take a few classes together, join some of the same clubs, and get to know each other's friends. Maybe they visit each other's hometowns and meet each other's families and high school friends. Whitney and Madeline may each have little habits that annoy the other, but they choose not to let these annoyances get in the way of a good friendship. When Whitney gets ill, perhaps Madeline will sacrifice a date to stay home and take care of her sick roommate. Other ways that people maintain their relationships include continuing mutually acceptable levels of affection, self-disclosure, favors, and support.

▷ Dissolving Relationships

The less highly developed a relationship is the more likely it is to dissolve over time (Parks, 2007). Many relationships with acquaintances, casual friends, co-workers, and neighbors eventually end because these are not relationships that have been sufficiently developed. Over time, though, even a developed relationship may become less satisfying to one or both relational partners. As a result, they may choose not to maintain it, letting it dissolve. As relationships dissolve, the levels of the seven dimensions decrease; we may begin to acknowledge that the relationship is dissolving when we recognize that there is less interdependence, depth, breadth, commitment, and frequency of communication. The parties may maintain the relationship at a less developed level, or the relationship may continue to dissolve until the partners end it altogether. In some relationships both partners are dissatisfied, while in others the process of disengaging is initiated by one partner. Regardless, the communication process in dissolving relationships is marked by three stages: the recognition of dissatisfaction, the process of disengaging, and ending.

The first sign that a relationship is dissolving is the recognition by one or both of the partners that the relationship is dissatisfying. The partners may feel less connected to each other, begin to share fewer activities, and communicate less frequently. They may begin to emphasize each other's faults and downplay virtues. Subjects that once involved deep, private, and frequent communication may become off-limits or sources of conflict. As the relationship begins to be characterized by an increase in "touchy" subjects and more unresolved conflicts, partners become more defensive and less willing to foster a positive communication climate. If Whitney and Madeleine have found themselves arguing about the cleanliness of their room, frequency of visitors, and unrepaid loans of money, they may begin to avoid talking about these subjects at all with each other, leading to discomfort and unhealthy avoidance of each other when these topics are likely to come up.

If the relationship continues to be dissatisfying, people begin to disengage from each other, or drift apart. They become less willing to sacrifice for each other, and they show less willingness to forgive. Their communication patterns

INTER-ACT WITH ● TECHNOLOGY

In days gone by, some people ended relationships by sending "Dear John (or Jane)" letters. Have you ever chosen to end a relationship using technology (like telephoning, text messaging, or e-mailing) rather than a face-to-face encounter? Why did you choose to end the relationship this way? What factored into your decision? What does this tell you about how technology affects how we end our relationships?

change from a pattern of sharing of ideas and feelings to a pattern of mostly small talk and other "safe" communication to finally a pattern of no significant communication at all. It may seem strange that people who once had so much to share find themselves with nothing to talk about. They may begin to avoid each other altogether and seek out other people with whom to share interests and activities instead. They may depend less on each other and more upon other people for favors and support. Hostility need not be present; rather, this stage is likely to be marked by indifference. Even though Whitney and Madeline have been very close during their first year at college, they may drift apart over time. Maybe one of them has betrayed the trust of the other and the tension has led to their becoming more annoyed with each other's faults. If this has happened, they will increasingly spend less time together, share fewer activities, talk about less important topics, and interact less frequently with each other.

If the relationship can't be maintained at a less developed level, it will end. A relationship has ended when the people no longer interact with each other at all. People give many reasons for terminating relationships, including poor communication, lack of fulfillment, differing lifestyles and interests, rejection, outside interference, absence of rewards, and boredom (Cupach & Metts, 1986). Unfortunately, while these reasons may be valid, people may sometimes look for reasons to end the relationship, blaming each other rather than finding equitable ways of bringing the relationship to an acceptable conclusion. When this happens people are likely to use strategies of manipulation, withdrawal, and avoidance (Baxter, 1982). Though misguided and inappropriate, manipulation involves being indirect and failing to take any responsibility for ending the relationship. Manipulators may purposely sabotage the relationship in hopes that the other person will break it off. Withdrawal and avoidance, also less than competent ways of ending relationships, involve taking a passive approach, which leads to a slow and often painful death of a relationship.

The most competent way to end a relationship is to be direct, open, and honest. It is important to clearly state your wish to end the relationship while being respectful and sensitive to the resulting emotions. If two people have had a satisfying and close relationship, they owe it to themselves and to each other to be forthright and fair about communicating during the final stage of the relationship. Perhaps Whitney and Madeline decide, separately, that their friendship has reached an end and that they both want to room with different people next year. As effective communicators, they should discuss this sensitive topic with each other without blame or manipulation, acknowledge that their relationship is less close than it once was, and mutually agree to move in with new roommates the following year.

Even when the participants agree that their relationship is over, they may choose to make a **relationship transformation**, which is continuing to interact and influence a partner through a different type of relationship after one type of relationship has ended. Romantic relationships may transform into friendships; best friends may become casual friends. Even when people end their marriage

Relationship transformation— continuing to interact and influence a partner through a different type of relationship after one type of relationship has ended.

through divorce they may continue on friendly terms or develop a type of "business" relationship where child-rearing practices and expenses are coordinated (Parks, 2007). Perhaps Whitney and Madeline are no longer roommates, and their intimate relationship has been damaged by arguing and mistrust, but they may continue to talk when they run into each other on campus.

◑ Understanding Relational Dialectics

A dialectic is defined as a tension between conflicting forces (Encarta Dictionary, 2009). Similarly, **relational dialectics** refers to the conflicting pulls that exist in relationships as well as within each of the individuals in a relationship. At any one time, one or both people in a relationship may be aware of these tensions. Three dialectics that are common to most relationships are the tugs between autonomy and connection, openness and closedness, and novelty and predictability (Baxter & Montgomery, 1996; Baxter & West, 2003). How these tensions are experienced and dealt with can alter the stage and life cycle of a relationship. We'll describe each of the dialectics and then discuss how you can effectively manage these tensions.

Relational dialectics—the conflicting pulls that exist in relationships as well as within each of the individuals in a relationship.

▷ Common Dialectical Tensions

Autonomy is the desire to act and make decisions independent of the partner or one's relationship. **Connection** is the desire to link one's actions and decisions with another person. Imagine that Joel and Shelly have been dating for about a

Autonomy—the desire to act and make decisions independent of one's partner or one's relationship.

Connection—the desire to link one's actions and decisions with another person.

How does this image demonstrate the tension between connection and autonomy?

year. At this point in their relationship, Shelly wants to spend most of her free time with Joel and enjoys talking with him before acting or making decisions, but Joel has begun to feel "hemmed in." For example, he wants to be able to play basketball with the guys without having to clear it first with Shelly. At the same time, however, he doesn't want to hurt Shelly's feelings or ruin the closeness in their relationship. At this point in the relationship, Shelly is at peace and may not recognize any tension between autonomy and connection in the relationship. On the other hand, Joel is feeling the tension between wanting to be more autonomous without jeopardizing his connection to Shelly. If Joel begins to act autonomously, he may relieve his own tension, yet he may create tension in the relationship.

Openness is the desire to share intimate ideas and feelings with one's partner and in one's relationship. **Closedness** is the desire to maintain privacy. This openness-closedness dialectic is also referred to as the disclosure-privacy dialectic. Let's say that Shelly discloses quite a bit to Joel. She believes that it is important to divulge her feelings and reactions to Joel, and she expects him to do the same. In other words, the open quadrant of Shelly's Johari window in her relationship with Joel is quite large. Joel, however, is a more private person. He does disclose to Shelly, but not as much as she would like. His secret quadrant of the Johari window is larger than Shelly would like it to be. The fact that Shelly and Joel differ in their preferred levels of self-disclosure is one source of tension in their relationship. But Shelly does not want complete openness all the time. She realizes that it is appropriate to be closed, or to refrain from self-disclosure with Joel, at times. So she seeks both openness and closedness in this relationship. Likewise, Joel, while wanting more closedness than Shelly does, still wants some openness. So, like Shelly, he wants both opposite forces to occur simultaneously in this relationship. In Chapter 10 we will discuss the theory of privacy management and identify the skills and strategies you can use to handle this dialectic.

Novelty is the desire for originality, freshness, and uniqueness in a partner's behavior or in one's relationship. **Predictability** is the desire for consistency, reliability, and dependability. People in relationships frequently experience tension between their desires for novelty and predictability. For example, because Shelly and Joel have been dating for a year, much of the uncertainty is gone from their relationship. But they do not want to eliminate uncertainty altogether. With no uncertainty at all, a relationship becomes so predictable and so routine that it is boring. While Shelly and Joel know each other well, can predict much about each other, and have quite a few routines in their relationship, they also want to be surprised and have new experiences with each other. Shelly and Joel may differ in their needs for novelty and predictability. Shelly may yearn for Joel to surprise her with a mystery date, or she may shock Joel by spontaneously breaking into their favorite song in the middle of the mall. At this point in their relationship, Joel may be comfortable operating by the routines they have established and may

Openness—the desire to share intimate ideas and feelings with one's partner and in one's relationship.

Closedness—the desire to maintain privacy.

INTER-ACT WITH ▶ TECHNOLOGY

Do dialectical tensions arise in online relationships? If so, how are they resolved? Are the tensions or the processes for resolving them different than in face-to-face relationships? If you have had an online relationship, you might consider this question in light of your own experience. If you haven't had an online relationship, talk with someone you know who has. Explain the three types of dialectical tensions and then ask this person to describe what he or she experienced.

Novelty—the desire for originality, freshness, and uniqueness in a partner's behavior or in one's relationship.

Predictability—the desire for consistency, reliability, and dependability.

be embarrassed and shocked by Shelly's song. Here is another tension between the two that must be managed in their relationship. But they must also cope with the fact that they each need some amounts of both novelty and predictability in the relationship.

It is important to remember that dialectical tensions exist in all relationships—not just romantic ones—and they are ongoing and changing. In other words, relationship dynamics are always in flux. Sometimes these dialectical tensions are active and in the foreground; at other times they are not prominent and are in the background. Nevertheless, when these tensions are experienced, they change what is happening in the relationship (Wood, 2000).

▷ Managing Dialectical Tensions

After reading about the preceding dialectical tensions discussed, you may be asking the question, "How can I cope with dialectical tensions in my relationships?" How do people satisfy opposite needs at the same time in relationships? Several researchers (Baxter & Montgomery, 1996; Wood, 2000) have studied how people actually manage the dialectical tensions in their relationships. People report using four strategies to manage these dialectics: temporal selection, topical segmentation, neutralization, and reframing.

Temporal selection is the strategy of choosing one side of a dialectical contradiction while ignoring the other for a period of time. For example, perhaps you and a friend realize that you have spent too much time apart lately (autonomy), so you make a conscious decision to pursue connection. That is, you agree that over the next few months, you will make a point of spending more time together. You schedule lots of activities together so you can be more connected. Over time, however, you may feel that you are spending too much time together, and so you may find yourself canceling dates. Seesawing back and forth like this is one way to temporarily manage a relational dialectic.

Topical segmentation is the strategy of choosing certain areas in which to satisfy one desire while choosing other areas to satisfy the opposite desire. For instance, if you and your mother want more openness in your relationship you may choose to be open about certain topics or aspects of life, such as feelings about school, work, or politics, but be closed about your sex lives. This segmentation satisfies both parties' needs for balance in the openness-closedness dialectic.

Neutralization is the strategy of compromising between the desires of one person and the desires of the other. Neutralization is a strategy that partially meets the needs of both people in the relationship but does not fully meet the needs of either. For example, a couple might pursue a moderate level of novelty and spontaneity in their lives, which satisfies both of them. The amount of novelty in the relationship may be less than what one person would ideally want and more than what the other would normally desire, but they have reached a middle point comfortable to both.

Reframing is the strategy of changing perceptions about the level of dialectical tensions. Reframing involves putting less emphasis on the dialectical contradiction,

Temporal selection—the strategy of choosing one side of a dialectical contradiction while ignoring the other for a period of time.

Topical segmentation—the strategy of choosing certain areas in which to satisfy one desire while choosing other areas to satisfy the opposite desire.

Neutralization—the strategy of compromising between the desires of one person and the desires of the other.

Reframing—the strategy of changing perceptions about the level of dialectical tensions.

looking at your desires differently so that they no longer seem quite so contradictory. For instance, maybe you are tense because you perceive that you are more open and your partner is more closed. As a result, you think about how much you disclose to him and how little he discloses to you. You might even discuss this issue with your partner. Perhaps during the conversation you begin to realize the times that you have held back (closedness), as well as the instances where he was open. After the conversation, you no longer see such a strong contradiction. You see yourselves as more similar than different on this dialectic. You have reframed your perception of the tension.

In most cases when you are developing, maintaining, or trying to repair a dissolving relationship, it is helpful if you can openly talk with your partner about the tensions that you are feeling and come to an agreement about how you will manage the dialectic going forward. Through self-disclosure and feedback, you and your partner may be able to negotiate a new balance that both of you find satisfying. At times, however, partners will be unable to resolve the tensions in their relationship. When this happens, it is likely that one or both of them will experience dissatisfaction with the relationship, and the relationship may dissolve or end.

Turning point—any event or occurrence that leads to a major change in a relationship.

◐ Turning Points in Relationships

Not only do relationships move through stages during their life cycles and experience dialectical tensions, but they also undergo episodes of major change. A **turning point** is any event or occurrence that leads to a major change in a relationship. For example, studies of romantic relationships (Baxter & Bullis, 1993; Baxter & Erbert, 1999) have identified going on a first date, experiencing a first kiss, meeting the family, dealing with an old or new rival, engaging in sexual activity, going on vacation together, deciding to date exclusively, having a big fight, making up, separating, living together, or getting engaged as important turning points. A study of online romantic relationships (McDowell, 2001) identified the first phone call and first face-to-face meeting as important turning points unique to developing relationships in cyberspace.

Turning points shape the direction and intimacy of any relationship. They are crucial junctures that affect the nature of the relationship and its future. The changes created by turning points can move a relationship to greater intimacy, or they may result in the dissolving or end of a relationship. For example, Will and Mikela have been dating for three months and seem to be heading toward a committed relationship. Then Mikela goes to dinner with Will's parents and witnesses how both Will and his father demean Will's mother. Because of this encounter, Mikela begins to notice that Will has little regard for the opinions of women. Quickly she decides that while Will is attractive, smart, and easy to be with, she doesn't want to be in a long-term relationship with someone who doesn't respect women.

All types of relationships experience turning points. In parent-child relationships, turning points often signal a change in the level of the child's dependence. So a child's first day of school, a religious coming-of-age ceremony, earning a driver's license, graduating from high school, beginning or graduating from college, and permanently moving out of the family home are common turning points that mark a significant change in this type of relationship. It is important for you to recognize potential turning points in your relationships. By anticipating turning points and discussing them with your partner both before and after they occur, you can better understand what the turning point means to each of you and how it may affect your relationship. For example, in a dating relationship, meeting your partner's parents will be a turning point. But if you are the first person your partner has introduced to mom and dad, the turning point may signal something different than if your partner routinely brings dates home to meet the family. So talking about this event will allow both of you to understand its significance to your relationship.

▼ Theoretical Perspectives on Relationships

What determines whether we will try to build a lasting relationship with another person? Why do some relationships never move beyond a certain level or begin to deteriorate? Two theories, interpersonal needs theory and exchange theory, offer insights that help us to answer these questions.

▷ Interpersonal Needs Theory

Relationships, like communication itself, exist in part because they satisfy basic human needs. **Interpersonal needs theory** is the theory that proposes that whether a relationship is started, developed, or maintained depends on how well each person meets the interpersonal needs of the other. Psychologist William Schutz (1966, pp. 18–20) has identified three basic interpersonal needs that all of us have: affection need, inclusion need, and control need.

Affection need is the need to express and to receive love. The people you know probably run the gamut of needing to show and express affection both verbally and nonverbally. At one end of the spectrum are the "underpersonal" individuals—those who avoid close ties, seldom show strong feelings toward others, and shy away from people who show or want to show affection. At the other end of the spectrum are the "overpersonal" individuals—those who thrive on establishing "close" relationships with everyone. They think of all others as intimates, confide in persons they have just met, and want everyone to consider them close friends. Somewhere in between these two extremes are "personal" people—those

OBSERVE AND ANALYZE ▼

Turning Points in Relationships

Select one long-term relationship in which you have been or are currently involved. Identify what you consider to be the turning points in that relationship. For each turning point, indicate whether, in your opinion, the turning point was positive and led to a deepening of the relationship or negative and led to lessening relationship intimacy. For each turning point, indicate whether you discussed the turning point with the other person.

Interpersonal needs theory—theory that proposes that whether a relationship is started, developed, or maintained depends on how well each person meets the interpersonal needs of the other.

Affection need—need to express and to receive love.

who can express and receive affection easily and who derive pleasure from many kinds of relationships with others.

Inclusion need—need to be in the company of other people.

Inclusion need is the need to be in the company of other people. According to Schutz, everyone has a need to be social. Yet people differ in the amount of interaction with others that will satisfy this need. At one extreme are "undersocial" persons—those who usually want to be left alone. Occasionally, they seek company or enjoy being included with others if specifically invited, but they do not require a great deal of social interaction to feel satisfied. At the other extreme are "oversocial" persons—those who need constant companionship and feel tense when they must be alone. If a party is happening, they must be there; if there is no party, they start one. Their doors are always open—everyone is welcome, and they expect others to welcome them. Of course, most of us do not belong to either of these extreme types. Rather, we are sometimes comfortable being alone and at other times need and enjoy interactions with others. The inclusion factor relates closely to the autonomy-connection dialectic discussed earlier. People with a strong need for inclusion are likely to want more connection with the relationship partner, while people with weaker needs for inclusion probably would want more freedom or autonomy.

Control need is the need to influence the events and people around us. As with the other two interpersonal needs, people vary in terms of how much control they need to have over events and people. At one extreme are persons who need no control, who seem to shun responsibility and do not want to be in charge of anything. These "abdicrats," as Schutz calls them, are extremely submissive and are unlikely to make decisions or accept responsibility. At the other extreme are persons who like to be—indeed, who feel they must be—in charge. Such "autocrats" need to dominate others at all times, and they become anxious if they cannot. They may usurp responsibility from those who actually have the authority in a given situation, and they may try to determine every decision. Again, most people fall somewhere between these two extremes. These "democrats" need to lead at certain times, but at other times they are content to follow the lead of others. Democrats can stand behind their ideas, but they also can be comfortable submitting to others, at least some of the time.

How can this theory help us understand communication in relationships? Relationships develop and are sustained in part because the partners choose to meet each other's interpersonal needs. This can be difficult in relationships where individuals have different levels of needs. Through verbal and nonverbal communication behavior, we display cues that reveal the level of our immediate interpersonal needs. As you interact with others, you can detect whether their needs for affection, inclusion, and control seem different from yours. We also can talk to each other about relationship needs and negotiate ways to satisfy partners' different levels of needs.

Suppose that Emily and Dan have been seeing each other regularly and both see their relationship as close. If in response to Dan's attempt to hold hands with Emily while they are watching television Emily slightly stiffens, it might suggest that Emily doesn't have quite the same need for affection as Dan. It should be emphasized that people's needs do differ; moreover, people's needs change over time. Differences in these and other needs may reflect the dialectical tensions in relationships. When other people's needs at any given time differ significantly from ours and we fail to understand that, we can misunderstand what's going wrong in our relationships and experience relationship dissatisfaction.

▷ Exchange Theory

Another way of analyzing our relationships is on the basis of exchange ratios. **Exchange theory**, originated by John W. Thibaut and Harold H. Kelley, is the theory that proposes that relationships can be understood in terms of the exchange of rewards and costs that takes place during interactions (Thibaut & Kelley, 1986, pp. 9–30). **Rewards** are the outcomes that are valued by a person. Some common rewards are good feelings, prestige, economic gain, and fulfillment of emotional needs. **Costs** are the outcomes that a person does not wish to occur. These include time, energy, and anxiety.

According to Thibaut and Kelley, people seek interaction situations in which their behaviors will yield an outcome of high reward and low cost. For example,

Control need—the need to influence the events and people around us.

Exchange theory—theory that proposes that relationships can be understood in terms of the exchange of rewards and costs that takes place during interactions.

Rewards—outcomes that are valued by a person.

Costs—outcomes that a person does not wish to occur.

when Hunter and Jack spend the afternoon together, Jack talks mainly about himself and does not listen to Hunter. Hunter has a choice about whether to continue spending time with Jack or leave. What Hunter does will depend in part on his cost/reward analysis of the interaction. While he perceives costs in spending time with Jack, he also enjoys being out of the house and spending time with a friend. Perhaps he would enjoy watching the ballgame together, even though he finds Jack's communication behavior today to be annoying. If Hunter sees more rewards in spending the afternoon with Jack than he sees costs, he will continue the interaction. If Hunter believes that the costs of being with Jack today exceed the rewards, then he is likely to leave.

This analysis can be extended from single interactions to relationships. If, over an extended period, a person's net rewards (reward minus cost) in a relationship fall below a certain level, that person will come to view the relationship itself as unsatisfactory or unpleasant. But if the net rewards are higher than the

LEARN ABOUT YOURSELF ▽

Take this short survey to learn something about yourself. Answer the questions based on your first response. There are no right or wrong answers. Just be honest in reporting your true behavior. For each question, select one of the following numbers that best describes your behavior:

1 = Strongly Agree
2 = Agree Somewhat
3 = Neutral
4 = Disagree
5 = Strongly Disagree

_____ 1. I talk to people because it makes me feel less lonely.
_____ 2. I talk to people because I am concerned about them.
_____ 3. I talk to people because I want someone to do something for me.
_____ 4. I talk to people because it is reassuring to know someone is there.
_____ 5. I talk to people to show others that I care about them.
_____ 6. I talk to people to influence them.
_____ 7. I talk to people because I need someone to talk to or be with.
_____ 8. I talk to people to show others encouragement.
_____ 9. I talk to people to tell others what to do.

Scoring the Survey: This is a test of interpersonal needs: inclusion, affection, and control. To get an inclusion score, add your scores for items 1, 4, and 7. The lower your score (range of 3–15), the stronger your need to be included by others. To get an affection score, add your scores for items 2, 5, and 8. The lower your score (range of 3–15), the stronger your need to express and receive affection. To get a control score, add your scores for items 3, 6, and 9. The lower your score (range of 3–15), the stronger your need to control others.

Adapted from Rubin, R. B., Perse, E. M., & Barbato, C. A. (1988). Conceptualization and measurement of interpersonal communication motives. *Human Communication Research, 14,* 602–628.

level viewed as minimally satisfactory, the person will regard the relationship or interaction as pleasant and satisfying.

Thibaut and Kelley suggest that the most desirable ratio between cost and reward varies from person to person and within one person from time to time. One reason people differ in their assessments of costs and rewards is that they have different definitions of what is satisfying. If people have a number of relationships they perceive as giving them a good cost/reward ratio, they will set a high satisfaction standard and will probably not be satisfied with low-outcome relationships. By contrast, people who have few positive interactions will be satisfied with relationships and interactions that people who enjoy high-outcome relationships would find unattractive. For instance, Calvin may continue to go out with Erica even if she treats him very poorly because, based on his experiences in other relationships, the rewards he gets from being with Erica are on par.

The ratio of costs to rewards determines how attractive or unattractive a relationship or an interaction is to the individuals involved, but it does not indicate how long the relationship or interaction will last. Although it seems logical that people will terminate a relationship or an interaction in which costs exceed rewards, circumstances sometimes dictate that people stay in a relationship that is plainly unsatisfactory. Thibaut and Kelley's explanation for such a situation involves what they call the **comparison level of alternatives**, the other choices a person perceives as being available that affect the decision of whether to continue in a relationship. A person who feels dissatisfied will tend to leave a relationship or interaction if there is a realistic alternative that seems to promise a higher level of satisfaction. But if there are no such alternatives, the person may choose to stay in the situation because, unsatisfactory though it is, it is the best the person believes can be attained at that time. Thus, if Joan has four or five men she gets along well with, she is less likely to put up with Charley, who irritates her. If, however, Joan believes that Charley is the only man who can provide the companionship she is seeking, she will be more inclined to tolerate his irritating habits.

Comparison level of alternatives— other choices a person perceives as being available that affect the decision of whether to continue in a relationship.

Like Schutz's interpersonal needs theory, Thibaut and Kelley's exchange theory helps illuminate important aspects of relationship development. Yet critics of this theory point out an important limitation. Exchange theory suggests that people consciously and deliberately weigh the costs and rewards associated with any relationship or interaction. In other words, people rationally choose to continue or terminate relationships. Thus, the theory assumes that people behave rationally from an economic standpoint: They seek out relationships that benefit them and avoid those that are costly (Trenholm, 1991, p. 72). In fact, although people may behave rationally in most situations, rational models such as Thibaut and Kelley's cannot always explain complex human behavior. Nevertheless, it can be useful to examine your relationships from a cost/reward perspective. Especially if a relationship is stagnating, you may recognize areas where costs are greater than rewards, either for you or for the other person. If so, you may be able to change some aspects of the relationship before it deteriorates completely.

Communal relationships—
relationships in which we allow the costs to exceed the rewards and yet still consider the relationships to be satisfactory.

You may discover that it is fruitful to use both the interpersonal needs theory and the exchange theory when examining your relationships. What you (or your partner) count as "costs" and "rewards" may depend significantly on what your particular needs are. If your needs differ, you may misunderstand the other person's perceptions of rewards and costs. Looking at relationships in this way might help resolve misunderstandings and make you less defensive. That is, if you understand the other person's needs and can take his or her perceived costs and rewards into account, you may understand the situation better and in a way that is less destructive to your own self-esteem.

While we usually hope that rewards will exceed costs in relationships, communal relationships change that balance. **Communal relationships** are relationships in which we allow the costs to exceed the rewards and yet still consider the relationships to be satisfactory. These relationships tend to be our very closest relationships with others, and as a result, we are less likely to regularly keep count of costs and rewards. We may consider these relationships so important that we will endure a situation of costs far exceeding rewards. We are more concerned about the welfare of the other or about maintaining the relationship, despite the uneven cost/reward ratio. You may maintain a relationship with a close friend, for example, if that friend has had a number of crises in her life and is unable to meet your emotional needs in the relationship. Maybe you give more to this person than you get in return, but your genuine concern for your friend's welfare keeps you in the relationship, despite the costs to you. Relationships between parents and adult children or between adult siblings may be described as communal in that they may persist even if one person bears more of the costs and the other person reaps more of the rewards. For many people, maintaining nuclear family relationships takes precedence over an exchange theory analysis.

◐ Summary

One of the main purposes of interpersonal communication is developing and maintaining relationships. Relationships may be impersonal or personal. People have three types of personal relationships. Acquaintances are people we know by name and talk with but with whom our interactions are limited in quality and quantity. Friends are people with whom we voluntarily spend time. We expect responsiveness, self-disclosure, emotional support, and conflict management from our friends. Close or intimate friendships are those in which we may share our deepest feelings, spend great amounts of time together, share activities and favors, and feel interdependence. People can examine the balance of disclosure and feedback in their relationships by drawing a Johari window to see whether both parties are sharing information in ways that help the relationship to develop.

Relationship development is based on increasing levels of interdependence, depth, breadth, commitment, predictability, communication codes, and communication frequency. Relationships go through life cycles whose stages include a beginning stage, developing stage, maintaining stage, and perhaps dissolving stage.

Relationship dialectics are tensions that occur as a result of conflicting relationship needs. Common relationship dialectics involve tensions between autonomy and connection, openness and closedness, and novelty and predictability. We manage contradictory needs through temporal selection, topical segmentation, neutralization, and reframing. Relationships experience turning points or events that occasion a major change in the relationship.

Two theories are especially useful for explaining the dynamics of relationships. Schutz sees relationships in terms of their ability to meet the interpersonal needs of affection, inclusion, and control. Thibaut and Kelley see relationships as exchanges: People evaluate relationships through a cost/reward analysis, weighing the energy, time, and money invested against the satisfaction gained. However, in communal relationships, the levels of caring and genuine concern for each other can allow costs to exceed rewards.

A QUESTION OF ETHICS ▽ What Would You Do?

Grant and Amy have been in a committed relationship for two years. They maintain their relationship by spending almost all of their free time together and having a common circle of friends. They are each other's best friends, share many hobbies and interests, and confide in each other on virtually all topics. A few months ago, Grant met Devon online through Facebook because they had a friend in common. They began to talk more frequently online and occasionally would call each other to chat by phone. They have met a few times for coffee. Their relationship seems to be developing such that they share personal information, seem to connect with each other easily, interact quite frequently, and expect that the relationship will continue. Amy and Devon do not know about each other.

1. What are the issues of communication and ethics facing Grant?
2. What should Grant communicate to Amy? To Devon?

◙ Chapter Resources

Communication Improvement Plan: Relationships ▽ Find more on the web @ www.oup.com/us/interact12

Do you have a relationship that you would like to change? Do you want to develop, maintain, or end the relationship? Using information in this chapter, write a communication plan to accomplish your goal. You can find a communication improvement plan worksheet on our website at www.oup.com/us/interact12.

Key Words ▾

Inter-Act with Media:
Communicating in Relationships ▾ Find more on the web @ www.oup.com/us/interact12

Television

Grey's Anatomy (2005–). Ellen Pompeo, Patrick Dempsey.

Brief Summary: In season one, Meredith (Pompeo) and Derek's (Dempsey) relationship begins when they meet in a bar the night prior to Meredith starting a hospital internship. During their fling, neither knows that they will work together at Seattle Grace Hospital. Once they realize their professional connection, they futilely try to avoid each other. Derek's physician wife joins the staff and serves as another obstacle. Meredith dissolves her relationship with Derek while he deals with his marriage, though Derek cannot stay away. Once Derek divorces, he deepens his commitment to Meredith. By this point, Meredith's emotional baggage, combined with lack of trust in Derek, causes her to distance herself. By season four, the two maintain a purely collegial relationship; however, as Derek starts dating again, Meredith pursues therapy and decides that she wants a full future with him. Through four seasons, this couple's relationship follows all of the relationship stages, vacillating between coming together and apart and dealing with major and minor dialectical tensions along the way.

IPC Concepts: Communication patterns during stages of relationships, de-escalating and dissolving a relationship, relational dialectics, managing dialectical tensions.

I Think I Love My Wife (2007). Chris Rock (director). Chris Rock, Kerry Washington, Gina Torres, Edward Herrmann.

Brief Summary: Richard Cooper (Rock) has a successful career, a seven-year marriage to wife Brenda (Torres), and two children. As Richard struggles with boredom because of a lack of intimacy with his wife, he finds himself fantasizing about other women and struggles with the contemplation of an affair with an old free-spirited friend. Rather than regularly communicating about their needs as a couple, Richard and Brenda tend to the business of the household and raising their children. The couple blames each other for their lack of intimacy, and Brenda makes excuses for her own lack of physical affection, even in counseling. Although the couple ultimately reconciles their shared need for intimacy, their dynamic is indicative of novelty versus predictability in long-term relationships and dialectical tensions that can bring about change.

IPC Concepts: Intimates, relational dialects, dialectical tensions, turning point, interpersonal needs theory, affection, exchange theory, comparison level of alternatives.

What's on the Web

Find links and additional material, including self-quizzes, on the companion website at www .oup.com/us/interact12.

4

Verbal Communication

After you have read this chapter, you should be able to answer these questions:

- ▷ What is the relationship between language and perception?

- ▷ How do people assign meaning to words?

- ▷ How does culture affect language use?

- ▷ What is the difference between denotative and connotative meaning?

- ▷ What is the theory of muted groups?

- ▷ How can you improve your language usage so that it is more specific?

- ▷ How can you use the skills of dating information, indexing generalizations, and communication accommodation?

- ▷ How can you phrase messages so that they demonstrate sensitivity?

"Welcome to Introduction to British Literature," announces Professor Singelton. "You should have purchased the eleven texts we will be deconstructing this semester."

"Deconstructing? What's he talking about?," whispers Adam to his friend in the seat beside him.

The Professor continues, "When reading each text, you must be fastidious in your focus and analysis, paying attention to the paradigmatic concepts as well as the minutiae. Your failure to do both will have a deleterious effect on your grade and, as magnanimous as I consider myself, I will not be benevolent to students without impeccable attention to the written word."

Adam thinks that this class is impossible, decides to drop it later today, and texts his girlfriend, "hav 2 drop lit."

第1旅客ターミナル　出発
Terminal 1 Departures

定刻	変更	行先/経由地	航空会社	便名	航空会社	便名	ゲート	備考
16:20		香港		CX521		AA6115	17	出発済み
16:25		シンガポール		SQ5901			A63	第2ターミナル
16:40		ニューヨーク		UA800	ANA	NH7800	41	最終案内
16:45		サンフランシスコ		UA852	ANA	NH7016	31	最終案内
16:55		ヒューストン		NW6006			D97	第2ターミナル
17:00	16:55	ソウル		KE2			26	搭乗中
17:00		サンフランシスコ		UA9690			B71	第2ターミナル
17:05		シンガポール		UA891	ANA	NH7051	37	搭乗中
17:06		ロスアンゼルス		UA9686			D85	第2
17:15		釜山		NH29			21	定刻
17:15		シアトル		UA876	ANA	NH7030	44	定刻
17:20		ロスアンゼルス		AA7210			D96	
17:20	20:00	ニューアーク		NW6008			D94	時刻変更
17:25		ロスアンゼルス		AA170	JAL	JL5016	18	定刻
17:25		サンフランシスコ		AA7220			A61	

定刻	変更	行先/経由地	航空会社	便名	航空会社	便名	ゲート	備考
17:30		シンガポール		NW5		CO5875	23	定刻
17:30		サイパン/名古屋		NW77			24	定刻
17:35		上海		NW25			24	定刻
17:35		シカゴ		UA882	ANA	NH7008	45	定刻
17:35		バンコク		UA9711			D98	第2ターミナル
17:40		ソウル		UA837	ANA	NH7047	42	定刻
17:45		北京		NW11			28	定刻
17:45		広州		NW9			22	定刻
17:50		サンノゼ		AA128	JAL	JL5006	11A	定刻
17:50		シンガポール		AA7215			B73	第2ターミナル
18:00		ソウル		AA7229			C85	定刻
18:00		ホーチミン		AA7247			C84	第2ターミナル
18:00		ソウル		NW7		CO5007	27	定刻
18:05		ハノイ		AA7241			C88	第2ターミナル
18:05		香港		NW1			25	定刻

第1旅客ターミナル　出発
Terminal 1 Departures

航空会社	便名	航空会社	便名	ゲート	備考
	UA801			33	定刻
	SQ12			14	定刻
	UA881	ANA	NH7055	35	定刻
	CX505		AA6113	11B	定刻
	UA853			43	定刻
	AA7217			A84	第2ターミナル
	NW27		CO5027	23	時刻変更
	UA7252			D97	第2ターミナル
		ANA	NH7024	37	定刻
		Asiana	OZ6604	37	定刻
		ANA	NH7049	31	定刻
		JAL	JL5004	15	定刻
				25	時刻変更
		ANA	NH5837	12	共同運航便
		ANA	NH6255	37	定刻

便名	ゲート	備考
NH7012	41	定刻
TG5604	41	定刻
JL5014	16	定刻
JL5002	16	定刻
NW30	28	定刻
	24	定刻
AF2278	14	定刻
	B71	第2ターミナル
	A85	第2ターミナル
JL5055	17	定刻
	A61	第2ターミナル

サービス終了

ould you understand what Professor Singleton has said? Sometimes, for a variety of reasons, the way we form our messages makes it difficult for others to understand what we mean—the meaning of our words cannot be transferred to others.

In this chapter, we will investigate verbal communication to see how the language we use to form our messages affects how accurately and easily we are understood. We begin by defining the word "language" and how language works. After that, we introduce six skills that you can use to improve your verbal messages. Finally, we discuss how new technologies are changing verbal communication.

◐ The Nature and Characteristics of Language

Language works in a variety of interconnected ways. To explain how it works, let's start by clarifying what we mean by the word "language"; then we'll discuss how language affects what we see and shapes what we think, how people ascribe meaning to the words they use and hear, how language is related to culture, and the characteristics of language that affect our interpersonal exchanges.

▷ Definition of Language

Language—a system of words, sounds, and gestures common to a group of people used to communicate messages.

Language is a system of words, sounds, and gestures common to a group of people used to communicate messages. As Thomas Holtgraves (2002, p. 8) reminds us, "Language is one of those things that we often take for granted. It's almost like breathing—necessary for life but not something we pay much attention to unless problems develop. But unlike breathing, language has profound implications for our social existence. It plays a role in virtually every aspect of our dealings with others. Understanding what we are doing when we use language can aid our understanding of what it means to be a social being."

As this definition of language indicates, in order for language to transmit meaning, there must be a common speech community, words that make up the language, and a system of grammar to group the words into meaningful phrases. A **speech community** is a group of people who share a common language. There are between three thousand and four thousand speech communities in the world, with the number of native speakers ranging from over a hundred million to communities with only a few remaining native speakers. The five largest speech communities, in order, are Chinese, Spanish, English, Arabic, and Hindi (Columbia Encyclopedia, 2008). **Words** are arbitrarily chosen symbols used by a speech community to name things. Each speech community uses different words to

Speech community—a group of people who share a common language.

Words—arbitrarily chosen symbols used by a speech community to name things.

symbolize the same phenomena. These words may be inherited and adapted from other languages (for instance, many English words originate from Greek and Latin), or they may have been invented for and remain original to that language. **Grammar** is the set of rules by which words are put together to structure messages. As they vary in the words they use, speech communities also vary in their rules of grammar. While some languages follow very similar and straightforward grammatical rules (such as the related "romance languages" of French, Italian, Spanish, and Portuguese), others follow very different rules (languages such as English, Finnish, and Icelandic are known for being particularly complex grammatically).

▷ Language and Perception

Our use of symbols to name things is what makes us human. For animals, reality just is (Burke, 1968). In other words, when an animal sees something, the animal perceives the object just as it appears in nature. The animal does not link a word or a term to the object. When your dog sees your car, your dog experiences the object directly, perhaps conjuring memories of going to the veterinarian or to the park. The dog does not link the word "car" to the object. But for humans, reality is always filtered through symbols. For everything we see, there is a word that we cannot help but associate with the thing. This point may seem trivial, but you will see its relevance for shaping our behavior when we get to the portion of this chapter dealing with the characteristics of language.

The **Sapir–Whorf hypothesis**, named after two theorists, Edward Sapir and Benjamin Lee Whorf, is the theory stating that language shapes how people think and perceive (Littlejohn & Foss, 2005). Your language allows you to perceive certain aspects of the world by naming them and allows you to ignore other parts of the world by not naming them. Sapir and Whorf elaborated on this observation by noting that not only does the language itself shape thoughts and perceptions, but so does the culture that uses the language. For example, in English we have only one word for "snow." But in Eskimo speech communities there is a multitude of words to describe what we call "snow." Why? Because differentiating between snow types is more central to survival in Eskimo culture. Similarly, if you work in a job such as fashion or interior design, perceiving subtle differences in colors is important to your success as a member of one of these professional subcultures. So if you are a designer, you are likely to develop a larger vocabulary that allows you both to see and to describe subtle differences in hue and tint.

How do we know what words mean?

Grammar—the set of rules by which words are put together to structure messages.

Sapir–Whorf hypothesis—a theory stating that language shapes how people think and perceive.

Knowing various words for shades of white—such as ecru, eggshell, cream, ivory, pearl, bone china, white, and antique white—actually helps you see differences in shades of white and be more successful in achieving your design goals.

In addition, there are phenomena that a speech community cannot fully perceive until a word is coined to capture the concept. We can now think about "cyberspace" and "date rape." The phenomena those terms refer to existed before the expressions were coined. But as a speech community, we became better able to perceive and talk about these phenomena once they had been named. Sometimes, new words are deliberately created so that we perceive something differently. The management of many larger companies, which used to refer to planned employee firings as "layoffs" or "downsizing," now prefers to use the term "rightsizing." Notice how the first words focus our attention on the loss of people's livelihoods while the third term shapes our perception to focus on the needs of the organization. Though we may take language for granted, it is vitally important in shaping our reality.

INTER-ACT WITH ● TECHNOLOGY

wiki, lol, blog, cookie, emoticon, flame, imho, MP3, URL, zip

These words are terms that are commonly used in the world of computers and electronic communication. How good are you at decoding these terms? To what extent do you use these sorts of terms in your own communication? Are any of your relationships impeded by this kind of tech talk? Have you ever felt excluded from a conversation because you didn't understand some of the technical terms that were being used?

▷ Language and Meaning

At first glance the relationship between language and meaning seems simple. You select the words, structure them using standard rules of grammar, and transmit your message to people in your speech community. The extent to which those in your community share your vocabulary (if they share culturally accepted words and/or if they have accepted newly invented words into their vocabulary) will determine how well they will perceive your meaning. However, the process is more complex than that. To understand how meaning is transmitted, you first need to understand the concepts of the denotation and connotation of words and how denotation and connotation work together to form meaning.

Denotation is the direct, explicit meaning of a word found in a dictionary. However, denotative meanings are a problem because dictionary definitions vary, dictionary definitions can change over time, and dictionaries use words to define other words. The result is that in addition to words being defined differently in various dictionaries, they may also have multiple meanings that change over time, and they are limited in that the only way to make a definition is to use other words. In addition, meaning may vary depending on the syntactic context (the position of a word in a sentence and the other words around it) in which the word is used. For instance, in the same comment a person might say, "I love vacationing in mountain areas. Mornings are really cool. By getting out early you can see some really cool animals." Most listeners would understand that "mornings are really cool" refers to temperature and "see some really cool animals" refers to animals that are uncommon or special.

Connotation is the feelings or evaluations we personally associate with a word. We bring many emotional reactions to words based on our experiences, and therefore the meaning we get from words is based on more that dictionary definitions. For example, think of the different meanings that people bring to the word "family,"

Denotation—the direct, explicit meaning of a word found in a dictionary.

Connotation—the feelings or evaluations we personally associate with a word.

based on their positive or negative experiences growing up in their unique family situation. A "family" may be a harmonious group consisting of mother, father, children, and relatives by both blood and marriage. Or "family" may mean a nontraditional family, such as a gay or lesbian couple raising either birth or adopted children. Or it may mean an extended group of tightly connected individuals, such as a family of co-workers or a family of close friends. There may be even greater variation of connotative meaning with more strictly emotion-based words such as love, freedom, harmony, hate, oppression, and so on.

Two theories explain how people arrive at the meaning of words using denotation and connotation: symbolic interactionism and coordinated management of meaning.

Symbolic interactionism is the theory stating that the meaning of words results from social interaction (Blumer, 1986; Leeds-Hurwitz, 1995). In other words, the denotation of words cannot be understood without socially influenced connotations. The theory is based on three premises. First, humans have their own personal meanings for words. So it doesn't matter what you meant for a person to understand when you use a word. What will determine their response to what you say is how they personally understood what you said. Second, meaning arises through the process of interaction with others, so meaning is a social product. Third, based on their interactions, humans, through self-talk, interpret what an interaction or word means. For instance, when Tina says, "We bought an SUV. I think it's the biggest one Chevy makes," Kim might think, "Gas guzzler. Why in the world would anyone buy something that does so much environmental harm?" and Alexia might think, "Power and visibility. I'd love to be able to afford that. It has great pick up and it sits so high on the road" (Blumer, 1986, pp. 2–6).

Let's look at a quick example of this theory in action. As a child you learned the meaning of words through your social interactions with your family and later through your friends and school. In an effort to save you from a burn, your mother may have told you, "Don't touch the stove, it is *hot*." While you may have heard the word *hot* before, if you touched the stove, your concept of *hot* probably changed and your internal conversation may have gone something like this: "WOW *hot* burns and it's not something I want to do again." As a teenager, however, when you heard your friend refer to Clark as *hot*, you didn't pull your hand away because the context of that interaction would have helped you to interpret a different meaning. So you interpreted your friend's remark as a comment on Clark's physical attractiveness. In summary, then, from a social interaction perspective, the meanings you experience are made as you interpret your interactions with the world.

Coordinated management of meaning is the theory explaining how people come to any agreement on the rules of meaning in an interaction (Philipsen, 1995), thus building on the theory of symbolic interactionism. Obviously, if all we had were unique idiosyncratic ideas about the meaning of words and messages, communication between people would be impossible. So this theory explains the processes through which people begin to align or coordinate meaning.

Symbolic interactionism—theory stating that the meaning of words results from social interaction.

Coordinated management of meaning—theory explaining how people come to agree on the rules of meaning in an interaction.

The theory assumes that when you enter an interaction, you do not know exactly what to expect from that interaction. You do not know what rules of meaning the other person will be using. So in each exchange, you need to coordinate the rules of meaning for that interaction with the other person. The theory of coordinated management of meaning says that one individual may subtly propose enacting a certain type of communication (episode), but only when the other person accepts that proposal has the meaning of the symbols in that exchange been coordinated.

Imagine for instance that Kacie subtly proposes a "friendly competition" episode of communication with Josh. There are certain behaviors, language, and nonverbal symbols that people generally associate with friendly competition. When Kacie enacts those behaviors, such as bragging, one-upping, and putting-down Josh in what she perceives as a friendly manner, he can accept or reject the type of communication she has offered. If he responds with messages of friendly competition, then he has tacitly agreed with Kacie to enact a certain episode and they have together coordinated the meaning of their verbal and nonverbal symbols. In other words, they have agreed to similar rules and a similar interpretation of this exchange. It is important to note that only the communicators can coordinate the meaning of a communication episode. This explains why observers may misinterpret or get the wrong meaning from a situation of which they are not a part. Have you ever interpreted a couple's judgmental language and angry behavior as their "having an argument," while the participants themselves would describe the same exchange as "playful banter"?

▷ Language and Culture

Cultures differ not only in the languages spoken but also in how messages are expected to be worded. Cultures may be either high- or low-context cultures and either low- or high-power distance cultures.

A **low-context culture** is a culture in which messages are expected to be direct, specific, and detailed. Speakers are expected to say exactly what they mean and get to the point. There is a strong reliance on verbal means of communicating, and people can be forceful in persuading others. Generally, the United States, Germany, and Scandinavia are low-context cultures. A **high-context culture**, on the other hand, is a culture in which messages are indirect, general, and ambiguous. People are more likely to talk around an issue rather than to be direct. There is more emphasis on nonverbal communication, and speakers often use silence as a means of communication. Speakers are expected to be cautious and tentative in their use of language. Generally, Native American, Latin American, and Asian countries are high-context cultures (Chen & Starosta, 1998).

Such cultural variations in language can have a noticeable effect on the interactions between people of different cultural backgrounds. Imagine Isaac, a

OBSERVE AND ANALYZE ●

Language and Meaning

Answer the questions for each word or phrase that follows. Then ask a friend to do the same without seeing your answers.

Expensive car: How much does it cost?
Staying up late on a weeknight: What time did you go to sleep?
Spending a lot of time preparing for a speech in class: How much time did you prepare?
He's rich: How much money does he have?
She's liberal: What are her views on immigration, abortion, capital punishment, and global trade?
He's got one of those little cars: What make and model is the car?
They're tree-huggers: What environmental practices do they follow?

Compare the similarities and differences in the interpretation of these phrases between the two of you. Based on the meaning that you and your friend gave to these words, what can you conclude about the coordinated management of meaning? About language denotation and connotation?

Low-context culture—culture in which messages are expected to be direct, specific, and detailed.

High-context culture—culture in which messages are indirect, general, and ambiguous.

How might culture affect the conversation between the children in this picture?

member of a low-context culture, and Zhao, a member of a high-context culture, trying to conduct business together:

Isaac: *Let's get right down to business here. We're hoping that you can provide 100,000 parts per month according to our six manufacturing specifications spelled out in the engineering contract I sent you. If quality control finds more than a 2 percent margin of error, we will have to terminate the contract. Can you agree to these terms?*

Zhao: *We are very pleased to be doing business with you. We produce the highest quality products and will be honored to meet your needs.*

Isaac: *But can you supply that exact quantity? Can you meet all of our engineering specifications? Will you consistently have a less than 2 percent margin of error?*

Zhao: *We are an excellent, trustworthy company that will send you the highest quality parts.*

Isaac is probably frustrated with what he perceives as general, evasive language on Zhao's part, while Zhao may be offended by the direct questions, specific language, and perceived threat in the message. As global business and travel become more commonplace, we must understand the effect of culture on our communication.

Power distance is the amount of difference in power between people, institutions, and organizations in a culture. A **high power-distance culture** is a culture in which power is distributed unequally. Some people in a high power-distance culture are perceived as having a great deal of power while others have very little.

INTER-ACT WITH ▶ TECHNOLOGY

In what ways is the communication of members of low- and high-context cultures affected when they use various technologies to communicate? For example, if high-context culture members rely on nonverbal behaviors and silence to send and interpret messages, how do e-mail and text messaging affect the shared meaning? In what ways is the communication of members of high- and low-context cultures affected when they use other technologies to communicate?

Power distance—the amount of difference in power between people, institutions, and organizations in a culture.

High power-distance culture—culture in which power is distributed unequally.

Low power-distance culture— culture in which power is distributed equally.

Thus a person with a title, rank, or status would be treated with much formality and respect. Formal terms of address like Mr. or Mrs., proper and polite forms of language, as well as nonverbal signals of status differences, would be evident in an exchange with such a person. The high-status person would control the interaction and others would listen without question. A **low power-distance culture** is a culture in which power is distributed equally. There is little perceived difference in power between people, regardless of actual titles, ranks, or status. In an exchange between two people in a low power-distance culture, the participants would address each other by first names rather than as Mr. or Mrs., the communication would be informal and casual, neither person would control the exchange, and each person could question or confront the other.

▷ Characteristics of Language

Now that we know what language is, how it is perceived, how meaning is transmitted, and how that meaning is affected by culture, let's discuss some of the general characteristics of language, which must be understood if we are to see how words affect our interpersonal communication. In this section we will explain the seven characteristics of language: how it is arbitrary, ambiguous, abstract, self-reflexive, changeable, revealing, and hierarchical.

1. Language is arbitrary. We have already explained that the words used to represent things in all languages are arbitrary symbols. Our understanding of the machine that transports us from one place to another via the road would not be changed at all if we named it a "rul" rather than a "car." There is no physical connection between the word and its referent. However, while the words used to represent objects, ideas, or feelings are arbitrary, for a word to have any meaning it must be recognized by members of the speech community as standing for a particular object, idea, or feeling. Different speech communities use different word symbols for the same phenomenon, but as long as all members of the speech community accept the use of a particular word, it carries meaning. For instance, the season for planting is called "spring" in English-speaking communities and "printemps" in French-speaking communities, but the meaning of these words is nonetheless understood within either community.

2. Language is ambiguous. No matter how specific you try to be with your words, there can always be multiple interpretations. We have already acknowledged that dictionary definitions of words can vary and that words carry with them varying connotations, or emotional meanings that different people bring to words. Because the meaning of words is not in the words themselves but in the people who use them, there cannot be total agreement between the sender and receiver in any communication. Even the notion of clarity in language can be misleading because what is clear to you cannot be transferred to the mind of the other. To speak about clarity of communication implies a transfer of meaning. In other words, some speakers think that if they can just be clear enough in their language, then others will get their meaning. We should not think of interpersonal communication as the transference of meaning from one person's brain to the other person's brain, however. As we have discussed, communication is a more complex process than that. Instead, we should think of it as people working together to achieve similarity of meaning and consensus of interpretation, but not exactness.

3. Language is abstract. A great number of the words we use are abstract. That is, they don't describe an exact, concrete thing. For instance, a word may describe a concept that cannot be visualized, such as "truth," or it may describe a category of similar items, but not a specific item. Suppose you told your friend that you were about to buy a new car. "Car" is a category. At this point your friend might say, "What kind of car are you thinking about?" Now you're being asked to be more specific, thus demonstrating that "car" is actually a more ambiguous word than you might at first think. What could you say? Let's look at the potential continuum of the word "car" from its most general meaning to its most specific meaning, as illustrated in Figure 4.1. The more abstract a word is, the greater the chance there is that the meaning of the word will not be shared by communicating partners. If Rema refers to her "pet," a fairly concrete word, her co-worker Margi may think of a dog, cat, snake, bird, or hamster. Even if Rema specifically mentions her dog, Margi still has many possibilities for interpretation, including dogs of various breeds, sizes, colors, and temperaments. If words that refer to tangible objects like cars and pets vary in abstraction, imagine all the possibilities of meaning for nontangible concepts such as honesty, patriotism, or justice.

4. Language is self-reflexive. Not only does language refer to other things, but it can also refer back to itself. In other words, it is self-reflexive. We can use language to talk about language itself and about its possible uses—and as a result of that reflexivity of language, humans are able to explore concepts that animals cannot explore. For instance, humans have the capacity to think and talk about themselves, to speak hypothetically, to talk about past and future events,

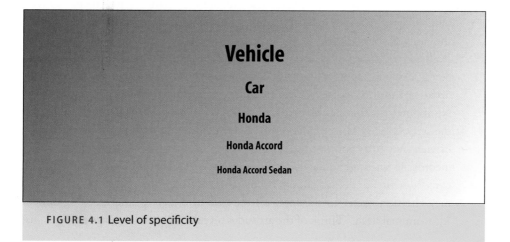

Vehicle

Car

Honda

Honda Accord

Honda Accord Sedan

FIGURE 4.1 Level of specificity

and to communicate about people and things that are not present. Language enables us to learn from others' experiences, to share a common heritage, and to develop a shared vision for the future. In addition, language, coupled with the ability to reflect upon ourselves, allows for a higher-order communication, or communication about communication. Think of the possibility for improving interpersonal communication when people can comment on the very process of communicating.

    5. Language is changeable. Language changes over time in a number of ways. First, new words are constantly being invented. Younger generations invent new words or assign different meanings to the words they learn. For instance, terms such as "bling" (flashy jewelry and decorations) have come into common usage and may not be understood by older generations. In addition to new words created by young people, new inventions spur new words. Think of words related to technology that have entered our vocabulary: "wiki," "laptop," "MP3," "blog," "blackberry," "DVD," "IM," and "text message" are just a few recently invented technological terms. Second, terms used by older generations, such as "cellophane" for "plastic wrap" or "piazza" for "porch," may fade from use over time and may even be removed from dictionaries. Third, members of the speech community will often invent new meanings for old words to differentiate themselves from other subgroups of the language community. For instance, among teenagers in some parts of the country "stupid" means "cool," as in "That's a really stupid shirt," and "played" means "boring," as in "This party is played; let's go." Meanwhile, other groups have invented new terms to replace words that demean or stereotype. For example, the word "housewife" is no longer used, as it assumes not only that all stay-at-home married people are women but also that a wife's only role in life is to maintain a house. Finally, as our society becomes increasingly multicultural, the English language gradually adopts what were once foreign words, such as "petite," "taco," "gelt," "kindergarten," "lasagna," and thousands of others.

    6. Language is revealing. Language is not neutral. Most people do not realize the extent to which our word choice reveals our attitudes, judgments, or feelings. Imagine, for example, that Shana routinely saves 60 percent of the money she earns. She lives in a very modest apartment, drives an old car, makes her own clothes, and rarely buys material possessions. What word comes to your mind to describe Shana's approach to money? Do you call her thrifty, budget-conscious, or frugal? Or do you select words such as tightwad, penny-pincher, or stingy? Notice how the first set of words tends to have a more positive connotation, while the second set of words conveys a negative connotation. By the word you use, a listener may infer your attitude toward the habit of saving versus spending one's income. If you see Hallie taking more time than others to make a decision, you could describe Hallie as either "thoughtful" or "dawdling." Likewise, someone may choose to refer to the food on the grill as either "prime filet mignon" or "dead animal flesh." Think of the attitudes revealed in such language as "She's just a stewardess" versus "She's a flight attendant"; "He's fat" versus "He's heavy-set"; or "The professor is brutal" versus "The professor is a hard but fair grader."

7. Language is hierarchical. Kenneth Burke tells us that language allows for comparisons and judgments and that with comparisons come social orderings (1968). For instance, once we are able to compare, then notions of better and worse inevitably follow. When people compare anything with anything else and notice difference, seldom is that difference seen as merely a difference. Instead, there is a natural tendency in humans to judge or evaluate difference in some way. This tendency to judge difference creates hierarchy, with some things (and people) seen as better or worse than others.

There is an even more complex relationship between language and social hierarchies, which can be explained by the theory of muted groups (Griffin, 1997). The **theory of muted groups** is the theory stating that whoever is dominant in a social hierarchy has the power to shape everyone's perceptions via language. Thus the views of the world of those who are subordinate will be repressed by language, and these people will be silenced—that is, their voices will be muted. The novel *1984* by George Orwell illustrates the theory of muted groups well by showing that when those in power control the language, they also control thought and action. In Orwell's novel, those in power have created Newspeak, an official language in which war means peace, freedom means slavery, and ignorance means strength. By changing the traditional meanings of words, those in power are able to prevent an entire population from rebelling against an oppressive totalitarian state.

> **Theory of muted groups**—theory stating that whoever is dominant in a social hierarchy has the power to shape everyone's perceptions via language.

You may be wondering how the theory of muted groups extends beyond Orwell's classic book to affect your life today. All around you are examples of powerful groups and individuals (the government, the media, your parents, your teachers) using language to impose their views of the world, thereby making it difficult or impossible for your view of the world to be heard. Imagine a teenager whose parents define her purchasing behavior as "wasteful spending." Once those words are invoked, all discussions of money between the teen and her parents will center around the issue of whether her spending is wasteful. It will be difficult for the teen to speak positively about her spending because the conversation will inevitably focus on the concept of wastefulness. In essence her voice will be muted. If initially her behavior was described as "wise spending," then the parents would have been more likely to let the conversation be framed by this term. The shaping of language happens frequently in the corporate world. When corporations popularize the term "frivolous lawsuit," this is likely to make it difficult for plaintiffs with legitimate lawsuits to move public perceptions toward the idea that their complaint has merit. In addition, the hierarchical shaping of language also occurs frequently at the government level. Those in power can define war as a "peace-keeping effort," a reformer as an "agitator," or a less industrialized nation as "underdeveloped," thereby curtailing social criticism from within and maintaining an image of power over other nations.

○ Improving Your Language Skills

There are many concrete skills that can improve our use of language in interpersonal situations. These include using specific language, adapting your language to your listeners, providing dating information, indexing generalizations, practicing speech accommodation, and demonstrating linguistic sensitivity.

▷ Using Specific Language

When we use specific language, we reduce ambiguity and abstractness. This often helps speakers and listeners to assign similar meaning to what has been communicated. Compare the speaker's use of language in the following two descriptions of a near miss in a car: "Some nut almost got me a while ago" versus "An hour ago, a older man in a banged-up Honda Civic ran the light at Calhoun and Clifton and almost hit me broadside while I was in the intersection waiting to turn left." In the second description, the speaker used language that was much more specific, so the speaker and listener are likely to have similar perceptions of the situation, which the first description would not have made possible.

Often, as we try to express our thoughts, we tend to generalize, leading to an ambiguous message, but we can get a message across better if we use specific language. **Specific language** is language in which concrete and precise words, as well as details and examples, are used to clear up ambiguity in the message. What can we do to speak more specifically? We speak more clearly when we select words that most accurately or correctly capture the sense of what we want to communicate. For example, at first I might say, "Waylon was angry at the meeting today." Then I might think, "Was he really showing anger?" So I say, "To be more accurate, he wasn't really angry. Perhaps he was more frustrated or impatient with what he sees as lack of progress by our group." What is the difference between the two statements in terms of words? By carefully choosing words, you can show shades of meaning. Others may respond quite differently to your description of a group member according to whether they think the person is showing anger, frustration, or impatience. The interpretation others get of Waylon's behavior is very much dependent on the words you select. Let's look closer at what we mean by concrete words, precise words, details, and examples.

Concrete words are words that help clear up ambiguity by appealing to our senses. For example, instead of saying that Jill "speaks in a weird way," we might be more specific by saying that Jill mumbles, whispers, blusters, or drones. Each of these words creates a clearer sense of the sound of her voice. **Precise words**, meanwhile, are words that narrow a larger category to a smaller group within that category. For instance, if Nevah says that Ruben is a "blue-collar worker," she has named a general category. You might picture an unlimited number of occupations that fall within this broad category. If, instead, she is more precise and says he's a "construction worker," the number of possible images you can picture is reduced; now you can select your image only from a specific subcategory, construction worker. So your understanding is likely to be closer to the meaning

Specific language—language in which concrete and precise words, as well as details and examples, are used to clear up ambiguity.

Concrete words—words that help clear up ambiguity by appealing to our senses.

Precise words—words that narrow a larger category to a smaller group within that category.

Nevah intended. To be even more precise, she may identify Ruben as "a bulldozer operator," further limiting your choice of images and aligning your understanding with the meaning she intended to present to you. In the examples that follow, notice how the use of concrete and precise words in the right-hand column improves the clarity of the messages in the left-hand column.

The senator brought *several things* with her to the meeting.	The senator brought *recent letters from her constituency* to the meeting.
He lives in a *really big house*.	He lives in a *fourteen-room Tudor mansion*.
The backyard has *several different kinds of trees*.	The backyard has *two large maples, an oak, and four small evergreens*.
Morgan is a *fair grader*.	Morgan *uses the same standards for grading all students*.
Many students *aren't honest* in class.	Many students *cheat on tests* in class.
Judy *hits* the podium when she wants to emphasize her point.	Judy *pounds on* the podium when she wants to emphasize her point.

While choosing concrete and precise words enables us to improve clarity, there are times when a word may not have a more specific or concrete synonym. So another way to achieve specificity is to use a detail or an example to clarify. Suppose Linda says, "Rashad is very loyal." Since the meaning of loyal (faithful to an idea, person, company, and so on) is an abstract word, Linda might add, "I mean he never criticizes a friend behind her back" to avoid ambiguity and confusion. By following up her use of the abstract concept of loyalty with an example, Linda makes it easier for her listeners to "ground" their idea of this personal quality and see more accurately how it applies to Rashad.

In most situations, an effective communicator attempts to use specific language to reduce ambiguity and misunderstanding. But there are situations in which a speaker may choose to use vague language when interacting with another person. **Strategic ambiguity** is being purposefully vague or offering a response that is not precisely on topic when communicating. There are many reasons a person may choose to be ambiguous, but most have to do with protecting themselves, protecting another person, or protecting the relationship between the speaker and the listener. For example, if a new co-worker asked your opinion about your manager, with whom you have a difficult working relationship, you might use strategic ambiguity when you reply, perhaps saying, "Most people feel that she's a hardworking person." By couching your answer as a group opinion, you have provided accurate information, withheld your personal opinion, have not actually been deceptive, and have protected yourself. Research shows that there can be positive benefits to strategically ambiguous messages in relationships. Teenagers, for instance, frequently choose to be more clear, specific, and definite when revealing information to peers than when doing so with parents. Teens may be purposefully vague in communicating with parents in order to preserve family harmony and advance teens' natural drive toward independence (Sillars, 1998).

OBSERVE AND ANALYZE ◯

Concreteness and Precision

Revise each of the following sentences to include words that are more concrete and precise.

The food was great.
Mary's stuff is really nice.
The new building is awful.
She's really cool.
Stay away from Don—he's a real jerk.
He was really on me for being late.
Jones assigns a lot of outside reading for the course.
I like sweet potatoes, they're tasty.
At the PGA, lots of players had trouble with the weather.

Strategic ambiguity—being purposefully vague or offering a response that is not precisely on topic when communicating.

▷ Adapting Your Language to Your Listeners

There are times when we use words that our listeners do not understand. Sometimes these words are so familiar to us that we forget that others are unaware of their meaning. To be a better communicator, however, you should adapt your language to your listeners by (1) using vocabulary the listener understands, (2) using jargon sparingly, and (3) using slang only when speaking with others who know that vocabulary.

The first way to adapt your language to your listeners is to use vocabulary that the listener is likely to understand. People vary in the extent to which they know and use a large variety of words. If you have made a conscious effort to expand your vocabulary, are an avid reader, or have spent time conversing with others who use a large and varied selection of words, then you probably have a large vocabulary. The larger your vocabulary, the more choices you, as a speaker, have from which to select the words you want. Having a larger vocabulary, however, can present challenges when you are communicating with people whose vocabulary is more limited. For example, if Carl, an interior designer, phones his client Jim and says he has chosen an "ecru brocade fabric" for the couch in Jim's office, Jim might not picture a beige-toned cloth with a raised design.

As a speaker, therefore, you must try to adapt your vocabulary to the level of your partner so that your words will be understood. One strategy for assessing another's vocabulary level is to listen to the types and complexity of words the other person uses—that is, to take your signal from your communication partner. So if Carl noticed Jim describing colors in very basic terms, Carl might want to explain the meaning of the more precise words he uses to describe colors. Adjusting your vocabulary to your partner is part of the concept of behavioral flexibility, which we discussed in Chapter 1. When you have determined that your vocabulary exceeds that of your partner, you can use simpler synonyms for your words or use word phrases composed of more familiar terms. Adjusting your vocabulary to others does not mean talking down to them, however. It is merely polite behavior and effective communication to try to select words that others understand. Think of your frustration in situations when speakers repeatedly used words that you could not comprehend.

As listeners, we can use other strategies to better understand others' words. You can work to improve your own vocabulary. By learning new words, you will be in a better position to understand others, and you will have more choices of words to specifically and precisely express your thoughts. You can also question the speaker so that you come to understand any unfamiliar words the speaker has used. So when Carl tells Jim that the fabric is ecru, Jim might ask, "Is ecru an earth-toned color?" By asking for specifics, he can get clarification of the unfamiliar word.

The second way to adapt to your listeners is to use jargon sparingly. **Jargon** refers to technical terminology whose meaning is understood only by a select group of people based on their shared activities or interests. Members of a

Jargon—technical terminology whose meaning is understood only by a select group based on their shared activities or interests.

group may form a special speech community with much group-specific jargon when they share the same hobby or occupation. For example, medical practitioners speak a language of their own that people in the medical field understand and those outside of the medical field do not. The same is true of lawyers, engineers, government employees, educators, and people in virtually all occupations. If you are an avid computer user, you may know a lot of computer-related terms that those who do not use computers do not know. Likewise, there are special terms associated with sports, theater, wine tasting, and science fiction, to name just a few hobbies. Imagine a person interested in environmental concerns speaking about "PCBs" "brown-fields," and "eco-terrorism" with someone who does not understand this jargon. The key to effective use of such specialized terms is to employ them only with people who speak the same jargon. When people understand the same jargon, then its use facilitates communication. Jargon becomes a shorthand way of expressing yourself within the jargon-based community. If you must use jargon with people outside that occupation or special interest group, remember to explain the terms you are using. Without explanation to outsiders, jargon becomes a type of foreign language.

The final way to adapt your language to your listeners is to use slang appropriately. **Slang** is informal vocabulary developed and used by particular groups in society. It is casual and playful alternate vocabulary deliberately used in place of standard terms, but it also performs an important social function. Slang bonds those who use the same words, emphasizing a shared experience. But slang simultaneously excludes others who don't share the terminology. The simultaneous inclusion of some and exclusion of others is what makes slang so popular with youth in all cultures. Young people often invent slang words that other youth understand but adults do not understand, thus forming a bond. Although slang words serve a variety of functions, they tend not to last long because they either get adopted into standard language or are dropped from usage because too many outsiders come to understand them. Slang may emerge from teenager life, urban life, college life, gang life, or other contexts. Using slang appropriately means using it with people who understand the slang but avoiding it with people who may not be familiar with the slang words you use. If your communication purpose is to be understood, then you must give careful consideration to the words you use.

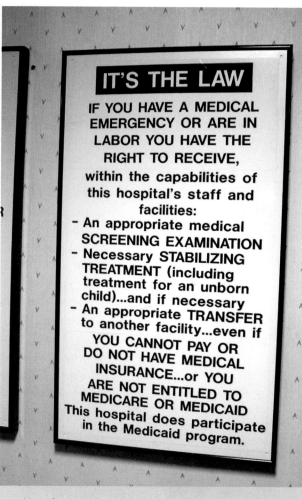

IT'S THE LAW

IF YOU HAVE A MEDICAL EMERGENCY OR ARE IN LABOR YOU HAVE THE RIGHT TO RECEIVE, within the capabilities of this hospital's staff and facilities:
- An appropriate medical SCREENING EXAMINATION
- Necessary STABILIZING TREATMENT (including treatment for an unborn child)...and if necessary
- An appropriate TRANSFER to another facility...even if YOU CANNOT PAY OR DO NOT HAVE MEDICAL INSURANCE...or YOU ARE NOT ENTITLED TO MEDICARE OR MEDICAID

This hospital does participate in the Medicaid program.

How does jargon improve or hinder communication?

Slang—informal vocabulary developed and used by particular groups in society.

Dating information—information about time or time period used in communications to improve clarity.

▷ Providing Dating Information

Another way to improve your communication skills is to always consider the importance of providing dating information to others. **Dating information** is information about time or time period used in communications to improve clarity. Providing dating information is important because we draw conclusions based on the information we are given. If the information is inaccurate, the conclusions drawn from that information are likely to be inaccurate as well. A common source of inaccuracy is giving the impression that information is current when in fact it is not. For instance, Parker says, "I'm going to be transferred to Henderson City. Do you know anything about the city?" to which Laura replies, "Yes I do. Let me just say that they've had some real trouble with their schools." On the basis of Laura's statement, Parker may worry about the effect the move will have on his children. What he doesn't know is that Laura's information about this problem in Henderson City is five years old! Henderson City may still have problems, but then again, it may not. Had Laura replied, "I know that five years ago they had some real trouble with their schools. I'm not sure what the situation is now, but you may want to check," Parker would have understood the information more clearly.

Nearly everything changes with time. Some changes are imperceptible; others are so extensive that old information becomes inaccurate, obsolete, and even dangerous. We can make our messages clearer by using the skill of dating to indicate when the information we are conveying is accurate. To date information, we (1) consider or find out when the information was true and (2) verbally acknowledge this time frame. This seems like a simple skill to put into practice—and it is. But often, we just don't think about the implications of communicating using old

SKILL BUILDERS ○ **Adapt Language to Listeners**

SKILL	USE	PROCEDURE	EXAMPLE
Using vocabulary, jargon, and slang that listeners understand	To avoid words that listeners do not understand	1. Use simpler synonyms or familiar terms for words. 2. Explain jargon terms to listeners who may not understand them. 3. Use slang words only with listeners who understand it.	Instead of saying, "Jose is in his penultimate year of work," Larry can say, "Jose is in his next to last year of work." Sally can say, "Your asset-to-liability ratio, which is a calculation of how much money you have compared to how much money you owe, is really quite good." Judy can say a rock star is "hot" when talking with a friend but describe the star as "cute" when talking with her aunt.

data. We have no power to prevent change. But we can increase the effectiveness of our messages if we verbally acknowledge the reality of change by dating the statements we make. Consider each of the examples that follow. The statements on the left are undated generalizations; those on the right are carefully dated generalizations.

Cancún is really popular with the college crowd.	When we were in Cancún *two years ago*, it was really popular with the college crowd.
Professor Powell brings great enthusiasm to her teaching.	Professor Powell brings great enthusiasm to her teaching—at least she did *last quarter* in communication theory.
The Beast is considered the most exciting roller coaster in the country.	*Years ago*, The Beast was considered the most exciting roller coaster in the country.
You think Mary's depressed? I'm surprised. She seemed her regular high-spirited self when I talked to her.	You think Mary's depressed? I'm surprised. She seemed her regular high-spirited self when I talked with her *the day before yesterday*.

▷ Indexing Generalizations

Still another skill to improve the clarity of your communications is to index any generalizations you make. **Indexing generalizations** is the mental and verbal practice of acknowledging individual differences when voicing generalizations. Generalizations allow people to use what they have learned from their experiences and apply their knowledge to other situations. For instance, when Glenda, a third grade teacher, learns that three of her students who have been absent frequently are at or near the bottom of her class in reading, she generalizes that students who fail to attend school regularly are likely to do poorly in reading. Although the capacity to generalize carefully is important to all of us when we make decisions, the misuse of generalization contributes to perceptual inaccuracies because it ignores individual differences. Thus, just because Alex and Manuel are better at math than Alicia does not mean that boys (or men) in general are

Indexing generalizations—the mental and verbal practice of acknowledging individual differences when voicing generalizations.

SKILL BUILDERS ◑ Dating Information

SKILL	USE	PROCEDURE	EXAMPLE
Including a specific time referent to clarify a message	To avoid the pitfalls of language that allow you to speak of a dynamic world in static terms	1. Before you make a statement, consider or find out when the information was true. 2. If not based on present information, verbally acknowledge when the statement was true.	When Jake says, "How good a hitter is Steve?" Mark replies by dating his evaluation: "When I worked with him two years ago, he couldn't hit the curve."

better at math than girls (or women) or that Alex and Manuel are better than Alicia in any other respect.

To avoid making misleading generalizations and to help us make generalizations that may be true, we need to practice indexing, a skill that is borrowed from mathematics, where it is used to acknowledge individual elements within a group (X1, X2, X3, etc.). We mentally index by acknowledging that whether we have observed one, five, or ten or more similar outcomes to the same situation, we can't always be sure that a generalization based on those outcomes is valid. Thus, just because we learn that Brent frequently spends a lot of money at expensive restaurants does not necessarily mean that Brent is rich. So, if we were to say, "Brent eats at expensive restaurants, so he must be rich," we should add, "of course not all people who choose to spend their earnings at expensive restaurants are rich."

All people generalize at one time or another, but by using indexing, we can avoid the misunderstandings that generalized statements can create. Here are two steps to help you use the skill of indexing: (1) Consider whether what you want to say is about a specific object, person, or place or whether it is a generalization about a class to which the object, person, or place belongs. (2) If what you want to say is based on a generalization, qualify your statement appropriately so that your assertion does not go beyond the evidence that supports it. In the examples that follow, the statements on the left are overgeneralizations, whereas those on the right are carefully indexed, clearer, statements.

Because men are physically stronger than women, Max is probably stronger than Barbara.	*In general*, men are physically stronger than women, so Max is probably stronger than Barbara.
State has got to have a good economics department; the university is ranked among the top twenty in the nation.	Because State is among the top twenty schools in the nation, the economics program should be a good one, *although it may be an exception*.

SKILL	USE	PROCEDURE	EXAMPLE
Mentally or verbally accounting for individual differences when generalizing	To avoid "allness" in speaking	1. Before you make a statement, consider whether it pertains to a specific object, person, or place. 2. If you use a generalization, inform the listener that it does not necessarily apply in the situation being discussed.	"He's a politician and I don't trust him, although he may be different from most politicians I know."

Jack is sure to be outgoing; Don is, and they're brothers.

Jack is likely to be outgoing because his brother Don is, *but Jack could be different.*

Your Chevrolet should go fifty thousand miles before you need a brake job; Jerry's did.

Your Chevrolet may well go fifty thousand miles before you need a brake job; Jerry's did, *but, of course, all Chevrolets aren't the same.*

▷ Practicing Communication Accommodation

Practicing communication accommodation is such an important part of improving language clarity that a theory has grown around it. **Communication accommodation theory** is the theory explaining how people adjust their language patterns to accommodate their partners during communication (Giles & Coupland, 1991). The researchers who developed this theory observed that when we talk with someone we adapt our language in one of two ways. We may practice **convergence** (adapting to the language style of our partner) or we may practice **divergence** (consciously speaking in a language style different from that of our partner). When we want to signal that we are part of a group or show closeness to another person, we use language and language patterns that are more like those of the other. When we want to distance ourselves from a group or another person, we use language and language patterns that are different.

The features we alter when practicing communication accommodation can include our verbal communications (grammar, slang, jargon, and profanity) and/or our nonverbal communication features, including volume, tone of voice, accents,

Communication accommodation theory—theory explaining how people adjust their language patterns to accommodate their partners during communication.

Convergence—adapting to the language style of our partner.

Divergence—consciously speaking in a language style different from that of our partner.

Do you find yourself using "baby talk" when interacting with toddlers?

pronunciation, and rate of speaking (we will explore these in the next chapter). For example, an elementary school teacher who uses simple words with a lot of vocal variations and a slow rate of speech when talking with her young students is using convergence to make her communication more like theirs. A college professor who feels that being in a position of authority in the classroom is important, on the other hand, may accentuate the differences between her students and herself by using complex vocabulary, correct grammar, no slang, and a formal tone of voice.

Research has shown an interesting connection between culture and communication accommodation (Larkey, 1996). Perceptions of status, authority, and cultural identity affect how communication accommodation occurs. Those considered lower in status in a society are expected to adjust their communication to be more similar to higher-status speakers, not vice versa. For instance, European American males are less likely to practice communication convergence. They typically maintain their language style as standard; others, such as women and minorities, accommodate to that style. Indeed, the unwillingness of a lower-status communicator to adjust to the higher-status speaker can be seen as a sign of disrespect because it seems to signal a desire to remain separate. In the "Spotlight on Scholars" feature of this chapter, Professor Ronald L. Jackson II discusses the complex ways that people practice communication accommodation in relation to the negotiation of status and cultural identity.

Jackson also discusses the concept of codeswitching as it relates to cultural identity, so let's explore that concept first. **Codeswitching** is the use of two languages or linguistic styles simultaneously or interchangeably (Woolard, 2004). A bilingual speaker may smoothly incorporate aspects of both languages while communicating. For instance, native Spanish speakers who have strong fluency in English may use elements of both languages when speaking. Many residents of Quebec, Canada, switch between English and French because their province has two primary languages. Codeswitching has also come to refer to the alternating use of two linguistic styles rather than distinct languages. As a type of codeswitching, some African Americans may combine words, expressions, sounds, and other linguistic choices based on dominant societal norms with verbal and nonverbal language from their racial or cultural backgrounds. Codeswitching may help a cultural group retain a sense of cultural identity while simultaneously signaling that they also have membership in dominant, majority, or workplace cultures.

Codeswitching—the use of two languages or linguistic styles simultaneously or interchangeably.

▷ Demonstrating Linguistic Sensitivity

The final way to use language in a clearer way is to demonstrate that you are linguistically sensitive. It is important to be aware of potential language differences between people and to remember how our language reveals our attitudes and creates and reinforces hierarchy. By realizing that people differ in the language they use and the ways they interpret words, we can try to be more sensitive in our use of language. **Linguistic sensitivity** is choosing to use language that respects others and avoiding language that others perceive as offensive. Some of the mistakes in language that we make result from using expressions

Linguistic sensitivity—choosing to use language that respects others and avoiding language that others perceive as offensive.

Ronald L. Jackson II
Associate Professor of Communication and Culture, Penn State University, on
The Negotiation of Cultural Identity

Ronald L. Jackson II recognized in his early adolescence that something peculiar was happening with the people all around him. His mother would adjust her language, voice, and mood when talking with a friend versus talking with the bill collector. His teacher would use different words and change her level of enthusiasm when talking about politics versus family. And everyone seemed to lower their voices to a whisper and exercise caution in finding just the right words when talking about their most personal views regarding race. Although changing one's language patterns has been understood historically as codeswitching, this type of codeswitching had a lot to do with cultural identity. It could be more accurately characterized as a negotiation between oneself and others with the "bargaining chip" being one's cultural identity. Throughout his career Jackson has been concerned primarily with questions of cultural self-definition, and more specifically with the ways in which people shift their language and behavior when they come in contact with cultural others.

In 1991, Jackson earned his B.A. in communication, and two years later his M.A. in organizational communication from the University of Cincinnati. Subsequently, at the age of twenty-five, Jackson completed his Ph.D. in rhetoric and intercultural communication at Howard University. His dissertation examined the social construction and negotiation of racial and cultural identity in university settings. He derived his dissertation data from two predominately white universities and two predominately black universities and compared racial perceptions and cultural self-definitions among white and black students in different race contexts. This study was later published as his first book, *Negotiation of Cultural Identity*, in 1999. Since then, he has authored four monographs, edited four books, and penned approximately three dozen articles and book chapters. His latest projects are the two-volume *SAGE Encyclopedia of Identity* and the edited volume *Global Masculinities* (with Murali Balaji).

Jackson's body of research includes the development of the "cultural contracts theory." He argues that "cultural contracts" are the daily ways in which human beings negotiate the social world by adding, deleting, exchanging, and resisting modifications to core dimensions of one's multiple identities (e.g., religious, personal, political, cultural, racial, gender, etc.). Jackson identifies three types of cultural contracts: ready-to-sign (assimilation/accommodation), quasi-completed (adaptation), and co-created (mutual validation). Those who "carry" ready-to-sign contracts expect others to assimilate to them; if that happens, a "ready-to-sign" contract is consummated. Those who carry quasi-completed contracts tend to believe they are acting fairly and only seek a give-and-take relationship; however, one person tends to have more power than another and the fairness collapses intermittently, leading to a partial commitment to equality. This sometimes happens in interracial workplace relationships. Those who carry co-created contracts are those who are comfortable negotiating the terms of the contract and use language of equal status in the relationship, regardless of power.

The complexity of identity negotiation reveals itself when you consider the fact that any two people at any given time may have different or similar core identity dimensions that they feel are threatened within an interaction. This initial "threat" is often the result of a perception that the other person wants you to be more like him or her, and therefore feels you must change a part of how you define yourself. Threats to secondary identities tend to constitute low threats, while threats to core identities tend to constitute high threats. The higher the threat, the more individuals are likely to insulate themselves and prepare to resist. When people have enough power to successfully resist, they will likely feel less threatened and the ability to retain the integrity of the core will be higher. On the other hand, those with low power tend to be unsuccessful at resisting high threats to the core without some negative consequences. For example, imagine that a new Jewish employee is told he has to work during Yom Kippur. He asks for a vacation day, but his supervisor refuses to allow him off work and further states that if he tries to take off for any religious holidays, he might as well not show up for work the next day. In this case, the new employee only has a few options: comply, resist, or quit. Assuming being Jewish is a core dimension of his identity, his power is low in this organization, and he does not need this particular job, he will likely resist or quit. Though very simplistic, this example shows how a small conflict represents a critical incident for an individual within a stream of ongoing identity negotiations occurring within personal/private and professional/public contexts.

that are perceived by others as sexist, racist, or otherwise biased—that is, any language that is perceived as belittling any person or group of people. The most prevalent linguistic styles that are insensitive are those that use generic, nonparallel, or prejudicial language.

Generic language is language that may apply only to one sex, race, or other group that is used in a way that assumes it represents everyone. This usage is a problem because it linguistically excludes a portion of the population.

One example of generic language is the sexist use of masculine pronouns to refer to all people. English grammar traditionally called for the use of the masculine pronoun *he* to stand for the entire class of humans regardless of gender. Under this rule, the sentence "When a person shops, *he* should have a clear idea of what *he* wants to buy" was considered correct. However, in modern English grammar, we are aware that the sentence is sexist because the use of the word *he* inherently excludes females. Despite traditional usage, it is hard to picture people of both sexes when we hear the masculine pronoun *he*. To be linguistically sensitive means avoiding such sexist usage in one of two ways. First, use plurals. For instance, instead of saying, "Because a doctor has high status, his views may be believed regardless of topic," you could say, "Because doctors have high status, their views may be believed regardless of topic." Alternatively, you can use both male and female pronouns: "Since a doctor has high status, his or her views may be believed regardless of topic." Stewart, Cooper, Stewart, and Friedley (1998, p. 63) cite research to show that using *he or she* and to a lesser extent *they* alerts listeners to the importance of gender balance both in language and in life.

Another example of generic language is the traditional use of the generic word *man*. "Generic man" refers to the use of *man* as part of a word when the referent is to all humans. Many words that are inherently sexist in that they apply to only one gender have become a common part of our language. Consider the term *man-made*. What this really means is "produced by human beings," but its underlying connotation is "made by a male human being." Some people try to argue that just because a word has "man" within it does not really affect people's understanding of meaning. But research has demonstrated that people usually visualize men (not women) when they read or hear these words. Moreover, when job titles end in "man," their occupants are assumed to have stereotypically masculine personality traits (Gmelch, 1998, p. 51). In past generations this masculine generalization may have been appropriate, but that is no longer the case. In place of most sexist expressions, people now use or create suitable alternatives. For instance, use *police officer* instead of *policeman*, and substitute *synthetic* for *man-made*. Instead of saying *mankind*, change the construction—for example, go from "All of *mankind* benefits" to "All the *people in the world* benefit."

In addition to generic language, nonparallel language should also be avoided. **Nonparallel language** is language in which unnecessary asides are added to a sentence to point out someone's sex, race, or other characteristics. Because it treats groups of people differently, nonparallel language is also belittling. Two common forms of nonparallel language are marking and unnecessary association.

Generic language—language that may apply only to one sex, race, or other group that is used in a way that assumes it represents everyone.

Nonparallel language—language in which unnecessary asides are added to a sentence to point out someone's sex, race, or other characteristics.

Marking is the unnecessary addition of sex, race, age, or other designations to a general description of someone. For instance, *doctor* is a word representing a person with a medical degree. To describe Sam Jones as a doctor is to treat Jones linguistically as an equal member of the class of doctors. For example, you might say, "Jones, a doctor, contributed a great deal to the campaign." If, however, you said, "Jones, a woman doctor" (or a black doctor, or an old doctor, or a disabled doctor), you would be marking. Marking is offensive to many people because it is trivializing the person's role by laying emphasis on an irrelevant characteristic. For instance, if you say, "Jones is a really good female doctor," you may be intending to praise Jones, but your listeners may interpret the sentence as meaning Jones is a good doctor for a woman, but not necessarily as good as a male doctor. If it is relevant to identify a person by sex, race, age, or other characteristic, do so, but leave markers out of your labeling when they are irrelevant. One test of whether a marker is relevant and appropriate is to use the opposite sex, race, age, or other marker in the sentence. It would be relevant to specify "female doctor," for example, only if in that context it would be equally relevant to specify "male doctor."

Unnecessary association is emphasizing a person's association with another person when the second person is not relevant to the discussion. For example, if you hear a speaker say something like "Gladys Thompson, whose husband is CEO of Acme Inc., is the chairperson for this year's United Way campaign," you could argue that the association of Gladys Thompson with her husband further adds to her credentials. But more likely the association may be interpreted as implying that Gladys Thompson is important not because of her own accomplishments but because of her husband's accomplishments. A more flagrant example of unnecessary association would be the following: "Don Jones, twelfth grade teacher at Central High School and husband of Brenda Jones, local state senator, is chairperson for this year's minority scholarship campaign." Here Brenda Jones' occupation and relationship to Don Jones is clearly irrelevant. In either case, the pairing takes away from the person who is supposed to be the focus. So, avoid noting the association one person has with others when the association is irrelevant.

Prejudicial language is language that blatantly denigrates, stigmatizes, or marginalizes others based on their race, sex, ethnicity, sexual orientation, religion, age, ability, or other factors. You've heard children shout, "Sticks and stones may break my bones, but words will never hurt me." This rhyme may be popular among children because, even though they know it is untrue, it gives them a defense

Marking—the unnecessary addition of sex, race, age, or other designations to a general description of someone.

Unnecessary association—emphasizing a person's association with another person when the second person is not relevant to the discussion.

Prejudicial language—language that blatantly denigrates, stigmatizes, or marginalizes others based on their race, sex, ethnicity, sexual orientation, religion, age, ability, or other factors.

Do you think that children of celebrities have trouble avoiding unnecessary association remarks?

I Am . . .

by Dolores V. Tanno

How do you behave when you are asked to talk about yourself, especially when you are perceived as "different," whether that difference is by sex, religion, or ethnicity? Delores V. Tanno, University of Nevada, Las Vegas, describes how each ethnic self-reference communicates a story, and multiple stories provide significance to determining who "I am."

Over the course of my life one question has been consistently asked of me: "*What are you?*" I used to reply that I was American, but it quickly became clear this was unacceptable because what came next was, "No, really what are you?" In my more perverse moments I responded, "I am human." I stopped when I realized that people's feelings were hurt. Ironic? Yes, but the motive behind the question often justified hurt feelings. I became aware of this only after asking a question of my own: "Why do you ask?"

Confronting the motives of people has forced me to examine who I am. In the process I have had to critically examine my own choices, in different times and contexts, of the names by which I am placed in society. The names are "Spanish," "Mexican American," "Latina," and "Chicana."

"I am Spanish." Behind this label is the story of my childhood in northern New Mexico. New Mexico was the first permanent Spanish settlement in the Southwest, and New Mexicans have characterized themselves as Spanish for centuries. My parents, grandparents, and great-grandparents consider themselves Spanish; wrongly or rightly they attribute their customs, habits, and language to their Spanish heritage, and I followed suit. In my young mind, the story of being Spanish did not include concepts of racial purity or assimilation; what it did do was allow me to begin my life with a clearly defined identity and a place in the world. For me, the story of being Spanish incorporates into its plot the innocence of youth, before the reality of discrimination became an inherent part of the knowledge of who I am.

"I am Mexican American." When I left New Mexico, my sense of belonging did not follow me across the state border. When I responded to the question, "What are you?" by saying, "I am Spanish," people corrected me: "You mean Mexican, don't you?" My initial reaction was anger; how could they know better than I who I was? But soon my reaction was one of puzzlement, and I wondered just why there was such insistence that I be Mexican. Reading and studying led me to understand that the difference between Spanish and Mexican could be found in the legacy of colonization. Thus behind the name "Mexican American" is the story of classic colonization that allows for prior existence and that also communicates duality. As Richard A. Garica argues: "Mexican in culture and social activity, American in philosophy and politics." As native-born Mexican Americans we also have dual visions: the achievement of the American Dream and the preservation of cultural identity.

"I am Latina." If the story behind the name Mexican American is grounded in duality, the story behind the name "Latina" is grounded in cultural connectedness. The Spaniards proclaimed vast territories of North and South America as their own. They intermarried in all the regions in which they settled. These marriages yielded offspring who named themselves variously as Cubans, Puerto Ricans, Colombians, Mexicans, and so forth, but they connect culturally with one another when they name each other Latinas. To use the name *Latina* is to communicate acceptance and belonging in a broad cultural community.

"I am Chicana." This name suggests a smaller community, a special kind of Mexican American awareness that does not involve others (Cubans, Puerto Ricans, etc.). The name was the primary political as well as rhetorical strategy of the Chicano movement of the 1960s. Mirande and Enriquez argue that the dominant characteristic of the name "Chicana" is that it admits a "sense of marginality." There is a political tone and character to "Chicana" that signifies a story of self-determination and empowerment. As such, the name denotes a kind of political becoming. At the same time, however, the name communicates the idea of being American, not in a "melting pot" sense that presupposes assimilation, but rather in a pluralistic sense that acknowledges the inalienable right of existence for different peoples.

What, then, am I? The truth is I am all of these. Each name reveals a different facet of identity that allows symbolic, historical, cultural, and political connectedness. These names are no different than other multiple labels we take on. For example, to be mother, wife, sister, and daughter is to admit to the complexity of being female. Each name implies a narrative of experiences gained in responding to circumstances, time, and place and motivated by a need to belong.

In my case, I resort to being Spanish and all it implies whenever I return to my birthplace, in much the same way that we often resort to being children again in the presence of our parents. But I am also Mexican American when I balance the two important cultures that define me; Latina when I wish to emphasize cultural and historical connectedness with others; and Chicana whenever opportunities arise to promote political empowerment and assert political pride.

It is sometimes difficult for people to understand the "both/and" mentality that results from this simulta-

neity of existence. We are indeed enriched by belonging to two cultures. We are made richer still by having at our disposal several names by which to identify ourselves. Singly the names Spanish, Mexican American, Latina, and Chicana communicate a part of a life story. Together they weave a rhetorically powerful narrative of ethnic identity that combines biographical, historical, cultural, and political experiences.

Excerpted from Tanno, D. V. (2001). Names, narratives, and the evolution of ethnic identity. In A. Gonzalez, M. Houston, & V. Chen (Eds.), *Our Voices—Essays in Cultural Ethnicity and Communication* (3rd ed., pp. 25-28). Los Angeles: Roxbury Publishing Company.

against cruel name-calling. However, whether we admit it, words do hurt, sometimes permanently.

Great personal damage has been done to individuals throughout history as a result of prejudicial labeling. Of course, we all know that it is not the words alone that are so powerful; it is the context of the words—the situation, the feelings of the participants, the time, the place, or the tone of voice. You may recall circumstances in which a friend called you a prejudicial name and you did not even flinch, yet you can probably recall other circumstances in which someone made you furious by using the same term. It may be permissible for members of a culture to use prejudicial language, for instance a racial slur, when referring to a friend who is also a member of that subculture. But it is inappropriate for a nonmember to use that language, and some members may be offended even if the speaker is from the same group. One way to avoid using prejudicial language is to describe groups of people using the words they prefer to have used. These may change with time and may even vary between members of a group. So if you are in doubt, it's a good thing to ask or not use the term at all.

⚇ The Effects of Technology on Verbal Communication

Traditionally oral communication was viewed as synchronous, while written messages were considered asynchronous. New communication technologies, however, have blurred the distinctions between oral and written messages. The advent of instant messaging, text messaging, and chat technologies has created a context in which conversations, traditionally the domain of oral messages, can be held through the synchronous exchange of short written notes. Since their introduction, instant messaging, texting, and chatting have grown in popularity.

According to the Pew Internet and American Life Project (2008), 62 percent of all Americans are part of a wireless, mobile population that regularly participates in digital communication away from home, including the use of cell phones, personal digital assistants (PDAs), and the Internet. We can expect that the numbers of people using these new technologies to communicate on a daily basis will continue to grow.

These new communication technologies are giving rise to new written or text "dialects" that are condensed forms of the parent language of speech communities. These dialects have been called Weblish, netlingo, e-talk, techspeak, or wired style. But the most popular term is **netspeak**, language in which the rules of style, grammar, spelling, and abbreviations are varied in technology-moderated communication. In an instant message (IM), text, or chat using netspeak, the structure of messages in the written parent language is modified, words are spelled phonetically or abbreviated, and whole phrases may be represented by the first or first and second letters in each word. These changes are designed so that the exchange of written messages can mimic the "real-time" nature of oral conversations (Thurlow, Lengel, & Tomic, 2004). So your friend might send an IM or text reading "wen wud u b hm," which you would decode as "When would you be home?" In an online chat, your partner may use abbreviations like lol (laugh out loud), jk (just kidding), and bbl (be back later). While these messages can look like gibberish to some people, they are quickly comprehended by members of the speech community who are fluent in the netspeak

Netspeak—language in which the rules of style, grammar, spelling, and abbreviations are varied in technology-moderated communication.

A QUESTION OF ETHICS ▼ What Would You Do?

Pam and Christine had been best friends in high school and had decided to room together when they both chose to go to State U for college. Late in the fall semester Pam began seeing Matt, who was in a fraternity. Early on, Pam and Matt had tried fixing Christine up with a series of Matt's fraternity brothers, but none of the relationships had panned out. Matt's friends each thought that Christine was just a little too "needy" and expected them to quickly form a serious relationship with her. So after a time, Matt told Pam he wouldn't help her fix Christine up any more.

As Matt and Pam's relationship intensified, Christine, who had not made many other friends at school, became more and more demanding of Pam. She wanted to know what Pam's schedule was and where Pam was going. She wanted to know the details of Pam's relationship with Matt. She asked about Matt's friends and why she hadn't heard from them. Pam felt very conflicted. She really treasured her friendship with Christine and didn't want to hurt her feelings, but she also felt that she had a right to some privacy. So when Christine would ask her a question, she found herself giving deliberately vague answers.

On Thursday when Christine asked her what she was doing that weekend, Pam said, "Well, there are a number of things going on campus and I think I'll probably hang around and see what looks good," even though she knew that she and Matt would be going to the football game and then to a fraternity party afterward. Later that day as Pam and Christine were walking across campus toward their dorm after class, they ran into Matt, who smiled broadly at Pam and said, "How about if I pick you up about 11 on Saturday so we can get a bite to eat before the game?" After they left Matt, Pam noticed that Christine was acting cold and distant, answering her questions with one-word answers. When they got to their room, Christine slammed her books down on her desk, jerked her coat off, threw it on the floor, and sat down at her desk with her back to Pam.

1. Was it ethical for Pam to withhold her plans for the weekend from Christine?
2. Was it ethical for Christine to expect Pam to share information about her relationship, her plans, and what she knew about Matt's friends?
3. What can be done to repair the relationship?

dialect. Netspeak is now so common that netspeak "words" have been compiled in dictionaries (Jones, 2006) and books have been published to educate non "speakers" on "netiquette."

While netspeak is now widely used for instant messaging, text messaging, and chatting, experts still recommend that you use traditional spelling and follow the common rules of grammar in your e-mail messages. Over the past ten years, in business and the professional life, e-mail has begun to replace paper memos, notes, and letters as a way of documenting problem resolutions and decisions. So e-mail is now considered a more formal form of written communication than it once was. To avoid costly misunderstandings, e-mail messages should be written in full sentences that adhere to the traditional grammar of the language. We should also use concrete and precise words and provide details and examples. Because e-mails are often viewed as work products that reflect your competence, you should also spell-check and carefully proofread e-mails before sending them. Finally, make sure that the subject line of your e-mail accurately reflects the topic of the message (Brown, 2007).

❍ Summary

Language is the system of words, sounds, and gestures common to a group of people used to communicate messages. For language to work, there must be a speech community, words, and grammar. Through language, we discuss things outside our immediate experience, we reflect upon ourselves, and we talk about language itself.

You will be a more effective communicator if you understand that language affects perception in that it shapes what we are able to see and not see. You also need to understand that meaning is shaped by a complex series of interactions with others; it is not the simple transmission of messages from one person's brain to another's. When you are involved in a communication exchange, you must coordinate with the other person, so that you agree on the rules that shape the meaning of that interaction. The two levels of meaning attached to all words further complicate the interpretation of words. The denotation of a word is its dictionary meaning, which is complicated by the problem of many words having more than one dictionary meaning. The connotation of a word is the emotional significance the word has for the listener in a particular situation. Culture also has an effect on the understanding of language. Expectations of low-context and high-context cultures and high- and low-power distance cultures affect language use.

The seven characteristics of language are that it is arbitrary, ambiguous, abstract, self-reflexive, changeable, revealing, and hierarchical . You can improve your language skills by using specific language (concrete words, precise words, details, and examples) while considering the use of strategic ambiguity, by adapting your language to your listeners, by providing dating information, by indexing generalizations, by practicing communication accommodation, and by demonstrating linguistic sensitivity. Communication technologies are increasingly altering verbal communication.

◯ Chapter Resources

Communication Improvement Plan: Verbal Communication ◯ Find more on the web @ www.oup.com/us/interact12

How would you like to improve your use of language as discussed in this chapter?

- Using specific language
- Adapting language to listeners (vocabulary, jargon, and slang)
- Providing dating information
- Indexing generalizations
- Practicing communication accommodation
- Demonstrating linguistic sensitivity (avoiding sexist and prejudicial language)

Pick one of these topics, and write a communication improvement plan. You can find a communication improvement plan worksheet on our website at www.oup.com/us/interact12.

Key Words ◯

Language, *p. 90*
Speech community, *p. 90*
Words, *p. 90*
Grammar, *p. 91*
Sapir-Whorf hypothesis, *p. 91*
Denotation, *p. 92*
Connotation, *p. 92*
Symbolic interactionism, *p. 93*
Coordinated management of meaning, *p. 93*
Low-context culture, *p. 94*
High-context culture, *p. 94*

Power distance, *p. 95*
High power-distance culture, *p. 95*
Low power-distance culture, *p. 96*
Theory of muted groups, *p. 99*
Specific language, *p. 100*
Concrete words, *p. 100*
Precise words, *p. 100*
Strategic ambiguity, *p. 101*
Jargon, *p. 102*
Slang, *p. 103*
Dating information, *p. 104*
Indexing generalizations, *p. 105*

Communication accommodation theory, *p. 107*
Convergence, *p. 107*
Divergence, *p. 107*
Codeswitching, *p. 108*
Linguistic sensitivity, *p. 108*
Generic language, *p. 110*
Nonparallel language, *p. 110*
Marking, *p. 111*
Unnecessary association, *p. 111*
Prejudicial language, *p. 111*
Netspeak, *p. 114*

Skill Practice ◯ Find more on the web @ www.oup.com/us/interact12

Skill Practice exercises challenge you to master the material you have read in this chapter. For additional Skill Practice activities, visit our website at www.oup.com/us/interact12.

Concrete, Precise

1. For each word listed, find three words or phrases that are more specific, or more concrete.

implements	building	nice	education
clothes	colors	chair	bad
happy	stuff	things	car

2. Make the following statements clearer by editing out words that are not precise, specific, or concrete:

"You know I love basketball. Well, I'm practicing a lot because I want to get better."

"Paula, I'm really bummed out. Everything is going down the tubes. You know what I mean?"

"Well, she just does these things to tick me off. Like, just a whole lot of stuff—and she knows it!"

"I just bought a beautiful outfit—I mean, it is really in style. You'll love it."

"I've really got to remember to bring my things the next time I visit."

Inter-Act with Media: Verbal Communication ◉ Find more on the web @ www.oup.com/us/interact12

Television

Grey's Anatomy, episode: "Crash into Me, Parts One and Two" (2007). Chandra Wilson, Cress Williams, T. R. Knight.

Brief Summary: A brief verbal exchange at breakfast marks a turning point for Dr. Miranda Bailey's (Wilson) marriage. Miranda's husband, Tucker (Williams), tells her, "You're never here" while a distracted Miranda tends to hospital paperwork. She responds by saying, "I'm here . . . in the mornings. . . . I'm here at night." Tucker responds by clarifying that she's "there" between midnight and 6 A.M. and then saying, "We need to talk." Miranda asks Tucker to meet her for lunch, but as the episode continues, an emergency surgery delays her. Miranda tells intern George (Knight) to ask Tucker to wait, which he does, for hours. When George relays another message that Miranda will be gone even longer, Tucker tells George to tell Miranda that he's done waiting. This couple's verbal communication is fraught with ambiguous language and connotation, given that their perception of how much Miranda is "here" and how long Tucker will wait for her to be there varies greatly.

IPC Concepts: Coordinated management of meaning, connotation, characteristics of language, ambiguous language.

Cinema

The Savages (2007). Tamara Jenkins (director). Laura Linney, Philip Seymour Hoffman, Philip Bosco.

Brief Summary: Siblings Wendy (Linney) and Jon Savage (Hoffman) come together to care for their aging father, Lenny (Bosco), who suffers from dementia. Wendy and Jon lacked closeness with their father, but they band together to make difficult decisions about putting him in a nursing home. While filling out the application, advance directive questions arise that must be discussed with Lenny. They start the conversation in a restaurant after giving their father a new hearing aid. Wendy leads the discussion but stalls, unable to ask the question about Lenny's wishes. Jon asks directly, "What if you were in a coma? Would you want a breathing machine to keep you alive?" Lenny asks agitatedly, "What kind of question is that?" Jon tells him that the question is "just in case," then stammers that it is procedural. Lenny says, "For who?" and Jon names the nursing home, which Lenny thought was a hotel. Then Lenny screams, "Pull the plug!" Jon stammers, but then asks, "Then what do we do with you?" After more mutters and back-and-forth talk, Lenny calls them idiots and yells, "You bury me!" The difficult content reflected in this exchange would understandably lead to less direct language. The siblings could not have anticipated Lenny's incredulity over their lack of concrete questioning and his precise language in response.

IPC Concepts: Ambiguous language, choosing specific language, using concrete and precise words, adapt language to listener.

What's on the Web

Find links and additional material, including self-quizzes, on the companion website at www.oup.com/us/interact12.

5

Communicating through Nonverbal Behaviors

"Carlo, I don't think our relationship means very much to you. You just like the convenience of having a girlfriend, but you are not really committed to us as a couple."

"Whoa, where did that come from? What do you mean, Cecily? I've never said that. You mean everything to me."

"It's not *what* you say. It's what you *show* in how you act."

"What do you mean, 'how I act?'"

"Well, Carlo, for one thing, you don't look at me the way you used to. When I stop by, you don't look happy to see me. And you used to enjoy cuddling on the couch while we watched a movie. Lately you've been acting like I'm crowding you. Last night you got up from the couch and moved to the chair to sit alone. It's these types of things that let me know how you are really feeling."

"How can you say that, Cecily? Every day I tell you that I love you. I buy you presents. I don't go out with other girls. Don't those things say what I feel?"

"Well maybe. . . . But lately you've been spending so much time with your brother and your friends it seems as if I don't really matter. And before, when we were out in public together, you'd hold my hand or put your arm around my waist as we walked, showing everybody that we're a couple. But recently you've been walking a few steps ahead of me as though you were alone. And all of these signals taken together lead me to believe that you just don't care much anymore. I don't think I'm imagining this. You like the idea of having a girlfriend, but I'm not sure you're really into me."

Nonverbal communication behavior—bodily actions, use of vocal qualities, and other behaviors that typically accompany a verbal message.

We've all heard—and said—"actions speak louder than words." Cecily is sensitive to how Carlo's actions have changed, and she is concerned about what these changes signal in their relationship. What are Carlo's actions communicating? They are communicating quite a lot. Actions are so important to our communication that researchers have estimated that as much as 65 percent of the social meaning we convey in face-to-face interactions is a result of nonverbal behavior (Burgoon, Buller, & Woodall, 1996). In other words, the meaning we assign to any communication is based on both the content of the verbal message and our interpretation of the nonverbal behavior that accompanies and surrounds the verbal message. As we can see from the interaction between Cecily and Carlo, interpreting these nonverbal actions is not always the easiest thing to do. Was Cecily making incorrect assumptions, or was she correctly interpreting Carlo's behavior? It's hard to be sure.

In the last chapter, we discussed language, the verbal side of interpersonal communication. In this chapter, we provide a framework for understanding and improving nonverbal communication behaviors. In the broadest sense, the term "nonverbal communication" is commonly used to describe all human communication events that transcend spoken or written words (Knapp & Hall, 2006). More specifically, **nonverbal communication behavior** describes the bodily actions, use of vocal qualities, and other behaviors that typically accompany a verbal message.

We begin this chapter by describing the characteristics and functions of nonverbal communication. Next, we identify the types of nonverbal communications, including body motions (kinesics), nonverbal sounds (paralanguage), spatial cues (proxemics), and self-presentation cues. Then, we discuss the ways that these types of nonverbal communication may vary based on cultural and gender factors. Finally, we offer suggestions for improving the ways you send and interpret nonverbal communications.

◐ Characteristics and Functions of Nonverbal Communication

To lay a foundation for a complete discussion of the specific elements of nonverbal communication, we need to consider its many characteristics and functions.

▷ Characteristics of Nonverbal Communication

Nonverbal communication can be broken down into five distinct characteristics: It is intentional or unintentional, primary, ambiguous, continuous, and multi-channeled. Let's look at these characteristics more closely.

1. Nonverbal communication can be *intentional* or *unintentional*. Sometimes we are aware of what we communicate nonverbally, but more often than not we are not consciously aware of it. For example, perhaps Zach smirks when he is nervous, taps his foot when he is impatient, speaks forcefully when he is angry, or stands tall when he is confident. He may be unaware of all of these mannerisms, but people close to him may be quite aware of his habits. This is why many react to seeing themselves on videotape by saying things like, "I didn't know that I sounded like that, walked like that, gestured like that, or made those facial expressions." People interpret nonverbal cues as intentional, acting as if such cues are intended, even if they are transmitted unconsciously or unintentionally (Burgoon, 1994).

2. Nonverbal communication is *primary*. When we communicate with others, we base our interpretation of the speaker's feelings and emotions almost totally on the nonverbal aspects of the interaction. In other words, nonverbal communication is primary, taking precedence over verbal communication. In a classic study of nonverbal communication and emotion, psychologist Albert Mehrabian (1972) found that about 93 percent of the emotional meaning of messages is conveyed nonverbally. Think about it, 93 percent! In addition, nonverbal communication is perceived to be more believable than verbal communication. It is easy to deceive others with our preplanned words. Nonverbal behavior, however, is harder to fake because it is more spontaneous. For instance, when Janelle frowns, clenches her fists, and forcefully says, "I am NOT angry!" her sister Renée knows that Janelle is in fact angry. Renée ignores the verbal message and believes the nonverbal behaviors, which indicate that Janelle is angry. Have you ever encountered a situation where your gut-level response to another was discomfort or distrust? The other person's verbal messages may have seemed friendly or kind, but your reaction was based on nonverbal cues. Though you may not have been consciously aware of what in the person's nonverbal behaviors bothered you, you were reacting to them more than to the verbal message.

3. Nonverbal communication is frequently *ambiguous*. Since most nonverbal behaviors are not codified, a particular nonverbal behavior can have many meanings depending on the user's personality, family influences, culture, the context of communication, or the relationship of the nonverbal behaviors to the verbal message. For example, when Ashley fidgets by tapping her fingers and moving in her seat, her behavior may mean she is nervous, bored, energetic, impatient, excited, hyperactive, or feeling the effects of some cold medication she took before class. Any one of these meanings may be accurate. You may display your anger by frowning or by being poker-faced, you may speak louder or softer, you may speak quickly or slowly, you may aggressively stare at someone or avoid eye contact altogether, or you may cry. In short, it is difficult to interpret nonverbal behaviors accurately, especially when you do not know someone well. However, when we are in a relationship with someone, we learn to "read" our partner's nonverbal behaviors and we become more accurate at decoding what their behaviors mean.

4. Nonverbal communication is *continuous*. You can never stop communicating nonverbally. This is why nonverbal communication is often called nonverbal behavior. Any time you are behaving, intentionally or not, and someone else notices that behavior and attaches meaning to it, you have communicated nonverbally. For instance, when Austin yawns and nods off during a meeting at work, his co-workers will notice this behavior and make assumptions about Austin. Some may think he is rude; others may believe he is bored. Paul may correctly recognize that his friend Austin is exhausted from studying for exams. In any of these cases, however, Austin may not realize it, but even in a situation in which he thinks he has removed himself from active communication, he is nonetheless constantly communicating through his nonverbal behaviors.

5. Nonverbal communication is *multi-channeled*. When interpreting someone's nonverbal communication, we may use a variety of cues to make that interpretation, including the vocal tone, body position, gestures, facial expressions, and general appearance of the other person. In other words, nonverbal communication is transmitted through a variety of channels. For example, when Alisha meets her new neighbor Mimi, she will notice many things at once, including Mimi's smile, twinkling eyes, fast rate of speech, erect posture, designer suit, perfume, and apartment decor. Not only do we notice a variety of nonverbal behaviors to interpret someone's meaning, but rarely do we perceive these behaviors in isolation. Rather, we interpret all of these behaviors together with any verbal messages that accompany them to determine the real meaning that the speaker intended.

In negotiations, he appeared to have ice in his veins, but his tail betrayed him.

▷ Functions of Nonverbal Communication

In addition to having the specific characteristics we just discussed, nonverbal communication serves five primary functions: It provides information, regulates interaction, expresses or hides emotion and affect, presents an image, and expresses status, power, and control. While we will describe each function separately in this section, it is important to recognize that in an interaction, some of these functions overlap, and nonverbal communication may fulfill more than one of these functions at the same time.

1. Nonverbal communication *provides information*. Our nonverbal behaviors provide information by repeating, substituting for, emphasizing, or contradicting our verbal messages. Let's look at each way our nonverbal behaviors provide information in turn. First, we may use nonverbal cues to *repeat* what we have said verbally. For instance, if you say "no" and shake your head at the same time, you have used a nonverbal cue to repeat what you have said verbally. Second, some nonverbal cues can *substitute* for the words. A wave, for example, can stand in place of the word "hello" or "goodbye." As another example, in some cultures, curling your index finger and motioning toward yourself can substitute for the words "Come here," while in other cultures the same gesture can mean "Go away" or "good-bye." You could make a lengthy list of nonverbal symbols that take the place of words or phrases that you use frequently. Third, nonverbal cues can *emphasize* the verbal message by accenting, complementing, or adding information to the words. For instance, a teacher may smile, clap, or pat a student on the back when saying, "Good job on the test." In this case, facial expression, body motions, and voice volume emphasize the verbal statement of praise. Finally, nonverbal cues may *contradict* the verbal message. The nonverbal behavior may provide information, but in contradicting the verbal message, the nonverbal information leads to confusion rather than clarity. For example, when Sadie says in a quiet, monotone voice, "I am really interested in your project," while avoiding eye contact and moving away, her nonverbal message has contradicted her verbal message. The result of contradictory verbal and nonverbal messages is a mixed message, but because one of the characteristics of nonverbal behavior is its primacy over verbal messages, people are likely to rely more on the nonverbal cues to figure out a mixed message than the words.

2. Nonverbal communication *regulates interaction.* We manage a conversation through subtle and sometimes obvious nonverbal cues. We use shifts in eye contact, slight head movements, posture changes, raised eyebrows, and nodding to tell another person when to continue, to repeat, to elaborate, to hurry up, or to finish what he or she is saying. Think of the times you have used nonverbal cues in an attempt to end a conversation. You may have decreased the amount of eye contact you gave the other person, given abrupt or abbreviated responses, shown less animated facial expression, or turned away from the other person. Students in a classroom regularly signal to the instructor that class time is nearly over by packing away their laptops, putting on their coats, fidgeting in their seats, or mumbling to each other. Effective communicators learn to adjust what they are saying and how they are saying it on the basis of the nonverbal cues of others.

3. Nonverbal communication *expresses or hides emotion and affect.* We have already explained that most of the emotional aspects of communication are conveyed through nonverbal means. Think of how you nonverbally show others that you care for them. You may smile, hug, kiss, sit closer to, gaze at, or spend more time with those about whom you care deeply. Alternatively, you can use nonverbal behavior to mask your true feelings. In either case, more often than not, we show our true emotions nonverbally rather than describing our emotions with words. Sometimes we try to hide our emotions or feelings, but they may unintentionally leak out nonverbally. Blushing when one is embarrassed is a prime example of the inadvertent display of emotion.

4. Nonverbal communication *presents an image.* In Chapter 2, we discussed how people try to create impressions of themselves through appearance and actions. Much of impression management occurs through the nonverbal channel. People may carefully develop an image through clothing, grooming, jewelry, and other personal possessions that they display. For example, when you see someone briskly walking down the street wearing a Bluetooth headset, what do you think? How people handle, use, accessorize, and wear their cell phones communicates something about them and their lifestyles (Kleinman, 2007). Not only do people use nonverbal communication to communicate a personal image, but they may also use nonverbal cues to signal their relationship status. For instance, in the opening conversation of this chapter, one of Cecily's complaints is that when Carlo chooses to walk alone without holding her hand, he is sending the message that he and Cecily are not a couple. Sometimes the image presented is not accurate, however. For example, couples in a distressed marriage may publicly project a positive image by holding hands or being attentive to each other through facial expressions (Patterson, 1994).

5. Nonverbal communication *expresses status, power, and control.* Many nonverbal behaviors are signs of dominance, regardless of whether the person displaying them intended to convey power and control. Think of how a high-level manager conveys status and how subordinate employees acknowledge that status through nonverbal behavior. The manager may dress more formally, have a larger and more expensively furnished office, and walk and speak authoritatively. Subordinates may show respect to the manager by using eye contact and listening attentively when the manager speaks, by not interrupting, and by seeking permission (appointments) to enter the manager's office. As another example, imagine a parent who says to a child, "Look at me when I'm speaking to you." The parent expects that the child will nonverbally accept parental dominance by using steady eye contact as a sign of respect. Further, expressions such as, "She's looking down her nose at me" or "He's treating me like I'm a child" show the role of nonverbal behavior in expressing status, power, and control.

○ Types of Nonverbal Communication

Nonverbal behaviors can be classified into four general categories or types. These categories are body language (body motions used in communication, such as eye contact, facial expressions, gestures, posture, and touch), paralanguage (nonverbal sounds such as pitch, volume, rate, quality, and intonation that accompany words), spatial usage (the use of acoustic space, territory, and artifacts during communication), and self-presentation cues (use of physical appearance cues, time cues, and smell cues).

▷ Body Language

Of all the categories of nonverbal behavior, you are probably most familiar with **body language**, nonverbal communication through body movements. **Kinesics**

Body language—nonverbal communication through body motions.

Kinesics—the study of body language.

is the study of body language. Body language includes eye contact, facial expression, gesture, posture, and haptics (touch).

1. Eye contact. Eye contact (also referred to as gaze) is how and how much we look at the people with whom we are communicating. Eye contact conveys many meanings, and these meanings vary by culture. Eye contact can signal whether you are paying attention, and it can convey a range of emotions, such as anger, fear, or affection. For instance, we describe people in love as looking "doe-eyed." Intense eye contact may also signal dominance (Pearson, West, & Turner, 1995). As a result we comment on "looks that could kill," and we talk of someone "staring another person down." Moreover, through our eye contact, we monitor the effect of our communication. By maintaining eye contact, you can see how someone is responding to your message.

The amount of eye contact used in communication differs from person to person, from situation to situation, and from culture to culture. Studies show that in Western cultures, talkers hold eye contact about 40 percent of the time and listeners nearly 70 percent of the time (Knapp & Hall, 2006). In Western cultures people also generally maintain better eye contact when they are discussing topics with which they are comfortable, when they are genuinely interested in another person's comments or reactions, or when they are trying to influence the other person. Conversely, they tend to avoid eye contact when they are discussing topics that make them uncomfortable, when they are uninterested in the topic or the person talking, or when they are embarrassed, ashamed, or trying to hide something.

In addition, the use of eye contact can signal status or aggression. In many Eastern cultures (and some American subcultures), a person will avoid direct eye

Eye contact—how and how much we look at the people with whom we are communicating.

contact when talking to someone of higher status to show respect. Violating this cultural expectation is seen as rude or aggressive. In Western cultures, holding a gaze for too long, or staring at someone, tends to be interpreted as a sign of dominance or aggression. Indeed, in some segments of society, a prolonged stare may be an invitation to a physical fight. Yet, ironically, not giving someone eye contact at all can also be seen as a sign of dominance. The dominant person in an exchange, such as a boss, an interviewer, a teacher, or a police officer, has the freedom to maintain eye contact or look away at will, but the subordinate person in the situation is expected to give steady and respectful eye contact.

2. Facial expression. Facial expression is the arrangement of facial muscles to communicate emotional states or reactions to messages. The three sets of muscles that are manipulated to form facial expressions are those of the brow and forehead; those of the eyes, eyelids, and root of the nose; and those of the cheeks, mouth, remainder of the nose, and chin. Our facial expressions are especially important in conveying the six basic emotions of happiness, sadness, surprise, fear, anger, and disgust. In fact, facial expressions are so important to interpersonal communication that people have invented a system of conveying facial expressions online, using **emoticons**, which are typed or graphic symbols that convey emotional aspects of online messages (Walther & Parks, 2002). Facial expressions are also useful for conveying feedback during an interpersonal exchange. Think of the times you have used a quizzical look to signal that you do not understand someone or a frown to convey your disagreement.

3. Gesture. In addition to eye contact and facial expression, we also use gestures to communicate nonverbally. **Gesture** is the movement of hands, arms, and fingers to describe or to emphasize. Thus, when a person says "about this high" or "nearly this round," we expect to see a gesture accompanying the verbal description. Likewise, when a person says, "Put that down" or "Listen to me," a pointing finger, pounding fist, or some other gesture often reinforces the point. Individuals and cultural groups vary, however, in the amount of gesturing they use to accompany their spoken messages. In some cultures gesturing is more central to communication, and within cultures some people "talk with their hands" far more than others in the same cultural group. Some gestures, called **emblems**, substitute completely for words. A hitchhiker's upward-pointing thumb, for example, is an emblem because it is a gesture that needs no words to accompany it. Likewise, a finger placed vertically across the lips automatically means, "Be quiet." Emblems have automatic meanings in a particular culture but can vary greatly across cultures. Other gestures, called **adaptors**, are unconscious and respond to a physical need. For example, you may scratch an itch, yawn, adjust your glasses, or rub your hands together when they are cold. You do not mean to communicate a message with these gestures, but others do notice them and attach meaning to them.

4. Posture and body orientation. Posture also conveys nonverbal messages. **Posture** is the position and movement of the whole body. **Body orientation**, meanwhile, refers to posture in relation to another person. Like eye contact, it can be described as direct or indirect. Facing another person squarely is called

Facial expression—arrangement of facial muscles to communicate emotional states or reactions to messages.

Emoticons—typed or graphic symbols that convey emotional aspects of online messages.

Gesture—movement of hands, arms, and fingers to describe or to emphasize.

Emblems—gestures that can substitute completely for words.

Adaptors—gestures that are unconscious and respond to a physical need

Posture—position and movement of the whole body.

Body orientation—posture in relation to another person.

direct body orientation. When two people's postures are at angles to each other, this is called indirect body orientation. The combination of posture and body orientation can convey information about attentiveness, respect, and power. For example, think of how you would sit in a job interview. You are likely to sit up straight and face the interviewer directly because you want to communicate your interest, respect, and confidence, while the interviewer may also sit up straight, face you directly, and possibly lean forward to signal dominance. Interviewers tend to interpret a slouched posture and indirect body orientation as disinterest, disrespect, and lack of confidence, while interviewees may interpret a slouched, indirectly oriented, and back-leaning interviewer as not only disinterested and disrespectful but also a pushover. Yet in other situations, such as talking with friends, a slouched posture and indirect body orientation may be appropriate and may not carry any messages about attention, respect, or power. This difference in meaning based on various situations shows the ambiguous nature of nonverbal communication. It is rare that any one posture or body orientation absolutely means any one thing.

5. Touch. Formally known as haptics, **touch** is putting part of the body in contact with something. It is the first form of nonverbal communication that we experience in our lives because as infants we lack the capacity to understand verbal messages and most nonverbal messages, responding only to messages of love and comfort through touch. Touching behavior is a fundamental aspect of nonverbal communication in general and of self-presentation in particular. We use our hands, our arms, and other body parts to pat, hug, slap, kiss, pinch, stroke, hold, embrace, and tickle, communicating a variety of emotions and messages. Our touching can be gentle or firm, perfunctory or passionate, brief or lingering. Like many of the other types of body motion, touch can convey messages about power. Usually, the higher-status person in a situation is the

Touch—formally known as haptics, touch is putting part of the body in contact with something.

one to initiate touch. Managers are more likely to touch their employees than vice versa, and faculty members are more likely to touch their students than vice versa. There are three types of touch: spontaneous touch, ritualized touch, and task-related touch.

Spontaneous touch is touch that is automatic and subconscious. Patting someone on the back when you hear that he or she has won an award, for example, is spontaneous touch. In addition, there are many forms of **ritualized touch**, touch that is scripted rather than spontaneous. Handshakes or high-five slaps of the hands, for example, are forms of ritualized touch that have rather definite meaning as greeting rituals and are expected in certain situations. **Task-related touch** is touch used to perform a certain unemotional function. For instance, a doctor may touch a patient during a physical examination, or a personal trainer may touch a client during a workout at the gym. We do not attach the same meanings to task-related touch as we do to spontaneous or ritualized touch. We see task-related touch as part of the professional service we are receiving. There is also a type of touch that combines spontaneity and task-related touch to convey messages of closeness. For example, someone who, in public, adjusts your coat collar for you or removes some lint from your clothing is not only doing a task-related favor for you but is also signaling, perhaps inadvertently, a degree of closeness between the two of you that they would not signal to a complete stranger or a casual acquaintance.

People differ in their touching behavior and in their reactions to unsolicited touch from others. Some people, because of individual preference, family background, or culture, like to touch and be touched; other people do not. Although American culture is relatively non-contact-oriented, the kinds and amounts of touching behavior within our society vary widely. Touching behavior that seems innocuous to one person may be perceived as overly intimate or threatening to another. Moreover, the perceived appropriateness of touch differs with the context. Touch that is considered appropriate in private may embarrass a person when done in public or with a large group of people.

▷ Paralanguage

The second category of nonverbal communication is paralanguage. **Paralanguage** (also known as vocalics) is communication through nonverbal sounds. The five vocal characteristics that comprise paralanguage are pitch, volume, rate, quality, and intonation. By controlling these five major vocal characteristics, we can complement, supplement, or contradict the meaning conveyed by the language of our message. While we use the five characteristics to add shade to messages, vocal interferences can have the effect of disrupting message flow.

1. Pitch. Pitch is the highness or lowness of a person's vocal tone. People raise and lower vocal pitch to emphasize ideas, indicate questions, or show nervousness. They may also raise the pitch when they are nervous or lower the pitch when they are trying to be forceful. Voices that are lower in pitch tend to convey more believability and credibility.

Spontaneous touch—touch that is automatic and subconscious.

Ritualized touch—touch that is scripted rather than spontaneous.

Task-related touch—touch used to perform a certain unemotional function.

Paralanguage—communication through nonverbal sounds.

Pitch—highness or lowness of a person's vocal tone.

2. Volume. Volume is the loudness or softness of a person's vocal tone. Whereas some people have booming voices that carry long distances, others are normally soft-spoken. Regardless of their normal volume level, however, people do vary vocal volume depending on the situation or topic of discussion. For example, people may talk loudly when they wish to be heard in noisy settings, they may raise their volume when they are angry, or they may speak more softly when they are being romantic or loving.

3. Rate. Rate is the speed at which a person speaks. People tend to talk more rapidly when they are happy, frightened, nervous, or excited, and they tend to talk more slowly when they are problem solving out loud or trying to emphasize a point.

4. Quality. Quality is the sound of a person's voice. Each human voice has a distinct tone: Some voices are raspy, some smoky, some have bell-like qualities, and others are throaty. But regardless of voice quality, each of us may use a slightly different quality of voice to communicate a particular state of mind. We may accompany a complaint with a whiny, nasal vocal quality; a seductive invitation with a soft, breathy quality; and anger with a strident, harsh quality.

5. Intonation. Intonation is the variety, melody, or inflection of a person's voice. Some voices have little intonation and sound monotonous. Other voices have a great deal of melody and may have a childlike melody to them. People prefer to listen to voices with a moderate amount of intonation.

6. Vocal interferences. While pitch, volume, rate, quality, and intonation add nonverbal shades of meaning to words, **vocal interferences** are extraneous sounds or words that interrupt fluent speech. These vocalized sounds add little or no meaning to the verbal message and may even interfere with understanding. They are sometimes used as "place markers" designed to fill in momentary gaps in a verbal message while we search for the right word or idea. These place markers indicate that we are not done speaking and that it is still our "turn." The use of an excessive number of fillers can lead to the impression that you are unsure of yourself or confused in what you are attempting to say. The most common interferences that creep into our speech include "uh," "er," "well," and "OK," as well as the extraneous use of "you know" and "like."

▷ Spatial Usage

Spatial usage is a third category of nonverbal communication. **Spatial usage** is nonverbal communication through the use of the space and objects around us. We communicate nonverbally through our use of the physical space around us (informal space), our use of the space in which we can be heard (acoustic space), our use of the spaces that we own and protect (territory), and our use of objects to decorate our space (artifacts).

1. Informal space. Informal space is the space around the place a person occupies at a given moment. **Proxemics** is the study of informal space. Managing informal space requires an understanding of attitudes toward physical distance.

Volume—loudness or softness of a person's vocal tone.

Rate—speed at which a person speaks.

Quality—sound of a person's voice.

Intonation—variety, melody, or inflection of a person's voice.

Vocal interferences—extraneous sounds or words that interrupt fluent speech.

Spatial usage—nonverbal communication through the use of the space and objects around us.

Informal space—space around the place a person occupies at a given moment.

Proxemics—the study of informal space.

Have you ever been speaking with someone and become aware that you were uncomfortable because the other person was standing too close to you? Or maybe you've found yourself starting a conversation and then moving closer to someone as you begin to share an embarrassing story. If you have experienced either of these situations, you are already aware of the way that the space between conversational partners influences their interaction. Edward T. Hall (1969) suggests that in the dominant U.S. culture, four distinct distances are comfortable, depending on the nature of the conversation. These distance zones, based on Hall's research, represent descriptions of what most people consider appropriate or comfortable distances in various situations:

- *Intimate distance,* up to eighteen inches, is appropriate for private conversations between close friends.
- *Personal distance,* from eighteen inches to four feet, is the space in which casual conversation occurs.
- *Social distance,* from four to twelve feet, is where impersonal business such as a job interview is conducted.
- *Public distance* is anything more than twelve feet and is the distance between people in public.

Of greatest concern to most people is the intimate distance—the distance we regard as the appropriate distance between people when we have a very personal conversation with close friends, parents, and younger children. People usually become uncomfortable when "outsiders" violate this intimate distance. For instance, in a movie theater that is less than one-quarter full, people will tend to leave one or more seats empty between themselves and people they do not know. If in such a setting a stranger sits right next to you, you are likely to feel uncomfortable or threatened, and you may even move away. Intrusions into our intimate space are acceptable only in certain settings and then only when all involved follow the unwritten rules. For instance, people will tolerate being packed into a crowded elevator or subway car, making physical contact with people they do not know, provided those involved follow the "rules." The rules may include standing rigidly, looking at the floor, and not making eye contact with others. In essence, we cope with this space violation by turning other people into objects. Only occasionally will people who are forced to invade each other's intimate space acknowledge the other as a person. Then they are likely to exchange sheepish smiles or otherwise acknowledge the mutual invasion of intimate distance.

In the "Spotlight on Scholars" box for this chapter, we feature Judee Burgoon, who has focused a great deal of her research on the effects of such intrusions into our intimate space. Her findings develop and test what she calls "expectancy violation theory."

2. Acoustic space. Because of mobile communication technology, a new concept of space has emerged in recent years. Informal space is now measured both visually, as we described earlier, and acoustically, by sound. **Acoustic space** is the area over which one's voice or music can be heard (Kleinman, 2007). Mobile

Acoustic space—area over which one's voice or music can be heard.

Judee K. Burgoon
Professor of Communication, University of Arizona, on
Nonverbal Expectancy Violation Theory

With eight books and more than 250 articles and book chapters to her credit, Judee K. Burgoon is a leading scholar who has helped to shape how we now think about nonverbal communication. Her fascination with nonverbal behavior dates back to a graduate school seminar assignment at West Virginia University, where she was asked to make sense of what was known about proxemics, the study of space. From that assignment, she says, "I just got hooked. Nonverbal is more elusive and difficult to study and I've always enjoyed a challenge!"

In the early 1970s, scholars believed that the road to interpersonal success lay in conforming one's behaviors to social norms about the distances that are appropriate for certain types of interactions and the types of touch that are appropriate for certain people in certain relationships. Thus, people would be successful in their interactions as long as they behaved according to these norms. Encouraged by one of her professors to "look for the counterintuitive," Burgoon's research showed that there were situations where violations of these norms resulted in positive, rather than negative, consequences. For example, in settings where two people were not well acquainted and one of them began "flirting" by moving closer to the other, thus "violating" that person's space, the other person did not always react by moving away from the violator as expected. In fact, at times the person seemed to welcome the violation and at times may even have moved closer. Similarly, she noticed that touching behavior that violated social norms was sometimes rejected and at other times accepted.

To explain what she saw happening, Burgoon developed and began to test what she named "expectancy violation theory," which is based on the premise that we have strong expectations about how people ought to behave when they interact with us. Whether they meet our expectations affects not only how we interact with them, but also how competent, credible, and influential we perceive them to be and what we think of our relationship. She found that how we interpret a violation depends on how we regard that person. If we like the person, we are likely to read the nonverbal violation as positive ("Gee, she put her arm around me—that means she's really interested in me"). Conversely, if we don't like the person, we are likely to read the same nonverbal violation as negative ("He better take his arm off of me—this is a clear case of harassment"). And,

because we have become sensitized to the situation, the violations will be subject to strong evaluations ("Wow, I really like the feel of her arm around my waist" versus "He's making me feel really uncomfortable"). As Burgoon continued to study violations, she discovered that when a person we really like violates our expectations, we are likely to view the interaction as even more positive than we would have if the person had conformed to our expectations. Over the years, in numerous research studies, Burgoon and her students have provided strong support for expectancy violation theory.

Burgoon's scholarship has developed in a number of branches. Her first work, focusing narrowly on proxemics, grew with expectancy violation theory to include all of nonverbal behavior and continues to branch. Presently, she is studying what determines how people adapt their behaviors when they experience any type of communication violation. Why and when do they reciprocate the violation (e.g., if someone shouts, you shout back) or compensate for it (e.g., if someone comes too close to you, you step back)? At the same time, Burgoon is focusing on a specific type of expectancy violation: deception. Here she is trying to sort out the role that nonverbal behavior plays in deceitful interactions and, as director of the Center for Identification Technology Research, in identifying people from their characteristic nonverbal behaviors. Finally, she has begun a new study whose purpose is to identify expectations for mediated forms of communication and what constitutes positive violations. Whatever branch her research takes, Judee Burgoon brings the same readiness to challenge the current thinking that has been the hallmark of her work.

In addition to having taught a number of courses, Burgoon has served as director of graduate studies in communication and has mentored graduate students in communication and management. Helping students learn how to conduct research and formulate theory gives her great satisfaction. "Mentoring others is among the major gratifications of doing research. The fun is to teach others what I was taught: Always challenge the current assumptions." For complete citations of many of her recent publications in these areas, see the references for this chapter at the end of the book.

phone conversations and car or headphone music that is excessively loud can be seen as a form of acoustic invasion of space. This is why some communities have ordinances prohibiting loud music from cars and restaurants, hospitals and theaters have rules against cell phone use, and public transportation passengers are increasingly bold about asking other passengers to turn down their music and keep their cell phone conversations to themselves.

3. Territory. Territory is the space over which we claim ownership. Sometimes we do not realize the ways in which we claim space as our own. For example, when Rheanne decides to eat lunch at the company cafeteria, the space at the table she occupies unconsciously becomes her territory. If during lunch Rheanne leaves her territory to get butter for her roll, she is likely to leave her coat on her chair and her tray of food on the table, subconsciously indicating that the chair and the space around her tray are "hers." If, when she returns, Rheanne finds that someone at the table has moved a glass or a dish into the area that she regards as her territory, she is likely to feel resentful.

In other instances, we purposefully and directly communicate our territory to others using visible markers. People use locks, signs, and fences to communicate ownership of their territory. For instance, Graham may have "his chair" in the family room because he has always used this chair and has positioned it in a certain way (he may even have verbally announced that it is his chair). As a result, other members of the family will avoid using it. Likewise, Regan may assert the kitchen as her territory by creating an organizational scheme for where various types of food, utensils, plates, and so on should go, and she will expect her roommates to know that she is the one who has decided where objects are placed. She is likely to be upset if anyone rearranges the kitchen layout.

Territoriality may also have a power dimension to it. For instance, higher-status people generally claim larger, more prestigious, and more protected territory (Henley, 1977). A top-level executive may have a large, expensively decorated, top-floor office with a breathtaking view, as well as one or more people to protect the space from intruders. An entry-level employee in the same organization may have a small cubicle that is neither private nor protected. Think of all the messages that we get from the amount and type of territory that someone claims. For instance, in a family, who shares bedrooms and who gets the largest one? Who sits where when the family members are watching TV? Who generally sits at the "head" of the dinner table? Not only do territoriality concerns permeate family, work, and friendship groups, but the power dimension is also played out in political and social areas. For example, consider where subsidized housing or environmentally harmful facilities are located in your community—usually in areas that are economically poor.

4. Artifacts. Artifacts are the possessions we use to decorate our territory and communicate about our space. People own objects not just for their function but also because they find the objects pleasing in some way. As a result, other people looking at these artifacts come to understand something about the owners. Think

Territory—space over which we claim ownership.

Artifacts—possessions we use to decorate our territory and communicate about our space.

of all the types of cars and the images that different cars project about their owners. Someone driving a beat-up 1987 Ford is likely to convey a different image than someone driving a brand new Lexus. People who walk down a street talking on a cell phone or listening to an MP3 player through personal headphones also send messages about themselves and their image.

Think what your home, apartment, or room says about you. You probably accumulated the objects in that space over a period of time, but taken together, they provide information to others about who you are and what you think is important, beautiful, and so on. We select and place furnishings and decorations to achieve certain effects. The chairs and couch in your living room may approximate a circle that invites people to sit down and talk. Or the seating in a room may be theater style and face the television, thereby discouraging conversation. A supervisor's office with a chair facing the supervisor across the desk encourages formal conversation. It says, "Let's talk business—I'm the boss and you're the employee." A supervisor's office with a chair at the side of the desk (absence of a physical barrier) encourages more informal conversation. It says, "Don't be nervous—let's just chat."

The colors we use in our territory can also be subtle nonverbal signals of the mood that underlies what will happen. Color stimulates both emotional and physical reactions. For instance, red excites and stimulates, blue comforts and soothes, and yellow cheers and elevates moods. Knowing this, professional interior designers may choose blues when they are trying to create a peaceful, serene atmosphere for a living room, whereas they may decorate a playroom in reds and yellows.

OBSERVE AND ANALYZE ◯

Intruding on Personal Space

Find a crowded elevator. Get on it and face the back. Make direct eye contact with the person you are standing in front of. Note their reaction. On the return trip, introduce yourself to the person who is standing next to you and begin an animated conversation. Note the reaction of others around you. Get on an empty elevator and stand in the exact center. Do not move when others board. Note their reactions. Be prepared to share what you have observed with your classmates.

▷ Self-Presentation Cues

The final category of nonverbal communication is self-presentation cues. In Chapter 2 we discussed that you manage others' perceptions of you by how you present yourself. This includes not only your explicit messages but also the nonverbal cues that you present to others based on your physical appearance, your use of time, and your use of smells and scents. Let's have a look at each of these self-presentation cues in turn.

1. Physical appearance. First, we learn a great deal about others and make judgments about others based on their physical appearance—how they look. You control some parts of your physical appearance, while other parts you inherit from your family. Your physical appearance includes your gender, race, body type, and facial features, as well as the choices you make about your clothing, personal

"The boss finally noticed me today. He said I should wear deodorant."

grooming, and body decorations. In our sex- and race-conscious society, your gender, race, and ethnicity are used by others to form impressions of who you are. The size and shape of your body are also taken into consideration when people are trying to figure out who you really are, with some body types held in higher regard than others. American society places much emphasis on physical appearance, and entire industries are devoted to changing one's physical appearance through cosmetic surgery, weight loss, and grooming products. In addition, many people go to great lengths to select clothing to manage the impressions they portray. Brands and styles of clothing convey certain images. How you wear your hair and whether and how you use makeup and decorate yourself also convey something about you to others, though the exact "message" will depend on another person's frame of reference. For example, magenta tinted and spiked hair coupled with a large tattoo and nose piercing may be read by one person as, "Wow, she's a real individual" and by another as, "She's crying out for attention." Since choice of clothing and personal grooming will communicate messages about you, it is important to determine what messages you want to send and then dress and groom accordingly. You may want or need to modify your preferred look to meet the expectations of a particular situation or group of people. For example, you will generally want to dress conservatively for job interviews, court appearances, and funerals, and in some settings your appearance may be dictated by your employer or school.

2. Use of time. Time perception, how people view and structure their time, is also part of your nonverbal self-presentation. **Chronemics** is the study of the way the perception of time differs by individual and by culture. Some people and cultures are **monochronic**, following a linear and sequential perception of time. Consequently, they do one thing at a time, adhere strictly to schedules, value punctuality, and resist interruptions. For instance, when Margarite, who perceives time in a monochronic way, is interrupted by her sister, who is excited to share some good news, Margarite may scream, "Get out of here right now, You know it's my study time!" Other people and cultures are **polychronic**, following a nonlinear and flexible perception of time. As a result, they are comfortable doing several things at once, having flexible schedules or none at all, and disregarding deadlines and appointment times to satisfy relationship needs (Chen & Starosta, 1998). People who take a polychronic approach to time may not even perceive interruptions as such; instead, they may be pleased to have the opportunity to do one more thing in a period of time. For example, Lee, who perceives time in a polychronic way, may show up for a noon lunch with Raoul at 12:47 and not think of that as a problem because his co-worker stopped him to ask for help with a project. It is important to note that monochronic and polychronic perceptions of time are general tendencies of certain cultures and individuals, not absolutes, and that one system is not better than the other. Keep in mind that other people and cultures may approach time differently than you do.

Time perception—how people view and structure their time.

Chronemics—study of the way the perception of time differs by individual and by culture.

Monochronic—linear and sequential perception of time.

Polychronic—nonlinear and flexible perception of time.

INTER-ACT WITH ○ TECHNOLOGY

Sign into MySpace. Visit the page of someone you don't know. Do not read any of the text that is written. Instead, just look at the pictures the person has chosen to post. After carefully observing the pictures quickly, list twenty words that you believe describe this person. Then indicate what you think this person's interests are and write down other information about them that you have inferred from viewing these pictures. Now read the text that accompanies the page. Did you learn anything that would cause you to change your description of this person?

Another way people perceive and communicate time nonverbally involves **time orientation**, the time period on which people focus their attention. Are you a person who is focused on the past, the present, or the future? Some people and cultures think mostly about the past, others focus on the present, and others emphasize the future (Chen & Starosta, 1998). One's orientation to time tends to be a psychological state that is manifested in nonverbal behavior. Someone with a *past orientation* emphasizes tradition, relives the past, and is nostalgic about earlier times. If you have a *present orientation,* you live for the moment, concentrate on the here and now, and focus on what you are doing or feeling right now. Having a *future orientation* means looking ahead and planning what will happen later. While it is rare for someone to have only one of these orientations, many people are oriented in one direction more than the others. One style is not necessarily better than another. Relationship challenges may develop, however, if one person greatly emphasizes one orientation to time and the partner focuses on a different orientation. For instance, imagine if Bettina and Nadia are business partners who have different time orientations. Bettina thinks quite a bit about the future, wants to develop a five-year plan, and saves money for the long-range goal of expanding the business. Nadia focuses on the present by spending large

Time orientation—time period on which people focus their attention.

LEARN ABOUT YOURSELF ⊘ Orientation to Time

Take this short survey to learn something about your perception of time. Answer the questions based on your first response. There are no right or wrong answers. Just be honest in reporting your true behaviors. For each question, select one of the following numbers that best describes your behavior:

1 = Always False
2 = Usually False
3 = Sometimes True, Sometimes False
4 = Usually True
5 = Always True

_____ 1. I do many things at the same time.
_____ 2. I stick to my daily schedule as much as possible.
_____ 3. I prefer to finish one activity before starting another one.
_____ 4. I feel like I waste time.
_____ 5. I would take time out of a meeting to take a social phone call.
_____ 6. I separate work time and social time.
_____ 7. I break appointments with others.
_____ 8. I prefer that events in my life occur in an orderly fashion.
_____ 9. I do more than one activity at a time.
_____ 10. Being on time for appointments is important to me.

Scoring the Survey: To find your score, first reverse the responses for the odd-numbered items (if you wrote a 1, make it a 5; 2 = 4; leave 3 as is; 4 = 2; and 5 = 1). Next add the numbers for each item. Scores can range from 10 to 50. The higher your score, the more monochronic you are. The lower your score, the more polychronic you are.

Adapted from Gudykunst, W. B., Ting-Toomey, S., Sudweeks, S., & Stewart, L. P. (1995). *Building Bridges: Interpersonal Skills for a Changing World.* Boston: Houghton Mifflin.

amounts of money to create a professional business environment, making quick decisions, and taking immediate action. The partners' different orientations to time lead them to behave differently, with Bettina behaving cautiously, slowly, and deliberately and Nadia engaging in risk taking, as well as spontaneous and impulsive behavior. Their different orientations to time and their resulting behaviors may result in conflicting interests, making it very difficult for them to make joint business decisions.

3. Use of smells and scents. Your intentional or unintentional odor and intentional use of scents either on your body or in your territory also sends messages to others. **Olfactory communication** is nonverbal communication through smells and scents. If you do not think that smells and scents have the power to communicate, think of the burgeoning industry in the United States designed to manufacture and market scent-related products. We buy not only perfumes and colognes but also scented soaps, shampoos, air fresheners, candles, cleaning products, and pet products, to name a few. Often we go to great lengths to affect the smells associated with our bodies, our cars, and our homes. Aromatherapy is used to relieve stress and alter mood (Furlow, 1996). The meanings attached to certain odors and scents are very firmly based in culture, as we will see in the next section.

Olfactory communication— nonverbal communication through smells and scents.

◐ Cultural and Gender Variations in Nonverbal Communication

Throughout this chapter we have alluded to the fact that the meanings conveyed by nonverbal behaviors differ by culture and by gender. Let's now look at some of the specific differences, following the four categories of nonverbal communication outlined in the preceding sections.

▷ Variations in Body Language

The use of body motions, as well as the meanings they convey, differs among cultures and by gender. Several cultural differences in body motions are well documented.

First, eye contact is a major variant. The majority of people in the United States and other Western cultures expect those with whom they are communicating to "look them in the eye." In their review of the research on this topic, however, Samovar, Porter, and McDaniel (2007) conclude that direct eye contact is not universally considered appropriate. For instance, in Japan people direct their gaze to a position around the Adam's apple and avoid direct eye contact. Chinese people, Indonesians, and rural Mexicans lower their eyes as a sign of deference—to them, too much direct eye contact is a sign of bad manners. Middle Easterners, in contrast, look intently into the eyes of the person with whom they are talking for longer periods—to them direct eye contact demonstrates keen interest. Likewise, there are differences in use of eye contact among co-cultures and by gender within the United States. For instance, African Americans tend to use more continuous eye contact than European Americans when they are speaking, but less when they are listening (Samovar, Porter, & McDaniel, 2007). A recent study of black kinesics (Johnson, 2004) reports that some African Americans may be reluctant to look authority figures in the eye because to do so would be a sign of disrespect carried over from the days of slavery and Jim Crow, when for African Americans to look directly at whites signaled an inappropriate assumption of equality. Meanwhile, women tend to use more frequent eye contact during conversations than men do (Cegala & Sillars, 1989). Moreover, women tend to hold eye contact longer than men regardless of the sex of the person with whom they are interacting (Wood, 2007). It is important to note that these differences, while often described as biological differences, are also related to societal status. For example, historically women in the United States have had lower status than men which may partially explain the differences between men and women in eye contact that we observe today. People, whether male or female, will use more eye contact when they are displaying behaviors considered to be feminine than they will when they are displaying behaviors considered to be masculine.

Second, the use of facial expressions varies across cultures and by gender. Studies show that there are many similarities in nonverbal communication across cultures, especially in facial expressions. For instance, several facial expressions seem to be universal, including a slight raising of the eyebrow to communicate recognition and wriggling one's nose paired with a disgusted facial look to show social repulsion (Martin & Nakayama, 2006). In fact, at least six facial expressions (happiness, sadness, fear, anger, disgust, and surprise) carry the same basic meaning throughout the world (Samovar, Porter, & McDaniel, 2007). However, the choice of whether to display emotions through facial expressions varies across cultural and gender lines. For instance, in some Eastern cultures, people have been socialized to downplay emotional behavior cues like frowning and smiling, whereas members of other cultures have been socialized to amplify their displays of emotion through facial expressions. In addition, research has shown that gender plays a role in the choice of displaying emotion through facial expressions. Women and men communicating in ways socially perceived as feminine tend to smile more frequently and, conversely, tend to smile less frequently when communicating in so-called masculine ways, for instance, when being authoritative.

Third, the use of gesture varies greatly across cultures and by gender. Gender differences in the use of gesture are so profound that people have been found to attribute masculinity or femininity on the basis of gesture style alone (Pearson, West, & Turner, 1995). For instance, women are more likely to keep their arms close to the body and less likely to lean forward, they play more often with their hair or clothing, and they tap their hands more often than men. Men who frequently gesture in ways considered feminine are often labeled as effeminate, while women who gesture in ways considered masculine are considered to be "butch." Across cultures, people also show considerable differences in the meaning of gesture. For instance, the forming of a circle with the thumb and forefinger, which signifies "OK" in the

United States, means zero or worthless in France, is a symbol for money in Japan, and is a vulgar gesture in Germany and Brazil (Axtell, 1998). When communicating with people from cultures other than your own, be especially careful about the gestures you use, as they are by no means universal.

Finally, according to Gudykunst and Kim (1997), differences in touching behavior are highly correlated with culture and gender. In some cultures, lots of contact and touching is normal behavior, while in other cultures, individual space is respected and frequent touching is not encouraged. As Gudykunst and Kim further argue, "People in high-contact cultures evaluate 'close' as positive and good, and evaluate 'far' as negative and bad. People in low-contact cultures evaluate 'close' as negative and bad, and 'far' as positive and good" (p. 235). Latin America and Mediterranean countries are high-contact cultures, northern European cultures are medium to low in contact, and Asian cultures are for the most part low-contact cultures. The United States, which is a country of immigrants, is generally perceived to be in the medium-contact category, though there are wide differences among individual Americans because of variations in family heritage. Meanwhile, in terms of gender, women tend to touch others less than men do because they generally value touching more than men do. Women view touch as an expressive behavior that demonstrates warmth and affiliation, whereas men view touch as instrumental behavior; for instance, touching females is considered as leading to sexual activity (Pearson, West, & Turner, 1995).

▷ Variations in Paralanguage

There are a few cultural and gender variations in use of paralanguage as well. In the Middle East, speaking loudly signifies being strong and sincere. People from Hong Kong use high-pitched, expressive voices. What we call vocal interferences in the United States are not considered to be interferences in China, where using fillers signals wisdom and attractiveness (Chen & Starosta, 1998). In the United States, there are stereotypes about what are considered to be masculine and feminine vocalics. Masculine voices are expected to be low pitched and loud, with moderate to low intonation, while feminine voices are expected to be higher pitched, softer in volume, and more expressive. The voice characteristic of breathiness is associated with femininity. While both sexes have the option to portray a range of masculine and feminine vocalics, most people probably do conform to the expectations for their sex. One voice feature, pitch, does have a physical basis to it. Men's vocal cords, on average, are larger and thicker than women's, and this accounts for the lower pitch of men's voices and the higher pitch of women's voices. Despite this physical reason for voice pitch differences between the sexes, societal expectations about masculinity and femininity still play a part. Before puberty, the vocal cords of males and females do not differ. Yet, even before there is a physical reason for sex differences in pitch, little boys frequently speak in a lower pitch than little girls do (Wood, 2007).

▷ Variations in Spatial Usage

We create problems in our relationships when our use of space violates the expectations of our partner or when our partner's use of space violates our expectations. Violations may be caused by cultural and gender differences in how space is used. As you would expect, the spatial environments in which people feel comfortable depend on cultural background. In the United States, where many people live in single-family homes or in large apartments, we expect to have greater personal space. In other countries, where population densities in inhabited regions are high, people live in closer quarters and can feel "lonely" or isolated in larger spaces. In Japan and Europe, most people live in spaces that by our U.S. standards would be called cramped. Similarly, people from different cultures have different ideas about what constitutes appropriate distances for various interactions. Recall that in the dominant culture of the United States, the boundary of personal or intimate space is about eighteen inches. In Middle Eastern cultures, however, men move much closer to other men when they are talking (Samovar, Porter, & McDaniel, 2007). Thus, when an Egyptian man talks with an American man, one of the two is likely to be uncomfortable. Either the American will feel uncomfortable and invaded or the Egyptian will feel isolated and too distant for serious conversation. But we don't have to go off the North American continent to see variations in the way uses of space may differ. In the "Diverse Voices" box in this chapter, notice how Latin American and Anglo American spatial usage differs.

Unfortunately, there are times when one person intentionally violates the space expectations of another, usually in the context of gender variations regarding personal space. When the violation is between members of the opposite sex, it may be considered sexual harassment. For instance, Glen may, through violations of informal space, "come on" to Donnice. If Donnice does not welcome the attention, she may feel threatened. In this case, Glen's nonverbal behavior may be construed as sexual harassment. To avoid perceptions of harassment, people need to be especially sensitive to others' definitions of intimate space.

Likewise, the objects and artifacts that people treasure and display in their territories differ by culture. What constitutes art is a function of culture, as are certain decorating aesthetics. Chinese and Japanese approaches to interior design follow Feng Shui, the ancient Chinese approach of arranging objects to achieve harmony in one's environment. Rooms arranged according to these principles communicate messages that are different from rooms arranged according to other design principles.

Even the meanings that we assign to colors vary by culture, mostly because of religious beliefs. In India, white, not black, is the color of mourning, and Hindu brides wear red. In Latin America, purple signifies death, and in Japan, green denotes youth and energy.

▷ Variations in Self-Presentation Cues

The self-presentation cues of physical appearance, time perception and orientation, and olfactory communication also vary widely by culture and across gender lines.

Latin American and Anglo American Use of Personal Space in Public Places

by Elizabeth Lozano

How we use space and how we expect others to treat the space around us are determined by our culture. In this excerpt the author focuses our attention on the ways in which the body is understood and treated by Latin Americans and Anglo Americans and the cultural differences that become apparent when these two cultural groups find themselves sharing common space.

It is 6:00 P.M. The Bayfront, a shopping mall near a Miami marina, reverberates with the noise and movement of people, coming and going, contemplating the lights of the bay, sampling exotic juice blends, savoring the not-so-exotic foods from Cuba, Nicaragua, or Mexico, and listening to the bands. The Bayfront provides an environment for the exercise of two different rituals: the Anglo American visit to the mall and the Latin American paseo, the visit to the outdoor spaces of the city.

Some of the people sitting in the plaza look insistently at me, making comments, laughing, and whispering. Instead of feeling uneasy or surprised, I find myself looking back at them, entering this inquisitive game and asking myself some of the same questions they might be asking. Who are they, where are they from, what are they up to? I follow their gaze and I see it extend to other groups. The gaze is returned by some in the crowd, so that a play of silent dialogue seems to grow amidst the anonymity of the crowd. The crowd that participates in this complicity of wandering looks is not Anglo American. The play of looks described above has a different "accent," a Hispanic accent, which reveals a different understanding of the plaza and public space.

The Anglo American passers-by understand their vital space, their relationship with strangers, and their public interactions in a different manner. If I address them in the street, I better assume that I am confronting them in an alley. But when I am walking by myself along the halls of a Hispanic mall, I am not alone. I do not expect, therefore, to be treated by others as if they were suddenly confronting me in a dark alley. I am in a crowd, with the crowd, and anyone there has access to my attention.

Anglo Americans are alone (even in the middle of the crowd) if they choose to be, for they have a guaranteed cultural right to be "left alone" on their way to and from anywhere. To approach or touch someone without that person's consent is a violation of a fundamental right within Anglo-Saxon, Protestant cultural tradition. This is the right to one's own body as private property. Within this tradition, touching is understood as an excursion into someone else's territory. With this in mind then, it is understandable that Anglo Americans excuse themselves when they accidentally touch someone or come close to doing so. To accidentally penetrate someone else's boundary (especially if that person is a stranger) demands an apology, and a willingness to repair the damage by stepping back from the violated territory.

One can see how rude a Latin American might appear to an Anglo American when the former distractingly touches another person without apologizing or showing concern. But within Latino and Mediterranean traditions, the body is not understood as property. That is, the body is not understood as belonging to its owner. It does not belong to me or to anyone else; it is, in principle, public. It is an expressive and sensual region open to the scrutiny, discipline, and sanction of the community. It is, therefore, quite impossible to be "left alone" on the Latin American street. For Latin Americans, the access to others in a public space is not restricted by the "privacy" of their bodies. Thus, the Latin American does not find casual contact a form of property trespassing or a violation of rights. Walking the street in the Anglo United States is very much an anonymous activity to be performed in a field of unobstructive and invisible bodies. Since one is essentially carrying one's own space into the public sphere, no one is actually ever in public. Given that the public is private, no intimacy is granted in the public space. Thus while the Latin American public look or gaze is round, inquisitive, and wandering, the Anglo American is straight, nonobstructive, and neutral.

Civility requires the Anglo American to restrict looks, delimit gestures, and orient movement. Civility requires the Latin American to acknowledge looks, gestures, and movement and actively engage with them. For the Latin American, the unavoidable nature of shared space is always a demand for attention and a request to participate. An Anglo American considers "mind your own business" to be fair and civil. A Latin American might find this an unreasonable restriction. What takes place in public is everybody's business by the very fact that it is taking place in public.

One can understand the possible cultural misunderstandings between Anglo Americans and Latin Americans. If Anglo Americans protest the "impertinence" of Latin Americans as nosy and curious, Latin Americans would protest the indifference and lack of concern of Anglo Americans. The scene in the Miami mall could happen just as easily in Los Angeles, Chicago, Philadelphia, or New York, cities in which Latin Americans comprise an important segment of the population.

The influence of this cultural heritage is going to have growing influence in the next few decades on the Anglo American scene, as Hispanics become the largest ethnic and linguistic minority in the United States. The more knowledge we can gain from what makes us culturally diverse, the more we will be able to appreciate what unifies us through the mixing and mutual exchanges of our cultures.

Excerpted from Lozano, E. (2007). The cultural experience of space and body: A reading of Latin American and Anglo American comportment in public. In A. Gonzalez, M. Houston, & V. Chen (Eds.), *Our Voices: Essays in Culture, Ethnicity, and Communication: An Intercultural Anthology,* 4th edition (pp. 274–280). New York: Oxford University Press.

First, standards of physical appearance and beauty vary widely by culture and gender. For example, in India and Pakistan, both females and males who are more heavy-set in appearance are considered more attractive than is socially acceptable in the United States, where being thin and/or physically fit is considered the standard of physical attractiveness. Conversely, in Japan, even more emphasis is placed on being thin than in the United States, which has resulted in a severe occurrence of anorexia and bulimia among teenage girls, rivaling an already serious problem in America. In terms of body decoration, cultures vary widely as to how much or how little decoration is considered appropriate. Within the United States, women's clothing and accessories are more decorative, while men's clothing and accessories are more functional. Think of the variety of clothing and accessories aimed at women: shoes and purses in every color and style; jewelry for ears, neck, wrists, ankles, toes, and clothing; decorations for the hair; decorative belts and scarves; patterned hose and colorful socks; not to mention the enormous variety of clothing itself. While the accessory options for men are increasing, the emphasis on decorative accessories for men remains minimal.

Second, with regard to time, cultures differ in terms of time perception and time orientation. Some cultures, like China, are oriented very much toward the past, while the orientation in the United States is considered to be toward the present and near future. In addition, the dominant culture of the United States is monochronically oriented. We compartmentalize our time and schedule one event at a time. In this culture, being even a few minutes late may require you to acknowledge your lateness. Being ten to fifteen minutes late usually requires an apology, and being more than thirty minutes late is likely to be perceived as an insult, requiring a great deal of explanation (Gudykunst & Kim, 1997). People from other cultural backgrounds, such as Latin America, Africa, Asia, and the Middle East, tend to view time polychronically. Cultural differences in perception of time can cause misunderstandings. For instance, a naive U.S. sales representative with a business appointment in Latin America may be very frustrated with what he or she

OBSERVE AND ANALYZE ▽

Cultural Differences in Nonverbal Behavior

Interview or converse with two international students from different countries. Try to select students whose cultures differ from each other and from the culture with which you are most familiar. Develop a list of questions related to the material discussed in this chapter. Try to understand how people in the international students' countries differ from you in their use of body language, paralanguage, space, and self-presentation cues. Write a short paper explaining what you have learned.

regards as a "cavalier" attitude toward time; likewise, a Latin American person with a business appointment in the United States may be frustrated by the perceived rigidity of time schedules here.

Finally, while cultural and gender variations are not great with regard to the olfactory aspect of nonverbal communication, there are some points worth noting. The fact that certain scents are marketed differently to men and women in colognes and perfumes does show different expectations or stereotypes about male and female preferences. In some cultures, artificial scents from colognes and perfumes are considered annoying, while in other cultures, such as the dominant United States culture, natural body odors are offensive.

◉ Improving Nonverbal Communication Skills

Because nonverbal communication varies by situation, culture, and gender, it is difficult to prescribe exactly how you should communicate nonverbally. In this section, however, we provide some general suggestions that you can implement to help you be more effective at sending and receiving messages nonverbally.

▷ Sending Messages

As we explained in Chapter 1, encoding consists of the cognitive thinking processes you use to transform ideas and feelings into symbols and to organize them into a message. To improve your sending of nonverbal messages, consider the following guidelines.

1. Be conscious of the nonverbal behavior you are displaying. Remember that you are always communicating nonverbally. Some nonverbal cues will always be subconscious, but you should work to bring more of your nonverbal behaviors into your conscious awareness. It is a matter of just paying attention to what you are doing with your eyes, face, posture, gestures, voice, use of space, and appearance, as well as your handling of time and scents. If you initially have difficulty paying attention to your nonverbal behaviors, ask a friend to point out the nonverbal cues you are displaying.

2. Be purposeful or strategic in your use of nonverbal communication. Sometimes, it is important to control what you are communicating nonverbally. For instance, if you want to be persuasive, you should use nonverbal cues that demonstrate confidence and credibility. These may include direct eye contact, a serious facial expression, a relaxed posture, a loud and low-pitched voice with no vocal interferences, and professional-style clothing and grooming. If, on the other hand, you want to communicate empathy and support, you might select different nonverbal behaviors, including moderate gaze, caring facial expressions, posture in which you lean toward the other, a soft voice, and touch. While there are no absolute prescriptions for communicating nonverbally, there are strategic choices we can make to convey the messages we desire.

3. Make sure that your nonverbal cues do not distract from your message. Sometimes, when we are not aware of what nonverbal cues we are displaying or when we are anxious, certain nonverbal behaviors will hinder our communication. Fidgeting, tapping your fingers on a table, pacing, mumbling, using vocal interferences, and using physical adaptors can hinder the other person's interpretation of your message. It is important to control extraneous nonverbal cues that get in the way of effective interpersonal communication.

4. Make your nonverbal communication match your verbal communication. When we presented the functions of nonverbal communication earlier in this chapter, we explained how nonverbal communication may contradict verbal communication, causing a mixed message to occur. Effective interpersonal communicators try to avoid mixed messages. Not only is it important to make your verbal and nonverbal communications match, but various aspects of nonverbal communication should match each other also. If you are feeling sad, your voice will be softer and less expressive, but you should not let your face contradict your voice with a smile. People get confused and frustrated when they receive inconsistent messages.

5. Adapt your nonverbal behavior to the situation. Situations vary in their formality, familiarity, and purpose. Just as you would select different language for different situations, you should adapt your nonverbal messages to the situation. Assess what the situation calls for in terms of body motions, paralanguage, spatial usage, artifacts, physical appearance, and use of time and scents. Of course, you already do some situational adapting with nonverbal communication. You wouldn't dress the same way for a wedding as you would to walk the dog. You would not treat your brother's territory the same way you would treat your doctor's territory. But the more you can consciously adapt your nonverbal behaviors to what seems appropriate to the situation, the more effective you will be as a communicator.

▷ Receiving Messages

Decoding is the process the receiver uses to transform the messages that are received into the receiver's own ideas and feelings. To improve your receiving of nonverbal messages, consider the following guidelines.

1. When interpreting others' nonverbal cues, do not automatically assume that a particular behavior means a certain thing. Except for emblems, there is no universal meaning of nonverbal behaviors. And even the meaning of emblems varies culturally. There is much room for error when people make quick interpretations or draw rapid conclusions about an aspect of nonverbal behavior.

2. Consider cultural, gender, and individual influences when interpreting nonverbal cues. We have shown how nonverbal behaviors vary widely based on culture and gender. The more you know about intercultural and gender aspects of nonverbal communication, the more accurate you will be in interpreting others' nonverbal cues. Note also that some people are totally unique in their display of nonverbal behaviors. You may have learned over time that your friend grinds her teeth when she is excited. You may never encounter another person who uses this behavior in this way, but this nonverbal behavior must be considered when dealing with this individual. Remember from Chapter 2 the importance of getting to the psychological level of prediction based on a person's uniqueness.

3. Pay attention to multiple aspects of nonverbal communication and their relationship to verbal communication. You should not take nonverbal cues out of context. In any one interaction, you are likely to get simultaneous messages from a person's eyes, face, gestures, posture, voice, spatial usage, and touch. Even in electronic communication, where much of the apparatus of nonverbal communication is absent, facial expression and touch can be communicated through emoticons, paralanguage through capitalization of words, and perceptions/orientations of time through the timing and length of electronic messages. All nonverbal cues will occur in conjunction with words. By taking into consideration all of the channels of communication, you will more effectively interpret the messages of others.

4. Use perception checking. As we discussed in Chapter 2, the skill of perception checking lets you see if your interpretation of another person's message

A QUESTION OF ETHICS ❍ What Would You Do?

After the intramural mixed-doubles matches on Tuesday evening, most of the players adjourned to the campus grill to have a drink and chat. Although the group was highly competitive on the courts, they enjoyed socializing and talking about the matches for a while before they went home. Marquez and Lisa, who had been paired together at the start of the season, sat down with another couple, Barry and Elana, who had been going out together for several weeks. Marquez and Lisa had played a particularly grueling match that night against Barry and Elana, a match that they lost largely because of Elana's improved play.

"Elana, your serve today was the best I've seen it this year," Marquez said.

"Yeah, I was really impressed. And as you saw, I had trouble handling it," Lisa added.

"And you're getting to the net a lot better too," Marquez added.

"Thanks, guys," Elana said in a tone of gratitude, "I've really been working on it."

"Well, aren't we getting the compliments today," sneered Barry in a sarcastic tone. Then after a pause, he said, "Oh, Elana, would you get my sweater? I left it on that chair by the other table."

"Come on Barry, you're closer than I am," Elana replied.

Barry got a cold look on his face, moved slightly closer to Elana, and said emphatically, "Get my sweater for me, Elana—now."

Elana quickly backed away from Barry as she said, "OK Barry—it's cool," and she then quickly got the sweater for him.

"Gee, isn't she sweet?" Barry said to Marquez and Lisa as he grabbed the sweater from Elana.

Lisa and Marquez both looked down at the floor. Then Lisa glanced at Marquez and said, "Well, I'm out of here—I've got a lot to do this evening."

"Let me walk you to your car," Marquez said as he stood up.

"See you next week," they said in unison as they hurried out the door, leaving Barry and Elana alone at the table.

1. Analyze Barry's nonverbal behavior. What was he attempting to achieve?
2. How do you interpret Lisa's and Marquez's nonverbal reactions to Barry?
3. Was Barry's behavior ethically acceptable? Explain.

is accurate or not. By describing the nonverbal behavior you have noticed and tentatively sharing your interpretation of it, you can receive confirmation or correction of your interpretation. For instance, suppose a person smiles and nods her head when you tell her about a mistake she has made. Before you conclude that the person agrees with your observation and accepts your criticism, you might say, "From the smile on your face and your nodding, I get the impression that you had already recognized a problem here, or am I off base?" It may be helpful to use perception checking when faced with gender or cultural variations in nonverbal behavior. It is especially important to use perception checking when you receive mixed messages from others.

◗ Summary

Nonverbal communication refers to how people communicate through bodily actions and vocal qualities typically accompanying a verbal message. The characteristics of nonverbal communication are that it varies in intentionality, it is ambiguous, it is primary, it is continuous, and it is multi-channeled. The functions of nonverbal communication are that it provides information, regulates interactions, expresses or hides emotions, presents an image, and conveys power.

There are many types of nonverbal communication. Perhaps the most familiar type of nonverbal communication is body language, how a person communicates using eye contact, facial expression, gesture, posture, and touch. A second type of nonverbal communication is paralanguage, which includes our use of pitch, volume, rate, quality, and intonation to give special meaning to the words we use. Whereas these vocal characteristics help us interpret the meaning of a verbal message, vocal interferences ("ah," "um," "you know," and "like") often impede a listener's ability to understand. A third type of nonverbal communication is spatial usage. People communicate through the use of physical space, acoustic space, posture and body orientation, and territory. We also communicate through artifacts, such as personal possessions and the ways we arrange and decorate our space. The final type of nonverbal communication is self-presentation cues, including personal appearance, use of time, and choice of scents and smells.

The many types of nonverbal communication we may use may vary depending on the individual's culture and gender. As a result, our body language, paralanguage, spatial usage, and self-presentation cues may differ considerably.

You can improve your encoding of nonverbal communication by being conscious of the nonverbal behavior you are displaying, being purposeful or strategic in your use of these cues, making sure that your nonverbal cues do not distract people from your message, making your nonverbal communication match your verbal communication, and adapting your nonverbal behaviors to the situation. You can improve your decoding of nonverbal communication by not misinterpreting others' nonverbal cues; considering cultural, gender, and individual differences; paying attention to aspects of nonverbal communication and their relationship to verbal communication; and perception checking.

● Chapter Resources

Communication Improvement Plan:
Nonverbal Communication ● Find more on the web @ www.oup.com/us/interact12

Would you like to improve your use of the following types of nonverbal behavior discussed in this chapter?

Body language: Eye contact, facial expressions, gesture, posture and body orientation, touch
Paralanguage: Pitch, volume, rate, quality, intonation, vocal interferences
Spatial usage: Informal space, acoustic space, territory, artifacts
Self-presentation cues: Physical appearance, use of time, use of smells and scents

Pick the area in which you would like to improve, and write a communication improvement plan. You can find a communication improvement plan worksheet on our website at www.oup.com/us/interact12.

Key Words ●

Nonverbal communication behavior, *p. 120*
Body language, *p. 124*
Kinesics, *p. 124*
Eye contact, *p. 125*
Facial expression, *p. 126*
Emoticons, *p. 126*
Gesture, *p. 126*
Emblems, *p. 126*
Adaptors, *p. 126*
Posture, *p. 126*
Body orientation, *p. 126*

Touch, *p. 127*
Spontaneous touch, *p. 128*
Ritualized touch, *p. 128*
Task-related touch, *p. 128*
Paralanguage, *p. 128*
Pitch, *p. 128*
Volume, *p. 129*
Rate, *p. 129*
Quality, *p. 129*
Intonation, *p. 129*
Vocal interferences, *p. 129*
Spatial usage, *p. 129*

Informal space, *p. 129*
Proxemics, *p. 129*
Acoustic space, *p. 130*
Territory, *p. 132*
Artifacts, *p. 132*
Time perception, *p. 134*
Chronemics, *p. 134*
Monochronic, *p. 134*
Polychronic, *p. 134*
Time orientation, *p. 135*
Olfactory communication, *p. 136*

Inter-Act with Media ● Find more on the web @ www.oup.com/us/interact12

Television
Ugly Betty, episode: "Pilot" (2006). America Ferrera, Eric Mabius, Alan Dale.

Brief Summary: Betty Suarez's (Ferrera) mantra is that she's "an attractive, confident business-woman." However, with her makeup-less face, frumpy clothes, and braces, a job at *Mode* maga-zine—a fashion "Bible" akin to *Vogue*—would appear an unlikely career fit for endomorphic Betty. Surprisingly, Betty's looks serve as the *exact* reason for her hiring: Her lack of beauty makes Betty someone that her boss, handsome Daniel Meade (Mabius), will not pursue, ac-cording to his father, publishing mogul Bradford Meade (Dale). To force her to quit, Daniel ex-ploits Betty's "ugliness" by asking her to wear a skimpy leather outfit to stand in for a missing model. This tactic works. Later, remorseful Daniel goes to Betty's home and begs her to return. He realizes that Betty's outer appearance does not reflect her relentless work ethic, talent, and intelligence.

IPC Concepts: Functions of nonverbal communication, self-presentation cues, physical appearance.

Cinema

21 (2008). Robert Luketic (director). Jim Sturgess, Kate Bosworth, Laurence Fishburne, Kevin Spacey.

Brief Summary: MIT student Ben Campbell (Sturgess), bound for Harvard Med, needs tuition money, and his $8/hour retail job isn't solving the problem. When his professor Micky Rosa (Spacey) invites him to join an undercover student card-counting team in Vegas, he initially balks, but then signs on. He soon learns the lingo of counting, but more importantly, he memorizes the nonverbal signals required for communication among the team. Folded arms mean that a table is hot; a touch to the eye means, "We need to talk"; a hand to the forehead means that the deck is cooling off. The most serious gesture—fingers through the hair—means, "Get out now." Inevitably, Ben is caught by Cole Williams (Fishburne), chief of security, who, unbeknownst to Ben, has an old vendetta with Rosa. When Ben cuts a deal with Williams so he can get Rosa, Ben and his team must change their outward appearance. Before leaving for the final game, glances pass between Rosa and the team and among Ben and the team. Since Rosa doesn't know he's being set up by Ben and Williams, the glances all occur under the guise of completely different meanings. Nonverbal communication provides several functions in this film in terms of exchanging messages, deception cues, and appearance.

IPC Concepts: Functions of nonverbal communication, gesture, eye contact, touch, physical appearance.

What's on the Web

Find links and additional material, including self-quizzes, on the companion website at www .oup.com/us/interact12.

6

Communication across Cultures

After you have read this chapter, you should be able to answer these questions:

▷ What is culture?

▷ What is culture shock?

▷ What is intercultural communication?

▷ What four dimensions can help identify the similarities and differences between cultures?

▷ How does the communication of people from individualistic cultures differ from that of people in collectivist cultures?

▷ How does the communication of people from high uncertainty-avoidance cultures differ from that of people from low uncertainty-avoidance cultures?

▷ How does the communication of people from high power-distance cultures differ from that of people from low power-distance cultures?

▷ How does the communication of people from masculine cultures differ from that of people from feminine cultures?

▷ What is a dominant culture, and what are the various co-cultures that exist within the United States?

▷ What barriers do we face when communicating interculturally?

▷ How can you improve your intercultural communication?

"Alex, I don't think we should serve beer at our party on Friday."

"What, no beer? You've got to be kidding me. Look Frieda, all of the guys expect there to be beer at an Oktoberfest party. I mean, that's what good Germans drink. How can we serve brats and metts and sauerkraut without beer?"

"Well, I'm just thinking about Brendan and Sean, and your other Irish friends."

"Huh? What, I don't follow you, Frieda, what about Brendan and Sean? They love beer."

"Well, that's just the point, isn't it? You know the Irish, they love their beer and their wine, and their whiskey. But they don't know when to stop. What if they wind up binge drinking, pass out, and end up in the ER?"

How accurate are Frieda's assumptions about the Irish? How accurate are Alex's assumptions about what good Germans drink? Most of us have stereotypes about other cultures that we have learned from family, friends, schooling, and the media. These stereotypes not only influence what we think of people from other cultures but can also affect how we communicate with people from other cultures.

Our twenty-first-century reality is that contact between cultures is accelerating. Mass migrations, the globalization of trade, and the Internet are all making it more likely that you will interact with others who come from cultures that are different from your own. While some people celebrate this trend and enjoy meeting diverse people, others feel overwhelmed and may fear that they will lose their own local culture and its traditions. Regardless of your personal feelings about these changes, to be an effective communicator you will need to understand what culture is and how communication differs between cultures. Relying on old cultural stereotypes—which may never have been accurate—is unlikely to aid you in developing and maintaining effective relationships with others who come from different cultures.

In this chapter, we examine how culture affects our own communication behaviors and how it influences our perception of the communication we receive from others. We begin by explaining basic concepts of culture, culture shock, and intercultural communication. Then we describe the four dimensions that help us identify the similarities and differences between cultures. After that, we examine the dominant culture and co-cultures that exist within the United States. Next, we identify the barriers that arise from cultural difference. Finally, we offer guide-

lines that can make you a more competent communicator when communicating with someone from a culture other than your own.

○ Culture, Culture Shock, and Intercultural Communication

You will recall in Chapter 1 that we defined **culture** as the system of beliefs, values, and attitudes shared by a particular segment of the population (Samovar, Porter, & McDaniel, 2007, p. 20). Historically, a culture was shared by a society of people who inhabited a particular geographic area. Therefore, to meet someone from a different culture required that you travel to that area. But the United States has always been different. As a nation of immigrants, the United States has always been by definition a multicultural society. Today its citizens include recent immigrants (many from Asia, Latin America, Eastern Europe, and Africa) as well as the descendants of earlier voluntary immigrants, the descendants of Africans brought here against their will as slaves, and native peoples. Globally, we are in a period of massive migration not only into the United States but all over the world. As a result, more and more of us are finding ourselves interacting with others who come from cultural backgrounds that differ from our own. When we interact with those who are culturally different from us, misunderstandings are likely to arise, particularly since what is considered appropriate communication behavior varies by culture.

People are so familiar with their own language, gestures, facial expressions, conversational customs, and norms that they may experience anxiety when these familiar aspects of communication are disrupted. Yet this occurs frequently when we interact with people from different cultures. **Culture shock** is the psychological discomfort of adjusting to a new cultural situation (Klyukanov, 2005). Because culture shock is caused by an absence of shared meaning, you are likely to feel it most profoundly when you are thrust into another culture through travel, business, or international study. But it can also occur when you come in contact with people from other cultures within your home country. For example, Brittney, who is from a small town in Minnesota, may experience culture shock when she visits Miami for the first time. She may be overwhelmed by the distinct Latino flavor of the city: by hearing Spanish spoken among people on the street, by the prevalence of Latin beat music, by the prominence of outdoor advertisements written in Spanish, and by the way people look and are dressed. Brittney is likely to be disoriented not only because of the prominence of the Spanish language but also because the beliefs, values, and attitudes of the people she encounters might seem quite foreign to her.

As a result of Brittney's culture shock, she will likely not be an effective communicator with those of Latino descent while in Miami, and she will need to learn how to be a more effective intercultural communicator. **Intercultural communication**

Culture—the system of beliefs, values, and attitudes shared by a particular segment of the population.

Culture shock—the psychological discomfort of adjusting to a new cultural situation.

Intercultural communication— interactions that occur between people whose cultures are so different that the communication between them is altered .

refs to interactions that occur between people whose cultures are so different that the communication between them is altered (Samovar, Porter, & McDaniel, 2007, p. 10). In other words, when communicating with people whose beliefs, values, and attitudes are culturally different from our own, we are communicating across cultural boundaries, which can lead to misunderstandings that would not ordinarily occur between people who are culturally similar. It is important to recognize that not every exchange between persons of different cultures exemplifies intercultural communication. For example, when Brittney is on the beach in Miami and joins a group of Latinos in a friendly game of beach volleyball, their cultural differences are unlikely to affect their game-related exchanges. However, should Brittney decide to join the group for a night of club-hopping, she is likely to experience conversations where cultural difference leads to difficulty in understanding or interpreting what is said. As a first step toward effective intercultural communication, both she and the individuals in the group she is with need to identify their cultural similarities and differences.

◉ Identifying Cultural Similarities and Differences

Some aspects that identify a member of a particular culture may be easy to spot. We may be able to figure out what culture people are from based on their language, how they dress, or their personal artifacts, such as religious markers worn as jewelry or placed in the home. For example, when people meet Shimon, they can discern from his side curls, his yarmulke, and his black clothes that he is a Hassidic Jew. But while these things may help you to identify someone as belonging to a specific culture, they may not really help you to understand the values shared by members of that culture. Appearance alone does not explain who people are inside, how they perceive the world, and how they interact with others. For example, beyond how one dresses, what does it really mean to be a Hassidic Jew? How are Hassidic Jews similar to other cultural groups, and how do they differ from other cultural groups? The work of Geert Hofstede gives us a way to understand how cultures are similar and different from one another and to understand how that variation affects communication. When he was a manager in the personnel research department at IBM Europe, Hofstede (1980) conducted a large-scale research project that studied fifty countries and three regions. His work identified four dimensions of culture that affect communication: individualism-collectivism, uncertainty avoidance, power distance, and masculinity-femininity. Figure 6.1 shows where the United States falls on each of these dimensions. As you read through this section and learn more about each dimension, refer back to this figure.

▷ Individualism-Collectivism

The first dimension of culture that affects communication is **individualism-collectivism**, the extent to which people in a culture are integrated into groups.

Individualism-collectivism—the extent to which people in a culture are integrated into groups.

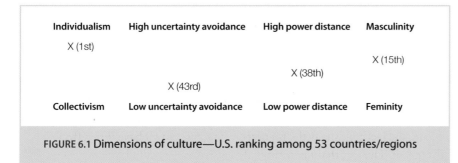

Individualism	High uncertainty avoidance	High power distance	Masculinity
X (1st)			
			X (15th)
		X (38th)	
	X (43rd)		
Collectivism	Low uncertainty avoidance	Low power distance	Feminity

FIGURE 6.1 Dimensions of culture—U.S. ranking among 53 countries/regions

In Chapter 2, we briefly discussed the effects of individualism-collectivism on our self-perceptions, but let's explore it now in more depth.

An **individualistic culture** is a culture that emphasizes personal rights and responsibilities, privacy, voicing one's opinion, freedom, innovation, and self-expression (Andersen, Hecht, Hoobler, & Smallwood, 2003). In individualistic cultures, people's connections to groups are loose. People in individualistic cultures place primary value on the self and on personal achievement, which explains the emphasis on personal opinion, innovation, and self-expression. They consider the interests of others only in relationship to how those interests affect the interest of the self. If you come from an individualistic culture, you may consider your family and close friends when you act, but only because your interests and theirs align. People in individualistic cultures also view competition between people as desirable and useful. Because of this, personal rights, freedom, and privacy are in place to ensure fair competition. According to Hofstede (1997), individualistic cultures include those in the United States, Australia, Great Britain, Canada, and northern and eastern European countries.

In contrast, a **collectivist culture** is a culture that emphasizes community, collaboration, shared interests, harmony, the public good, and avoiding embarrassment (Andersen, Hecht, Hoobler, & Smallwood, 2003). In collectivist cultures, from early in life, people are integrated into strong, close-knit groups, which will protect them in exchange for loyalty. Collectivist cultures place primary value on the interests of the group and group harmony. An individual's decision is shaped by what is best for the group, regardless of whether it serves the individual's interests. Collectivist societies are highly integrated, and the maintenance of harmony and cooperation is valued over competitiveness and personal achievement. According to Hofstede (1997), collectivist cultures are found in South and Central America, East and Southeast Asia, and Africa.

The values of individualism and collectivism influence many aspects of communication, including, most notably, our self-concept and self-esteem formation, approaches to conflict, and working in groups (Samovar, Porter, & McDaniel, 2007).

First, individualism and collectivism affect self-concept and self-esteem. For example, in the United States, an individualistic culture, our self-concept and

Individualistic culture—a culture that emphasizes personal rights and responsibilities, privacy, voicing one's opinion, freedom, innovation, and self-expression.

Collectivist culture—a culture that emphasizes community, collaboration, shared interests, harmony, the public good, and avoiding embarrassment.

self-esteem are rooted in how successfully we have advanced our own interests without respect to how our actions have affected others. In collectivist cultures, on the other hand, what affects self-concept and self-esteem is not individual achievement but whether the group thrives based on one's actions. For example, if Marie is raised in an individualistic culture and she is the highest-scoring player on her basketball team, she will feel good about herself and identify herself as "winner," even if her team has a losing season. But if Marie is from a collectivist culture, the fact that she is the highest-scoring player will have little effect on her self-esteem. The fact that her team had a losing season will likely cause her to feel less personal esteem.

Second, people coming from each of these cultural perspectives view conflict differently. The emphasis that is placed on the individual leads members of individualistic cultures to value and practice assertiveness and confrontational argument, while members of collectivist cultures value accord and harmony and thus practice collaboration or avoidance in arguments. In the United States, we teach assertiveness and argumentation as useful skills and expect them to be used in interpersonal and work relationships, politics, consumerism, and other aspects of civic life. By contrast, in the collectivist culture of Japan, to maintain harmony and avoid interpersonal clashes Japanese business has evolved an elaborate process called *nemawashii,* a term that also means "binding the roots of a plant before pulling it out." In Japan, any subject that might cause conflict at a meeting should be discussed in advance so that the interaction at the meeting will not seem rude or impolite (Samovar, Porter, and McDaniel 2007). In collectivist so-

How comfortable would you be in a collectivist culture like this? What if you didn't feel like exercising?

cieties, a style of communication that respects the relationship is more important than the information exchanged (Jandt, 2001). In collectivist societies, group harmony, sparing others embarrassment, and a modest presentation of oneself are important ways to show respect and avoid conflict. A person does not speak directly if it might hurt others in the group.

Finally, individualism and collectivism influence how people work in groups. Because members of collectivist cultures see group harmony and the welfare of the group to be of primary importance, they strive for consensus on group goals and may at times sacrifice optimal outcomes for the sake of group accord. In individualistic cultures, however, optimal outcomes should always be attained, regardless of whether that results in group disharmony. Your cultural assumptions affect how you work to establish group goals, how you interact with other group members, and how willing you are to sacrifice for the sake of the group. Groups whose members come from both individualistic and collectivist cultures may experience difficulties because of their varying cultural assumptions.

▷ Uncertainty Avoidance

The second dimension of how culture influences communication, according to Hofstede, is **uncertainty avoidance**, the extent to which the people in a culture avoid unpredictability regarding people, relationships, and events. Cultures differ in how they deal with unpredictability. A **low uncertainty-avoidance culture** (such as the United States, Sweden, and Denmark) is a culture characterized as being accepting and having a low need to control unpredictable people, relationships, or events. People in low uncertainty-avoidance cultures are comfortable with unpredictability and so put little cultural emphasis on reducing unpredictability. They tend to accept the unpredictability and ambiguity in life easily and tend to be tolerant of the unusual, prize initiative, take risks, and think that there should be as few rules as possible. People from these cultures are also more comfortable accepting multiple perspectives on "truth" rather than searching for one "Truth." A **high uncertainty-avoidance** culture is a culture characterized as having a low tolerance for and a high need to control unpredictable people, relationships, or events. These cultures create systems of formal rules and believe in absolute truth as a way to provide more security and reduce risk. They also tend to be less tolerant of people or groups with deviant ideas or behaviors. Because their culture emphasizes the importance of avoiding uncertainty, they often view life as hazardous and experience anxiety and stress when confronted with unpredictable people, relationships, or situations. Nations whose cultures are marked by high uncertainty avoidance include Japan, Portugal, Greece, Peru, and Belgium (Samovar, Porter, & McDaniel, 2007). How our culture has taught us to view uncertainty affects our communication with others. It shapes how we use language and develop relationships with others.

First, uncertainty avoidance affects the use of language. People from high uncertainty-avoidance cultures use and value specific and precise language because they believe that through careful word choice we can be more certain of

Uncertainty avoidance—the extent to which the people in a culture avoid unpredictability regarding people, relationships, and events.

Low uncertainty-avoidance culture—a culture characterized as being accepting and having a low need to control unpredictable people, relationships, or events.

High uncertainty-avoidance culture—a culture characterized as having a low tolerance for and a high need to control unpredictable people, relationships, or events.

what a person's message means. Imagine a teacher declaring to a class, "The paper must be well-researched with evidence cited and professional in format and appearance." Students from high uncertainty-avoidance cultures would find the teacher's remarks to be too general and vague. They would most likely experience anxiety and, to reduce their uncertainty, would probably ask a lot of questions about what kind of research is appropriate, how to cite evidence, how much evidence is needed, what writing style to use, and the desired length of the paper. These students would welcome a specific checklist or rubric that enumerated the exact criteria by which the paper would be graded. By contrast, students from a low uncertainty-avoidance cultural background would be annoyed by an overly specific list of rules and guidelines, viewing it as a barrier to creativity and initiative. As you can imagine, a teacher with students from both of these backgrounds faces a difficult challenge when trying to explain an assignment.

Second, uncertainty avoidance influences how people approach new relationships and how they communicate in developing relationships. As you might expect, people from high uncertainty-avoidance cultures are wary of strangers and may not seek out new relationships or relationships with people they perceive as different from them, since this would be unpredictable. They generally prefer meeting people through friends and family, and they refrain from being alone with strangers. When developing relationships, people from high uncertainty-avoidance cultures tend to guard their privacy, to refrain from self-disclosure early in a relationship, and to proceed more slowly through relationship development. Members of low uncertainty-avoidance cultures, on the other hand, are likely to initiate new relationships with people who differ from them and enjoy the excitement of disclosing personal information in earlier stages of relationship development.

▷ Power Distance

The third dimension of how culture affects communication is power distance. In Chapter 4, we introduced the concept of power distance and discussed its effect on language use. Let us elaborate on the concept and show several ways that it affects interpersonal communication. To repeat the definition, **power distance** is the amount of difference in power between people, institutions, and organizations in a culture. A culture can be either a high power-distance culture or a low power-distance culture. A **high power-distance culture** is a culture in which power is distributed unequally. In these cultures the power imbalances are endorsed as much by less powerful members as they are by those with power. While no culture has power distributed perfectly equally, in high power-distance cultures more inequality is seen, and it is viewed as natural. High power-distance cultures include most Arab countries of the Middle East, Malaysia, Guatemala, Venezuela, and Singapore, among other countries. A **low power-distance** culture is a culture in which power is distributed equally, or at least mostly equally. In cultures characterized as having low power distance, inequalities in power, status, and rank are underplayed and muted. People know that some individuals have

Power distance—amount of difference in power between people, institutions, and organizations in a culture.

High power-distance culture—a culture in which power is distributed unequally.

Low power-distance culture—a culture in which power is distributed equally.

more clout, authority, and influence, but lower-ranking people are not in awe of, are not more respectful toward, and do not fear people in higher positions of power. Even though power differences exist, these cultures value democracy and egalitarian behavior. Austria, Finland, Denmark, Norway, the United States, New Zealand, and Israel are examples of countries whose dominant cultures are characterized by low power distance.

Our cultural beliefs about power distance naturally affect how we interact with others in authority positions. If you were a student, an unskilled worker, or an average citizen in a high power-distance culture, you would not challenge a person in authority because you would expect to be punished for doing so. You would expect the more powerful person to control any interaction, you would listen with attention to what that person said to you, and you would do what was ordered without question. When talking with a more powerful person, you would also address that person formally by using his or her title as a sign of respect. Formal terms of address such as Mr., Mrs., and Dr.; proper and polite forms of language; and nonverbal signals of your status differences would be evident in the exchange. In contrast, if you come from a low power-distance culture, because differences in status are muted, you are more comfortable challenging those in authority. When interacting with a higher-power person, you feel comfortable directing the course of the conversation, and you question or confront powerbrokers if you need to. You do not feel compelled to use formal titles when addressing more powerful people.

In feminine cultures like Sweden, people, regardless of sex, assume a variety of roles. Did your family tend to have a masculine or a feminine culture?

Masculinity-femininity—the extent to which notions of "maleness" and "femaleness" are valued in a culture.

Masculine culture—a culture in which people are expected to adhere to traditional sex roles.

Feminine culture—a culture in which people regardless of sex are expected to assume a variety of roles based on the circumstances and their own choices.

OBSERVE AND ANALYZE ▽

Observing Dimensions of Culture

Interview someone who was born and raised in a country other than yours. During the discussion, explain the cultural dimensions of (a) individualism-collectivism, (b) uncertainty avoidance, (c) power distance, and (d) masculinity-femininity. Solicit an example from this person of each of these four dimensions so that you can determine where his or her culture falls on each one of the dimensions. Then analyze what you have learned about these four cultural dimensions as a result of this activity.

Dominant culture—a culture within a society whose attitudes, values, beliefs, and customs hold the majority opinion.

▷ Masculinity-Femininity

The final dimension of how culture affects communication is **masculinity-femininity**, the extent to which notions of "maleness" and "femaleness" are valued in a culture. Cultures differ in how strongly they value traditional sex role distinctions. A culture that Hofstede called a **masculine culture** would be a culture in which people are expected to adhere to traditional sex roles. Hofstede called these cultures "masculine" because, for the most part, groups that maintain distinct sex-based roles also value masculine roles more highly than feminine ones. If you come from a masculine culture like the ones that are dominant in Mexico, Italy, and Japan, you are likely to value men when they are assertive and dominant and to value women when they are nurturing, caring, and service-oriented. When you encounter people who don't meet these expectations, you are likely to be uncomfortable. Overall, if you come from a masculine culture, you will see masculine behaviors to be more worthwhile, regardless of your own sex. As a result, you are likely to value the traditionally masculine characteristics of performance, ambition, assertiveness, competitiveness, and material success more than you value traditionally feminine traits such as service, nurturing, relationships, and helping behaviors (Hofstede, 2000). A **feminine culture** is a culture in which people regardless of sex are expected to assume a variety of roles depending on the circumstances and their own choices. If you are from a feminine culture, like Sweden, Norway, or Denmark, not only will you feel free to act in ways that are not traditionally assigned to people of your sex, but you will also value those traits that have traditionally been associated with feminine roles (Hofstede, 1998).

Whether you come from a masculine or a feminine culture has a significant effect on how much behavioral flexibility you demonstrate. People from masculine cultures have strict definitions of what behavior is appropriate for people of a particular sex. As a result, they learn and are rewarded only for those behaviors that are seen to be appropriate for their sex. Men in these cultures are unprepared to engage in nurturing and caring behaviors, such as empathizing and comforting, and women are unprepared to be assertive or argue persuasively. Both men and women in feminine cultures learn and are rewarded for demonstrating both traditionally masculine and feminine behaviors. As a result, people from feminine cultures are more flexible in their communication behavior. Both men and women learn to nurture, empathize, assert, and argue, although any single individual may still lack skill in one or more of these behaviors.

◑ Dominant Cultures and Co-Cultures

Although the United States is a multicultural society, there are many attitudes, values, beliefs, and customs that the majority of people hold in common and that the minority feel they must follow. The **dominant culture** is the culture within a society whose attitudes, values, beliefs, and customs hold the majority opinion. Like the dominant culture of any country, the dominant culture of the United States has evolved over time. It once strictly reflected and privileged the values of white, western European, English-speaking, Protestant, heterosexual men. Before the 1960s, people coming to the United States from other cultural backgrounds were expected to assimilate into this dominant cultural perspective and to sublimate or abandon their native culture. In many cases, immigrants arriving from other countries changed their names to sound more "American"; they were expected to learn English as quickly as possible, and talk was expected to follow the norms of conversation from the dominant culture. But since the 1960s the United States has experienced a cultural revolution that has resulted in the adjustment of the dominant cultural perspective so that it is more reflective of the diverse cultures with which its citizens identify. We have come to understand and expect that different people may follow different communication patterns and that to be competent communicators we need to be able to adjust to diversity.

While we continue to have a dominant culture of shared beliefs, many Americans identify more strongly with groups whose values, attitudes, beliefs, and customs differ from those of the dominant culture. These groups, called **co-cultures**, are groups of people living within a dominant culture who are clearly different from the dominant culture. Co-cultural groups form around shared demographic characteristics and often share the same **cultural identity**, a sense of self that people form based on the cultural groups with which they most closely align themselves. Research has shown that cultural identity is determined by the importance we assign to our membership in a cultural group (Ting-Toomey et al., 2000). You may identify more closely with one of the co-cultural groups into which you fit, or you may consciously or unconsciously ignore or reject any or all of your co-cultural associations and choose to identify with the dominant cultural group. For example, many young working-class women work hard to distance themselves from their social class because they know that the dominant culture sees working-class women as aggressive, lacking values, and sexually promiscuous. On the other hand, working-class men often take pride in their working-class language and status (Skeggs, 1997).

Let's explore each of the co-cultural groups in turn, groups that are distinguished in terms of gender, race, ethnicity, sexual orientation and gender identity, religion, social class, and generation.

▷ Gender

Men and women have different cultural identities because they are biologically different from each other and because they are socialized differently throughout their lives (through clothes, games, toys, education, roles, etc.). Women and men communicate differently in a number of ways because of these cultural differences. For instance, research shows that women are primarily concerned with personal relationships when they communicate. They talk more about relationships and feelings, tend to include others in conversations, and actively respond

Co-cultures—groups of people living within a dominant culture who are clearly different from the dominant culture.

Cultural identity—a sense of self that people form based on the cultural groups with which they most closely align themselves.

to others. Men more often focus on tasks or outcomes when they communicate. They talk more about content and problem solving, tend to emphasize control and status, and are less responsive to others (Wood, 2007).

▷ Race

Traditionally the term "race" has been used to classify people based on biological characteristics, such as skin and eye color, hair texture, and body shape. However, scientific justifications for such divisions have proven elusive, and the classification system itself has changed drastically over time (Hotz, 1995). Despite the difficulty of scientifically defining race, people have experienced the social effects of perceived race and have formed communities and cultures based on racial experiences. As a result, race is an important cultural signifier for many people, and racial identity can influence communication in a number of ways. As Ronald Jackson described in the "Spotlight on Scholars" box in Chapter 4, African Americans may codeswitch by altering their linguistic and nonverbal patterns to conform to the dominant culture, or they may adopt communication forms unique to their race, depending on the topics or co-participants in a conversation (Bonvillain, 2003). Other co-cultures based on gender, ethnicity, or social class may also change their communication from time to time to be more similar to that of the dominant culture.

▷ Ethnicity

Ethnicity—classification of people based on shared national characteristics such as country of birth, geographic origin, language, religion, ancestral customs, and tradition.

Like race, ethnicity is an inexact distinction. **Ethnicity** is a classification of people based on shared national characteristics such as country of birth, geographic origin, language, religion, ancestral customs, and tradition. People vary greatly in terms of the importance they attach to their ethnic heritage and the degree to which it affects their attitudes, values, and behaviors. You may be a third-generation American from an Italian heritage and this may affect your verbal and nonverbal mannerisms, your religion, the foods you eat, and many other aspects of your identity. Your roommate, who is also a third-generation Italian, on the other hand, may be more assimilated to American culture, rarely thinking of or identifying herself as from an Italian background. She may not adhere to any of the cultural communication norms common to those of this ethnic background.

Language or mother tongue is an obvious influence of ethnicity on communication. Immigrants bring with them the language of their original country and may or may not speak English when they arrive. Even after they learn English, many immigrants choose to speak their mother language at home, live in proximity to other people from their home country, and interact with them in their native language. Although the United States is considered an English-speaking country, it now has the third-largest Spanish-speaking population of any country in the world, and 70 percent of Latinos in the United States mainly speak Spanish at home (Carlo-Casellas, 2002). To accommodate Spanish speakers, many businesses and government agencies now offer automated phone services with bilingual menus and employ bilingual customer service professionals.

How were you encouraged to maintain your ethnic identity?

▷ Sexual Orientation and Gender Identity

In the United States, as in most other countries, the dominant culture values and privileges heterosexuality and identity with one's birth gender. While public displays of affection between heterosexual couples go unnoticed, homosexual couples holding hands or kissing in public may be regarded as displaying offensive behavior, as is blurring gender lines. Over the past forty years, gay activism has resulted in the modification of some of the most extreme beliefs held about homosexuals and transgender people by members of the dominant culture. But discrimination based on sexual orientation and gender identity still occurs. As a result, many gay, lesbian, bisexual, and transgender people participate in and identify with nonheterosexual communities whose distinct attitudes, values, customs, rites, rituals, and language markers provide social support that is absent in the dominant culture. Choices about physical appearance as self-presentation cues expressed through nonverbal communication, for instance, may vary based on sexual orientation.

▷ Religion

A **religion** is a system of beliefs, rituals, and ethics shared by a group and based on a common perception of the sacred or holy. Although the dominant culture of the United States values religious freedom and diversity, historically it has reflected Judeo-Christian values and practices. All observant practitioners of a religion participate in a co-culture. Those who strongly identify with a religious group that is outside the Judeo-Christian tradition will have different orientations that shape

Religion—a system of beliefs, rituals, and ethics shared by a group and based on a common perception of the sacred or holy.

relationships and their communication behaviors. For example, Buddhism advises individuals to embrace rather than resist personal conflict. Adversity, emotional upheaval, and conflict are seen as natural parts of life (Chuang, 2004). So a Buddhist is apt to communicate openly and calmly during an interpersonal conflict and embrace the positive aspects of conflict in strengthening interpersonal ties.

▷ Social Class

Social class is a level in the power hierarchy of a society whose membership is based on income, education, occupation, and social habits. Most Americans are uncomfortable talking about social class and identify with the middle class even though they may really be members of more elite or lower classes (Ellis, 1999). But social classes exist in the United States just as they exist in all societies. Your social class often determines where you live and with whom you come in contact. As a result, over time members of a social class develop and reinforce their cocultures with distinct values, rituals, and communication practices. For example, aspects of verbal communication, including grammar, vocabulary, and the use of slang, may be influenced by social class.

▷ Generation

The time period in which we are born and raised can have a strong formative influence on us. People of the same generation form a cultural cohort group whose personal values, beliefs, and communication behaviors have been influenced by the common life experiences and events they encountered as they aged. People who grew up influenced by the Great Depression tend to be frugal; those alive during World War II value sacrifice of self for cause and country. Baby Boomers, who include large numbers of people who came of age during the counterculture of the 1960s, are likely to judge, question, and be competitive and driven to get ahead. Those we call Generation X, who experienced latch-key childhoods and the consequences of widespread divorce, value self-sufficiency and are adaptable, creative, and savvy with technology. Millennials (also called Generation "Y" or the Echo Boomers) never knew life without technology, were exposed to school and world violence at an early age, experienced corporate failures and globalization, and grew up during a time when children were put on pedestals by their parents. They are adept at using technology to multitask, have a high sense of morality, are cautious about issues of safety, and appreciate diversity. Whether in family relationships or in the workplace, when people from different generations interact, their co-cultural orientations can create communication difficulties. For example, when members of different generations work together, miscommunication, misunderstandings, and conflict are likely to occur more than when people work with others of the same generation. Generally, people from earlier generations are less likely to question authority figures like parents, teachers, religious leaders, or bosses. They demonstrate their respect by using formal terms of address such as referring to people as Mr., Ms., Dr., Sir, and so forth. People who

Social class—level in the power hierarchy of a society whose membership is based on income, education, occupation, and social habits.

came of age in the 1960s or later, on the other hand, tend to be more skeptical of authority and less formal in dealing with authority figures. They are more likely to question their managers and to openly disagree with decisions that are made by those in authority (Zemke, Raines, & Filipczak, 2000).

◑ Barriers to Effective Intercultural Communication

Now that we have developed an understanding of culture and the variations that can exist among cultures and co-cultures, we are in a better position to appreciate the specific barriers that cultural differences give rise to, including anxiety, assuming similarity or difference, ethnocentrism, stereotyping, incompatible communication codes, and incompatible norms and values.

▷ Anxiety

It is normal to feel some level of discomfort or apprehension when we recognize that we are different from most everyone else or when entering a cultural milieu whose customs are unfamiliar. Most people experience fear, dislike, and distrust when first interacting with someone from a different culture (Luckmann, 1999). For example, when Marissa, who is from a barrio in Los Angeles, is about to leave to attend a small liberal arts college in New England, she may be nervous and

INTER-ACT WITH ◐ TECHNOLOGY

Do a technology survey of your extended family. Who in the family is most likely to adopt new electronic technologies? What electronic technologies is each person in your family competent at using? In the area of technology, who are the teachers and who are the learners? How does each generation's comfort with technology affect their approach to electronic communication?

When you have found yourself in the midst of others from a different culture, what was your initial feeling?

question whether her decision to attend school in the northeast is a good one. Although the other students may be friendly enough during orientation week, it may become clear to Marissa that she doesn't really have much in common with them. While the other students may easily share stories of spring break trips they have taken with their families and joke about the cars they have wrecked, Marissa may find that she has little to contribute to the conversation, since her family has always visited her grandmother in Mexico during vacations and she has never had a driver's license. When she hesitantly mentions her quinceañera party, she may be greeted with blank stares and even an insensitive comment. At first, the other women may listen to Marissa politely, but Marissa's increasing nervousness may cause her to stumble over her words and do a poor job of explaining this coming-of-age tradition that is so important to her community. Most of us are like Marissa when we are anxious. We don't do a good job of sharing our ideas and feelings, and our anxiety becomes a barrier to our ability to communicate effectively.

▷ Assuming Similarity or Difference

When people cross into an unfamiliar cultural environment, they often assume that the norms that have always applied in their familiar situation will apply in a new situation. When traveling internationally from the United States, for example, many people expect to eat their familiar hamburgers and fries provided with rapid and efficient service. Likewise, they may be annoyed with shops and restaurants closing during midday in countries that observe the custom of siesta. It can be just as great a mistake to assume that everything about an unfamiliar culture will be different. With time Marissa is likely to find that the other students really aren't as different from her friends at home as she thinks, and school is still school even when there is snow on the ground. As she makes friends, she may learn that while Rachel, who is Jewish, didn't have a quinceañera party, she did have a bat mitzvah celebration, and Kate, who is Irish Catholic, had a big confirmation party. Since our assumptions guide our communication behaviors, incorrectly assuming similarities that are not accurate or differences that do not exist can lead to miscommunication. The wisest way to overcome this barrier is not to assume anything, but to be aware of the feedback you receive. This feedback will provide cues to the real similarities and differences that exist between your cultural expectations and those of your interaction partners.

▷ Ethnocentrism

Ethnocentrism is the belief that one's own culture is superior to others. The stereotype of the immigrant in the host country, loudly complaining about how much better everything is back home, is the classic example of ethnocentrism. In varying degrees, ethnocentrism is found in every culture (Haviland, 1993) and can occur in co-cultures as well. An ethnocentric view of the world leads to

Ethnocentrism—the belief that one's own culture is superior to others.

attitudes of superiority and messages that are directly and subtly condescending in content and tone. As you would expect, these messages are offensive to receivers from other cultures or co-cultures and get in the way of intercultural communication.

▷ Stereotyping

Stereotyping is assigning attributions to people that ignore individual differences and assume that everyone in a cultural group is the same. Basing our interactions on stereotypes can lead to misunderstandings and can strain relationships. For example, when Laura anticipates meeting Joey, who she has heard is gay, she may expect him to be effeminate in his mannerisms and interested in fashion. So she embarrasses him and herself when early in their conversation in an attempt to find common ground she asks him for advice on what type of cologne to buy her boyfriend and he replies, "What is your problem? I may be gay, but I'm not that Carson Kressley dude from *Queer Eye*!" Likewise, thinking that a Chinese

Stereotyping—assigning attributions to people that ignore individual differences and assume everyone in a cultural group is the same.

LEARN ABOUT YOURSELF ◗ Ethnocentrism

Take this short survey to learn something about yourself. Answer the questions based on your first response. There are no right or wrong answers. Just be honest in reporting your true beliefs. For each question, select one of the following numbers that best describes your beliefs.

1 = Strongly Agree
2 = Agree Somewhat
3 = Neutral
4 = Disagree
5 = Strongly Disagree

_____ 1. My country should be the role model for the world.
_____ 2. Most other countries are backward in comparison to my country.
_____ 3. People in my culture have just about the best lifestyle of anywhere.
_____ 4. People in other cultures could learn a lot from people in my culture.
_____ 5. Other cultures should try to be more like my culture.
_____ 6. I respect the customs and values of other cultures.
_____ 7. I am interested in the customs and values of other cultures.
_____ 8. Each culture should preserve its uniqueness.
_____ 9. People from my culture act strange and unusual when they go to other cultures.
_____ 10. Although different, most countries have equally valid value systems as ours.

Scoring the Survey: To find your scores, add up your responses for items 1, 2, 3, 4, and 5. Then add up separately your responses for items 6, 7, 8, 9, and 10. Each score can range from 5 to 25. Each score measures ethnocentrism. On the first score, the lower the number, the higher your ethnocentrism. On the second score, the higher the number, the higher your ethnocentrism.

Adapted from Neuliep, J. W., & McCroskey, J. C. (1997). "The development of a U.S. and generalized ethnocentrism scale," *Communication Research Reports*, *14*, 385398.

student in your class will get the best grade in the course because all Chinese students excel intellectually; assuming that Alberto, who is Mexican, is working in the United States as an illegal, undocumented worker; or anticipating that all European Americans are out to take advantage of people of color are all examples of stereotyping. When we interact based on stereotypes, we risk creating messages that are inaccurate and damage our relationships. Likewise, when we listen with our stereotypes and prejudices in mind, we may misperceive the intent of the person with whom we are talking.

▷ Incompatible Communication Codes

When our conversational partners, people in our group, or audience members speak a different language than we do, it is easy to see that we have incompatible communication codes. But even when people speak the same language there will be cultural variations that result from the co-cultures to which they belong. For example, people from Great Britain take a "lift" to reach a higher floor, while Americans ride an "elevator." Or less powerful co-cultural groups will often purposefully develop "in-group" codes that are easily understood by co-culture members but unintelligible to those from the outside. Just try to have a conversation about your computer problem with your friend Sam, who is a "techno geek." As an insider, Sam is likely to talk in a vocabulary that is as foreign to you as if he were speaking Icelandic. To get past incompatible communication codes, we may use nonverbal signing in an effort to overcome the language barrier. As we have seen, however, there are significant differences in the use and meaning of nonverbal behaviors, so those codes may also be incompatible. For example, in some cultures belching after eating signifies that the meal did not agree with the diner, while in other cultures it is a compliment to the cook. In some cultures, the gesture used in the United States to mean "OK" is obscene.

▷ Incompatible Norms and Values

All cultures base their communication behaviors on cultural norms and values. Sometimes the norms and values held by two people from different cultures create a barrier that makes it difficult for them to understand each other. For example, Jeff and Tabito have been best friends since elementary school. They have shared everything: schoolwork, summer vacations, sports, and camping trips. Now that they are in high school, their interests seem to be changing. One day Jeff tells Tabito that he has some pot, and he offers to share it with Tabito. Tabito simply says "no" and offers no explanation, leaving Jeff confused by Tabito's behavior. To Jeff, a fourth-generation American whose family is individualistic in its cultural orientation, it's no big deal. He figures, "Even if we get caught, it's not like we're selling it, and neither of us has ever been in trouble before, so all we'd get is a slap on the wrist." He doesn't consider how an arrest might affect his family and chides Tabito by saying, "Come on, don't wimp out on me now." What Jeff does not understand is that Tabito, who comes from a first-generation Japanese American family, holds the collectivist values of his parents. Being caught with drugs would bring great disgrace upon his whole family, and him. The collectivist goal of maintaining the reputation of his family is much more important to him than having fun with a friend. Because Tabito and Jeff don't recognize that their cultural backgrounds have led them to have different expectations, they don't discuss it. But both feel the strain that it puts on their conversation and relationship.

○ Intercultural Communication Competence

Effective intercultural communicators can overcome cultural barriers by doing a number of things, including tolerating ambiguity, remaining open-minded, and being altruistic; acquiring knowledge about other cultures; and developing culture-specific skills.

▷ Tolerate Ambiguity, Remain Open-Minded, and Be Altruistic

Succeeding as an intercultural communicator, according to Neuliep (2006), involves motivation and flexibility toward interacting with people from different cultures. In other words, be receptive to the learning process by tolerating ambiguity, remaining open-minded, and being altruistic.

1. Tolerate ambiguity. Communicating with strangers creates uncertainty, and when we recognize that a stranger also comes from a different culture, we can become anxious about what he or she will expect of us. People beginning intercultural relationships must be prepared to tolerate a high degree of uncertainty about the other person and to tolerate it for a long period of time. If we enter an intercultural interaction with belief that it is OK for us to be unsure about how to proceed, we are likely to pay closer attention to the feedback we receive from the other person and can then work to adjust our behaviors and messages so that together we can achieve understanding. Accepting the ambiguity in the interaction can help us work hard to make the conversation successful, and we are much less apt to become frustrated or discouraged by the inevitable false starts and minor misunderstandings. For example, Jerome has read the Partner Assignment List posted on the bulletin board outside of the lab and has discovered that his lab partner has an Indian-sounding name, but he has resolved to try hard to make the relationship a success. So when he meets Meena in class and finds out that she is an exchange student from Mumbai, he works diligently to attune his ear to her accent and is pleased to discover that while her accent is at first difficult to understand, her command of English is as good as his. Over the semester, Jerome labors to understand Meena's English and is rewarded; she has a much better grasp of chemistry than he does, and he appreciates her willingness to tutor him as they work on assignments.

OBSERVE AND ANALYZE ○

Communicating within Co-Cultures

Attend an event of a co-cultural group on campus or in your community. Consider visiting an ethnic festival, a house of worship that is very unfamiliar to you, or a senior center. Observe the behavior of others and communicate with as many people as possible. Then write a paper describing the experience and discussing the concepts of intercultural communication, culture shock, ethnocentrism, and stereotyping. Provide specific examples of any of these concepts you experienced.

2. Remain open-minded. An open-minded person is someone who is willing to receive the ideas and opinions of others unemotionally. Open-minded people are aware of their own cultural values and recognize that other people's values are different. They resist the impulse to judge the values of other cultures in terms of those of their own culture. In other words, they resist ethnocentrism. By remaining open-minded during the process of learning to be an effective intercultural communicator, such people are more able than others might be to adjust their thinking as they learn until a high degree of intercultural understanding is achieved.

3. Be altruistic. Altruism is a display of genuine and unselfish concern for the welfare of others. The opposite of altruism is **egocentricity**, a selfish interest in one's own needs to the exclusion of everything else. Egocentric people are self-centered, while altruistic people are other-centered. Altruistic communicators do not neglect their own needs, but they recognize that for an intercultural exchange to be successful, both parties must be able to contribute what they want and take what they need from the exchange. In this chapter's "Diverse Voices" box, "What Do You Say?" June Lorenzo describes a painful conversation she had regarding the word "squaw." As you read the excerpt, try to imagine how the conversation might have differed had all of the participants acted altruistically.

Altruism—display of genuine and unselfish concern for the welfare of others.

Egocentricity—selfish interest in one's own needs to the exclusion of everything else.

▷ Acquire Knowledge about Other Cultures

The more we know about other cultures, the more likely we are to be competent intercultural communicators (Neuliep, 2006). There are various ways to learn about other cultures: by observing, taking on formal study, and cultural immersion.

1. Observe another culture. You can simply watch as members of another culture interact with each other. As you watch, you will notice how the values, rituals, and communication styles of that culture are similar to and different from your own and from other cultures with which you are familiar. Passive observers study the communication behaviors that are used by members of a particular culture and are able to become better intercultural communicators as a result.

2. Formally study another culture. You can learn even more about another culture by reading accounts written by members of that culture, reading ethnographic research studies, taking courses, or interviewing a member of the culture about his or her values, rituals, and so on. Formal study and observation can go hand-in-hand and work off of each other to help you achieve greater intercultural understanding.

3. Immerse yourself in another culture. The best way to learn a great deal about another culture is by actively participating in it. When you live or work with people whose cultural assumptions are different from yours, you not only acquire obvious cultural information but also learn the nuances that escape passive observers and are generally not accessible through formal study. One reason that study abroad programs often include homestays is to ensure that students become immersed in the culture of the host country. We hope that you will consider participating in a study abroad experience. The international or global studies office at your college or university can point you to a variety of study abroad opportunities and may even guide you to scholarships or grants to help pay your expenses.

▷ Develop Culture-Specific Skills

To be effective in intercultural situations you may need to adapt the communication skills that you will learn in this course to the demands of a particular culture. To this end, three of the specific skills that you will study and that will be most useful are listening, empathy, and flexibility.

1. Practice listening. Listening is an effective way to improve your communication with people from other cultures. Because language and nonverbal communication vary across cultures, it is vitally important that you focus closely on the other person and listen attentively. It is important to note that there are cultural differences in how people engage in listening and the value that cultures place on listening. In the United States, we listen closely for concrete facts and information and often ask questions while listening. In other cultures, such as Japan, Finland, and Sweden, listeners are more reserved and do not ask as many questions (Samovar, Porter, & McDaniel, 2007). For many cultures in the Far East, listening is much more valued than speaking. Regardless of your cultural background, however, becoming a more skillful listener will help you in your intercultural encounters. In Chapter 8, you will learn more about the skills associated with active listening.

A QUESTION OF ETHICS ▼ What Would You Do?

Tyler, Jeannie, Margeaux, and Madhukar were sitting around Margeaux's dining room table working on a group marketing project. It was 2:00 A.M. They had been working since 6:00 P.M. and still had several hours of work remaining.

"Oh, the agony," groaned Tyler, pretending to slit his own throat with an Exacto knife. "If I never see another photo of a veggie burger it will be too soon. Why didn't we choose a more 'appetizing' product to base our project on?"

"I think it had something to do with *someone* wanting to promote a healthy alternative to greasy hamburgers," Jeannie replied sarcastically.

"Right," Tyler answered. "I don't know what I could have been thinking. Speaking of greasy hamburgers, is anyone else starving? Anyone up for ordering a pizza or something?"

"Sorry, but no one will deliver up here so late," Margeaux apologized. "But I have a quiche that I could heat up."

"Oh, oui, oui," Tyler quipped.

"You wish," Margeaux said. "It came out of a box."

"Sure, it sounds great, thanks," Jeannie said. "I'm hungry too."

"It doesn't have any meat in it, does it?" asked Madhukar. "I don't eat meat."

"Nope, it's a cheese and spinach quiche," Margeaux answered.

Tyler and Margeaux went off to the kitchen to prepare the food. Tyler took the quiche, which was still in its box, from the refrigerator. "Uh-oh," he said. "My roommate is a vegetarian, and he won't buy this brand because it has lard in the crust. Better warn Madhukar. He's a Hindu, so I imagine it's pretty important to him."

"Shhh!" said Margeaux. "I don't have anything else to offer him, and he'll never know the difference anyway. Just pretend you didn't notice that."

1. What exactly are Margeaux's ethical obligations to Madhukar in this situation?
2. What should Tyler do now?

What Do You Say?

by June Lorenzo

Cultural sensitivity involves understanding that certain words may be offensive to some racial or ethnic groups, but not to others. In this excerpt, the author describes the challenge of communicating her emotions about the name of a geographic location offensive to Native Americans.

Like our brothers and sisters in the African American, Hispanic, and Asian communities, Native Americans struggle with the "name game"—that those in power (get to) name and describe those who are not. In December 1996, I learned that the Arizona legislature was considering legislation which would change the name of a local landmark because of its offensive meaning. At the time, I was at a gathering of Native American Christians in Phoenix. We gladly received this news as an indication that the Phoenix community was demonstrating some cultural sensitivity.

However, on my return to Washington, D.C., the following day, I overheard a conversation between two other Phoenix passengers as we waited for our luggage. The conversation went something like this:

"Did you hear that they're thinking of changing the name of Squaw Peak?"

"Yeah, it's supposed to be offensive or something."

"Yes, apparently the word 'squaw' means woman and that is offensive to some people" (chuckle chuckle). "I don't know what the big deal is."

"Oh you never know how far they're going to go. . . . The next thing you know they'll discover Indian burial grounds on my land, and then I'll have to move out of my home" (chuckle chuckle).

As I found myself in a dilemma, my blood rose. I had a thirty-second conversation with myself: "What do I say? Do I have a right to say anything? Who am I to say something to them? If I turn around and they see that I am a Native person, will they be embarrassed? Worse yet, what if they don't care? Will I be embarrassed? Will I even think of something intelligent to say? Shall I just say nothing? No—I can't just stand here and ignore these words! This is offensive to me!"

Before I lost my nerve, I turned around and faced an Anglo woman and an Anglo man. I decided that I'd first try to join their conversation: "Actually, the name used to be 'squaw tit' but that was changed to its present name," I said, sharing information I had received in Phoenix. My intent was not to be funny, but their response was laughter. I decided to try again. "Actually the word means vagina. It was a French word used to describe Indian women, and I think it is offensive."

"Yes, but it just means woman, and I don't think it was French. And I don't think it was intended to be derogatory at the time," snapped the woman (as if she knew what the thinking of "the time" was).

I was unprepared for her indignation. Still, I opted to stick with my "be-patient-with-people-who-may-not-know" strategy and volunteered more information: "I believe it was a word used by the French to describe women in the upper Mid-west," I continued, hoping I would appeal to her conscience. "There was a time when we did not think names like Black Sambo or the image of Aunt Jemima was offensive. If we can change these, then we surely can change names like Squaw Peak."

"Yeah—we should spend our tax dollars on things like that!" replied the man sarcastically.

I began to wonder what I had gotten myself into. "Maybe, but hopefully it demonstrates more sensitivity."

"Maybe we're becoming too sensitive," he insisted. "Will this money be spent on changing road signs," he said. The woman nodded in agreement.

I turned around to check for my luggage. I was fuming inside. I stood there for a moment, trying to calm down and asking myself whether I should say anything more. What do you say to words like these? Simply "these people don't get it" and dismiss it as ignorance? Rationalize that they are total strangers and therefore don't really matter?

Regardless of the exact meaning of the word squaw, the point is that it is extremely offensive to Native women (at a minimum). That is sufficient. If we inform people of how offensive squaw and other terms are, will it make a difference? Do those in power refrain from taking actions of support if they are not personally hurt? Because of cultural differences, how can they experience the hurt caused by the use of such derogatory terms? Representative Jack Jackson, the Navajo sponsor of the bill, was criticized as "oversensitive" and "politically correct."

In the airport, I decided to say nothing more. But, if I could be honest about my feelings, what would I say? I would express to them how hurtful their comments and laughter were to me as a Native woman. I would tell them that every time I hear comments like theirs, I have to do battle inside myself. I have to tell myself, "No. This is not a truth about myself. It is a statement of their insensitivity."

As a member of a people who have struggled with genocide and systematic oppression in this country, as a person who inherited generations of self-hate from attempts to assimilate Indian people, I would tell them that it has taken years of work to say that I am a Native person and feel pride. I would say that I and my people are as fully human as they are and deserve respect.

But I would also say that despite the racism I experience in my life, I want to believe in the good of all people. This is what my people have taught me. I want to believe that the two people in the airport had no idea how hateful their words were.

Authors' postscript: It is a common misperception that the English word "squaw" was derived from the Iroquois or Mohawk language. Rather, linguists, including specialists on Indian languages, agree that as early as 1624 the word was borrowed from the Algonquians who lived in the area of Massachusetts. In that lan-

guage it simply meant "younger woman." Nevertheless, historically the word "squaw" has been used by whites as a derogatory reference to American Indian women and as such now has racist overtones. In his article "The Sociolinguistics of the 'S-word': 'Squaw' in American Placenames," William Bright, noted professor emeritus of linguistics at UCLA, suggests that "we don't need sociolinguistic reasons to eliminate 'squaw' from official maps, simple courtesy is enough" (Bright, 2002). Although Ms. Lorenzo seems to couch some of her arguments in sociolinguistic terms, it is evident that the racist connotations of the term "squaw" are her gravest concern. In April 2003, Governor Janet Napolitano of Arizona used her leadership to change the name of Squaw Peak to Piestewa Peak in honor of Lori Piestewa from the Hopi Tribe, who was killed in battle in Iraq. Lori Piestewa is believed to be the first Native American woman to give her life in combat for the United States. Nevertheless, the battle over offensive place names continues to this day.

Excerpted from "What Do You Say?" *The Other Side,* March–April 1998, vol. 34, no. 2, p. 48.

2. Practice intercultural empathy. Intercultural empathy means imaginatively placing yourself in another person's cultural world to attempt to experience what he or she is experiencing (Ting-Toomey, 1999). The native American saying, "Don't judge another person until you have walked two moons in his moccasins," captures this idea. By paying close attention to other person and focusing on the emotions displayed, we can improve our empathic skills. We will elaborate on how to communicate empathy in Chapter 9.

3. Develop flexibility. You can also learn concrete strategies for becoming more flexible in your intercultural communications. When you adjust your communication to fit the other person and the situation, you are behaving flexibly. With flexibility, you can use a wide variety of communication skills during an interaction and modify your behavior within and across situations. As we explained in Chapter 1, being flexible means analyzing a situation, making good decisions about how to communicate in that situation, and then modifying your communication when things are not going well.

> **Intercultural empathy**—imaginatively placing yourself in another person's cultural world to attempt to experience what he or she is experiencing.

▽ Summary

People of different cultures are increasingly coming into contact with each other. Culture is the system of beliefs, values, and attitudes shared by a particular segment of the population. Culture shock refers to the psychological discomfort people have when they attempt to adjust to a new cultural situation. Intercultural communication involves interactions that occur between people whose cultures are so different that the communication between them is altered.

Cultural norms and values vary in systematic ways, and we can understand how similar or different one culture is from others by understanding where the culture is regarding the dimensions of individualism-collectivism, uncertainty avoidance, power distance, and masculinity-femininity.

A shared system of meaning exists within the dominant culture, but meanings can vary within co-cultures based on gender, race, ethnicity, sexual orientation and gender identity, religion, social class, and generation.

Barriers to intercultural communication include anxiety, assumptions about differences and similarities, ethnocentrism, stereotyping, incompatible communication codes, and incompatible norms and values.

To develop intercultural communication competence, we should learn to tolerate ambiguity, remain open-minded, and be altruistic. We can acquire knowledge of other cultures by observing another culture, formally studying another culture, and immersing ourselves in another culture. Useful skills for intercultural communication competence are listening, empathy, and flexibility.

◉ Chapter Resources

Communication Improvement Plan:
Intercultural Communication ◉ Find more on the web @ www.oup.com/us/interact12

How would you like to improve your ability to communicate across cultures, as discussed in this chapter?

- Tolerate ambiguity
- Remain open-minded
- Be altruistic
- Observe another culture
- Formally study another culture
- Immerse yourself in another culture
- Practice listening
- Practice intercultural empathy
- Develop flexibility

Pick the area in which you would like to improve, and write a communication improvement plan. You can find a communication improvement plan worksheet on our website at www.oup.com/us/interact12.

Key Words ◉

Culture, *p. 151*
Culture shock, *p. 151*
Intercultural communication, *p. 151*
Individualism-collectivism, *p. 152*
Individualistic culture, *p. 153*

Collectivist culture, *p. 153*
Uncertainty avoidance, *p. 155*
Low uncertainty-avoidance culture, *p. 155*
High uncertainty-avoidance culture, *p. 155*

Power distance, *p. 156*
High power-distance culture, *p. 156*
Low power-distance culture, *p. 156*
Masculinity-femininity, *p. 158*
Masculine culture, *p. 158*

Inter-Act with Media
Communication across Cultures ⊙ Find more on the web @ www.oup.com/us/interact12

Television

Prison Break, episode: "Pilot" (2005). Wentworth Miller, Dominic Purcell.

Brief Summary: Engineer Michael Scofield (Miller) holds up a bank intentionally so he can go to prison and help free his innocent brother (Purcell), who is on death row for murder. As Michael masterminds their escape in a prison that he once helped construct, he must negotiate and forge relationships with inmates who represent myriad racial backgrounds. Although Michael's brother warns him that stereotypes still prevail in prison—Caucasian inmates believe they are superior to inmates of color—Michael believes that "the right deals transcend race." He cuts a deal with an African American inmate, but then is coerced to choose sides when the leader of a "family" of Caucasian inmates wants Michael to join their group. Michael attempts to communicate in a straightforward way, regardless of whom he encounters. On his first day in prison, he and his Latino cellmate chat about a universal topic: relationship issues. However, this extreme co-cultural environment shows that even when groups are forced to follow the same rules and norms, issues of race, ethnicity, social class, and stereotypes prove to be complicating factors.

IPC Concepts: Culture shock, co-cultures, race, ethnicity, sexual orientation, social class, stereotypes.

Cinema

Borat: Cultural Learnings of America for Make Benefit Glorious Nation of Kazakhstan (2006). Larry Thomas (director). Sacha Baron Cohen, Ken Davitian.

Brief Summary: Borat (Cohen), a Kazakh TV personality, travels to the United States to report on American culture and his interactions with American people. In Borat's country, family and extended family live close to one another, women are viewed as lesser citizens, and children possess guns. Borat's initial communication with Americans breeds culture shock—both for Borat and for those with whom he comes into contact. First, Borat is used to greeting men and women alike with a kiss on each cheek. Clearly, this violates the American ideal of personal distance. The faux pas continue to spiral: Borat struggles to learn what is appropriately humorous in America. He meets with a humor coach and has trouble determining how to add the common American vernacular "Not!" to the end of a sentence. At a rodeo, Borat offends the audience with his ethnocentrism: He sings Kazakhstan's national anthem to the tune of the U.S. national anthem, and his lyrics indicate his country's superiority—even in potassium! While the cultural differences are satirically portrayed, Borat's adjustment to American culture could be experienced by any person visiting for the first time.

IPC Concepts: Culture shock, intercultural communication, uncertainty avoidance, collective and individualistic cultures, masculine-feminine culture, ethnocentrism, communicating within co-cultures.

What's on the Web

Find links and additional material, including self-quizzes, on the companion website at www .oup.com/us/interact12.

7

Holding Effective Conversations

After you have read this chapter, you should be able to answer these questions:

- ▶ What is a conversation?

- ▶ What are the parts of a conversation?

- ▶ How do casual social conversations and problem consideration conversations differ?

- ▶ What are the six characteristics of conversations?

- ▶ What are conversational rules?

- ▶ What is the cooperative principle?

- ▶ What are the guidelines you should follow to be a more effective conversationalist?

- ▶ What issues emerge from conversations via technology?

- ▶ What are significant cultural variations in conversation?

"Hello, are you flying all the way to Los Angeles or getting off this plane in Denver?"

"I'm going to California."

"Are you going there for business or vacation?"

"I have a sales meeting to attend there."

"What do you do for a living? I'm in financial services. You know, most people do not even have personal financial advisors. They don't save enough for retirement, they don't purchase adequate life insurance, they don't pay attention to their investments, and . . ."

"Excuse me, I have to look over these reports on route. Enjoy the flight."

"Do you have a personal financial advisor? Are you married? Do you have a family? I can give you my card or recommend my company."

"I'm really not interested. Good luck in your work."

Conversations are the stuff of which our relationships are made. All relationships begin with a conversation, be it face-to face, on the phone, or online. Steve Duck, a leading researcher on relationships, claims that talking is one of the primary activities among friends (2007). When conversations go well, they are interesting, informative, stimulating, and just good fun. Yet many conversations are awkward, uncomfortable, and do not follow the guidelines for holding effective conversations, as our opening dialogue between the two airplane passengers illustrates. By understanding how conversations work, we can see how their effectiveness and value depend on the willingness of participants to share, and we can learn to use conversational skills to increase the informative value and enjoyment of participating.

In this chapter, we explore what exactly conversations are and how they work. We start by defining the word "conversation" and describing the structure and types of conversations. Then we discuss the six characteristics of conversations: formality, turn-taking, topic change, talk time, scriptedness, and audience. Next, we explain how conversational rules are applied in our interactions, including the rules associated with the cooperative principle. Then, we present guidelines to help you become a more effective conversationalist. Finally, we summarize how culture and technology affect conversations.

◑ Definition, Structure, and Types of Conversations

As a start, let's first define exactly what a conversation is, then explore the basic structure that all conversations follow, and finally pinpoint the various types of conversations. With this basic understanding of conversations, we can then move on to more specific topics.

▷ Definition of Conversation

Conversation—an interactive, locally managed, sequentially organized, and extemporaneous interchange of thoughts and feelings between two or more people.

A **conversation** may be defined as an interactive, locally managed, sequentially organized, and extemporaneous interchange of thoughts and feelings between two or more people. Why this complex definition? We use all of the adjectives in the definition because conversations differ from other forms of communication like speeches, interviews, group meetings, or debates in these particular ways. First, unlike speeches, conversations are *interactive;* that is, they involve at least two people who take turns speaking and listening. Second, unlike group meetings, conversations are *locally managed,* meaning that only those involved in the conversation determine the topic or topics discussed, who will speak, the order of speaking, the length of time each will speak in a turn, and how many turns each will take. Third, like other forms of communication, conversations are *sequentially organized;* that is, they have openings, bodies, and closings. But unlike all of the other forms of communication listed here, the choice and sequence of topics is not preplanned. Fourth, unlike all of the other aforementioned communications, conversations are largely *extemporaneous,* meaning the participants have not prepared or memorized what they will be saying (Svennevig, 1999).

LEARN ABOUT YOURSELF ⬗

Take this short survey, which will help you get a better idea of how conversations work by exploring an actual conversation you have had. Pick a recent conversation (satisfactory or unsatisfactory) you had with a friend, colleague, family member, or anyone else, and then answer the following questions. There are no right or wrong answers, so answer the questions using your first instincts. For each question, select one of the following numbers that best describes your attitudes toward the conversation you chose to explore.

1 = Strongly Agree
2 = Agree Somewhat
3 = Neutral
4 = Disagree Somewhat
5 = Strongly Disagree

_____ 1. I would like to have another conversation like this one.
_____ 2. I was very dissatisfied with this conversation.
_____ 3. During this conversation, I was able to present myself as I wanted the other person to view me.
_____ 4. The other person expressed a lot of interest in what I had to say.
_____ 5. We talked about things I was not interested in.
_____ 6. I was annoyed by the other person's interruptions of me.
_____ 7. Turn-taking went smoothly in this conversation.
_____ 8. There were many uncomfortable moments during this conversation.
_____ 9. I did not get to say what I wanted to in this conversation.
_____10. I was very satisfied with this conversation.

Scoring the Survey: To find your score, first reverse the responses for the odd-numbered items (if you wrote a 1, make it a 5; 2 = 4; leave 3 as is; 4 = 2; and 5 = 1). Next add the numbers for each item. Scores can range from 10 to 50. The lower (closer to 10) your score, the more satisfied you were with the conversation. The higher (closer to 50) your score, the less satisfied you were with the conversation. Keep your score in mind as you work through this chapter and learn how to improve your conversational skills. If your conversation got a low satisfaction score, what could the participants have done to improve the conversation? If your conversation got a high satisfaction score, what did the participants do right?

Note: After an important conversation, it would be useful for both you and your partner to complete this survey separately, then compare and discuss your scores.

Adapted from Hecht, M. L. (1978). Measures of communication satisfaction, *Human Communication Research, 4,* 350–368.

▷ Structure of Conversations

Now that we have a clear idea of what a conversation is, let's have a look at how all conversations are structured. All conversations have identifiable beginnings (openings), middles (bodies), and ends (conclusions). How obvious or formal each part is will vary depending on how long the conversation lasts, how well the participants know each other, and the context of the conversation.

First, all conversations have a beginning, or opening. All conversations begin when one person starts to talk while another listens and then responds in a way that indicates an interest in pursuing the interaction. So, people who wish to converse must indicate their availability and willingness to talk and find a topic that is mutually acceptable (Holtgraves, 2002). For example, suppose Adrianna and Luise (who don't know each other) are waiting for a bus. If neither is busy with another activity, both are of course available. After a few minutes of standing there, Adrianna says, "Beautiful day, isn't it?" to which Luise replies, "Yeah," and then looks up the street for the bus. Although Luise is available, she shows no willingness to talk—so unless Adrianna pursues it, there will be no conversation. But if in response to "Beautiful day, isn't it?" Luise says, "Sure is—a great day to be outdoors, isn't it?" she indicates a willingness to continue the conversation. In essence, all conversations begin with two utterances, spoken by different people. The first person initiates a topic, and the second reacts to the first in a way that suggests that he or she is interested or uninterested in continuing the interaction.

When you know your conversational partner and the topic you want to talk about is not controversial, you probably don't even think about the ways you go about initiating conversations. However, many of us find it very stressful when we begin a conversation with a stranger or someone we don't know very well. While the ways in which you can begin these conversations is limited only by your imagination, Figure 7.1 presents five ways to initiate a conversation with someone with whom you have little or no intimacy. Notice that each approach concludes by asking a question. The skillful use of questions is an effective strat-

Introduce yourself.	"Hi, my name is Gordon. What's yours?"
Refer to the physical context.	"Don't you just love classrooms that have outlets so you can plug in your laptop? Are all the rooms on campus like this?"
Refer to your thoughts or feelings.	"I'm so stressed by this class. I wasn't very good at math in high school. What about you? Are you dreading this class, too, or are you OK in math?"
Refer to another person.	"I don't believe I've met you before. Do you work with Erin?"
Use humor or make a light-hearted remark.	"My husband dragged me here—that's my excuse and I'm sticking to it. What's yours?"

FIGURE 7.1 Five ways to open a conversation

egy for initiating, sustaining, and directing a conversation (Dickson & Hargie, 2006). Don't be afraid to use humor to open conversations, as researchers have found that a shared laugh can ease the initial awkwardness between strangers (Fraley & Aron, 2004).

Second, all conversations include a middle, or body. The body of a conversation is the substantive part, and it may include several types of message exchanges, including small talk, gossip, and information and idea messages.

Small talk is message exchanges on inconsequential topics that meet the social needs of participants with low amounts of risk. We are all familiar with small talk and use it to initiate conversations with strangers, break the ice with new acquaintances, or even begin conversations with intimates. Topics for small talk are comfortable and nonconfrontational and include the weather, uncontroversial news topics, harmless facts and predictions, and the like. For instance, Adrianna and Luise may engage in small talk as they wait for their bus, since Adrianna has introduced the weather as a topic. Or, as they are waiting for a play to begin, Tom and Elena may chat about the upcoming playoff games, speculating on which teams will make the cut.

Gossip is message exchanges about other people who are not present in a conversation. Statements such as, "Do you know Armando? I hear he has a really great job"; "Would you believe that Mary Simmons and Tom Johnson are going together? They never seemed to hit it off too well in the past"; and "My brother Omar is really working hard at losing weight. I saw him the other day, and all he talked about was the diet he's on" are all examples of gossip. Gossip can be a harmless way to pass conversational time. All of the preceding examples are relatively harmless forms of gossip (assuming the people talked about have not expressed a desire to keep such information private). However, gossip can also be unethical and malicious. Gossip that discloses information that is private or inaccurate is unethical. Perhaps the most malicious kind of gossip is that which purposefully hurts or embarrasses a person who is not present. Before sharing gossip, ask yourself if you would say what you are planning to say about someone if that person were present.

Information and idea exchanges are message exchanges that focus on sharing important facts, opinions, and beliefs. Information and idea exchanges are common between new acquaintances and friends alike, but tend to carry more import than small talk. For example, rather than talking about the weather or about an upcoming event, Jin may talk with Gloria about the U.S. role in the Middle East or Dave may seek Hugo's views on cloning. Although the discussion of foreign policy and cloning is "deeper" than small talk about sports or cars, these types of exchanges may be appropriate during early stages of a relationship because through them you learn what other people value and how they think. Based on idea and information exchanges, you can assess how much effort you want to put into developing and sustaining a relationship.

Finally, all conversations have an ending, or conclusion. Conversations are usually ended when one person indicates a need or desire to disengage from the

Small talk—message exchanges on inconsequential topics that meet the social needs of participants with low amounts of risk.

Gossip—message exchanges about other people who are not present in a conversation.

Information and idea exchanges—message exchanges that focus on sharing important facts, opinions, and beliefs in a conversation.

interaction. For instance, you might say, "Oh, look what time it is . . . " or "This has been great, we'll have to get back together and talk some more." Sometimes, the conclusion is not formally discussed; the parties just stop talking. After an unusually long pause indicating closure, one of the participants might say, "Well, it's been great talking with you." At other times, one or the other participant will attempt to extend the conversation with a new approach, such as, "Just a second, I wanted to ask you . . ." A statement like this may lead to a lengthy additional exchange or may result in a minimal response before the person who wished to disengage reiterates the closure statement and ends the conversation. In a face-to-face conversation, nonverbal signs of leaving, such as putting on a coat, gathering one's belongings, or moving away from the person, may be used to signal the conclusion. Effective conversationalists recognize when a conversation partner is trying to end an interaction and show their respect by quickly finishing what they need to say.

▷ Types of Conversations

Although there may be many ways to categorize conversations by type, two types of conversations are common and easy to recognize: casual social conversations and problem consideration conversations.

Casual social conversations are interactions between people whose purpose is to enhance or maintain a relationship through spontaneous exchanges about general topics. For instance, when four friends have dinner together, they may have conversations on multiple topics, some in which all four participate and others in which two sets of two converse on different topics. During dinner they might focus most of their talk on one topic, such as a controversial election, or they might bounce around talking about several topics, sometimes circling back to make comments about previously discussed topics. During casual social conversations, participants may engage in small talk, gossip, and information and idea exchange. These message exchanges may be interwoven throughout the conversation. Figure 7.2 illustrates a casual social conversation, with commentary. Note that the purpose of the conversation between Donna and Juanita is not to solve problems but simply to enhance and maintain the relationship between the participants.

Problem consideration conversations, on the other hand, are interactions between people in which the purpose for at least one of the participants is to elicit cooperation in solving a problem or meeting a specific goal. For example, Allie and Barbara are roommates who are supposed to split the household chores. Lately Allie has noticed that Barbara hasn't been doing the dishes, cleaning the bathroom, or dusting when it is her turn, so when they are driving to the grocery store, Allie decides to broach the subject. She has a problem-solving purpose or goal in mind for the conversation—to get Barbara to agree to do her share of the chores.

A problem consideration conversation is more structured than a casual social conversation because it requires the participants to deliberate and reach a con-

Casual social conversations—interactions between people whose purpose is to enhance or maintain a relationship through spontaneous exchanges about general topics.

Problem consideration conversations—interactions between people in which the purpose for at least one of the participants is to elicit cooperation in solving a problem or meeting a specific goal.

Conversation	Commentary
As they look around the theater, Donna says, "They really did an Art Deco thing with this place didn't they?"	Donna introduces a possible topic.
"Yeah. . . . Hey," Juanita says as she surveys the audience, "it looks as if this is going to be a sellout."	Juanita acknowledges Donna's statement, chooses not to discuss it, and introduces a different topic.
"Certainly does. I see people in the last row of the balcony."	Donna accepts the topic and extends discussion with a parallel comment.
"I thought this would be a popular show. It was a hit when it toured Louisville . . . and I hear the attendance has been good all week."	Juanita continues the topic by providing new information.
Agreeing with Juanita, Donna adds, "Lots of people I've talked with were trying to get tickets."	Donna and Juanita continue the topic for two more turns.
"Well, it's good for the downtown."	
"Yeah," Donna says as she glances at the notes on the cast. After a few seconds she exclaims, "I didn't know Gloria VanDell was from St. Louis!"	Donna acknowledges Juanita's reply and then introduces a different topic.

FIGURE 7.2 Casual social conversation

clusion. These conversations are more orderly than casual social conversations and can have as many as five distinguishable parts. First, the conversation may begin with a greeting followed by very brief exchange on casual topics in order to develop rapport. Second, one person introduces the problem to be discussed and the reason or need for the conversation. Third, both participants engage in a series of speaking turns to share information and opinions, generate alternative ideas for solutions, and present the advantages and disadvantages of different options. Because conversations are spontaneous, they are unlikely to follow a linear textbook problem-solving format. In the midst of this discussion, they may digress by changing the topic to something unrelated to the problem at hand before circling back to identifying and evaluating alternatives. But although the discussion may not be linear, certain messages will need to be exchanged by both parties. Fourth, as the partners approach the end of their conversation, one person will usually try to obtain closure by summarizing what has been agreed to. The other person will either accept the summary as accurate or will amend it to clarify the areas of agreement as well as disagreement, if any. At times conversational partners skip this step, but doing so is risky because one partner will act on what he or she perceives has been agreed to, and that may not match the other partner's perception. Finally, the partners will either disengage, transition to another problem, or move back to a casual social conversation topic. The formal closing often includes showing appreciation for the conversation, such as, "I'm glad we took some time to share ideas. I think we'll be far more effective if the two of us are on the same page." The closing might also leave the door open for later conversation, such as, "If you have any second thoughts, give me a call."

⊙ Characteristics of Conversations

Rarely do we consciously think about the individual characteristics that make up conversations. Conversations often are so routine or habitual that we do not think about these individual elements. However, they are nonetheless a part of every conversation. The six characteristics to a conversation are formality, turn-taking, topic change, talk time, scriptedness, and audience.

▷ Formality

One of the characteristics of conversations is formality. **Formality** refers to the degree to which a conversation must follow rules and procedures. Two factors, status and familiarity, influence the formality of a conversation. Regarding status, the greater the status difference between the participants in a conversation, the greater the formality of the conversation. For example, if you were speaking to the president of your college or your company, the conversation would be a highly formal one. Both participants would shake hands rather than hug or slap hands when greeting, you would allow the person of higher status to select the topics, you would be careful not to interrupt the person of higher status or to use profanity, and certain topics of conversation would be off-limits to both of you. Regarding familiarity, the greater the familiarity between the participants in a conversation, the more informal the conversation. For example, when speaking with a close friend, a degree of close physical contact is expected, both participants may select topics, interruptions are acceptable, and—depending on the sensitivity of the participants to profanity and intimate topics—both are likely to be allowable.

Status and familiarity often go hand-in-hand in certain situations, which may involve careful negotiation and awareness of context. For example, if you are speaking to a new neighbor, even though the two of you are strangers, there are fewer formalities to attend to because you are equal in status. Each of you can feel free to select and change topics, interruptions or mild profanity may be used, and both of you can speak about a greater range of topics than in a conversation with the company president. However, the low level of familiarity will lead you both to avoid physical contact other than handshakes and to stay away from the overuse of profanity and the discussion of sensitive topics, such as politics and religion. Similarly, if you are good friends with your boss, both of you need to balance status with familiarity. The degree of physical contact can be higher than with strangers, but you still need to avoid sensitive topics in a social context, such as what you think of each other's working styles, and you still need to avoid being overly informal in a work context, such as interrupting your boss when he or she gives you an assignment.

Formality—degree to which a conversation must follow rules and procedures.

▷ Turn-Taking

A second characteristic of conversations is turn-taking. **Turn-taking** refers to alternating between speaking and listening in a conversation. A turn can be one word or a long monologue. Researchers note that in ordinary conversation, people often speak at the same time, and turns are not always easy to identify. As Ford, Fox, and Thompson (2002) point out, however, the fact is that participants in interaction treat the concept of "turn" as "relevant, real, and consequential in an individual's speaking time/space" (p. 8). For instance, when two people try to take a turn speaking at the same time, various behaviors can occur that demonstrate a mutual understanding of the importance of turn-taking. One person may back down and let the other person speak. Or both may back down through a polite negotiation where each says, "I'm sorry. You go ahead." Or both may continue trying to speak until the more persistent one wins a turn and the other finally backs down. The point here is that turn-taking is a complicated type of exchange that can be compared to a dance, but it is nonetheless understood by all communicators. Some people lead and some follow, the movements may be slow or fast, and we don't know when or where it will end.

Turn-taking is more predictable when two people are conversing because when one person stops speaking, it is the other person's turn to speak. But turn-taking can be challenging when a conversation involves three or more people. R. K. Sawyer's book *Creating Conversations* (2001) lists some unwritten norms of turn-taking in group conversations. For instance, it is understood that a speaker can select the next person to talk by directing a question to that person. Or it is taken for granted that we can become the next person to talk by being the first person to make an utterance once the first speaker has finished. Moreover, we nonverbally signal our desire to be the next speaker—and those cues are considered acceptable—by nodding, saying "uh hum," leaning forward, smiling, or giving eye contact or by using a combination of nonverbal cues. Sometimes the speaker may nonverbally signal the next turn-taker by turning toward that person, nodding, smiling, or touching. Furthermore, it is generally understood that interruptions are inappropriate and should be avoided. There are times and situations, however, when interruptions are inevitable and appropriate. We will discuss appropriate interruptions later in this chapter.

A unique approach to turn-taking is emerging through the use of instant messaging. Instant messaging allows a person to converse in real time with many people at once. However, not all of those people are conversing with each other. Therefore, the conventional rules of turn-taking do not apply. Let's say that Anika is instant messaging with five different friends one afternoon. She may pose a question to her friend Howie, but before the question appears on Howie's computer or smartphone screen, he may already have sent a question on a different topic to her. This defies the typical process of conversation, where you are expected to answer a person's question before you can ask a question of your own. Anika may be taking turns conversing online with five different people on five or more different topics at the same time, yet keeping track of what conversations go

Turn-taking—alternating between speaking and listening in a conversation.

with what people. If instant messaging remains as popular as it is today, it may, in time, affect the very process by which we conduct face-to-face conversations.

▷ Topic Change

Topic change—method by which people introduce new topics into a conversation.

A third characteristic of conversations is topic change. **Topic change** is the method by which people introduce new topics into a conversation. In casual social conversations, topics are introduced and changed quite randomly. Unlike in structured meetings, when we engage in casual conversation, we do not have an agenda that lists the order of topics or indicates how long we will converse on each topic. Topic change is negotiated informally and spontaneously between the participants. For instance, imagine that Hector and Desirée are chatting casually before class. Desirée may introduce a topic based on common ground between the two of them, such as an upcoming exam in the class. They may converse about that for a short while before subtle nonverbal cues signal that this topic is winding down. Each person's voice may become softer and less animated, and there may be shorter remarks and more pauses between turns. Hector may notice this and make a conscious decision to introduce a new topic, such as another student in the class. They may converse on that topic until nonverbal cues indicate the need for a further change. Or Desirée may abruptly change the topic in the middle of the discussion of the other classmate by asking, "Have you had lunch yet?" Topic change can be gradual, following a natural progression from one topic to the next, or it can be quite abrupt and unpredictable, changing from one unrelated issue to the next. It is best when all participants contribute equally to topic selection, though as we described earlier, higher-status people in a conversation usually have more control over topics discussed.

▷ Talk Time

Talk time—the share of time participants each have in a conversation.

A fourth characteristic of conversations is talk time. **Talk time** is the share of time participants each have in a conversation. Conversations are most satisfying when

SKILL BUILDERS ▽ Turn-Taking

SKILL	USE	PROCEDURE	EXAMPLE
Engaging in appropriate turn-taking	Determining when a speaker is at a place where another person may talk if he or she wants	1. Take your share of turns. 2. Gear turn length to the behavior of partners. 3. Give and watch for turn-taking and turn-exchanging cues. Avoid giving inadvertent turn-taking cues. 4. Observe and use conversation-directing behavior. 5. Limit interruptions.	When John lowers his voice as he says, "I really thought they were going to go ahead during those last few seconds," Melissa, noticing that he appears to be finished, says, "I did, too. But did you notice . . ."

all participants feel that they have had their fair share of talk time. Generally, we should balance speaking and listening in a conversation, and all participants should have roughly the same opportunity for talk time. However, like other elements of a conversation, talk time is affected by the status of the people conversing. We tend to defer to higher-status people and allow them to have more talk time out of respect. In addition, talk time is affected by the conversational styles of the participants. Some people are more outgoing and others more naturally quiet, so talk time need not be completely equal among participants. The key is to give everyone who wants to talk the opportunity to do so.

In general, however, talk time in conversation should be as equal as possible. People are likely to tune out or become annoyed at conversational partners who make speeches, filibuster, or perform monologues rather than engage in the ordinary give-and-take of conversation. Similarly, it is difficult to carry on a conversation with someone who makes one- or two-word replies to questions that are designed to elicit meaningful information. Turns do vary in length depending on what is being said, but if your statements average much longer or much shorter than those of your conversational partners, you need to adjust. If you discover that you are speaking more than your fair share, try to restrain yourself by mentally checking whether everyone else has had a chance to talk once before you talk a second time. On the other hand, if you find yourself being inactive in a conversation, you should try to increase your participation level. If you have information to contribute, you're cheating yourself and your partner or group when you do not share it. In a group conversation, you can help others who are unable to get enough talk time by saying something like, "Donna, I get the sense that you've been wanting to comment on this point" or "Tyler, you haven't had a chance to comment on this. What do you think?"

▷ Scriptedness

A fifth characteristic of conversations is scriptedness. Some types of conversation have happened so often and are so routine that they follow a basic script (Berger, 2002). **Scriptedness** involves the use of routine conversational phrases from past encounters applied appropriately to a new situation. For example, think of the habitual ways that we greet others or say good-bye. If Kimiko and Jesse, who have not seen each other for a while, bump into each other while jogging, the conversation is likely to sound like this:

Jesse: Hey, it's been a long time. How are you doing?
Kimiko: Yes, it's been forever since we've seen each other. I'm doing fine. How about you?
Jesse: I'm good. Can't complain. How is work going?
Kimiko: Work's keeping me busy. Are you still with KDC Software?

Notice how there is a reciprocal exchange of routine topics in a greeting conversation. Jesse greets Kimiko and asks a question; after acknowledging the greeting and answering the question, Kimiko asks the same question of Jesse. Certain

Scriptedness—the use of routine conversational phrases from past encounters applied appropriately to a new situation.

topics are standard in a greeting conversation. We are likely to chat about health, work, school, and common friends rather than world politics, serious crises, or our financial status. Notice also how turns are very short. Greeting conversations have a quick give-and-take to them. Other scripted conversations might relate to giving and receiving compliments or the annual phone call to your great aunt to thank her for your birthday present.

Sometimes we script a very important conversation, perhaps a problem consideration conversation, by rehearsing our remarks and anticipating what our partner might say. For example, it would be appropriate to have a mental script ready when asking your boss for a raise or when breaking up with your intimate partner. We do more planning in conversations of these types because the goal and outcomes are much more important than they are in casual social conversations. Note, however, that although it is important to prepare mental scripts as a guide for challenging conversations, you should be flexible about using them so that you do not sound stilted, rehearsed, or unable to adapt to what other people say in reply to you.

There is a unique type of conversational scripting that occurs between two individuals who have been interacting for a long time. **Co-narration** (Sawyer, 2001) involves two people finishing each other's sentences in a conversation because they know each other's style of conversation very well. For example, perhaps Dana and Armand have lived together for many years and often tell stories from their shared experiences in a collaborative fashion. When Armand says, "In 1999, we went out West for a trip," Dana joins in and says, "It was spring and we drove our RV." Armand adds, "That RV always gave us trouble because . . ."

Co-narration—two people finishing each other's sentences in a conversation because they know each other's style of conversation very well.

Co-narration is expected of identical twins, but it is also experienced by others who are intimate. Do you know any couples that co-narrate?

and Dana finishes, "the engine would overheat when you drove fast." They are collaboratively telling a story and altering the rules of turn-taking. Because this conversation is so routine and follows a basic two-person script, Armand and Dana do not perceive that they are interrupting each other.

▷ Conversational Audience

The final characteristic of conversations is conversational audience. Naturally, for a conversation to occur, it must have an audience of at least one person other than the speaker. **Conversational audience** refers to both the intended and unintended participants in a conversation. Most of the time, we are well aware of who is participating in a conversation and who is not. This is obvious in a two-person interaction, but it is less clear in a conversation among a group of people at a party. For example, imagine that you are speaking in a group conversation at a party. As people move in and out of the circle of conversation, you may notice a couple of people at the edge of the group listening and appearing interested in joining in. In a way, these outsiders are also the audience for the conversation; they are candidates to join the discussion, and those actively involved in the conversation may or may not allow this. You or another participant may move to widen the circle so that the newcomers can join, or you or another participant may address a remark to them, thereby bringing them into the conversation. Alternatively, you or another participant may tighten the distance between the conversational partners, or move to another space, so that the candidates continue to be excluded.

Eavesdropping is another way that people become an audience to others' conversations. In some situations, we become unwilling eavesdroppers, as it becomes impossible not to overhear what others are discussing. For example, servers in restaurants cannot help but hear parts of conversations at their tables. Likewise, some people speak loudly in the dentist's waiting room or at the gym and we cannot help becoming part of the audience. This is especially true with the prevalent use of cell phones today. Some people speak loudly on cell phones in public, and it is inevitable that an audience of more than one will hear the one-sided conversation. In other situations what we inadvertently overhear from another conversation interests us to the point where we become willing eavesdroppers. Sometimes we may signal our interest in becoming part of the conversation, while at other times we may be content simply to listen without making our silent participation known.

◉ Rules of Conversations and the Cooperative Principle

Although conversations may seem to have little form or structure, they are actually conducted based on implicit **rules,** which are "unwritten prescriptions that indicate what behavior is required, preferred, or prohibited in certain contexts" (Shimanoff, 1980, p. 57). These unwritten rules specify what kinds of messages

Conversational audience—intended and unintended participants in a conversation.

OBSERVE AND ANALYZE ◉

Characteristics of Conversations

During the next week, summarize one conversation that you consider to be effective and satisfying. Also, summarize one conversation that you consider to be ineffective and unsatisfying. For each conversation, analyze the conversational characteristics of formality, turn-taking, topic change, talk time, scriptedness, and conversational audience. Which of these conversational characteristics distinguish effective from ineffective conversations? What can you conclude about holding effective conversations?

Rules—unwritten prescriptions that indicate what behavior is required, preferred, or prohibited in certain contexts.

and behaviors will be seen as appropriate in a given physical or social context or with a particular person or group of people. We use these rules to guide our own behaviors and as a framework within which to interpret the behaviors of others.

What makes a rule a rule? As we answer this, let's use one of the most basic conversational rules as an example: "If one person is talking, then another person should not interrupt." This socially accepted rule contains within it all of the parts of our definition. First, rules specify appropriate human behavior, or what to do or not to do—what is *required, preferred, or prohibited*. Second, rules are *prescriptions*. A rule tells you what to do or say to be successful or effective and leaves little room for interpretation. If you choose to break the rule, you risk being viewed as an incompetent conversationalist, or you risk damaging your relationships. For example, if you interrupt, you may be viewed as rude, and the speaker may glare at you or verbally upbraid you. Third, rules are based on *contexts*. This means that conversational rules that apply in some situations may not apply under different conditions. To use our example, most of the time the rule is, "Don't interrupt." But if there is a true emergency—like a fire—this rule doesn't apply. Because rules are contextual, some conversational rules differ by culture. So, when we communicate with people of different cultural backgrounds, we may unintentionally break the conversational rules that guide their behavior and vice versa. For example, cultures differ in how eye contact should be used during conversations. In some cultures, the rule is to look directly at a speaker during a conversation, while in others the rule is to avoid direct eye contact with a speaker. Figure 7.3 presents several general rules of conversation that are observed in many cultures.

Not only are there general conversational rules, but effective conversations depend on participants cooperating with each other by following the cooperative principle. The **cooperative principle** is the principle stating that contributions

Cooperative principle—principle stating that contributions to a conversation should be cooperative—in line with the shared purpose of the conversation.

The following are common conversational rules observed in many cultures. Notice that many rules that we use are framed in an "if . . . then" format:

- If your mouth is full of food, then you must not talk.
- If someone is talking, then you must not interrupt.
- If you are spoken to, then you must reply.
- If another does not hear a question you ask, then you must repeat it.
- If you are being spoken to, then you should direct your gaze to the speaker.
- Or, from a different cultural perspective, if you are being spoken to, then you should look at the floor.
- If more than two people are conversing, then each should have equal time.
- If your conversational partners are significantly older than you, then you should refrain from using profanities and obscenities.
- If you can't say something nice, then you don't say anything at all.
- If you are going to say something and you don't want it to be overheard, then drop the volume of your voice.

FIGURE 7.3 Common conversational rules

to a conversation should be cooperative—in line with the shared purpose of the conversation. For example, when Barry asks, "Who's going to pick up Mom from work today?" and his brother answers, "I've got a big test tomorrow," Barry will assume that his brother is cooperating in the conversation and will interpret his brother's remark as, "I can't; I have to study," rather than as a random, unrelated comment. The rules of conduct that cooperative conversational partners follow are known as **maxims.** Communication scholars have identified four maxims: the quality maxim, the quantity maxim, the relevancy maxim, and the manner maxim (Grice, 1975). In addition, we propose two others: the morality maxim and the politeness maxim.

1. The **quality maxim** is the requirement to cooperate by providing information that is truthful in a conversation. When we purposely lie, distort, or misrepresent, we are not acting cooperatively in the conversation. Being truthful means not only avoiding deliberate lies or distortions but also taking care to avoid misrepresentation. For example, if a classmate asks you what the prerequisites for Bio 205 are, you should share them if you know them, but you should not guess and offer your opinion as though it were fact. If you don't know or if you have only a vague recollection, you follow the quality maxim by honestly saying, "I'm not sure." In this way, you are sharing with your classmate what he or she expects you to share.

2. The **quantity maxim** is the requirement to cooperate by providing a sufficient or necessary amount of information to satisfy the informational needs of others in a conversation. You violate this maxim if you provide more information than is needed so that you undermine the informal give-and-take that is characteristic of good conversations or when you give so little information that your partner has difficulty continuing the conversation. For instance, when Sam asks Randy how he liked his visit to St. Louis, Randy's answer, "Fine," is uncooperatively brief because it makes it difficult for Sam to continue the conversation. On the opposite extreme, should Randy launch into a twenty-minute monologue that details everything he did, including recounting what he ate each day, he would also be violating the quantity maxim.

3. The **relevancy maxim** is the requirement to cooperate by providing information that is related to the topic currently being discussed in a conversation. Comments that are only tangential to the subject or seek an abrupt subject change when other conversational partners are still actively engaged with the topic are uncooperative. For example, Hal, Corey, and Li-Sung are in the midst of a lively discussion about the upcoming 5K walk/run for the local homeless shelter when Corey asks whether either Hal or Li-Sung has taken Speech 101. Since Corey's change of subject disrupts a discussion that is still ongoing, he is violating the relevancy maxim.

4. The **manner maxim** is the requirement to cooperate by being specific and organized when communicating one's thoughts in a conversation. We cooperate with our conversational partners when we choose specific language and organize

Maxims—rules of conduct that cooperative conversational partners follow.

Quality maxim—the requirement to cooperate by providing information that is truthful in a conversation.

Quantity maxim—the requirement to cooperate by providing a sufficient or necessary amount of information to satisfy the informational needs of others in a conversation.

Relevancy maxim—the requirement to cooperate by providing information that is related to the topic currently being discussed in a conversation.

Manner maxim—the requirement to cooperate by being specific and organized when communicating one's thoughts in a conversation.

our words in a manner that allows our partners to easily understand our meaning. For example, when D'wan asks Rob how to download a computer file, Rob will comply with the manner maxim by explaining the process one step at a time, using language that D'wan can understand. Obviously, observing the manner maxim doesn't mean that you must have a specific outline for every comment you make. Conversations, after all, are informal. But following the manner maxim does mean that you need to organize what you say thoughtfully and clearly so that others don't have to work too hard to understand you.

5. The **morality maxim** is the requirement to cooperate by meeting moral/ethical expectations in a conversation. Although the quality maxim requires truthfulness, this maxim extends moral and ethical principles further. For example, in the United States, violations of the morality maxim would include repeating information that had been disclosed confidentially, purposefully deceiving someone about the truthfulness or accuracy of another's statements, or persuading someone to do something that the speaker knows is wrong or against the other person's personal interests.

6. The **politeness maxim** is the requirement to cooperate by showing respect and courtesy to others during a conversation. In our conversations, we should attempt to observe the social norms of politeness in the dominant culture and not purposefully embarrass others or ourselves during the interaction.

When we are talking with others, we assume that they are following the maxims outlined in the cooperative principle, and they assume that we are as well. But the truth is that most of us violate one or more of these maxims when we talk. Sometimes we lie to avoid hurting someone's feelings or to protect our self-image. We sometimes say too much or too little or insert irrelevant comments. And often what we say is disorganized and uses a vocabulary with which our partner is unfamiliar (Holtgraves, 2002). Nevertheless we rely on the cooperative principle to help us achieve effective conversations as often as we can.

❍ Guidelines for Effective Conversationalists

Conversations have a life of their own and move spontaneously according to the wishes of the participants. As a result, it is difficult to identify a single skill or set of skills that will enable you to be an effective conversationalist. There are, however, several general guidelines you can follow as you work to be a better conversational partner: Develop an other-centered focus, engage in appropriate turn-taking, maintain conversational coherence, practice politeness, balance appropriateness and efficiency, protect privacy, and engage in ethical dialogue. Let's look at each of these guidelines in turn.

▷ Develop an Other-Centered Focus

Skilled conversationalists listen carefully to their partners, ask questions of their partners, and introduce topics that are of interest to their partners. This other-

---

Morality maxim—the requirement to cooperate by meeting moral/ethical expectations in a conversation.

Politeness maxim—the requirement to cooperate by showing respect and courtesy to others during a conversation.

centered focus is also demonstrated by full involvement in the conversation. For example, looking at partners rather than watching others who are entering or leaving the room, silencing cell phones and not responding to vibration, and not "multitasking" when someone is talking to you are ways to be other-centered. If you are focused on others, you can still talk about yourself when the conversation naturally moves to your interests or when your conversational partner asks you for information.

▷ Engage in Appropriate Turn-Taking

Another way to be an effective conversationalist is to follow the politeness maxim by taking turns. Skillful turn-takers use conversation-directing behaviors to balance turns between those who speak freely and those who may be more reluctant to speak. Similarly, effective turn-takers remain silent and listen politely when the conversation is directed to someone else. By paying attention to the turn-taking process, without being too preoccupied with it, you can become skilled at smooth turn-taking.

One of the crucial skills of turn-taking is learning not to interrupt others. Some people are chronic interrupters and do not realize it. Pay attention to your turn-taking behavior to make sure that you do not abruptly seize the floor from others. Culture and status do affect the perceived appropriateness of interruptions, however. In some cultures, it is acceptable for participants in a conversation to take their turns via interruptions. Likewise, higher-status people in most cultures typically have freedom to interrupt those lower in status. A physician on a tight schedule may repeatedly interrupt a patient with questions to understand the patient's symptoms, and that is considered appropriate. However, a patient who frequently interrupts a physician is likely to be seen as rude. In addition, interrupting for "clarification" or "agreement" (confirming) is generally considered to be interpersonally acceptable (Kennedy & Camden, 1983, p. 55). For instance, interruptions that are likely to be accepted include relevant questions or paraphrases intended to clarify, such as, "What do you mean by 'presumptuous?'" or "I get the sense that you think presumptuous behavior is especially bad," and reinforcing statements such as, "Good point, Max" or "I see what you mean, Suzie." Interruptions that are likely to be viewed as disruptive or impolite include those that change the subject or seem to minimize the contribution of the interrupted person.

▷ Maintain Conversational Coherence

Conversational coherence is the extent to which the comments made by one person relate to those made previously by others in a conversation (McLaughlin, 1984, pp. 88–89). It is based on the relevancy maxim and is important in maintaining effective conversations. Littlejohn and Foss (2007) discuss conversational coherence as a way to create clear meaning in conversation. The more directly messages relate to those that precede them, the more coherent or meaningful the conversation. In other words, what we say should be related

Conversational coherence—the extent to which the comments made by one person relate to those made previously by others in a conversation.

to what was said before. If what we want to say is only tangentially related or is unrelated to what was said before, then we should yield our turn to someone else who may have more relevant comments. If there are only two people conversing, then the listener should respond to the speaker's message before introducing a change in topic.

▷ Practice Politeness

Politeness, or relating to others in ways that meet their need to be appreciated and protected, is universal to all cultures and contributes greatly to effective conversation (Brown & Levinson, 1987). One way of showing politeness is to engage in face-saving. **Face-saving** means helping others to preserve their self-image or self-respect. Put another way, face-saving means helping another person to avoid embarrassment. There are many ways that we engage in face-saving during conversations. One way is to avoid potentially embarrassing topics. For example, if Chad knows that Charlie just lost his job, Chad is not likely to bring up that topic in a casual conversation among a group of friends at the coffee shop. To say, "Hey, Charlie my man, I hear you just got canned at work," would cause embarrassment to everyone. Another way to engage in face-saving is to choose our words carefully. For example, suppose your professor returns a set of papers and you believe the grade you received does not accurately reflect the quality of the paper. You could say, "You didn't grade my paper fairly. It deserves a much higher grade." However, saying something like this, which implies that the professor was wrong, is likely to threaten the professor with a loss of face and lead to defensive behavior. You might, instead, say something diplomatically worded, like, "I would appreciate it if you could look at my paper again. I honestly thought I did a better job than what the grade shows. I've marked the places on the paper where my comments come from our textbook, and I've noted the textbook pages. I'm not sure why these sections were marked wrong. I wonder if you would consider re-grading the paper or at least helping me understand the reasons for this grade."

▷ Balance Appropriateness and Efficiency

In every effective conversation, people must balance two primary considerations: the need to be appropriate and the need to be efficient (Kellerman & Park, 2001). **Appropriateness** refers to being polite and following situational rules of conversation. **Efficiency** means being direct in the interest of achieving conversational goals in a relatively short amount of time. Depending on the situation, the balance of appropriateness and efficiency will vary. For example, imagine that Vince is meeting a very important client regarding a major business deal. While there are business goals that he would like to achieve in this conversation, there are rules that he must follow to balance appropriateness and efficiency. He cannot begin by asking the client to sign a contract because that would be efficient but not appropriate. Instead, he may begin with small talk by asking about the client's company and sharing information about his company. Then Vince may

Politeness—relating to others in ways that meet their need to be appreciated and protected.

Face-saving—helping others to preserve their self-image or self-respect.

Appropriateness—being polite and following situational rules of conversation.

Efficiency—being direct in the interest of achieving conversational goals in a relatively short amount of time.

move the conversation to a deeper level by discussing how the client likes to conduct business. Only after gradual, polite conversation can Vince directly get to the point of asking for the client's business. In a different situation, however, concern for efficiency may outweigh concern for appropriateness. For instance, if Vince calls a supplier to his company, it is both appropriate and efficient for him to ask a question immediately about when the supplies were shipped. He need not work up to the question gradually and cautiously.

In short, the balance of appropriateness and efficiency in a conversation will vary based on the relationship of the participants, the topics being discussed, the context of the conversation, and the channel by which the conversation is occurring. Formal situations or conversations with strangers usually call for more appropriateness and less efficiency. Think of all the rules of conversation you must follow during a job interview, at a funeral, or with an acquaintance at a fancy restaurant, for example. In contrast, informal situations, routine interactions, and conversations with close friends and family usually call for more efficiency and less appropriateness. For instance, think of how you can get right to the point when conversing with your best friend or with the pharmacist at your local drugstore. Keep in mind the dual challenges of following social norms and achieving your goal in a conversation when balancing appropriateness and efficiency. It is important to make a conscious decision about what levels of politeness and directness are needed and then to make comments that reflect both goals.

▷ Protect Privacy

To be an effective conversationalist, protect privacy by paying attention to who may be an audience to your conversation and keeping confidences. Regarding your audience, think about both your need for privacy and the need of others not to have to overhear your personal conversations. To do so, you may choose to move a private conversation to a more private location, speak more softly, have the conversation at another time, and not impose your cell phone conversation on others. Regarding keeping confidences, keep in mind the morality maxim. If someone reveals private information in a conversation and asks you not to share this information with others, it is important to honor this request.

▷ Engage in Ethical Dialogue

The final guideline followed by effective conversationalists is to engage in ethical dialogue. According to Johannesen (2000), ethical dialogue or conversation is characterized by authenticity, empathy, confirmation, presentness, equality, and supportiveness.

Authenticity is communicating information and feelings that are relevant and legitimate to the subject at hand directly, honestly, and straightforwardly. To sit in a discussion, disagreeing with what is being said but saying nothing, is inauthentic. It is also inauthentic to agree verbally with something that you really do not believe in.

Authenticity—communicating information and feelings that are relevant and legitimate to the subject at hand directly, honestly, and straightforwardly.

Empathy—demonstrating an understanding of another person's point of view without giving up one's own position or sense of self.

Confirmation—expressing a warm affirmation of others as unique persons without necessarily approving of their behaviors or views.

Presentness—willingness to become fully involved with another person by taking time, avoiding distractions, being responsive, and risking attachment.

Equality—treating conversational partners as peers, regardless of the status differences that separate them from other participants.

Supportiveness—encouraging the other participants in a conversation to communicate by praising their worthwhile efforts.

Empathy is demonstrating an understanding of another person's point of view without giving up one's own position or sense of self. Comments such as, "I see your point" or "I'm not sure I agree with you, but I'm beginning to understand why you feel that way" demonstrate empathy. Because of the importance of empathy in making effective responses, we will consider it in more detail in later chapters.

Confirmation is expressing a warm affirmation of others as unique persons without necessarily approving of their behaviors or views. Examples of confirmation might include, "Well, Keith, you certainly have an interesting way of looking at things, and I must say, you really make me think through my own views" or "Well, I guess I'd still prefer that you didn't get a tattoo, but you really have thought this through."

Presentness is the willingness to become fully involved with the other person by taking time, avoiding distractions, being responsive, and risking attachment. The most obvious way to exhibit presentness in a conversation is by listening actively. You can also demonstrate presentness during a conversation by asking questions that are directly related to what has been said.

Equality is treating conversational partners as peers, regardless of the status differences that separate them from other participants. To lord one's accomplishments, one's power roles, or one's social status over another during conversation is unethical.

Supportiveness is encouraging the other participants in a conversation to communicate by praising their worthwhile efforts. You will recall from our discussion of relationships in Chapter 3 that positive communication climates are characterized by an exchange of messages that are descriptive, open, and tentative, as well as equality oriented.

When we engage in ethical dialogue, we improve the odds that our conversations will meet our needs and the needs of those with whom we interact.

○ Conversations via Technology

Thus far in this chapter, we have assumed that conversations typically occur face-to-face. This mirrors the historical fact that conversations were for a long time oral interactions that occurred in face-to-face settings or over the phone. But increasingly our interpersonal interactions are either technologically mediated (via cell phone calls or text messages) or occur in cyberspace (via e-mail, blog postings, IMs, chat rooms, etc.). As the speed with which we can send and receive written messages has increased from the days of "snail mail," exchanges of short written messages have begun to approximate what we have traditionally thought of as conversations. Similarly, as telephone technology has allowed us mobility, when and where we hold conversations has changed as well. As a result of the widespread use of these technologies, today traditional understandings of conversations are changing regarding awareness of audience, degree of conversational spontaneity, abruptness of disengagement, multiplicity of conversations, acceptance of interruptions, and notions of privacy, all of which we will explore

further in this section. Quite simply, in technology-meditated and cyberspace communication, conversational rules are seen as less important than in face-to-face communication (Shedletsky & Aitken, 2004, p. 126).

▷ Awareness of Audience

In more traditional conversations, we know who our conversational partner is when we begin the interaction. But when we send e-mails or text messages, post to a blog, or develop a profile on a social networking site, we can't always be sure who our conversational partner will be. For example, you may text your Mom about your weekend plans, but if your younger brother happens to pick up your Mom's phone, he may answer you pretending to be her. Likewise, you may send an e-mail to a friend thinking your communication is a private one between friends, only to find that your friend has forwarded the message to several other people. Moreover, posting a message on a blog or setting up a profile on a social networking website such as MySpace or Facebook functions like an invitation to conversation with unexpected people. In fact, regarding social networking sites, Sylvia Engdahl, editor of the book *Online Social Networking* (2007), believes: "You can't set up a profile and walk away. You have to approve new friend requests, respond to messages, post your latest action alerts, send out bulletins and keep your profile up to date. You are not creating a billboard, but are starting a conversation" (p. 163). Your profile is tantamount to inviting thousands or hundreds of thousands of people into conversation with you.

▷ Degree of Conversational Spontaneity

In traditional conversations, most of the body of the interaction involves unscripted, informal, spontaneous exchanges. But e-mails and especially blogs do not conform strictly to these expectations. Since e-mails and blogs are locally managed, sequential, and somewhat interactive, they fit within the broad definition of a conversation. But both e-mails and blogs are written forms of communication, and people often edit their comments before sending them or posting them online. So the comments are not as extemporaneous—unscripted, informal, or spontaneous—as traditional conversations. Just as conversations include small talk, gossip, and information and idea exchange, so too do e-mails and blogs. E-mails are frequently used to solve problems and share information. Blogs facilitate topic-based information and idea exchanges about political topics, personal interests, and current events. In addition, according to Geert Lovink (2008), "blogs spread rumor and gossip and mimic conversations in cafes, bars and corridors" (p. 10). However, these forms of conversation are often carefully scripted and sometimes formally written and, therefore, not spontaneous.

▷ Abruptness of Disengagement

Your oral conversations have clear endings with commonly understood disengaging behaviors, but in your cyber conversations, disengaging may be truncated or

OBSERVE AND ANALYZE ❽

Analysis of a Media Conversation

Analyze a conversation between two people in a television show or movie. Evaluate the communicators according to the guidelines for effective conversationalists. To what extent do the two people show an other-centered focus, take turns appropriately, maintain conversational coherence, practice politeness, balance appropriateness and efficiency, protect privacy, and engage in ethical dialogue? Provide examples of the characters either using or violating these guidelines.

even nonexistent. For example, have you ever been in a chat room or interacting with someone in a role-playing game only to have him or her simply "disappear" or abruptly end the interaction by typing "bye"? These abrupt departures can be disconcerting because we expect our cyber partners to abide by the expectations for ending conversations that are used in face-to-face interactions. But the cyberspace environment is different, and increasingly such forms of conversational disengagement behaviors are acceptable.

▷ Multiplicity of Conversations

While there may be more than one conversation taking place in a face-to-face conversational group at any one time, all participants recognize when multiple conversational topics are being discussed and who the participants in side conversations are. With the advent of cyber and technology-mediated conversations, however, it is not always apparent to everyone which conversations are taking place with whom. For example, imagine Janey and her project group are e-mailing each other before class starts. While they are trying to decide when to meet, Janey disengages from that conversation and takes a cell phone call from her roommate, Chris. Chris really wants to talk with one of her classmates, Sam, whose phone number he doesn't have, so Janey sends a text message to Chris with Sam's phone number. In the meantime, one of the other members of the group begins e-mailing his Mom to get her work schedule for the following week so he knows which days he will need to pick up his younger sister at school. Meanwhile, two

Does it bother you when someone you are talking with interrupts your conversation to answer a cell phone call, check for IMs and e-mails, or engage in other technology-mediated communication?

other members of the group have a quick side instant message conversation about an upcoming test in calculus. Just then their instructor sends a group e-mail and one member of the group replies to all asking the instructor about the project guidelines. Meanwhile, Sam and Chris have called each other and made a date to have dinner on Saturday. While this may seem like conversational chaos, it is an increasingly normal and acceptable occurrence.

▷ Acceptance of Interruptions

Traditionally, it was considered socially rude to interrupt a face-to-face conversation with one person or group to answer a phone or respond to a competing invitation to converse. Social etiquette dictated that you finish a conversation with one person before beginning another, and people who were physically present took priority over those who were not, unless it was an emergency. Today, especially among younger people, the opposite appears to be the case. Multiple conversations abound, occurring between people who are present and those who may be continents away. People who are not present and wish to "converse" are favored over those who are present, and people think nothing of interrupting important face-to-face interactions to answer their cell phones, respond to text messages, and so on.

▷ Notions of Privacy

The notion of conversations as private or semi-private communications is also being eroded by mediated and cyber technologies. You have probably had the unpleasant experience of becoming the audience for another person's loud cell phone conversation, or you may have been unable to avoid someone sitting next to you sending a text message or e-mail. Some mobile technology users don't seem to notice people or events around them when they are in public spaces. They are seemingly engaged in private conversations when talking on cell phones, e-mailing, or text messaging, yet they are in public places. Thus, the distinctions between public and private spaces for communication have become blurred.

INTER-ACT WITH ⬤ TECHNOLOGY

Locate a blog kept by a famous person you admire. Read at least one week of postings on the blog. To what extent does this blog seem to be a traditional conversation? What elements are conversational? What elements don't seem conversational? How has reading the blog changed your opinion of the blog owner? What is your impression of the people who have responded to this blog?

⬤ Cultural Variations in Conversations

Throughout this chapter, we have assumed a Western cultural perspective on having effective conversations, specifically the perspective of low-context cultures. But just as various verbal and nonverbal rules vary from low-context to high-context cultures, so do the guidelines for effective conversation. Gudykunst and Matsumoto (1996, pp. 30–32) explain four differences in conversational patterns between people from low-context and high-context cultures.

First, while low-context culture conversations are likely to include greater use of such categorical words as *certainly, absolutely,* and *positively,* high-context culture conversations are likely to see greater use of qualifiers such as *maybe, perhaps,* and *probably.*

Conversational Ballgames

by Nancy Masterson Sakamoto

Nancy Masterson Sakamoto is professor of American studies at Shitennoji Gakuen University, Hawaii Institute, and coauthor of Mutual Understanding of Different Cultures (1981). A former English teacher and teacher trainer in Japan, she co-wrote (with Reiko Naotsuka) a bilingual textbook for Japanese students called *Polite Fictions: Why Japanese and Americans Seem Rude to Each Other* (1982). "Conversational Ballgames" is a chapter from *Polite Fictions*.

After I was married and had lived in Japan for a while, my Japanese gradually improved to the point where I could take part in simple conversations with my husband and his friends and family. And I began to notice that often, when I joined in, the others would look startled, and the conversational topic would come to a halt. After this happened several times, it became clear to me that I was doing something wrong. But for a long time, I didn't know what it was.

Finally, after listening carefully to many Japanese conversations, I discovered what my problem was. Even though I was speaking Japanese, I was handling the conversation in a western way.

Japanese-style conversations develop quite differently from western-style conversations. And the difference isn't only in the languages. I realized that just as I kept trying to hold western-style conversations even when I was speaking Japanese, so my English students kept trying to hold Japanese-style conversations even when they were speaking English. We were unconsciously playing entirely different conversational ballgames.

A western-style conversation between two people is like a game of tennis. If I introduce a topic, a conversational ball, I expect you to hit it back. If you agree with me, I don't expect you simply to agree and do nothing more. I expect you to add something—a reason for agreeing, another example, or an elaboration to carry the idea further. But I don't expect you always to agree. I am just as happy if you question me, or challenge me, or completely disagree with me. Whether you agree or disagree, your response will return the ball to me.

And then it is my turn again. I don't serve a new ball from my original starting line. I hit your ball back again from where it has bounced. I carry your idea further, or answer your questions or objections, or challenge or question you. And so the ball goes back and forth, with each of us doing our best to give it a new twist, an original spin, or a powerful smash.

And the more vigorous the action, the more interesting and exciting the game. Of course, if one of us gets angry, it spoils the conversation, just as it spoils a tennis game. But getting excited is not at all the same as getting angry. After all, we are not trying to hit each other. We are trying to hit the ball. So long as we attack only each other's opinions, and do not attack each other personally, we don't expect anyone to get hurt. A good conversation is supposed to be interesting and exciting.

If there are more than two people in the conversation, then it is like doubles in tennis, or like volleyball. There's no waiting in line. Whoever is nearest and quickest hits the ball, and if you step back, someone else will hit it. No one stops the game to give you a turn. You're responsible for taking your own turn.

But whether it's two players or a group, everyone does his best to keep the ball going, and no one person has the ball for very long.

A Japanese-style conversation, however, is not at all like tennis or volleyball. It's like bowling. You wait for your turn. And you always know your place in line. It depends on such things as whether you are older or younger, a close friend or a relative stranger to the previous speaker, in a senior or junior position, and so on.

When your turn comes, you step up to the starting line with your bowling ball, and carefully bowl it. Everyone else stands back and watches politely, murmuring encouragement. Everyone waits until the ball has reached the end of the alley, and watches to see if it knocks down all the pins, or only some of them, or none of them. There is a pause, while everyone registers your score.

Then, after everyone is sure that you have completely finished your turn, the next person in line steps up to the same starting line, with a different ball. He doesn't return your ball, and he does not begin from where your ball stopped. There is no back and forth at all. All the balls run parallel. And there is always a suitable pause between turns. There is no rush, no excitement, no scramble for the ball.

No wonder everyone looked startled when I took part in Japanese conversations. I paid no attention to whose turn it was, and kept snatching the ball halfway down the alley and throwing it back at the bowler. Of course the conversation died. I was playing the wrong game.

This explains why it is almost impossible to get a western-style conversation or discussion going with English students in Japan. I used to think that the problem was their lack of English language ability. But I finally came to realize that the biggest problem is that they, too, are playing the wrong game.

Whenever I serve a volleyball, everyone just stands back and watches it fall, with occasional murmurs of encouragement. No one hits it back. Everyone waits until I call on someone to take a turn. And when that person speaks, he doesn't hit my ball back. He serves a new ball. Again, everyone just watches it fall.

So I call on someone else. This person does not refer to what the previous speaker had said. He also serves a new ball. Nobody seems to have paid any attention to what anyone else has said. Everyone begins again from the same starting line, and all the balls run parallel. There is never any back and forth. Everyone is trying to bowl with a volleyball.

And if I try a simpler conversation, with only two of us, then the other person tries to bowl with my tennis ball. No wonder foreign English teachers in Japan get discouraged.

Now that you know about the difference in the conversational ballgames, you may think that all your troubles are over. But if you have been trained all your life to play one game, it is no simple matter to switch to another, even if you know the rules. Knowing the rules is not at all the same thing as playing the game.

Even now, during a conversation in Japanese I will notice a startled reaction, and belatedly realize that once again I have rudely interrupted by instinctively trying to hit back the other person's bowling ball. It is no easier for me to "just listen" during a conversation than it is for my Japanese students to "just relax" when speaking with foreigners. Now I can truly sympathize

with how hard they must find it to try to carry on a western-style conversation.

If I have not yet learned to do conversational bowling in Japanese, at least I have figured out one thing that puzzled me for a long time. After his first trip to America, my husband complained that Americans asked him so many questions and made him talk so much at the dinner table that he never had a chance to eat. When I asked him why he couldn't talk and eat at the same time, he said that Japanese do not customarily think that dinner, especially on fairly formal occasions, is a suitable time for extended conversation.

Since westerners think that conversation is an indispensable part of dining, and indeed would consider it impolite not to converse with one's dinner partner, I found this Japanese custom rather strange. Still, I could accept it as a cultural difference even though I didn't really understand it. But when my husband added, in explanation, that Japanese consider it extremely rude to talk with one's mouth full, I got confused. Talking with one's mouth full is certainly not an American custom. We think it very rude, too. Yet we still manage to talk a lot and eat at the same time. How do we do it?

For a long time, I couldn't explain it, and it bothered me. But after I discovered the conversational ballgames, I finally found the answer. Of course! In a western-style conversation, you hit the ball, and while someone else is hitting it back, you take a bite, chew, and swallow. Then you hit the ball again, and then eat some more. The more people there are in the conversation, the more chances you have to eat. But even with only two of you talking, you still have plenty of chances to eat.

Maybe that's why polite conversation at the dinner table has never been a traditional part of Japanese etiquette. Your turn to talk would last so long without interruption that you'd never get a chance to eat.

Excerpted from Sakamoto, N. M. (1995). Conversational ballgames. In R. Holton (Ed.), *Encountering Cultures* (pp. 60–63). Englewood Cliffs, N.J.: Prentice-Hall.

Second, low-context cultures strictly adhere to the relevancy maxim by valuing relevant comments that are perceived by listeners to be directly to the point. In high-context cultures, however, individuals' responses are likely to be more indirect, ambiguous, and apparently less relevant because listeners rely more on nonverbal cues to help them understand a speaker's intentions and meaning.

Third, in low-context cultures, the quality maxim operates through truth-telling. People are expected to communicate their actual feelings verbally, regardless of how this affects others. Effective conversationalists in high-context cultures, however, employ the quality maxim differently. They define quality as maintaining harmony, and so conversationalists will sometimes send messages that mask their true feelings.

Finally, in low-context cultures, periods of silence are perceived as uncomfortable because when no one is speaking, little information is being shared. In high-context cultures, silences in conversation are often meaningful. When three or four people sit together and no one talks, the silence may indicate agreement, disapproval, embarrassment, or disagreement, depending on the context.

In this chapter, you have learned a number of guidelines for conducting effective conversations. But because of cultural variations, there are some types of conversation that may defy adhering to such guidelines. In other words, different cultures have different standards as to what constitutes an effective conversation. For example, Sawyer (2001) describes a conversational type in which several participants of Jewish background may converse by yelling, confronting, interrupting, abruptly changing topics, and being quite emotional. This style of conversation may occur among some people from southern European and Middle Eastern cultural backgrounds as well. People who are not familiar with this conversational style may perceive that an argument is taking place. But for the participants, this is not the case. Such behavior is considered to be part of having a lively, engaging conversation. To follow rules of politeness, turn-taking, topic change, and conversational coherence would be uninvolving and ineffective to them. Instead, as a good conversationalist, you would be expected to discuss

A QUESTION OF ETHICS ▽ What Would You Do?

Tonia is her Uncle Fred's only living relative, and he has been her favorite relative for as long as she can remember. About three years ago, Fred was diagnosed with lung cancer that eventually led to surgery and a round of chemotherapy and radiation. At that time, Fred made out his will, naming Tonia as his executor and giving her his medical power of attorney. Recently, he also signed a waiver so that his medical team would be able to disclose all of his medical information to Tonia even though he has been feeling great.

Uncle Fred has worked hard all of his life and has talked about, dreamed about, and saved to take a trip to visit his mother's hometown in northern Italy. Last week he called Tonia very excited and told her that he had just finished making all of his reservations and was scheduled to leave for Italy in two weeks. While Tonia was really happy for him, she wondered if his doctor had approved his trip.

Unwilling to "rain on his parade," Tonia nonetheless phoned the doctor to see if Uncle Fred had told him about the trip. She was alarmed to find not only that

Uncle Fred had not mentioned the trip to his doctor but also that Fred's latest follow-up CT scan showed that the cancer was growing aggressively. The doctor believed that Fred needed to cancel his trip and immediately begin another round of chemotherapy. When Tonia asked the likelihood that the treatments would bring the cancer back into remission the doctor said, "To be perfectly honest, there is only a 10% chance that the chemo will work. But without treatment the cancer is sure to kill him in less than six months." Then the doctor implored Tonia to talk with her uncle and convince him to cancel his plans and begin treatment.

1. Is it ethical for Tonia to try to convince her uncle to stay and have chemotherapy?
2. Should Tonia agree to talk with her uncle? If so, what ethical issues will she confront?
3. If she chooses to have this conversation with her uncle, how can Johannesen's guidelines for ethical dialogue help her create an effective conversation?

multiple topics at once; jump into the conversation without waiting for a turn; speak in a loud, emotional tone; and disagree strongly with others. So be aware that there are cultural norms but no such thing as absolute rules regarding conversation. By understanding and appreciating cultural variation in conversations, we can avoid judging others' conversational styles when they do not conform to our own rules. There are many ways to have a conversation.

In the "Diverse Voices" box in this chapter, Nancy Masterson Sakamoto discusses how having a conversation can be a very different experience in Japan than it is in the United States.

○ Summary

Conversations are interactive, locally managed, sequentially organized, and extemporaneous interchanges of thoughts and feelings between two or more people. After some opening exchanges, the body of a conversation develops. It is likely to involve various types of information, including small talk (message exchanges on inconsequential topics that meet the social needs of participants with low amounts of risk), gossip (message exchanges about other people who are not present in a conversation), and information and idea exchanges (message exchanges that focus on sharing important facts, opinions, and beliefs in a conversation).

The two types of conversations are casual social conversations and problem consideration conversations. Casual social conversations occur between people when they desire to enhance or maintain a relationship. Problem consideration conversations occur when the goal of at least one of the participants is to solicit the cooperation of the other in meeting a goal.

The characteristics of a conversation include formality, turn-taking, topic changes, talk time, scriptedness, and audience.

Conversations are guided by rules, which are unwritten prescriptions that indicate what behavior is required, preferred, or prohibited. Effective conversations are also governed by the cooperative principle, which suggests that contributions to a conversation should be cooperative—in line with the shared purpose of the conversation. The cooperative principle gives rise to maxims relating to quality, quantity, relevancy, manner, morality, and politeness.

Good communicators follow the guidelines for conducting effective conversations, which include focusing on others, taking turns appropriately, avoiding interruptions, maintaining conversational coherence, practicing politeness, balancing appropriateness and efficiency, protecting privacy, and engaging in ethical dialogue.

Changes that have arisen from our traditional notions of conversations as a result of technology include awareness of audience, degree of conversational spontaneity, abruptness of disengagement, multiplicity of conversations, acceptance of interruptions, and notions of privacy. It is also important to realize that there are cultural variations in the conduct of conversations.

◔ Interaction Dialogue: Conversations

Conversations that are likely to be casual social or problem-solving interactions tend to follow unwritten rules. Conversations are most effective when they adhere to the quality, quantity, relevancy, manner, morality, and politeness maxims. Skills of effective conversation include focusing on the other, appropriately taking turns, maintaining conversational coherence, practicing politeness (including helping others save face), balancing appropriateness and efficiency, considering privacy needs, and engaging in ethical dialogue.

Here's a transcript of Susan and Sarah's conversation, with analysis of the conversation in the right-hand column. As you read the dialogue, determine the type of conversation that is taking place. Look for the signs of effective conversation just mentioned. You may want to write down some of your observations before you read the analysis in the right-hand column.

Susan and Sarah are close friends who share the same religious background and the occasional frustrations related to their family beliefs.

Conversation	Analysis
Susan: So how are you and Bill getting along these days?	Susan initiates the conversation with a meaningful question.
Sarah: Oh, not too well, Suze. I think we've got to end the relationship. There are so many issues between us that I just don't have the same feelings.	Sarah answers the question and gives "free information" about her changed feelings and the presence of multiple problems.
Susan: Yeah, you know, I could tell. Is there one specific thing that's a problem?	Susan poses a question that focuses on Sarah and suggests the potential for problem consideration.
Sarah: Yes, and it's ironic because early on I didn't think it would be a problem, but it is. You know he's not Jewish, and since we've started talking about marriage, I've realized that it is a problem. While Bill's a great guy, our backgrounds and beliefs just don't mesh. I never realized how important my Jewishness was to me until I was faced with converting. And Bill feels similarly about the issue.	Sarah accepts Susan's willingness to discuss a problem by sharing specific information that becomes the topical focus of the rest of the conversation—information that meets Grice's conversational maxims.
Susan: I think I'm kind of lucky, well, in the long run. Remember in high school my parents wouldn't let me go out with anybody who wasn't Jewish? At the time I resented that and we both thought they were reactionary, but now I'm kind of glad. At the time my parents said, "You never know what's going to come out of a high school relationship." Well, they	Susan shifts the topic a bit by speaking about her experiences. This seems to violate the relevancy maxim, but in so doing, she lays the groundwork for later exchanges.

never got that far, but it did force me to think about things.

Sarah: Yes, I remember that. You hated it. It's amazing to realize your parents can actually be right about something.

Susan: Right, it was the pits at the time, but at least it spared me the pain you and Bill are going through. It must be awful to be in love with someone that you realize you don't want as a life partner.

Sarah: Exactly, but I'm glad that my parents didn't restrict my dating to Jewish guys. I've learned a lot by dating a variety of people, and I know that I've made this decision independently. Bill's a great guy, but for me to be me, I need to partner with a Jewish man—and Bill knows he can't be that. Making this choice has been hard, but it's helped me to grow. I guess I understand myself better.

Susan: So where have you guys left it? Are you going to still see each other? Be friends?

Sarah: We hope so. But right now, it's too fresh. It hurts to see him, so we're trying to give each other some space. It will really be tough when I hear he's seeing someone else. But I'll get by.

Susan: Well, you know I'm here for you. And when you're ready there are some real hotties at Hillel. I'll be glad to introduce you.

Sarah: Thanks Suze. So how's your new job?

Susan: Oh, it's great. I really like my boss and I've gotten a new assignment that fits right in with my major. Plus my boss has been flexible in assigning my hours. I just wish that it wasn't so far away.

Sarah: I thought it was downtown.

Susan: It is, but it takes me over an hour because I have to change buses three times.

Sarah: Wow—are you at least able to study while you ride?

Susan: Not really. I get carsick.

Sarah shows that she recalls what was said. She keeps the conversation flowing.

Susan confirms that her parents' wisdom spared her pain. She then makes a statement that stimulates further discussion from Sarah.

Sarah agrees, but then explains her perception of the value of being free to date a variety of people.

Here Sarah confirms that it was her decision not to partner with a man outside her religion. But she also confirms that the decision was difficult.

Susan pursues the topic by asking questions to probe the consequences of Sarah's decision.

These questions lead Sarah to disclose the difficulties she's experienced as a result of her decision.

Here Sarah opens the door for Susan's support. Susan picks up on Sarah's need by stating that she stands by her and is willing to help.

Sarah's thanks serve as a close to the topic. She then asks a question suggesting a change of topic.

Although Susan could probe further, she accepts the change of topic by giving information to support her generalization of "It's great."

Sarah continues the side issue by asking another question.

Susan shows why she can't study.

◖ Chapter Resources

Communication Improvement Plan: Conversation ◗ Find more on the web @ www.oup.com/us/interact12

How would you like to improve your conversational skills as discussed in this chapter?

- Developing an other-centered focus
- Engaging in appropriate turn-taking
- Maintaining conversational coherence
- Practicing politeness
- Balancing appropriateness and efficiency
- Protecting privacy
- Engaging in ethical dialogue

Pick one of these topics, and write a communication improvement plan. You can find a communication improvement plan worksheet on our website at www.oup.com/us/interact12.

Key Words ◗

Conversation, *p. 176*
Small talk, *p. 179*
Gossip, *p. 179*
Information and idea exchanges, *p. 179*
Casual social conversations, *p. 180*
Problem consideration conversations, *p. 180*
Formality, *p. 182*
Turn-taking, *p. 183*
Topic change, *p. 184*
Talk time, *p. 184*
Scriptedness, *p. 185*

Co-narration, *p. 186*
Conversational audience, *p. 187*
Rules, *p. 187*
Cooperative principle, *p. 188*
Maxims, *p. 189*
Quality maxim, *p. 189*
Quantity maxim, *p. 189*
Relevancy maxim, *p. 189*
Manner maxim, *p. 189*
Morality maxim, *p. 190*
Politeness maxim, *p. 190*
Conversational coherence, *p. 191*

Politeness, *p. 192*
Face-saving, *p. 192*
Appropriateness, *p. 192*
Efficiency, *p. 192*
Authenticity, *p. 193*
Empathy, *p. 194*
Confirmation, *p. 194*
Presentness, *p. 194*
Equality, *p. 194*
Supportiveness, *p. 194*

Skill Practice ◗ Find more on the web @ www.oup.com/us/interact12

Skill Practice exercises challenge you to master the material you have read in this chapter. For additional Skill Practice activities, visit our website at www.oup.com/us/interact12.

Identifying Parts of Problem-Solving Conversations

Identify each part of the problem-solving conversation structure in the following script.

April: Hi, Yolanda. How are you doing?

Yolanda: Oh, can't complain too much.

April: I'm glad I ran into you—I need to check something out with you.

Yolanda: Can we do this quickly? I've really got to get working on the speech I'm doing for class.

April: Oh, this will just take a minute. If I remember right, you said that you'd been to The Dells for dinner with Scot. I'd like to take Rob there to celebrate his birthday, but I wanted to know whether we'd really feel comfortable there.

Yolanda: Sure. It's pretty elegant, but the prices aren't bad and the atmosphere is really nice.

April: So you think we can really do dinner on fifty or sixty dollars?

Yolanda: Oh, yeah. We had a salad, dinner, and a dessert and our bill was under sixty even with the tip.

April: Thanks, Yolanda. I wanted to ask you 'cause I know you like to eat out when you can.

Yolanda: No problem. Gotta run. Talk with you later—and let me know how Rob liked it.

Inter-Act with Media ○ Find more on the web @ www.oup.com/us/interact12

○Search

Television

Two and a Half Men, episode: "We Called It Mr. Pinky" (2005). Charlie Sheen, Jon Cryer.

Brief Summary: The first expression of "I love you" between partners can have myriad results. Here is how this conversation ensues between Charlie Harper and his girlfriend of two months:

Girlfriend: "I think I love you, Charlie Harper."
Charlie: "Thank you."

(Girlfriend walks out the door, then knocks. Charlie opens the door.)

Girlfriend: "Wait a minute. Did you just say 'thank you?'"
Charlie: "Did I?"
Girlfriend: "I said 'I think I love you' and you just said thank you."
Charlie: "Thank you? It's an expression of appreciation . . . 'thank you.'"
Girlfriend: "That's it? You don't have anything to add?"
Charlie: "Thank you . . . so very much."
Girlfriend: "That's great. I open my heart to you and you couldn't care less."
Charlie: "Well that's not fair, I could care less! A lot less! Come on, what do you want me to do, lie to you?"

(Girlfriend tells Charlie to drop dead and adds other choice words.)

Clearly, Charlie's response did not satisfy what his girlfriend wanted to hear, but he did follow the cooperative principle. Based on the maxims, Charlie was ethical in his disclosure, offering honesty about his feelings. He clarified his girlfriend's concerns over his use of the phrase "thank you," and he remained polite, rather than becoming evasive or angry.

IPC Concepts: Problem consideration conversations, turn-taking, the cooperative principle, maxims, ethical dialogue.

Cinema

Into the Wild (2007). Sean Penn (director). Emile Hirsch, Marcia Gay Harden, William Hurt, Jena Malone, Hal Holbrook.

Brief Summary: Twenty-two-year-old Christopher McCandless (Hirsch) was a real-life adventurer who defied his privileged but troubled family life after graduating from college. Bound for Alaska by way of South Dakota, the Colorado River, and California, McCandless traveled a largely solo journey through the wilderness, but he encountered and conversed with a number of unique people along the way. One such interaction occurred between McCandless and elderly Ron Franz (Holbrook). Each loners, McCandless and Franz connect quickly on a deeply interpersonal level. Each shares his history and insights about life and human relationships. In a pivotal exchange, Franz asks McCandless what he's running from and McCandless turns the question back on Franz. McCandless tells Franz he needs to "get back in the world" and "make a radical change in lifestyle." Referring to previous conversations about McCandless' family, Franz later offers his own advice to forgive them. Before parting, Franz asks if he can adopt McCandless and become his grandfather. McCandless agrees to discuss the request when he returns from his trip. While this conversation will never happen, the attentive, thoughtful exchanges between these men represent the characteristics of authentic other-centered, ethical dialogue.

IPC Concepts: Guidelines for effective conversationalists, conversational coherence, turn-taking, other-centered focus, appropriateness and efficiency, ethical dialogue.

What's on the Web

Find links and additional material, including self-quizzes, on the companion website at www .oup.com/us/interact12.

Listening Effectively

8

After you have read this chapter, you should be able to answer these questions:

- ▶ What is listening?

- ▶ What skills can you use to attend more effectively?

- ▶ What are techniques you can use to understand better?

- ▶ How can you remember and retain information more accurately?

- ▶ What skills can you use to improve your ability to evaluate information critically?

- ▶ What are the techniques you can use to respond more appropriately?

- ▶ What are the five types of listening?

- ▶ What are the guidelines for listening in high-technology environments?

"Can you print out a copy of this quarter's consumer data on the 18-ounce packaging? I need to review it before the 9 o'clock meeting with the marketing folks."

"No, the data needed cleaning and we have been told . . ."

"I can't believe it. I had a hard copy of that research when I left the office last night. I've got to get myself prepared for this meeting "

"Ethan, it's OK . . ."

"You know, I think the janitorial crew has been taking stuff from my office at night. This is not the first time that things have disappeared from the top of my desk. I think they use our computers too."

"Ethan, I'm trying to tell you that . . ."

"I can't even find my electronic copy. I think it's an attachment to an e-mail from Jack from last week, but I've got a conference call right now."

"Ethan, chill out. You're not listening. Haven't you heard?"

"Chill out? Not listening! I'm dead meat if I can't explain the data in less than an hour."

"Ethan, I've been trying to tell you. The 9 o'clock meeting with marketing has been postponed until tomorrow."

"Well, why didn't you tell me?"

re you a good listener—even when you're under pressure like Ethan? Or do you sometimes find that your mind wanders and you interrupt when others are talking to you? How often do you forget something that someone says to you? Do you sometimes feel that other things get in the way of your listening effectiveness? Have any of your close friends or intimates ever complained that you just don't seem to listen to them? Do your responses clearly reflect your listening?

Listening is a fundamental communication skill that affects the quality of our conversations and shapes the course of our relationships. First, listening creates reality. "We listen and create reality based on what we hear in each moment" (Ellinor & Gerard, 1998, p. 99). Second, listening plays an important role in the enactment, development, and maintenance of a variety of social and personal relationships (Halone & Pecchioni, 2001). Third, of the basic communication skills (reading, writing, speaking, and listening) we use listening the most. "From 42 to 60 percent (or more) of our communication time is spent listening, depending on whether we are students, managerial trainees, doctors, counselors, lawyers, or nurses" (Purdy, 1996, p. 4). Unfortunately, after forty-eight hours, many listeners can remember only about 25 percent of what they heard (Steil, Barker, & Watson, 1983). Considering its importance and how little attention most of us pay to it, listening may be the most underrated of all communication skills.

In this chapter we first provide a definition of listening. We then look at the five listening processes of attending, understanding, remembering, critically evaluating, and responding. Next, we briefly discuss the five types of listening. Finally, we talk about applying listening to mediated and cyber interactions.

◉ Definition of Listening

Listening—the process of receiving, constructing meaning from, and responding to spoken and/or nonverbal messages.

What is listening? The International Listening Association favors the following definition: "**Listening** is the process of receiving, constructing meaning from, and responding to spoken and/or nonverbal messages" (Brownell, 2006, p. 50). While you may assume that listening is a natural and innate process, there are a number of challenges to effective listening. For instance, anxiety about having to listen can produce listening apprehension, which interferes with your ability to be an effective listener. You may wonder what would cause anxiety about listening. If you are in a listening situation that you consider to be important, such as an interview or job training, you may feel undue stress about having to absorb all of the important information. Or your anxiety may escalate if you find yourself in a situation where the material you need to absorb is difficult or confusing. You may have experienced listening apprehension while trying to grasp the information for a difficult course in which your grade is on the line. Likewise, your anxiety may increase when you have to listen closely to a message but are not feeling well, are tired, or are feeling a great deal of stress. Apprehensiveness can also result from the fear of misinterpreting or not being able to adjust psychologically to what you hear (Brownell, 2006). Finally, listening to bad news raises our anxiety levels and causes us to fail to catch the full meaning of what is being said. Whatever the reasons for listening apprehension, anxiety negatively affects our concentration. When we are anxious, our ability to process, understand, and remember information is reduced.

Listening problems also arise from simply not being a well-trained listener. Listening involves skills that, though mostly unconscious, can be improved with practice once you are aware of how the listening process works. The bulk of this chapter is devoted to improving your listening skills in each of the five areas that make up the listening process: attending, understanding, remembering, critically evaluating, and responding. Let's have a look at each of these processes.

LEARN ABOUT YOURSELF ❖ Listening Effectiveness

How frequently do you find yourself engaging in each of the following listening behaviors? On the lines below, indicate 5 for frequently, 4 for often, 3 for sometimes, 2 for rarely, and 1 for never.

_____ 1. I listen differently depending on whether I am listening for enjoyment, understanding, or evaluation.

_____ 2. I stop listening when what the person is saying to me isn't interesting to me.

_____ 3. I consciously try to recognize the speaker's purpose.

_____ 4. I pretend to listen to people when I am really thinking about other things.

_____ 5. When people talk, I differentiate between their main points and supporting details.

_____ 6. When the person's manner of speaking annoys me (such as muttering, stammering, or talking in a monotone), I stop listening carefully.

_____ 7. At various places in a conversation, I paraphrase what the speaker said in order to check my understanding.

_____ 8. When I perceive the subject matter as very difficult, I stop listening carefully.

_____ 9. When the person is presenting detailed information, I take good notes of major points and supporting details.

_____10. When people use words that I find offensive, I stop listening and start preparing responses.

Scoring the Survey: In this list, even-numbered items indicate negative listening behaviors, so to score yourself, reverse the scoring of the even-numbered items (if you wrote a 1, make it a 5, 2 = 4, leave 3 as is, 4 = 2, and 5 = 1). Odd-numbered items on this list indicate positive listening behaviors. Leave the numbers you originally wrote down. Sum up your scores. There are 50 points possible. If you score over 40, you are effective in your listening. If you score below 40, identify the questions for which you got a low score. You will want to pay particular attention to the sections of this chapter that relate to these areas.

◐ Attending

The listening process begins with **attending**, the process of willfully striving to perceive selected sounds that are being heard (O'Shaughnessey, 2003). To get a clearer idea of what attending is, stop reading for a minute, and try to become conscious of all of the sounds you hear around you. Perhaps you notice the humming of an electrical appliance, the rhythm of street traffic, the singing of birds, footsteps in the hall, a cough from an adjoining room. Yet while you were reading, you were probably unaware of most of these sounds. Although we physically register any sounds emitted within our hearing range, we exercise psychological control over the sounds to which we attend. Improving your listening, then, begins with attending—learning to attend, or "pay attention," to what you hear in a more focused manner. To improve your attending skills, get physically and mentally ready to attend, make the shift from speaker to listener a complete one, resist tuning out, and avoid interrupting.

▷ Get Physically and Mentally Ready to Attend

To get ready to attend, good listeners prepare physically and mentally. Physically, good listeners create an environment conducive to listening, and they adopt a listening posture. It is easier to pay attention to what someone is saying when you have eliminated possible sources of distraction. For example, turning down your iPod before you answer the phone creates a better environment for you to focus on the caller's message. You can also improve your attention if you align your body so your senses are primed to perceive messages. Moving toward the speaker,

adopting a more upright stance, and making direct eye contact with the speaker are all physical actions that stimulate your senses and prepare you to perceive. For instance, when the professor tells the class that the next bit of information will be on the test, effective listeners are likely to sit upright in their chairs, lean slightly forward, cease any extraneous physical movement, and look directly at the professor. Their body is poised to attend to what will be said.

Likewise, because attending is a willful act, it requires mental preparation. Effective listeners will psychologically focus on what the speaker is saying by ignoring competing stimuli. They consciously block out miscellaneous thoughts that pass through their minds, such as errands they need to complete later in the day or emotional distractions. Attending to competing thoughts and feelings rather than the message is one of the leading causes of poor listening.

▷ Make the Shift from Speaker to Listener a Complete One

In conversation, you are called on to switch back and forth from being a speaker to being a listener frequently, and as a result you may find it difficult at times to make these shifts completely. If, instead of listening, you spend your time rehearsing what you're going to say as soon as you have a chance, your attending effectiveness will suffer. Especially when you are in a heated conversation, take a second to check yourself: Are you preparing your next remark instead of listening? Shifting completely, from the role of speaker to that of listener, requires constant and continuous effort.

▷ Resist Tuning Out

Far too often, we stop attending before the person we are conversing with has finished speaking because we think we "know what they are going to say." Yet until the other person has finished speaking and we are finished attending to what he or she is saying, we don't have all of the data needed to understand the message. "Knowing" what a person is going to say is really only a guess. So, effective listeners cultivate the habit of waiting for the speaker to finish before they stop attending to the message.

In addition, we often let certain mannerisms and words used by the people we converse with interfere with our ability to attend to their messages. Can you think of a time when someone's gestures or vocal quality distracted you from paying attention to what he or she was saying? Are there any words or ideas that create bursts of semantic noise for you, causing you to stop listening attentively? If so, you need to become aware of this "noise" and recommit yourself to attending to the message.

▷ Avoid Interrupting

One of the most common interferences with attending is interrupting. In a study by Halone and Pecchioni (2001), college students cited interrupting as the behavior that most interferes with really listening to what another person is saying. Recall that in the previous chapter we

INTER-ACT WITH ○ TECHNOLOGY

Cell phones have brought a new level of convenience to communication. These days you can work on your computer, drive, or cook dinner while you are on the phone. But have these devices affected your ability to attend to what you are listening to? The next time you are using one of these devices, be conscious of how well you are attending. Which of the attending guidelines should you apply to improve your listening skills under these conditions?

Experimenting with Attending Skills

Select an information-oriented program on your local public television station (such as *NOVA, News Hour with Jim Lehrer,* or *Wall Street Week*). If possible, record it before you watch it. Watch at least fifteen minutes of the show while lounging in a comfortable chair or while stretched out on the floor with music playing in the background. After about fifteen minutes, stop the playback and quickly outline what you have learned. Now, make a conscious decision to follow the guidelines for improving your attending skills during the next fifteen minutes of the show. Turn off the music and sit in a straight-back chair as you watch the program. Your goal is to increase your attentiveness so that you can absorb the information from the program as effectively as possible, so you need to eliminate distractions and put yourself in an attentive position. After this fifteen-minute segment, you should again outline what you remember. Watch the program a second time and make note of how your attentiveness affected your memory.

Compare your notes from the two listening sessions. Is there any difference between the amount and quality of the information you retained? Be prepared to discuss your results with your classmates. Are their results similar or different? Why?

Understanding—the process of accurately decoding a message so that you share its meaning with the speaker.

discussed the importance of appropriate turn-taking. It is especially important when trying to attend that you let the other person finish before you take your turn to speak. This is quite challenging when there is a group of people talking, when you are in a heated conversation, or when you are excited and enthusiastic about what you have just heard. With concentration and practice, however, you can become better at waiting until a speaker is finished while attending to what he or she is saying before you begin talking.

◐ Understanding

The second part of the listening process is understanding what is being said. **Understanding** is the process of accurately decoding a message so that you share its meaning with the speaker. Having attended to and perceived the message being sent, you are now ready to understand, or "make sense" of, it. To improve your understanding skills, identify the speaker's purpose and key points, interpret nonverbal cues, ask clarifying questions, and paraphrase what you hear.

▷ Identify the Speaker's Purpose and Key Points

Even in casual social conversations, speakers have some purpose or point they are trying to make. Sometimes people's thoughts are spoken in well-organized messages whose purposes and key ideas are easy to follow and identify. Other times, however, we must work harder to grasp the essence of what the speaker is trying to get across. If you can't figure out the speaker's purpose or key ideas, you will have trouble understanding the message. As you listen, ask yourself, "What does the speaker want me to understand?" and "What is the point being made?" For example, if Manuel spends two minutes talking about how much he likes the Cubs and asking Corella about her interest in baseball, casually mentioning that he has tickets for the game this weekend, Corella may recognize that he would like her to go with him.

When the speaker's purpose is to persuade you to think or do something, you will also want to identify what specific arguments the speaker is intending to make. For instance, when Marlee, who is running for class president, asks Joanna what she thinks about the plans for the new arts center and begins to talk about some of the pros and cons of the plan, Joanna understands that beneath the surface of what Marlee is saying, Marlee is persuading Joanna to vote for her.

▷ Interpret Nonverbal Cues

In Chapter 5 we noted that up to 65 percent of the meaning of a message is transmitted nonverbally. Therefore, to understand what a speaker means, you need to interpret not only what is said verbally but also the nonverbal behaviors that accompany what is said. For instance, if Deborah says to Gita, "Go on, I can walk home from here," what do these words mean? Without understanding the message cues transmitted through her tone of voice, body language, and facial expression, Gita can't really tell if Deborah truly prefers to walk or if she's just being polite but would really like a ride. So, whether you are listening to a co-worker explaining her stance on an issue, a friend explaining the process for hanging wallpaper, or a loved one explaining why he or she is upset with you, you must look to how something is said as well as to what is said if you want to understand the real message.

Sometimes there is a message in silence—the most subtle form of nonverbal communication—that needs to be understood. In the "Diverse Voices" box in this chapter, author Donal Carbaugh explains how silence creates a nonverbal connection among members of the Blackfeet community.

▷ Ask Clarifying Questions

An easy way to get to better understand what a speaker says to you is to ask a clarifying question. A **clarifying question** is a response designed to get further information or to remove uncertainty from information already received. It also encourages the speaker to continue speaking. In addition to helping the listener, good clarifying questions help speakers sharpen their thinking about the points they make. Although you may have asked clarifying questions for as long as you can remember, you may notice that at times your questions either don't lead to your getting the information you want or provoke an unwanted response—perhaps the other person becomes irritated, flustered, or defensive. You can increase the chances that your questions will get you the information you want and reduce unwanted responses if you observe the following guidelines.

Listening means paying attention to nonverbal as well as verbal cues. What message is the speaker conveying through nonverbal cues?

Clarifying question—response designed to get further information or to remove uncertainty from information already received.

1. Be specific about the kind of information you need to increase your understanding. Suppose Maria calls you and says, "I am totally frustrated. Would you stop at the store on the way home and buy me some more paper?" At this point, you may be a bit confused and need more information to understand what Maria is telling you. Yet if you respond by simply saying, "What do you mean?" you are likely to add to the confusion because Maria, who is already uptight, won't know precisely what it is you don't understand. To be more specific and increase your understanding, you might ask Maria one of these three types of question:

- *Questions to clarify the important details.* "What kind of paper would you like me to get, and how much will you need?"
- *Questions to clarify the use of a term.* "Could you tell me what you mean by 'frustrated?'"
- *Questions to clarify the cause of the feelings the person is expressing.* "What is it that's frustrating you?"

American Indian Students and the Study of Public "Communication"

by Donal Carbaugh

In this excerpt, the author describes listener-active silence as a form of communication in a Native American community. In what ways can silence communicate separateness or connection with others?

Some Blackfeet people, upon some occasions, use a cultural model of "communication" that presumes, sui generis, a patterned way of living. A primary mode of this "communication," from the Blackfeet view, is what might be called a "deeply communicative silence," a listener-active form of non-verbal co-presence in which all is presumably interconnected.... That form of "communication" [is] something taught by "grandparents," and discussed in this way: you are "able to communicate spiritually and physically . . . you are in tune with something long enough, to a point that you know it inside-out."...

This Blackfeet model of "communication," when realized, involves a scene of "harmony," of silently connective co-presence, a nonlinguistic togetherness in which one is knowingly integral to and communing with the actual persons, animals, spirits, and things with which one dwells. This is both an ideal for "communication" that is especially apparent in some special Blackfeet ceremonies (e.g., sweat lodge rituals), and, it is a desirable condition of "every day" communicative action. For this kind of "communication" to be forceful in social living, it presumes (and thus recreates) an unspoken consensus of interconnection that is largely non-verbal and non-linguistic, yet shared and publicly accessible, if one just listens.

This cultural model of "communication" creates a special significance for nonlinguistic channels of messages, and an important duty for communicants as listeners. Participants in this communication must therefore become active *listeners,* and observers of that which they are already a part....

Through this mode, the Blackfeet are saying something about people being already connected (or seeking a holistic connectedness), about people, spirits—and ancestors—being an inherent part of this grand picture, about natural features and animals being figured into this interconnected realm, with all of this providing a cultural scene of Blackfeet "communication." A primary mode of some Blackfeet communication is thus to "communicate spiritually and physically" through a listener-active silence with a cultural premise

(a belief and value) of this mode being the inheritance of a holistic world of intricate interconnections....

In the alternate model of communication . . . called a "whiteman" or "white people's" model, . . . the primary mode of communication is not a listener-active silence, but verbal speaking. The "white people's" primary mode of action is verbal and is based at least partly upon these "other" cultural premises: Speaking makes something public that was heretofore private, personal, or internal; speaking helps create (or construct) social connections among those who were presumably different or separate; and, connecting through speech is the principal way a society is made, and made to work. From the "white people's" view, the primary mode of communication is verbal speaking, with this mode being important for the actual "constructions" of personal, social, and societal life (Carbaugh, 1988).

A secondary mode of communication in the "white people's" system is silence. Communicative silence is figured upon the primary mode of verbal speaking and its premises. Silence plays upon the primary mode, however, by risking its negation, or by signaling the absence of the very premises that are presumably being activated in "white people's" actions of verbal speaking. Silence as a communicative action can mean, to "white people," a negation of one's personal being (as in "the silent treatment"), a failure to "connect" with others in "relationship," and a sign that social institutions have been ruptured or broken or corrupted (e.g., "a conspiracy of silence"). Without speaking, and with silence, one can hear (or feel) being amplified not an interconnectedness as among the Blackfeet, but a separateness, and disconnectedness that is present between presumably different individuals or peoples. Silence, then, is a prominent way to accentuate the different, separate, and even disconnected states of affairs which are so often presumed as a basis for many public American (i.e., multicultural) events and scenes.

Excerpted from Carbaugh, D. (2002). American Indian students and the study of public "communication." In J. N. Martin, T. K. Nakayama, & L. A. Flores (Eds.), *Readings in Intercultural Communication* (pp. 138–148). New York: McGraw-Hill.

Determine whether what you actually need is more details, clarification of a word or idea, or information about feelings, then phrase your question accordingly.

2. Deliver questions in a sincere tone of voice. Ask questions with a tone of voice that is sincere—not a tone that could be interpreted as affected, bored, sarcastic, cutting, superior, dogmatic, or judgmental. We need to remind ourselves constantly that the way we speak can be even more important than the words we use.

3. Limit questions or explain that you need to ask multiple questions. Sometimes asking several clarifying questions in a row can seem like an interrogation. If you can, limit the number of clarifying questions you ask to the most appropriate ones. But if you need to ask several clarifying questions, you might explain why you are asking them. For instance, Vanessa could say to her Dad, "I really want to understand what you are saying, so I need to ask a few questions to get more information. Is that OK?"

4. Put the "burden of ignorance" on your own shoulders. To minimize unplanned or unwanted reactions, phrase your clarifying questions in a way that puts the burden of ignorance on your own shoulders. Preface your questions with a short statement that suggests that any problem of misunderstanding may be the result of *your* listening skills. For instance, when Drew says, "I've really had it with Malone screwing up all the time," you might say, "Drew, I'm sorry, I'm missing some details that would help me understand your feelings better. What kinds of things has Malone been doing?"

Here are two more examples that contrast inappropriate with more appropriate questioning responses.

Tamara: They turned down my proposal again!
Art: *(inappropriate)* Well, did you explain it the way you should have? (This question is a veiled attack on Tamara in question form.)
   (appropriate) Did they tell you why? (This question is a sincere request for additional information.)
Renée: With all those executives at the party last night, I really felt weird.
Javier: *(inappropriate)* Why? (With this abrupt question, Javier is making no effort to be sensitive to Renée's feelings or to understand them.)
   (appropriate) What is it about your bosses being there that made you feel weird? (Here the question is phrased to elicit information that will help Javier understand and may help Renée understand as well.)

Note how the appropriate, clarifying questions are likely to get the necessary information while minimizing the probability of an unplanned or unwanted reply. The inappropriate questions, on the other hand, may be perceived as an attack.

▷ Paraphrase What You Hear

Instead of asking clarifying questions, another way to assure your understanding of what others say is to paraphrase what you hear. A **paraphrase** is an attempt to verify one's understanding of a message by putting it into one's own words and

Paraphrase—attempt to verify one's understanding of a message by putting it in one's own words and sharing it with the speaker.

sharing it with the speaker. Paraphrasing is not mere repetition of what the speaker has said; rather, it is a message that conveys and seeks to verify the ideas and emotions you have perceived from the speaker's communication. It describes, in your own words, the understanding that has been sparked in your mind by the speaker's statement. For example, during an argument with your sister, after she has stated her concern about your behavior, you might paraphrase what she said as follows: "So you are saying that you think I try to act superior to you when I talk about my successes at work." Your sister can respond by saying, "Yes, exactly! It feels like you are trying to put me down when you do that." Or she may correct your paraphrase by saying, "No, I'm not feeling that you are trying to act superior to me. It just makes me feel bad about the fact that I'm not doing so well at work right now."

There are three types of paraphrases. A **content paraphrase** conveys one's understanding of the denotative meaning of a verbal message, a **feelings paraphrase** conveys one's understanding of the emotional meaning behind a speaker's verbal message, and a **combined paraphrase** conveys one's understanding of both the denotative and emotional meaning behind a speaker's verbal message. Usually speakers choose to use a content or feelings paraphrase. Whether a content or feelings paraphrase is most useful for a particular situation depends on whether you perceive the speaker's emphasis to be on the subject of the statement or on his or her feelings about what was said. Sometimes, however, we don't distinguish clearly between content and feelings, and our responses might well be a combination of both. All three types of paraphrase for the same statement are shown in the following example.

> *Statement:* "Five weeks ago, I gave the revised paper for my independent study to my project advisor. I felt really good about it because I thought the changes I had made really improved my explanations. Well, yesterday I stopped by and got the paper back, and my advisor said he couldn't really see that this draft was much different from the first."

Content paraphrase—paraphrase that conveys one's understanding of the denotative meaning of a verbal message.

Feelings paraphrase—paraphrase that conveys one's understanding of the emotional meaning behind a speaker's verbal message.

Combined paraphrase—paraphrase that conveys one's understanding of both the denotative and emotional meaning behind a speaker's verbal message.

SKILL BUILDERS ▽ Questioning

SKILL	USE	PROCEDURE	EXAMPLE
Phrasing a response designed to get further information or to remove uncertainty from information already received	To help get a more complete picture before making other comments; to help a shy person open up; to clarify meaning	1. Be specific about the kind of information you need to increase your understanding of the message. 2. Deliver questions in a sincere tone of voice. 3. Limit questions or explain that you need to ask multiple questions. 4. Put the burden of ignorance on your own shoulders.	When Connie says, "Well, it would be better if she weren't so sedentary," Jeff replies, "I'm not sure I understand what you mean by 'sedentary'—would you explain?"

Content paraphrase: "So you really thought that you had provided more depth and detail to your explanations, but Professor Delgato didn't notice."

Feelings paraphrase: "You seem really frustrated that Professor Delgato didn't notice the changes you'd made."

Combination: "So Professor Delgato told you that he didn't notice the work you had done. What a bummer. No wonder you sound so disgusted."

Common sense suggests that we need not paraphrase every message we receive, nor would we paraphrase after every few sentences. So when should you use the skill of paraphrasing to better understand what you hear? We suggest that you paraphrase in the following circumstances:

- When you need a better understanding of a message in terms of content, feelings, or both
- When misunderstanding the message will have serious consequences
- When the message is long and contains several complex ideas
- When the message seems to reflect emotional strain
- When you are talking with people whose native language is not English

◗ Remembering

The third part of the active listening process is **remembering**, the process of moving information from short-term memory to long-term memory. Too often people forget almost immediately what they have heard. Several things make remembering difficult. First, we often filter out messages through habit. For example, you can probably think of times when you were unable to recall the name of a person to whom you were introduced just moments earlier. This is caused simply by the bad habit of not concentrating on the importance of remembering names. Second, we are selective in our memories and find it easier to recall messages that support our position and forget information that contradicts our beliefs. For instance, you

Remembering—process of moving information from short-term memory to long-term memory.

SKILL BUILDERS ◗ Paraphrasing

SKILL	USE	PROCEDURE	EXAMPLE
Verifying one's understanding of a message by putting it in one's own words and sharing it with the speaker	To increase listening efficiency; to avoid message confusion; to discover the speaker's motivation	1. Listen carefully to the message. 2. Notice what ideas and feelings seem to be contained in the message. 3. Determine what the message means to you. 4. Create a message in your own words that conveys these ideas and/or feelings.	Grace says, "At two minutes to five, the boss gave me three letters that had to be in the mail that evening!" Bonita replies, "I understand; you were really resentful that your boss dumped important work on you right before quitting time, when she knows that you have to pick up the baby at daycare."

may watch a debate on television and recall the arguments for your point of view and forget some equally valid arguments that went against your beliefs. Third, we are more likely to remember information at the beginning or end of a message and forget what comes in between. The **primacy effect** is the tendency to remember information that we heard first over what we heard in the middle, and the **recency effect** is the tendency to remember the information that we heard last over what we heard in the middle. To get a better idea of both, think about speeches you have heard and how speakers almost always start with an attention-grabbing-introduction and summarize their entire speech at the conclusion. This is because listeners are likely to remember clearly only the beginning and end of the speech. Finally, at times, we are unable to remember information because we repress information that is somehow painful. For instance, you may clearly recall the most enjoyable moments from your high school days and forget the details about the time you spent a week stressed out and struggling with your research paper assignment.

To overcome these difficulties and become better at remembering, you can use several skills: Repeat what was said, create mnemonics, and take notes.

▷ Repeat What Was Said

Repetition, saying something two, three, or even four times, helps you store information in long-term memory (Estes, 1989, p. 7). As opposed to paraphrasing, which as we have seen is repeating something back to the speaker once to aid the understanding process, the key to repetition is repeating something back multiple times to aid the remembering process. If information is not reinforced, it will be held in short-term memory for as little as twenty seconds and then forgotten. So, when you are introduced to a stranger named Jack McNeil, if you mentally say, "Jack McNeil, Jack McNeil, Jack McNeil, Jack McNeil," you increase the chances that you will remember his name. Likewise, when a person gives you the directions, "Go two blocks east, turn left, turn right at the next light, and it's in the next block," you should immediately repeat to yourself, "Two blocks east, turn left, turn right at light, next block—that's two blocks east, turn left, turn right at light, next block."

▷ Create Mnemonics

Constructing mnemonics also improves the remembering process by helping listeners put information in forms that are easily recalled. A **mnemonic device** is any artificial technique used as a memory aid. One of the most common ways of forming a mnemonic is to take the first letter of each of the items you are trying to remember and form a word. For example, an easy mnemonic for remembering the five Great Lakes is HOMES (Huron, Ontario, Michigan, Erie, Superior). When you want to remember items in a sequence, try to form a sentence with the words themselves or assign words using the first letters of the words in sequence and form an easy-to-remember statement. For example, when you studied music the first time, you may have learned the notes on the

Primacy effect— tendency to remember information that we heard first over what we heard in the middle.

Recency effect—tendency to remember information that we heard last over what we heard in the middle.

Repetition—saying something two, three, or even four times.

Mnemonic device—any artificial technique used as a memory aid.

What are the advantages and disadvantages of taking notes during a meeting?

lines of the treble clef (EGBDF) with the saying, "Every good boy does fine." Or to help students remember the colors of the spectrum in sequence, science teachers often ask their students to remember the name "Roy G. Biv" (standing for "red, orange, yellow, green, blue, indigo, violet").

▷ Take Notes

Although note-taking is not an appropriate way to remember information when you are engaged in casual interpersonal encounters, it represents a powerful tool for increasing your recall of information when you are involved in telephone conversations, briefing sessions, interviews, and business meetings. Note-taking provides a written record that you can go back to, and it also enables you to take a more active role in the listening process (Wolvin & Coakley, 1996). In short, when you are listening to complex information, take notes.

What constitutes good notes will vary depending on the situation. Useful notes may consist of a brief list of main points or key ideas plus a few of the most significant details. Or the notes may be in the form of a short summary of the entire concept (a type of paraphrase), written after the message has been delivered. For lengthy and rather detailed information, however, good notes are best written in outline form, including the overall idea, the main points of the message, and key developmental material, organized by category and subcategory. Good outlines are not necessarily very long. In fact, many classroom lectures can be reduced to a one-page or shorter outline.

○ Critically Evaluating

Critically evaluating—process of interpreting what you have understood to determine how truthful, authentic, or believable you judge the meaning to be.

The fourth part of the active listening process is critically evaluating. **Critically evaluating** is the process of interpreting what you have understood to determine how truthful, authentic, or believable you judge the meaning to be. This may involve judgments about the accuracy of facts, the amount and type of evidence supporting a position, and how a position relates to your own values. For instance, when a person tries to convince you to vote for a particular candidate for office or to sign a petition to add a skateboard park to the neighborhood, you will want to listen critically to the message. Are the facts presented to you true? Have you been provided with the supporting information you need to make a judgment? Do you fundamentally agree with the basic idea? Improving your critical evaluation skills requires that you separate facts from inferences and probe for information.

▷ Separate Facts from Inferences

Facts—statements whose accuracy can be verified or proven.

Inferences—claims or assertions based on the facts presented.

Facts are statements whose accuracy can be verified or proven; **inferences** are claims or assertions based on the facts presented. Separating facts from inferences requires us to be able to tell the difference between a verifiable observation and an opinion related to that observation. Too often people treat inferences as factual. Let's clarify this distinction with an example. If we can document that Cesar received an A in geology, then saying that Cesar received an A in geology is a fact. If we go on to say that Cesar studied very hard, that statement is an inference. Cesar may have studied hard to receive his grade, but it is also possible that geology comes easily to Cesar or that Cesar had already learned much of the material in his high school physical science course.

Separating facts from inferences is important because inferences may be false, even if they are based on verifiable facts. Making sound judgments entails basing our inferences on facts whose correctness we have evaluated. So, when we encounter such statements as, "Better watch it; Carl is really in a bad mood today. Did you see the way he was scowling?"; or "I know you're hiding something from me; I can tell it in your voice"; or "Olga and Kurt are having an affair—I've seen them leave the office together nearly every night," we know that each one contains an inference. Each of them may be true, but none is necessarily true.

▷ Probe for Information

Probing questions—questions by which we search for more information or try to resolve perceived inconsistencies in a message.

Sometimes, after listening to a message, we need to encourage the speaker to delve deeper into the topic to be able truly to evaluate the message critically. Or we may need to challenge the information to see if it holds up under scrutiny. To do this, we can ask **probing questions**, questions by which we search for more information or try to resolve perceived inconsistencies in a message. For example, suppose that Jerrod's landlord was talking with him about the need to sign a lease.

Before signing such an important, legally binding document, Jerrod should ask the prospective landlord such probing questions as the following:

> "You said that I would need to sign a lease, but you did not state the term of the lease. What's the shortest lease I could get?"
> "Your ad in the paper said that utilities would be paid by the landlord, but just now you said that the tenant pays the utility bill. Which way will it work with this apartment?"

With both of these questions, Jerrod is expecting the landlord to supply information that Jerrod needs before he can critically evaluate the suitability of the apartment.

When asking probing questions, your nonverbal communication is especially important. You must pay attention to your tone of voice and body language so you do not appear arrogant or intimidating. Too many probing questions accompanied by inappropriate nonverbal cues can lead the other person to become defensive.

◗ Responding

The final part of the listening process is **responding**, the process of reacting to what has been heard while listening and after listening. One can listen without exhibiting any external activity that would indicate listening is taking place (Bostrom, 2006). But it is the responsibility of the listener to give cues to the speaker that listening is taking place. The listening process is not complete without responses on the part of the listener to indicate that he or she hears the speaker, understands the message, and is willing to comment on what has been understood. Although responding sounds like a part of the speaking process rather than the listening process, it is actually the last step of listening—taking what you have attended to, understood, remembered, and critically evaluated and transitioning back to the speaker. To improve your responding skills, provide back-channel cues and reply when the message is complete.

Responding—process of reacting to what has been heard while listening and after listening.

▷ Provide Back-Channel Cues

One way to indicate that you are listening is to provide **back-channel cues**, verbal and nonverbal signals demonstrating listener response to the speaker. Think of all the ways that you respond while listening to another person. You may nod, smile, laugh, frown, or say "uh huh," "yeah," or other verbal utterances. These are all forms of back-channel cues. They are useful and appropriate when they provide feedback to the speaker without becoming distractions.

Back-channel cues—verbal and nonverbal signals demonstrating listener response to the speaker.

▷ Reply When the Message Is Complete

In addition to using back-channel cues, listeners should also respond to the speaker when the message is complete. Besides asking questions or paraphrasing what was said, you might respond to a message by agreeing or disagreeing with what was said, expanding on the ideas, challenging some of the message, offering advice, or indicating empathy or support. For example, imagine that your friend tells you, "I need to look for a better job and I'm probably going to quit school. I'm in a major financial mess with credit card debt, monthly living expenses of $1200, and back-owed child support payments. And on top of all of this, my hours at work are being cut back. I'm in deep trouble here and pretty stressed out. I don't know what to do. Got any ideas?" If you just change the subject your friend is likely to be offended, but even a topic change is a type of response. Let's look at other ways you might respond after the speaker has finished talking:

Paraphrase: "So you're having trouble paying your bills at the same time that your paycheck is being reduced."

Question: "What's the difference between your bills and your take-home pay each month?"

Agreement: "Yeah, it makes sense to look for a higher-paying job."

Challenge: "Do you think it's smart to quit college when a degree is your ticket to a high-paying job eventually?"

Advice: "You may want to meet with a debt consolidator who can help you work on a long-term plan for getting back into good financial shape."

Support: "Wow, off the top of my head I can't really think of any, but I'm willing to talk with you about things and maybe together we can figure this thing out."

As you can see, some responses are aimed at helping you to develop a clearer understanding of the original message while others focus on helping the speaker. Rarely is one response perfect and all others inappropriate. But, as we discussed in Chapter 1, it is important that you develop behavioral flexibility so that you are skilled at responding in a variety of ways.

You have now seen that listening involves five processes, and you have learned some ways to improve your effectiveness at attending, understanding, remembering, critically evaluating, and responding. In our "Spotlight on Scholars" feature for this chapter, Judi Brownell talks further about listening effectiveness. She describes the complexity of listening and its importance to interpersonal relationships and a variety of workplace organizations, and she alerts us to the increasing listening challenges resulting from technology, which we will also explore further later in this chapter.

◗ Types of Listening

Now that we have examined the listening process and discussed listening skills, we can categorize the various types of listening situations in which you may find yourself. Scholars have identified at least five different types or levels of listening: appreciative listening, discriminative listening, comprehensive listening, critical-evaluative listening, and empathic listening (Purdy, 1997). Let's have a look at each.

1. Appreciative listening is listening that focuses on the enjoyment of what is said. With appreciative listening, you do not have to focus as closely or as carefully on specifics as you do in other listening situations. You might use appreciative

Appreciative listening—listening that focuses on the enjoyment of what is said.

Judi Brownell
Professor of Organizational Communication and
Dean of Students at Cornell University, on
Listening Effectiveness

Judi Brownell's attention was first drawn to listening when she observed a high school teacher attempting to improve his students' listening effectiveness. She vividly recalls the occasion when this frustrated eleventh-grade English teacher, unhappy with the scores his students had just received on the listening portion of their standardized examination, yelled loudly, "Listen!! You have to listen!!" as if his words alone would somehow change their performance. She remembers thinking, as she witnessed the students' blank stares, that there really had to be some more effective method of teaching students listening than simply shouting at them!

The topic emerged again soon after, this time in a quite different setting. Brownell was asked to provide listening training for the middle and senior management of a large technology organization. A recent needs assessment had indicated that employees' most frequent complaint about their workplace environment was that their managers "didn't listen." Brownell recalls the tension in the first training sessions as she confronted managers, who were convinced that they did not need listening improvement and who resented being required to take time away from their jobs to attend her listening program. Brownell immediately determined that she needed more information before the sessions could continue. In an effort to clarify employees' perceptions and to specify better what they meant when they said that their managers "didn't listen," Brownell designed an assessment survey that was given not only to the frustrated employees but also to the managers in the listening training program. When she had the data from these surveys analyzed, she realized that employees in different departments meant quite different things when they described "not listening."

Using factor analysis (a statistical method that finds similarities between survey items), Brownell developed the HURIER model of listening, which she used in the listening program and later expanded as the basis for her textbook on listening. She discovered that listening was comprised of six factors: hearing, understanding, remembering, interpreting, evaluating, and appropriateness of response. Further, when she compared the managers' listening self-reports with the average responses of the employees, she found that managers almost always overestimated the effectiveness of their listening behaviors. Presenting seminar participants with these companion scores served as an effective motivational tool. The model also allowed Brownell to focus the training sessions on the listening skills that were most needed by session participants. Since its development, numerous other researchers have applied and modified

the HURIER model and companion survey. It has proven useful in giving trainers and teachers a way to approach listening instruction beyond just shouting, "Listen!!"

Brownell has applied her model as a consultant to companies in the service industries, where her work has helped organizations improve their service quality, organizational culture and learning, and management of workforce diversity. In the hospitality industry, in particular, a diverse workforce and increasing globalization make listening skills essential. Customers, line employees, supervisors, and middle and senior managers all benefit by developing a listening focus. Brownell calls organizational cultures that support this emphasis "listening environments." She has written extensively on how managers can create these environments by modeling desired behaviors and by recognizing and rewarding listening excellence. She believes that organizations can remain competitive only to the extent that they remain responsive and "listen" in the face of constant change.

Brownell is also studying listening as a key leadership competency. Her previous research revealed that listening is an important skill for new employees as they try to figure out the organization's values and their job requirements. Her current work demonstrates how listening remains a critical competence in the workplace even for senior managers who must gather large quantities of information to make informed and fair decisions.

Dr. Brownell's international travel and teaching (including recent courses and seminars in Norway, Hong Kong, New Zealand, and France) have convinced her that listening is important for bridging cultural differences as well. She is exploring the role listening plays in cultural intelligence (the ability to recognize and respond in culturally appropriate ways to the messages of others). Brownell recognizes that the challenges of listening are becoming increasingly complex as technology expands the quantity of information that must be processed and the reach of messages that are sent. She is designing creative ways to assess and teach listening competencies that address the new technologies. Brownell is particularly interested in how trust is developed in virtual environments and the impact of technology on how listeners perceive the credibility of messages from senders. She firmly believes that, given the fast pace of technology, communicators cannot lose sight of elements such as integrity and character that enable individuals to build and maintain all-important personal relationships.

listening during a casual social conversation while watching a ball game with friends or when listening to your son describe the fish he caught on an outing with his grandpa.

Discriminative listening—listening that focuses on gaining an accurate understanding of the message.

2. Discriminative listening is listening that focuses on gaining an accurate understanding of the message. This involves attending closely and keeping a close eye out for verbal and nonverbal nuances. You might choose discriminative listening when you are helping a customer who is explaining a service problem or when meeting with your doctor who is explaining the results of your recent physical.

Comprehensive listening—listening that focuses on learning and remembering information.

3. Comprehensive listening is listening that focuses on learning and remembering information. You should use comprehensive listening whenever an instructor gives a lecture or when a work colleague teaches you a new procedure.

Critical-evaluative listening—listening that focuses on being able to judge or evaluate the information heard.

4. Critical-evaluative listening is listening that focuses on being able to judge or evaluate the information heard. In a critical-evaluative listening situations, your goal is not only to understand a message but also to be able to think critically about its merits. In doing so, you may need to listen "between the lines" to try to determine what is not being said outright. You might use this type of listening when talking to a salesperson or listening to an apology from someone who has violated your trust.

Empathic listening—listening that focuses on understanding the feelings of others.

5. Empathic listening is listening that focuses on understanding the feelings of others. This is also called therapeutic listening since it is used in most counseling settings. You might choose this style when someone talks with you about a recent personal loss or when counseling an employee at work.

◯ Listening in Cyberspace

Advances in technology provide us with greater opportunities for communication, but they also present us with additional communication demands, including challenges to attending, understanding, and remembering information.

For instance, computers can now translate data into sounds that mimic the human voice, allowing us to receive vocal rather than written messages on our computers and increasingly putting us in contact with computer-generated voices when we deal with call centers or other voice-menu computer systems. However, when listening to computer-generated speech in complicated menu options, listening stress may occur as we try to following the sequence of directions given us or try to comprehend and remember the amount of information provided without actual human contact. The listening skills of paraphrasing and probing, for instance, cannot be used in these listening contexts as they can in face-to-face interactions, and the problem of tuning out increases when listening to computer-generated speech.

In addition, technology bombards us with massive amounts of information and creates new forms of listening. The sheer amount of messages that we receive electronically makes the task of effective listening extremely stressful. In a single day, we may need to listen to a seemingly endless barrage of voice-mail messages, e-mail messages, text messages, and instant messages, all of which we have to attend to, understand, remember, evaluate, and respond to.

While much of the information in this chapter pertains to technology-mediated listening and online listening as well as to listening to actual speech, the unique challenges of listening to computerized voices and messages from multiple channels at once has led to scholarly research on the topic of listening in cyberspace. R. Anderson (1997) was one of the first experts in computer-mediated communication to offer suggestions for being an effective listener in cyberspace. Brownell (2006) also provides suggestions for listening in high-technology environments. We've boiled down their advice into four cyberspace listening guidelines.

1. Give extra effort to attending and understanding. Because of the speed of online chatting in real time, as well as the brevity of messages and the limited range of nonverbal cues listeners are provided with, it is easy to make mistakes when paying attention to and interpreting these types of messages. It is important to focus carefully by asking questions and paraphrasing statements before jumping to conclusions during cyberspace interactions or you may risk misunderstandings and bad feelings.

2. Practice critical evaluation. A study of teenage interactions in cyberspace showed that deceptions about age, appearance, occupation, and life circumstances do occur online. The study also revealed that people develop identification with others more quickly online than in face-to-face interactions (Pew Internet and

American Life Project, 2001). Because it is easy to fake identities online or to post inaccurate and misleading information, it is important to be able to evaluate critically the information you receive as you "listen" online. Ask clarifying and probing questions after receiving online messages, and be sure to separate facts from inferences.

3. Don't become overdependent on cyberspace listening. Because of the convenience of interacting in cyberspace, some people become so immersed in online interactions that they sacrifice face-to-face interactions. Resist the tendency to allow the keyboard increasingly to replace your ability to communicate with people face-to-face. Research has revealed that people heavily involved in online relationships tend to be shyer than those who do not (Ward & Tracey, 2004). Both online and face-to-face interactions have their place, but one should not replace the other.

4. Consciously choose what online information you want to attend to. Judi Brownell (2006) reminds us that we may feel overwhelmed by the amount of information available online, but we do not have to listen to all of the available messages we receive in cyberspace. We can select what to pay attention to and what to ignore.

◐ Summary

Listening is the process of receiving, constructing meaning from, and responding to spoken and/or nonverbal messages. The five parts of the active listening process are attending, understanding, remembering, critically evaluating, and responding.

A QUESTION OF ETHICS ◐ **What Would You Do?**

Janeen always disliked talking on the telephone—she thought that it was an impersonal form of communication. Thus, college was a wonderful respite because when her friends would call her, instead of staying on the phone she could quickly run over to their dorm or meet them at the campus coffeehouse.

One day, during reading period before exams, Janeen received a phone call from Barbara, an out-of-town friend. Before she was able to dismiss Barbara with her stock excuses, Janeen found herself bombarded with information about old high school friends and their whereabouts. Not wanting to disappoint Barbara, who seemed eager to talk, Janeen tucked her phone under her chin and began straightening her room, answering Barbara with the occasional "uh huh," "hmm," or "Wow, that's cool!" As the "conversation" progressed, Janeen began reading through her mail and then her notes from class. After a few minutes she realized there was silence on the other end of the line. Suddenly very ashamed, she said, "I'm sorry, what did you say? The phone . . . uh, there was just a lot of static."

Barbara replied with obvious hurt in her voice, "I'm sorry I bothered you; you must be terribly busy."

Embarrassed, Janeen muttered, "I'm just really stressed, you know, with exams coming up and everything. I guess I wasn't listening very well, you didn't seem to be saying anything really important. What were you saying?"

"Nothing 'important,'" Barbara answered. "I was just trying to figure out a way to tell you. I know that you were friends with my brother Billy, and you see, we just found out yesterday that he's terminal with a rare form of leukemia. But you're right, it obviously isn't really important." With that, she hung up.

1. In what ways have ethics been impacted by ineffective listening skills in this scenario? In what other situations might ineffective listening have an impact on ethics?
2. Besides tuning in better, what attending skills could Janeen have used in this situation? What type of listening was required of Janeen here?
3. Although Barbara was the one hurt by Janeen's comment about the "importance" of the call, how could she have better attended to Janeen's responses?

Attending is the process of willfully striving to perceive selected sounds that are being heard. To improve your attending skills, get physically and mentally ready to attend, make the shift from speaker to listener a complete one, resist tuning out, and avoid interrupting. Understanding is the process of accurately decoding a message so that you share its meaning with the speaker. To increase your understanding skills, identify the speaker's purpose and key points, interpret nonverbal cues, ask clarifying questions, and paraphrase what you hear. Remembering is the process of moving information from short-term memory to long-term memory. To be more skilled at remembering, repeat what was said, use mnemonic devices, and take notes. Critically evaluating is the process of interpreting what you have understood to determine how truthful, authentic, or believable you judge the meaning to be. To improve your critical evaluation skills, separate facts from inferences and probe for information. Responding is the process of reacting to what has been heard while listening and after listening. To improve your responding skills, provide back-channel cues and reply when the message is complete.

The five types of listening are appreciative, discriminative, comprehensive, critical-evaluative, and empathic listening. Listening skills are affected by technology and cyberspace.

◑ Inter-Action Dialogue: Listening Effectively

Good listening requires getting ready to listen, listening actively, and responding after listening.

In the dialogue between Gloria and Jill below, pay attention to the types of listening demonstrated as well as to how the five parts of the listening process present themselves.

Gloria and Jill meet for lunch on campus.

Conversation

Gloria: I'm really hungry—I don't know whether I've been working out too hard or what.

Jill: I know. There are some days when I can't figure out what happened, but I just feel starved.

Gloria: Thanks for meeting me today. I know you're up to here in work, but . . .

Jill: No problem Gloria. I feel bad that we haven't gotten together as much as we used to, so I've been really looking forward to seeing you.

Gloria: Well, I need to talk with you about something that's been really bothering me. (She notices that Jill is fumbling with something in her purse.) Jill—are you listening to me?

Jill: I'm sorry, Gloria. For a minute I couldn't find my cell phone. I wanted to turn it off while we talked, and then I worried that I might have dropped it. But everything's OK. I apologize—that was rude of me. (She then sits up straight and looks directly at Gloria.) I'm ready.

Gloria: Well, you know I'm working with Professor Bryant on an independent research project this term.

Jill: I recall you mentioning something about it, but remind me of the details.

Gloria: Last semester when I took her course on family communication I wrote a term paper on how shared dinnertime affected family communication. Well, she really liked it and asked me if I wanted to work with her on a study this term. She said I could get credit.

Jill: How?

Gloria: I had permission to sign up for four credit hours of independent study.

Jill: That sounds good—so what's the problem?

Gloria: Well, since she videotapes actual family discussions and then interviews family members, I thought I'd get to help with some of the interviews. But so far all I've been assigned to do is transcribe the tapes and do some library research.

Jill: So you're disappointed because you're not being challenged?

Gloria: It's more than that. I thought Dr. Bryant would be a mentor: there'd be team meetings, we'd talk over ideas and stuff. But I don't really even get to see her. Her graduate assistant gives me my assignments, and he doesn't even stop to explain why I'm being asked to do stuff. I'm not really learning anything.

Jill: So, if I understand, it's not only the type of assignments you're getting but it's also that instead of really being involved, you're being treated like a flunky.

Gloria: Exactly.

Jill: So when she asked you to work on her study, did she ever sit down and discuss exactly what the independent study would entail?

Gloria: Not really. I just signed up.

Jill: Well since the term began, have you had any contact with Dr. Bryant?

Gloria: No. Do you think I should make an appointment to see her?

Jill: I think so, but if you did, what would you say to her?

Gloria: Well, I'd just tell her how disappointed I am with how things are going. And I'd explain what I hoped to learn this term and ask if she could help me understand how the assignments I'd been given were going to help me learn about family communication research.

Jill: So the purpose of your meeting wouldn't be to get different assignments, but to understand what you are supposed to be learning from the assignments you've done so far?

Gloria: Right. But I think I'd also like her to know that I really expected to have more contact with her.

Jill: Well, it sounds as if you're clear on what you'd like to ask her.

Gloria: Yes, but I don't want to get her angry with me. Four credit hours is a lot and it's too late to drop the independent study.

Jill: So you're concerned that she would be offended and take it out on your grade.

Gloria: A little. But that's probably ridiculous. After all, she's a professional, and all the students I know who have gone to see her say that she's really understanding.

Jill: Well, then what do you want to do?

Gloria: Hmm. . . . I'm going to make an appointment to see her. In fact, I'll stop by her office on my way to my next class. Jill, thanks for listening. You've really helped me.

○ Chapter Resources

Communication Improvement Plan: Listening ○ Find more on the web @ www.oup.com/us/interact12

Would you like to improve your use of the following skills discussed in this chapter?

• Questioning
• Paraphrasing

Pick a skill, and write a communication improvement plan. You can find a communication improvement plan worksheet on our website at www.oup.com/us/interact12.

Key Words ○

Listening, *p. 208*	Remembering, *p. 217*	Probing questions, *p. 220*
Attending, *p. 210*	Primacy effect, *p. 218*	Responding, *p. 221*
Understanding, *p. 212*	Recency effect, *p. 218*	Back-channel cues, *p. 221*
Clarifying question, *p. 213*	Repetition, *p. 218*	Appreciative listening, *p. 222*
Paraphrase, *p. 215*	Mnemonic device, *p. 218*	Discriminative listening, *p. 224*
Content paraphrase, *p. 216*	Critically evaluating, *p. 220*	Comprehensive listening, *p. 224*
Feelings paraphrase, *p. 216*	Facts, *p. 220*	Critical-evaluative listening, *p. 224*
Combined paraphrase, *p. 216*	Inferences, *p. 220*	Empathic listening, *p. 224*

Skill Practice ○ Find more on the web @ www.oup.com/us/interact12

Writing Questions and Paraphrases

Provide an appropriate question and paraphrase for each of the following statements. To get you started, the first conversation has been completed for you.

1. **Luis:** It's Dionne's birthday, and I've planned a *big* evening. Sometimes, I think Dionne believes I take her for granted—well, I think after tonight she'll know I think she's something special!

   Question: What specific things do you have planned?

   Content paraphrase: If I'm understanding you, you're planning a night that's going to cost a lot more than what Dionne expects on her birthday.

   Feelings paraphrase: From the way you're talking, I get the feeling you're really proud of yourself for making plans like these.

2. **Angie:** Brother! Another nothing class. I keep thinking one of these days he'll get excited about something. Professor Romero is a real bore!

   Question:

   Content paraphrase:

   Feelings paraphrase:

3. **Jerry:** Everyone seems to be talking about that movie on Channel 5 last night, but I didn't see it. You know, I don't watch much that's on the "idiot box."

   Question:

   Content paraphrase:

   Feelings paraphrase:

4. **Kaelin:** I don't know if it's something to do with me or with Mom, but lately she and I just aren't getting along.

Question:

Content paraphrase:

Feelings paraphrase:

5. **Aileen:** I've got a report due at work and a paper due in management class. On top of that, it's my sister's birthday, and so far I haven't even had time to get her anything. Tomorrow's going to be a disaster.

Question:

Content paraphrase:

Feelings paraphrase:

Inter-Act with Media ❖ Find more on the web @ www.oup.com/us/interact12

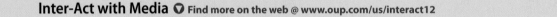

Television

Hell's Kitchen, season 4 (2008). Gordon Ramsey.

Brief Summary: In this reality competition, world-renowned chef Gordon Ramsey leads a crew of fifteen hopefuls who vie for the title of executive chef at one of Ramsey's international restaurants. In this episode, finalists Christina and Petrozza compete against each other with their voted-off colleagues serving as their sous chefs for the final meal service. To form an effective work team and accurately fulfill orders, all chefs must comprehensively listen to each other. The fast-paced nature of the kitchen makes listening a challenge. For example, when cleaning the kitchen prior to service, Petrozza innocently asks Jen if she needs help. Jen retorts, "If I need help sweeping, I wouldn't trust me to work a line." Jen's inference into Petrozza's statement stems from her resentment that she's not a finalist. Later, Petrozza tells Bobby that he needs an appetizer immediately, but when Bobby delivers cold strudel, Petrozza asks Bobby to please "touch everything before it comes to him." Bobby listens, acknowledges his mistake, and delivers a hot dish.

In the competing kitchen, Christina assigns Matt to help LouRoss, who fell behind on salads. Matt paraphrases each of LouRoss' instructions on the salad, which LouRoss finds annoying. To the camera, Christina criticizes Matt, indicating that he should not need such assistance constructing a salad. *Hell's Kitchen* reveals that in the workplace, varied levels of skill and personalities often prohibit effective listening and responding.

IPC Concepts: Attending, understanding, comprehensive listening, paraphrasing, critically evaluating information.

Cinema

The Nanny Diaries (2007). Shari Springer Berman, Robert Pulcini (directors). Scarlett Johansson, Laura Linney, Paul Giamatti, Nicholas Reese Art.

Brief Summary: After graduating from college, Annie Braddock (Johansson) struggles over her career path, despite her mother's encouragement to find a high-powered job in New York. After young Grayer (Art) slams into Annie while running in the park, his mother (Linney) mistakes Annie's name for "nanny" and assumes that she is one. Annie takes a year away from her job search to nanny for Grayer, calling his ultra-wealthy and parentally detached parents "Mr. and Mrs. X." Annie's first encounter in the park with Mrs. X involves selective listening when she mistook her name, but the listening snafus continually unfold. On one occasion, Mrs. X bursts into Annie's room and fires an intricate to-do list at her, without clarifying understanding or inviting questions. In another exchange, Mrs. X asks how Grayer is doing, and when Annie attempts to elaborate, she interrupts, saying, "Good enough then" and retreats from the room. When Mrs. X returns from a spa vacation, Annie tries to tell her that Grayer became very ill in her absence. Mrs. X asks about his whereabouts. Annie tells her he's sleeping. Mrs. X replies, "Then he can't be that sick, can he?" and proceeds to instruct Annie about the laundry. In the end, Mrs. X fires Annie and brings a "nanny-cam" recording for evaluation to a parenting class. There, Mrs. X and the other mothers are forced to listen to Annie's perception about Mr. and Mrs. X's uninvolved parenting style.

IPC Concepts: Attending, discriminative listening, comprehensive listening, critical-evaluative listening, understanding.

What's on the Web

Find links and additional material, including self-quizzes, on the companion website at www .oup.com/us/interact12.

9

Empathizing with and Supporting Others

After you have read this chapter, you should be able to answer these questions:

▷ What is empathizing?

▷ What are three approaches to empathy and ways to improve our ability to empathize?

▷ What is the process of supporting others?

▷ What are the characteristics of effective and ineffective supporting?

▷ What are the four supportive interaction phases?

▷ What are the five supportive message skills?

▷ How is support communicated in cyberspace?

▷ What are gender and cultural similarities and differences in supporting?

"Stacey, I'm so glad you're home. I'm really depressed and I really need to talk with you. I got three letters of rejection in the mail today from the graduate schools I applied to. I know graduate school admissions are very competitive, but I had great scores on the GRE, a 3.65 GPA, and two internships. One of the programs was a stretch—it's the top program in the country, but I thought the other two were safety schools. I'm just totally shocked. Now what am I going to do? You know I've had my heart set on grad school and becoming a professor!"

"Oh, Patti, that's so awful. I guess you'll have to start using the career center and go into the world of work like the rest of us. Hey, you'll never guess who just contacted me through Facebook—Jay from when I worked at the mall. Remember, he ran the cell phone kiosk outside my store?"

"Uh, thanks for the support Stacey. I'm having the worst day of my life and you're more interested in some guy who used to work near you? Remind me not to count on you for support. Thanks a lot!"

"Patti, chill. I was just trying to change the subject and get your mind off of the rejection letters. I mean, cheer up. It's not the end of the world. You're so smart. You'll get a great job."

Can you recall a situation in which you shared with a friend how hurt you were about an incident that happened to you? Did you feel that your friend really listened? Did your friend seem to understand and try to help you? Or was your conversation like the one between Stacey and Patti? Notice how Stacey's first response ("That's so awful") was followed by what is referred to as an "escape" strategy—when one person seems to dismiss the importance of another's concerns by changing the subject (Barbee & Cunningham, 1995). How should Stacey have responded in order to be helpful and comforting? Research indicates that what Patti needed from Stacey were comforting responses that provided solace and helped to solve the problem (Cunningham & Barbee, 2000). Patti would have perceived these responses as supportive rather than dismissive.

The importance of providing support for your friends and family members when they need it cannot be overstated. Research has linked messages of comfort and support with longer life, reduced incidence of disease, better recovery from illness, improved ability to cope with chronic illness, and better overall mental health (Albrecht & Goldsmith, 2003). For example, supportive communication has been shown to have a significant impact on cancer survival rates (Ahuja, 2007; Carpenter, 2006) and beneficial effects on cardiovascular, endocrine, and immune system health (Uchino, Cacioppo, & Kiecolt-Glaser, 1996). In addition, supportive communication can contribute to healthier relationships, with such benefits as marital satisfaction, healthy family interactions, strong friendships, and amicable work relationships (Goldsmith, 2004). Demonstrating closeness and caring can be beneficial to relationships and lack of supportive communication can be damaging to them.

In this chapter, we will examine effective supportive communication. We begin by explaining the concept of empathy and describing how to improve your ability to empathize. Then we discuss emotional support and the characteristics of effective and ineffective supporting. After that, we talk about the four phases of supportive interaction. Next, we describe the five skills you will want to learn so that you can provide effective support to others. Finally, we examine the increasing use of the online environment to give and receive support, as well as how gender and cultural differences and similarities play a role in supporting others.

❍ Empathizing

The foundation of supporting others is empathy. **Empathizing** is the cognitive process of identifying with or vicariously experiencing the feelings, thoughts, or attitudes of others. Scholars recognize that empathy is an important element in understanding and maintaining good interpersonal relationships (Omdahl, 1995). When you empathize, you attempt to understand and/or experience what another understands and/or experiences; in effect, you "put yourself in the other person's shoes." It obviously requires effort to empathize with someone who is very different from you or to empathize with someone who is experiencing something that is out of your realm of experience. But your effectiveness at supporting

Empathizing—cognitive process of identifying with or vicariously experiencing the feelings, thoughts, or attitudes of others.

LEARN ABOUT YOURSELF ❍ Empathic Tendency

Take this short survey to learn something about yourself. Answer the questions based on your first responses. Be honest in reporting your true feelings. There are no right or wrong answers. For each question, select one of the following numbers that best describes your true feelings.

1 = Always
2 = Often
3 = Sometimes
4 = Rarely
5 = Never

_____ 1. I try to consider the other person's point of view.
_____ 2. When I am upset with someone, I try to put myself in his or her shoes for a while.
_____ 3. I find it difficult to see things from the other person's point of view.
_____ 4. I try to imagine how it would feel to be in another person's place.
_____ 5. I dislike listening to other people's feelings.
_____ 6. I can easily identify with another person's feelings.
_____ 7. I would rather talk about myself than the other person in a conversation.
_____ 8. I get impatient when people talk about their own concerns and problems.
_____ 9. I like to help others feel better.
_____ 10. People spend too much time talking about their own feelings and problems.

This is a test of empathic tendency—your capacity to feel empathy for others.

Scoring the Survey: The questions have been divided into two separate sets of scores. Each score set ranges from 5 to 25 points. The lower (closer to 5) your total score for set 1, the more you tend to feel empathy toward others. The lower (closer to 5) your total score for set 2, the less you tend to feel empathy toward others. Whatever your scores, this chapter will help you to become better at empathizing with others.

Add scores for questions 1, 2, 4, 6, and 9   Total for set 1:_____
Add scores for questions 3, 5, 7, 8, and 10   Total for set 2: _____

or comforting someone is based on your ability to empathize with what he or she is experiencing. In this section, we discuss the three types of empathy and the steps you can take to improve your ability to empathize.

▷ Three Types of Empathy

Scholars who study empathy have identified three different types of empathy: empathic responsiveness, perspective taking, and sympathetic responsiveness (Weaver & Kirtley, 1995). These three categories represent different levels of empathy.

The deepest level of empathy is empathic responsiveness. **Empathic responsiveness** is experiencing an emotional response parallel to another person's actual or anticipated display of emotion (Omdahl, 1995; Stiff, Dillard, Somera, Kim, & Sleight, 1988). For instance, when Jackson tells James that he is in real trouble financially, and James not only senses the stress and anxiety that Jackson is feeling but also feels stress and anxiety himself, we would say that James has experienced empathic responsiveness. Empathic responsiveness is most common when there is a close or intimate relationship between the person in need of support and the person called upon to provide it. Because of a strong relational bond, you may identify more easily with the emotions of a close friend, family member, or intimate partner and experience those emotions along with the other person. Conversely, if you have just recently met someone and he or she asks for your support, it may be more difficult for you to experience empathic responsiveness.

Perspective taking—imagining yourself in the place of another person—is the most common type of empathy (Zillmann, 1991). While empathic responsiveness is actually feeling what another person feels, perspective taking is a way of approximating as best we can how another person feels. When perspective taking, we imagine ourselves in the situation described by another person in need of our support, anticipate how we would feel in that same situation, and then assume that the other person's feelings are similar to our own. In our example, if James personalizes Jackson's message by picturing himself in serious financial debt, brings to mind the emotions he might experience if this were to occur, and then assumes that Jackson must be feeling the same way, then James is empathizing by perspective taking. If we have been in a similar situation with the person with whom we seek to empathize, we will be better at perspective taking. If we have not been in a similar situation, perspective taking will require more effort. Although perspective taking is difficult for many of us (Holtgraves, 2002), with conscious effort, we can learn to imagine ourselves in the place of another.

The least deep level of empathy is sympathetic responsiveness. **Sympathetic responsiveness** is feeling concern, compassion, or sorrow for another person because he or she is in a distressing situation. Some scholars call this "emotional concern" (Stiff et al., 1988), while others use the nonacademic term "sympathy" (Eisenberg & Fabes, 1990). Sympathetic responsiveness differs from the other two types of empathy in that you don't attempt to experience the feelings of another person; rather, you focus on intellectually understanding what the speaker has said about what has happened and the emotions that accompany the re-

Empathic responsiveness—experiencing an emotional response parallel to another person's actual or anticipated display of emotion.

Perspective taking—imagining yourself in the place of another person.

Sympathetic responsiveness—feeling concern, compassion, or sorrow for another person because he or she is in a distressing situation.

counting. Rather than identifying with the emotions of the speaker, your feelings will be concern, compassion, or joy or sorrow for that person. You can use sympathetic responsiveness when the person you are listening to is recounting an experience or an emotional response that is unimaginable to you. In our example, if James always pays his bills on time and can't imagine being in financial difficulty, he can empathize with Jackson through sympathetic response. He understands that Jackson is stressed and worried, but instead of trying to feel Jackson's emotions directly or imagining how he himself would feel in a similar situation, James instead feels concern and compassion for his friend Jackson.

▷ Empathy Improvement Skills

Although people vary in their innate ability to empathize, most of us can increase our ability to empathize. Those of us who are overly self-absorbed or "I"-oriented can find it difficult to see the world from others' points of view. However, if we are to increase our interpersonal effectiveness, we need to exert extra effort to develop our capacity to empathize.

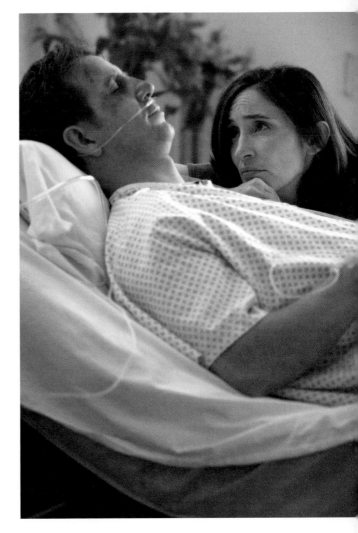

Though it may seem trite, the first step to improving your empathy skills is to take the time and make the effort to understand what other people are saying to you, especially when they ask you for your support. This does not mean that you need to have a deep, personal relationship with others to empathize with them. It means closely attending to what others are saying and what they seem to feel about what they are saying. Understanding others focuses your attention on the other, not on the self. In this chapter's "Diverse Voices" box, "Black and White," Linda Howard describes what she has experienced as a person who is multiethnic and biracial. As you read this excerpt from an interview with Ms. Howard, see how well you can understand and empathize with what she thinks and feels.

How well you empathize also depends on how clearly you observe and "read" the nonverbal messages others send. How accurately can you read others' emotions through their nonverbal behaviors? Research studies have shown that when people concentrate, they can do quite well. People are especially adept at recognizing such primary emotions as happiness, sadness, surprise, anger, and fear (greater than 90 percent accuracy) and rather good at recognizing contempt, disgust, interest, determination, and bewilderment (80 to 90 percent accuracy) (Leathers, 1997). The research also suggests that recognizing facial expressions is the key to perceiving emotion (Leathers, 1997). To improve your observation of nonverbal behaviors, try the following: When another person begins a conversation with you, develop the habit of silently posing two questions and

Black and White

by Linda Howard

Today we tend to label people as black, white, Asian, Hispanic, and so on. But what if you are biracial and/or multiethnic? Linda Howard is a recent high school graduate who has been awarded a four-year scholarship to a prominent university in New England. Based on the following transcript of an interview with her, in what ways can you empathize?

My parents are Black and White American. I come from a long heritage. I am of French, English, Irish, Dutch, Scottish, Canadian, and African descent.

I don't really use race. I always say, "My father's Black, my mother's White, I'm mixed. But I'm American; I'm human. That's my race; I'm part of the human race."

It's hard when you go out in the streets and you've got a bunch of White friends and you're the darkest person there. No matter how light you are to the rest of your family, you're the darkest person there and they say you're Black. Then you go out with a bunch of Black people and you're the lightest there and they say, "Yeah, my best friend's White." But I'm not. I'm both.

I don't always fit in—unless I'm in a mixed group. That's how it's different. Because if I'm in a group of people who are all one race, then they seem to look at me as being the other race . . . whereas if I'm in a group full of [racially mixed] people, my race doesn't seem to matter to everybody else. . . . Then I don't feel like I'm standing out. But if I'm in a group of totally one race, then I sort of stand out, and that's something that's hard to get used to.

It's hard. I look at history and I feel really bad for what some of my ancestors did to some of my other ancestors. Unless you're mixed, you don't know what it's like to be mixed.

I've had people tell me, "Well, you're Black." I'm not Black; I'm Black and White. I'm Black and White American. "Well, you're Black!" No, I'm not! I'm both. It's insulting, when they try and . . . bring it right back to the old standards, that if you have anybody in your family who's Black, you're Black . . . I mean, I'm not ashamed of being Black, but I'm not ashamed of being White either; and if I'm both, I want to be part of both. And I think teachers need to be sensitive to that.

See, the thing is, I mix it at home so much that it's not really a problem for me to mix it outside.

I don't think [interracial identity] is that big of a problem. It's not killing anybody, at least as far as I know, it's not. It's not destroying families and lives and stuff. It's a minor thing. If you learn how to deal with it at a young age, as I did, it really doesn't bother you the rest of your life, like drugs. . . .

I think we're all racist in a sense. We all have some type of person that we don't like, whether it's [a person] from a different race, or from a different background, or [a person with] different habits.

But to me a serious racist is a person who believes that people of different ethnic backgrounds don't belong or should be in their space and shouldn't invade our space: "Don't come and invade my space, you Chinese person. You belong over in China or you belong over in Chinatown."

Racists come out and tell you that they don't like who you are. Prejudiced people [on the other hand] will say it in like those little hints, you know, like, "Oh, yes, some of my best friends are Black." Or they say little ethnic remarks that they know will insult you but they won't come out and tell you, "You're Black. I don't want anything to do with you." Racists, to me, would come out and do that.

Both racists and prejudiced people make judgments, and most of the time they're wrong judgments, but the racist will carry his one step further. . . . A racist is a person that will carry out their prejudices.

I had a fight with a woman at work. She's White, and at the time I was the only Black person in my department. Or I was the only person who was at all Black in my department. And she just kept on laying on the racist jokes. At one point, I said, "You know, Nellie, you're a racist pig!" And she got offended by that. And I was just joking, just like she'd been joking for two days straight—all the racist jokes that she could think of.

I've got a foot on both sides of the fence, and there's only so much I can take. I'm straddling the fence, and it's hard to laugh and joke with you when you're talking about the foot that's on the other side.

She couldn't understand it. We didn't talk for weeks. And then one day, I had to work with her. We didn't say anything for the first like two hours of work. And then I just said, "Smile, Nellie, you're driving me nuts!" and she smiled and laughed. And we've been good friends ever since. She just knows you don't say ethnic things around me; you don't joke around with me like that because I won't stand for it from you anymore. We can be friends; we can talk about anything else—except race.

Excerpted from "Case Study: Linda Howard, 'Unless You're Mixed, You Don't Know What It's Like to Be Mixed.'" In Nieto, Sonia. (2000), *Affirming Diversity: The Sociopolitical Context of Multicultural Education* (3rd ed., pp. 50-60). Boston: Allyn & Bacon. Copyright © 2000 by Pearson Education. Adapted by permission of the publisher.

paraphrasing the answers to yourself: "What emotions do I believe the person is experiencing right now?" and "What are the cues the person is giving that I am using to draw this conclusion?" Consciously raising these questions can help you focus your attention on the nonverbal aspects of messages, where most of the information regarding the person's emotional state is conveyed. To ensure that you understand another's emotions accurately, use the skill of perception checking.

Finally, after attending and observing both verbal and nonverbal behaviors, employ one of the three types of empathy: empathic responsiveness, perspective taking, or sympathetic responsiveness. The type of empathy you employ will depend on how close you are with the person asking for your support and your level of experience with the situation described to you.

◖ Supporting

As we discussed in Chapter 8, effective listening precedes effective speaking, with effective listening strategies transitioning into effective spoken messages. The same is true of effective empathizing and supporting. To provide appropriate support to another person, you must first empathize effectively and then transition into an effective supporting response. **Supporting** is helping people feel better about themselves and their behaviors. A **supporting response** is a statement whose goal is to validate, show approval, encourage, soothe, console, cheer up, or bolster confidence. Research on supporting responses suggests that people

Supporting—helping people feel better about themselves and their behaviors.

Supporting response—statement whose goal is to validate, show approval, encourage, soothe, console, cheer up, or bolster confidence.

SKILL BUILDERS ◖ Empathizing

SKILL	USE	PROCEDURE	EXAMPLE
The cognitive process of identifying with or the vicarious experiencing of the feelings, thoughts, or attitudes of others	To prepare yourself for providing an appropriate supporting response	1. Show respect for the person by actively attending to what the person says. 2. Concentrate on understanding both the verbal and nonverbal messages conveyed to you, using paraphrasing and perception checking. 3. Experience an emotional response by employing one of the three types of empathy: empathic responsiveness, perspective taking, or sympathetic responsiveness.	When Daryl says, "I was really hurt when Sarah returned the ring I had given her," Mary listens closely to what Daryl says, observes his verbal and nonverbal behaviors, and experiences an emotional response to Daryl's message by either sharing Daryl's feelings directly, imagining herself in Daryl's situation, or feeling concern, compassion, or sorrow for Daryl in a more generalized manner.

OBSERVE AND ANALYZE ▼

Empathizing Effectively

1. Describe the last time you effectively empathized with another person. Write a short summary of the episode. Be sure to cover the following: What was the person's emotional state? How did you recognize it? What were the nonverbal cues? Verbal cues? What type of relationship do you have with this person? How long have you known the person? How similar is this person to you? Have you ever had a real or vicarious experience similar to the one the person was reporting? Did you use empathic responsiveness, perspective taking, or sympathetic responsiveness? Why? What was the outcome of this communication episode?

2. During the next two days, make a conscious effort to use the three steps toward being a more empathic person in your interactions with others. Attend to others when they ask for support, observe their verbal and nonverbal behaviors by using paraphrasing and perception checking, and employ one of the three types of empathy, depending on the situation. At the end of each day, assess your progress. How well did you do on each step? Where do you need to continue to exert effort?

who use a relatively high percentage of sophisticated supporting strategies are perceived as more sensitive, concerned, and involved (Burleson & Samter, 1990; Kunkel & Burleson, 1999; Samter, Burleson, & Murphy, 1987). They show that they care about people and what happens to them, and they demonstrate that the listener empathizes with a person's feelings, whatever their direction or intensity (Burleson, 1994). Supporting responses should not be used to simply tell people what they want to hear. Rather, effective supporting responses must be in touch with the facts. Let's look briefly at two supporting responses, one that supports positive feelings and another that supports negative feelings.

▷ Supporting Positive Feelings

We all like to treasure our good feelings. When we share them, we don't want them dashed by listeners' inappropriate or insensitive responses. Supporting positive feelings is generally easy, but it still requires some care. Consider the following example:

Kendra: *(hangs up the telephone, does a little dance step, and turns to Selena)* That was the bank. He said that I've been approved for the loan. Can you believe it? I'm going to have my own pottery studio.

Kendra's statement requires an appropriate verbal response. To provide one, Selena must appreciate the feeling people get when they receive good news, or she must envision how she would feel under the same circumstances. Selena responds:

Selena: Kendra, way to go, girl! That's terrific! I am so happy for you. You've worked so hard—you deserve this.

In this case, Selena's response gives her approval for Kendra to be excited. Her response also shows that she is happy because Kendra seems happy. Supporting responses like Selena's are much needed. Think of the times when you have experienced an event that made you feel happy, proud, confident, or amused and you needed to express those feelings. Didn't it make you feel even better when others recognized your feelings and affirmed your right to have them?

▷ Supporting Negative Feelings

When a person has had an unfortunate experience and is in the midst of or is recalling unpleasant emotional reactions, supporting negative feelings provides much-needed comfort. By acknowledging the person's feelings and affirming the person's right to those feelings, you can help the person work through his or her feelings. Providing appropriate responses to negative feelings can feel awkward and difficult. But when people are in pain, or when they are feeling justifiably angry, they need to be comforted by appropriate supporting statements, so we need to practice those supporting skills. An appropriate comforting statement in response to negative feelings demonstrates empathy, sensitivity, and a willingness to be actively involved if need be. Consider the following example:

Bill: My sister called today to tell me that Mom's biopsy came back positive. She's got cancer, and it's untreatable.

Dwight: Bill, you must be in shock. I'm so sorry that this is happening. Is there anything I can do for you?

Notice how Dwight begins by empathizing: "Bill, you must be in shock." He continues with statements that show his sensitivity to the seriousness of the situation: "I'm so sorry that this is happening." Finally, he shows that he wants to be involved: He is willing to take time to talk about Bill's negative emotions, and he asks whether he can do anything to help.

We offer the exchanges between Kendra and Selena and between Bill and Dwight as an introduction to supporting skills. Later in the chapter, we'll see that these are just two examples of how to provide support. For now, take a look at how one of the leading scholars on supporting responses, Brant Burleson, who is featured in this chapter's "Spotlight on Scholars" box (page 242), has explored supporting responses in his work.

● Characteristics of Effective and Ineffective Supporting

A great deal of research has been written about understanding what types of messages are perceived by receivers as supportive and what types of messages are perceived as unsupportive. According to Goldsmith (2004), whether a particular message is perceived as supportive can depend on who delivers the message, what the context of the interaction is, what nonverbal communication accompanies the message, and how

We can support others not only with our verbal messages but also by joining in celebrations of important milestones. How does attending someone's graduation show support?

the message is worded. For example, suppose Emily confides in someone else that she thinks she might be pregnant and her boyfriend doesn't know. The response, which on the surface seems straightforward and innocuous, is, "You'd better go talk to him." First, who delivers the message determines whether the message is viewed as supportive. It may be seen as caring and useful advice if Emily would typically expect silence or a negative message from the person she tells. On the other hand, it may seem unsupportive if it comes from a friend, parent, or other family member, since Emily would expect them to focus on her needs first, not those of her boyfriend. Second, the context of the interaction influences the perception of support.

Brant Burleson

Professor of Communication, Purdue University, on

Comforting

Over the years, Brant Burleson and his colleagues have provided a great deal of scholarship that informs our understanding of supporting responses. To better understand just why some comforting messages help people feel better while others don't do anything—or even make people feel worse—Burleson has dedicated his career as an educator and researcher to this topic.

The seeds of Brant Burleson's interest in comforting behaviors were sown during his undergraduate days at the University of Colorado at Boulder, where he was taught that all communication was rooted in persuasion. This proposition did not square with Burleson's own experiences. As a child of the 1950s who came of age during the emotion-filled 1960s, Burleson had witnessed a great deal of debate and conflict. But he had also seen people engaging in acts of altruism, comforting, and supporting. These acts, he reasoned, were not aimed at changing anyone's opinions or behaviors but were simply offered to help other people. So when he entered graduate school at the University of Illinois, Burleson began to study formally how individuals comfort one another. He wanted to establish scientifically whether comforting messages were important and whether they made a difference. Since graduate school, Burleson's work has done much to affirm that they are both important and have an impact.

In his research, Burleson has carefully defined "comforting strategies" (his term for "supporting responses") as messages that have the goal of relieving or lessening the emotional distress of others. Initially, he limited his work to looking at how we comfort others who are experiencing mild or moderate sadness or disappointment that happens as a result of everyday events. More recently, however, he has expanded his study to include comforting strategies in situations involving extreme depression or grief because of extraordinary events, such as the death of a loved one. Most of his work focuses on the verbal strategies that we use when we comfort (while some of his colleagues, such as Susanne Jones, have examined nonverbal comforting behaviors). Burleson's care in defining the "domain" of his work is important. By carefully stating the type of emotional distress he is concerned with, and by clearly identifying the limits of his work, Burleson en-

ables those who read his work to fully understand the types of comforting strategies to which his findings apply.

Early on, Burleson worked with James L. Applegate to develop a way of judging the sophistication of particular comforting strategies. He and Applegate determined that sophisticated comforting strategies are those that acknowledge, elaborate, legitimize, and explore the feelings of others. In contrast, unsophisticated comforting strategies are those that lack sufficient empathy, do not provide elaborations, tend to contradict rather than legitimize feelings, and tend to explore facts rather than feelings.

Lately, Burleson and others who study comforting strategies have turned their attention to understanding the results of those strategies more fully. Early research judged comforting strategies only on the extent to which they reduced immediate emotional distress. But more recent research shows that the effects of comforting strategies extend beyond this simple instrumental outcome. Effective comforting helps the people comforted to cope better in the future, improves personal relationships, and may even enhance physical health. Moreover, skilled comforting strategies also benefit the comforter. Burleson believes that when we effectively comfort others, we increase our own self-esteem, are viewed positively both by those we comfort and those who see us effectively comfort others, and are likely to have better long-term relationships than ineffective comforters. There is a growing list of research studies that provide further support for his theory.

Burleson's most recent research examines how recipients of comforting messages cognitively process and respond to these messages. This research seeks to explain why the effects of comforting messages sometimes vary depending on the culture and gender of the recipients, the personalities of the recipients, and other aspects of the comforting situation. Study of how people process the messages they receive will help determine when using sophisticated comforting strategies is particularly important and when it may be less important. For complete citations of some publications by Burleson and his colleagues, see the references list for this chapter at the end of the book.

If the comment occurred in the later stages of a lengthy conversation, Emily may see it as supportive. But if "You'd better go talk to him" is the first thing that is said, or even worse, is all that is said to her, Emily may view it as curt and unsupportive. Third, the nonverbal communication accompanying the response determines how the message is viewed. As you can imagine, Emily would interpret a harsh tone of voice, avoidance of eye contact, or a disapproving facial expression as unsupportive, whereas she would interpret a soothing vocal delivery, direct and sympathetic eye contact, or a smile as supportive. Finally, variations in the wording of a message can determine how it is received. Consider how the following alternative wordings might affect how Emily receives the overall message that she should consider her boyfriend's role:

"You might want to talk to him."
"I suggest you talk to him."
"Have you considered talking to him?"
"You might feel better by talking to him."
"Please tell me you're going to talk to him."
"I can't believe you haven't talked to him yet."
"March yourself over there and talk to him."

In general, effective supporting responses are helpful because they create and maintain an environment that feels safe and encourage the person needing support to talk through a distressing situation. Ineffective support messages are not helpful because they threaten the emotional well-being of the person needing comfort, discourage the person in need from talking through the situation, or impose the listener's interpretation of the situation on the person needing comfort. In his research, Burleson (2003) identified a number of effective and ineffective types of supporting responses. Effective supporting responses are those that:

1. Clearly state that the speaker's aim is to help the other ("I'd like to help you, what can I do?" or "You know that I'm going to be here for you for as long as it takes").

2. Express acceptance, love, and affection for the other ("I love you and understand how upset this makes you" or "I understand that you just can't seem to accept this").

3. Demonstrate care, concern, and interest in the other's situation ("What are you planning to do now?" or "Tell me more. What happened then?").

4. Indicate that the speaker is available to listen and support the other ("If you need to talk more, please call" or "Sometimes it helps to have someone to listen, and I'd like to do that for you").

"Of course I'm listening to your expression of spiritual suffering. Don't you see me making eye contact, striking an open posture, leaning towards you and nodding empathetically?"

5. State that the speaker is an ally ("I'm with you on this" or "Well, I'm on your side—this isn't right").

6. Acknowledge the other's feelings and situation as well as express sincere sympathy ("I'm so sorry to see you feeling so bad; I can see that you're devastated by what has happened" or "You have my sympathy; I couldn't work for a jerk like that either, no wonder you're frustrated").

7. Assure the other that feelings of distress are legitimate ("With what has happened to you, you deserve to be angry" or "I'd feel exactly the same way if I were in your shoes").

8. Encourage the other to elaborate on the story ("Uh huh, yeah" or "I see. How did you feel about that?" or "Well, what happened before that? Can you elaborate?").

On the other hand, according to Burleson, ineffective supportive messages are those that:

1. Condemn and criticize the other's feelings and behaviors ("I think you're wrong to be angry with Paul" or "That's dumb. Why do you feel like that?").

2. Imply that the other's feelings are not warranted ("You have no right to feel that way. After all, you've dumped men before" or "Don't you think you're being a bit overdramatic?").

3. Tell the other how to feel or advise the other to ignore justifiable feelings about the situation ("You should be really happy about this" or "Hey, you should just act as if you don't care").

4. Take attention away from the other and focus on the self ("I know exactly how you feel because when I . . .").

5. Are the result of an intrusion ("I know we've just met, but I know how to help you here").

⬢ Supportive Interaction Phases

Although we can attempt to support a person with a single supporting response, supporting someone usually involves a longer conversation. A **supportive interaction** is a conversation or series of conversations in which support is provided. Support may be offered numerous times in a single conversation, and/or supportive interaction may involve numerous conversations spanning days, weeks, or even months. Regardless of the length of the supportive interaction, the role of the supporter is to give emotional care to someone who is having difficulty achieving a cognitive reappraisal and so continues to need comfort. For example, in our chapter opening conversation, Patti had been anticipating getting into graduate school. Because this is so important to her, it is likely to take her weeks, if not months, to "talk out" her feelings and develop a reappraisal that allows her to accept the disappointment. So too, a person facing financial ruin or grieving the death of someone they loved is likely to need ongoing supportive interac-

OBSERVE AND ANALYZE ⬇

Emotional Support

Recall the last time you received emotional support from a partner. Describe the situation. Did you feel better because of this conversation? Which of the characteristics of effective support and ineffective support were used in the messages of your partner? Does this explain how comforted you felt? Next, consider each of the characteristics again. Which of these do your messages often exhibit?

Supportive interaction—
conversation or series of conversations in which support is provided.

tions. Whether a distressed person is comforted in one conversation or requires many conversations, Barbee and Cunningham (1995) have identified four well-ordered phases through which supportive interactions progress: support activation, support provision, target reaction, and helper responses.

1. Phase one: support activation. Supportive interactions begin when something happens to trigger an initial supportive response. Support activation can be triggered by the words or behaviors of the person needing support/comforting. For instance, in the chapter opener, Patti overtly seeks support when she self-discloses to Stacey, "I'm really depressed and I really need to talk with you." Alternatively, a relational partner who perceives a need to support the other can trigger support activation. For example, if Brianne comes home, walks into the kitchen, and finds her mother slumped over the sink silently sobbing into her arm, she is likely to activate support by rushing over, putting her arms around her mom, and asking, "Mom are you all right? What's happened?" Support, then, can be activated either by the person needing comforting or by one who has offered to be the comforter.

2. Phase two: support provision. During the second phase of a supportive interaction, comforters enact messages that are designed to provide support to the partner by focusing on the emotions being displayed or on the problem that has been expressed. In the chapter opener, Stacey failed to provide adequate support right away. However, in our other example, once Brianne's mother shares that the reason she is crying is because she's lost her job, Brianne may provide solace by saying, "I'm so sorry, I can understand why you're terrified about how we'll pay this month's rent." In this way Brianne provides support for her mother's feelings.

3. Phase three: target reaction. Once a comforter has responded to the person needing support, that person will react to what the helper has said or done. This reaction will indicate how successful the helper's message was at comforting the partner. For instance, Patti's response to Stacey's change of subject in our chapter opening conversation is an example of target reaction. Rather than being comforted by Stacey's offer of escape from the topic, Patti is obviously distressed with Stacey's response and tells her so. In our other example and by contrast, Brianne's mother may be somewhat soothed by the solace Brianne has offered. So she may calm down a bit and respond, "I'm not just worried about the rent; there's the car payment, and I just finished paying off the credit card bill. I don't know if I can face going into debt again."

4. Phase four: helper responses. The final step in supportive interactions consists of any continuing messages from the comforter, or helper, regarding what the partner has initially expressed. If the partner remains in need of comforting, the interaction will cycle back to a previous phase and continue until one of the partners changes the subject or ends the conversation. For example, in our chapter opening conversation, Stacey will now need to attend to Patti's statements more closely until Patti reaches a point of stability. On the other hand, if the person in need of support has reached a more stable emotional level, the helper may respond by changing the focus of the conversation. For instance, since Brianne's first message provided the needed support, her mother regained some of her composure and disclosed her fears about going into debt, so the helper responses phase may not be necessary. Brianne might refocus the discussion by helping to solve the family's financial problems.

As you have probably experienced during your own supportive interactions, these conversations are not always smooth. There may be false starts, interruptions, topic changes, and other disruptions during the course of the interaction. And the messages themselves will vary from very brief nonverbal cues to short verbal messages to lengthy narratives complete with subplot digressions. Nonetheless, you will be more effective in supporting others if the messages you use during phases two and four incorporate the supportive message skills presented next.

○ Supportive Message Skills

According to Burleson (2003), most people could benefit from training in emotional support skills. Based on his research, Burleson has identified five supportive message skills. Three of these skills allow you to demonstrate your sensitivity to the emotional needs of your partner. He refers to these as clarifying supportive intentions, buffering face threats (through positive and negative facework), and using other-centered messages. The other two skills enable you to help your partner to problem-solve, and he refers to these as framing information and advice-giving. Occasionally, you may find that using a single one of these skills will provide the necessary support. It is more likely, however, that you will need to use a combination of the skills as you provide support. Let's take a look at each of these individual skills in turn.

▷ Clarifying Supportive Intentions

When people are experiencing emotional turmoil, they can have trouble reaching out to and fully trusting those from whom they seek support. As a result, comfort givers may need to engage in clarifying supportive intentions. **Clarifying supportive intentions** is openly stating that one's goal in a supportive interaction is to help the person in need of support. This skill is vitally important and is often a prelude to using other support skills. It is vitally important because those in need of support are often in a vulnerable position and may be guarded about their emotions. Through clarifying supportive intentions, you let people in need of support know that your motive is simply and solely to help them, you let them know that someone is "on their side," and you provide a context for their understanding of your comments. To clarify supportive intentions, follow these guidelines: (1) Directly state your intentions by emphasizing your desire to help, (2) remind your partner of your commitment to your relationship (if necessary),

Clarifying supportive intentions— openly stating that one's goal in a supportive interaction is to help the person in need of support.

(3) indicate that helping is your only motive, and (4) phrase your clarification in a way that reflects helpfulness. Let's consider a more complete example:

David: (noticing Paul sitting in his cubicle with head in his lap and his hands over his head) Paul, is everything OK?

Paul: (sitting up with a miserable but defiant look on his face) Like you should care. Yeah, everything's fine.

David: Paul, I do care. You've been working for me for five years. You're one of our best analysts, so if something's going on, I'd like to help, even if all I can do is to listen.

Will this statement be enough to convince Paul to open up? Maybe it will. But if not, David can restate and amplify his supportive intentions, hoping that a second expression will be effective:

Paul: Look, you've got a lot to do without listening to my sad story. I can take care of this myself, so just forget it.

David: Paul, I do have lots to do, but I always have time to listen and to help you. I don't want to pry, I just want to help.

With his second response, David has clarified his supportive intentions following all of the guidelines described earlier. He directly states his desire to help ("I'd like to help, even if all I can do is to listen" and "I always have time to listen and to help you"), he reminds his partner of his commitment to the relationship ("You've been working for me for five years. You're one of our best analysts"), he indicates that helping is his only motive ("I don't want to pry, I just want to help"), and he phrases his clarification in a way that reflects helpfulness (he uses the word "help" several times).

People needing comfort can feel vulnerable and may not be comfortable about disclosing until you have given them several reassurances of your supportive intentions. But you also need to be sensitive to your partner's right to privacy. Repeated statements of supportive intentions can become counterproductive if your partner feels coerced and ends up disclosing information that he or she would have just as soon withheld. Supporters need to be sensitive to the fine line that exists between helping someone to "open up" and invading that person's privacy by focusing on your own curiosity. Even if your only motive is to help the other person, there will be times when your own curiosity must be unsatisfied. Thus, if Paul insists a third time that he'd rather not open up, David should not pursue the matter further, perhaps leaving off with a statement like, "OK, I understand that you may not want to talk, but if you change your mind, feel free to drop by my office." In this way, he has provided emotional support without knowing the full details of Paul's situation.

People who need to be comforted may feel vulnerable and may be hesitant about disclosing until you have given several reassurances of your supportive intentions. But how can you tell if someone just needs reassurance or if he or she wishes to maintain privacy?

▷ Buffering Face Threats

We must consider the effect that supportive responses may have on the self-image of the person receiving the support. Recall from our discussion of face-saving in Chapter 7 that every person wants to save face or preserve a public self-image (Goffman, 1959; Brown & Levinson 1987). Once you've clarified your intentions to provide support, you may discover that the very act of providing emotional support can be threatening to the face needs of your partner in two ways. First, providing emotional support can threaten face needs if your partner is concerned with needs for inclusion, respect, appreciation, and approval because of a distressing situation. For example, Leon's mother wants her son to respect her. So she is likely to be embarrassed and ashamed when telling her son that she has a drinking problem. Second, providing emotional support can threaten people's face needs if they feel that our support is a threat to their freedom and privacy. In short, support messages carry an altruistic meaning that signals you want to help, but they also carry a potentially threatening hidden meaning that says, "You are needy." As a result, those in need of support may try to save face by denying they actually need help. For example, if Marta tells Cindy that she'd like to help her, Cindy may say, "I can take care of this myself, so just forget it." Here Cindy is reacting to the **face-threatening act (FTA)**—a statement of support that a person in need may interpret as a threat to his or her public self-image—that Marta unwittingly committed.

Because supportive messages are also FTAs that question another's respectability/approval or freedom/privacy, comforters need to "buffer" or cushion the effect of their words by utilizing both positive and negative facework skills. Research on facework has categorized **positive facework** as providing messages that affirm a person or a person's actions in a difficult situation to protect his or her

Face-threatening act (FTA)—statement of support that a person in need may interpret as a threat to his or her public self-image.

Positive facework—providing messages that affirm a person or a person's actions in a difficult situation to protect his or her respectability and approval.

SKILL BUILDERS ◐ **Clarifying Supportive Intentions**

SKILL	USE	PROCEDURE	EXAMPLE
Openly stating that your goal in the conversation is to help your partner	To let people in need of support know that your motive is simply and solely to help them, to let them know that someone is "on their side," and to provide a context for their understanding of your comments	1. Directly state your intentions, emphasizing your desire to help. 2. Remind your partner about your ongoing relationship. 3. Indicate that helping is your only motive. 4. Phrase your clarification in a way that reflects helpfulness.	After listening to Sonja complain about flunking her geology midterm, her friend Deepak replies: "Sonja, you're a dear friend, and I'd like to help if you want me to. I did well enough on the midterm that I think I could be of help; maybe we could meet once a week to go over the readings and class notes together."

respectability and approval and **negative facework** as providing messages that offer information, opinions, or advice to protect a person's freedom and privacy.

To perform positive facework, provide messages that (1) convey positive feelings about what your partner has said or done in the situation, (2) express your admiration for your partner's courage or effort in the situation, (3) acknowledge how difficult the situation is, and (4) express your belief that your partner has the qualities and skills to endure or succeed. In the examples we have been looking at, David would be performing positive facework if he were to say to Paul (assuming Paul self-discloses that his wife has left him), "I know it's a terrible situation, but you are always amazing at pulling through in times of stress and this is certainly not your fault, so hang in there." In Brianne's conversation with her mom, she could perform positive facework by acknowledging how difficult it must be to be fired, saying how much she admires her mom's determination to stay out of debt and indicating her firm belief that her mother is talented and resourceful enough to quickly find a new job.

To perform negative facework, form messages that (1) ask for permission before making suggestions or giving advice, (2) verbally defer to the opinions and preferences of your partner, (3) use tentative language to hedge and qualify opinions and advice, and (4) offer suggestions indirectly by describing similar situations or hypothetical options. The first, yet most often overlooked, step when performing negative facework is to ask whether your partner wants to hear your opinions or advice before you offer such assistance. For example, you might say, "Would you like to hear my ideas on this?" At times, our partners are not interested in having us solve their problems, but instead want someone with whom to commiserate. If you brazenly offer unsolicited opinions or advice, your attempts to offer support may be seen as FTAs to your partner and may undermine the

Negative facework—providing messages that offer information, opinions, or advice to protect a person's freedom and privacy.

SKILL BUILDERS ○ Positive Facework

SKILL	USE	PROCEDURE	EXAMPLE
Providing messages that affirm a person or a person's actions in a difficult situation	To protect the other person's respectability and approval	1. Convey positive feelings about what your partner has said or done in the situation. 2. Express your admiration for your partner's courage or effort in the situation. 3. Acknowledge how difficult the situation is. 4. Express your belief that your partner has the qualities and skills to endure or succeed.	Anja has learned that Ken has suffered his brother's anger because of an intervention Ken initiated to help his brother. Anja says: "I really respect you for the way you have acted during this. It takes a lot of guts to hang in there like you've been doing, especially when you've been attacked for doing so. I know that you've got the skills to help you get through this."

very support you are trying to provide. Second, even when your partner has indicated that he or she is receptive to hearing your opinions and advice, word your messages carefully. Your opinions and advice should be conveyed in a way that acknowledges that your partner is a competent decision maker who is free to accept or reject the advice. Messages such as, "This is just a suggestion; you are the one who has to make this decision" express deference to your partner's opinions and preferences. Third, your messages should use language that hedges and qualifies your opinions and advice, making it easier for your partner to disagree with what you have said. For instance, you might say, "I'm not sure this will work or that you would want to proceed this way, but if I were in a situation like this, I might think about doing . . ." Finally, your supportive messages will be less threatening if you offer suggestions indirectly by relating what others have done in similar situations or by offering hypothetical suggestions. For instance, you might say, "You know, when my friend Tom lost his job, he . . ." or "Maybe one option to try might be . . ."

▷ Using Other-Centered Messages

In their "theory of conversationally induced reappraisals," Burleson and Goldsmith (1998) suggest that people experience emotional stress when they believe that their current situation is at odds with their life goals. These authors believe that to reduce emotional distress and move forward, people must "make sense" of what has happened to them by reevaluating the situation and determining how

SKILL BUILDERS ◉ Negative Facework

SKILL	USE	PROCEDURE	EXAMPLE
Providing messages that offer information, opinions, or advice	To protect the other person's freedom and privacy	1. Ask for permission before making suggestions or giving advice. 2. Verbally defer to the opinions and preferences of your partner. 3. Use tentative language to hedge and qualify opinions and advice. 4. Offer suggestions indirectly by describing similar situations or hypothetical options.	Judy has learned that Gloriana has been badly hurt by rejection from a best friend. Judy says: "Would you like any advice on this?" Gloria says that she would, and Judy then offers suggestions: "These are just a few suggestions, and I think you should go with what you think is best. Now, I'm not sure that these are the only way to go, but I think . . ." After stating her opinions, Judy says, "Depending on what you want to accomplish, I can see a couple ways that you might proceed . . ."

it relates to their goals with the help of a comforter. The role of the comforter is to use other-centered messages to create a supportive conversational environment in which the emotionally distressed person can talk through his or her situation and arrive at a solution. **Other-centered messages** are messages that focus on the needs of the person in need of support through active listening, expressions of compassion and understanding, and talk encouragement.

For many of us, other-centered messages are difficult to master. We may have been raised in families or come from cultures that have taught us not to dwell on problems or pry into the business of others. Consequently, even when a friend or intimate starts the conversation, our gut reaction may be to change the topic or make light of the situation. In our rush to help another person, we may also inadvertently change the focus to ourselves. For instance, in this chapter's opening conversation, when Stacey switched topics and began discussing her friend Jay, she might have thought she was being helpful by taking Patti's mind off of her troubles, or she might have been trying to relieve her own discomfort. Regardless, her topic change was not supportive. It took the focus away from Patti and didn't allow Patti the "space" to work through her painful situation. Therefore, it is important to focus on the person in need of support using other-centered messages.

When creating other-centered messages follow these guidelines: (1) Ask questions that prompt your partner to elaborate on what happened ("Really, what happened then?"); (2) emphasize your willingness to listen to an extended story ("You've got to tell me *all* about it, and don't worry about how long it takes. I want to hear the whole thing from start to finish"); (3) use vocalized encouragement ("Uh huh . . . ," "Wow . . . ," "I see . . .") and nonverbal encouragement (head nods, leaning forward, etc.) to communicate your continued interest without interrupting your partner; (4) affirm, legitimize, and encourage exploration of the feelings expressed by your partner ("Yes, I can see that you're disappointed. Most people would be disappointed in this situation. Is this as difficult as when . . . ?"); and (5) demonstrate that you understand and connect with what has happened, but avoid changing the focus to yourself ("I know that I felt angry when my sister did that to me. So what happened then?"). For example, to return to Patti and Stacey again, instead of changing the subject or as a follow-up to her initial misstep, Stacey might say, "I'm sorry this has all happened in one day, Patti. Why don't you tell me more about how you're feeling? I'm all ears and want to help you through this." During Patti's elaboration, Stacey should indicate that she's listening by vocally and/or nonverbally signaling her encouragement, and when Patti seems finished with her initial elaboration, she might say, "I see exactly what you're saying and I empathize, believe me. I was in a similar situation when I first applied to colleges—it seemed like I was just getting rejected left and right. But then I got in here, which I never expected. I'm sure you'll be accepted at one of the schools you applied to soon—you'll probably get into the one you least thought would take you, considering your great grades and honors. I think you've just been hit with an awful lot in one day."

Other-centered messages— messages that focus on the needs of the person in need of support through active listening, expressions of compassion and understanding, and talk encouragement.

▷ Framing Information

Framing information—providing support by offering information, observations, and opinions that enable the receiver to better understand or see his or her situation in a different light.

Especially when people's emotions are running high, they are likely to perceive events in very limited ways. **Framing information** is providing support by offering information, observations, and opinions that enable the receiver to better understand or see his or her situation in a different light. Many times by sharing information, observations, and opinions, we provide a different "frame" through which someone can "see" a situation—thus supplying a different (and perhaps less painful) way of interpreting what took place. Consider the following situation:

Travis returns from class and tells his roommate, Abe, "Well, I'm flunking calculus. It doesn't matter how much I study or how many of the online problems I do, I just can't get it. This level of math is above me. I might as well just drop out of school before I flunk out completely. I can ask for a full-time schedule at work and not torture myself with school anymore." In this example, Travis has not only described his situation but has also interpreted it in a limited way to mean that he is not smart enough to handle college-level math courses. Yet there

SKILL BUILDERS ⊙ Other-Centered Messages

SKILL	**USE**	**PROCEDURE**	**EXAMPLE**
Focusing on the needs of the person in need of support through active listening, expressions of compassion and understanding, and talk encouragement	To help partners in their efforts to reevaluate an emotionally distressing event	1. Ask questions that prompt your partner to elaborate on what happened. 2. Emphasize your willingness to listen to an extended story. 3. Use vocalized encouragement and nonverbal encouragement to communicate your continued interest without interrupting your partner as the account unfolds. 4. Affirm, legitimize, and encourage exploration of the feelings expressed by your partner. 5. Demonstrate that you understand and connect with what has happened but avoid changing the focus to you.	Angie begins to express what has happened to her. Allison says: "Really, what happened then?"As Angie utters one more sentence and then stops, Allison says: "Tell me *all* about it, and don't worry about how long it takes. I want to hear the whole thing from start to finish." During Angie's discussion, Allison shows her encouragement: "Go on . . . ,""And then . . . ?," and she nods her head, leans forward, and so on. To affirm, Allison says: "Yes, I can see that you're disappointed. Most people would be disappointed in this situation. Is this as difficult as when . . . ?" Allison then continues: "I know that I felt angry when my sister did that to me. So what happened then?"

could be information that Travis doesn't have or hasn't thought about that would lead to other interpretations. For example, Abe might remind Travis that he has been putting in a lot of hours at work this term, so perhaps his work schedule is interfering with his schoolwork. Or Abe might tell Travis that he heard that the calculus instructor likes to scare the class by grading really hard initially, but that he curves the grades at the end of the semester. In this way, Abe provides Travis with ways of reframing what has happened in light of alternative interpretations. There are interpretations other than inability to understand math that may account for Travis' poor grade.

Framing statements are supportive when they soothe your partner's feelings by helping him or her look at what has happened in ways that are less threatening to his or her self-esteem. To form framing messages: (1) Listen to how your partner is interpreting events; (2) notice information that your partner may be overlooking or overemphasizing in the interpretation; and (3) clearly present relevant, truthful information, observations, and opinions that enable your partner to reframe what has happened. Notice how the framing statements in the next two examples provide comfort by suggesting less painful interpretations for events.

> **Karla:** I'm just furious with Deon. All I said was, "We've got to start saving money for a down payment or we'll never get a house," and he didn't say a word; he just got angry and stomped out of the room.
>
> **Shelby:** Yes, I can see what you mean, and I'd be frustrated too. It's hard to work through issues when someone up and leaves. But perhaps Deon feels guilty

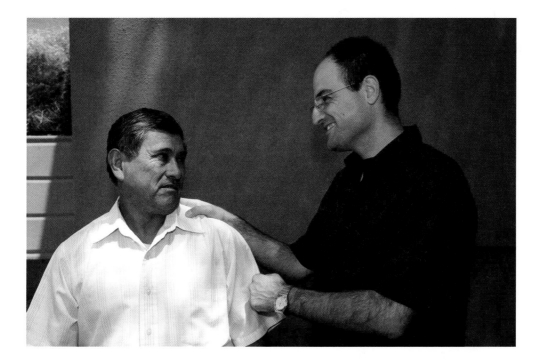

about not being able to save. You know his dad. Deon was raised to believe that the measure of a man is his ability to provide for his family. So, when you said what you did, unintentionally, you may have hurt his male ego.

Micah: I just don't believe Magdalena anymore. We had my annual evaluation last week and she says my work is top-notch, but I haven't had a pay raise in over two years.

Khalif: I can see that you're discouraged. No one in my department has gotten a raise either. But have you forgotten that we're still under that salary freeze? At least Magdalena is continuing to do performance reviews, so you know where you stand and what you should be eligible for when the freeze is over.

▷ Advice-Giving

Advice-giving—presenting relevant suggestions and proposals that a person could use to satisfactorily resolve a situation.

Sometimes we can support others by simply giving them advice. **Advice-giving** is presenting relevant suggestions and proposals that a person could use to satisfactorily resolve a situation. Advice can comfort our partners when we offer it in a well-established supportive climate. Unfortunately, we often rush to provide advice before we really understand the problem or before we have developed a rapport that allows our partner to see the advice as helpful. In general, advice-giving (and to a lesser extent, framing information) should not be expressed until our supportive intentions are understood, facework has been performed, and we have sustained an other-centered focus in an interaction. Only when we believe that our partners have had enough time to understand, explore, and make their own sense out of what has happened to them should we offer advice to help them with unresolved issues.

SKILL BUILDERS ▽ Framing Information

SKILL	USE	PROCEDURE	EXAMPLE
Offering information, observations, and opinions that enable the receiver to better understand or see his or her situation in a different light	To support others when you believe they have made interpretations based on incomplete information or have not considered other viable explanations	1. Listen to how your partner is interpreting events. 2. Notice information that your partner may be overlooking or overemphasizing in the interpretation. 3. Clearly present relevant, truthful information, observations, and opinions that enable your partner to develop a less ego-threatening explanation of what has happened.	**Pam:** "Katie must be really angry with me. Yesterday she walked right by me at the market and didn't even say 'Hi.'" **Paula:** "Are you sure she's angry? She hasn't said anything to me. And you know, when she's mad I usually hear about it. Maybe she just didn't see you."

Research has found that many people offer advice as the first response to hearing another person's problem, but advice may not be the appropriate response to many situations (Goldsmith, 2000). The same research has also reported that a particular piece of advice is more likely to be positively received when it is requested than when it is unsolicited. When our advice is not sought, it is often perceived as butting in.

Keeping this caveat in mind, follow these guidelines for advice-giving: (1) Ask for permission to give advice, (2) word the message as one of many suggestions in a way that the recipient can understand, (3) present any potential risks or costs associated with following the advice, and (4) indicate that you will not be offended should your partner choose to ignore your recommendation or look for another choice. For instance, suppose Shawn is aware that his boss relies on him to help solve major problems that confront the firm for which they both work. Yet on two occasions when positions that pay much more than Shawn's have opened up, his boss has recommended others who have done much less for the firm. When Martino becomes aware that Shawn is very concerned and doesn't know what to do about the situation, he first asks for permission to give advice by saying, "Shawn, we've helped each other a lot over the years. May I offer some advice?" When Shawn nods, Martino goes on, "I know you have many choices—one of which is to get a different job. But if I were in your shoes, before I did anything radical I would make a point of seeing the boss and carefully stating what you've told me about his reliance on you and how you appreciate his confidence in you. Then I'd describe my disappointment at not being promoted and ask him why he hasn't suggested you for these jobs." Keeping in mind the risks and that his advice is not the only

---

SKILL BUILDERS ○ Advice-Giving

SKILL	USE	PROCEDURE	EXAMPLE
Presenting suggestions and proposals a partner could use to satisfactorily resolve a situation	To comfort our partners after a supportive climate has been established and our partners are unable to find their own solutions	1. Ask for permission to give advice. 2. Word the message as one of many suggestions in a way that the recipient can understand. 3. Present any potential risks or costs associated with following the advice. 4. Indicate that you will not be offended should your partner choose to ignore your recommendation or look for another choice.	After a friend has explained a difficult situation she faces, Felicia might say something like the following: "I have a suggestion if you'd like to hear it. As I see it, one way you could handle this is to talk to your co-worker about this issue. This is just one idea—you may come up with a different solution that's just as good. So think this one over, and do what you believe is best for you."

option, Martino goes on to say, "Now this could irk him, but it seems to me that you might need to run that risk under the circumstances." Finally, Martino indicates that he won't be offended if Shawn doesn't take his advice or chooses another option by saying, "Still, it's your decision and there are probably other ways to go about it. But I believe my suggestion is worth thinking about."

○ Supporting in Cyberspace

When we face stress and crises in our lives, typically we turn to friends and family who can offer us support and comfort through face-to-face interpersonal communication. But increasingly people are seeking and finding new avenues of support online. A search for support groups through Yahoo!Groups found over 35,000 online support groups (Bambina, 2007). Via the Internet, you can receive empathic and supportive messages around the clock from strangers, as well as from friends and family.

Online support groups now exist for virtually any type of health, relationship, or financial crisis that a person may be experiencing. Whether you are seeking support for child rearing or hoping to connect with others dealing with elderly parents, struggling with a gambling addiction or weight loss, support groups are available to you twenty-four hours a day, seven days a week. For example, medical support groups that are diagnosis specific allow people sharing the same diagnosis to encourage one another. A study of online cancer support groups found survivors providing each other not only with disease relevant information but also with emotional support and advice. Frequent participants also form companionship networks in which smaller numbers of people chat, tease, express humor, and develop sociable rapport. Online support groups such as these not only provide empathy, encouragement, advice, and useful information but also seem to "provide patients with a safe outlet for expressing feelings with others who have a common experience rather than placing an additional emotional burden on family members and friends" (Bambina, 2007).

Support during periods of bereavement is also widely available online. The personal Facebook or MySpace page of someone who has died can become a public book of condolences, with poems, quotes, and other expressions of support. In the case of public tragedies, such as Hurricane Katrina or the Virginia Tech massacre, hundreds or even thousands of people may leave messages of hope and comfort on Web sites designed just for this purpose. In addition, online obituary services have made guest books available for obituaries published by newspapers. Friends and strangers alike can sign into these guest books to write messages of condolence and remembrance for someone deceased. Since e-mail addresses often accompany the posted messages, mourners can contact message authors for private online conversations that offer sympathy, support, and comfort.

Not only are people receiving peer-based informal cyber support, but in recent years online therapy also has developed as a means for clinicians to provide Web-based services and treatments via e-mail, discussion boards, chat rooms, and videoconferencing. Online therapy is increasingly considered to be an effective alternative for people who otherwise could not afford therapy, for those who are confined to their homes because of disability or lack of transportation, and for those who are isolated in rural areas or where therapists are not physically located (Jerome, DeLeon, James, Folen, Earles, & Gedney, 2000).

Cyber support has several advantages when compared to face-to-face support (Bambina, 2007; Walther & Parks, 2002). First, it creates a social distance that frees some people to disclose problems that they would be uncomfortable talking about in face-to-face settings. Online, people can even remain anonymous and receive comfort from strangers, which allows them to save face.

Second, cyber support provides an increased ability to receive support from a variety of people who have experienced the same situation as the person seeking help. While friends and loved ones can try to put themselves in your place when you are dealing with an uncommon problem, being able to chat with people who are in your exact situation can provide much comfort and emotional support. For those coping with uncommon chronic or terminal diseases, online support groups may be the only way to find others who can truly empathize.

Third, cyber support can be especially important for people who are extremely introverted, shy, or prone to loneliness (Segrin, 1998). For people who have difficulty initiating social activity and making friends, relationships developed online may be the primary means of receiving supportive messages.

Fourth, supportive communication online is often easier to manage. As comforters, we can carefully choose our words and craft our messages so that they comply with the guidelines for effective supporting. And, unlike in our face-to-face interactions, we can choose when to enter and exit supportive interactions in cyberspace.

Fifth, online supportive interactions with strangers can allow us to cross age, status, and education boundaries. Unlike in face-to-face interactions, cyberspace communication can empower a younger person to give advice to someone older or a less educated individual to provide information to more educated people. In other words, support online often erases barriers of power and status by focusing less on who is giving the support and more on the content of the supportive communication itself.

Finally, online support with either strangers or friends frees us from the confines of physical place, time, and appearance. We can receive online therapy or participate in an online forum at any time of the day or night when other professionals or friends would not be available, and these sources of support are available to the physically immobile. No travel is involved, and you need not be concerned with your physical appearance.

INTER-ACT WITH TECHNOLOGY

Read at least fifteen postings of any online support group. Identify examples of empathic responsiveness, perspective taking, sympathetic responsiveness, clarifying supportive intentions, buffering face threats, other-centered messages, framing information, and advice-giving. What conclusions can you draw about giving and receiving supportive messages online?

Gender and Cultural Similarities and Differences in Supporting

It is popular to believe that men and women differ in the value they place upon emotional support, with the common assumption that women expect, need, and provide more comfort than men do. One view holds that men and women differ intrinsically in the amount of support they need, while another view holds that their differences are the result of how they have been socialized. Yet Burleson (2003) reports on a growing body of research indicating that both men and women of various ages place a high value on emotional support from their partners in a variety of relationships (family relationships, same-sex friendships, opposite-sex friendships, and romantic relationships). Studies also find that men and women have similar ideas about what messages are more or less effective at reducing emotional distress. Both men and women find messages that encourage them to explore and elaborate on their feelings to provide the most support. The one major gender difference is that, while both men and women value other-centered support messages, research has found that men are less likely to use other-centered messages when providing support. According to

A QUESTION OF ETHICS ▽ What Would You Do?

Kendra and Emma are roommates and have been best friends since grade school. For the past three years, Kendra had been dating Emma's older brother Dominic. Dominic finished college recently and moved to Chicago, about an hour away from where Kendra and Emma go to school. This past weekend, Dominic invited Kendra to visit him, and she went. She even told Emma that she was sure he was going to ask her to marry him. Emma gently tried to discourage her from expecting that, but Kendra remained convinced that this was the purpose for the invitation.

Far from proposing, Dominic spent the weekend watching TV and picking fights with Kendra. By the end of the weekend, Kendra was miserable, hurt, and worried about their relationship, so to test him she tossed out, "Well, it just seems like you aren't very glad to see me, so maybe we should just forget it and start seeing other people." She was dumbfounded when Dominic replied, "Well, if that's what you want, OK." Then, he turned his attention back to the football game on TV. In shock, Kendra quickly gathered her things and left.

By the time she got back to the apartment she shared with Emma, she was a mess. Crying and screaming, she called Dominic every name she could think of as she walked in the front door. When Emma raced into the room, Kendra shouted, "I can't believe you let me go up there and be so humiliated! What kind of a friend are you? You're just like your brother—mean."

Shocked by Kendra's outburst, Emma asked, "Kendra, what are you talking about? What happened? Is Dominic OK?"

"Oh sure, you worry about Dominic, but what about me? Sure, take your brother's side. I don't know

what else I should have expected from you. You were probably in on it. It's just not fair."

"Wait a minute, Kendra, in on what? What happened?"

"Dominic broke up with me."

"He did? I can't believe it."

"Well . . . no, but, yeah, well kind of . . ."

"Kendra, you're not making any sense. Did Dominic break up with you or not? Tell me. What happened?"

"Well, he made it pretty clear that he didn't really want to be with me anymore."

"Kendra, did he or did he not break up with you?"

"Well, he certainly didn't propose marriage."

"Is that what this is about? Kendra, what made you think he was ready to propose? He just finished school, he has a ton of college debt, and he's still looking for a job. He can't help it if you got it in your head that he was going to propose. But I can't believe that he broke up with you. So what really happened?"

"Emma, I don't want to talk about it, especially not with you. Now would you please just leave me alone? Your family has done enough damage to me today."

With that Kendra stomped into her bedroom and slammed and locked the door.

1. What ethical guidelines were violated in this encounter?
2. Is it ethical for Kendra to expect Emma to support her if this means disowning her brother?
3. How can Emma support Kendra and not violate the ethical call to speak the truth?

Kunkel and Burleson (1999), this suggests that "we need more efforts directed at enhancing men's abilities in the comforting realm—both in school and in the home" (p. 334).

Research has also been directed toward understanding cultural differences in supportive situations. While studies have found some differences, Burleson (2003) reports that for members of all social groups, solace strategies—especially other-centered messages—are the most sensitive and comforting ways to provide emotional support.

⊙ Summary

Supporting others begins with being able to empathize. Empathizing is the cognitive process of identifying with or vicariously experiencing the feelings, thoughts, or attitudes of others and is shown through empathic responsiveness, perspective taking, and sympathetic responsiveness. Empathizing requires taking the time to empathize, observing and reading the nonverbal messages sent by others by asking questions and paraphrasing, and employing one of the three types of empathy.

Supporting is helping people feel better about themselves and their behaviors. A supporting response is a statement whose goal is to show approval, encourage, soothe, console, cheer up, or bolster confidence. We can support people's positive feelings or negative feelings. According to Burleson, effective supporting messages (1) clearly state that the speaker's aim is to help the other; (2) express acceptance, love, and affection for the other; (3) demonstrate care, concern, and interest in the other's situation; (4) indicate that the speaker is available to listen and support the other; (5) state that the speaker is an ally; (6) acknowledge the other's feelings and situation as well as express sincere sympathy; (7) assure the other that feelings of distress are legitimate; and (8) encourage the other to elaborate on the story. Ineffective supporting messages, on the other hand, (1) condemn and criticize the other's feelings and behaviors; (2) imply that the other's feelings are not warranted; (3) tell the other how to feel or advise the other to ignore justifiable feelings about the situation; (4) take attention away from the other and focus on the self; and (5) are the result of an intrusion.

Although we can attempt to comfort a person with a single supporting response, complete support more often involves a supportive interaction, a conversation or ongoing interaction in which support is provided. Supportive interactions often go through four phases: support activation, support provision, target reaction, and helper responses.

Research has identified five supportive message skills: clarifying supportive intentions, buffering face threats with positive and negative facework, using other-centered messages, framing information, and advice-giving.

Online therapy, support groups, and social networking sites may be effective vehicles for achieving and providing support. The desire to be comforted appears to be universal, with little substantial differences reported between men and women or across cultures.

○ Inter-Action Dialogue: Empathizing and Supporting

Providing emotional support to someone requires empathizing, clarifying supportive intentions, positive and negative facework, use of other-centered messages, framing information, and advice-giving. The following conversation between James and Rob illustrates these skills.

Rob and James meet after class.

Conversation

Rob: Hey man, what's up? You look rough.

James: Well, I'm not feeling very good. But I'll get by.

Rob: Well, tell me what's bothering you—maybe I can help. I've got the time.

James: Come on—you've got better things to do than to listen to my sad story.

Rob: *(sitting down and leaning toward James)* Hey, I know you can take care of it yourself, but I've got the time. So humor me, spill it. What's got you so down?

James: It's my old man.

Rob: Uh huh.

James: You know I hardly ever see him, what with him living out west and all.

Rob: That's hard.

James: *(lowering his voice and dropping his head)* And, you know, I thought that now that my mom remarried and has a whole bunch of stepkids and grandkids to take care of that maybe I could go out to California to college and, you know, live with my dad.

Rob: Yeah, that's understandable. So, did you call him? What did he say?

James: Oh, I called him and he said it was fine. Then he said we "could share expenses." Share expenses? I can't even afford the bus ticket out there. And I was hoping he'd pay for the college.

Rob: Ouch.

James: Rob, my dad's always had lots of money. Been living the good life. At least that's what he's been telling me all these years. He never sent the support money, but that's because he said he was "building his business." My mom's always been putting him down, but I believed him. Now I don't know what to think. What a fool I was.

Rob: Hey, you're no fool. Why wouldn't you believe him? But it sounds like he's been lying to you, and now you're really disillusioned. Is that it?

James: Yeah, I guess. You know, I always thought that when I was a man the two of us could, you know, get together. I love my mama. She's my hero. She raised me. But I always was proud of my dad with his business and all, and I just wanted to spend time with him. Get to know him.

Rob: I can relate. My dad died when I was young, but I'd sure like to have known him better. So have you told your mom about any of this?

James: No.

Rob: What do you think she'd say?

James: Oh, she'd probably just hug me and tell me to let it be.

Rob: Can you do that?

James: Maybe.

Rob: Do you want my advice?

James: Sure, why not.

Rob: Well, it's your decision, and I'm sure that there are other ways to handle it, but my advice is, do what your mom says—let it go. If he wants to see you, let him call you. You've got a great family here.

James: Maybe you're right. I'm so tired of being let down. And my stepdad is a good guy. He's been taking me to the gym and we play a little ball in the driveway. He's not my dad, but even with all the other kids around, at least he makes time to be with me. I guess getting close to my dad is just not meant to happen. And I guess I don't really need him. If he can't even help with college then why would I want to leave here? I mean, I have great friends . . . right?

Rob: Right.

◉ Chapter Resources

Communication Improvement Plan: Empathizing and Supporting ◉ Find more on the web @ www.oup.com/us/interact12

Would you like to improve your use of the following skills discussed in this chapter?

- Empathizing
- Clarifying supportive intentions
- Positive and negative facework
- Other-centered messages
- Framing information
- Advice-giving

Pick a skill, and write a communication improvement plan. You can find a communication improvement plan worksheet on our website at www.oup.com/us/interact12.

Key Words ◉

Empathizing, *p. 235*

Empathic responsiveness, *p. 236*

Perspective taking, *p. 236*

Sympathetic responsiveness, *p. 236*

Supporting, *p. 239*

Supporting response, *p. 239*

Supporting interaction, *p. 244*

Clarifying supportive intentions, *p. 246*

Face-threatening act (FTA), *p. 248*

Positive facework, *p. 248*

Negative facework, *p. 249*

Other-centered messages, *p. 251*

Framing information, *p. 252*

Advice-giving, *p. 254*

Skill Practice ◉ Find more on the web @ www.oup.com/us/interact12

Skill Practice exercises challenge you to master the material you have read in this chapter. For additional Skill Practice activities, visit our website at www.oup.com/us/interact12.

Buffering Face Threats

Choose one of the following situations, and write a multiturn script in which you use the five skills of supportive messages to support the speaker. Identify which message skills are present in each of your turns.

1. Your best friend walks into the restaurant, flops down in the booth, and sighs, "My manager is trying to fire me or get me to quit. He told me that my error rate was higher than average, so he wants me to drive all the way downtown to headquarters and take another ten hours of training on my own time."

2. As you turn the corner at work, you spy your co-worker, Janet, leaning against the wall, silently sobbing into her hand.

3. Your sister (or brother) storms in the front door, throws her (or his) backpack on the floor, and stomps upstairs. You slowly follow.

Inter-Act with Media ⊙ Find more on the web @ www.oup.com/us/interact12

Television

30 Days, season 3 (2008). Morgan Spurlock (creator/executive producer).

Brief Summary: Morgan Spurlock's reality show places Spurlock or a voluntary participant in a particular experience for thirty days—situations representing differing perspectives or opinions from their own. Spurlock begins the third season as a coal mine apprentice and learns about the dangers involved in the job. Then, after witnessing a fellow player become paralyzed during a game, retired NFL player Ray Crockett lives in a wheelchair for thirty days, attending rehabilitation and support groups for paraplegics. In another episode, "Kati," a married mother of two who is staunchly opposed to same-sex couples raising children, co-habitates with partners Dennis and Thomas Patrick and their four adopted sons. Finally, gun control advocate Pia Lalli stays with father Ken Ekermeyer and son Zach, whose lives revolve around recreational gun use. Spurlock and Crockett experienced empathy for others, Spurlock with the miners stricken with black lung and Crockett with the paraplegics he befriended. Conversely, Kati and Lalli's perspective-taking and empathic response was challenged by situations diametrically opposing their own intrinsic beliefs.

IPC Concepts: Empathizing, empathic responsiveness, perspective taking, sympathetic responsiveness, improving ability to empathize.

Cinema

No Reservations (2007). Scott Hicks (director). Catherine Zeta-Jones, Abigail Breslin, Aaron Eckhart.

Brief Summary: Master chef Kate (Zeta-Jones) runs her life and her kitchen with controlling and perfectionist sharpness. When her sister unexpectedly dies, leaving Kate her nine-year-old niece, Zoe (Breslin), Kate's impersonal nature results in an inability to provide emotional support to the child; she doesn't even share her own pain of losing her sister. Kate initially resorts to what she knows best: cooking Zoe gourmet, but un-child-friendly, meals. Instead of delving into Zoe's feelings and sharing her own, Kate escapes to the restaurant. When she later brings Zoe to work, Zoe warms up to lighthearted Nick (Eckhart), the new chef Kate believes was hired to replace her. Kate and Nick forge a professional and personal relationship, softening Kate's hard demeanor and allowing her to have fun with her niece. Zoe enjoys Kate, but when she suddenly disappears to her mother's gravesite, Kate sees that Zoe is still raw from her mother's death. Zoe admits fear that she will forget her mother. Kate finally provides supportive words, reassuring Zoe that she will not forget her mother and that they can visit the gravesite whenever Zoe wishes. Had Kate provided more supportive interaction immediately upon Zoe's arrival, the two could have comforted each other and possibly gained a more rapid emotional attachment.

IPC Concepts: Supporting responses, characteristics of effective and ineffective emotional support messages, supportive interaction phases, face threats, other-centered messages.

What's on the Web

Find links and additional material, including self-quizzes, on the companion website at www .oup.com/us/interact12.

Managing Personal Information

Disclosure and Privacy

After you have read this chapter, you should be able to answer these questions

▶ What is the disclosure-privacy dialectic?

▶ What is communication privacy management (CPM) theory?

▶ What are the five criteria we use to develop disclosure-privacy rules?

▶ How do disclosure and privacy affect relationships?

▶ How can you own your feelings and opinions?

▶ When and how should you display and describe feelings?

▶ Why and how can you manage privacy?

▶ What is personal feedback?

▶ How can you provide constructive criticism and praise?

▶ Why and how can you ask for feedback?

"Hector, I'm so upset! Janelle just told me how happy she is that you and I might be moving in together this summer. I thought we agreed not to tell anyone until I get a chance to tell my parents. Did you tell Tony and then Tony told Janelle?"

"I'm sorry, Rita. I didn't mean to say anything to Tony, but he kept asking me about being the fourth guy in their apartment, and I didn't want to leave him stranded. I told him that you and I might get a place, but he swore not to tell anybody."

"You know that if you tell Tony anything, he's going to tell Janelle. He tells her everything. And she couldn't keep a secret if her life depended on it."

"I really trusted Tony to keep that information private. I feel so bad."

"Private? Once you tell one person our private information, it isn't private. You and I had an agreement on this. Not only does everyone know our private plans now, but I'd better see my parents tonight before my mom hears it from Janelle's mom at work tomorrow."

When it comes to sharing personal information, we are constantly in a balancing act between disclosure and privacy. Sometimes you are the only one who knows your private information, and sometimes your private information is held by others whom you trust to maintain your confidentiality. When you disclose private information, the person you share it with then has to decide whether to keep the information private or reveal it to others. As we saw with Hector and Rita, there can be misunderstandings or violated expectations about disclosure and privacy. The communication of personal information is a complex matter affected by many factors, and it can impact our relationships.

In this chapter we begin by discussing the dialectic of disclosure and privacy. Then we turn to the theory of communication privacy management (CPM) and discuss what criteria affect our disclosure and privacy rules. Next, we explain how disclosure and privacy affect relationships and the effects of technology on privacy boundaries. After that, we present skills for self-disclosure and privacy management. Finally, we focus on giving personal feedback to others and how to ask for feedback about ourselves.

❍ The Disclosure-Privacy Dialectic

You will recall from Chapter 3 that in any relationship, both people may experience opposite pulls, or dialectics. One of these dialectics is the tension between openness and closedness. This is also called the **disclosure-privacy dialectic**, the tension between sharing personal information and keeping personal information confidential. Let's look closer at the two parts of the dialectic.

Disclosure is revealing confidential or secret information. While it includes **self-disclosure**, sharing your own biographical data, personal ideas, and feelings, it is a larger concept because it includes disclosing confidential information about others as well (Petronio, 2002). For example, suppose Jim tells Benjamin that he was a bed-wetter until he was in the sixth grade and has never told anyone else about it for fear of being teased. Jim has engaged in self-disclosure to Benjamin because he has revealed information about himself. If several months later Benjamin is in a conversation in which people are sharing their childhood secrets and Benjamin comments that Jim used to be a bed-wetter, Benjamin is engaged in disclosure, not self-disclosure, because he is disclosing Jim's private information, not his own.

Privacy is the opposite of disclosure. It is withholding confidential or secret information to enhance autonomy and/or minimize vulnerability (Margulis, 1977, p. 10). The concept of privacy rests on the assumption that people own their personal information and have the right to control it by determining whether that information may be communicated to others (Petronio, 2002). Like Jim, you have personal information that you can choose to reveal or conceal from others. Over time and as your relationship with another person devel-

Disclosure-privacy dialectic— tension between sharing personal information and keeping personal information confidential; also called the openness and closedness dialectic.

Disclosure—revealing confidential or secret information.

Self-disclosure—sharing your own biographical data, personal ideas, and feelings.

Privacy—withholding confidential or secret information to enhance autonomy and/or minimize vulnerability.

ops, you and your partner will share sensitive information with each other. Then, either of you may choose to reveal that sensitive information to others outside of the relationship or maintain it within the privacy of your relationship. If your partner has your permission to share a piece of your personal information with others, or if you no longer care that others know a piece of your personal information, then it is unlikely to affect your relationship if your partner discloses it to others. However, if you have not given your partner permission to disclose that information and/or if you still expect that information to be held privately within your relationship, then if your partner discloses it to others, the disclosure is likely to damage trust and undermine your relationship. Therefore, when Jim hears that Benjamin has "outed" him as a former bed-wetter, he may feel embarrassed, hurt, and violated because Benjamin has breached his privacy.

Because the disclosure-privacy dialectic occurs within an individual and within a relationship, tensions may occur because each person has different self-disclosure and privacy needs as well as different expectations of what should be held privately within the relationship or disclosed outside of the relationship. To further complicate things, these needs and expectations often vary with time. If Jim and Benjamin are both sixteen when Jim self-discloses his bed-wetting history, Jim may see this as a very risky disclosure and be much more sensitive should Benjamin breach his privacy. But he may be less sensitive about Benjamin's disclosure years later when they are both thirty-five because Jim may no longer view this disclosure as threatening. In short, the revealing or withholding of personal information is a very complex matter, so much so

When you share private information you run the risk of your partner sharing it with others. Have you ever had someone disclose information you had shared but thought would be held in private? How did you handle this breach of confidentiality? What was the long-term effect on your relationship?

that a number of theories have been developed to help us better understand it. We will explore those theories in the next three sections so that you can make more informed choices about when it is appropriate to disclose information and when it is appropriate to retain privacy.

◉ Communication Privacy Management Theory

Communication privacy management (CPM) theory is a theory that provides a framework for understanding the decision-making processes people use to manage disclosure and privacy. The theory was developed by Sandra Petronio, who

Communication privacy management (CPM) theory—theory that provides a framework for understanding the decision-making processes people use to manage disclosure and privacy.

is featured in this chapter's "Spotlight on Scholars" box, and it asserts that each of us has developed rules about privacy and disclosure to guide our behaviors as we make choices to disclose or conceal personal information about ourselves and about others. Over time, we come to rely on the rules that we have developed in previous situations and relationships to guide our choices in new situations and relationships. These rules are designed to help us maximize the benefits of disclosure while minimizing risks. Benefits of disclosure may include self-expression, relationship development, and social control. Risks include loss of face, lowering of status, and loss of control (Petronio, 2002). To control the risks, we usually try to place boundaries around the information we share. In terms of self-disclosure, we develop rules as to what we normally do or do not share. In terms of relationships, we negotiate rules with our partners about how the private information we have shared within the relationship will or will not be disclosed to others outside of the relationship, or we simply assume that our partners understand what rules apply (Petronio, 2002).

LEARN ABOUT YOURSELF ◐ Personal Disclosure

Take this short survey to learn something about yourself. You should be thinking of a specific partner when completing this survey. Answer the questions based on your first response. There are no right or wrong answers. Just be honest in reporting your true behaviors and feelings in your relationship with the partner you've chosen. For each question, select one of the following numbers that best describes your own behavior or your views about your partner's behavior.

1 = Strongly Agree
2 = Agree Somewhat
3 = Neutral
4 = Disagree Somewhat
5 = Strongly Disagree

_____ 1. I often talk about my feelings.
_____ 2. I often reveal undesirable things about myself.
_____ 3. I like to show my innermost self.
_____ 4. I do not hesitate to disclose personal things about myself.
_____ 5. I feel safe sharing any personal information.
_____ 6. My partner shares personal information with me.
_____ 7. My partner reveals personal feelings to me.
_____ 8. I am completely sincere in revealing my own feelings.
_____ 9. My partner expresses personal beliefs and opinions.
_____ 10. I can be honest about anything.

This is a test of your personal disclosure in a relationship.

Scoring the Survey: Add all of your scores for the ten items. Your total score will range from 10 to 50. The lower (closer to 10) your score, the more you and your relational partner engage in personal disclosure. The higher (closer to 50) your score, the less you and your relational partner engage in personal disclosure.

Adapted from: Derlega, V. J., Metts, S., Petronio, S. & Margulis, S. T. (1993). *Self-Disclosure*. Newbury Park, CA: Sage.

Sandra Petronio
Professor of Communication and Bioethics,
Indiana University–Purdue University, Indianapolis, on
Disclosure

Petronio's interest in disclosure began with her dissertation at the University of Michigan. As she investigated the large volume of research literature on "self-disclosure" she found that for every one finding, two or three contradictory findings appeared. The frustration she felt as a result led her to develop a theoretical framework to better understand the dynamics of disclosure. As she endeavored to make sense of the already-published literature concerning disclosure and to build a comprehensive understanding, it became clear that the concept of disclosure was more complex than it appeared. In fact, one of her more significant breakthroughs came when she determined that there was a discernible difference between the content of disclosure and the process of disclosure. In other words, what people disclosed was very different from how people disclosed personal information. Petronio realized that this difference was key to developing a theory that could gave depth and breadth to the notion of disclosure and address some of the existing problems. Out of this awareness, she began to craft the theory of communication privacy management (CPM).

CPM is an evidenced-based theory that describes how people make decisions about disclosing (giving access) or protecting (denying access) information they believe is private. Five principles define how people make these decisions and what happens when they either reveal or conceal information.

The first principle was the most difficult, and most important, for Petronio to ascertain. This principle says that *private information is defined as something people believe they own and therefore believe they have the right to control.*

This first principle led to a question: How do people exercise that control? To envision this next step, the second principle, it was helpful for Petronio to think about private information housed within a boundary. Control reflects decisions people make to both keep information within a privacy boundary and give access to that information. In the second principle, Petronio argues that this *control is accomplished through the use of privacy rules.* In other words, disclosing and, alternatively, keeping the privacy boundary closed are accomplished through rules that people use to manage the ebb and flow of information to others. For example, if you say, "Don't tell anyone, but . . . " you have stated a privacy rule for how you want to control third-party disclosure about your private information.

The third principle made a significant contribution to the way we now understand disclosure, in particular, and privacy overall. Petronio argues that *once a decision is made to disclose private information, the recipient of that information becomes a co-owner or shareholder of the information.* This principle allows us to see that people do more than just "self-disclose," as much of what people manage includes information that others give to them for safe keeping. This means that not only do people manage their own personal privacy boundaries, but they also co-manage privacy boundaries with other people. Therefore, we have both personal privacy boundaries, where our information resides, and collective boundaries, where we work with others to regulate the flow of co-owned information.

The fourth principle argues that to have smooth, synchronized management of co-owned privacy boundaries, where all of the co-owners have agreed about third-party access, we need to *coordinate privacy rules for permeability (how much can be told), rules for linkage (who else can know), and rules for ownership (how much control any one co-owner can have to make decisions about third-party disclosures or access).*

The fifth principle contends that because we do not live in a perfect world, *there are times when we do not have smooth synchronized management of co-owned privacy boundaries, and therefore we are likely to encounter boundary turbulence, or privacy violations, intrusions, and dilemmas.*

From the late 1970s to the present, Petronio has continuously worked to grow CPM theory. She believes that to be viable, theories must continue to expand and develop. Besides Petronio herself, others have widely applied CPM theory and extended its applicability to health issues, group dynamics, e-commerce, governmental issues, new technologies, mental health, family issues, and interpersonal relationships.

▷ Criteria for Disclosure and Privacy Rules in CPM Theory

Why do people differ in the rules that they use to manage privacy and disclosure? Petronio suggests that we use five criteria as we are developing our own rules about disclosure and privacy: culture, gender, motivation, context, and risk-benefit analysis.

The Disclosure-Privacy Dialectic

Think about a recent encounter you had in which you consciously decided to disclose information that you would normally keep private. What rule that you had previously followed did you violate to make this decision? What was the result of this disclosure? Did the benefits you received by making the disclosure outweigh the risks you took? In retrospect, if you had to do it over again, would you make the same decision about disclosure? Explain. Now consider a time when you decided to maintain your privacy by not disclosing something to your partner. What rule did you use to make this decision? What was the result of maintaining your privacy? What risks did you take by not disclosing, and what benefits did you receive? In retrospect, if you had to do it over again would you make the same choice? Explain.

1. Culture. First, our rules about privacy and disclosure are influenced by how our culture values privacy. In some cultures, a person's privacy is highly respected, and people who choose to disclose information that is generally regarded as confidential violate the cultural norms. Members of these cultures are less likely to disclose personal information to anyone but close intimates. As you might expect, individualistic cultures value privacy more than collectivist cultures do. So, British and German people, for instance, are less inclined to disclose and more likely to be protective of their privacy. While the United States is an individualistic culture where privacy is also valued, it is also less formal than other individualistic cultures (Samovar & Porter, 2001, p. 82). As a result, Americans tend to disclose more about themselves than people from many other individualistic cultures do, especially European cultures. For example, Sharon, who is English, was raised to place a high value on privacy. She came to the United States to attend college and was assigned Maria as a dorm mate. Marie, who was raised in the tell-all informal pop culture of the United States, tends to make Sharon very uncomfortable as she breezily chats about her dysfunctional family, her romantic relationships, and her religious beliefs. The rules that Sharon uses to manage privacy are very different from those guiding Maria's behavior. So, Sharon's discomfort with Maria's level of disclosure may in part be because of differences in cultural background.

2. Gender. Second, men or women who strongly identify themselves as masculine or feminine are likely to use rules for disclosure and privacy that correspond to sex role stereotypes (Snell, Belk, & Hawkins, 1986). The male stereotype throughout much of the world encompasses the characteristics "strong and silent" and competitive. Consequently, men may keep their feelings to themselves and avoid disclosing private information that might be used against them in a competitive situation. For example, if Horst sees himself as very masculine or macho, he probably won't disclose that as a child he studied ballet, fearing that if he told even his best friend this secret, he would be ridiculed. The female stereotype throughout much of the world, meanwhile, is that women are nurturing and sensitive. Therefore, women who identify with these characteristics are more likely to disclose personal information. For example, if Ashley considers herself to be very feminine, she may easily disclose her feelings or reveal information about someone else as a way of strengthening her self-image and relationships with others. People whose identities are not as strongly based on gender roles are less likely to base their disclosure-privacy rules on gender stereotypes.

3. Motivation. Third, people differ in how eager they are to disclose to someone. You may be motivated to disclose because at a particular moment you value companionship rather than solitude or because you are attracted to or are fond of a particular person (Petronio, 2002). For instance, Jacquie, who is a new student attending freshman orientation, may be more likely to disclose personal information to new acquaintances in an effort to establish a friendship quickly, whereas Ian, who is a stressed-out pre-law student, is more likely to maintain privacy to keep people at arm's length while he finishes his thesis. Likewise, Mick, who is attracted to Dania, is more likely to disclose personal information to Dania than to Tasha, whom he is not as interested in romantically. Not only are you more likely to disclose depending on these factors, but these factors are also likely to influence the rules you use when making decisions about disclosing private information about others. For instance, many people have no qualms about sharing embarrassing private information they have learned about someone they don't like, but most of us are motivated to maintain the confidentiality of our loved ones.

4. Context. Fourth, privacy and disclosure rules, like other communication rules, are influenced by the circumstances in which people find themselves. For example, you may disclose private information to a therapist or counselor to help you cope with a difficult situation. Likewise, in times of crisis, you may need to adjust your need for privacy and open up to people to whom you would not normally disclose. Just as supportive communication improves one's mental and physical health, research also shows that disclosure during times of stress contributes to

What type of disclosures might you share at a large family gathering like this one? What disclosures would be inappropriate? How do your family's cultural norms about disclosure affect the answers you gave?

physical and mental health (Pennebaker, 1995; Tardy, 2000). Moreover, circumstances related to a relationship may influence you to disregard the privacy needs of another person, such as if Sal tells Giovanni that he's extremely depressed and, to help a potentially dangerous situation, Giovanni tells one or two of Sal's close friends about this disclosure.

5. Risk-benefit analysis. Finally, one of the most important criteria that people use to make decisions about disclosure and privacy is risk-benefit analysis. In risk-benefit analysis, we weigh what advantages we might gain by disclosing or maintaining private information against the dangers of disclosing or maintaining private information. Common benefits of disclosing information include building a relationship, coping with stress, and emotional or psychological catharsis. Benefits of maintaining privacy include control and independence. Common risks of disclosing information include loss of control, vulnerability, and embarrassment. Risks of maintaining privacy include social isolation and being misunderstood by others. As an example entailing a variety of benefits and risks of disclosing information and maintaining privacy, consider the following: Joe gets in an accident at school, is arrested for DUI, is given a severe warning with community service, and not only completes his community service but also becomes a full-time volunteer. Should Joe confide in his sister, a strong opponent of drunk driving, about what happened? On the one hand, if Joe does disclose, he risks losing his sister's respect for being irresponsible and endangering others while driving drunk. On the other hand, he may benefit by demonstrating to his sister that he has not only paid his dues but has also gone above and beyond to help other people through volunteering, in addition to undergoing an emotional catharsis. Meanwhile, if Joe maintains his privacy, he benefits by keeping control of the situation and saving face about the DUI. But the risk is that he may feel dishonest with and isolated from his own sister.

◉ Effects of Disclosure and Privacy on Relationships

Although there are many ways that disclosure and privacy decisions effect relationships, the three most important are the ways these decisions affect intimacy, expectations for reciprocity, and information co-ownership.

▷ Effects of Disclosure and Privacy on Intimacy

The effects that disclosure and privacy have on intimacy in interpersonal relationships (relationships with friends, family, or romantic partners) are not straightforward. You might think that as relationships develop, people move in a clear-cut way toward greater and deeper disclosure. This was the position of early researchers Irwin Altman and Dolman Taylor (1973) and their social penetration theory. **Social penetration theory** was a theory holding that over time relationships move from lesser to greater intimacy based on the increasing number of

Social penetration theory—theory holding that over time relationships move from lesser to greater intimacy based on the increasing number of topics that relational partners discuss and the degree of personal information disclosed on those topics.

topics that relational partners discuss and the degree of personal information disclosed on those topics. You may think, as Altman and Taylor initially did, that over time the pattern for disclosure would be to consistently move from shallow disclosures to deeper, more personal ones. But their further research has shown that, because of the dialectical tensions in relationships, levels of disclosure cycle between deep disclosure and attempts to reestablish privacy boundaries (Altman, 1993). This can create problems if one partner craves greater intimacy, while at the same time the other partner needs to reestablish privacy.

Though Altman and Taylor link disclosure to increased intimacy in relationships, some research shows that disclosure of personal information may not in fact always lead to greater intimacy because not all disclosure is necessarily aimed at deepening the relationship. For example, people may disclose information as a cathartic release to relieve guilt or stress, such as when one partner in a romantic relationship discloses an infidelity or a close friend reveals a dark secret from the past. Once we share such private information, we may feel a release from stress or guilt, but depending on the nature of that private information, it may or may not serve to deepen the level of intimacy in the relationship. In fact, it may serve to damage or even end the relationship.

Focusing on privacy rather than disclosure, other research shows that by opting for privacy, we may preserve the intimacy and positive feelings in a relationship (Hendrick, 1981) and avoid conflict with our relational partners (Roloff & Ifert, 2000). Individuals may choose privacy over disclosure for many legitimate reasons, including protecting the other person's feelings, avoiding unnecessary conflict, being sensitive to the face needs of the other person, and protecting the relationship. For example, imagine that Will knows that his partner Celeste gets extremely anxious about their financial security. In the past, Celeste's worrying has caused her to lose sleep over minor unpaid bills. So when Will hears a rumor that there is a slight possibility that he could lose his job through downsizing, he may decide not to disclose this information to Celeste. Will's decision to keep this information private is based on his desire to protect Celeste from what may turn out to be unnecessary anxiety. In a few weeks, if Will learns that his job is secure, his decision to maintain privacy will have saved Celeste from worrying and had a positive effect on the relationship. If he finds out that he is going to be laid off, he will have to decide when and how to disclose the bad news to Celeste. People with life-threatening illnesses may also choose to maintain privacy rather than disclose the information for fear that disclosing this information may frighten a relational partner into withdrawal. Similarly, people whose religious, social, political, or sexual orientations conflict with the value systems of others may choose to keep their orientations private (Petronio, 2002). For example, for many gay, lesbian, and bisexual people, the decision to "come out" to their parents can be extremely risky and may lead to estrangement.

Sometimes in newly developing relationships, people may avoid disclosing certain topics for the express purpose of slowing down the growth of intimacy in the relationship. If a casual dating relationship seems to be moving too quickly toward greater emotional attachment, the relational partners may, for a certain period of time, avoid communicating on topics such as the state of the relationship, expectations of each other in the relationship, prior romantic relationships, and extra-relationship activity (Knobloch & Carpenter-Theune, 2004). For instance, if Carrie feels that her new relationship with Sam is getting too serious too fast, she may consciously chose to limit what she allows them to talk about and make sure that her time together with Sam is activity driven, not conversation driven.

▷ Effects of Disclosure and Privacy on Reciprocity

Reciprocity—mutual exchange of information.

The degree of reciprocity in a relationship is also affected by disclosure and privacy. **Reciprocity** is the mutual exchange of information, whether one partner's level of disclosure is matched by a similar level of disclosure by one's partner. Earlier scholars assumed that disclosure by one person in a relationship would typically be reciprocated by a disclosure by the other (Jourard, 1971). More recent research (Dindia, 1988, 2000), however, has questioned this assumption. Instead of occurring in a turn-by-turn sequence, it appears that there can be long time lags between the disclosure of one partner and the reciprocating disclosure of the other partner. One person may not be ready to disclose his or her feelings, even though the relational partner has revealed private information that seems to call for a similar disclosure from the other partner. For example, after a fourth date, Kristoff may blurt out, "Nancy, I love you and I know that I'm going to marry you!" However, Nancy, who thinks she may love Kristoff but wants to make sure that she genuinely loves him and is not just taken with the prospect of being in love, may not voice her feelings for many more months. Nevertheless, the two of them continue to see each other, building common history and sharing other personal information, even though Nancy does not reciprocate to the same degree when Kristoff expresses his love.

▷ Effects of Disclosure and Privacy on Information Co-ownership

Information co-ownership—mutual protection of private information.

A third way that decisions about disclosure and privacy effect relationships has to do with information co-ownership. **Information co-ownership** is the mutual protection of private information, how partners treat the private information that each has shared with the other. When you disclose secret information to your partner, you expect that your partner will respect your privacy and will not disclose your private information to others. Similarly, over the course of your relationship, you and your partner may share private experiences and make decisions that would typically be considered private, and each of you will expect the other to protect these types of information. Therefore, whether we actually hold this information in confidence or share it with others outside of the relationship may have an effect on the relationship. For example, if a friend has told you some private information and asked you not to tell others, you and your friend have become the co-owners of that information. You risk damaging the trust and intimacy of that friendship if you reveal the information to others. Likewise, families also co-own different types of private information and establish rules about communicating that information outside of the family. Some families may be very private about disclosing negative information about the family or its members. We are all familiar with the rule of "not airing dirty laundry in public." Taboo topics usually include personal, legal, or financial information, and all family members are instructed to avoid communicating with non-family members about those topics, lest private information be revealed (Afifi & Guerrero, 2000).

◗ The Effects of Technology on Privacy Boundaries

As people increasingly use technology to develop and maintain their relationships, the decisions they make about what to disclose and what to keep private, as well as the rules that guide those decisions, are changing. Both mobile communication technology and the Internet are affecting the disclosure-privacy dialectic.

Mobile communication technology has blurred the distinction between public and private communication (Kleinman, 2007). Cell phones and other wireless technologies allow people to carry on private conversation in public spaces. Today, while standing in line at the grocery store, you may overhear someone on a cell phone call revealing that she has asked her partner for a divorce or is pregnant but hasn't yet told her husband. People in these situations may not recognize that they are disclosing private information to complete strangers as well as to the person they have called. Or they may not care that strangers are privy to information that they would keep secret from people they know. They may even gain a certain level of excitement from breaking the unwritten boundary rules of privacy/disclosure.

Likewise, Internet technology is changing what people view as private and public. While paper diaries are still considered private thoughts to be guarded from others (reading someone else's diary continues to be taboo), today online diaries in the form of blogs are purposely made accessible to friends, acquaintances, and often thousands of strangers on the Web. There is a danger here, however. Teenage diarists often seem unaware of the long-term threats to their privacy that these disclosures may cause. They report that online journals connect them to a broader community, help them navigate friendships and romance, and allow them to vent (Bahrampour, 2007). But parents, teachers, and police often warn of the dangers of revealing too much information online by posting personal thoughts, as well as photographs, videos, and other information, which can be monitored by potential employers (who may not hire someone with a frivolous personal Web page), enemies (in a recent case, cruel messages left on a preteen's personal Web page led to her suicide), identity thieves, and even stalkers. So when using newer

INTER-ACT WITH ◗ TECHNOLOGY

Some people have violated their own privacy by being unprepared to make wise disclosure-privacy decisions when confronted with new technologies. What are your own rules that guide your disclosure versus privacy decisions on social networking sites, in blogs, in e-mails, and when talking in public on your cell phone? Notice how these rules differ from each other and from your face-to-face disclosure-privacy rules. Analyze the risks you take when your rules for technology-mediated disclosure are different from your rules for face-to-face disclosure. Do you think that it's OK for the rules to differ depending on the channel of communication? Be prepared to discuss in class your answer to this last question.

While personal blogging has become popular, there are risks inherent in keeping an online diary of your personal thoughts. Do you blog? If so, do you censor what you write with an eye toward the future?

technologies, it is important to continue to be aware of the costs as well as the rewards inherent in disclosing personal information.

⊙ Self-Disclosure and Privacy Management Skills

Once we have made a decision about what to do with a particular bit of our private information, we then need to either self-disclose or protect this information. If we are not skillful at determining how best to self-disclose information and how best to keep information private, we can harm our relationships. In this section you will learn skills you can use to form effective self-disclosure messages, as well as skills you can use to maintain your privacy effectively.

▷ Owning Feelings or Opinions

Owning feelings or opinions—skill of making "I" statements rather than generalizations to identify yourself as the source of a particular idea or feeling.

A basic skill of self-disclosure, **owning feelings or opinions** (also known as crediting yourself), means making "I" statements rather than generalizations to identify yourself as the source of a particular idea or feeling. An "I" statement is any statement that uses a first-person pronoun such as *I, my, me,* or *mine.* "I" statements help the listener understand fully and accurately the nature of the message being self-disclosed. Instead of owning their feelings and opinions and honestly self-disclosing them as such, people often express their thoughts and feelings in impersonal or generalized language or attribute them to unknown or universal sources. Consider the following paired statements:

"Lots of boys wet the bed."	"I was a bed-wetter."
"Everybody thinks Colin is unfair in his criticism."	"Colin hurt my feelings with his criticism, which I perceived as unfair."
"Nobody likes to be laughed at."	"Being laughed at embarrasses me."
"John flirts with all the girls."	"John has been flirting with me."

Being both accurate and honest in our self-disclosures requires taking responsibility for our own feelings and opinions. We all have a right to our reactions. If what you are self-disclosing is truly your opinion or an expression of how you really feel, let others know by taking responsibility for it.

▷ Displaying and Describing Feelings

At the heart of intimate self-disclosure is sharing your feelings with someone else, which is a risky business. Yet all of us experience feelings and have to decide whether to deal with them and then how to deal with them. Obviously, one option is to withhold or mask our feelings, maintaining privacy over them. But if we decide to share our feelings, there are two ways to do so effectively: displaying them or describing them.

Displaying feelings is the skill of accurately showing emotions through facial expressions, body language, or paralanguage. Although displays of feelings may be accompanied by verbal messages, the feelings themselves are acted out in nonverbal behaviors. Spontaneous cheering over a great play at a sporting event, recoiling when you bang your head against the car doorjamb, or grinning widely when you get a perfect score on an exam are all displays of feelings. Displays of feelings often serve as an escape valve for very strong emotions and allow you to "get it out of your system." Unfortunately, we often damage our ability to disclose effectively when we unnecessarily use negative displays of feelings or display feelings that don't match our verbal messages. These displays are either uncomfortable for others who witness them or may cause misunderstandings and mixed messages. For example, if Kiyoshi consistently displays negative feelings, he is likely to be perceived as someone who only shares negative experiences, a "downer." Likewise, if his nonverbal displays of feelings often contradict his verbal messages, he is likely to be seen as

Displaying feelings—skill of accurately showing emotions through facial expressions, body language, or paralanguage.

SKILL BUILDERS ❖ Owning Feelings and Opinions

SKILL	USE	PROCEDURE	EXAMPLE
Making an "I" statement rather than a generalization to identify yourself as the source of an idea or feeling	To help others understand that the feeling or opinion is yours	When an idea, opinion, or feeling is yours, say so.	Instead of saying, "Maury's is the best restaurant in town," say, "I believe Maury's is the best restaurant in town."

hard to understand at best and dishonest at worst, thus damaging his interpersonal relationships. Therefore, aim to display your feelings positively as often as is appropriate, or, if you are sharing a negative emotion, display your feelings in a way that matches your verbal messages.

Describing feelings—skill of explaining emotions one feels in a precise and unemotional manner.

When sharing feelings, you can do so more effectively by describing feelings accurately in addition to displaying them accurately. **Describing feelings** is the skill of explaining emotions one feels in a precise and unemotional manner. Many times people think they are describing their feelings when they are actually being emotionally out of control. For instance, an outburst like, "Who the hell asked you for your opinion?" is not an effective description. Therefore, try to keep your level of emotion down when describing feelings. When the skill of describing feelings is used effectively to explain how someone has angered, slighted, or hurt you, it increases the likelihood of having a positive interaction with someone rather than an argument, and it decreases the chances of creating defensiveness. When we describe our feelings, we can teach other people how we would like them to treat us without making an overt demand. For example, when LeRoy carefully and quietly tells Tony that he is annoyed that Tony borrowed his iPod without asking, Tony, who didn't mean to offend LeRoy, is more likely both to respond without defensiveness and to ask LeRoy's permission the next time. When the skill of describing feelings is used effectively to show affection or approval, it can have beneficial effects on the relationship. For example, when Paul's nana tells him straightforwardly and without gushing how much she enjoys his e-mails, Paul is likely not only to have good feelings about his nana but also to write to her more frequently.

Describing feelings is a complex skill. Simply beginning a sentence with "I feel" doesn't guarantee that you will end up actually describing a feeling. In many cases statements that begin with "I feel . . ." actually end up evaluating, blaming, or scapegoating someone or something. Consider a statement in which Jay starts by saying, "I feel like you insulted me when you said . . ." While Jay may believe that he has described a feeling, he has actually practiced blaming. The key to describing feelings is describing your own feelings, not labeling the person who made you feel that way or making assumptions about that person's intentions. Stop and think—if a person says something that you perceive as insulting, how might you *feel?* Perhaps you feel hurt, rejected, betrayed, or embarrassed. If so, then the descriptive statement might be "I felt hurt (or rejected, betrayed, or embarrassed) when you said . . ." Let's look at one more example. Suppose that your brother screamed at you for something you did. If you said, "I feel that you're angry with me," your statement echoes what the other person said, but does not describe your present feelings. To describe your feelings more effectively, you might instead say, "When you talk to me in an angry tone of voice, I feel scared (or hurt, pained, distressed)."

Describing feelings is a three-step process: (1) Identify what has triggered the feelings (a trigger is anything that causes a feeling or reaction); (2) identify the particular emotion you are experiencing accurately—this sounds easier than it sometimes is, but Table 10.1 provides a vocabulary of emotions to help you develop your ability to identify specific feelings; and (3) use an "I" statement to own, rather than project, the feeling. Here are two examples of describing feelings effectively:

> "Thank you for your compliment [trigger]; I [owning the feeling] feel gratified [specific feeling] that you noticed the effort I made."
>
> "When you criticize my cooking on days that I've worked as many hours as you have [trigger], I [owning the feeling] feel very resentful [specific feeling]."

If you are new to describing feelings, practice your skills by describing positive feelings: "You know, taking me to that movie really cheered me up" or "When you offered to help me with the housework, I really felt relieved." As you become more comfortable describing your positive feelings, you can try describing negative feelings attributable to environmental factors: "It's so cloudy; I feel gloomy" or "When we have a thunderstorm, I get really anxious." Finally, you can move to negative descriptions resulting from what people have said or done to you: "When you step in front of me like that, I really get annoyed" or "When you use a negative tone of voice while saying that what I did pleased you, I really feel confused."

▷ Managing Privacy

Maintaining privacy during interpersonal interactions can be awkward, especially when others are urging you to self-disclose. **Managing privacy** is the skill of making a conscious decision to withhold information or feelings from others. Because reciprocal self-disclosures are part of relationship development, your partner may expect you to respond to his or her self-disclosure with a self-disclosure of your own. Or you may encounter someone who asks you personal questions that you do not want to answer. In both cases, you will want to respond in a way that maintains your privacy while damaging the relationship as little as possible.

Managing privacy—skill of making a conscious decision to withhold information or feelings from others.

SKILL BUILDERS ◗ Describing Feelings

SKILL	USE	PROCEDURE	EXAMPLE
Explaining emotions one feels in a precise and unemotional manner	To self-disclose either positively or negatively to someone honestly and without resorting to strong emotion	1. Indicate what has triggered the feeling. 2. Identify what you are feeling—think specifically. Am I feeling amused? Pleased? Happy? Ecstatic? 3. Own the feeling by using an "I" statement.	"As a result of not getting the job, I feel depressed and discouraged." "Because of the way you stood up for me when I was being put down by Leah, I'm feeling very warm and loving toward you."

TABLE 10.1 ▼ **A List of More Than 200 Words That Can Describe Feelings**

Words related to *Angry*

agitated	annoyed	bitter	cranky
enraged	exasperated	furious	hostile
incensed	indignant	infuriated	irked
irritated	mad	offended	outraged
peeved	resentful	riled	steamed

Words related to *Helpful*

agreeable	amiable	beneficial	caring
collegial	compassionate	constructive	cooperative
cordial	gentle	kindly	neighborly
obliging	supportive	useful	warm

Words related to *Loving*

adoring	affectionate	amorous	aroused
caring	charming	fervent	gentle
heavenly	passionate	sensitive	tender

Words related to *Embarrassed*

abashed	anxious	chagrined	confused
conspicuous	disconcerted	disgraced	distressed
flustered	humbled	humiliated	jittery
overwhelmed	rattled	ridiculous	shamefaced
sheepish	silly	troubled	uncomfortable

Words related to *Surprised*

astonished	astounded	baffled	bewildered
confused	distracted	flustered	jarred
jolted	mystified	perplexed	puzzled
rattled	shocked	startled	stunned

Words related to *Fearful*

afraid	agitated	alarmed	anxious
apprehensive	bullied	cornered	frightened
horrified	jittery	jumpy	nervous
petrified	scared	shaken	terrified
threatened	troubled	uneasy	worried

Words related to *Disgusted*

afflicted	annoyed	nauseated	outraged
repelled	repulsed	revolted	sickened

TABLE 10.1 ◗ A List of More Than 200 Words That Can Describe Feelings—continued

Words related to *Hurt*

abused	awful	cheated	deprived
deserted	desperate	dismal	dreadful
forsaken	hassled	ignored	isolated
mistreated	offended	oppressed	pained
piqued	rejected	resentful	rotten
scorned	slighted	snubbed	wounded

Words related to *Belittled*

betrayed	defeated	deflated	demeaned
diminished	disparaged	downgraded	foolish
helpless	inadequate	incapable	inferior
insulted	persecuted	powerless	underestimated
undervalued	unfit	unworthy	useless

Words related to *Happy*

blissful	charmed	cheerful	contented
delighted	ecstatic	elated	exultant
fantastic	giddy	glad	gratified
high	joyous	jubilant	merry
pleased	satisfied	thrilled	tickled

Words related to *Lonely*

abandoned	alone	bored	deserted
desolate	discarded	empty	excluded
forlorn	forsaken	ignored	isolated
jilted	lonesome	lost	rejected
renounced	scorned	slighted	snubbed

Words related to *Sad*

blue	crestfallen	dejected	depressed
dismal	dour	downcast	gloomy
heavyhearted	joyless	low	melancholy
mirthless	miserable	moody	morose
pained	sorrowful	troubled	weary

Words related to *Energetic*

animated	bold	brisk	dynamic
eager	forceful	frisky	hardy
inspired	kinetic	lively	peppy
potent	robust	spirited	sprightly
spry	vibrant	vigorous	vivacious

You can use four privacy management strategies when you are being pressed to disclose something that you are not comfortable sharing: changing the subject, masking feelings, telling "white lies," and establishing boundaries.

1. Changing the subject. If you are being pressed to self-disclose something you don't choose to share, simply change the subject. Partners who are sensitive will recognize this as a signal that you don't want to self-disclose. For example, when Pat and Eric are leaving economics class, Pat says to Eric, "I got an 83 on the test, how about you?" If Eric doesn't want to share his grade, he might redirect the conversation by saying, "Hey, that's a B. Good going. Did you finish the homework for calculus?"

2. Masking feelings. When you have decided that sharing your feelings is too risky, you may choose to conceal the verbal or nonverbal cues that would ordinarily enable others to decipher the emotions you are feeling. Alternately you can mask your feelings through deception by enacting cues that signal emotions other than those you are feeling. A good analogy to masking feelings is "poker face," a neutral look that is impossible to decipher and stays the same whether the player's cards are good or bad. An example of masking feelings is if Alita laughs along with the others in a room as Manny makes fun of her—this display may mask her feelings of betrayal and embarrassment. On occasion, masking your feelings can be an effective strategy. However, if we overly rely on this strategy, we can experience interpersonal communication problems because we are turning our feelings inward and not revealing them to others. Likewise, we risk stunting the growth of our relationships, since our partners won't really know or understand us.

3. Telling "white lies." You probably have heard that telling a "white lie" is making a false or misleading statement in a situation in which telling the truth would embarrass or hurt either an individual or a relationship. For example, if Pat asks Eric about his grade on the test and Eric responds, "I'm not sure. I got a few tests back this week" (even though he knows full well what his grade was), Eric is telling a "white lie." Although lying should be avoided in most cases, "white lies" are considered acceptable because they are used to prevent damaged emotions, maintain healthy relationships, and help either you or a partner save face.

4. Establishing boundaries. Changing the subject, masking feelings, and telling "white lies" are strategies that manage privacy in one-time situations, but they will damage your relationships if

© Mike Baldwin / Cornered

It was like he could read my mind.

you employ them habitually or repeatedly. Therefore, you should also become proficient at the strategy of establishing boundaries to directly respond to people who expect you to self-disclose information you would prefer to keep private without using deception. To establish a boundary: (1) Recognize why you are choosing not to share the information, (2) identify your own privacy policy that guides your decision, and (3) form an "I"-centered message in which you briefly establish a boundary by diplomatically telling the person of your privacy policy and that you wish to keep that information private. For example, if Pat asks Eric about his test grade, instead of changing the subject or telling a "white lie," as in the earlier examples, Eric might reply, "I know that everyone's different and I don't mean to be rude, but it's my policy not to ask other people about their grades and not to discuss my own."

● Giving Personal Feedback

So far in this chapter we have focused on disclosure in terms of self-disclosure, what we choose to reveal about ourselves to others. Now let's turn to **personal feedback**, which is disclosing information about others to them. Sometimes in our interactions and relationships, it is appropriate to comment on another person's behavior by giving personal feedback. In some relationships we will need to consider carefully whether it is our place to give feedback; in other relationships we may be expected or required to provide it. For example, you may weigh whether it is your place to tell a friend that she has had too much to drink. But if you are a bartender in a state with dramshop laws (laws that hold bars liable for the actions of patrons who drink too much), giving patrons this type of feedback will be part of your job. Similarly, managers, parents, and social workers are expected to give personal feedback to employees, children, and clients. As a result, improving our skills in providing personal feedback about both positive behaviors and accomplishments and negative behaviors will have broad use.

We can use three skills to give personal feedback. First, effective personal feedback involves describing behavior. Second, when we identify negative or harmful behavior, we provide constructive criticism. Third, when we highlight positive behavior and accomplishments, we give praise.

▷ Describing Behavior

When giving personal feedback, many of us have a strong impulse to form our messages based on generalized conclusions we have reached about what someone has said or done. It is common to overhear personal feedback like "You're so stupid"; "Don't act like a jerk"; or "You're really cool." These statements and countless others like them are evaluative and vague. Rather than evaluating behavior, effective personal feedback uses **describing behavior**, the skill of accurately recounting the specific behaviors of others without drawing conclusions about

Personal feedback—disclosing information about others to them.

OBSERVE AND ANALYZE ●

The Vocabulary of Emotions

Look at each word in Table 10.1; say "I feel . . . ," and try to experience the feelings the word describes. Next make a list of those feelings that you recognize as ones that you have personally experienced. Then recall recent situations where you could have used each of these words. Write the message that would have been appropriate for each situation. In those situations, did you choose the exact work you wanted to use, or were you inexact in your word choice?

Describing behavior—skill of accurately recounting the specific behaviors of others without drawing conclusions about those behaviors.

those behaviors. Describing behavior, in short, is the other-centered equivalent to describing feelings, which we discussed earlier in this chapter. Consider the following situation. Miguel and you are discussing the performance of the college football team. After you have interrupted Miguel for the third time, he could say either, "You're so rude with your interruptions" or "Do you realize that you interrupted me three times before I had the chance to finish a sentence?" Which form of personal feedback would you feel better about receiving? The first message is clearly an evaluative generalization, and most of us would be embarrassed and might even become defensive upon hearing it. The second message, however, is an accurate description of the behavior. Since most of us already know that interrupting is not "good form," this feedback, describing the behavior but not voicing an evaluation of it, is more sensitive to the interrupter's face needs and therefore is less likely to cause embarrassment or defensiveness.

Like describing feelings, describing behavior may seem simple, but it can be very difficult to do because it requires us to move backward in the perceptual process. We have to stop short of the temptation of basing our description on the overall impression we got and step back to identify the specific stimuli on which our overall impression was based. Miguel may have come to the overall impression that your interruptions fit the pattern he associates with the word "rude." But to describe your behavior diplomatically, he must go back, recall, and verbalize your specific actions that led him to this impression.

The following guidelines will help you to describe behavior effectively: (1) Identify the overall impression you are experiencing, (2) recall the specific behaviors that have led you to this impression, and (3) form a message in which you report only what you have seen or heard without drawing a conclusion about these behaviors.

The skill of describing behavior is useful in a variety of feedback situations. Once you have described someone's behavior, you may want to voice your reac-

SKILL BUILDERS ▾ Describing Behavior

SKILL	USE	PROCEDURE	EXAMPLE
Accurately recounting the specific behaviors of others without drawing conclusions about those behaviors	Avoiding conflict or defensiveness when providing personal feedback by sticking to the facts, not your emotional responses	1. Identify the overall impression you are experiencing. 2. Recall the specific behaviors that led you to this impression. 3. Form a message in which you report only what you have seen or heard without drawing a conclusion about these behaviors.	Instead of saying, "She is such a snob," say, "She has walked by us three times now without speaking."

tion to the behavior. When your reaction is negative, you can provide constructive criticism, and when your reaction is positive, you can provide praise, as we will see next. Describing behavior also is used when you wish to work collaboratively to resolve an interpersonal conflict, as we will see in Chapter 12.

▷ Providing Constructive Criticism

Research on reinforcement theory has found that people learn faster and better through positive rewards such as praise (which we will describe in the next section), but there are still times when you will need to provide personal feedback on negative behaviors. **Constructive criticism** is the skill of diplomatically describing the specific negative behaviors or actions of another and the effects those behaviors/actions have on others. While it's best to give this type of personal feedback when a person specifically asks for it, we sometimes need to address the behaviors of people who haven't asked for feedback.

Constructive criticism—skill of diplomatically describing the specific negative behaviors or actions of another and the effects those behaviors/actions have on others.

Although the word "criticism" can mean "harsh judgment," the skill of constructive criticism is not based on judgment. Rather, it is grounded in empathy and understanding. When we provide another person with constructive criticism, our intention is to help. Therefore, we should begin the constructive criticism process by trying to empathize with the other person and by forecasting how he or she will react to the feedback. Then we should work to formulate a message that accurately communicates our meaning while attending to the face needs of the message recipient. Unfortunately, most of us are far too quick to criticize others and are not really all that constructive when we do so. At times we overstep our bounds by trying to help others "become better people" even when they aren't interested in hearing from us. Even when the time is right for providing negative feedback, we may not always do a good job of expressing it. While research shows that well-given constructive criticism can actually strengthen relationships and improve interactions in the long run, criticism that is not empathetically grounded or is otherwise poorly communicated is likely to hurt relationships and lead to defensive interactions (Tracy, Dusen, & Robinson, 1987). To be effective at providing constructive criticism, you should adopt the guidelines that follow.

1. Begin by describing the behavior or action. Follow the guidelines for describing behavior that we discussed earlier. Describing behavior lays a foundation for criticism by describing what behavior or action needs to change. In addition, by describing the behavior or action, you show that you are focused on the behavior or action rather than on attacking the person, which would result in his or her losing face. For example, suppose DeShawn asks Raul, "What did you think of my presentation of a fund-raising plan for the fraternity?" Instead of saying, "It's not going to make us much money," as a constructive critic, Raul might say, "Well, I think the idea of the guys doing spring cleanup work for a daily fee is really creative, but I think the plan to have us sell magazines could be a problem. The rowing team just did that last month and only made one-third of their goals.

They found that college students don't have extra money for magazine subscriptions." This criticism does not attack DeShawn's self-esteem, and it tells him what specifically may need to change.

2. Whenever possible, preface a negative statement with a positive one. One way to address the face needs of the recipient is to begin your comments by praising some related behavior. Of course, common sense suggests that superficial praise followed by crushing criticism will be seen for what it is. But criticism that is prefaced with valid praise can reduce defensiveness. Recall in the preceding situation the comment, "I think the idea of the guys doing spring cleanup work for a daily fee is really creative." Here the praise that is provided is relevant and balances the negative feedback that follows.

3. Be as specific as possible. The more specifically you describe the behavior you are going to criticize, the more effectively a person will be able to understand what needs to change and how to change it. In our example, it would not have been helpful for Raul to simply say, "Some of your ideas won't work." This comment would have been so general that DeShawn would have had no idea what Raul believed needed to change. Instead, Raul provided specific comments about how college students don't usually have enough funds for magazine subscriptions. He brought in an example about the rowing team's efforts.

4. When appropriate, suggest how the person can change the behavior or action. Since the focus of constructive criticism is helping, it is appropriate to

SKILL BUILDERS ◗ Providing Constructive Criticism

SKILL	**USE**	**PROCEDURE**	**EXAMPLE**
Diplomatically describing the specific negative behaviors or actions of another and the effects those behaviors/actions have on others	To help people see themselves as others see them	1. Begin by describing the person's behavior or action. 2. Whenever possible, preface negative statements with positive ones. 3. Be as specific as possible. 4. When appropriate, suggest how the person can change the behavior or action.	Carol says, "Bob, I've noticed something about your behavior with Jenny. Would you like to hear it?" After Bob assures her that he would, Carol continues, "Although you seem really supportive of Jenny, there are times when Jenny starts to relate an experience and you interrupt her and finish telling the story. You did this a few times while Jenny was trying to talk about her trip to Colorado and she looked a little hurt. She's pretty sensitive about being interrupted, so you might want to try to let her finish her stories the rest of this evening or she might get upset."

provide the person with suggestions that might lead to positive change. So in responding to DeShawn's request for feedback, Raul might also have added, "Maybe we could find out what school supplies or personal care products are most often purchased and sell those instead." By including a positive suggestion, you not only help the person but also show that your intentions are constructive.

▷ Providing Praise

Too often, the positive things people say and do or the accomplishments that they achieve are not acknowledged by others. Yet our self-concept and, consequently, our behaviors are shaped by how others respond to us. **Praising** is the skill of sincerely describing the specific positive behaviors or accomplishments of another and the positive effects those behaviors/accomplishments have on others. By praising we provide others with personal feedback affirming that what they have said or done is commendable. We do so for the sole purpose of sincerely informing others, not to get on their good side or manipulate them. Praise can reinforce positive behavior and help another person to develop a positive self-concept.

For praise to be effective, you need to focus the praise on specific behaviors and accomplishments and word the message to be consistent with the significance or value of the accomplishment or behavior. For example, if a child who tends to be forgetful remembers to return the scissors he borrowed, that exact behavior should be praised so that it will be reinforced. Saying, "You're so wonderful, you're on top of everything" reinforces nothing because this is an overly general statement that doesn't identify the particular behavior or accomplishment. An effective praise message might simply say something like, "Thanks for putting the scissors back where they belong—I really appreciate that." This response acknowledges the accomplishment by describing the specific behavior and the positive feeling of gratitude that the behavior has caused. The following are two more examples of appropriate praising:

> **Behavior:** Sonya selected and bought a group wedding present for a friend. The gift is a big hit.
> **Praise:** "Sonya, the present you chose for Steve was really thoughtful. Not only did it fit our price range, but Steve really liked it."

Praising—skill of sincerely describing the specific positive behaviors or accomplishments of another and the positive effects those behaviors/accomplishments have on others.

OBSERVE AND ANALYZE ⊙

Expressing Criticism

Think about the last time you criticized someone's behavior. Which, if any, of the guidelines for constructive criticism did you follow or violate? Did you describe the behavior or action accurately? Did you preface negative comments with positive ones? Did you provide specific details? If called for, did you offer advice on how the person might change his or her behaviors or actions? If you were to offer the same criticism again, what would you say differently?

Accomplishment: Cole receives a letter inviting him to a reception at which he is to receive a scholarship award for academic accomplishments and community service work.

Praise: "Congratulations, Cole. I'm so proud of you! It's really great to see that the effort you put into studying, as well as the time and energy you have devoted to the Second Harvest Food Program and Big Brothers, is being recognized and valued."

While praising doesn't "cost" much, it is valuable and generally appreciated. Not only does praising provide information and acknowledge the worth of another person, but it can also deepen a relationship by increasing its openness. To increase the effectiveness of your praise, use the following guidelines: (1) Make note of the specific behavior or accomplishment that you want to reinforce, (2) describe the specific behavior and/or accomplishment, (3) describe the positive feelings or outcomes that you or others experience as a result of the behavior or accomplishment, and (4) phrase your response so that the level of praise appropriately reflects the significance of the behavior or accomplishment.

◐ Asking for Personal Feedback

Having now focused on the skills involved in self-disclosure and maintaining privacy, as well as disclosing to others, let's conclude by discussing how we can ask others to disclose to us, to provide us with personal feedback.

SKILL BUILDERS ◐ Praise

SKILL	USE	PROCEDURE	EXAMPLE
Sincerely describing the specific positive behaviors or accomplishments of another and the positive effects those behaviors/accomplishments have on others	To help people see themselves positively	1. Make note of the specific behavior or accomplishment that you want to reinforce. 2. Describe the specific behavior and/or accomplishment. 3. Describe the positive feelings or outcomes that you or others experience as a result of the behavior or accomplishment. 4. Phrase the response so that the level of praise appropriately reflects the significance of the behavior or accomplishment.	"Marge, that was an excellent writing job on the Miller story. Your descriptions were particularly vivid."

We can deepen our relationships and gain self-knowledge by asking our relational partners for personal feedback. Such information from others helps us to identify our strengths and weaknesses or to correct our mistakes. Although the most obvious way of getting feedback is to ask for it directly, sometimes people are reluctant to do so because they feel threatened or embarrassed. Instead, people rely on others' nonverbal cues. Yet even when we interpret nonverbal cues accurately, these clues cannot help us understand *why* our behaviors have generated the reactions they did. Nor will such cues help us decide what changes are needed for us to improve. By using the verbal skill of asking for feedback, we can accomplish both of these objectives. So, how do you prepare to receive personal feedback from others?

1. Think of personal feedback as being in your best interest. No one likes to be criticized, and some people are embarrassed by praise, but through personal feedback we often learn and grow. When you receive a different appraisal from the one you expected, you have learned something about yourself that you did not previously know. Whether you will do anything about the feedback is up to you, but the feedback you have solicited allows you to consider aspects of your behavior that you might not have identified on your own.

2. Before you ask, make sure that you are ready for an honest response. If you ask for feedback, don't expect others to lie to you just to make you feel better. If you don't want an honest response, don't ask the question. For example, if you

Asking for feedback at work can help you to become more effective at your job. Do you find it difficult to ask for help at work? If so, how can you overcome your reluctance?

ask a friend, "What do you think of my speaking skills?" expect an honest reply, even if it is negative, such as, "Well, you tend to ramble a bit." If others realize that typically when you request personal feedback you are actually fishing for a compliment, honest appraisals will not be forthcoming in the future.

3. Take the initiative to ask for personal feedback. Taking the initiative in asking for personal feedback prepares you psychologically to deal with what is said. Also, if you don't take the initiative, others are not likely to know that you need input.

4. Specify the kind of personal feedback you are seeking. Rather than asking very general questions about ideas, feelings, or behaviors, ask specific questions. If you say, "Colleen, is there anything you don't like about my ideas?" she is likely to not know how to respond. But if you say, "Colleen, do you think I've given enough emphasis to the marketing possibilities?" you will encourage Colleen to speak openly to the specific issue.

5. Avoid loaded questions. You can't expect honest personal feedback if you phrase your questions in a way that begs an answer. For example, if you say, "I did a great job on that, didn't I?" or "I did a mediocre job on that, right?" obviously the person you ask is going to recognize that you want affirmation.

6. Try to avoid negative verbal or nonverbal reactions to the feedback. Suppose you ask your roommate how he likes your rearrangement of the furniture. If when he replies, "It's going to be harder for everyone to see the TV when we have people over to watch a DVD," you get an angry look on your face or exclaim,

SKILL BUILDERS ○ Asking for Feedback

SKILL	USE	PROCEDURE	EXAMPLE
Asking others for their reaction to you or to your behavior	To get information that will help you understand yourself and your effect on others	1. Think of personal feedback as being in your best interest. 2. Before you ask, make sure that you are ready for an honest response. 3. Take the initiative to ask for personal feedback. 4. Specify the kind of personal feedback you are seeking. 5. Avoid loaded questions. 6. Try to avoid negative verbal or nonverbal reactions to the feedback. 7. Paraphrase what you hear. 8. Show gratitude for the feedback you receive.	Lucy asks, "Tim, when I talk with the boss, do I sound defensive?" Tim replies, "I think so—your voice gets sharp and you lose eye contact, which makes you look nervous." "So you think that the tone of my voice and my eye contact lead the boss to perceive me as defensive?" "Yes." "Thanks, Tim. I've really got to work on this."

"Well, if you can do it any better, you can move the furniture!" your roommate will quickly learn not to give you personal feedback in the future, even when you ask for it.

7. Paraphrase what you hear. By paraphrasing the personal feedback you receive, you ensure that you do not overgeneralize what you have heard. For example, if Joshua asks his classmate to comment on his presentation but boils down the specific comments he receives to simply "good" or "bad," he is not going to learn anything constructive from the feedback he requested.

8. Show gratitude for the feedback you receive. Regardless of whether what you heard makes you feel good or bad, thank people for their feedback. No one likes to be asked to provide personal feedback and then ignored or even snubbed for providing what was asked.

⊙ Summary

As an interpersonal communicator, it is important to manage the dialectic tension between disclosure and privacy. Disclosure is revealing confidential information. Privacy is withholding confidential or secret information to enhance autonomy and minimize vulnerability.

Communication privacy management theory provides a framework for understanding the decision-making processes people use to manage disclosure and privacy. The theory asserts that each of us has developed rules about privacy

A QUESTION OF ETHICS ⊙ What Would You Do?

Fifteen-year-old Craig frequently self-discloses personal information to his older brother Marshall. In the past few months, Craig has told Marshall about some parties he has attended where alcohol has been present. When Marshall has asked Craig if he has been drinking at these parties, Craig has assured him that he has not. Nonetheless, Craig has asked Marshall not to tell their parents about these alcohol-related parties. Marshall has agreed to maintain Craig's privacy because Craig has refrained from drinking and because he likes his brother and does not want to get him in trouble with their parents.

Today when the brothers were chatting, Craig told a story about getting drunk at a party the night before. Craig said this behavior is just a natural part of growing up and that they were safely at a friend's house where everyone slept over and no one drove while under the influence of alcohol. He begged Marshall not to say anything to their parents because this information would cause their parents to worry and they would

likely punish Craig. Because the family is having some financial stress, Craig felt even more strongly that it would be inappropriate for Marshall to add to their stress by sharing Craig's information.

Analyze the factors that may contribute to the dialectical tension that Marshall would feel between disclosure and privacy.

1. What individual motivational, contextual, and risk-benefit issues might affect Marshall's decision to disclose or to maintain Craig's privacy?
2. If Marshall decides to disclose this information to their parents, how might that decision affect the relationship between the brothers? If he decides to keep this information from their parents, how might that decision affect Marshall's relationship with his parents?
3. What decision would you make in this situation if you were Marshall?

and disclosure to guide our behaviors as we make choices to disclose or conceal personal information about ourselves and about others. These rules are designed to help us maximize the benefits of disclosure while minimizing risks. Benefits of disclosure may include self-expression, relationship development, and social control. Risks include loss of face, lowering of status, and loss of control. We formulate our rules about what to disclose or keep private based on culture, gender, motivation, context, and risk-benefit analysis.

The three most important ways that disclosure and privacy affect relationships are in terms of intimacy, expectations for reciprocity, and information co-ownership.

Skills for self-disclosure include owning feelings or opinions, displaying feelings, and describing feelings. Skills for privacy management include changing the subject, masking feelings, telling "white lies," and establishing boundaries. Skills for giving personal feedback to others include describing behavior, providing constructive criticism, and providing praise. In addition to self-disclosing and disclosing to others, you may also need to ask for personal feedback to enhance relationships and self-knowledge.

● Inter-Action Dialogue: Disclosure

Relationships can move toward friendship and intimacy through appropriate disclosure and feedback. Effective self-disclosures own feelings and opinions and display and describe feelings. Giving effective feedback requires describing specific behaviors and how they affect others. When the effects are positive, praise statements are provided; when the effects are negative, constructive criticism can be provided. Read the dialogue between Maria and Mark that follows, and analyze the sharing and withholding behaviors of each.

Maria and Mark have coffee after seeing a movie.

Conversation

Maria: That was a great movie! The characters were so fascinating, and I loved the way we slowly learned about their childhood.

Mark: Yeah, I liked it too, but at times it hit a little too close to home.

Maria: Really? How do you mean?

Mark: Well, remember how as a little guy he spent so much time alone?

Maria: Yes, that made me feel kind of sad.

Mark: Oh? Well, my mom and dad both had full-time jobs and my dad often worked a second one as well. So since I was an only child and we didn't have any other family here, I spent a lot of time alone.

Maria: That must have been hard on you.

Mark: In a way, yes, but I think it helped me to become independent, resourceful, and very competitive at games and sports.

Maria: Gee, I guess I understand independent, but why do you say being alone helped you to become resourceful?

Mark: Well, usually no one was home when I came home from school and sometimes my mom had to work late, so I had to get my own supper.

Maria: So how did that make you resourceful?

Mark: When there were leftovers it wasn't too hard to reheat them, but when there weren't any I'd have to scrounge around in the cupboards and fridge. I wasn't allowed to use the stove or oven—just the microwave—so I sometimes had to be really creative.

Maria: Really? What did you make?

Mark: I was a master of microwave black beans and rice. If you're lucky I'll make them for you someday.

Maria: I think I'll pass. I ate enough beans and rice when I was growing up. My mom wanted us to identify with our "heritage" so she made a big deal of cooking recipes from her childhood a couple of times a week. Unfortunately, she's not a good cook, so we got pretty sick of it. Today, my favorite take-out is Thai—now that's cuisine!

Mark: I've never had Thai food. What's so great about it?

Maria: Well it's very spicy-hot, with lots of complex flavoring.

Mark: Does it have much MSG? I'm allergic to that.

Maria: I don't know. Hey, back to our previous topic. You said being alone also made you competitive. How?

Mark: Well, since I was alone and had no friends to play with, I'd work out ways to compete with myself.

Maria: Really, like what?

Mark: I'd play "Horse." You play basketball, don't you?

Maria: Sure. But what's "Horse"?

Mark: Well, Horse is usually played with two or more people: One person takes a shot; if he makes it, the other person has to attempt the same shot. If that person misses he gets an "h." If he makes it, then he takes a shot and his opponent now has to try to make it. The first one to get all five letters, h-o-r-s-e, loses.

Maria: So how did that make you competitive?

Mark: Well, I used to play against my alter ego. Only he was a left-hander! After awhile I was as good left-handed as I was right-handed. I think that's how I made first string on my high school basketball team. I'm not very fast, but I can shoot with either hand from about anywhere on the court.

Maria: So spending a lot of time alone wasn't all bad.

Mark: No. In truth I learned to enjoy my own company and I still like to be alone a lot. In fact, I have trouble enjoying just hanging out or partying with lots of people. It kind of seems like a waste of time. I enjoy smaller groups or one-on-one time, but the party scene leaves me cold.

Maria: Yes, I've noticed that when we're with the group, you don't have much to say. I used to think you thought you were better than us, but I guess I understand why you act that way now. Still, you might want to think about being more vocal. You're really an interesting guy, and I think others in the group don't know how to take you.

◐ Chapter Resources

Communication Improvement Plan: Developing Relationships through Disclosure and Feedback ◐ Find more on the web @ www.oup.com/us/interact12

Would you like to improve your disclosure or feedback skills, as discussed in this chapter?

- Owning feelings or opinions
- Displaying feelings
- Describing feelings
- Managing privacy
- Describing behavior
- Providing constructive criticism
- Providing praise
- Asking for criticism

Choose the skill(s) you want to work on, and write a communication improvement plan. You can find a communication improvement plan worksheet on our website at www.oup.com/us/interact12.

Key Words ◐

Skill Practice ◐ Find more on the web @ www.oup.com/us/interact12

Skill Practice exercises challenge you to master the material you have read in this chapter. For additional Skill Practice activities, visit our website at www.oup.com/us/interact12.

Providing Personal Feedback
For each of the following situations, write an appropriate feedback message.

1. You have been driving to school with a fellow student whose name you got from the transportation office at school. You have known him for only three weeks. Everything about the situation is great (he's on time, your schedules match, and you enjoy your conversations), except he drives ten to fifteen miles per hour faster than the speed limit, and this scares you.

2. A good friend of yours has fallen into the habit of saying "like" and "you know" more than once every sentence. While you know she has a good vocabulary and is a dean's list student, she comes across as uneducated. She is about to graduate and has begun on-campus job interviews. Thus far she has been disappointed because every employer with whom she has spoken has rejected her. She asks why you think she is having such a hard time.

3. After being on your own for five years, for financial reasons you have returned home to live with your parents. While you appreciate your parents' willingness to take you in, you are embarrassed to be living at home. Your mother has begun to treat you the way she did when

you were a child. Specifically, she doesn't respect your privacy. She routinely enters your room without knocking and opens your drawers under the guise of putting away your clean clothes. Yesterday you found her looking at your bank statement, which was in an envelope on your desk. You are becoming resentful of these intrusions.

4. Your professor in this class has asked you for feedback on his or her teaching style. Based on your experience in this class, write a message of praise and one of constructive criticism.

Inter-Act with Media ◐ Find more on the web @ www.oup.com/us/interact12

Television

The Office (U.S.), episode: "Cocktails" (2007). Steve Carell, John Krasinski, Jenna Fischer, Melora Hardin, David Denman.

Brief Summary: Michael (Carell) and his boss, Jan (Hardin), go public with their romantic relationship at a house party with Dunder Mifflin executives. Upon initial introductions, Michael blurts out, "Jan and I are lovers." Jan and Michael then argue throughout the party. On the way home, Jan expresses that taking their relationship public was a mistake. Michael becomes emotional and owns his feelings by admitting that he wants "the house, the picket fence, the ketchup fights, the tickling, and the giggling."

In a subplot of this episode, sharing of personal information abounds: Pam (Fischer), who was formerly engaged to warehouse worker Roy (Denman), reveals that she and colleague Jim (Krasinski) kissed prior to her breaking off their engagement. Roy goes ballistic over this indiscretion, and any hope for a reunion ends. Both examples reveal that regardless of stage, sharing personal information holds risks for deepening or dissolving a relationship.

IPC Concepts: Balancing self-disclosure and privacy, owning feelings or opinions, displaying and describing feelings, managing privacy, describing behavior.

Cinema

Little Children (2007). Todd Field (director). Kate Winslet, Patrick Wilson, Jennifer Connelly.

Brief Summary: Sarah, an emotionally bored and drab-looking housewife, spends days with her three-year-old daughter Lucy at the park with mothers who typify the suburbanite persona. While Sarah differs from the women in appearance, the women share one commonality: their fascination with Brad, an attractive father who visits the park daily with his son. None of the women interact with Brad; rather, they call him "the Prom King" and hypothesize about why he is available during the daytime hours. When the mothers dare Sarah to get Brad's phone number, he makes small talk at first but then tells her to "ask what the person who wears the pants in the family does." He discloses failing the bar exam repeatedly and that he possibly should find something else to do with his life. Sarah realizes that Brad is lonely since he shared personal information so quickly and easily.

IPC Concepts: Appropriate self-disclosure, managing privacy.

What's on the Web

Find links and additional material, including self-quizzes, on the companion website at www.oup.com/us/interact12.

11

Using Interpersonal Influence Ethically

After you have read this chapter, you should be able to answer these questions:

▷ What is interpersonal influence?

▷ What is power?

▷ What are the six principles of power?

▷ What are the five types of power?

▷ What is persuasion?

▷ What are the three components of persuasive messages?

▷ What are seven compliance-gaining strategies?

▷ What is assertiveness?

▷ How can you be assertive rather than passive or aggressive?

▷ What are the skills for formulating assertive messages?

"Stella, we agreed to talk tonight about the job offers we both have, our careers, and where we're going to live after we get married. Since I'm an engineer and you're a social worker, one thing we can count on is that I will make more money. So I think it's obvious that we will want to live wherever my job takes me."

"Whoa, wait a minute, Vince. I know that we want a good life and that we want to have enough money to start a family, but for me, it's not all about money. I think it's important to be near our family and friends, and it's also important to consider whether we are going to like the place we live."

"But Stella, you know that I have a great offer in Tempe, Arizona. Now I know you don't like heat or the desert, and it's far away from our friends and family, but I didn't go through five years of engineering classes and three different internships to turn down an offer like this."

"Vince, are we having an honest conversation? Is this who you really are? It seems to me that you've already decided what we are going to do, and it appears that nothing I say is going to change your mind. Do you really think that just because I will earn less than you that I don't get a say in this decision and any others we might need to make? Well, if you do you're wrong; I have both the power and the right to influence this and any other decisions we make. If you don't agree, then we really need to reconsider whether we should get married. Bottom line, if you want me to be your wife, then you're going to have to learn that we will make all of our life decisions together with both of our needs in mind after we have an honest conversation."

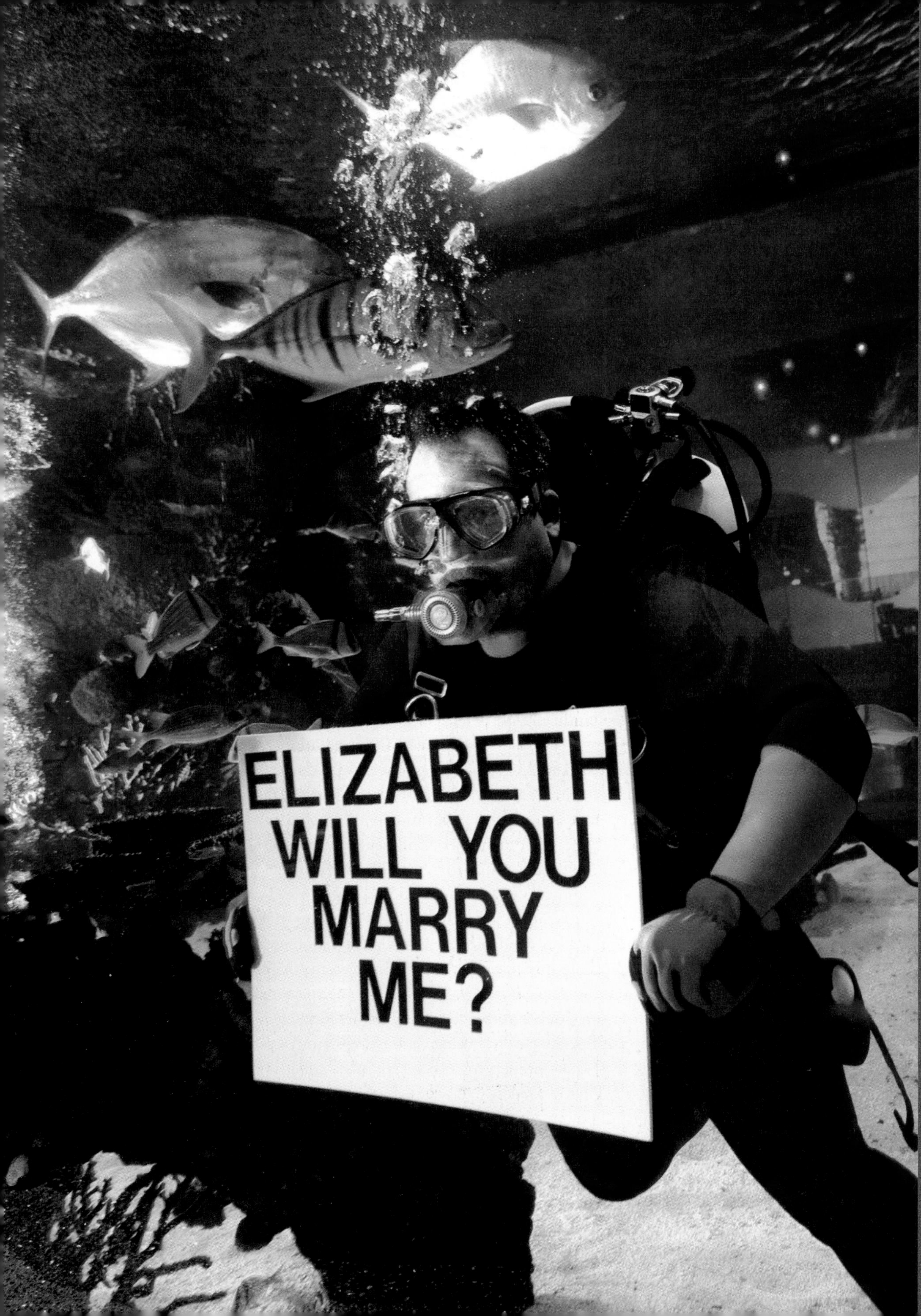
ELIZABETH
WILL YOU
MARRY
ME?

Think about a long-term intimate relationship you have had. Did you and your partner always agree on every joint decision you needed to make? Probably not. So to make decisions you most likely needed to talk through the issues. During your conversations each of you probably attempted to explain your preferred solutions, hoping that you could influence your partner's positions. Now think of a specific time that you and your partner had to make an important decision. Were you successful in your attempts to influence the outcome? Did you consider how you should proceed? Did you think about your partner's interests when making your point? Did your message acknowledge this? In the vignette you just read, Vince appears to have forgotten that Stella had a legitimate expectation that she and Vince would exchange ideas about their future and collaborate on the decision that they made. Instead, Vince took for granted that Stella would see things the way that he did. When she didn't, his message conveyed the idea that his needs were more important and that his perspective was the only one of value. As Vince's behavior showed, when our influence attempts do not take into account the needs of our partners, they become manipulative or coercive. Unfortunately, unethical people use manipulative messages in attempts to force others to do things that are against their own best interests. When these people are successful, they enjoy a short-term benefit, but their short-term success may cause long-term damage to their relationship. Conversely, ethical influence can help strengthen relationships and ensure that both partners' needs are met.

Interpersonal influence—practice of preserving or changing the attitudes or behaviors of others.

Interpersonal influence is the practice of preserving or changing the attitudes or behaviors of others (Dillard, Anderson, & Knobloch, 2002, p. 426). Interpersonal influence is a core element of human interaction because whenever people communicate, they intentionally or unintentionally influence each other (Parks, 2007). In addition to helping to reach decisions, the most common uses of interpersonal influence are to give advice, to gain assistance, to share activities, to obtain permission, to change attitudes, and to alter relationships (Dillard & Marshall, 2003). All of these uses of influence are part of daily communication, so understanding and learning to use ethical interpersonal influence skills is fundamental to interpersonal communication competence.

Thinkers and scholars across human history, going back to the Greek philosophers Socrates, Plato, and Aristotle and the Roman orator Cicero, have studied and written about influencing others. Over the years, their ideas have been elaborated upon and refined. Today, the study of interpersonal influence essentially focuses on three areas: power (the potential for influencing others), persuasion (the art of influencing others using various skills), and assertiveness (the overriding skill used when influencing others). In this chapter, we will examine each of these areas. First, we identify five sources of interpersonal power and explain six principles of power. Then, we discuss the components of persuasive messages and seven common compliance-gaining strategies. Finally, we define assertiveness and its opposites (passive and aggressive behaviors), explain how to build assertiveness skills, and identify cross-culture differences in assertive behaviors.

◒ Power

We turn to the concept of power first because before you can influence others, you must first have a basis from which to do so. **Power** is the potential that one person has to influence the attitudes, beliefs, and behaviors of others. Many communication scholars believe that power is prevalent in all relationships, regardless of whether we are consciously aware of how power issues affect our communication (Guerrero, Andersen, & Afifi, 2007). We begin our study of power by looking at five sources of power. Then we will describe the six principles that explain power dynamics in interpersonal relationships.

Power—potential that one person has to influence the attitudes, beliefs, and behaviors of others.

▷ Sources of Power

John French and Bertram Raven (1968) proposed that to be effective in influencing others, people must use their power, which comes from one or more sources. Based on their research, they identified five sources of power in relationships: coercive power, reward power, legitimate power, expert power, and referent power. Other research has sharpened our understanding of these types of power (Hinken & Schriesheim, 1980).

1. Coercive power. Coercive power is the potential to influence based on the ability to physically or psychologically hurt another. The easiest way to understand coercive power is to consider the examples of the playground bully and the abusive spouse. A playground bully may get his or her way by taunting another child psychologically or because he or she has demonstrated physical aggressiveness. Similarly, an abusive spouse may get his or her way because his or her partner has experienced and fears further verbal or physical abuse. Although these are two of the most extreme examples of coercive power, this type of power can also be more benign. A person can have coercive power and yet never intentionally attempt to use it to influence others. Nonetheless, the potential for influence is there. For example, a person of imposing physical stature may unintentionally be perceived as threatening to others and therefore exert influence over others. This is humorously illustrated in the old vaudeville joke: "Where does a gorilla sit when it enters the room? Anywhere it wants to." Similarly, a person may exert psychological power unintentionally if he or she has a powerful personality—always speaking forthrightly, having a booming voice, and so on.

Coercive power—potential to influence based on the ability to physically or psychologically hurt another.

2. Reward power. Reward power is the potential to influence based on the ability to provide monetary, physical, or psychological benefits that others desire. Examples of reward power include the financial power parents have over children ("If you clean your room, you'll get your allowance"), the physical power people have over people who physically desire them ("Since you told me I look sexy, I'll kiss you"), and the psychological power siblings have over each other ("If you don't tell mom that I went to that party, I won't pick on you anymore"). Your reward power is based not only on how much another person values the rewards you control but also on how likely you are to bestow the rewards upon them. For

Reward power—potential to influence based on the ability to provide monetary, physical, or psychological benefits that others desire.

Legitimate power—potential to influence granted to a person who occupies a legal position of authority.

Expert power—potential to influence others based on the real or perceived command of a subject area with which others are less familiar but have a need to know.

example, if Wendy really wants to attend the sold-out White Stripes concert, and her brother Mitchell has an extra ticket to this concert, if Mitchell asks Wendy to take his turn doing the dishes after dinner, she may comply, hoping to ingratiate herself to Mitchell so that he will "reward" her by taking her to the concert.

3. Legitimate power. Legitimate power is the potential to influence granted to a person who occupies a legal position of authority. The power is called "legitimate" because it is bestowed in some official way and because the person with the power may be upheld by laws or rules that dictate how that power is used. Elected officials (regardless of whether you voted for them or agree with their selection) are the most obvious example of legitimate power. Other people have legitimate power because they happen to hold a position of authority. For example, teachers have legitimate power with respect to their students, parents with their minor children, managers with employees, and nonelected government officials with citizens. If your teacher tells you that you must attend every class meeting, if your parents tell you that you must get a summer job, if your boss tells you that you must complete your report by Friday, or if you are speeding and a police car signals you to pull over, you must comply or risk negative consequences because of the legitimate authority of others over you.

4. Expert power. Expert power is the potential to influence others based on the real or perceived command of a subject area with which others are less familiar but

In the doctor-patient relationship the doctor is normally thought to have expert power. How is the availability of medical information on the Internet changing this?

have a need to know. For example, if you want to get a divorce and your friend is a family law attorney, she has the potential to influence your decisions about your divorce settlement because of her expertise. Since she doesn't have children and has little other experience with kids, however, she has little expert power over your child-rearing decisions. In your classes, your instructors can influence your thinking because they usually have more subject-specific knowledge and expertise than you do. Similarly, when a physician tells you to take medication for your high blood pressure, you are probably persuaded because your doctor has medical expertise and you do not.

At times we can be blinded by the perception of expert power. Another person may not actually possess the knowledge we desire, but if we believe people know more than we do, they may influence us. For instance, when shopping for a water heater, a person can be intimidated into buying a specific model by an aggressive sales associate. All salespeople are not water heater experts; rather, they are hired to sell, and their product knowledge may actually be sketchy. As salespeople gain experience with a line of goods, they may acquire expert product knowledge that is valuable to their clients. We are always grateful to have a knowledgeable sales associate when we have to buy an expensive item like a TV or computer. But that expertise is not always a given, even if we believe it to be.

5. Referent power. Referent power is the potential to influence based on having the respect and admiration of others. Let's face it, we want to be liked and impress those we find respectable or admirable. As a result, we are likely to allow them to influence us. If your best friend raves about a little-known movie showing at the local retrospective movie house, you are likely to go see it, even though you've never heard of it and don't know any of the actors in it. Likewise, corporations often hire celebrities to endorse products knowing that they can draw on the referent power of the star to stimulate sales of their product. Thus Pepsi hired P. Diddy to advertise Diet Pepsi not because he has reward, coercive, legitimate, or expert power, but because of his referent power. We are also attracted to those we find agreeable. Simply being a person who has strong interpersonal skills, such as listening, supporting, and holding conversations, is likely to increase your referent power.

> ▷ **Principles of Power**

Research has identified at least six basic principles: (1) Power is a perception, not a fact; (2) power exists within a relationship; (3) power represents an exchange of and sometimes a struggle over resources; (4) the person with less to lose has greater power; (5) the partner with more power can make and break the rules for the relationship; and (6) power is not inherently good or bad (Guerrero, Andersen, & Afifi, 2007).

The first principle states that *power is a perception, not a fact*. While you may perceive yourself to be powerful, able to reward or coerce your partner, if your partner doesn't perceive you as having power, you don't. For example, in our opening vignette, Vince thought he had the upper

Referent power—potential to influence based on having the respect and admiration of others.

> **OBSERVE AND ANALYZE** ▽

Sources of Power

Observe several conversations between two characters on television or in a movie in which one person is trying to influence another. Note examples of each of the five types of power. In fictional conversations, which source of power is most common? Least common? Then analyze several advertisements on the Internet, television, or radio and note examples of each of the five sources of power. In media advertisements, which source of power is most common? Least common? Are there similarities or differences in the sources of power underlying influence in fictional dialogue and media ads?

hand, that he was more powerful than Stella, because he could reward her with his money. But it turns out that money wasn't as important to Stella as he thought it was. Therefore, he didn't actually have the power he thought he had in the relationship. The second principle is closely related to the first and holds that *power exists within a relationship.* Power is not a personality trait or a behavior that you can learn and perform. Rather, the sources of power available to you are specific to each relationship you have and can change over time. For example, Joshua, who has taken a class on personal finance, may be perceived by his younger sister to be an "expert" on consumer credit and she may take his advice when selecting a credit card. But Joshua is unlikely to be perceived as an expert in finance by his older brother, who is a stockbroker. In some relationships, power is unequally distributed, with one person having more power than the other person, while in other relationships it is more balanced.

The third principle is that *power is based on resources.* If the resources you have to offer are easily available to your partner outside of your relationship, you will have less power than if the resources you control are relatively unavailable outside of your relationship. This is why during a downturn in the economy, a person will tolerate poor management, a hostile work environment, the lack of a raise, and the reduction of benefits on the job. The resources to complain or quit are not available in such situations, but those resources will return when the economy improves, with employees demanding raises, improved benefits, and changes to management and the work environment. In our opening vignette, Vince assumed he had power because of the financial resources he could offer, but since Stella didn't think money was as important as being close to family and friends, his resources didn't represent power after all. The fourth principle is related to the third and holds that *the person with less to lose has greater power.* In our opening vignette, Vince initially assumed that Stella had more to lose because as a social worker she didn't make as much money. However, Stella turned that power relationship around when she not only said that money didn't matter to her but also gave an ultimatum to Vince, implying that if her terms were not met she was willing to walk away from the relationship. As a result, Vince actually ended up having more to lose than Stella did.

The fifth principle is related to the third and fourth and states that *the person with more power can make and break the rules for the relationship.* For example, there are many situations in families or in workplaces where parents or managers make and break the rules that children and employees must follow. In families, children have to eat what is put on their plates, but parents may opt out of eating a vegetable they don't like. In workplaces, employees are docked pay for coming late to work, but a manager may habitually arrive five to ten minutes late with no negative consequences. In our opening vignette, Vince thought he had the power to make or break the rules of the relationship, but Stella's implication that she would rather walk out of the relationship than capitulate to Vince's demands meant that she gained the power to set the rules.

The last principle holds that *power is not inherently good or bad.* The power dynamic within a relationship can both enhance success and strengthen relationships and compromise individuality and cripple relationships. In a relationship where power is balanced, the partners may communicate well and the relationship may flourish by drawing on the power sources of both partners. Or the relationship may flounder amid a sea of influence stalemates, with neither partner willing to concede to the influence of the other. When power is unbalanced in a relationship, the relationship may be effective and satisfying to both partners if the more powerful individual is sensitive to the needs and concerns of the less powerful partner. Or the relationship may become abusive as the more powerful partner utilizes power to achieve selfish goals at the expense of the less powerful partner. In and of itself, power is neither good nor bad, but the use of power can lead to positive or negative outcomes. Whether the power dynamic in a relationship is healthy or sick will depend on the communication skills of both partners and the ethical use of power by the more powerful partner.

◒ Interpersonal Persuasion

Persuasion is the art of skillfully and ethically influencing the attitudes or behaviors of others by crafting verbal arguments using reasoning, credibility, and emotional appeals. Persuasion is ethical because it relies on verbal arguments rather than force and allows others freedom to resist the influence attempt (Trenholm, 1989). We begin by explaining the components of persuasive messages. Then we will look at seven strategies you can use to form messages whose purpose is to get someone to act in a specific way.

Persuasion—art of skillfully and ethically influencing the attitudes or behaviors of others by crafting verbal arguments using reasoning, credibility, and emotional appeals.

▷ Components of Persuasive Messages

Persuasion involves (1) providing good reasons, (2) being a credible source, and (3) appealing to emotions. Once you understand these components of persuasive messages, you will be better able to put into practice the persuasion strategies we will introduce in the next section.

1. Providing good reasons. Because people pride themselves on being "rational"—that is, they seldom believe or do anything without a reason—you increase the likelihood of persuading them if you can provide them with reasons rather than just claiming something. **Reasons** are statements that provide valid explanations or justifications for a belief or action. They answer the question "Why?" by providing information to back up the position you are taking. **Claims**, on the other hand, are simple statements of belief or opinion. They don't answer the "Why?" question. You can probably think of many times that you made a claim and the person you were talking to in effect said, "I can't accept what you've said on face value—give me some reasons!" Let's look at a simple example to help you understand the relationship between claims and reasons. Suppose you're talking with a friend about movies. You might ask, "Have you seen *Ironman*?" If your friend says "No," you might then make the claim, "It's great. You really need to see it." If your friend asks "Why?" you might explain, "Well, first, it shows a very

Reasons—statements that provide valid explanations or justifications for a belief or action.

Claims—simple statements of belief or opinion.

intelligent superhero. And the dialogue between Ironman and his personal assistant is really witty." Your reasoning could be diagrammed as follows:

> ***Claim:*** You need to see *Ironman.* (Why?)
> ***Reason 1:*** Because it shows intelligent characters.
> ***Reason 2:*** Because some of the dialogue is really witty.

Ethical communicators give good reasons to back up their claims so that their partners are able to weigh and evaluate for themselves the substance of the influence attempt. Having heard the reasons given, they may accept or reject the influence based on how they evaluate the reasons. Now let's consider what makes a reason a good or effective reason.

- **Good reasons are relevant to the claim.** As you think of the reasons that you might provide to support a claim, you'll find that some reasons are better than others because they relate more directly to the issue at hand. For example, the reasons just offered for seeing *Ironman*—"a very intelligent superhero" and "witty dialogue"—are relevant reasons. These are likely to be criteria that people look for in movies.
- **Good reasons are well supported.** In addition to making your reasons relevant, any time you're trying to persuade by using reasons, you need to support the reasons you present. For instance, once you say, "You should see *Ironman* because it shows a very intelligent superhero and has witty dialogue," your friend may find those reasons relevant but still want additional information that justifies your reasons. As a result, you'll also need to provide specific support or evidence. In support of "very intelligent superhero," you may have to elaborate that Ironman "is the corporate head of a major defense contracting business and can create computer applications

Richard Petty
Professor of Psychology, the Ohio State University, on
Attitude Change

As an undergraduate political science major, Richard Petty got so interested in how people change their attitudes that he chose to minor in psychology, where he could not only take more courses in attitude change but also learn empirical research methods. He then decided to go on to graduate work in psychology at the Ohio State University, where he could focus on studying attitude change and persuasion. Like many scholars, the subject of his doctoral dissertation laid the foundation for a career of research. Petty chose attitude change induced by persuasive messages.

When Petty began his research, the psychological scholarship of the previous forty years had been unable to demonstrate a relationship between people's attitudes and behaviors. Petty believed that the relationship between attitude change and behavior had been obscured by the complexity of the variables involved in assessing attitude change. Now Petty is in the forefront of scholars who have demonstrated that attitude change and behavior are, in fact, related.

During the last twenty years, Petty has published scores of research articles on his own and with colleagues on various aspects of influence, seeking to discover under what circumstances attitudes affect behavior. His work with various collaborators has been so successful that he has gained international acclaim. Many of his works have been published worldwide, and his elaboration likelihood model (ELM) theory of persuasion, which he developed in collaboration with John Cacioppo, has become the most cited theoretical approach to attitude and persuasion.

According to the ELM theory, attitude change is likely to occur through one of just two relatively distinct "routes to persuasion." The first route, known as the central route, is through a person's careful and thoughtful consideration of the true merits of the reasons presented in support of a claim. The second route, called the peripheral route, is via non-reason-based cues in the persuasion context (for instance, the charisma or attractiveness of the person doing the persuading) that induce change without necessitating scrutiny of the central merits of the claim. Following their initial speculation about these two routes to persuasion, Petty and Cacioppo developed, researched, and refined their ELM theory.

ELM is about the processes responsible for attitude change and the strength of the attitudes that result from those processes. ELM hypothesizes that what is persuasive to a person and how lasting any attitude change based on that persuasion is depend on how motivated and able people are to assess the merits of a speaker, an issue, or a position. People who are highly motivated are likely to study available information about the claim. As a result, they are more likely to arrive at a reasoned attitude that is well articulated and bolstered by information received via the central route. For people who are less motivated to study information related to the claim, attitude change can result from a number of less resource-demanding processes that do not require the effort of evaluating the relevant information. Less motivated people are affected more by information through the peripheral route, but their attitude changes are likely to be weaker in endurance. ELM explains why some attitude changes are related to behavior but others are not. Specifically, attitude changes that result from considerable thought also result in behavior change, but attitude changes that result from simple peripheral cues (e.g., agreeing simply because the source is an expert) may not.

So what can we learn about influencing others from Petty's research? First, we must recognize that attitude change results from our choices of influence tactics in combination with the choices made by our conversational partners about how deeply they wish to probe into the information. We should strive to present rational influence strategies based on good reasons and supporting evidence when we expect that our conversational partner will think deeply about what we are saying. Likewise, we should draw on our credibility and use emotional influence factors when listener thinking is expected to be superficial. Finally, we must remember that the attitudes changed by considerable mental effort will tend to be stronger than those that were changed after little thought.

Where is Petty going from here? He will certainly continue working on aspects of attitude change because, as he says, "I never finish a project without discovering at least two unanswered questions arising from the research." In addition, he's interested in finding out how people behave when their judgments may have been inappropriate or biased. That is, sometimes it becomes salient to people that they were inappropriately biased by the mere attractiveness of the message source rather than by the substance of what was said.

Petty teaches both graduate and undergraduate courses in attitudes and persuasion, research methods, and theories of social psychology. Petty has written scores of research articles and several books, all dealing with aspects of attitude, attitude change, and persuasion. For titles of several of his publications, see the references for this chapter at the end of the book.

for robotics design," and in support of "witty dialogue," you may need to quote a particularly good line of dialogue you remember.

- **Good reasons are meaningful to the person you're trying to persuade.** There are times when you know something about your conversational partner that calls for you to give more weight to one particular reason than to another. As a result, you also need to tailor your reasoning to make your reasons meaningful to the person you are trying to persuade. For instance, suppose the friend to whom you recommended seeing the movie *Ironman* loves expensive sports cars. In this case, you might want to mention not only the intelligent superhero and witty dialogue but also the scenes in which sports cars appear.

2. Being a credible source. Good reasons alone may be persuasive, but they are even more powerful when presented by a credible source. **Credibility** is the extent to which the target believes in the speaker's expertise, trustworthiness, and likability. In effect, how persuasive you are may depend on whether your conversational partner has confidence in who you are as a person. You may be able to recall times when no matter how logical the information presented to you appeared to be, you didn't believe it because you lacked confidence in the person presenting it. On the flip side, of course, are situations in which people believe anything that a highly charismatic person says even when that person provides no good reasons and argues illogically. Why do we *ever* allow a person's charisma to be the sole factor in important decisions? In this chapter's "Spotlight on Scholars" box, Richard Petty, who has studied attitude change, argues that as receivers of information, we follow either a central route or peripheral routes as we consider persuasive messages. The central route requires us to weigh and consider the reasons and evidence carefully. However, we often reserve the central route for issues that are really important to us. Therefore, we may take the peripheral route to make most of our decisions, relying on the word of friends or charismatic others to make many of our decisions for us.

Let's consider the three factors of credibility—competence, trustworthiness, and likability—more closely:

- **Competence** is the perception that the speaker is well qualified to provide accurate and reliable information. The more people perceive you as knowledgeable on a particular subject, the more likely they will pay attention to your views on that subject. For example, if Reggie sees his friend Gloriana as unusually well informed on local political issues, he will consider her to be competent and may be persuaded to vote for a tax levy simply because Gloriana supports it.

- **Trustworthiness** is the perception that the speaker is dependable, honest, and acting for the good of others. A speaker's intentions or motives are particularly important in determining whether others will view the person as trustworthy. For instance, if you are trying on a pair of slacks and a sales clerk you know is working on commission says to you, "Wow, you

Credibility—extent to which the target believes in the speaker's expertise, trustworthiness, and likability.

Competence—perception that the speaker is well qualified to provide accurate and reliable information.

Trustworthiness—perception that the speaker is dependable, honest, and acting for the good of others.

look terrific in those," you may well question that person's trustworthiness. Conversely, if a fashionably dressed bystander looks over at you and comments, "I wish I looked as good in those; they really fit you well," you are likely to accept the trustworthiness of the statement because the bystander has nothing to gain by speaking with you.

- **Likability** is the perception that the speaker is congenial, friendly, and warm. Until proven wrong, we tend to believe people that we like. For example, Ron may let Miguel talk him into spending the night camping out in the desert with Miguel's Cub Scout troop simply because Ron likes Miguel. Likability should be considered carefully because of the danger of scam artists, unethical operators who cultivate likability to persuade others to do things that are not really in their best interests.

Likability—perception that the speaker is congenial, friendly, and warm.

Over time, you can influence how credible others perceive you to be. First, you can show that you know what you are doing and why you are doing it—that you are competent. In contrast, if you behave carelessly, take on too many tasks at one time, and do not double-check details, you're likely to be perceived as incompetent. Second, you can show that you care about the effects of what you say and do on others, offer to help others, and smile when you meet friends and strangers alike—that you are likable. Third, and perhaps most importantly, you can establish your credibility by behaving in ways that are ethical—demonstrating that you are trustworthy. Behaving ethically can sometimes be difficult. When you believe strongly in the rightness of your cause, you may well be tempted to say or do anything, ethical or not, to achieve your goals. But before you succumb to behaving unethically, even if you feel doing so is ultimately for a good cause, think of all of the people in the world who have ridden roughshod over moral or ethical principles to achieve their goals. Eventually their credibility is called into question. Even if they have achieved their short-term goals, the long-term effect is a lack of credibility. For example, consider political commentators Rush Limbaugh and Michael Moore, one of whom (Limbaugh) represents the extreme right wing and the other of whom (Moore) represents the extreme left wing. No doubt both commentators firmly believe in the moral correctness of their stances, but both have come under fire for manipulating the truth to make their arguments, the result being that neither is viewed as credible by political moderates. How you handle ethical questions says a great deal about you as a person. What is your code of ethics? The following behaviors are essentials of ethical persuasion.

- **Tell the truth.** Of all the aspects of trustworthiness, this may be the most important. If people believe you are lying to them outright or manipulating the truth in some way, they

"Everything's all screwed up. Nice job, people."

are likely to reject you and your ideas wholeheartedly. As a result, tell the truth at all times, and if you are not absolutely sure if information you report is true, say so. Many times an honest "I really don't know, but I'll find out" or "I'm not 100 percent sure, but the facts I do have lead me to believe this is true" will contribute far more to your reputation for trustworthiness than trying to stretch the truth.

- **Disclose the complete picture.** One way to stretch the truth is to leave out important details that, if revealed, would change people's conclusions. People can make something sound good or bad, better or worse, by leaving out pertinent details, but purposely putting a favorable spin on unfavorable information is unethical. For instance, if Hector's mother asks him, "Why don't you admit you broke the vase?" and Hector says he didn't break it (but leaves out the fact that his friend, who was not supposed to be in the apartment, did break it), Hector is stretching the truth through omission and in effect lying.

- **Resist personal attacks against those who oppose your ideas.** Deflecting attention away from yourself when asked tough questions and focusing it instead on irrelevant personal attacks against opponents is another way to manipulate the truth. For instance, if Philip is asked why he cheated on the exam by his teacher and Philip either accuses another student of cheating or blames the teacher for failing to prepare the class for the exam, Philip is using personal attacks to hide from the truth.

3. Appealing to emotions. The third and final component of persuasive messages is appealing to the emotions of those you are trying to persuade. Messages that provide good reasons and come from a credible source are likely to be persuasive. But when you're trying to influence others to act, you can increase the persuasiveness of your message by appealing to people's emotions (Jorgensen, 1998). Some who *believe* they should do something may be nonetheless reluctant to act on their belief without an additional appeal. For instance, Jonas may believe that people should donate money to worthy causes, but he may not do so; Gwen may agree that people should exercise for forty-five minutes, three times a week, but she may not do so. What motivates people who simply believe in something to act on that belief is often the degree of their emotional involvement. Emotions are the driving force behind action, the instrument that prods or nudges us from passive belief to overt action. So, understanding and using an emotional appeal can increase the effectiveness of our persuasive messages.

The effectiveness of emotional appeals depends on the mood and attitude of the person you are persuading and the persuasive language itself. For example, suppose you are trying to convince your brother to loan you money so that you can buy your textbooks for the semester without waiting for your grant money to be released. In addition to your rational approach, you may want to include several appeals to his emotions using specific examples and experiences, such as, "I'm sure you remember how tough it is to understand the lectures when you haven't looked at the book" or "Mom will be on my back if I don't do well in this class" or "I know you want to be a nice guy and help your little brother here." Or even better, you may want to phrase your emotional appeal in story form. For instance, instead of just saying, "I thought you might be interested in going hiking and rock climbing with me tomorrow—it will be fun," you might say, "I thought you might be interested in going hiking and rock climbing with me. I think it will be like old times when we would spend the whole day at the gorge. Just two brothers, 'bonding.' Remember how much fun we had on our hike to Clear Creek Canyon?"

▷ Compliance-Gaining Strategies

When we need to influence someone, we may craft elaborate messages using all three components of persuasion, or we may opt to use one or two **compliance-gaining strategies**—simple verbal arguments designed to get people to act in a way they are not naturally inclined to act, which draw heavily on one component of persuasion. In this section, we look at seven of the most common compliance-gaining strategies that you may consider using in your influence attempts. Scholars have identified hundreds of compliance-gaining strategies, and numerous efforts have been made to group these into categories (O'Hair & Cody, 1987; Kellerman & Cole, 1994). We will present the seven basic strategies identified by O'Hair and Cody (1987). As you will see, each of these strategies draws heavily on one component of persuasion in forming influence messages. The seven strategies are supporting-evidence, exchange, direct-request, empathy-based, face-maintenance, other-benefit, and distributive.

1. Supporting-evidence strategy. The **supporting-evidence strategy** is using influence messages that seek compliance by offering good reasons. These messages are based on claims but are backed up with strong support. For example, to get someone to not quit his or her job, you might say, "Let me give you what I think are the three best reasons for holding onto the job you have," or to get someone to loan you his or her notes for a class you missed, you might say, "I need to borrow your notes from last Tuesday's class. I missed class because I was sick. I had a temperature of 102° and couldn't keep anything in my stomach."

2. Exchange strategy. The **exchange strategy** is using influence messages that seek compliance by offering the target something he or she values if he or she complies with what is being requested. In other words, these strategies involve agreeing to do something for someone if he or she does something for you (Guerrero, Andersen, & Afifi, 2007). For example, if you want help with your history homework, you might say, "I'll help you with calculus if you help me with history," or if you want a discount on something, you might say, "I'll agree to the price if you'll throw in free delivery." In both cases, you imply that the underlying reason for the other person to comply is that you will both benefit from the action. Why will you comply with my request for history help? Because you want help with calculus. Why will you give me free delivery? Because then I'll

Compliance-gaining strategies— simple verbal arguments designed to get people to act in a way they are not naturally inclined to act, which draw heavily on one component of persuasion.

Supporting-evidence strategy— using influence messages that seek compliance by offering good reasons.

Exchange strategy—using influence messages that seek compliance by offering the target something he or she values if he or she complies with what is being requested.

Direct-request strategy—using influence messages that seek compliance by simply asking the target to comply.

Empathy-based strategy—using influence messages that seek compliance by causing the other to emotionally identify with your situation.

Face-maintenance strategy—using influence messages that seek compliance through indirection as a means of maintaining face for the influencer, the target, or both people.

Other-benefit strategy—using influence messages that seek compliance by identifying how complying will benefit the other person.

Distributive strategy—using influence messages that evoke negative emotions that can be neutralized by complying with the request.

buy your product. Notice that exchange messages are based on credibility. Your conversational partner is likely to comply only if he or she believes that you will carry out your part of the exchange.

3. Direct-request strategy. The **direct-request strategy** is using influence messages that seek compliance by simply asking the target to comply. For example, a friend might simply say, "Can I borrow your cell phone?" Or, while you are watching TV, your father may walk in and say, "Why don't you turn down the TV?" Direct requests are based primarily on credibility. In effect, a person making a direct request says, "You know I'm trustworthy or you like me or you respect me and so you'll comply." Research shows that direct-request strategies are most commonly used by people who feel powerful and supported (Levine & Boster, 2001).

4. Empathy-based strategy. The **empathy-based strategy** is using influence messages that seek compliance by causing the other to emotionally identify with your situation. This strategy is based on emotional appeals. For example, if you want to influence your roommate not to drink and drive you might say, "Please promise me you won't get behind the wheel when you have been drinking anymore. Imagine how I would feel having to call your parents and tell them that you're dead." Similarly, you might try to convince your professor to give you a make up exam by saying, "Come on, Professor Smith, you remember how hard it was to wake up for 8:00 classes when you were in college."

5. Face-maintenance strategy. The **face-maintenance strategy** is using influence messages that seek compliance through indirection as a means of maintaining face for the influencer, the target, or both people. For example, if I want to borrow your class notes but don't want to embarrass either you or me should you not want to lend them, I might say, "Gee, I really want to do well on our Econ midterm, but my notes are a mess; I wish I had a better outline to study from." The direct meaning embedded in this indirect message is, "I need to borrow your notes." My hope is that you will be persuaded to comply with this real but unstated influence message. But by phrasing my message indirectly, I won't be embarrassed or embarrass you if you do not comply with my request. Indirect messages are most effective when there is a positive relationship and when the influencer is liked, trusted, or respected by the target.

6. Other-benefit strategy. The **other-benefit strategy** is using influence messages that seek compliance by identifying how complying will benefit the other person. For example, Maxine's academic advisor tried to convince Maxine to study abroad by explaining, "For you study abroad would be the perfect way to get your language requirement finished and enjoy the sunshine of southern Spain while we're freezing and buried in three feet of snow!" This strategy draws on reasoning but presents reasons that the target will view as advantageous. Obviously the other-benefit strategy is most successful when used in close relationships where you understand what the target is likely to see as an advantage.

7. Distributive strategy. Finally, the **distributive strategy** is using influence messages that evoke negative emotions that can be neutralized by complying with the request (Guerrero, Andersen, Jorgensen, Spitzberg, & Eloy, 1995). Commonly, these messages are designed to induce fear, guilt, or shame for noncompliance. Some of these messages we've heard since childhood: "I'll tell . . ."; "Go have fun, don't worry about me"; and "Big boys don't cry" are just a few examples. Unfortunately they continue to be used in adulthood.

▷ Choosing a Compliance-Gaining Strategy

How should you choose which compliance-gaining strategy to use in a particular situation? Your choice depends on how effective you believe a particular strategy will be in a given situation (Miller, Cody, & McLaughlin, 1994). The better you are at assessing the situation, the more likely you are to craft a message that will be effective. Although there is no one "best" strategy, you may find the following guidelines useful in helping you make your decision.

1. Choose the strategy that is best tailored to your partner. Since people are unique, and because no strategy will work equally well for everyone, you have to think about the person you want to influence. Will this person respond more favorably to a direct or an indirect method? Will he or she appreciate a logical argument or be more likely to comply on the basis of an emotional appeal or on the basis of your credibility? Are you in a position to offer some reward?

2. Choose the strategy that would best protect the relationship. Sometimes a strategy may work, but at the same time may not be good for the relationship. If the relationship is one that you want to preserve, then you will want to select a strategy that will not be perceived as manipulative, such as a phony-sounding face-maintenance or empathy-based strategy. Moreover, you are likely to want to select a strategy that will be perceived as polite. For instance, if you put pressure on a person by using a threat of punishment or guilt-inducement, the person may comply but is likely to be resentful. Such distributive strategies are considered to be the least polite of all strategies (Kellerman & Shea, 1996) and may damage relationships as a result. Sometimes failing to win compliance is better than hurting the relationship.

3. Choose the strategy that is most comfortable for you. Sometimes a strategy may work without necessarily hurting the relationship, but it may be personally uncomfortable for you. Some compliance-gaining strategies are a better fit with our own personal communication styles than others. For example, a person who likes to work with others in a cooperative manner may be more comfortable using exchange strategies, and a person who is highly attuned to emotion may prefer to use empathy-based strategies. Since you are more likely to be effective with a strategy that fits you, all other things being equal, choose the one that best suits you.

In addition to these three guidelines for selecting a compliance-gaining strategy, Hample and Dallinger (2002) have found that people also take into consideration whether a compliance-gaining strategy is too distasteful or forceful, whether using it would make them look bad or threaten the other person, and whether it is relevant to the situation at hand.

▷ Overcoming Resistance to Compliance-Gaining Strategies

Not all attempts to gain compliance will be successful. Sometimes, even when we have stated well-reasoned, credible positions that appeal to the emotions of those we try to persuade, we nonetheless encounter resistance. As Knowles, Butler, and Linn (2001) point out, "Resistance is the most important component of any social influence attempt that fails to gain compliance" (p. 57). Too often when someone resists, our tendency is to continue to use the techniques we used in the first place. However, this only adds to a person's resistance. Instead of redoubling our persuasive efforts, one of the easiest ways of dealing with resistance is to ask the person you are trying to persuade to explain his or her reluctance to do what you are asking. If you listen closely, you will be able to understand his or her thinking. Then you may be able to adopt a different strategy that is more successful. Some research has shown that when an initial influence attempt is unsuccessful, people tend to use follow-up strategies that are more forceful, more aggressive, and sometimes more rude (Hample & Dallinger, 1998). When facing resistance to our influence attempts, it is important that we try new strategies that aren't necessarily more aggressive or intimidating. For example, don't always follow up an empathy-based strategy with a

Redoubling your persuasive effort is usually an ineffective means of changing someone's mind who has already rejected your appeals. How can asking that person to state his or her objections help you be more successful?

distributive strategy. Instead, try following it up with an exchange strategy or a supporting-evidence strategy. Of course, regardless of how many well-crafted messages you send, your partner may never accept your influence attempt. In these cases you will have to reassess the importance of your request against the value you place on your relationship.

○ Assertiveness

Many people who try the various compliance-gaining strategies we have outlined here remain ineffective at exerting influence in their relationships because they do not practice assertiveness. **Assertiveness** is the act of sending messages that declare personal preferences and defend personal rights while at the same time respecting the preferences and rights of others. To better understand assertiveness, in this section we will first take a look at the alternatives to assertiveness—passive behavior and aggressive behavior—before we detail the skills used to form assertive messages. Then we will compare and contrast situations in which passive, aggressive, and assertive responses might be used. Next, we will discuss the skills you can use to practice assertiveness. Finally, we will discuss assertiveness in cross-cultural relationships.

▷ Passive and Aggressive Behaviors

Passive behavior is behavior in which one is reluctant or unable to state opinions or share feelings that are in one's interests to express. Passive behavior is not influential, and those who use this method end up submitting to other people's demands, even when doing so is inconvenient, is against their best interests, or violates their rights. For example, suppose that when Sergei uncrates the new plasma television set he purchased at a local department store, he notices a deep scratch on the left side. If he is upset about the scratch but doesn't try to get the store to replace the expensive item, he is exhibiting passive behavior.

Aggressive behavior is behavior in which one states opinions or shares feelings too strongly, in a manner that shows little regard for the situation or for the feelings, needs, or rights of others. People exhibit aggressive behavior when they behave belligerently, violently, or confrontationally. Aggressive messages depend on coercive power; they can involve name-calling, threatening, judging, or fault-finding. For example, suppose that after discovering the scratch on his new television set, Sergei storms back to the store, confronts the first salesperson he finds, and loudly demands his money back while accusing the salesperson of intentionally selling him damaged merchandise. Such aggressive behavior may or may not result in getting the damaged set replaced, but it will certainly damage his relationship with the salesperson. Even in a professional scenario, most receivers of aggressive messages are likely to feel hurt by them (Martin, Anderson, & Horvath, 1996). While Sergei may not care about his relationship with the salesperson, if he is prone to aggression as a means of persuasion, he will likely damage other, more intimate, relationships.

Assertiveness—act of sending messages that declare personal preferences and defend personal rights while at the same time respecting the preferences and rights of others.

Passive behavior—behavior in which one is reluctant or unable to state opinions or share feelings that are in one's interests to express.

Aggressive behavior—behavior in which one states opinions or shares feelings too strongly, in a manner that shows little regard for the situation or for the feelings, needs, or rights of others.

Flaming—hostile interactions between Internet users.

Cyber stalking—use of information and communications technology, particularly the Internet, to harass others.

Passive-aggressive behavior—behavior in which one exhibits aggressive behavior, but in a passive manner.

Today, certain textual, visual, and audio forms of online messages have the potential to harm others because they utilize aggressive behavior (Kleinman, 2007). One such aggressive message is **flaming**, which is hostile interactions between Internet users. Flaming usually occurs in the social context of a discussion board, Internet relay chat (IRC), or even e-mail. Another type of online aggressiveness is **cyber stalking**, the use of information and communications technology, particularly the Internet, to harass others. The behavior includes false accusations, monitoring transmissions, threats, identity theft, damage to data or equipment, the solicitation of minors for sexual purposes, and gathering information for harassment purposes.

Another type of aggressive behavior is passive-aggressive behavior. **Passive-aggressive behavior** is behavior in which one exhibits aggressive behavior, but in a passive manner. Examples of passive-aggressive behavior include being stubborn, being unresponsive, intentionally refusing to help, and not owning up to one's responsibilities. In a quiet way, passive-aggressive behavior is almost more insidious than aggressive behavior because it doesn't allow the recipient of the behavior the opportunity to respond. For example, suppose instead of being aggressive, Sergei calmly and professionally complains to a salesperson about his scratched television set. If the salesperson promises to help rectify the situation but out of a dislike for customers in general does nothing, or if the salesperson refuses to acknowledge the store's responsibility and instead only offers, "Well, we don't like to accept returns but we'll do it this time," he or she is exhibiting passive-aggressive behavior.

Assertiveness, in contrast to passive behavior and aggressive behavior, is always focused simultaneously on both one's own interests and those of others. Unlike aggressive behavior, assertiveness respects the rights and dignity of others through the use of nonhostile verbal content and vocal attributes (Alberti & Emmons, 2001). Unlike passive behavior, assertiveness respects the rights and dignity of oneself through the vocalization of one's honest thoughts and feelings. The difference between assertiveness and passive or aggressive behavior is not in how individuals think and feel, but how their feelings work in conjunction with the thoughts and feelings of others. To return to our example, if Sergei chooses an assertive response upon discovering that he has bought a damaged TV, he will still feel angry. But instead of either doing nothing and living with the damaged merchandise, or verbally assaulting the salesperson, Sergei might choose to call the store, describe the condition of the TV set to a customer service representative, share his feelings on discovering the scratch, and state what he would like to see happen now, such as exchanging the damaged set for a new one or getting a refund. Sergei's assertive messages should accomplish his own goals without annoying or hurting anyone else.

▷ Assertive Message Skills

Assertiveness is difficult for many of us because effective assertiveness messages combine a number of interpersonal communication skills, including:

1. **Make "I" statements.** "I" statements allow you to own your thoughts and feelings. Because the purpose of assertive responses is to represent your position or needs, your message should include "I" statements like "I think . . . ," "My opinion is . . .", "I feel . . . ," and "I would like . . ."

2. **Describe behaviors and feelings.** If we want others to satisfy our needs, then we should provide them with specific descriptive information to justify our requests. We do this by describing the feelings we have and the behaviors and outcomes we desire.

LEARN ABOUT YOURSELF ● Assertiveness

Take this short survey to learn something about yourself. Answer the questions based on your first response. There are no right or wrong answers. Just be honest in reporting your true behavior. For each question, select one of the following numbers that best describes your behavior.

1 = Strongly Agree
2 = Agree Somewhat
3 = Neutral
4 = Disagree Somewhat
5 = Strongly Disagree

_____ 1. I am aggressive in standing up for myself.
_____ 2. If a salesperson has gone to a lot of trouble to show me merchandise that I do not want to buy, I have no trouble saying "no."
_____ 3. If a close and respected relative were bothering me, I would keep my feelings to myself.
_____ 4. People do not take advantage of me.
_____ 5. If food in a restaurant is not satisfactory to me, I complain and insist upon a refund.
_____ 6. I avoid asking questions for fear of sounding stupid.
_____ 7. I would rather make a scene than bottle up my emotions.
_____ 8. I am comfortable in returning merchandise.
_____ 9. I find it difficult to ask friends to return money or objects they have borrowed from me.
_____ 10. If I hear that a person has been spreading false rumors about me, I confront that person and talk about it.
_____ 11. I can yell at others when I feel that I have been wronged.
_____ 12. I get anxious before making problem-solving business phone calls.

This is a test of your passive, assertive, and aggressive behavior.

Scoring the Survey: Add your scores for items 3, 6, 9, and 12. Your score will range from 4 to 20. The lower (closer to 4) your score, the more you tend to engage in passive behavior.

Add your scores for items 2, 4, 8, and 10. Your score will range from 4 to 20. The lower (closer to 4) your score, the more you tend to engage in assertiveness.

Add your scores for items 1, 5, 7, and 11. Your score will range from 4 to 20. The lower (closer to 4) your score, the more you tend to engage in aggressive behavior.

Adapted from: Rathus, S. (1973). A 30-item schedule for assessing assertive behavior. *Behavior Therapy, 4*, p. 398.

3. **Maintain regular eye contact and a self-confident posture.** Our nonverbal behaviors should convey our convictions. Staring and standing over someone represents aggressive behavior, while repeatedly shifting your gaze away and shrinking back is a sign of passive behavior. A steady gaze and a relaxed, involved body posture, however, will assertively convey self-confidence.

4. **Use a firm but pleasant tone of voice.** Aggressiveness is signaled by yelling or using harsh vocal tones, while speaking softly in a tentative tone of voice or not saying anything at all signals passivity. Assertive messages should be conveyed at a normal pitch, volume, and rate.

5. **Speak fluently.** Avoid vocalized pauses and semantic noises, which may signal passivity.

6. **Be sensitive to the face needs of others.** The goal of assertive messages is to influence others without damaging your relationships. Messages should be formed in ways that both meet the face needs of others and present your own needs.

In addition, follow the following assertiveness guidelines: (1) Identify what you are thinking or feeling; (2) analyze the cause of these feelings; (3) choose the appropriate skills to communicate these feelings, as well as predict the outcome you desire; and (4) communicate these feelings to the appropriate person.

It's important to recognize that you will not always achieve your goals by being assertive and, just as with self-disclosure and describing feelings, that there are risks involved in being assertive. For instance, some people, not knowing the difference between assertiveness and aggressive behavior, may be inclined to label any assertive behavior as "aggressive." Nonetheless, people who have difficulty asserting themselves often do not appreciate the fact that the potential benefits

SKILL BUILDERS ❍ Assertiveness

SKILL	USE	PROCEDURE	EXAMPLE
Behaving in a way in which you declare your personal preferences and defend your personal rights while at the same time respecting the preferences and rights of others	To show clearly what you think or feel	1. Identify what you are thinking or feeling. 2. Analyze the cause of these feelings. 3. Choose the appropriate skills necessary to communicate these feelings, as well as predict the outcome you desire. 4. Communicate these feelings to the appropriate person. Remember to own your feelings.	When Gavin believes that he is being unjustly charged for his drink, he says, "I have never been charged for a refill on iced tea before—has there been a change in policy?"

far outweigh the risks. If you have trouble taking the first step to being more as-sertive, try beginning with situations in which your potential for success is high (Alberti & Emmons, 2001). Remember, our behavior teaches people how to treat us. When we are passive, people will ignore our feelings because we have taught them that it's OK for them to do that. When we are aggressive, we teach people to respond in kind. By contrast, when we are assertive, we can influence others to treat us as we would prefer to be treated.

▷ Distinguishing among Passive, Aggressive, and Assertive Responses

Now that you understand passive and aggressive behavior and the skills needed to form assertive messages, let's look at examples of each type of behavior in three different contexts.

1. At work. Tanisha works in an office that employs both men and women. Whenever the boss has an especially interesting and challeng-ing job to be done, he assigns it to a male co-worker whose desk is next to Tanisha's. The boss has never said anything to Tanisha or to the male employee that would indicate he thinks less of Tanisha or her abilities. Nevertheless, Tanisha is frustrated by the boss's behavior.

> *Passive:* Tanisha says nothing to her boss. She's very frustrated by consistently be-ing overlooked but makes no response.
>
> *Aggressive:* Tanisha storms into her boss's office and says, "I'm sick and tired of you giving Tom the plum assignments and leaving me the garbage jobs. I'm every bit as good a worker, and I'm not going to take this any more."
>
> *Assertive:* Tanisha arranges a meeting with her boss. At the meeting she says, "I don't know whether you are aware of it, but during the past three weeks, every time you had a really interesting job to be done, you gave it to Tom. To the best of my knowledge, you believe that Tom and I are equally competent—you've never said anything to suggest that you thought less of my work. But when you 'reward' Tom with jobs that I perceive as interesting and continue to offer me routine jobs, I get really frustrated. Do you understand my feelings about this?" In this statement, she has described both her perception of the boss's behavior and her feelings about that behavior.

If you were Tanisha's boss, which of her responses would you most likely respond to? Probably the assertive response. Which of her responses would be most likely to get her fired? Probably the aggressive response. And which of her responses would be least likely to have any affect at all? Undoubtedly the passive response.

2. With a friend. Reece is a doctor doing his residency at City Hospital. He lives with two other residents in an apartment they have rented. Carl, one of the other residents, is the player of the group: It seems that whenever he has time off, he has a date. But like the others, he's a bit short of cash. He doesn't feel at all bashful about borrowing clothes or money from his roommates. One evening

Carl asks Reece if he can borrow his watch—a new, expensive watch that Reece received as a present from his father only a few days before. Reece is aware that Carl does not always take the best care of what he borrows, and he is very concerned about the possibility of Carl's damaging or losing the watch.

Passive: "Sure."

Aggressive: "Forget it! You've got a lot of nerve asking to borrow a brand-new watch. You know I'd be damned lucky to get it back in one piece."

Assertive: "Carl, I know I've lent you several items in the past, but this watch is special. I've had it only a few days, and I just don't feel comfortable lending it to anyone. I hope you can understand how I feel."

What are likely to be the consequences of each of these responses? If he behaves passively, Reece is likely to worry the entire evening and harbor some resentment of Carl, even if he gets the watch back undamaged. Moreover, Carl will continue to think that his roommates feel comfortable lending him anything he wants. If Reece behaves aggressively, Carl is likely to be completely taken aback. No one has ever said anything to Carl before, so he has no reason for believing that his borrowing was becoming an issue. Moreover, Reece will damage the relationship. However, if Reece behaves assertively, he puts the focus on his own feelings and on this particular object—the watch—while at the same time he thinks of Carl's feelings. His response isn't a denial of Carl's right to borrow items, nor is it an attack on Carl. It is an explanation of why Reece does not want to lend this item at this time.

3. In a social situation. Margarita has invited two of her girlfriends and their dates to drop by her residence hall suite before the dance. Shortly after the group arrives, Nick, who has come with Ramona, Margarita's best friend, lights a cigarette. Margarita, who is allergic to smoke, knows that it is illegal to smoke in the dorm and that if they are caught she will get kicked out of the residence hall.

Passive: Margarita coughs and makes awful faces, but says nothing.

Aggressive: "Nick, can't you read? The sign out front says 'No Smoking,' so put that damn thing out. Didn't anyone ever tell you it's not polite to stink up someone else's place, and besides, I'm allergic to smoke. Are you trying to kill me?"

Assertive: "Nick, please put your cigarette out. You probably forgot that the dorm is a nonsmoking area and I could get kicked out of the dorm if someone smells it and tells the RA. You also need to know that I'm allergic to smoke."

Again, let's contrast the three behaviors. In this case, Margarita knows the consequences if the smoke is detected, and she knows the risk to her own health. But Margarita's passive behavior may not get Nick's attention. The aggressive behavior is hardly better. She knows nothing about Nick, but her outburst insults him as though he purposefully intended to harm her. If Nick is at all inclined to be belligerent, her method is only going to incite him and damage her relationship with Ramona. The assertive behavior accurately and pleasantly presents her position in a way that respects Nick's face needs.

▷ Assertiveness in Cross-Cultural Relationships

As with most communication skills, assertiveness is valued in some cultures more than in others. As Samovar and Porter (2001) point out, "Communication problems arise when cultures that value assertiveness come in contact with cultures that value accord and harmony" (p. 85). Thus, the standard of assertiveness considered appropriate in the dominant American culture can seem inappropriate to people whose cultural frame of reference leads them to perceive it as either aggressive or weak.

Asian cultures are quite different from American culture regarding assertiveness. It would be inaccurate to say that Asian cultures value passivity, but they do value a more cautious approach to communication than assertiveness to maintain accord and harmony. Research has shown that Japanese, Malaysian, and Filipino adults are less likely to engage in assertiveness than their Western counterparts (Niikura, 1999). For instance, "to maintain harmony and avoid interpersonal clashes, Japanese business has evolved an elaborate process called 'nemawashii,' a term that means binding

A QUESTION OF ETHICS ○ What Would You Do?

Cassandra and Pete have been very lucky. They both have well-paying jobs that they dearly love. During college they had both worked hard and saved money so that two years after graduating they had enough money to buy a house. Their first home has needed a lot of remodeling, but Cassie and Pete have found that they enjoy working together and learning how to do various projects. So far they have refinished the floors, repaired some drywall, removed the old wallpaper, and repainted every room in the house. Now it is time to tackle the kitchen.

The current kitchen is a mess. The cabinets are scratched and several doors are loose, the flooring is discolored and coming up in places, and the appliances are from the 1970s. The more they have discussed the kitchen, the more they have found that they disagree on what needs to be done. Pete wants them to tackle the project themselves and believes that they can make the kitchen serviceable by removing the current floor, putting down ceramic tile, painting the current cabinets, and buying new appliances, phasing in the purchases over several years. Cassie, who loves to cook, wants the kitchen to be the centerpiece of the home. She wants to hire a kitchen designer to plan and execute a complete kitchen remodel. Pete adamantly refuses to consider spending the twenty thousand dollars or more that this would take. Having stated his position, Pete considers the conversation over. During their most recent discussion of the issue, Pete walked out of the room, turned on the TV, and refused to say any more on the matter.

Recently, Cassandra decided to take a different approach. So she asked Pete, "Do you really love me?" to which Pete replied, "Of course I love you, do you really need to ask?"

"Well, I was wondering if for our anniversary we could take a couple of weeks and go to Europe? It would be expensive, but it would be such a wonderful treat."

"Hey, that's a great idea," Pete replied, "I'll talk to a travel agent tomorrow."

"Well, are you sure?" Cassandra asked, "I mean, it's going to cost a lot, since we already used up our frequent flier miles."

"Don't worry, babe, we've got the money in the bank, and you know I only live to make you happy."

"Really," Cassandra pounced, "then why can't we hire a designer and have the kitchen done first class? You know I hate to travel, but I love to cook. Why are you willing to pay for an expensive trip but not pay for my dream kitchen?"

1. What are the ethical issues that Cassandra and Pete have confronted in this situation?
2. Analyze the conversation between Cassandra and Pete. Was Cassandra's approach an ethical use of interpersonal influence, or was it a manipulative trap?

the roots of a plant before pulling it out. In this process, any subject that might cause disorder at a meeting is discussed in advance. Anticipating and obviating interpersonal antagonism allow the Japanese to avoid impudent and discourteous behavior" (Samovar & Porter, 2001, p. 85). In fact, in collectivist societies like those throughout Asia, "a style of communication in which respecting the relationship through communication is more important than the information exchanged" (Jandt, 2001, p. 37). Jandt goes on to explain that these societies use group harmony, avoidance of loss of face to others and oneself, and a modest presentation of oneself as means of respecting the relationship."One does not say what one actually thinks," Jandt continues, "when it might hurt others in the group" (p. 37). Consistent with these principles, research has shown Turkish adolescents as less likely to engage in assertiveness than Western adolescents (Mehmet, 2003).

On the other hand, in Latin and Hispanic societies, men are frequently taught to exercise a form of self-expression that goes far beyond the guidelines presented here for assertiveness. In these societies, the concept of "machismo" guides male behavior. Though not exactly aggressive, "machismo" is more focused on the self than on a balance between the self and the other.

Thus when we use assertiveness—as with any other skill—we need to be aware that no single standard of behavior ensures that we will achieve our goals. Although what is labeled appropriate behavior varies across cultures, the results of passive and aggressive behavior seem universal. Passive behavior fails to communicate problems, leading to resentment on the part of the person behaving passively toward others, while aggressive behavior also fails to communicate problems effectively, leading to the fear and misunderstanding of others toward the person exhibiting the aggressive behavior. When talking with people whose cultures, backgrounds, or lifestyles differ from your own, you may need to observe their behaviors and their responses to your statements before you can be sure how best to communicate with them in a persuasive manner.

❂ Summary

Interpersonal influence is the practice of preserving or changing the attitudes or behaviors of others.

Power is the potential that one person has to influence the attitudes, beliefs, and behaviors of others. There are six principles of power: (1) Power is a perception, not a fact; (2) power is based on relationships; (3) power is based on resources; (4) the person with less to lose has greater power; (5) the person with more power can make and break the rules for the relationship; and (6) power is not inherently good or bad. The types of power are described as coercive power, reward power, legitimate power, expert power, and referent power.

Persuasion is the art of skillfully and ethically influencing the attitudes or behaviors of others through verbal messages. The three components of persuasive messages are providing good reasons (reasons that are relevant to the claim, well-supported, and meaningful to the person you're trying to persuade), being a credible source (being competent, trustworthy, and likable), and appealing to emotions. Compliance-gaining strategies include supporting-evidence strategies, exchange strategies, direct-request strategies, empathy-based strategies, face-maintenance strategies, other-benefits strategies, and distributive strategies. To be effective at gaining compliance, choose the strategy that you believe is most likely to be effective, would best protect the relationship, and is most comfortable for you.

Assertiveness is behavior in which one declares personal preferences and defends personal rights while at the same time respecting the preferences and rights of others. It contrasts with passive behavior, which is behavior in which one is reluctant or unable to state opinions or share feelings that are in one's interests to express, and aggressive behavior, which is behavior in which one states opinions or shares feelings too strongly, in a manner that shows little regard for the situation or for the feelings, needs, or rights of others. Flaming and cyber stalking are two examples of aggressive behavior via the Internet. Passive-aggressive behavior is also a form of aggressive behavior, in which one exhibits aggressive behavior in a passive manner. Some of the skills for behaving assertively include owning your ideas, thoughts, and feelings; describing behaviors and feelings; maintaining eye contact and a self-confident posture; using a firm but pleasant tone of voice; speaking fluently; and being sensitive to the face needs of others. Assertiveness is not valued in all cultures, but is valued in most Western cultures.

◑ Inter-Action Dialogue: Interpersonal Influence

Interpersonal influence occurs when one person attempts to change another person's attitudes or behaviors. As you read the following dialogue, consider the types of power exerted in the exchange, the components of persuasive messages that are used (providing good reasons, being a credible source, appealing to emotions), the compliance-gaining strategies used, and how the speakers engage in assertiveness.

Paul's friend Hannah stops by his dorm to show him what she has done.

Conversation

Hannah: Hey Paul, take a look at my term paper.

Paul: *(quickly reading the first page)* Wow, so far this looks great. You must have put a lot of time into it.

Hannah: No, but it should be good, I paid enough for it.

Paul: What?

Hannah: I got it off the Internet.

Paul: You mean you bought it from one of those term paper sites? Hannah, what's up? That's not like you—you're not a cheater.

Hannah: Listen—my life's crazy. I don't have time to write a stupid paper.

Paul: What's stupid about the assignment?

Hannah: I think the workload in this class is ridiculous. The professor acts as if this is the only class we've got. There are three exams, a team project, and this paper. What's the point?

Paul: Well, I think the professor assigned this paper for several reasons, to see whether students really know how to think about the material they have studied and to help us improve our writing.

Hannah: Come on, we learned how to write when we were in elementary school.

Paul: That's not what I said. Sure you can write a sentence or a paragraph, but can you really express your own ideas about this subject? What the professor is doing is putting us in a position not only where we show our understanding of the material, but also where we have to show our ability to phrase our thoughts in a sophisticated manner. By writing a term paper we have the chance to develop our own thinking about a topic. We can read a wide variety of sources and then make up our own minds and in our writing explain our thoughts. And the neat thing is, we'll get feedback about how we did.

Hannah: Yes, but you're not listening—I just don't have time.

Paul: So you believe the best way to deal with the situation is to cheat?

Hannah: Man, that's cold. But I'm not the only one doing this.

Paul: Are you saying that since some people cheat it's OK for you to cheat? Like people take drugs or sleep around so it's OK for you?

Hannah: No, don't be silly, but I told you I'm up to here in work. I've got no time.

Paul: Right. So remind me what you did last night.

Hannah: You know. I went to Sean's party. I deserve to have a little social life. I'm only twenty after all.

Paul: Sure, point well taken. So what did you do the night before?

Hannah: Well, I worked until 8:00, then Mary and I grabbed a bite to eat and then went clubbing.

Paul: So, for two nights you chose to do no school work, but you had time to socialize? And you're saying you're "up to here in work." Hannah, I'm just not buying it. Your workload is no different from mine. And I manage to get my work done. It's not perfect—like your Internet paper. But it's mine. So who do you hurt when you cheat? Besides your own character, you hurt me. Thanks friend.

Hannah: Hey, chill. You've made your point. But what can I do now? The paper's due in two days and I haven't even begun.

Paul: Do you have to work tonight?

Hannah: No.

Paul: Well, then you still have time. It will be a couple of long, hard days, but I'll bring you coffee and food.

Hannah: What a friend. Well, OK, I guess you win.

Paul: Hey wait. Let's seal it by tearing up that bought paper.

Hannah: What! You mean I can't even borrow a few ideas from it?

Paul: Hannah!

Hannah: OK. OK. Just kidding.

❍ Chapter Resources

Communication Improvement Plan:
Influencing Ethically ❍ Find more on the web @ www.oup.com/us/interact12

Would you like to improve your use of the following skills discussed in this chapter?

- Persuasion
- Compliance-gaining
- Assertiveness

Pick a skill, and write a communication improvement plan. You can find a communication improvement plan worksheet on our website at www.oup.com/us/interact12.

Key Words ❍

Interpersonal influence, *p. 298*

Power, *p. 299*

Coercive power, *p. 299*

Reward power, *p. 299*

Legitimate power, *p. 300*

Expert power, *p. 300*

Referent power, *p. 301*

Persuasion, *p. 303*

Reasons, *p. 303*

Claims, *p. 303*

Credibility, *p. 306*

Competence, *p. 306*

Trustworthiness, *p. 306*

Likability, *p. 307*

Compliance-gaining strategy, *p. 309*

Supporting-evidence strategy, *p. 309*

Exchange strategy, *p. 309*

Direct-request strategy, *p. 310*

Empathy-based strategy, *p. 310*

Face-maintenance strategy, *p. 310*

Other-benefit strategy, *p. 310*

Distributive strategy, *p. 310*

Assertiveness, *p. 313*

Passive behavior, *p. 313*

Aggressive behavior, *p. 313*

Flaming, *p. 314*

Cyber stalking, *p. 314*

Passive-aggressive behavior, *p. 314*

Skill Practice ❍ Find more on the web @ www.oup.com/us/interact12

Skill Practice exercises challenge you to master the material you have read in this chapter. For additional Skill Practice activities, visit our website at www.oup.com/us/interact12.

Developing Assertive Responses

For each of the following situations, write a passive or aggressive response; then contrast it with a more appropriate assertive response.

1. You come back to your dorm, apartment, or house to type a paper that is due tomorrow, only to find that someone is using your computer.

Passive or aggressive response:

Assertive response:

2. You're working at a store part time. Just as your hours are up and you are ready to leave (you want to rush home because you have a nice dinner planned with someone special), your boss says to you, "I'd like you to work overtime if you would—Martin's supposed to relieve you, but he just called and can't get here for at least an hour."

Passive or aggressive response:

Assertive response:

3. During a phone call to your parents, who live in another state, your mother says, "We're expecting you to go with us when we visit your uncle on Saturday." You were planning to spend Saturday working on your résumé for an interview next week.

Passive or aggressive response:

Assertive response:

4. You and your friend made a date to go dancing, an activity you really enjoy. When you meet, your friend says, "If it's all the same to you, I thought we'd go to a movie instead."

Passive or aggressive response:

Assertive response:

Inter-Act with Media ◗ Find more on the web @ www.oup.com/us/interact12

Television

The Simpsons, episode: "That 90s Show" (2008). Dan Castellaneta, Julie Kavner.

Brief Summary: In this flashback episode, not-yet-married Marge and Homer live together, and Marge attends Springfield University. Marge's professor, Stefan August, is interested in Marge, though she doesn't immediately catch on. To lighten his authority presence, Professor August tells Marge that he's her "advisor" rather than her professor. He suggests that Marge is being held back by her high school fling with Homer. When Marge opens up a note from Homer saying, "I miss you," Professor August says that "I" is the subject and "you" is the object, which means that Homer thinks he owns Marge. Marge tells him that Homer pays for her college and incredulous Professor August reiterates Homer's ownership of her, which he likens to oppression. Marge and Homer break up temporarily and she dates Professor August. She finds out that the professor opposes marriage, which leads Marge back to Homer. Although Marge was not coerced into dating Professor August, he definitely influenced her with his opinions about her relationship with Homer.

IPC Concepts: Interpersonal influence, interpersonal power in relationships, legitimate power, giving good reasons, supporting evidence strategies, appeals to emotion.

Cinema

The Bucket List (2007). Rob Reiner (director). Jack Nicholson, Morgan Freeman.

Brief Summary: Carter Chambers (Freeman) and Edward Cole (Nicholson) have little in common, other than the fact that they are dying. While sharing a hospital room, Chambers accidentally drops a piece of paper containing a "bucket list," based on a long-ago professor's assignment of things to do before death. Cole calls the list, which includes making a million dollars and doing a good deed, "extremely weak" and adds his own items: traveling, skydiving, getting a tattoo, and so on. Cole suggests that they actually complete the items on the list, citing that he can financially support them. He further persuades Chambers by telling him that he will be "smothered by pity and grief" if he simply returns home to die. Instead, Cole suggests that they are well enough to "put some moves on." Chambers agrees to the adventure, but first endures an argument with his wife, whom he cannot convince that the travels are a good idea. Together, the men experience race car driving, skydiving, a safari, and worldwide travel before Chambers finds himself ready to return home. Prior to his death, he reminds Cole that the list is unfinished and tells him to complete it without him. It is Cole's assistant who ultimately completes the list for both men when he places their ashes atop Mount Everest.

IPC Concepts: Interpersonal influence, persuasion, good reasons, personal credibility.

What's on the Web
Find links and additional material, including self-quizzes, on the companion website at www .oup.com/us/interact12.

Managing Conflict

After you have read this chapter, you should be able to answer these questions:

▷ What is interpersonal conflict?

▷ What are the six types of conflict?

▷ What are withdrawing, accommodating, forcing, compromising, and collaborating?

▷ What are the destructive behaviors to avoid in a conflict?

▷ What are the productive skills to use when initiating conflict?

▷ What are the productive skills to use when responding to conflict?

▷ What are the productive skills to use when mediating a conflict?

▷ How can you recover from conflict management failures?

"LeRoy, how about if we work on the basement project this weekend?"

"Sorry, Phoebe, I've promised to help my brother move today, and tomorrow I want to work out at the gym and then watch the game."

"But the basement has been torn up for over a month now. I really want to get this renovation finished. You never want to work on it, and I have to live with the mess."

"That's not fair, Phoebe. You nagged me about redoing the basement. I was fine with it the way it was. I'm tired of you making me feel guilty every time I want to do something else."

"I'm not making you feel guilty. You're just lazy when it comes to doing anything around this house and you know it."

"I don't need this hassle. I'm out of here. I'll be back when you can calm down."

"LeRoy, don't just walk out on this. That's no way to behave. We need to talk this over and figure out a schedule for finishing the basement before your parents come to stay with us in June."

S ometimes in our relationships, we find ourselves in serious conflicts over core issues, while at other times, our conflicts occur over mundane, day-to-day issues. In either case, how we choose to deal with conflict will affect our relationships. For instance, the issue of working together on household projects that Phoebe and LeRoy are discussing may be resolved easily, or it may escalate into a serious disagreement that could damage their relationship.

Interpersonal conflict may be defined broadly as disagreement between two interdependent people who perceive that they have incompatible goals (Guerrero, Andersen, & Afifi, 2007, p. 307). Although many people believe that interpersonal conflict is a sign of a bad relationship, the reality is that conflicts occur in all relationships. In fact, conflicts are a normal and natural part of everyday life that can be beneficial to relationships because they prevent stagnation and provide a safety valve for expressing problems (Putnam, 2006). Whether conflict hurts or strengthens a relationship depends primarily on how those involved deal with it. Since conflict is inevitable, generally it should be managed in ways that maintain the relationship while satisfying the goals of both parties involved. Understanding conflict and developing conflict management skills will make you a more effective interpersonal communicator, able to deal with the inevitable conflict episodes you will face in most of your relationships.

While you may not personally like to deal with conflict, it is viewed as a normal part of any relationship in American culture. In other cultures, especially in Asian cultures, conflict is viewed as dysfunctional to relationships and damaging to social face (Ting-Toomey, 2006). However, in this chapter, we present information that is grounded in an American perspective. We begin by looking at the six types of interpersonal conflict. Then we discuss five styles people use to manage conflict, indicating when each approach can be used effectively. Next, we describe destructive behaviors to be avoided in conflicts. After that, we describe positive communication strategies that can be used to initiate, respond to, or mediate conflict episodes. Finally, we discuss how to recover from conflict management failures.

> **Interpersonal conflict**—disagreement between two interdependent people who perceive that they have incompatible goals.

⌄ Types of Interpersonal Conflict

Some conflicts are easier to manage than others. When we can identify the type of conflict that is occurring, we are better equipped to manage it. Conflicts generally fall into one of the following six broad categories: pseudoconflict, fact conflict, value conflict, policy conflict, ego conflict, and metaconflict. Table 12.1 summarizes these types of conflict and provides suggestions for resolving each type.

TABLE 12.1 ◯ Conflict Types and Resolution Strategies

Type	Dialogue	Resolution Strategy
1. Pseudoconflict Conflict that is caused by a perceptual difference between partners and is easily resolved	"I can't go to the party; I don't feel well." "Well if you're sick, then I'd rather stay home and make chicken soup for you."	Use perception checking, look for ways to satisfy both parties' needs, and observe badgering boundaries.
2. Fact conflict Conflict that is caused by a dispute over the truth or accuracy of a piece of information	"Parker said that the paper has to be in today." "No, it can be turned in Tuesday."	Disengage until you can consult an external source to determine real facts.
3. Value conflict Conflict that is caused by disagreements about deep-seated moral beliefs	"Tom, you've got to tell Jamison that you agree with him just to calm him down." "But I don't see the world the way he does, and I'm not going to say that I do."	Look for areas in which both parties agree, and work from there. If no agreement results, then respectfully agree to disagree.
4. Policy conflict Conflict that is caused by a disagreement over a plan or course of action	"Myrna, please write down any message you take." "Why? I remember to tell you without writing them down."	Identify the nature of the problem. Agree on a policy (a plan or course of action) that is most likely to provide the best solution.
5. Ego conflict Conflict that results when both parties in a disagreement insist on being the "winner" of the argument	"Gloria, I don't think that this design fits the assignment." "Oh, so you think that I'm incapable of doing this job?"	Look for ways to move the conflict away from an ego level and back down to a content level.
6. Metaconflict Conflict that is caused by disagreements about the process of communication itself during an argument	"Corina, you are out of control here. I'm sick of your yelling and stubbornness when we are fighting."	Set rules for how communication will occur during conflicts and follow them. If a conflict rule is broken, gently ask your partner to abide by the mutually developed rules.

▷ Pseudoconflict

A **pseudoconflict** is conflict that is caused by a perceptual difference between partners and is easily resolved. Pseudoconflicts usually occur in three situations. First, they can occur when communication partners ascribe different meanings to words. For example, if Suzanne tells Chris that she will be back "this afternoon," Chris may expect her to arrive shortly after 1:00 P.M. If Suzanne doesn't show up until 4:00 P.M., Chris may be irritated, but when they unravel the conflict and discover that the problem was a difference in how each perceived the words "this

Pseudoconflict—conflict that is caused by a perceptual difference between partners and is easily resolved.

afternoon," the conflict is quickly resolved. In this case, the pseudoconflict has been resolved through paraphrasing what each partner means by the words "this afternoon." Second, pseudoconflicts may happen when communication partners are confronted with goals or needs that appear to clash, when in reality both goals or needs can be accommodated. For instance, if Carl says to Cynthia, "Hey, the all-star game is on this evening," and Cynthia replies: "Wait a minute, we have tickets for the ballet tonight!" they may perceive a conflict. However, if the couple has TiVo, they actually have a pseudoconflict that can be easily resolved if Carl is willing to watch the game on a delayed basis. In this situation, the pseudoconflict has been resolved through clarification of goals and compromising. Finally, pseudoconflict may occur through badgering. **Badgering** is light teasing, taunting, and mocking behavior. This type of pseudoconflict may be harmless play, or it may be destructive when it moves beyond normal playfulness and has the unspoken goal of provoking a real conflict over some other issue or hurting someone. For example, Renee tells Tony that she can't go to the movies tonight because she doesn't want to go out in the rain and risk having her hair frizz before the wedding she is singing at tomorrow. Tony, knowing that Renee is a little vain about her appearance, playfully replies, "You're such a prima donna!" Renee may miss his attempt at humor and take his comment seriously. Hurt by what she perceives as his criticism, she may escalate the conflict by lashing out with an angry retort. In this case, the pseudoconflict could have been avoided if Tony, who knew about Renee's sensitivity, had respected this boundary and not badgered in reply. Likewise, had Renee recognized Tony's remark as a simple tease, she might have perceived it for the pseudoconflict it was.

Badgering—light teasing, taunting, and mocking behavior.

▷ Fact Conflict

Fact conflict, often referred to as simple conflict, is conflict that is caused by a dispute over the truth or accuracy of a piece of information. These conflicts are "simple" because the truth or accuracy of the information in dispute can be verified by consulting an external source. For example, if Jermaine says to Marge, "Paul asked if I would go with him to the community watch meeting next Wednesday," and Marge replies, "You can't do that; that's Parents' Night at school," and Jermaine counters, "No, Parents' Night is the following Wednesday," they have encountered a fact conflict. At this point, Marge and Ken can escalate the conflict into an argument, with allusions to Jermaine's bad memory and/or Marge's being a know-it-all. Or, if they recognize that this is a simple conflict over a fact, they can double-check the dates. If you find yourself in a fact conflict suggest that you consult a source where you can verify what is true or accurate.

Fact conflict—conflict that is caused by a dispute over the truth or accuracy of a piece of information.

▷ Value Conflict

While pseudoconflicts and fact conflicts can be managed easily, when the conflict stems from differences in value systems, the conflict management process is more difficult. A **value conflict** is a conflict that is caused by disagreements about deep-seated moral beliefs. Value conflict can occur either when we differ in

Value conflict—conflict that is caused by disagreements about deep-seated moral beliefs.

the degree of importance we place on a particular value we otherwise agree on or when we simply disagree on a value altogether. Suppose, for example, that Josh and Sarah are considering getting married. In their discussions, they have discovered that they have two serious areas of value conflict. First, Sarah, a conservative Jew, values the spiritual disciplines of keeping kosher and observing other daily home-based religious practices as well as weekly attendance at temple. She considers these fundamental to marriage. Josh, who was also raised in a Jewish home, believes that his Jewish values are expressed through his worldview and considers attending temple on major religious holidays to be a sufficient expression of his spirituality. In this case, they both value expressing their religious beliefs, but each assigns a different priority to daily religious observation. Second, Sarah is a committed vegetarian who feels that eating meat is morally reprehensible, while Josh is an avid meat eater. Here Sarah and Josh have two competing values that conflict. They view the consumption of meat completely differently. Many times, value conflicts are not resolvable, and we must simply be content to respect each other but "agree to disagree." However, if resolution is possible, it will begin with the recognition that the issue is a value conflict. In the Josh and Sarah scenario, it is important for both parties to realize that neither of them is "just being stubborn" or will come around to the "right" point of view about either issue given time and prodding. Instead, they must draw on the trust and mutual respect that they have established in their relationship and recognize that they have incompatible values on the issues before them. Then, recognizing these differences, they may be able to discuss the reasons they each feel the way they do and work to set respectful boundaries around these issues. For instance, they may find a compromise on both issues, with Sarah and Josh agreeing to keep kosher at home, but Sarah agreeing that Josh need not keep kosher when he is out. Similarly, they may agree that when they eat at home they will prepare vegetarian meals, but when they eat out, Josh will be free to eat meat.

▷ Policy Conflict

A **policy conflict** is a conflict that is caused by a disagreement over a plan or course of action. What is perceived to be an appropriate policy is both culturally based and situational, so this type of conflict is common to most relationships. Many times policy conflict stems from novel situations for which there is no existing relational policy. For instance, if Tyrone comes from a family in which children are given a great deal of freedom, while Cherise comes from a family in which children's activities are closely monitored and supervised, they are likely to have a conflict over child-rearing policy when they have their first child. At other times, a policy may have already been established, but a changing situation prompts a policy conflict. For instance, if Paul and Mary have been going out together for several months and the informal but never discussed "policy" has been for Paul to pay for meals and entertainment, this situation may need to change as the relationship deepens. Although Mary may understand the problem if Paul raises it, she may point out that she doesn't make as much money as

Policy conflict—conflict that is caused by a disagreement over a plan or course of action.

Paul and can't afford the expensive nights out Paul likes to plan, thus leading to a policy conflict. Because policy conflicts are based on highly personal considerations, there is no "right" or "wrong" way to resolve them; the policy that is to be followed depends on what both parties feel personally comfortable with. These conflicts can be successfully managed if the parties are willing to compromise.

▷ Ego Conflict

Ego conflict—conflict that results when both parties in a disagreement insist on being the "winner" of the argument.

An **ego conflict** is a conflict that results when both parties in a disagreement insist on being the "winner" of the argument. When both people already engaged in a conflict see that conflict as a measure of who they are, what they are, how competent they are, whom they have power over, or how much they know, an ego conflict may occur in addition to the already-present fact, value, or policy conflict. In these situations "winning" the conflict becomes the means of satisfying ego or self-esteem needs and may take precedence over resolving the underlying conflict. Ego conflicts can develop when a discussion of facts, values, or policy is undermined by personal or judgmental statements that prompt one or both speakers to ignore the central argument and defend themselves personally. Once your sense of self-worth has been threatened, your ability to remain rational can be impaired. Before you realize it, emotions come into play, words may be said that cannot be taken back, and an otherwise minor conflict can be blown out of proportion. When you recognize that you are experiencing ego conflict, you should use comments that save face for your partner to help de-escalate the conflict to the content level. For instance, suppose Darlene is upset that Grant's

Conflicts in which values or egos are at issue often escalate. How can we manage conflicts of these types?

brother hasn't returned a sleeping bag he borrowed. If she points this out to Grant, she is making a point about a policy conflict—the importance of family members and friends returning what they borrow. If, however, in raising this point of policy, Darlene overstates her case, perhaps accusing Grant of ignoring her request to get the item back "like you always do," Grant may feel prompted to protect his ego first and deal with the policy conflict second. He may say, "Darlene, why are you accusing me of ignoring you? I'm happy to respond to what you ask when you're reasonable about it. Maybe if you wouldn't nag me so much I'd pay more attention." To help avert the ego conflict, Darlene might de-escalate the conflict by replying, "Grant, I'm sorry I'm sounding like I'm nagging and I shouldn't have snapped at you. The point I was trying to make is that your brother hasn't returned the sleeping bag he borrowed over a month ago, we really need it for our camping trip next week, and I asked you twice to get it back from him. That's why I was getting anxious about it and snapped at you." Once the ego conflict is resolved, Darlene and Grant can return to the policy conflict, hopefully with Grant agreeing to call his brother right away and Darlene agreeing not to snap at him again about it as long as he makes the effort.

▷ Metaconflict

Metaconflict is conflict that is caused by disagreements about the process of communication itself during an argument (Guerrero, Andersen, & Afifi, 2007). In a metaconflict, we may accuse our partner of pouting, nagging, name-calling, not listening, showing too much emotion, fighting unfairly, or a variety of other negative behaviors related to the conflict communication process. Similar to ego conflict, once we engage in metaconflict, we then have two conflict issues to address: the original area of incompatibility and the conflict process itself. We may go back and forth between communicating about the issue at hand and how we are handling the conflict. Metaconflict complicates our interpersonal communication and makes a satisfactory solution to our conflict less likely. The best way to deal with metaconflict is to recognize it and then agree with our partner to follow rules about how to communicate during conflicts. For example, if Tasha and Marcus consistently "hit each other below the belt" when they argue about politics, with Tasha often accusing Marcus of being an "insensitive conservative" and Marcus often calling Tasha a "bleeding heart liberal," they may need to agree that when they have value conflicts over political issues in the future, neither of them may use such labels on the other.

Metaconflict—conflict that is caused by disagreements about the process of communication itself during an argument.

● Styles of Managing Interpersonal Conflict

Think about the last time you experienced a conflict. How did you react? Did you try to avoid it? Did you give in? Did you force the other person to accept your will? Did you compromise, getting part of what you wanted and giving the other person part of what he or she wanted?

OBSERVE AND ANALYZE ○

Conflict Episodes

Describe a conflict episode you have recently experienced. What type of conflict was it—pseudoconflict, fact conflict, value conflict, or policy conflict? Was ego conflict or metaconflict also involved? How did you act, and how did the other person behave? What was the outcome of the conflict? How did you feel about it then? Now? Was there a different way the conflict might have been handled that would have resulted in a better outcome?

Or did the two of you find a solution with which you were both completely satisfied? Such approaches differ in the amount of cooperation and assertiveness the participants display. Specifically, they differ in how much one person is willing to cooperate and how much one person is willing to be assertive. They range from not cooperating at all/being completely unassertive to cooperating fully/being fully assertive. The extent to which people are willing to cooperate when managing a conflict depends on how important they believe the relationship affected by the conflict is to them and how important the issue is to them. Let's take a closer look at the five styles people use when confronted with a conflict: withdrawing, accommodating, forcing, compromising, and collaborating (Lulofs & Cahn, 2000). As you read through this section, refer to Table 12.2, which outlines the characteristics, goals, and outlooks of each conflict management style.

▷ Withdrawing

Certainly one of the easiest ways to deal with conflict is to withdraw. **Withdrawing** is resolving a conflict by physically or psychologically removing oneself from the conflict. This style is both uncooperative and unassertive because at least one person involved in the conflict refuses to talk about the issue at all. A person may withdraw physically by leaving the site. For instance, as Eduardo and Justina get into an argument about their financial situation, Eduardo may withdraw physically by saying, "I don't want to talk about this," and walk out the door. On the other hand, psychological withdrawal occurs when one person simply ignores what the other person is saying. Using the same example, when Justina begins to talk about their financial situation, Eduardo may ignore her, acting as though she has not spoken.

Withdrawing—resolving a conflict by physically or psychologically removing oneself from the conflict.

TABLE 12.2 ◗ Styles of Conflict Management

Approach	Characteristics	Goal	Outlook
Withdrawing	Uncooperative, unassertive	To keep from dealing with conflict	"I don't want to talk about it."
Accommodating	Cooperative, unassertive	To keep from upsetting the other person	"Getting my way isn't as important as keeping the peace."
Forcing	Uncooperative, assertive	To get my way	"I'll get my way regardless of what I have to do."
Compromising	Partially cooperative, partially assertive	To get partial satisfaction	"I'll get partial satisfaction by letting the other person get partial satisfaction as well."
Collaborating	Cooperative, assertive	To solve the problem together	"Let's talk this out and find the best solution possible for both of us."

Considered from an individual satisfaction standpoint, withdrawing creates a lose/lose situation because neither party to the conflict really accomplishes what he or she wants. In our example, although Eduardo temporarily escapes from the conflict, he knows it will come up again. Meanwhile, Justina experiences frustration on two levels: Not only does she not get an answer to her question about how to pay the bills, but she also feels ignored and slighted. When used repeatedly, withdrawal hurts relationships in at least two ways. First, researchers have found that when conflict is avoided it eventually resurfaces and is usually more difficult to resolve at that time (Roloff & Cloven, 1990). Second, withdrawal leads to "mulling behavior," or stewing over issues and behaviors to the point where they become bigger than they actually are, leading to permanent ill feelings about the relationship.

Although withdrawing is an ineffective style most of the time from a relational satisfaction standpoint, there are at least three sets of circumstances in which withdrawing may be a useful strategy. First, withdrawal can be appropriate when neither the relationship nor the issue is really important to you. For example, consider Josh and Mario, who work in different departments of the same company. At company gatherings in the past, the two men have gotten into heated arguments about whether the Giants or the Cardinals is a better ball club. At the next gathering, Mario may withdraw by avoiding sitting near Josh or quickly changing the subject when Josh begins the argument anew. In this case, Mario judges that it simply isn't worth trying to resolve the disagreement with Josh—neither the issue nor the relationship is that important to him.

Second, withdrawing is a useful strategy when used to avoid a potential conflict before your partner is aware that the two of you disagree. When an issue is

What motivates people to withdraw? What is lost as a result?

No, I don't think you're a mental case, Mrs. Clydehopper. Then again, this is a furniture store, and I'm a salesperson...

unimportant to you but the relationship is important, you might simply choose to hide your objections to your partner's position and go along with what he or she says. Research suggests that when used this way avoiding or withdrawing can have a positive relationship effect (Caughlin & Golish, 2002). For instance, if you don't like your partner's taste in music and you are both throwing a party, but you would prefer not to embarrass your partner by making an issue over the music, knowing that he or she tends to be sensitive, you may be better off leaving well enough alone.

Third, withdrawing permits a temporary disengagement that allows strong emotional reactions to be checked. When both an issue and a relationship are important to you, you may find that temporarily withdrawing from the argument allows both of you to calm down and renew the discussion at a later time when you are able to approach the issue with a clear head. For example, when Pat and her father begin to argue heatedly over Pat's decision to quit school, Pat may say, "Hold it a minute, I'm getting way too emotional. Let me make a pot of coffee and calm down a bit; then we'll talk about this some more." A few minutes later, having calmed down, Pat may return, ready to approach the conflict in a more productive way.

▷ Accommodating

Accommodating is resolving a conflict by satisfying the other person's needs or accepting the other person's ideas while neglecting one's own needs or ideas. This approach is cooperative but unassertive. It preserves friendly relationships but fails to protect personal rights. People who are insecure in their relationships with others tend to accommodate to ensure the continuance of relationships they perceive as fragile. For instance, if Juan worries about the status of his relationship with Mariana, when he and Mariana discuss their vacation plans, Juan may accommodate Mariana's request to have another couple join them, even though he would rather she and he vacation alone.

Considered from an individual satisfaction standpoint, accommodating creates a lose/win situation. The accommodator chooses to lose while the other person gets what he or she wants. From a relational satisfaction standpoint, habitual accommodation creates two problems. First, accommodation may lead to poor decision making because important facts, arguments, and positions are not voiced by the accommodator. Second, habitual accommodation results in one

Accommodating—resolving a conflict by satisfying the other person's needs or accepting the other person's ideas while neglecting one's own needs or ideas.

person's taking advantage of the other, regardless of whether it is intentional. This can damage the accommodator's self-concept and lead to feelings of resentment that undermine the relationship.

There are also situations, of course, in which it is appropriate and effective to accommodate from a relationship satisfaction standpoint. When an issue is not important to you but the relationship is, accommodating is the preferred style. For example, if Hal and Yvonne are trying to decide where to go for dinner, and Hal says, "I really have a craving for some Thai food tonight," Yvonne, who prefers less spicy foods, may say, "OK, that will be fine with me," because Hal often accommodates her suggestions. It may also be useful to accommodate from time to time to build "social credits" or goodwill that can be used later. In addition, it should be noted that in some cultures, accommodating is almost always the preferred style when dealing with conflict, even when both the issue and the relationship are important to a person. In Japan, for instance, it is thought to be more humble and face-saving to accommodate than to risk losing respect through conflict (Lulofs & Cahn, 2000).

▷ Forcing

A third style of dealing with conflict is forcing. **Forcing** is resolving a conflict by satisfying one's own needs or advancing one's own ideas with no concern for the needs or ideas of the other person or for the relationship. Forcing can be done through physical threats, verbal attacks, coercion, or manipulation. If the other party accommodates, the conflict subsides. If, however, the other side responds forcibly, the conflict escalates. Forcing is uncooperative but assertive. The forcer wishes to exert his or her will over the other and will argue assertively to do so.

Considered from an individual satisfaction standpoint, forcing creates an I win/you lose situation. The person doing the forcing wins, but at the expense of the relational partner. Therefore, from a relational satisfaction standpoint, forcing usually hurts a relationship, at least in the short term.

However, there are times when forcing is an effective means of resolving conflict from a relational satisfaction standpoint. In emergencies, when quick and decisive action must be taken to ensure safety or minimize harm, forcing is useful; this tactic is often used by firefighters, paramedics, and police officers to ensure the safety of others, for example. In addition, when an issue is critical to your own or the other person's welfare and you know you are right, you may find forcing necessary. For example, if Felicia and her mother are arguing about Felicia borrowing the car to go to a party, Felicia's mother may simply say, "No, you're not using the car if you're planning to drink, and that's the end of the discussion." Although she is forcing, she has the welfare of her daughter in mind when doing so. Finally, if you are interacting with someone who is likely to take advantage of you if you do not force the issue, forcing is appropriate. For example, if David knows that his younger sister habitually sneaks out of the house when his parents are away and have left him responsible, it is appropriate for him to say, "You're not sneaking out tonight, and if you do, I'll tell mom and dad."

Forcing—resolving a conflict by satisfying one's own needs or advancing one's own ideas with no concern for the needs or ideas of the other person or for the relationship.

▷ Compromising

Compromising is resolving a conflict by mutually agreeing with one's partner to partially satisfy each other's needs or interests. Under this approach, both people give up part of what they really want or believe, or trade one thing they want or believe, to get something else. Compromising is an intermediate between assertiveness and cooperativeness: Each person has to be somewhat assertive and somewhat cooperative to get partial satisfaction. For example, if Heather and Paul are working together on a class project, both need to meet outside of class, and both have busy schedules, they may need to compromise on a time to meet.

From an individual satisfaction standpoint, compromising creates neither a lose/lose nor a win/win situation because both people in a sense "lose" something even as they "win" something else. From a relational satisfaction standpoint, compromise may be seen as neutral to positive because both parties gain some satisfaction. Compromising is appropriate when the issue is moderately important, when there are time constraints, and when attempts at forcing or collaborating have not been successful.

Although compromising is a popular and at least partially satisfying conflict management style, there can be significant problems associated with it. One problem of special concern is that one of the parties may "trade away" a better solution to reach a compromise with the other party. For instance, if roommates Manny and Humberto have a conflict over apartment selection, Manny may agree to pay extra rent for the larger apartment that is close to campus because Humberto cannot afford the higher rent. But in his haste to reach a compromise, Manny may have missed the even better option of their finding a third roommate to share the cost of the new apartment.

▷ Collaborating

The fifth and final style of managing conflict is **collaborating**, which is resolving a conflict by using problem solving to arrive at a solution that meets the needs and interests of both parties in the conflict. During collaboration people treat their disagreement as a problem to be solved, so they discuss the issues, describe their feelings, and identify the characteristics of an effective solution. Collaborating is both assertive and cooperative. It is assertive because both parties voice their concerns; it is cooperative because both parties work together to gain resolution.

From an individual satisfaction standpoint, collaborating creates a win/win scenario because both people's needs are met completely. From a relational satisfaction standpoint, collaboration is positive because both sides feel that they have been heard. They get to share ideas and weigh and consider information in a way that satisfies both parties individually and in terms of their relationship.

Managing conflict through collaboration requires some of the communication skills we have discussed previously. For example, participants must use accurate and precise language to describe their ideas and feelings, and they must empathetically listen to the ideas and feelings of the other person. In addition,

Compromising—resolving a conflict by mutually agreeing with one's partner to partially satisfy each other's needs or interests.

Collaborating—resolving a conflict by using problem solving to arrive at a solution that meets the needs and interests of both parties in the conflict.

they must follow five problem-solving steps: (1) Define the problem ("What's the issue being considered?"), (2) analyze the problem ("What are the causes and symptoms of the issue?"), (3) develop mutually acceptable criteria for judging solutions ("What goals will a good solution reach?"), (4) generate solutions ("What do you think about this idea?") and alternative solutions ("What is another approach we could take if that other idea doesn't work?"), and (5) select the solution or solutions that best meet the criteria identified ("What do you say we go with this solution and that one, too, since we both seem to agree that these are the most realistic ones?").

Let's consider these five steps as applied to a conflict example mentioned earlier: Justina and Eduardo's financial situation. To collaborate, both parties must honestly want to satisfy the other's concerns as well as their own. If they agree to collaborate, each may begin by following steps 1 and 2, defining and analyzing the problem from his or her perspective while the other listens with empathy and understanding. Justina may describe for Eduardo threats she has received from the landlord about possible eviction if the rent checks continue to be late and her anxiety about not paying the other bills on time. Eduardo may remind her that money is tight because he recently took a pay cut to start a new job that has more potential. From this baseline, they can work together on step 3, creating a list of guidelines or criteria a solution would have to meet for it to be acceptable to them both. After this, they might begin work on step 4, developing solutions

What is necessary to stimulate collaboration in resolving an issue of conflict?

and alternative solutions. Justina might suggest that the solution should be one that enables them to pay more than the minimum balances on their credit cards and get the payments in on time so that they avoid additional penalties. Eduardo might want the solution to be one that doesn't leave them without any way to

LEARN ABOUT YOURSELF ◑ Conflict Management

Take this short survey to learn something about yourself. Answer the questions based on your first response. There are no right or wrong answers. Just be honest in reporting your true behaviors. For each of the following questions, select one of the following numbers that best describes your behavior:

1 = Always
2 = Often
3 = Sometimes
4 = Rarely
5 = Never

_____ 1. I try to avoid conflicts whenever possible.
_____ 2. I will give up my own desires to end a conflict.
_____ 3. It is important to win an argument.
_____ 4. I am willing to compromise to solve a conflict.
_____ 5. It is important to discuss both people's point of view in a conflict.
_____ 6. I am stubborn in holding to my position in a conflict.
_____ 7. In conflicts, I give up some points in exchange for other points.
_____ 8. I try to avoid conflicts.
_____ 9. I give in to others during conflict.
_____ 10. It is important to regard conflicts as problems to be solved together.
_____ 11. I strongly assert my views in a conflict.
_____ 12. I withdraw from disagreements.
_____ 13. I try to find the middle-ground position in a conflict.
_____ 14. I will give in to the other person to end an argument.
_____ 15. I try to be cooperative and creative in finding a resolution to a conflict.

This is a test of your conflict management style.

Scoring the Survey: Add your scores for items 1, 8, and 12. Your score will range from 3 to 15. The lower (closer to 3) your score, the more you tend to use withdrawal as a conflict management style.

Add your scores for items 2, 9, and 14. Your score will range from 3 to 15. The lower (closer to 3) your score, the more you tend to use the accommodating style of conflict management.

Add your scores for items 3, 6, and 11. Your score will range from 3 to 15. The lower (closer to 3) your score, the more you tend to use the forcing style of conflict management.

Add your scores for items 4, 7, and 13. Your score will range from 3 to 15. The lower (closer to 3) your score, the more you tend to use the compromising style of conflict management.

Add your scores for items 5, 10, and 15. Your score will range from 3 to 15. The lower (closer to 3) your score, the more you tend to use the collaborating style of conflict management.

"have fun." Then, together they might brainstorm a list of possible alternative solutions. For example, Justina might propose that they save money by eating out only once a month and renting DVDs rather than going to movies. Eduardo might suggest that they have a yard sale to sell stuff they don't use any more and use the proceeds as a "fun fund." Once they have a satisfying list of options that they can both live with, they can then complete the collaborative problem-solving process by doing step 5, selecting the solution or solutions with which they are both happy. They might decide to go with three of the four ideas they came up with: paying more than the minimum credit card balances, eating out only once a month (but still going to the movies occasionally), and having the yard sale.

Collaboration is difficult. When two people commit themselves to trying, however, chances are they will discover that through discussion, they can arrive at creative solutions that meet their needs and ideas while simultaneously maintaining their relationship.

INTER-ACT WITH ⊙ TECHNOLOGY

Participate in an online discussion in which the topic of conversation is controversial. What kinds of behaviors (withdrawing, accommodating, forcing, compromising, or collaborating) do you tend to engage in most? Do your conflict management behaviors online differ from your behaviors in face-to-face conflicts? If so, what accounts for those differences?

⊙ Destructive Behaviors in Conflicts

Communicating during a conflict episode is quite challenging under any circumstances, but it can be unnecessarily complicated when partners use negative thinking and destructive behaviors. During a conflict episode, it is important to monitor your own communication so that you recognize and disrupt these negative behaviors when you see them developing. Five common behaviors that complicate effective conflict management are ascribing motives, counterblaming, engaging in demand-withdrawal, engaging in spiraling negativity, and practicing stubbornness.

▷ Ascribing Motives

One common behavioral error in conflict management is ascribing motives. **Ascribing motives** is a behavior in which one assumes that one knows what another person is thinking or why that person is behaving a certain way. In a conflict, the motives we ascribe are nearly always negative ones. We look for and come up with hidden malevolent motivations to explain the behavior of others. However, assuming we know what motivates others involves guesswork rather than actual knowledge. To make matters worse, sometimes when we ascribe negative motivations toward others, we extend our guesswork to attribute consistent negative behaviors to our conflict partners. Recall from Chapter 2 the discussion of dispositional attributions that inaccurately link causes of a person's behavior to personality characteristics or traits of the person. When explanations of conflict behavior include negative persistent attributions, the conflict becomes harder to manage (Guerrero, Andersen, & Afifi, 2007). For example, suppose that while Ben and Sol are having an argument about an unpaid debt, Sol says to Ben, "I know you're only taking your time paying me back because you have no respect for me!" Although Sol may legitimately

Ascribing motives—behavior in which one assumes that one knows what another person is thinking or why that person is behaving in a certain way.

feel that Ben sometimes treats him with a cavalier attitude, in fact Sol has no evidence to support his statement. Ben may simply be having a difficult time financially, and Sol's comment may damage the relationship by opening up personal conflicts that have nothing to do with the current conflict.

▷ Counterblaming

Another ineffective conflict management behavior is **counterblaming**, a behavior in which one moves the focus of an argument away from oneself by blaming the other person. Instead of resolving an argument, counterblaming only leads to an escalating back-and-forth series of attacks that if continued can lead to irreparable damage to a relationship. For example, suppose that Nicole initiates a conflict by saying to Stacey, "I can't believe you just took my green skirt and wore it without asking." Here Stacey should respond to the issue at hand (unauthorized borrowing); if she feels her actions were valid, she should defend herself: "But you said I could always borrow anything from you." If however, Stacey replies, "I would not have had to borrow your skirt for work today if you had done the laundry like you promised," she has chosen to engage in counterblaming. Nicole may either respond appropriately by saying, "Stacey, the issue is not why you needed to borrow the skirt, but that you did it without asking me" or she may take the bait and counterblame herself by saying, "I couldn't do the laundry because you didn't buy any laundry detergent when you went shopping, as usual." And Stacey may counterblame again: "Well, dimwit, how can I know that we need detergent when you don't bother to put it on the shopping list?" Notice how counterblaming strays increasingly away from the original issue and escalates into a series of more personal attacks that resolve nothing.

▷ Engaging in Demand-Withdrawal

Engaging in demand-withdrawal can become a recurring pattern of conflict communication in long-term relationships (Caughlin & Huston, 2006). **Demand-withdrawal** is a pattern of behavior in which one partner consistently demands while the other consistently withdraws. Typically, the person in the demanding position tends to be the less powerful person in the relationship and is dissatisfied with something, while the person in the withdrawing position is the more powerful in the relationship and is happy with the status quo (Sagrestano, Heavey, & Christensen, 2006). If one person consistently demands to resolve a conflict while the other consistently ignores those demands, the result is an unhealthy escalation with no chance of resolution. For instance, imagine that Angelina reintroduces her continuing concern about her husband's weight by saying, "Kevin, you really need to lose a few pounds. It's not good for your health to be overweight. It's all the pop you drink and the bedtime snacks," and Kevin, as usual acting as though he did not hear a word Angelina has said, looks up from the computer and says, "Hey, we could get a great deal on a digital camera on eBay." If whenever Angelina brings up the topic of his weight Kevin ignores her comments and changes the subject, the pattern of demand-withdrawal is likely to escalate, with Angelina's demands more forceful each time and Kevin's withdrawal more pronounced. The end result of this pattern will be a chronic conflict in their relationship. The only way to end such a pattern is for one or both partners to choose a new approach. However, in many relationships, once a pattern of demand-withdrawal is cemented, it is often never resolved.

▷ Engaging in Spiraling Negativity

Another destructive conflict management behavior is spiraling negatively. **Spiraling negativity** is a pattern of behavior in which both partners in an argument trade increasingly negative and/or hostile remarks. The pattern begins when one person interjects a hostile comment into a conflict conversation and the partner matches that negative comment with one of his or her own. The longer this pattern continues, the more it is likely to result in the degeneration of a conversation into name-calling and bitter accusations that could poison the entire relationship. Although it is natural to feel defensive when you believe you have been attacked, you can halt a negative spiral by describing your feelings and refocusing the discussion on the issue. For example, you might say, "What you just said really hurts my feelings, but I think we are not going to resolve this by making personal attacks. So I'd like us to refocus on the issues."

> **Spiraling negativity**—pattern of behavior in which both partners in an argument trade increasingly negative and/or hostile remarks.

▷ Practicing Stubbornness

A final ineffective conflict management behavior is stubbornness. **Stubbornness** is behavior that is characterized by unyieldingness and inflexibility. When one or both parties in a conflict obstinately cling to a position on an issue for the sake of maintaining face, they hinder effective discussion and fail to provide an avenue for resolution. While at times holding to your position is an ethical obligation, more frequently, people stubbornly refuse to acknowledge when a partner has made a good point. When you notice yourself stubbornly maintaining your own position for the sake of winning the debate, you can choose to modify your messages in a more flexible manner. Likewise, when you notice that your partner is being stubborn, you might point out that the real issue at stake is resolving the disagreement, not necessarily winning the argument.

> **Stubbornness**—behavior that is characterized by unyieldingness and inflexibility.

◐ Productive Conflict Management Skills

Your primary goal in managing conflict productively should be to be both appropriate and effective in your own behaviors. In the "Spotlight on Scholars" box in this chapter (page 345), we can see how the research of Professor Daniel Canary, at Arizona State University, has validated the importance of both appropriateness and effectiveness in conflict management. Essential to appropriate and effective conflict management is agreeing with your conflict partner upon the rules for how each of you

OBSERVE AND ANALYZE ◐

Changing Conflict Behaviors

Think of a recent conflict you experienced in which ineffective conflict behaviors developed. Analyze what happened using the concepts from this chapter. What type of conflict was it? What conflict management style did you adopt? What was the other person's style? Did any of the destructive conflict management behaviors creep into the conversation? How might you change what you did if you could "redo" this conflict episode?

will behave as you attempt to resolve the conflict (Roloff & Miller, 2006). During conflict the automatic reactions of both participants may be negative in style and tone, so agreed-upon rules can help both you and your partner to be more attentive, alert, focused, and mindful during conflict communication (Canary & Lakey, 2006). Rules should be developed together early in the conflict and should include such skills as staying on topic, owning thoughts and feelings, listening, and not imposing upon each other.

In the remainder of this chapter, we will describe the skills that you can use to resolve conflicts collaboratively. We begin by explaining how to effectively initiate a conflict when it becomes necessary for you to do so. Then we describe how you can effectively respond to a conflict initiated by someone else. Next, we present guidelines to help you mediate the conflicts of others. Finally, we provide tips to help you recover from conflict management failures.

▷ Communication Skills for Initiating Conflict

In some situations, you may need to be the person to initiate a conflict (that is, giving voice to a conflict you already perceive, not starting an argument) as the first step in resolving it. The following guidelines for initiating conflict (as well as those for responding to conflict in the next section) are based on work from several fields of study (Adler, 1977; Gordon, 1970; Whetten & Cameron, 2007).

1. Mentally rehearse what you will say before you confront the other person. Initiating a collaborative conflict conversation requires us to be in control of our emotions. Yet, by nature and despite our good intentions of keeping on track, our emotions can get the better of us, and in the heat of the moment we may say things we shouldn't. As a result, take a minute to practice, incorporating the guidelines listed here. Mentally rehearse a few statements you think will lead to productive conflict resolution.

2. Recognize and state ownership of the conflict. If a conflict is to be managed, it is important to acknowledge that you are angry, hurt, or frustrated about something that has occurred between you and your conflict partner. It is honest to own your own ideas and feelings by using "I" statements. For example, suppose you are trying to study for a major test in your most difficult course and your neighbor's music is so loud that your walls are shaking to the point where you can't concentrate. As this continues, you are likely to become agitated because you can't focus on your study. Who has a problem? Your neighbor? No. You have a problem. It's your study that is being disrupted, so to initiate the conflict you must decide to confront your neighbor. Remember, your goal is to seek collaboration in dealing with the problem. You could knock on your neighbor's door and shout, "Your music is too damn loud, turn it down—I'm trying to study!" However, this approach is almost guaranteed to arouse defensiveness in your neighbor and lead to an ego conflict. A more appropriate way of owning your problem would be to say, "Hi, I'm trying to study for an exam."

Daniel J. Canary

Professor of Communication in the Hugh Downs School
of Human Communication, Arizona State University, on

Appropriate and Effective Conflict Management

Dan Canary, citing the personal benefits of studying conflict, stated, "I learned how to control my own behavior and become more effective in my personal relationships." Canary's initial curiosity about effective conflict management behaviors was piqued when he was in graduate school at the University of Southern California. At the time he was a classmate of Brian Spitzberg (see the "Spotlight on Scholars" box in Chapter 1), who formulated the theory that relational competence is a product of behaviors that are both appropriate and effective, and Bill Cupach, who was studying conflict in relationships. Although Canary saw the connection between his work and theirs, it was several years later—after he experienced successful and unsuccessful resolution of significant conflict episodes in his own personal life—that he began in earnest to study how the way people behave during conflict episodes affects their relationships.

Communication scholars can become well known in a number of ways: (1) by developing a new theory that describes what really happens when we interact more clearly than those theories that came before; (2) by carrying out a series of research studies that test and elaborate on the theories developed by others; or (3) by organizing, integrating, and synthesizing the existing theories and research work in a particular area of study so that people who are not specialists can better grasp what is known. Dan Canary's reputation was made largely as a result of his ability to identify and build on connections among the theories and experimental data already available to scholars.

Canary's research studies are helpful in identifying the behaviors that make a person a competent conflict manager. Canary argues that although some conflict management behaviors are appropriate and others are effective, both types of behavior are necessary if one is to be perceived as a competent conflict manager. Drawing on Spitzberg's competence theory, Canary's research studies are designed to identify conflict behaviors that accomplish the goals of both appropriateness and effectiveness. The results of his studies consistently show that those who practice integrative conflict strategies—problem-solving, collaborative, and compromising approaches that display a desire to work with the other person—are perceived to be both appropriate and effective (i.e., competent). Furthermore, his studies have shown that when one partner in a relationship is thought to be a competent conflict manager, the other one trusts the partner more, is more satisfied with the relationship, and perceives the relationship to be more intimate.

Canary's research studies identify specific conflict management behaviors that are viewed as appropriate and/or effective. Canary has found that a person who acknowledges the arguments of others (e.g., "Uh huh, I can see how you would think that") and agrees with the arguments that others make to support their points (e.g., "Gee, that's a good point that I hadn't really thought about") is viewed as being an *appropriate* conflict manager. To be viewed as an *effective* conflict manager, however, requires a different set of behaviors. According to Canary's findings, conflict-handling behaviors that are viewed as effective included stating complete arguments, elaborating and justifying one's point of view, and clearly developing one's ideas. Canary noticed that in a conflict situation, what was viewed as appropriate alone had the potential to be ineffective, since appropriate behaviors seemed to involve some sort of agreement with the other person.

Canary reasoned that there must be ways to be both appropriate and effective in conflict situations. This led him to consider methods of sequencing or ordering messages in a conflict episode. His preliminary results have revealed that competent communicators (those perceived to be both appropriate and effective) will begin by acknowledging the other's viewpoint, or agreeing with part of the other's argument, before explaining, justifying, and arguing for their own viewpoint. Canary believes that in using this sequence, competent communicators help "frame" the interaction as one of cooperative problem solving rather than as a situation of competing interests where only one party can "win."

Many of Canary's major contributions to the study of conflict in personal relationships are included in two books: *Relationship Conflict* (co-authored with William Cupach and Susan Messman) is a synthesis of the diverse conflict literature and was written for graduate students and other scholars, and *Competence in Interpersonal Conflict* (also co-authored with Cupach) focuses on how readers outside of the academic community can increase their interpersonal conflict management competence in a variety of settings. For complete citations of these books and additional works by Canary, see the references for this chapter at the end of the book.

Canary teaches courses in interpersonal communication, conflict management, and research methods. His most recent research involves a quickly applied conflict rating system that people can use to observe conflict in an efficient yet valid way.

3. Describe the conflict in terms of behavior, consequences, and feelings (b-c-f) . Once you have owned the conflict as your problem, describe the conflict to your partner using the b-c-f—or behavior, consequences, and feelings—sequence: "When a specific behavior(s) happen(s), the specific consequences result, and I feel (a certain way)" (Gordon, 1971). It's important to include all three of these elements in your description for the other person to fully understand what is happening. Earlier in this book we discussed the importance of objectivity when using the skills of describing behavior and describing feelings. Notice that the b-c-f sequence also involves describing behavior and feelings. Therefore, when the b-c-f sequence is used in initiating a conflict, it also helps to communicate the problem in nonevaluative terms. To return to our loud music example, you would follow up on your ownership of the problem opening using the b-c-f sequence. For example, you might say, "When I hear your music [b], I get distracted and can't concentrate on studying [c], and then I get frustrated and annoyed [f]." The loudness of the music is the behavior, the consequences are distraction and inability to concentrate, and the feelings are frustration and annoyance. Note that like the ownership statement, all of the statements here are "I"-centered ("When I hear your music," rather than "When you play your music so loud"; "I get distracted," rather than "You distract me"; and "I get frustrated and annoyed," rather than "You frustrate and annoy me").

4. Avoid blaming or ascribing motives. Since your goal is to resolve your complaint without escalating the conflict, you want to make sure that you do nothing that might create defensiveness. So be careful to avoid making accusations or distorting what the other person has done. A blaming statement would be saying, "You're being really inconsiderate of others in the building." Although this doesn't ascribe motives, it accuses the other person and puts him or her in a defensive position. You want the focus to be on what is happening to you. A statement ascribing motives would be to say, "You're obviously trying to drive everyone in the building crazy, aren't you?" You have no way of knowing what the other person's motives are, so you are likely to only agitate the other person with an assumption like this. In actuality, your neighbor is probably not intentionally undermining your study time, but rather trying to enjoy her leisure time.

5. Keep it short. Since problem solving requires interaction, it is important that you quickly draw the other person into the conversation. The longer you talk, the more likely you are to deviate from using "I"-centered statements, stray from the b-c-f formula, blame, and/or ascribe motives. In addition, you will allow more time for the other person to become defensive. Effective turn-taking rather than dominating the exchange during the early stages of conflict conversation will nurture the problem-solving climate.

6. Be sure the other person understands your problem. Even when you take the greatest care in briefly describing your needs, others may become defensive, try to rationalize, or immediately counterattack. They may get the general drift of the message but misunderstand the seriousness of the problem, or they may not understand at all. As a result, sometimes you may need to rephrase or restate what you have said. For example, suppose that when you approach your neighbor about the loud music, she says, "Oh come on, everyone plays loud music in this neighborhood, and there have been times when I have even heard your loud music." You might reply, "Yes, I understand it's a noisy neighborhood, and loud music normally doesn't bother me. And I'm sorry if I've disturbed you in the past—I didn't mean to. But I'm still having a problem studying right now. It's a really important exam." Notice that this doesn't accuse the noisy neighbor of not listening or of continuing to be insensitive. It merely attempts to get the focus back on the problem that you are having.

7. Phrase your preferred solution in a way that focuses on common ground. Once you have been understood and you understand the other's position, make your suggestion for change. This suggestion is more likely to be accepted if you can tie it to a shared value, common interest, or shared constraint. In our example, you might say, "I think we both have had times when even little things got in the way of our being able to study. So even though I realize I'm asking you for a special favor, I hope you can help me out by turning down your music for a couple of hours."

▷ Communication Skills for Responding to Conflict

It is more difficult to create a collaborative climate when responding to conflict initiated by another person than it is to initiate a conflict appropriately. Because most people do not use the behavior-consequences-feelings sequence to initiate conflict and instead express their feelings in inappropriate, evaluative terms that threaten others, it can be difficult for the parties on the other end of the conflict to overcome their defensiveness and respond appropriately in turn. For instance, suppose you were not the one to initiate a conflict over loud music, that instead of being the person annoyed by loud music, you were the one playing your music loudly. If in initiating the conflict, your neighbor knocks on your door and says, "Turn down that damn music! Quit being such a jerk to others," you might very well respond to the "you"-centered and blaming conflict initiation by slamming

---

SKILL BUILDERS ◗ Behavior, Consequences, and Feelings (b-c-f) Sequence

SKILL	USE	PROCEDURE	EXAMPLE
Describing a conflict in terms of behavior, consequences, and feelings (b-c-f)	To help the other person understand the problem completely	1. Own the message, using "I"-centered statements. 2. Describe the behavior that you see or hear. 3. Describe the consequences that result from the behavior. 4. Describe your feelings that result from the behavior.	Jason says, "I have a problem that I need your help with. When I tell you what I'm thinking and you don't respond (b), I start to think you don't care about me or what I think (c), and this causes me to get very angry with you (f)."

your door and not turning down your music. Your most difficult task as a responder is to take an ineffectively initiated conflict and turn it into a productive, problem-solving discussion. The following guidelines will help you to respond effectively in these situations.

1. Put your "shields" up. When someone is overly aggressive in initiating a conflict, you need to learn to put your mental "shields" up to enable you to listen and improve your capacity to respond effectively rather than becoming defensive or counterattacking. One method that can help you do this is to remind yourself that the other person should be the one to own the problem, not you. In all likelihood, the anger being vented toward you is caused by accumulated frustration, only part of which directly relates to the current conflict. So put those shields up, take your time responding, and while you are doing so, think of your options for turning the attack into a problem-solving opportunity.

2. Respond empathetically with genuine interest and concern. A person who initiates a conflict, even with a bold order like "Turn down that damn music!" will be watching you closely to see how you react. If you make light of the other person's concerns, become defensive, or counterattack, you will undermine the opportunity to solve the problem in a cooperative manner. Even if you disagree with the complaint, for effective collaboration to occur, you must show respect to the person by being attentive and empathetic. Sometimes you can do this by allowing the other person to vent while you listen. Only when the other person has calmed down can you begin to problem-solve. In our example, you might well start by saying, "I can see you're angry. Let's talk about this."

3. Ask questions to clarify issues and paraphrase your understanding of the problem. Since most people are unaware of the b-c-f sequence, you may want to form a paraphrase that captures your understanding of the b-c-f issues or ask questions to elicit this information. For instance, let's suppose that in addition to saying "Turn down that damn music! Quit being such a jerk to others," your neighbor also ascribes motives by saying, "You're deliberately disrupting everyone!" If information is missing, as with this initiating statement, then you can ask questions to fill in the missing information, such as "I'm not sure what you're upset about. Are you studying right now, is that the issue?" Then, once you have all of the information you need, use a paraphrase that reflects the b-c-f framework: "OK, so I take it you are upset (f) because my music is loud (b) and that's interrupting your ability to study (c). Is that right?" It can also be helpful to ask the person not only if you have paraphrased correctly, but also if there is anything else that has not been mentioned. Sometimes people will initiate a conflict episode in relation to minor issues without mentioning what really needs to be considered.

4. Seek common ground by finding some aspect of the complaint with which to agree. Regardless of whether someone has initiated a conflict with you effectively, once you have gotten to the point of clarifying the problem, your next step is to seek common ground as the first step in resolving the conflict. This does not mean that you must give in completely to the other person. Nor does it mean that you should feign agreement with the other person. However, using your skills of supportiveness, you can look for points on which you both can agree. Adler (1977) says that you can agree with a message without accepting all of its implications. You can agree with part of it, you can agree with it in principle, you can agree with the initiator's perceptions of the situation, and/or you can agree with the person's feelings. For example, once you and your neighbor have come to a mutual understanding that the conflict is your loud music interrupting study time and causing frustration, you could either agree with the entire statement ("I totally agree with you and I'm sorry"), agree in part ("I know it's hard to study for a tough exam"), agree in principle ("I know it's good to have a quiet place to study"), agree with the initiator's perception ("I can see that you're having trouble studying with loud music in the background"), or agree with the person's feelings ("I can see that you're frustrated and annoyed"). You do not need to agree with the initiator's conclusions ("Your music is causing me to have difficulty studying") and concede completely. But by agreeing to some aspect of the complaint, you create common ground from which a problem-solving discussion can proceed. For example, you may not agree that your music is actually all that loud, but at least you can find some area of common ground.

5. Ask the initiator to suggest solutions. Finally, as soon as you are sure that the two of you have agreed on what the problem is, at least in part, ask the initiator for ways to handle the conflict. In response to the loud music conflict, the initiator's solutions may be for you to turn the music down or for you to turn it off completely. Since the initiator has probably spent time thinking about what needs to be done, your request for a solution signals a willingness to listen and cooperate. You may find that one of the suggestions seems reasonable to you (turning the music down so you can still listen, instead of turning it off). If none of the suggestions are reasonable, you may be able to craft an alternative that builds on one of the ideas presented ("I'd be happy to turn the music down, but most people are done with their exams, so you might also think about working in the designated quiet area if someone else starts playing their music loud"). In any case, asking for suggestions communicates your trust in the other person, strengthening the problem-solving climate.

▷ Communication Skills for Mediating Conflict

In some situations, you may be called upon to mediate or referee a conflict between other people rather than be one of the participants engaged directly in the conflict—to take on the role of mediator. A **mediator** is a "neutral and impartial guide, structuring an interaction that enables the conflicting parties to find a mutually acceptable solution to their problems" (Cupach & Canary, 1997, p. 205). Mediating conflict draws on a variety of basic interpersonal communication skills: Mediators must be assertive and persuasive, as well as effective at listening, paraphrasing, and questioning. At times they will use interpreting responses to reframe issues in ways that reduce defensiveness. As a mediator, you can provide a useful service for friends and family as you help them repair relationships and

Mediator—a neutral and impartial guide, structuring an interaction that enables the conflicting parties to find a mutually acceptable solution to their problems.

It is often useful to have help in mediating conflict. What is a mediator likely to do to help people resolve conflict?

work to create more positive communication by observing the following guidelines (Cupach & Canary, 1997; Whetten & Cameron, 2007).

1. Make sure that the people having the conflict agree to work with you. Sometimes people say they want a mediator when in reality they just want to stall discussion or resolution. If one or both of the parties doesn't really want your help, then you are not likely to be able to do much good. You may be able to clarify this by saying, "I'm willing to help you work on this, but only if both of you want me to." Depending on the willingness of both parties, you can either mediate or bow out gracefully.

2. Help the people identify the real conflict. Many times people seem to be arguing over one thing, when in actuality the true source of conflict has not been stated. When the source of the conflict is not clear and you have taken on the role of mediator, it is important that you help the parties identify the real issue by asking clarifying questions and paraphrasing.

3. Maintain neutrality. Perhaps the most important role of the mediator is to remain impartial. When you paraphrase, be sure to paraphrase the points of view of both parties, listen empathetically to both parties, and be very careful never to show favoritism. Any perception of favoritism will test the patience of one of the parties and destroy the opportunity for successful mediation.

4. Keep the discussion focused on the issues rather than on personalities. Because problem solving is nurtured in a supportive communication climate, the mediator must help participants to make descriptive statements, not ego-centered, blaming, or insulting comments that stray the focus onto the personalities of the people involved in the conflict. This can be done through asking questions that elicit b-c-f statements and by setting ground rules that encourage statements that are problem-oriented and not person-oriented, descriptive and not evaluative. If, during the discussion, one of the parties begins acting egocentric, accusing the other party, or insulting the other party, the mediator can simply remind the violator of the previously agreed-upon ground rules.

5. Work to ensure equal talk time. It is important for the mediator to control the conversation in a way that allows both parties to have an equal chance to be heard. The quality of the conversation is increased if each person has equal input because both parties feel that what they have to say is meaningful and important. A mediator can do this by directing questions to the more reticent, or withdrawn, party and by encouraging turn-taking to signal to the more assertive party that equal talk time is essential. For instance, you could say, "We've heard your concerns, Erin; now I'd like us to hear how Ed sees this issue."

6. Focus the discussion on helping the parties find a solution. A mediator is not a judge. Mediators should not let themselves be placed in the position of assessing guilt or making decisions. While some interpersonal conflicts involve issues of right and wrong, most arise from differences in perspective. Therefore, if asked for a personal opinion, the mediator might say, "I'm not in a position to judge. What I want to do is help find a way to handle this issue that both of you can feel good about." In this way, the mediator focuses the participants on managing the conflict between them rather than bringing the mediator into it.

7. Use paraphrasing and perception checking to make sure both parties fully understand and support the agreed-upon solution. Sometimes mediators make the mistake of believing that when one party suggests a reasonable solution to which the other party voices no disagreement, the dispute has been resolved. Silence cannot automatically be interpreted as agreement, however. A good mediator paraphrases the suggested solution and asks each party whether he or she understands it fully and supports it. It is also important that mediators check their perceptions of the nonverbal messages that participants send. While a participant may voice agreement, his or her nonverbal behaviors may be shouting hesitancy. If the mediator suspects that a participant's agreement is half-hearted, this should be explicitly explored through a perception check. Once convinced that both parties are satisfied with the proposed solution, the mediator can move to the final step in the process.

8. Establish an action plan and follow-up procedure. Unfortunately, some mediators stop short, assuming that once a solution has been agreed upon in principle, the participants can work out the details unassisted. But taking the essential final step of making sure that the parties have an action plan, with clearly agreed-to responsibilities, is part of effective mediating. The action plan should specify what each party is to do and how results will be measured and monitored. A mediator can move participants to this final stage by praising them for reaching agreement on a general solution framework and asking each party to describe the

The Power of *Wastah* in Lebanese Speech

by Mahboub Hashem

Mahboub Hashem teaches communication at Fort Hayes State University. His research interests are in the areas of interpersonal and intercultural communication.

" Do you have any *wastah*?" This was the only question that many of my Lebanese friends and relatives asked me when I applied for one of the Chair of Administrative Affairs positions at the Lebanese University [some years ago]. I replied that I ranked among the top five in the competency exam and they needed to hire at least ten people, so why would I need a *wastah*? They simply shrugged and warned, "Wait and you'll see."

To make the story short, I was passed over and more than 10 other people were hired. Every one of those who were hired had some type of *wastah*. I was hired three years later only after I had acquired strong *wastah,* which included several influential individuals, among them Suleiman Frangieh, the President of Lebanon at that time. . . .

By examining the *wastah* phenomenon in Lebanon and how it is practiced, one may be able to shed some light on this very important communicative behavior not only in Lebanon but also in the rest of the Middle East. This essay addresses the power of *wastah* (i.e., mediation), considered to be one of the most important communication patterns in the Lebanese cultural system. . . .

Wastah has been the way of life in Lebanon since before it became a republic. The term *wastah* means many things to many Lebanese people, including clout, connections, networking, recommendations, a "go-between" for two parties with different interests, and a type of contraception to prevent pregnancy.

Wastah can be used within various contexts, such as family, clan, government organizations, neighbors, villages, and nations. It is usually necessary to get a job, a wife, a date, a passport, a visa, a car, or any other commodity. It can also resolve conflicts, facilitate government decisions, or solve bureaucratic problems. For instance, I once had to wait three hours until I could find an influential person to help me pay the annual tag fee for my car. The common perception in the Arab world, particularly in Lebanon, is that "one does not do for oneself what might better be done by a friend or a friend's friend."

How Does the Process of *Wastah* Work?

Wastah is mostly used to find jobs for relatives or close friends and to solve conflicts. The extended family acts as an employment agency by searching for a *wasit* to help get a job, preferably one with high social status in the family. The *wasit* is supposed to be well "wired up," an insider who can make things happen (Hall, 1984). He must also be able to use the language of persuasion . . . with the elite of the religious and political groups of the nation.

In conflict situations, the *wasit*'s job is to conciliate rather than to judge. Conciliation is intended to lead disputants toward a compromise through mutual concessions, as well as to re-establish their relationship on the basis of mutual respect. The *wasit* tries to talk to each disputant separately, then brings them together to reach a possible compromise that presumes to save face for everyone involved and their extended families.

Lebanese people prefer mediators from the same family or business, depending on the type and context of the conflict. . . . [T]he role of a *wasit* is to create a supportive climate of communication wherein conflicting parties can modify their behaviors. When a conflict is between members from two different clans, however, a *wasit* on each side tries to prevail over his or her own clan members. These mediators then come together to conciliate.

For instance, when a conflict occurred between my father and a man named Tony Ayoub, one elderly person from the Hashem clan and another one from the Ayoub clan came together to mediate and negotiate a possible settlement. Then each of the two met with their clan member to discuss the results of their meeting(s) and what the two believed to be a fair solution. After several private meetings between the two mediators, my father and Tony were asked to personally participate in the final one to announce the settlement of the problem. The common ground among mediators of different families is the mutual desire to keep the government out of the clans' affairs as much as possible. Hence, mediators seem better qualified than government agencies to resolve certain conflicts. . . .

The knowledge of these styles and how they are used in various cultures promotes more awareness and understanding of ourselves and others and can consequently lead to more effective intercultural relationships.

Excerpted from Hashem, M. (2004). The power of *Wastah* in Lebanese speech. In A. González, M. Houston, & V. Chen (Eds.), *Our Voices* (pp. 150–154). Los Angeles: Roxbury Publishing Company.

specific behaviors or changes in behavior that they will need to perform in the future to make the solution an actuality.

▷ Recovering from Conflict Management Failures: Understand and Forgive

There are times when no matter how hard you try, you will be unable to manage the conflict successfully in a way that meets the needs of both parties. Some conflicts are extremely complex and may not be resolvable even using the communication skills we have described here (Sillars & Weisberg, 1987). In such situations, it is important that at the least you understand why the conflict was not resolved successfully and that you practice forgiveness.

First, when the relationship is important to you, it is useful to analyze the inability of both parties to manage the conflict. You can begin this process by questioning yourself about the conflict: What went wrong? Did one or more of you become competitive? Or defensive? Did you use a style that was inappropriate to the situation? Did you initiate or respond inappropriately? Did either or both of you fail to implement the problem-solving method adequately? By analyzing your

A QUESTION OF ETHICS ⊙ What Would You Do?

Maria and José had been shopping at the outlet mall. After loading their purchases into the trunk of the car, they decided to move the car to a parking space closer to the next group of shops. Maria was backing out; she glanced in the rearview mirror and cried, "She's going to hit us!" She began to honk her horn, but the other vehicle, an SUV, continued backing up and banged into Maria's rear bumper. Maria and José immediately hopped out of the car to check out the damage.

Three conservatively dressed women, with their hair covered by scarves, appeared to be daughter, mother, and grandmother. They slowly exited the SUV. José shouted, "What's wrong with you! Couldn't you see us or hear the horn?" Maria told José to shut up and turned to the driver, a young woman about her own age, and said, "Good grief! Just give me your information!" Rima, the other driver, turned to José and politely told him that she hadn't seen them or heard the horn. Then she turned to Maria and said that she needed to call her husband and immediately retreated into the SUV, pulling her cell phone out of her purse as she closed the door.

Maria exploded. She began banging on Rima's window, shouting, "Why do you need to talk to your husband? He wasn't here! What does he have to do with this!" At this point the second woman, who appeared to be Rima's mother, quietly asked Maria not to yell,

but her request had no effect. After a few moments, Rima opened the door and asked Maria to speak with Rima's husband, who was on the phone. Maria yelled that she had no intention of speaking to anyone and again demanded that Rima produce her license and insurance information. Rima then directed her mother and grandmother to get back in the car and said that she was going to call the police. The three women sat in the SUV until a police car arrived.

After talking with Maria and José, the officer who had responded to the call explained to Rima that police don't intervene in traffic accidents on private property if there are no injuries unless there is a problem with the parties exchanging information. Rima and her mother cut him off and told him that Maria had verbally assaulted them, using bad words and threatening them. The police officer replied that Maria's behavior might have been unfortunate, but her request had been legal and was actually the proper procedure at the scene of this type of accident. Rima responded that she had never had an accident before and had called her husband to find out what she should do. Had Maria simply been patient, none of this would have happened.

1. In this situation, was it ethical for each person to use the conflict style chosen?
2. Which of Johannesen's characteristics of ethical dialogue (see Chapter 7) were violated in this incident?

behavior and that of your partner, you will become more aware of how you can continue to improve your conflict management skills and become more aware of how to handle areas of incompatibility in your relationships in the future.

Second, regardless of whether you are able to effectively manage a conflict, it is important to forgive the person with whom you were in conflict, especially if that person is a friend or family member who is a major part of your life. Forgiving is the act of excusing the hurt that someone has caused you and forgoing revenge to repair or restore a relationship. Forgiveness paves the way for reconciliation, through which you can rebuild trust in a relationship and work toward restoration. Forgiving is not the same as forgetting, nor does forgiving automatically restore trust. But forgiving is a process through which you can put what has happened during the conflict in the past so that you and your relationship can move beyond the damage that the conflict has caused (Lulofs & Cahn, 2000).

⭕ Summary

Interpersonal conflict is disagreement between two interdependent people who perceive that they have incompatible goals. Even in good relationships, conflicts are inevitable.

There are six types of interpersonal conflict: pseudoconflicts, which are caused by perceptual differences and are easily resolved; fact conflicts, which are caused by informational disagreement; value conflicts, which are caused by disagreements over deep-seated moral beliefs; policy conflicts, which are caused by disagreements over how to deal with plans or courses of action; ego conflicts, which are the result of one party insisting on being the "winner" of an argument; and metaconflicts, which are caused by disagreements over the process of communication itself.

We manage conflict by withdrawing, accommodating, forcing, compromising, or collaborating. Each of these strategies can be effective under certain circumstances. When we are concerned about maintaining long-term relationships, collaboration is the most appropriate strategy.

Destructive behaviors in conflicts include ascribing motives, counterblaming, engaging in demand-withdrawal, engaging in spiraling negativity, and practicing stubbornness.

You can increase the likelihood that conflict will be effectively resolved if you and your partner agree to certain rules prior to talking about your disagreement. To initiate a collaborative conflict management conversation, you should mentally rehearse what you will say before you confront the other person; recognize and state ownership of the conflict; describe the conflict in terms of behavior, consequences, and feelings (b-c-f); avoid blaming or ascribing motives; keep it short; be sure the other person understands your problem; and phrase your preferred solution in a way that focuses on common ground.

When seeking collaboration when responding to another person's initiation of conflict, you should put your "shields" up, respond empathetically with genuine interest and concern, ask questions to clarify issues and paraphrase your understanding of the problem, seek common ground by finding some aspect of the complaint to agree with, and ask the initiator to suggest solutions.

When you mediate a conflict, you should make sure that the people having the conflict agree to work with you, help the people identify the real conflict, maintain neutrality, keep the discussion focused on the issues rather than on personalities, work to ensure equal talk time, focus the discussion on helping the parties find a solution, use paraphrasing and perception checking to make sure both parties fully understand and support the agreed-upon solution, and establish an action plan and follow-up procedure.

Finally, learn from failures in conflict management. Even when you cannot resolve a conflict, you can try to understand why the conflict was not resolved successfully and forgive the other person so that you can get on with your life.

◐ Inter-Action Dialogue: Interpersonal Conflict

Interpersonal conflict occurs when two interdependent people perceive that they have incompatible goals. As you read the following dialogue between Brian and Matt, consider the types of conflict, styles of managing conflict, and skills that promote successful conflict management.

Brian and Matt share an apartment. Matt is consistently late in paying his share of expenses. Brian has tolerated this for over six months, but he has finally had enough and decides to confront Matt.

Conversation

Brian: Matt, I need to talk with you.

Matt: What's up?

Brian: Well, I have a problem. When I got home from class today, I tried to call my mom, and guess what? The phone's been disconnected.

Matt: You're kidding.

Brian: No, I'm not. And when I went next door and called the phone company, you know what they said?

Matt: I can guess.

Brian: They said the bill hadn't been paid and that this was the fourth month in a row that the bill was over two weeks late.

Matt: Look man, I can explain.

Brian: Like you explained not paying the utility bill on time last month? We were just lucky that it was a cool week and that we didn't fry without air conditioning. The candlelit dinner was charming and all that, but I really resented having to go to the library to study for my test. Matt, I just can't go on like this. I mean, I gave you my share of the phone bill three weeks ago. I always give you my half of the utility bill the day it arrives. And I'm sick and tired of having to nag you for your share of the rent. For the last four months I've had to cover your share by taking money out of what I am saving to buy Angie's engagement ring. I know that you eventually pay me back, but I lose the interest and it's just not fair.

Matt: Gosh, I didn't know that you were so upset. I mean it's not like I don't pay. I always make good, don't I?

Brian: Yes, so far that's true, but every month it's later and later before you pay me back. And I'm not a lending agency. Why do you expect me to loan you money each month? We work at the same place, make the same money, and we've both got the same expenses. If I can come up with the rent and other expenses on time, you can too.

Matt: Listen man, I apologize about the phone bill. I thought I'd mailed it. So, I'll check it out with the phone company tomorrow morning. And the utility bill was just a mistake. I lost the bill and didn't realize it hadn't been paid. I know that I've not always had the money for the rent when you asked, but you usually ask me for it a week or more before it's due. You are really good at saving ahead, but I'm not. You say we have the same expenses, but that's not true. I have a car loan and you don't. And since I got that ticket last year, my car insurance has skyrocketed. Some months I'm living really close to the edge. I know it's no excuse, but I want you to understand that I'm not just some deadbeat who's trying to suck off of you.

Brian: Matt, I'm sorry I said that we have similar expenses. You're right, yours are higher. And if I understood you correctly, our problems with the utility company and the phone company weren't caused by you not having the money but were because somehow the bills just slipped through the cracks?

Matt: Yeah. I'm never very organized but right now things are chaos. Between work, school, and the stuff that's going on with my family I don't know if I'm coming or going.

Brian: Well, I can understand that you are under a lot of pressure. And I hope you can understand that when you don't pay bills on time, it's not just you that suffers. Angie and I want to buy a house before we get married, so I'm really careful about paying bills on time so that I have a good credit rating. That's why I ask you for the rent so early. When you forget to pay the utility and phone bills, not only do we lose service, but since both of our names are on the bill, we both take a hit in our credit ratings. A poor credit rating will make it harder for me to get a loan. And it also will make it harder for you to get credit later. I know that you wouldn't intentionally do anything to hurt me, but the fact is, you have.

Matt: Whoa, I never really thought about it this way. Man, I'm sorry.

Brian: Apology accepted. So how can we work this out?

Matt: Well, you seem to have thought more about it than I have, do you have any ideas?

Brian: Yeah, as a matter of fact, a couple of alternatives come to mind. One, we could agree on a date each month to sit down and pay the bills together. That way, I'd know that the bills had been written and sent, and you could control my tendency to bug you for your half of the rent before it really needs to be sent. Or, with each paycheck we could each put a certain amount into a joint account. Then when the bills come in I would just write the checks out of that account, and you wouldn't have to bother with it at all.

Matt: Maybe we could do a combination of those things.

Brian: What do you mean?

Matt: Well, I don't want to totally turn control over to you. I mean, I really need to learn how to be responsible for getting stuff done on time. But I'm really jammed for time right now. So how about if we set the date for paying the bills but also set up the joint account? That way, if something comes up and I don't have the time to sit down with you and pay the bills, you can still get them done on time. But when I do have time, we can do it together. I think I can probably learn some good budgeting habits from you.

Brian: That's fine as long as you put in your share each pay period. I really get a kick out of managing my personal finances, and I'd be glad to show you what I do. What I do may not work for you, but you might get some ideas that you can adapt to your style. In any case, I'm glad we talked. I was really getting pissed at you and now I'm feeling like things are going to be OK. So when can we get together to set our bill-paying "date" and set up the joint account?

● Chapter Resources

Communication Improvement Plan:
Conflict Management ● Find more on the web @ www.oup.com/us/interact12

Would you like to improve the following aspects of your conflict resolving behaviors, as discussed in this chapter?

• Initiating conflict
• Responding to conflict
• Mediating the conflicts of others

Pick an aspect, and write a communication improvement plan. You can find a communication improvement plan worksheet on our website at www.oup.com/us/interact12.

Key Words ●

Interpersonal conflict, *p. 328*
Pseudoconflict, *p. 329*
Badgering, *p. 330*
Fact conflict, *p. 330*
Value conflict, *p. 330*
Policy conflict, *p. 331*
Ego conflict, *p. 332*

Metaconflict, *p. 333*
Withdrawing, *p. 334*
Accommodating, *p. 336*
Forcing, *p. 337*
Compromising, *p. 338*
Collaborating, *p. 338*
Ascribing motives, *p. 341*

Counterblaming, *p. 342*
Demand-withdrawal, *p. 342*
Spiraling negativity, *p. 343*
Stubbornness, *p. 343*
Mediator, *p. 349*

Skill Practice ● Find more on the web @ www.oup.com/us/interact12

Skill Practice exercises challenge you to master the material you have read in this chapter. For additional Skill Practice activities, visit our website at www.oup.com/us/interact12.

Identifying Types of Conflict
Label the following as S (pseudoconflict), F (fact conflict), V (value conflict), P (policy conflict), or E (ego conflict).

a. Joe wants to live with Mary, but Mary wants the two of them to get married.

b. Stan believes that because he is an insurance salesman, Jerry should not dispute his position on annuities.

c. George defends his failure to present an anniversary gift to Agnes by asserting that their anniversary is not today (May 8) but May 18.

d. Martin calls to announce that he is bringing the boss home for dinner. His wife replies, "That will be impossible. The house is a mess and I need to go shopping."

e. Jane says, "Harry, pick up your clothes. I'm not your maid!" Harry replies, "I thought we agreed that it's your job to take care of the house. I take care of the yard."

Answers: a. V; b. E; c. F; d. S; e. P

Inter-Act with Media ❂ Find more on the web @ www.oup.com/us/interact12

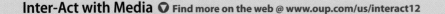

Television

ER, episode: ". . . As the Day She Was Born" (2008). Mekhi Phifer, Scott Grimes, Troy Evans.

Brief Summary: In one of this episode's subplots, resident Dr. Gregory Pratt (Phifer) begins a management seminar focusing on conflict resolution and then finds himself acting as a referee between bickering chief resident Dr. Archie Morris (Grimes) and desk clerk Frank Martin (Evans). The arguing begins over Frank's claim that hospital accreditation standards prevent food in the front desk area; in response, Dr. Morris yells, "Hostile work environment!" Later, the quibbling continues over trivial behavior—loud breathing and pen-tapping—and then leads to name-calling. Dr. Pratt steps in and encourages the men to begin their concerns with "I feel . . . " Soon, the exchange reveals the *true* conflict: Frank feels hurt over not being invited to Dr. Morris' recent party. Dr. Morris claimed that he "didn't think Frank liked sushi and karaoke." The conflict dissolves with a hug and offer to buy coffee.

IPC Concepts: Badgering; counterblaming; communication skills for initiating, responding to, and mediating conflict.

Cinema

Waitress (2007). Adrienne Shelly (director). Keri Russell, Jeremy Sisto, Cheryl Hines, Adrienne Shelly.

Brief Summary: Jenna (Russell) is a small-town diner waitress stuck in a volatile marriage to Earl (Sisto). Rather than dealing directly with Earl's emotional immaturity, jealousy, and possessiveness, Jenna accommodates his behavior with half-hearted but continual reassurance of her love and commitment. She perpetually withdraws and redirects herself into her true passion: baking "to-die-for" pies and naming them based on her life's turmoil. When she finds herself unexpectedly pregnant, Jenna creates the "I don't want Earl's baby" pie. The impending baby causes Earl to become increasingly selfish and controlling, resulting in further withdrawal from Jenna. She attempts to leave unsuccessfully and ultimately begins an affair. Although Jenna's conflicts are not necessarily resolved, she finally discovers and asserts her true needs after the birth of her daughter.

IPC Concepts: Ego conflicts, styles of managing conflict, withdrawal, accommodating, forcing, ascribing motives, understanding unresolved conflicts.

What's on the Web

Find links and additional material, including self-quizzes, on the companion website at www .oup.com/us/interact12.

13

Communicating in Intimate Relationships

Close Friends, Life Partners, and Families

After you have read this chapter, you should be able to answer these questions:

▶ What are intimate relationships, platonic relationships, and romantic relationships?

▶ What are the characteristics of intimate relationships?

▶ What are the three types of intimate relationships?

▶ How is intimacy communicated in male-male, female-female, and female-male platonic relationships?

▶ What factors define long-term relationships?

▶ What are the types of couple relationships?

▶ What are the characteristics of successful long-term relationships?

▶ What is a family?

▶ What are the functions of family communication?

▶ What are two dimensions of family communication patterns?

▶ What are the strengths and challenges of intergenerational family communication?

▶ What are five ways to improve family communication?

▶ What are relational uncertainty and possessiveness, and how can you resolve these problems?

"Hi, Bethany, I'm home."

"Well whoopee. Big deal. I mean, after all, you're an hour late."

"Sorry hon, but something came up at work at the last minute and I had to take care of it before I could leave, so I missed the train and had to wait for the next one. But I'm home now."

"Great, but Evan, dinner was ready an hour ago and the pork chops are pretty well dried out by now. And this is the fourth time this month that you've been late without even bothering to call or text me. It's not like I don't have other things I could be doing besides cooking dinner for you and having it ruined. I've got about four hours of studying to get done. Had I known that you were going to be late, I wouldn't have made dinner and then waited thinking you'd walk in the door at any minute. Don't you ever think of anyone but yourself? You say you want to start a family. You say you love me, but you don't even show up for dinner when you're supposed to or have the courtesy to let me know that you'll be late. If you can't be trusted with stuff as simple as this, how am I ever supposed to trust that you will be there for me and for any kids we might have?"

People, it seems, are designed to be in relationships. Our understanding of the importance of relationships starts early on when we bond with our parents and family members. As we grow into maturity, most of us develop relationships with people who are likely to be there when we need them. Those we are close with stand by us regardless of the circumstances, listen to us when we are joyful about something, and comfort us without judgment in our times of need. You may have a large number of friends and acquaintances, but if you are lucky, you may also have a handful of close relationships with both same-sex and opposite-sex intimates whom you trust with your innermost secrets.

Yet some people find themselves unable to establish and maintain intimate relationships. Some people are lonely, without the close relationships they desire, because they lack the ability to disclose with and support others. On the other hand, other people do develop satisfying intimate relationships, but then fail to maintain them for a variety of reasons, sometimes for reasons beyond their control. In our opening vignette, the conflict between Evan and Bethany illustrates how difficult maintaining intimacy can be. Yet we know that the key to maintaining intimacy is continual effective interpersonal communication.

In this chapter we will explore the role effective communication plays in intimate relationships. We begin by defining intimate relationships and describing the characteristics of intimate relationships. Then, we identify various different types of intimate relationships and discuss the nature and role of communication in each type. Finally, we present two problems that may occur in intimate relationships and discuss how communication can help to resolve them.

Intimate relationship—close and caring personal relationship in which both partners have detailed knowledge of each other's history, personality, and aspirations as a result of observations and mutual disclosures that have occurred over an extended period of time.

Platonic relationship—intimate relationship in which the partners are not sexually attracted to each other or do not choose to act on their sexual attraction to each other.

◎ Definition and Characteristics of Intimate Relationships

An **intimate relationship** is a close and caring personal relationship in which both partners have detailed knowledge of each other's history, personality, and aspirations as a result of observations and mutual disclosures that have occurred over an extended period of time. An intimate relationship can be platonic or romantic. **Platonic relationships** are intimate relationships in which the partners are not sexually attracted to each other or do not choose to act on their sexual attraction to each other. Healthy normal intimate family relationships between parents and children and between siblings are platonic, as are close friendships. Conversely, **romantic relationships** are intimate relationships in which the partners act on their sexual attraction to each other. Notice the definition of a romantic relationship is one in which there is both intimacy and sexual attraction that is acted on in some fashion. While intimate relationships may or may not be sexual, people also have sexual relationships that are not intimate.

To get a better understanding of what intimate relationships are, let's have a look at the characteristics that make up both platonic and romantic intimate relationships: warmth and affection, trust, self-disclosure, commitment, and shared symbols and rituals.

▷ Warmth and Affection

Perhaps the first, if not the most, important characteristic of intimacy is mutual warmth and affection. Intimates like each other and enjoy spending time together. Through their nonverbal and verbal behaviors, they demonstrate their delight in being together. Platonic intimates may smile at one another, enjoy recounting previous encounters, share private jokes, and enjoy spending long stretches of time just talking together. Romantic intimates not only enjoy these behaviors but also enjoy demonstrating their affection through sexually oriented behavior such as touching, kissing, and so on.

▷ Trust

Another important characteristic of intimate relationships is trust. **Trust** is confidence that your partner will not intentionally harm you (LaFollette, 1996, p. 116). Most of us recognize that trust almost always involves some level of risk. There is always a chance that your partner may disappoint you, as Evan disappointed Bethany in our opening scenario. As your trust in your partner grows, you are more likely to become dependent on each other and less likely to seek out other people to meet your needs. As this happens, you become more satisfied with the relationship and invest more of yourself in the other person (Rusbult, Olsen, Davis, and Hannon, 2001).

Research suggests that four factors lead to trust (Boon, 1994):

1. Dependability. Dependable partners can be relied upon at all times, under all circumstances. We view partners as dependable when experience tells us that they will be there for us when we need them and will do what is expected. Evan's late arrival from work indicated that he was not dependable, and, as a result, this caused Bethany to question whether she could trust him.

2. Responsiveness. Responsive partners think about the needs of their partners and act accordingly. At times this may require that one person sacrifice his or her interests for the good of the other. When Evan didn't bother to call or to text Bethany he was ignoring her need to know when she could expect him to be home.

3. Collaboration. Effective conflict-resolving partners optimally collaborate (or, if necessary, compromise) rather than engage in the less effective conflict-resolution

Romantic relationship—intimate relationship in which the partners act on their sexual attraction to each other.

Trust—confidence that your partner will not intentionally harm you.

strategies. Partners who withdraw or accommodate to preserve the short-term peace or force their position on their partner weaken the bond of trust between them. When partners can engage in open and constructive conflict, however, they are exercising their trust in each other—trust that they will be able to work out the conflict in beneficial ways.

4. Faithfulness. Faithful partners demonstrate a sense of loyalty to their partners and to their relationships. They honor the privacy wishes of their partners and do not reveal co-owned information without express permission; they defend the reputation and honor of their partners even when it is personally inconvenient; and, in intimate relationships, they do not engage in sexual behavior outside of the relationship.

▷ Self-Disclosure

A third pivotal characteristic of intimate relationships is self-disclosure. Without personal disclosure of private information you cannot have intimacy. In fact, some scholars believe that self-disclosure is the essence of intimacy (Mills & Clark, 2001). While we can learn some things about our partners and they about us through observation, only when we choose to share our histories, feelings, hopes, dreams, fears, and so forth with each other do we truly come to know and understand each other. Through self-disclosure, partners invest themselves in their relationships, providing each other with information that shows they trust, value, and care for each other. Out of this joint ownership of otherwise private information, partners develop a sense of "we-ness" that characterizes intimacy.

Nevertheless, even within intimate relationships, partners have the right to maintain some information as private. In fact, too much self-disclosure too soon may actually harm intimacy. For example, Marcel, who is a devout Catholic and has to fight his tendency to be jealous, may not be able to cope with knowing that his girl friend Rebecca had a teenage pregnancy. Should Rebecca choose to disclose this information too early, Marcel may unreasonably feel that Rebecca has been unfaithful and has violated his trust, even though the pregnancy occurred years before they met. In situations like this, maintaining one's privacy may be a wise decision because the disclosure of this information could short-circuit what would otherwise be a satisfying intimate relationship. When or if Rebecca decides to disclose her teenage pregnancy she will need to weigh the benefits of disclosing against the risks that sharing this information might pose.

▷ Commitment

Intimate relationships are also characterized by a deep level of **commitment**, the choice to obligate oneself and one's resources to an intimate partner. These resources include your time, your treasure, and your talents. For example, if Judy's husband Nick suddenly increases the number of weeknights he spends playing basketball at the gym from one to four, she may feel that the marriage is in

OBSERVE AND ANALYZE ⌄

Platonic versus Romantic Intimate Relationships

Compare a platonic relationship you have been in (or are still in) with a romantic relationship you have been in (or are still in). Compare each of these relationships in terms of the characteristics of intimate relationships described in this chapter. How are the platonic and romantic relationships similar? How do they differ? How typical is each relationship to others of its kind that you have experienced?

Commitment—choice to obligate oneself and one's resources to an intimate partner.

trouble because Nick is no longer willing to demonstrate commitment to the relationship. Note, however, that the level of commitment expected varies from relationship to relationship. While the level of commitment expected in a marriage is understandably high, particularly when there are children involved, the level of commitment expected in an intimate friendship may vary. For example, some intimate friends see each other only once or twice a year because they live far away from each other, but they perceive an ongoing level of commitment to keep the friendship going when they do get in touch.

▷ Shared Symbols and Rituals

A less obvious but important characteristic of intimate relationships is the shared use of symbols and rituals. As intimacy develops in a relationship, partners may celebrate, commemorate, publicize, or formalize their relationship through these symbols and rituals. Many intimate couples wear clothing or jewelry that symbolically commemorates and publicizes their relationship or engage in various rituals that celebrate their partnerships, such as the anniversaries of their meeting, first dates, and other significant relationship events. Justine and Silvia, who met when their children were in nursery school and just "clicked," now exchange birthday gifts and have ritualized a weekly date for coffee after Thursday morning car pool. Sonia wears the ring that Juan gave her when she became engaged, and they now celebrate the "monthivesaries" of their engagement by going out for dinner. Although the symbols and rituals will differ from relationship to relationship, intimates almost always develop symbols and rituals to remind themselves and others about the special nature of the relationship. Just as someone's behavior may signal a change in their level of commitment to the relationship, one partner's failure to honor the symbols or perform the rituals associated with the relationship can signal that the relationship is deteriorating. For example, if Josh forgets Sarah's birthday this year and then doesn't send her flowers on Valentine's Day either, Sarah is likely to perceive that Josh is no longer committed to the relationship.

While all intimate relationships are characterized by warmth and affection, trust, self-disclosure, commitment, and shared symbols and rituals, how these characteristics develop depends on the type of intimate relationship in which the participants are involved and the characteristics of the participants in those relationships. In the next three sections, we will describe how communication patterns differ in close friendships, long-term relationships (including marriages and other life partnerships), and families.

◑ Close Friendships

Intimate platonic friendships can be the most satisfying lifelong relationships in which we are involved. Regarding close friendships, research has found that the communication patterns that lead to intimacy differ depending on the sex of the partners. In general, it appears that men

INTER-ACT WITH ◑ TECHNOLOGY

How does the technology you use affect your intimate relationship? For three days keep a log of all the technology-mediated interactions you have. Note the type of technology, the nature of your relationship with the person, and whether you interrupted a face-to-face interaction to engage in the mediated one. Note how many of these interactions were with your intimates. Looking over your journal data, do you use technology to maintain your intimate relationships? Do you use text messaging, e-mail, and so on to keep in touch with intimates to whom you are not physically close? Do you interrupt face-to-face conversations to "talk" with intimates who are not present, or vice versa?

and women view intimacy in close friendships differently. Men tend to define close friendships in terms of joint activities, while women tend to define close friendships in terms of shared thoughts and feelings (Reis, 1998). Yet despite the apparent differences in behaviors, both men and women define intimacy using the same words: warmth, disclosure of personal feelings, and shared activities. Let's explore in more depth how communication is used to achieve intimacy in male-male, female-female, and female-male close friendships.

▷ Male-Male Friendships

Throughout history, platonic male friendships have been glorified as the epitome of camaraderie. Large numbers of popular books, movies, and television shows have portrayed male comradeship and romanticized the male bonding experience. Scholars have found that "buddy" books, films, and TV shows do accurately reflect how men in heterosexual male-male close friendships communicate. Practical help, mutual assistance, and companionship appear to be the benchmarks of intimacy in these relationships (Wood & Inman, 1993). Conversational topics can be classified as topical, relational, or personal. Men's conversations tend to be primarily topical, revolving around politics, sex, activities, work, and events (such as sports, music, or other events), rather than personal (having to do with one's own thoughts and feelings) or relational (having to do with exploring interpersonal relationships).

Generally, men don't spend time with their close male friends discussing relationships and personal issues. We can speculate that cultural ideals of manhood

Male friendship usually focuses on activities, and men regard practical help, mutual assistance, and companionship as benchmarks of caring.

and deep-seated biological imperatives for self-preservation and independence make it more difficult for men to self-disclose and thus become vulnerable to other men. So it may be that men have developed "an alternate path" to intimacy by relying on shared activities and favors rather than personal disclosures as a means of developing closeness (Wood & Inman, 1993). However, Julia Wood (2003) has suggested that men do self-disclose to other men, using covert intimacy. **Covert intimacy** is delivering messages signaling closeness, trust, and equality by using mild insults, competition, or put-downs (Wood, 2007). When used with a less intimate acquaintance these behaviors would signal hostility and would lead to distrust and relationship damage. But within the context of a well-established intimate male friendship, such exchanges usually signal affection. For example, Nick might playfully say to Alex, his boyhood friend and now roommate, "Hey idiot, has that girlfriend of yours realized yet that she can do better than you?" Alex might respond, "At least I have a girlfriend. When was the last time some girl was willing to go out with you?" It is through such covert intimacy that male friends can implicitly say that they care about each other.

Covert intimacy—delivering messages signaling closeness, trust, and equality by using mild insults, competition, or put-downs.

▷ Female-Female Friendships

Women's intimate friendships are marked by mutual self-disclosures. In contrast to male-male conversations, which we've learned are generally topical in nature, female-female conversations tend to span the three conversational categories—topical, relational, and personal. When women talk with one another, they talk not only about topics such as politics, sex, activities, work, and events but also about personal feelings, their own relationships, and the relationships of others.

It appears that female-female close friendships are rich when measured by many of the criteria of effective interpersonal communication. Nonetheless, women are not always satisfied with their female-female friendships. Because women self-disclose to each other to a larger degree, they also tend to get as deeply involved with the problems of others as they do with their own problems. Over time, this heavy emotional involvement can take its toll, leading to health problems attributable to stress and overdependence on others (otherwise known as co-dependence). In addition, some women experience a desire to overly self-disclose and/or disclose information about others, and, as we have seen, sometimes it is better to withhold information that may have the effect of damaging close friendships with others.

▷ Female-Male Friendships

Because men and women tend to achieve relational intimacy through different means, there are times when these differences can impede intimacy in female-male friendships. Nevertheless, both men and women frequently enjoy intimate female-male relationships. Interestingly, many men report that the relationships most meaningful to them are their friendships with women. Although men don't usually share as much intimate information with other men, they still have a need for the type of emotional closeness that comes from self-disclosure. As you would expect, research has found that men rate their female friends higher regarding nurturing and give their male friends lower ratings (Fitzpatrick & Bochner, 1981). In addition, men not only confide more to their best women friends but also report being closer to their women friends than to their male friends (Winstead, Derlega, & Rose, 1997).

For women, self-disclosure is the key to intimacy, so while women may enjoy sharing in activities with their male friends, they are unlikely to feel that there is real intimacy in the relationship if the man is unable or unwilling to self-disclose. In fact, women frequently criticize men for failing to express their feelings through such self-disclosing statements as, "Our friendship is really important to me. My life would be empty without you." On the other hand, women need to understand that for many men, intimacy is defined through practical help, mutual assistance, and companionship, so actions such as helping make repairs, cooking dinner, and so on need to be recognized as acts of intimacy. In the past, our society has valued women's preferences for verbal disclosures as the best measure of intimacy; recently more emphasis has been placed on how men's instrumental activity creates intimacy (Wood & Inman, 1993). Some say that women's expressive style and men's instrumental style are complementary approaches that work well together. Still others maintain that the optimal situation is one in which all people, regardless of gender, embrace both affective and activity-oriented modes of relating to friends (Fehr, 1996). Male-female relationships are likely to run more smoothly if participants recognize and value the differing approaches.

⊙ Long-Term Relationships, Marriages, and Other Life Partnerships

A substantial amount of research has been directed at understanding intimacy in long-term, committed romantic relationships, including marriages and other life partnerships. In good relationships of these types, people find perhaps better satisfaction than they do with any other types of intimate relationships. For example, in a survey of more than two thousand American married people, J. D. Bloch (1980) found that 40 percent of all respondents considered their spouses to also be their best friends. In a different study of married people, 88 percent of married men and 78 percent of married women named their spouses as the people "closest" to them (Fischer & Narus, 1981, p. 449).

Studies comparing heterosexual and homosexual life partners find no significant differences on any measures of relationship satisfaction. The few studies of committed relationships that have included older gay men and lesbians have found that relationships lasting twenty years or more are not uncommon. Research shows that most lesbians and gay men want long-term committed relationships and are successful at creating them (Peplau, 1993).

▷ Factors Defining Long-Term Relationships

Mary Anne Fitzpatrick, a leading scholar of marriage, has identified three factors that define long-term relationships: independence, ideology, and communication (Fitzpatrick, 1988; Fitzpatrick & Badzinski, 1994).

1. Independence. First, couples can be defined on the basis of their independence, the extent to which the partners share their feelings with each other. Some couples are independent, less reliant on their partners for emotional sharing and support. Other couples are interdependent, depending primarily on their partners for comfort, expressions of love, and fun.

2. Ideology. The second factor that defines long-term relationships is ideology, the extent to which the partners adhere to long-established belief systems. Some couples adhere highly to traditional belief systems and values, for example, believing in traditional sex roles, traditional rules about the institution of marriage, sexual fidelity, and the like. Other couples, meanwhile, are open to alternative belief systems, including identifying novel sex role relationships or choosing alternative long-term living arrangements.

3. Communication. The third factor that defines long-term relationships is one that Fitzpatrick originally called "conflict avoidance" but now calls "communication." According to this dimension, couple types differ in the extent to which they seek to avoid or engage in conflict as they interact.

▷ Types of Couple Relationships

Using these three characteristics, Fitzpatrick's research has identified three basic types of couple relationships, which she labels as traditional, independent, and separate.

1. Traditional couples. Traditional couples are couples who maintain a traditional ideology about their long-term relationships, are interdependent, and engage in conflict. In these types of couples, both partners follow the values accepted by their parents and grandparents. Their values place more emphasis on stability than on spontaneity, and they almost always chose marriage over alternative living arrangements. In addition, they hold to traditional customs related to marriage. For example, if married, the woman is likely to take her husband's last name, and both parties will always consider infidelity to be inexcusable. Traditional couples are interdependent, meeting many of their intimacy needs within the relationship. They are likely to face their conflicts rather than avoid them.

Traditional couples—couples who maintain a traditional ideology about their long-term relationships, are interdependent, and engage in conflict.

2. Independent couples. Independent couples are couples who share an ideology whose values differ from traditional ones, are interdependent, and engage in conflict. These relationships are called independent because they don't rely on traditional ideology. Instead, each partner desires a relationship that is unconventional when compared to traditional ones. For example, the partners may believe that their relationship should not constrain each partner's individual freedoms. While they are interdependent to experience intimacy they do not need to share physical space and may live in different cities without either feeling abandoned or lonely.

Independent couples—couples who share an ideology whose values differ from traditional ones, are interdependent, and engage in conflict.

They make keep separate schedules, with one working days while the other nights, without feeling relationship stress. Like traditional couples, independent couples are interdependent, relying on each other to meet their emotional needs, but they develop unconventional ways of achieving this. Also like traditional couples, independents engage in rather than avoid conflict.

3. Separate couples. Separate couples are couples who share a traditional ideology but are independent and avoid conflict. Separate couples are similar to traditional couples because they embrace traditional ideology. For example, they adhere to the customary sex roles and prefer marriage to other living arrangements. However, they differ from both traditional and independent couples in that they are emotionally distant, relying on other relationships to satisfy their emotional needs, and they prefer to avoid conflict. In many "arranged marriages" the couples fit this type.

While two-thirds of the married couples Fitzpatrick studied agreed about their relationship types, in the remaining one-third, the partners disagreed. When partners disagreed, the wife most frequently classified herself as a "traditional" and the husband more frequently saw himself as a "separate." Fitzpatrick called these types of couples "separate-traditionals." In these relationships, the husband and wife agree on the traditional ideology of marriage, but whereas the wife views the marriage as an interdependent relationship in which conflict is expressed, the husband views the relationship as one that is more emotionally distant and in which conflict should be avoided.

Separate couples—couples who share a traditional ideology but are independent and avoid conflict.

How does a traditional marriage differ from an independent one?

Mary Anne Fitzpatrick
Dean of the College of Arts and Sciences of the University of South Carolina, on
Couple Types and Communication

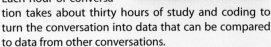

The notion that not all long-term relationships are exactly alike seems obvious. We all know of couples who seem to have relationships that "work" for them and that are similar in "feel" to those of other couples we know. At the same time, we know some couples whose relationships are very different from those of other people we know but seem to be equally effective for the people involved. As a doctoral student, Mary Anne Fitzpatrick became intrigued with the different relational patterns that she saw in long-term relationships. In her dissertation, she began work to uncover a typology or classification scheme that could describe these different relationships: the traditional, independent, and separate relationship types described in this chapter. Fitzpatrick's own observations of couples suggested to her that couples in which both partners were of the same type showed a consistent pattern of relating to one another, while couples in which both partners were not of the same type showed interrelationship problems.

In conducting her research, Fitzpatrick has demonstrated scholarly leadership through her methods. In all of her work, Fitzpatrick has been careful to study a broad range of couples from a wide cross-section of the population. While in some research it may be permissible to study only college students (who are easy to find at a university), Fitzpatrick believes that for theories about communication in relationships and families to be accurate, the population studied must be drawn from a broader base. So she is careful to recruit participants for her studies in a variety of settings and from a variety of backgrounds.

Fitzpatrick believes that her most useful work comes from studies in which she examines the actual conversations of couples and families. Using a research technique called "discourse analysis," Fitzpatrick and other scholars study, categorize, and summarize the flow of actual conversations. By studying the order, topics, and interaction processes through which conversations unfold, Fitzpatrick is able to understand how different types of couples negotiate their relationships. This technique is labor intensive. Each hour of conversation takes about thirty hours of study and coding to turn the conversation into data that can be compared to data from other conversations.

Finally, Fitzpatrick believes in involving her undergraduate students in her research. Along with her colleagues at the University of South Carolina and elsewhere, Fitzpatrick is committed to the concept of "scholarship in the service of teaching," meaning that the purpose of scholarship is twofold. First, through scholarship, we create better explanations that more accurately describe the world. These up-to-date explanations should be the substance of what is taught in the modern university. Second, a goal of university teaching is to strengthen the critical thinking and lifelong learning skills of graduates. So involving students in ongoing research projects equips them to be critical of other studies they read, able to sort out well-done studies from those that are less well executed. Further, it allows students to "get their hands dirty" and in so doing gives them practice in the research skills that they will need to use later to study problems and find valid answers on their own.

Recently, Fitzpatrick has extended her work to investigating how family relationships differ in families headed by different types of couples. She has already completed one project in which she provided evidence for her belief that there is a systematic relationship between types of couples and types of families. Fitzpatrick and her students also have coded conversation data from families with adolescent children. The data will be used to discover how different types of families communicate with one another and handle misunderstandings. For some of Fitzpatrick's major publications, see the references for this chapter at the end of the book.

Using these couple types and focusing on the actual conversations of couples, Fitzpatrick and her associates, as well as other scholars, have been able to understand how different couple types handle conflict, deal with compliance-gaining messages, display power and control, have casual discussions, and talk about the issues and themes that are important to a long-term relationship. What Fitzpatrick has concluded is that no couple type is better than any other type; rather, each type has different kinds of strengths and weaknesses. To provide more insight into Mary Anne Fitzpatrick and her work, we feature her in the "Spotlight on Scholars" box for this chapter.

▷ Characteristics of Successful Long-Term Relationships

To many of us the most important question to answer about long-term relationships is, What is the secret to a long and happy intimate romantic relationship? Researchers have found there are three common characteristics of married couples that have stayed together for more than fifty years (Dickson, 1995).

LEARN ABOUT YOURSELF ○ **Respect for Partner**

Take this short survey to learn something about yourself. Answer the questions based on your first response. There are not right or wrong answers. Just be honest in reporting your true feelings about a partner in an intimate relationship. For each question, select one of the following numbers that best describes your feelings.

1 = Always
2 = Often
3 = Sometimes
4 = Rarely
5 = Never

_____ 1. My partner is trustworthy.
_____ 2. My partner fosters a relationship of mutual care.
_____ 3. My partner shows interest in me.
_____ 4. My partner is sensitive and considerate of my feelings.
_____ 5. My partner provides unconditional love.
_____ 6. My partner is open and receptive.
_____ 7. My partner is honest and truthful.
_____ 8. My partner fosters good two-way communication.
_____ 9. My partner is committed to me.
_____ 10. My partner is understanding and empathic.

This is a test of your level of respect for a partner.

Scoring the Survey: Add the scores together for all ten questions. The score will range from 10 to 50.

The lower your score (closer to 10), the more you feel respect for your relationship partner. The higher your score (closer to 50), the less respect you feel for your relationship partner.

Adapted from Frei, J. R., & Shaver, P. R. (2002). Respect in close relationships: Prototype definition, self-report assessment, and initial correlates. *Personal Relationships, 9,* 121–139.

1. Mutual respect. The first characteristic of successful long-term relationships is mutual respect, when partners in the long-term relationship treat each other with dignity and value each other for what and who they are.

2. Comfortable level of closeness. The second characteristic of healthy long-term relationships is a comfortable level of closeness, when partners in a long-term relationship spend a mutually satisfying amount of time with each other. This does not mean that longtime partners need to be with each other all of the time. Whereas some partners desire constant companionship, others are happy with a relatively low level of closeness. The important point is that both partners continue to know each other through whatever level of closeness works for them. The fact is that many couples drift apart over time—that is, they quit seeking each other's company or come to prefer the company of different people. To counter this, couples must make an effort to remain close. For many couples, closeness is maintained through such rituals as celebrations, family traditions, and patterned routines (Werner, Altman, Brown, & Ginat, 1993, p. 115). Probably the most important element in maintaining closeness in a relationship is a patterned routine. For instance, some couples make sure that at least one night a week they go out together for dinner and a movie or just sit and talk. When people regularly make time to be together, it's easy for them to remember why they were drawn to each other in the first place. But if partners let their relationship drift, before long they may lose track of what brought them together.

3. Presence of a shared plan or life vision. The third characteristic of maintaining long-term relationships is the presence of a plan or life vision. Sometimes this is consciously negotiated. At other times it just seems to happen. The important point is that both partners agree on their long-term goals—and, of course, that the partners see each other in those long-term plans. Such partners talk about "we" and "us" rather than "I" or "me."

❍ Families

A **family** is a "group of intimates who through their communication generates a sense of home and group identity, complete with strong ties of loyalty and emotion, and experiences a history and a future" (Galvin, Byland, & Brommel, 2007). Families are not always made up of two opposite-sex married parents living with one or more of their children. Figure 13.1 describes both traditional family structures and other common family structures. See also this chapter's "Diverse Voices" box, "Performing Commitment" by Jacqueline Taylor, to learn more about a nontraditional but now increasingly common family structure.

In this section, we will explore family communication from a variety of angles, first describing three important functions of family communication, next discussing family communication patterns, then exploring intergenerational family communication, and finally talking about ways you can improve family communication.

Family—group of intimates who through their communication generates a sense of home and group identity, complete with strong ties of loyalty and emotion, and experiences a history and a future.

- Traditional family: Family consisting of two opposite-sex parents who are married and living with one or more children from the union of those two parents
- Single-parent family: Family in which one parent lives with the children; the other is not present in the home and may or may not be actively parenting the children
- Shared-custody family: Family in which the parents have divorced; the children live alternately with each parent
- Blended family: Family consisting of two adults and one or more children, some of whom were born to those parents in previous relationships
- Common-law family: Family consisting of unmarried opposite-sex partners living with the children of their union
- Gay and lesbian family: Family in which same-sex partners are raising children
- Extended family: Family consisting of multiple generations of related people living together
- Communal family: Family of unmarried people related by nongenetic factors who participate in a cooperative living arrangement

FIGURE 13.1 Common family structures

▷ Functions of Family Communication

Families are vitally important in terms of our ability to form intimate relationships throughout our lives because our first intimate relationships are typically with family members. Small children develop their first intimate relationships when they rely on their parents, and then, if they have siblings, they develop relationships as brothers and sisters. Family relationships may remain intimate ones. In many families, adult children remain close to their parents, and sisters or brothers continue to be each other's closest friends throughout their lives. However, during their teen years and beyond, many people develop closer friendships with people outside of the family. And many adults do not maintain intimate relationships with any members of their family.

As with other intimate relationships, family relationships are created and maintained through communication. When the family communication patterns are healthy, they serve three essential functions: They contribute to self-concept formation, they supply needed recognition and support, and they establish communication models for younger family members.

1. Healthy family communication contributes to self-concept formation. In Chapter 2, we discussed the role of communication in the formation of self-concept and discussed how family is instrumental in forming self-concept. Since much of one's initial self-concept is developed within family relationships, the family plays a critical role in how family members view themselves (Demo, 1987). When family communication includes praise and constructive criticism members develop positive self-concepts. On the other hand, when family communication patterns are pathological, characterized by name-calling, blaming, and negative hurtful feedback, the self-concepts of family members can be damaged. Therefore, family members have a major responsibility to interact with one another in ways that

Performing Commitment

by Jacqueline Taylor

Families are structured in different ways. In this excerpt, the author describes how mundane daily activities as well as rituals and public ceremonies serve as performances of commitment in her family.

For over 13 years I have created family within the context of my commitment to Carol, my partner and longtime companion. The law says we are not a couple, but two single women. No church or state has blessed or ratified our union. Although our property and our finances are by this time as entwined as our hearts and lives, the state does not apply its joint-property laws to us or give us the right to inherit from each other in the absence of a will. I cannot include her on the family insurance benefits my university offers. The only place we can purchase a family membership is at the women's bookstore.

Eight years ago we became mothers together, with the adoption of our first daughter, Lucy. One year later we adopted Grace. The law recognized us not as one family, but as two—two single mothers living in the same house with our two adopted children. No blood ties unite any of the four of us. We are a family not because but in spite of the social and legal structures that refuse to name us so. Because our status as a family has been ignored or denied by the laws and customs of our society, our existence as a family can never be taken for granted but must be constantly created and recreated. That our family differs in some significant ways from conventional notions of what constitutes a family means that our creation of family must simultaneously affirm and critique familial structures. . . .

The process of knitting ourselves into a family has taken years and has been characterized more by daily and, yes, mundane performances of commitment than by rituals and ceremonies. Yet we have also participated in public rituals that have helped us to construct ourselves.

The arrival of our babies was greeted by four different showers thrown by friends. Each of our workplaces and two sets of friends organized parties. The various communities we participate in have worked hard to fill the gap between what the law and convention define as family and what our experience reveals. The four of us create our own rituals, as well. . . .

Carol reminds me that the most important performance of commitment is the daily care and love we give to our daughters. Parents communicate commitment every day through the constant and repetitive tasks that children's survival depends on—changing diapers, wiping up spills, kissing "owies"—and later on, supervising homework, chauffeuring to sports and music lessons, listening to their stories. For heterosexual families perhaps this is enough. But we gay and lesbian (and adoptive) families create family outside the context of the social and legal structures that allow traditional families to take themselves for granted, and so we must do more.

Thus, we have learned to use language consciously, carefully, and repetitively to define ourselves to each other and our social world. "Family" we say, over and over. "Thank you for carrying that package. You are helping our family." "This party is just for our family." "In our family, we don't hit."

Our family doesn't fit anybody's mold. But we are a family, held together by ties of love, loyalty, commitment, and daily life. Because our family does not conform to traditional definitions of family, the performances that connect us to the social fabric and to one another take on even greater importance. Through the anniversaries, ceremonies, rituals, and holidays that mark our years and the repeated mundane actions of commitment that mark our days, we perform the bonds that make us kin. . . . [F]amily is a group of people who live together and love each other, bound by their shared commitment to the health, growth, and welfare of all.

Excerpted from Taylor, J. (2002). Performing commitment. In Martin, J. N., Nakayama, T. K., & Flores, L. A. (Eds.), *Readings in Intercultural Communication* (pp. 310–318). New York: McGraw-Hill.

will contribute to the development of strong self-concepts in all family members, especially younger children (Yerby, Buerkel-Rothfuss, & Bochner, 1995). Table 13.1 contrasts examples of statements among family members that lead to positive self-concepts with ones that lead to negative self-concepts.

2. Healthy family communication supplies needed recognition and support. A second responsibility of family members is to interact with each other in ways that recognize and support individuals within the family. Recognition and support enable family members to feel that they are important and guide them toward getting through the difficult times all of us sometimes face. The importance of this responsibility cannot be overstated. Family members are usually the people with whom we feel the safest, and we often turn to them when we need praise, comfort, and reassurance. Yet in many families this important responsibility is forgotten in the rush of day-to-day living. For example, if Judith, the youngest daughter in a family, comes home excited about the gold star she received for her spelling test, her mother and/or father need to take time to recognize the accomplishment, regardless of how busy they are or what problems they may have faced that day. Likewise, when adult family members come home from a rough day at work, spouses, siblings, and children need to behave in ways that show that their home is a safe haven, where the difficulties of the workaday world can be set aside. The point is that all family members need to be told when they are doing well and assured that they can rely on each other. When people can't get recognition and support from within the family, they go outside the family for it.

TABLE 13.1 ◯ **Family Communication Patterns and Self-Concept**

Communication Behavior	Positive Pattern Example	Negative Pattern Example
Feedback statements	"Jason, you put some of your toys away. Thank you. Now can you put the rest away too?"	"Jason, I told you to put your toys away, and you didn't finish the job. Why do I always have to yell at you to get you to finish anything?"
Support statements	"Drew, I don't understand why you want to quit school when you are so close to earning your degree, but I know that you have really thought through this, and I support your decision."	"Drop out of school? You've got to be kidding me. I always knew you didn't have any sense, but this just confirms it."
Affection statements	"Katie, you're my daughter and while we may not always agree, I need you to know that I will always love you."	"How do you expect me to love you when you act like that?"

3. Healthy family communication establishes communication models for younger family members. A third responsibility of family members is to communicate in ways that serve as models of good communication for younger family members. Interactions within the family teach children how to communicate with and relate to others (Turner & West, 2006). Parents serve as role models, regardless of whether they want to. The saying, "Do as I say, not as I do" hardly represents a workable model of behavior because it teaches only hypocrisy. Rather, parents should put modeling behavior into direct practice. For example, if Juanita sees her parents listening to, paraphrasing, and comforting each other, she will be more likely to practice the same behavior when she interacts with her friends and siblings and, later, not only with friends and siblings but also with other people in her life. If, however, she sees her parents ignoring, brushing off, or being unsympathetic to others, she will learn to behave similarly. Modeling behavior is especially important in teaching children how to manage conflict. Children react in vigorous ways when they believe they have been wronged. They will scream, cry, hit, punch, and scratch. As they become more sophisticated, they learn to manipulate, lie, and do whatever is necessary to get their own way. It's the parents' responsibility to socialize children, to teach them how to manage the conflict in their lives in productive ways. Simply telling children how to behave and then engaging in just the opposite behavior will only reinforce aggressive or passive conflict-management strategies. On the other hand, parents who model collaboration by discussing, weighing and considering, describing their feelings, and being supportive during their disagreements not only protect their own relationships but also model for their children how loving people work through conflict.

Recognition and support help family members feel valuable and help them get over difficult times they face. Recall an incident in your own life when a family member gave you support. How did that behavior affect your relationship?

▷ Family Communication Patterns

Have you ever spent time with another family and noticed that they seem to interact differently than members of your family interact? This is because communication in families typically differs along and within two dimensions: conversation orientation and conformity orientation (Fitzpatrick, 2006).

Conversation orientation—degree to which families create a climate of open communication and exchange of ideas.

Conformity orientation—degree to which families create a climate that stresses similarity of attitudes, values, and beliefs.

Communication in Your Family

For a few days, keep a diary of communication within your family: Report examples of language and nonverbal communication that raise or lower the self-concepts of individual family members, that recognize and support or fail to recognize and support family members, and that provide good or bad models of communication behavior. In general, does the family communication appear to be more positive or more negative? What do you see as the effects of family communication styles on individual members of the family and on the family as a unit? In addition, describe your family's communication pattern: high conversation/high conformity, high conversation/low conformity, low conversation/high conformity, or low conversation/low conformity. Are you satisfied with the way this pattern works in your family? If yes, how so? If no, how do you think it should change?

Conversation orientation is the degree to which families create a climate of open communication and exchange of ideas. Families with a high conversation orientation interact openly and freely with each other, talk about a wide range of topics, and willingly engage in conflict. Families with a low conversation orientation interact less openly and less freely with each other, limit themselves to a narrower range of topics, and tend to avoid conflict.

On the other hand, **conformity orientation** is the degree to which families create a climate that stresses similarity of attitudes, values, and beliefs. Families with a high conformity orientation consist of members who hold similar views and typically engage in interactions that focus on harmony and obedience to the parents. Families with a low conformity orientation consist of members who hold a variety of views and engage in interactions that focus on the uniqueness and independence of family members.

All family communication patterns consist of a combination of conversation orientation and conformity orientation. Essentially, there are four different patterns: (1) In a family with a high conformity orientation and a low conversation orientation, family members all share similar beliefs and values, but at the same time don't discuss or argue about them with each other; (2) in a family with a high conformity orientation and a high conversation orientation, family members all share similar beliefs and values and talk freely about them, even if conflict over the particulars of those views arises; (3) in a family with a low conformity orientation and a high conversation orientation, family members tend to disagree about beliefs and values, and they talk about their disagreements freely; and (4) in a family with a low conformity orientation and a low conversation orientation, family members share different views and don't talk or argue about their differences freely.

No one communication pattern is necessarily better than another. The challenge arises, however, when individuals with different family communication patterns create their own families and then find that their vastly different communication patterns must be coordinated or managed in some way. Imagine a blended family wherein one parent and set of children value individuality and practice open communication on any topic while the other parent and set of children value obedience and harmony and restrict communication. How would they negotiate these conflicting patterns? As with any differences in interpersonal communication styles, being able to identify and acknowledge such differences in family communication patterns is the fist step toward successful coordination. Couples creating new family situations should first understand what the different communication patterns are and then discuss how to negotiate a middle ground that works for all parties involved.

▷ Intergenerational Family Communication

When considering communication within families, it is important to understand not only the functions that healthy communication serves and the patterns of communication that occur in general but also how communication occurs between multiple generations.

Communication across the entire generational spectrum (in multiple directions between children, parents, and grandparents) can be a source of both great joy and much frustration in families. In studying intergenerational communication across the life span, Williams and Nussbaum (2001) found many factors accounting for the strength of whole-family relationships, concluding that these relationships remain satisfying when there is consistent contact, high levels of mutual affection, social support and tangible assistance, and a consensus of values, beliefs, and opinions. It is also important that family members know what topics not to discuss with other family members.

Communication between parents and their children can be challenging and frustrating as well. Adolescents and their parents often experience conflict around issues of control, autonomy, and responsibility. Adolescence is a period of great change, and, as a result, both the parents and the teens must be willing to adapt to and negotiate the changes.

Grandchildren and their grandparents may find it difficult to communicate with each other, too, because of different interests, different sets of values, geographic distance, the fast pace of contemporary life, and stereotypes surrounding youth and aging (Ryan, Pearce, Anas, & Norris, 2004). One of the most frequently reported communication problems between younger and elderly family members is how young adults speak to their elders. Gould (2004) found that younger family members often overaccommodate older relatives. They limit the topics introduced, speak in overly simple ways, talk too loudly, and tend to be repetitive in their remarks. Older adults recognize and resent this style of communication as limiting and patronizing. At the same time, younger family members may find their grandparents to be sometimes too rigid in their beliefs and out of pace with change. Yet intergenerational communication can be rewarding as older family members transmit cultural and family values to younger family members and younger family members carry on family traditions, thus providing their elders with a sense of fulfilled purpose and immortality.

▷ Improving Family Communication

Now that we have a better understanding of family dynamics and communication patterns, let's specifically discuss five guidelines that family members can use to improve communication within the family: opening the lines of communication, confronting the effects of power imbalances, recognizing and adapting to change, respecting individual interests, and managing conflicts equitably.

1. Opening the lines of communication. For a number of reasons, lines of communication within a family can become scrambled or broken, causing family members to feel isolated from one another. With the exception of requests and orders from other family members ("Clean up your room"; "Don't play the stereo so loudly"), many people actually spend very little time each day genuinely communicating with other family members. Instead, they spend the bulk of their time interacting with people outside of the home. The first step in opening the lines of communication is setting a time each day specifically for family members to talk to each other. One good time for families to talk is during the evening meal. Unfortunately, the rush of busy lives and ever-presence of distractions like voice-mail and text messages, television, and other media often compete for the attention of family members, even when they are physically together, and thus threaten such conversations. Recent national studies are showing that families are spending much less time together than they did a generation ago: Family dinners are down by one-third over the past twenty years, and family vacations have decreased by 28 percent ("Family Time," 2002). It may be difficult to set aside significant family time every day of the week, but the consequences of not doing so are becoming increasingly clear.

2. Confronting the effects of power imbalances. Family members are dependent on one another for many things. Children depend on their parents for food, shelter, clothing, and transportation, as well as love. Siblings depend on one another for friendship and support. And parents depend on their children for love, companionship, and validation. Because of the nature of these dependencies, the distribution of power within families is unequal. Society gives parents legitimate power over their children, and because parents usually control the family budget and are physically stronger than their children, they wield considerable reward and coercive power. Meanwhile, older children often have great amounts of coercive and referent power over their younger brothers and sisters in addition to the legitimate power given them by the parents. Moreover, in many families, children are not treated equally. For example, parents who realize that one of their children has certain gifts or talents that the others lack may allow this child privileges the others do not enjoy, or sometimes parents forget how they treated one child and treat a different child differently under the same circumstances. Not all power imbalances have damaging effects, but they all have effects of some kind that should be discussed openly. Each member of the family should feel free to inquire about any family power dynamic that is problematic for another family member or members. For instance, parents who enforce a curfew should explain why the curfew is in effect, not simply say, "Because I said so, that's why!" If parents give their children reasons for rules, their children are more likely to accept the rules and confide in their parents. Likewise, parents, children, and siblings should feel able to communicate openly about power imbalances among the children. If these imbalances are discussed, those with damaging effects can be changed.

3. Recognizing and adapting to change. Family members know each other so well that they may be quick to predict how a particular family member will think, feel, or act under many different circumstances. These predictions will not always be accurate, however, because people change gradually over time, and family members are often the last to recognize individual changes. Even as children grow and change in seemingly obvious ways, their brothers and sisters, and especially their parents, continue to see them as they once were, not as they are or are becoming. Recall our discussion in Chapter 2 of how social perceptions are not always accurate. This is true even when those perceptions come from family members who "know each other like the back of their hand." As a result, the skill of perception checking is as important among family members as it is when communicating with strangers. Moreover, the skills of dating information and indexing generalizations, discussed in Chapter 4, are also important skills for family members to master.

Recognizing and adapting to change appears to be especially difficult in families as children become teens and strive to achieve independence, while at the same time their parents may be experiencing the changes associated with midlife transition. Frequently, parents who are preoccupied with their own adult life transition find it difficult to reexamine and change their relationships with their teen children. They may continue to interact with their children in a habitual way and justify the behavior by asserting that children must earn the right to be treated like adults. Yet teenagers who are treated like children will probably rebel or act out, whereas those treated as adults are likely to reason and discuss.

Recognizing change has another dimension as well. Family members need to be alert to changes in other family members that may indicate stress or emotional distress. Unfortunately, family members are often unable to notice gradual behavioral changes that signal emotional problems until those problems become

What clues suggest that this family enjoys each other's company?

more serious. Family members who suspect difficulty should openly confront relatives about their behaviors. They might begin by saying something like, "I've noticed that you don't seem to be yourself. You've withdrawn from most of your activities, you aren't eating well, and you look really sad. Is there something happening that we can help you with?" Family members, like people in all relationships, need to use their supportive communication skills to help other family members adapt to change.

4. Respecting individual interests and accomplishments. Healthy family communication also respects individual interests and accomplishments. Chapters 8 and 9 discussed the importance of listening to, understanding, and supporting others. Certainly these skills apply to family relationships; yet family communication can often be marked by indifference or apathy when it comes to the interests of individual family members. Individual family members are sometimes overly concerned with differentiating themselves from other family members, for instance, children perceiving their parents as "uncool" and "unhip," siblings asserting their individuality in relation to their brothers and sisters, and parents seeing themselves as too grown up to associate themselves with the "juvenile" interests of their children. When family members express their individuality or accomplishments related to their individual interests, the first reaction of other family members should never be "Big deal" or "Whatever." When family members celebrate the accomplishments of their relatives and show a genuine interest in the interests and activities of others, they not only encourage individual expression but also offer support.

5. Managing conflicts equitably. Because interdependent family members have unique needs, and because power in families is unevenly distributed, situations that lead to conflict are inevitable. Yet families differ in their abilities to resolve conflicts in effective ways. In some families, conflict is avoided at all costs. Members learn to avoid conversing about subjects on which there is likely to be disagreement. Obviously, this approach does not work because no satisfactory resolution of problems can be reached through silence. The end result is not only lack of conflict resolution but also a continued lack of equality between family members. In other families, coercive or forcing behaviors are used to resolve conflicts. Such families often end conflict episodes by acceding to the wishes of the most powerful member (usually the parent), who might say, "As long as you're under my roof . . ." or "Because I'm the mother, that's why." This approach is ineffective, too, because forcing behaviors are often met with resistance rather than acquiescence. In fact, conflicts "resolved" by forcing may lead to family violence, a spiral of family conflict that escalates into attacks on family members (Yerby et al., 1995). These attacks can take many forms, including verbal aggression, psychological abuse, and physical abuse (including wife-battering and spousal abuse, child abuse and neglect, sibling abuse, abuse of elderly relatives, and violence by children). While there is strong evidence to suggest that the tendency to engage in abusive behavior is handed down from generation to generation, those who abuse others are also likely to lack appropriate communication skills, including those related to constructive conflict management (Sabourin, 1996). How can you keep relationships from becoming abusive? The best advice is to reread the material in Chapter 12 and try to apply it to your family relationships.

The effective approach to managing conflict is to be democratic. When family members find themselves in conflict, they may hold a family meeting to jointly work out the problem, with one or more of the neutral family members serving as mediator(s), or through a less formalized process. The operative rule in this approach to managing conflict is to view conflict not as a barrier but as an opportunity to promote win/win outcomes between family members.

○ Problems Associated with Intimacy

Intimacy in relationships is difficult to achieve and maintain. In this final section, we describe two problems related to intimacy, relational uncertainty and possessiveness, and then discuss how improved communication can help to alleviate these problems.

▷ Relational Uncertainty

Relational uncertainty is a feeling of doubt about the nature of a relationship. It may stem from three sources: an absence of clarity about the nature of the relationship, a tension between closeness and separation, and concern about the future.

1. Absence of clarity about the nature of the relationship. A first source of relational uncertainty is absence of clarity between partners about whether the relationship is platonic or romantic. There may be elements of both relationship types occurring simultaneously, and as a result one or both parties may be uncertain about how to define the relationship. This type of relational uncertainty is most prevalent as a relationship moves from casual dating to serious romantic attachment (Knobloch & Solomon, 2002) because it is rare for both partners to desire to move from a casual relationship to a serious romantic relationship at the very same time.

2. Tension between closeness and separation. A second source of relational uncertainty stems from a dialectical tension in which partners desire closeness one day and separateness the next. You will recall from the discussion of relational dialectics in Chapter 3 that competing tensions often pull people back and forth in their relationship needs. These variations can occur both within and between individuals.

Relational uncertainty—feeling of doubt about the nature of a relationship.

3. Concern about the future. A third source of relational uncertainty arises from concern about the future of a relationship, stemming from perceived distancing, unresolved conflicts, or life change events. At times, people in committed relationships begin to notice and become concerned about signs that the relationship has become more distant, with less sharing involved or less time spent on mutually enjoyable activities. At other times, partners may become concerned about unresolved (or irresolvable) conflicts, such as differences in money management philosophies or religious beliefs. At still other times, normal life transitions can also give rise to concern about the future. When a daughter marries, for instance, her mother may experience relational uncertainty about the future as new boundaries to their relationship are developed, or best friends may become uncertain about how their relationship will change as they prepare to leave for different colleges.

The best way to deal with relational uncertainty is to consciously acknowledge it to yourself and discuss your feelings of uncertainty with your partner. While such openness may be difficult, communicating directly about each other's feelings can be a useful way to reduce uncertainty and to sustain the relationship. For example, imagine that Dana and Jamie have been close friends their whole lives. Recently, Jamie has not been returning Dana's calls or responding to e-mails. They have not found the time to get together socially in quite a while either. Dana misses her close friendship with Jamie and feels uncertain about whether the two of them will remain close friends. To help lessen the uncertainty, Dana might ask Jamie directly, "Do you think that our friendship is drifting apart? It seems to me that we have not gotten together in about six months, and we seldom talk by phone or e-mail. I wonder what the future holds for our friendship." Jamie may clarify by responding, "Hey, I feel bad about not being able to get together or to even talk once in a while. I am swamped at work right now and I'm in the middle of trying to finish building the deck on my house before the weather turns cold. I don't want you to think that I'm blowing off our friendship. I hope that whatever happens in our separate lives, we can count on each other as friends."

▷ Possessiveness

Possessiveness is the desire to control another person to ensure that he or she is one's exclusive partner. Possessive behaviors can range from mild actions like holding a partner's hand at a party to ensure that you communicate to others that your partner "belongs" to you to physically or psychologically intimidating a partner into compliance with your "ownership" of him or her. Possessiveness is caused by **jealousy**, an intense feeling of suspicion that one's partner values, likes, or loves someone else more than oneself. It can occur in a variety of intimate relationships. Sibling rivalries are a form of jealousy that stem from children vying for parental attention and affection. Parents may become jealous of each other if they perceive favoritism on the part of their children, or par-

Possessiveness—desire to control another person to ensure that he or she is one's exclusive partner.

Jealousy—intense feeling of suspicion that one's partner values, likes, or loves someone else more than oneself.

ents may become jealous of the relationships that their older children develop with other adults. Platonic same-sex friendships can experience problems with jealousy when friends perceive that their partners are spending more time with others, and, of course, romantic relationships and life partnerships are also susceptible to jealousy. Like other feelings, jealousy is neither good nor bad. Jealousy can lead to an appropriate concern when there is a legitimate threat to your relationship, and it can motivate you to talk with your partner about your feelings. But jealousy can also be a destructive force that may ruin your relationship when it leads you to extreme possessiveness (Pelusi, 2006). According to one study, 57 percent of respondents cited a former friend's jealous feelings or critical attitude toward the respondent's other relationships as a "moderate to very important" reason for the breakup of their relationship (Marsh, 1988, p. 27).

Open, honest communication in the form of simple conversations between partners can reduce feelings of jealousy, prevent misunderstandings, and circumvent possessive behaviors. For example, if at a party Paul notices that his fiancée Jocelyn is spending most of the evening in a deep conversation with a very handsome man whom Paul does not know, he may feel jealous. To avoid his jealous

Jackie and Michael had been dating for a year and were talking about marriage when Michael's company transferred him to Columbus for six months. Two months into their separation, Jackie visited Michael's new city and had a chance to meet his co-workers at a party, including Veronica, a beautiful woman a few years younger than herself. Michael had talked to Jackie about all of his new colleagues, including Veronica, but she had had no idea how attractive Veronica was. In addition, as the evening went on, Jackie could sense that Michael and Veronica were forming a special friendship. She couldn't help but feel a twinge of jealousy for this woman who got to spend time with her boyfriend. Nevertheless, Michael seemed completely attentive to Jackie and they had a wonderful visit.

A couple of weeks later, while on a business trip to Columbus, Gwen, an acquaintance of Jackie's, happened to see Michael and Veronica having dinner together at a restaurant. The day after her return, Gwen ran into Jackie at the grocery store and casually remarked that she had seen Michael with Veronica. When Jackie commented that Michael and Veronica were co-workers, Gwen hesitantly replied, "Well, they certainly seem to

have a close working relationship." Jackie blanched. Trying to soothe her, Gwen said, "I'm sure there's an explanation for everything. I mean there could be lots of reasons for him to be holding her hand. I'm sorry I said anything." But Jackie did not feel better.

Later that evening when Michael called, Jackie immediately confronted him by saying sarcastically, "So, how's Veronica?"

When Michael replied, "What do you mean?" Jackie went on, "Don't give me any of your innocent 'what do I mean' stuff—you were seen and you know it!"

"Oh, Gwen," said Michael. "So you'll take the word of some nosy, trouble-making woman and judge me before you find out the real situation? If that's all the trust you have in me, then I'm not sure . . . "

"Oh, sure, defend yourself by blaming Gwen. But she did see you. You're right about one thing, this is about trust."

1. What ethical issues are involved in this situation?
2. What could/should Jackie have said to her friend Gwen and to Michael?
3. How could/should Michael have responded?

feelings turning into possessiveness, he may politely interrupt the conversation, ask Jocelyn to dance, and confess his jealous feelings by diplomatically saying, "Honey, I don't know who that guy is and what you're talking about with him, but I do know that I am feeling jealous." In doing so, he may find out that the man is actually an old friend of her brother's who recently lost his wife in an accident.

On the other side of the coin, you can circumvent unreasonable jealousy on the part of your partner by giving your partner feedback and describing his or her possessive behaviors in a diplomatic way. For instance, if Sarella and Cary have been seeing each other for several months and are getting serious, but Janette, who is Sarella's best friend and roommate, has begun to erase Cary's voice-mail messages to Sarella, she may need to speak with Sarella about what is happening. She might say, "Janette, during the past week I know that Cary has left three messages on the answering machine that weren't there when I got home. Can you help me understand what's happening?" This nonthreatening description may lead to a longer conversation in which Janette admits to feeling jealous and both of them come to a better understanding about the importance of their friendship.

Conversations like the ones just cited can alleviate jealousy and possessive behaviors by building and restoring trust before the relationship is permanently damaged. Unfortunately, sometimes jealousy and possessiveness become psychopathic, leading to stalking and harassment. If you find one of your intimates crossing the line between possessiveness and stalking, and conversations have not helped, you can suggest that the person seek professional help. For your own safety and peace of mind, it may be appropriate for you to distance yourself from the relationship.

○ Summary

An intimate relationship is a close and caring personal relationship in which both partners have detailed knowledge of each other's history, personality, and aspirations as a result of mutual disclosures that have occurred over an extended period of time. They can be platonic or romantic, and they are marked by a high degree of warmth and affection, trust (which includes dependability, responsiveness, collaboration, and faithfulness), self-disclosure, commitment, and shared symbols and rituals. Three types of intimate relationships are close friendships (same-sex and opposite-sex friendships), long-term relationships (including marriages and other life partnerships), and families.

Men and women differ in how they communicate in close friendships. Male-male communication tends to be topical, but men may communicate closeness thorough covert intimacy. Female-female communication tends to be relational and personal. Female-male communication tends to be impeded by a female desire for self-disclosure and a male desire to communicate through actions.

Strong and enduring intimacy often occurs in long-term relationships like marriages and other life partnerships. Long-term relationships are defined by independence, ideology, and communication. Long-term couple relationships generally fit into three types: traditional, independent, and separate. Successful long-term relationships are characterized by mutual respect, a comfortable level of closeness, and the presence of a plan or life vision.

The family is "a group of intimates who generate a sense of home and group identity, complete with strong ties of loyalty and emotion, and experience a history and a future." There is wide diversity in how families are structured. When family communication is healthy it contributes to self-concept formation, supplies needed recognition and support, and establishes communication models for younger family members. Family communication patterns differ along the dimensions of conversation and conformity orientations. There are many factors contributing to strong intergenerational family relationships, as well as challenges and frustrations in communication across generational lines. Family relationships are improved by opening the lines of communication, confronting the effects of power imbalances, recognizing and adapting to change, respecting individual interests, and managing conflicts equitably.

Problems in intimate relationships can stem from relational uncertainty or possessiveness. The best way to reduce relational uncertainty is to acknowledge it and discuss it with your partner. To reduce feelings of jealousy, engage in open, honest communications about your feelings. To curb possessiveness on the part of a partner, provide feedback and describe the possessive behaviors.

◗ Chapter Resources

Communication Improvement Plan:
Intimate Relationships ◗ Find more on the web @ www.oup.com/us/interact12

Would you like to improve your use of the following aspects of intimate relationship communication discussed in this chapter?

- Male-male communication
- Female-female communication
- Female-male communication
- Long-term relationship communication
- Family communication

Pick an aspect, and write a communication improvement plan. You can find a communication improvement plan worksheet on our website at www.oup.com/us/interact12.

Key Words ⊙

Inter-Act with Media ⊙ Find more on the web @ www.oup.com/us/interact12

Television

Sex and the City, episode: "The Agony and the 'Ex'-tacy" (2001). Sarah Jessica Parker, Kristen Davis, Cynthia Nixon, Kim Cattrall, Chris Noth.

Brief Summary: *Sex and the City* showcases the relationships among four women: Carrie Bradshaw (Parker), Miranda Hobbes (Nixon), Samantha Jones (Cattrall), and Charlotte York (Davis). In this episode, Carrie feels melancholy about turning thirty-five and not yet finding her soul mate. Her friends plan a restaurant party and Carrie waits for hours, not knowing that the attendees went to another eatery with a similar name. Depressed, Carrie returns home, but later, Charlotte shows up and encourages her to celebrate anyway with the other women at a coffeeshop. As the women sit together, Carrie discloses how alone she feels without a special someone in her life. Charlotte suggests, "Maybe we can be each other's soul mates and then we can let men just be these great, nice guys to have fun with." The episode concludes with Carrie agreeing that she has three soul mates "already nailed down." This long-running show consistently depicts the unique intimacies and commitment of female friendship.

IPC Concepts: Self-disclosure, characteristics of intimate relationships, female-female relationships.

Cinema

Lars and the Real Girl (2007). Craig Gillespie (director). Ryan Gosling, Emily Mortimer, Paul Schneider, Kelly Garner, Patricia Clarkson.

Brief Summary: Lars (Gosling) is a shy, introverted man who lives in brother Gus (Schneider) and sister-in-law Karin's (Mortimer) garage. Although Lars has acquaintances at work and women who seem to like him, his extreme social phobia prevents him from emotional and physical connections. When Lars orders "Bianca," a lifelike sex doll, from the Internet, he creates a full-fledged relationship with her. Gus and Karin seek help from a physician (Clarkson), who claims that Lars needs this delusion to work through the baggage that prevents him from bonding with others. Eventually, Gus, Karin, and the entire town play into the relationship, treating Bianca as a live woman. Throughout the charade, Gus deepens his communication with Lars, expressing his guilt for occurrences that he believes shaped Lars' life. Ultimately, through his relationship with fake Bianca, Lars takes baby steps to attempt real intimacies.

IPC Concepts: Family relationships, family communication and self-concept formation, improving family communication, problems associated with intimacy.

What's on the Web

Find links and additional material, including self-quizzes, on the companion website at www.oup.com/us/interact12.

14

Communicating in the Workplace

After you have read this chapter, you should be able to answer these questions:

▶ **What are the essential elements of a résumé?**

▶ **How can you write an effective cover letter?**

▶ **What should you do to prepare for a job interview?**

▶ **What are some typical questions asked by job interviewers?**

▶ **What should you do during and after an interview?**

▶ **How do managers and employees develop mutual and trusting exchanges?**

▶ **How can you communicate effectively with co-workers?**

▶ **What are the characteristics of an effective work team?**

▶ **What are the communication roles of team members?**

▶ **What communication technologies assist teamwork?**

▶ **What are the guidelines for running team meetings?**

▶ **What are the member responsibilities in a team meeting?**

▶ **What are some of the communication issues in a diverse workplace?**

"Mark, today's the monthly staff meeting at work, so I'll come out to meet you on the beach around 11:30. Have fun without me."

"Can't Grove and Associates get along without you for even one week, Adelaide? I can't believe that they expect you to bring your computer with you on vacation and do work from out here."

"Oh Mark, it's no big deal. You know that I'm part of this reorganization team and I really don't want them making any big decisions without my input. They'll put me on speakerphone at the meeting in Dallas this morning, then I'll post my data on projected savings from the closing of the St. Louis office. After that, it will be just a few e-mails here and there for the rest of the week."

"It's just the idea that there's never a break from work anymore. During our layover in the airport, you were on the phone with the St. Louis office, and both of your bosses were e-mailing you about work-related emergencies."

"But Mark, I like being able to communicate with people at work. It eases my mind to keep my work going when I'm away and to still be part of this reorganization team. I'm having a fantastic vacation and by staying in touch with work, things won't be so crazy when I get back into the office on Monday."

A dults spend approximately half of their waking hours at work, and as our example with Adelaide and Mark reminds us, mobile communication technology increasingly allows us to stay in touch with our workplace around the world and around the clock. Indeed, since mobile communication makes us reachable regardless of physical location or time of day, the dividing line between work and nonwork has become blurred (Kleinman, 2007). Thus, many of the relationships and much of the communication that adults maintain are with work colleagues. These relationships differ from friendships and family relationships because, for the most part, they serve different purposes and are not voluntary—you usually don't choose the people for whom and with whom you work.

In this chapter we'll explore the interpersonal communication challenges that we face at work. Of course, the first challenge is getting a job. As a result, we begin by discussing the hiring process, including how to write cover letters and résumés and how to conduct yourself during a job interview. Then, we explore how to manage relationships with managers and co-workers on the job. After that, we talk about various aspects of teamwork, including what characterizes an effective work team, what the communication roles of team members are, which technologies facilitate teamwork, how to run team meetings, and what the responsibilities of team members are. Finally, we discuss issues of diversity at work, including culture-based work styles, intergenerational differences, sexual harassment, and organizational romance.

⊙ The Hiring Process

You have probably already been through the job search process and know how stressful it can be. In this section, we describe strategies and tactics you can use to make your next job search more successful and less stressful, first by writing effective résumés and cover letters to get to the interview stage and then by conducting yourself effectively in an interview.

▷ Résumés and Cover Letters

Résumé—summary sheet outlining your work history, educational background, skills, and accomplishments.

Cover letter—short, well-written letter expressing your interest in a particular position.

Because interviewing is time consuming, most organizations do not interview all of the people who apply for a job. Rather, they use a variety of screening devices to eliminate people who don't meet their qualifications. Chief among these is evaluating the qualifications you present on your résumé and in the cover letter that accompanies it. A **résumé** is a summary sheet outlining your work history, educational background, skills, and accomplishments. A **cover letter** is a short, well-written letter expressing your interest in a particular position. The goal of your résumé and cover letter is to sell yourself and get an interview (Farr, 2008).

To write an effective résumé and cover letter that highlights your qualifications for a particular job, you need to know something about the job requirements and the company. All companies maintain Web sites that provide substantial information about the organization. In addition, the career center advisors at your college or university can assist you with your research, and you can learn a great deal about the company or companies you'd like to work for by researching them on the Web.

Once you know as much as possible about the company and about the particular job position you want to apply for, either prepare a résumé if you do not already have one or tailor your existing one to fit the qualifications of the job. Although there is no universal format for résumé writing, there is some agreement on what should be included. The following information should appear on your résumé:

1. Contact information. Centered at the top of your résumé should be your name, mailing address, telephone number, e-mail address, and a URL for your personal Web site, if you have one. As your contact information changes, change your résumé to match.

2. Career objective. Include a one- or two-line sentence, directly beneath your contact information, stating your specific short-term career goals, tailored to the position for which you are applying.

3. Education. Provide a list, in reverse chronological order (most recent school first), of the schools you have attended (including specialized military schools), including the names and locations of the schools, the degrees or certificates earned (or expected), the dates of attendance (if not the school of graduation), the year of graduation (or expected), your GPA (if 3.0 or higher), certificates or licenses earned, relevant seminars attended, study abroad experience, and any academic honors received.

4. Employment history. Include a list, again in reverse chronological order (most recent job first), of your paid and unpaid work experiences. List the name, city and state of each organization, your employment dates, your title, and a bulleted description, using specific action verbs, of the skills you used or learned, accomplishments you achieved, and recognitions you earned. If relevant, also include in your employment history:

- **Military background.** List the branch of the military for which you served, the dates of service, last rank held, significant commendations, and discharge status.
- **Relevant professional affiliations.** List the names of the organizations, dates of membership, and any offices held.
- **Community service.** List community service organizations and clubs, positions held, and years involved. Do not include specific religious or political organizations.

5. Personal information. Include only personal information directly relevant to the job or that demonstrates your versatility, such as areas of expertise, hobbies, and the like. Do not ever include a picture of yourself or provide your social security number, which might be an invitation to identity theft should your résumé get into the wrong hands. Also do not indicate your height, weight, age, sex, marital status, sexual orientation, health, race, ethnicity, religion, ability status, or political affiliation, as these are not only irrelevant to getting hired but also illegal for prospective employers to ask you about.

6. Special skills. List language fluencies, computer software applications, and other specialized qualifications that make you stand out in the workplace.

7. References. Do not include the names or contact information of your references on your résumé. Instead, say "available on request," and have their names, addresses, e-mail addresses, and phone numbers available on a separate sheet of paper to present at your interview. You should have at least three references—people who will speak well of your abilities, your work, and your character.

Notice that the list does not include any reference to salary, as this should be discussed in a subsequent interview. If the job ad requests salary requirements, provide a range based on research about the job and company and your bottom-line needs. Note also that it is becoming rather standard practice that résumés be just one page long, no matter your level of experience. This presents a challenge to include all relevant information in a captivating but concise way.

Increasingly job searches occur electronically. While you might find a local part-time job during college without using electronic resources, you are likely to need to understand electronic job searching when you seek your first career-related full-time job. Most large employers use either third-party résumé database services or have computerized applicant tracking systems to screen the résumés that they receive. Therefore, prepare not only a hard copy résumé but also an electronic résumé, or e-résumé. E-résumés should use plain text and not include any special formatting (bullets, tabs, centering, etc.) so that any employer can easily scan, store, retrieve, and read your résumé whatever their computer system. E-résumés also include a "keywords" list, or list of words the employer may be looking for, that will aid your chances of making the first cut in employment selection. It helps to use the same words on the keywords portion of your résumé that are also included in the job posting. Another strategy is to comb a company's Web site for terms related to technologies, skills, capabilities, and qualities the company values and use these as keywords in your résumé.

Electronic job searching also allows for the use of online portfolios. It is now possible for potential employers to review online supplemental information about you before scheduling an interview. Online portfolios typically include your résumé, work examples, video clips or photos of your work, or links to your work projects (Cram, 2007). Avoid including any irrelevant or frivolous information in your online portfolio, such as personal information, photos, and clippings. Today there are more ways than ever before for you to communicate to potential employers about your qualifications, work experience, and work products.

When you submit your résumé to a prospective employer, always include a cover letter. The cover letter should explain how you learned of the opening and why you are interested in the company, highlight just the skills and experiences on your résumé that demonstrate how you fit the requirements of the position, be focused on the employer's needs, and directly ask for an opportunity to interview for the position. Keep your cover letter short and to the point, make sure it is free of spelling and grammatical errors, and maintain professionalism throughout.

Figure 14.1 displays a sample cover letter and Figure 14.2 a sample résumé for a recent college graduate.

2326 Tower Place
Cincinnati, OH 45220
April 10, 2009

Mr. Kyle Jones
Acme Marketing Research Associates
P.O. Box 482
Cincinnati, OH 45201

Dear Mr. Jones:

    I am applying for the position of research assistant at Acme Marketing Research Associates that I learned about through the Office of Career Counseling at the University of Cincinnati. I am a senior mathematics major at the University of Cincinnati who is interested in pursuing a career in marketing research. I am highly motivated and eager to learn, and I enjoy working with all types of people. I am excited by the prospect of working for a firm like AMRA, where I can apply my leadership and problem-solving skills in a professional setting.

    As a mathematics major, I have developed the analytical proficiency that is necessary for working through complex problems. My courses in statistics have especially prepared me for data analysis, while my more theoretical courses have taught me how to construct an effective argument. Through my leadership training and opportunities, I have learned to work effectively in groups and have seen the benefits of both individual and group problem-solving approaches. My work as a student member of the strategic planning committee for a large day school introduced me to the skills associated with strategic planning. Finally, from my theatrical experience, I have gained the poise to make presentations in front of small and large groups alike. I believe that these experiences and others have shaped who I am and have helped me to develop many of the skills necessary to be successful. I am interested in learning more and continuing to grow.

    I look forward to having the opportunity to speak with you. I have enclosed my résumé with both my school address and phone number. Thank you for your consideration. I hope to hear from you soon.

Sincerely,

Elisa C. Vardin

FIGURE 14.1 Sample cover letter

Elisa C. Vardin
2326 Tower Place
Cincinnati, OH 45220
Phone: (513) 861-2497
E-mail: ElisVardin@UC.edu

Professional Objective:
A (job title) position utilizing intellectual abilities, quantitative capabilities, communication skills, and proven leadership to further the mission of a high-integrity marketing research organization.

Educational Background:
University of Cincinnati, Cincinnati, OH, B.A. in Mathematics, June 2009. GPA 3.36. Dean's List.

National Theater Institute at the Eugene O'Neill Theater Center, Waterford, CT. Fall 2007. Acting, voice, movement, directing, and playwriting.

Work and Other Business-Related Experience:
Reynolds & Dewitt, Sena Weller Rohs Williams, Cincinnati, OH. Summer 2008.

Intern at brokerage/investment management firm. Provided administrative support. Created new databases, performance comparisons, and fact sheets in Excel and Word files.

Mummers Theatre Guild, University of Cincinnati, Spring 2006–Spring 2009. Treasurer. Responsible for all financial/accounting functions for this undergraduate theater community.

Summerbridge Cincinnati, Cincinnati Country Day School, Cincinnati, OH. Summer 2007. Teacher in program for "at-risk" junior high students. Taught 7th grade mathematics, 6th and 7th grade speech communication, sign language; academic advisor; club leader. Organized five-hour diversity workshop and three-hour tension-reduction workshop for staff.

Strategic Planning Committee, Summit Country Day School, Cincinnati, OH. Fall 2004–2005. One of two student members. Worked with the board of directors developing the first strategic plan for a thousand-student independent school (pre-K through 12).

AYF International Leadership Conference, Miniwanca Conference Center, Shelby, MI. Summer 2000–2002. Participant in international student conference sponsored by American Youth Foundation.

Interests:
Musical theater: lifetime involvement, including leads and choreography for several shows. A cappella singing group: 2006–2009, director 2007–2009. Swing Club: 2004–2007, president and teacher of student dance club. Junior high youth group leader: 2003. Math tutor: 2004. Aerobics instructor: 2004–2007. University of Cincinnati Choral Society: 2006–2009. American Sign Language instructor: Winter 2005, 2006.

Technical Skills and Training: SAS, SPSS, Excel, Access, Word. Univariate and multivariate statistics (2 courses), regression analysis (2 courses).

References: Available on request.

FIGURE 14.2 Sample résumé

Interview—structured conversation with the goal of exchanging information needed for decision making.

▷ Interviews

An **interview** is a structured conversation with the goal of exchanging information needed for decision making. Careful handling of an interview includes getting ready for the interview, conducting yourself during the interview, and performing interview follow-up.

While your résumé and cover letter make you an attractive candidate for an employer, interview preparation will solidify your chances of receiving an offer. Several guidelines that can help you prepare for an interview follow.

1. Do your homework. If you haven't done extensive research on the position and company in preparation for writing/updating your résumé or writing your cover letter, do it before you go to the interview. Be sure you know the company's products and services, its areas of operation and ownership, and its financial health. Nothing puts off interviewers more than applicants who arrive at an interview knowing little about the company.

2. Based on your research, prepare a list of questions about the organization and the job. The employment interview should be a two-way street: You size up the company as the interviewer sizes you up. As a result, prepare and bring with you a number of specific questions to ask the interviewer. For example, "Can you describe a typical work day for the person in this position?" or "What is the biggest challenge in this job?"

3. Rehearse the interview. Several days before the interview, spend time reviewing the job requirements and determining how your knowledge, skills, and experiences meet those requirements. Practice answering questions commonly asked in interviews, such as those listed in Figure 14.3.

4. Dress appropriately and conservatively. You will want to make a good first impression, so it is important to be well groomed and neatly dressed for

How can you prepare to successfully present yourself in an interview?

School

How did you select the school you attended?

How did you determine your major?

What extracurricular activities did you engage in at school?

In what ways does your transcript reflect your ability?

How were you able to help with your college expenses?

Personal

What are your hobbies? How did you become interested in them?

Give an example of how you work under pressure.

At what age did you begin supporting yourself?

What causes you to lose your temper?

What are your major strengths? Weaknesses?

Give an example of when you were a leader and what happened.

What do you do to stay in good physical condition?

What was the last non-school-assigned book that you read? Tell me about it.

Who has had the greatest influence on your life?

What have you done that shows your creativity?

Position

What kind of position are you looking for?

What do you know about the company?

Under what conditions would you be willing to relocate?

Why do you think you would like to work for us?

What do you hope to accomplish?

What qualifications do you have that would make you beneficial to us?

How do you feel about traveling?

In what part of the country would you like to settle?

With what kinds of people do you enjoy interacting?

What do you regard as an equitable salary for a person with your qualifications?

What new skills would you like to learn?

What are your career goals?

How would you proceed if you were in charge of hiring?

What are your most important criteria for determining whether you will accept a position?

FIGURE 14.3 Sample interview questions

the interview. Although "casual" or "business casual" is common in many workplaces, some organizations still expect employees to be more formally dressed. If you don't know what the dress code is for the organization, call the Human Resources Department and ask. Even when the dress code is casual, you will want to be a little more conservatively attired than the average employee to show that you mean business. Men should wear collared shirts (not golf or tee shirts), dress slacks, and a tie. In a business casual setting, a sport coat should be worn or carried. In some situations, men will want to wear suits. Men should also be recently shaved, or with facial hair well groomed. If a man's hair is long, it should be pulled back into a ponytail; if short, it should be recently barbered. Women should wear suits, pant suits, or professional-looking dresses. Skirt length and necklines should be modest, and midriffs should be completely covered. Makeup should be unnoticeable. Hair should be clean and worn away from the face. Very long hair should be worn up or pulled back. When possible, wear clothing that covers body art and piercings to avoid having such personal fashion statements negatively influence an interviewer's perception of your qualifications.

5. Plan to arrive on time. The interview is the organization's first exposure to your work behavior. Therefore, you don't want to be late. Find out how long it will take you to travel to the interview by making a dry run several days before. Plan to arrive ten or fifteen minutes before your appointment, as you may be asked to fill out paperwork prior to the actual interview.

6. Bring supplies. Gather and bring extra copies of your résumé, cover letter, and references, as well as the list of questions you plan to ask. You will also want to have materials for taking notes—a pen and a note pad. Do not bring your laptop or personal organizer, as keyboarding during the interview will distract the interviewer.

While the interview itself can be a stressful experience, several guidelines can help you put your best foot forward.

1. Use active listening. When we are anxious, we sometimes have trouble listening carefully. As a result, you will need to work on attending, understanding, and retaining what is asked of you. Remember that the interviewer will be aware of your nonverbal behaviors, so be sure to make and keep eye contact as you listen, avoid slouching or sitting forward, refrain from fidgeting, and so on.

2. Think before answering. If you have prepared for the interview, you should be able to answer the questions posed smoothly. If you are initially stumped by a question, don't just dive in and "wing it": Take a moment to consider how you can answer the question in a way that portrays your skills and experiences in the best light. "Tell me about yourself" is not an invitation to give the interviewer your life history. When you are asked this question, think about what you're going to say and answer concisely.

3. Be enthusiastic. If you come across as bored or disinterested, the interviewer is likely to conclude that you would be an unmotivated employee. Show that you genuinely want the job.

4. Ask questions. As the interview is winding down, be sure to ask the questions you prepared that have not already been answered. You may also want to ask how well the interviewer believes your qualifications match the position and elaborate upon how you are qualified, if necessary.

5. Avoid discussing salary and benefits. The time to discuss salary is when you are offered the job. If the job description did not previously ask you to state your salary requirements and your interviewer tries to pin you down to an answer, you may end up boxing yourself into a lower salary than you deserve or putting yourself in the position of asking for too much. Simply say something like, "I would like to defer talking about salary until we know we have a match." Similarly, discussions of benefits are best held until an offer is made.

OBSERVE AND ANALYZE ◗

Interviewing

Recall a recent job interview. Describe the ways in which the experience was difficult for you. Suppose you were to engage in that same interview again: Which of the guidelines presented in the text would be most helpful for you?

When the interview is complete, you should take several important follow-up steps.

1. Write a thank-you note. It is appropriate to write a short note thanking the interviewer for the experience and re-expressing your interest in the job.

2. Self-assess your performance. Take time to critique your performance. How well did you do? What can you do to be better next time?

3. Contact the interviewer for feedback. If you don't get the job, you might call the interviewer and ask for feedback. Be sure to be polite and to indicate that you are calling simply to get some help on your interviewing skills. Actively listen to the feedback, using questions and paraphrases to clarify what the interviewer says. Be sure to thank the interviewer for helping you.

◯ Manager and Co-worker Relationships on the Job

Good communication skills are universally recognized as essential for successful interactions with colleagues at work (Whetten & Cameron, 2005). You will need to use your interpersonal communication skills to develop and maintain healthy relationships with others at work, including managers and co-workers. Let's have a look at communicating in these two types of work relationships before focusing on the more complex communication skills involved when working with teams.

▷ Communicating in Managerial Relationships

Communication in managerial relationships is a two-way process: Managers need to communicate effectively with employees, and employees need to communicate effectively with their managers. For managers to ensure that their employees are performing their jobs as effectively as possible, they must instruct employees, provide them with useful feedback about their job performance, and influence them to accomplish their tasks well. Instructing employees requires managers to be adept at describing behaviors, using clear and vivid language, and offering constructive criticism. Providing useful feedback to employees about their job performance requires managers to know how to praise and how to criticize in appropriate ways. Influencing employees to accomplish their tasks well requires managers to understand their employees' needs so that they can choose appropriate compliance-gaining strategies. For employees to do their jobs, they must communicate effectively with their managers, using the skills of listening, questioning, paraphrasing, asking for feedback, and being assertive. When both persons in a manager-employee relationship recognize the importance of communication and jointly assume responsibility for sharing meaning, communication breakdowns are less likely to occur, and the needs of both relationship members are likely to be met.

As with any other relationship, the one between a manager and an employee develops over a period of time. From the start, managers

Search the web for additional guidance on writing cover letters, crafting résumés, and participating in interviews. Consider the advice offered in comparison with the advice presented in this chapter. You will see that not all job search advice matches, but the general principles are consistent. Think critically about the sites that you visit. Are they nonprofit sites that seem to offer well-considered advice? Are they commercial sites that also offer useful advice? Or are they sites that have an agenda, such as trying to sell you something? Bookmark the websites that seem to offer the most genuinely useful advice, and save them for when you do your next job search.

look for employees who are willing to do more than what is normally expected of employees (Graen, 1976). As those individuals who do go "above and beyond" become more valuable to the manager over time, they establish a greater power base from which to negotiate. To maintain a "fair exchange" with these individuals, managers negotiate special "rewards" for employees performing duties beyond those formally expected of them. Although the rewards may be financial (e.g., bonuses), they are more likely to be in the form of choice task assignments, better office space, public praise for special assignments, access to information not usually shared with employees at that level, and closer interpersonal relationships with their managers. Employees often describe these types of relationships as mentoring relationships, indicating that the relationship has helped them to develop skills and expertise beyond what would normally be learned on the job. These skills in turn make them more valuable to the organization as a whole and will help them to advance in their careers. On the other side of the coin, individuals who perform their role assignments acceptably but without doing anything extra to help out the managers may receive good work evaluations, adequate raises, and fair treatment, but they will find it difficult to be promoted or to develop close working relationships with their managers. Thus, ambitious employees are likely to ask themselves, "How can I give 110 percent to this job?" rather than "How can I do what is expected of me?"

To establish a high-quality exchange relationship with your manager, you must begin by assessing the skills and expertise you possess that may be of value in helping your manager accomplish the work that falls outside the formal role prescriptions of your job. These skills may be those that are in short supply in your work unit or those that your manager lacks. For instance, if a company is considering a new computer application that is unfamiliar to your manager, you might determine that your existing computer skills and knowledge are talents you should incorporate into the job, even though the job description never specified that such skills were required when you applied for the job.

Once you are aware of what skills and expertise you can bring to an exchange relationship, you need to communicate your willingness to perform extra assignments that require your talents and knowledge. For example, if your manager, who might not wish to ask you directly for help, says something to you like, "I'm just swamped with work, and now Human Resources says they need to have these affirmative action forms filled out and returned by Monday," as a savvy employee, you need to see this as a call for help and an opportunity to prove your value. Rather than responding, "Yeah, HR always needs paperwork. Well, I've got to get back to my desk," you might establish an exchange relationship by responding with a supportive statement like, "Barb, I was on an affirmative action committee at my last job and probably have a good idea of what HR needs on those forms. Can I help fill them out?"

Once you've assessed your skills and knowledge and let your manager know that you are willing to use them on the job, the manager-employee communication relationship becomes one of ongoing development. Through skillful use of listening, perception checking, describing, questioning, and paraphrasing, you can control the manner in which your relationships with your managers develop. Without careful and attentive use of these skills, you are likely to have a distant and ineffective working relationship with your manager or, if you are in a managerial position, with your employees. In time, you and your manager will develop the essential bond in a close manager-employee relationship: mutual trust. Being willing to take on additional assignments will further your relationship, but only if you are willing to perform such assignments well and on time. Although doing this often means working more, you may be able to negotiate with your manager to be removed from other, mundane assignments.

▷ Communicating in Co-worker Relationships

Your co-workers are the other members of your work group, team, or department who are at the same job level as you. It has been shown that co-workers influence both the quality of our job performance and our satisfaction with our jobs (Jablin & Krone, 1994). Therefore, don't take co-worker relationships for granted; they are just as important as employee-manager relationships. Like other relationships, your relationships with your co-workers are developed through your communication experiences. Just as you cannot choose who your manager will be, you cannot select those people with whom you will work. As in manager-employee relationships, then, how well you get along with your co-workers depends on your communication competence. For example, if you choose to be insensitive to the needs and feelings of your

What kinds of communication skills are recognized as essential for successful interaction with colleagues at work?

co-workers, either not listening to them attentively or being insensitive to cultural differences, then you are likely to find that your relationships with fellow employees are ineffective and unsatisfying. Therefore, assess, establish, and develop your relationships with co-workers just as you would with a manager, and develop mutual trust and cooperation with co-workers through effective communication.

Co-worker trust and cooperation does not mean that co-workers must be close friends with each other or always agree with one another. Indeed, as the workforce becomes more diverse, it is likely that disagreements and misunderstandings between co-workers will become more frequent in many workplaces. As a result, co-workers must pay special attention to developing and maintaining healthy working relationships with one another through effective interpersonal communication. Skills like turn-taking, listening, resolving conflicts through collaboration, empathizing, and supporting are critical skills all workers must possess.

▷ Team Relationships on the Job

Today, most work that goes on inside organizations uses a team approach (Eisenberg & Goodall, 2004). Therefore, it is essential to be an effective communicator not only in employee-manager relationships and co-worker relationships but also in team relationships. A **team** is a formally established group with a clear purpose and appropriate structure in which members know each other's roles and work together to achieve goals (Conrad & Poole, 2005). Work teams can be short-lived or ongoing. They may comprise people in the same department, or their membership may be drawn from several functional areas of the organization. Teams may be tasked with making recommendations, making decisions, or implementing decisions that have been made by others. For example, a company might form a team to develop a new policy on e-mail archiving, to determine whether the current e-mail archiving system should be replaced, or to ensure that the new guidelines for e-mail archiving are communicated effectively throughout the company. Regardless of the type of work team, interpersonal communication plays a pivotal role in the overall effectiveness of the team effort.

In this section, we focus on effective team communication. First we list the characteristics of effective work teams. Then we outline the various communication roles of team members. After that, we discuss the communication technologies that facilitate teamwork. Next, we provide guidelines for setting up team meetings. Finally, we discuss member responsibilities in team meetings

> **Team**—formally established group with a clear purpose and appropriate structure in which members know each other's roles and work together to achieve goals.

▷ Characteristics of Effective Work Teams

Whether a work team operates in the same physical location, meeting face-to-face to accomplish its work, or operates as a virtual team spread across multiple locations using technology to facilitate communication, the characteristics of all effective work teams are the same. The hallmarks of effective teams have been studied across a variety of disciplines. In one study of fifty effective teams, Larson and LaFasto (1989) found that the following eight characteristics best characterize effective teamwork.

1. A clear group goal. It goes without saying that a team that understands and agrees on its goal is likely to be more effective than one that does not. Therefore, when managers are considering organizing a work team, it is their job to make sure that each member of the team clearly understands the overall goal to be accomplished. Sometimes, teams are given an abstract or overly general goal to reach, resulting in confusion and frustration. If you are assigned to a work team, you can use the skills of questioning and paraphrasing to make sure that you and other team members clearly understand what goal or goals you are expected to accomplish as a team. You may find that asking managers for a list of the "deliverables" that you are expected to produce is an effective way of making a seemingly abstract goal more concrete. For example, suppose you have been assigned to work on a team whose stated goal is to review the current absentee policy and make recommendations for changes. It will probably help the team to understand the scope of the assignment if the manager states that the recommendations should take the form of a report, complete with an analysis of absence data for the past two years, as well as an analysis of the absentee polices of competing companies and "best practice" exemplars.

2. Clear individual member roles. It makes no sense for everyone to perform the same role on a team. A major benefit of having many people working together as a team is that different people bring different strengths to the task. Sometimes people are selected for a team because their various skills are complementary. If team members are unsure of their roles or are competing to perform the same roles, then team functioning suffers. Consequently, when people are assigned to a team, or invited to join one, the convener of the group should describe the role envisioned for each individual. For example, if you were asking Jonathan to join a team whose goal is to enhance fund-raising among Greek organizations on campus, you might describe his role by saying, "We are hoping that you will share your experience in alumni relations to help this team develop strategies for raising money from former members of fraternities and sororities on campus." At the same time, you might clarify Ella's anticipated role by saying, "Since you are a public relations major, we hope that you can assist the team in creating a thematic image and some communication strategies for a fund-raising campaign."

3. Regular feedback about individual and group performance. Even when team members clearly know their roles, they still need regular feedback regarding their performance. Such feedback not only tells them about the quality of their work but also provides them with information about whether they need to adjust their work performance in any way—and if so, how to do that. Frequent open and honest communication among team members also becomes the vehicle for understanding, coordinating, and monitoring overall team performance. It ensures that an ongoing system of checks and balances and constructive criticism occurs. To establish the importance of feedback, the team leader should highlight feedback procedures at the first team meeting. Then, at the first follow-up meeting, he or she should say something like, "Let's talk about the area of expertise that each person has been bringing to our task and discuss how well we think we are each doing. Ella, we value the public relations expertise that you bring to the group. What's the group sentiment about our PR effort so far? Do we have a clear message for our fund-raising campaign, or do we need to develop this area further?" By explicitly communicating team expectations and progress related to each role, leaders allow individual members and the team as a whole to regularly assess performance.

4. A combination of expertise and people skills in team members. Ideally, team members have among them all of the expertise necessary to accomplish the tasks of the group and reach its overall goal. But sometimes experts lack the basic interpersonal skills that enable them to express what they know to others or to politely disagree with someone on the team who is less knowledgeable. Since it is important to the group's success that expertise be shared and divergent viewpoints be aired, it is essential that team members have "people skills," a wide variety of interpersonal skills that will help them facilitate meaningful discussions within the group. As a member of a team, you can help less verbal members to share their expertise by encouraging turn-taking, asking questions of quieter members, and pointing out where members disagree. You can also help less interpersonally skilled team members to express themselves better by paraphrasing and describing behaviors tactfully. The interpersonal communication skills presented throughout this textbook can be used to enhance the effectiveness of work teams.

5. Commitment to the team and its success. Commitment is making a personal decision to work enthusiastically with other team members to achieve the group's goals. It is not enough for team members to be committed to the goal itself; it is also important that they be committed to achieving the goal by working with each other. Early in the life of a group, it is helpful for the group members to spend time getting to know each other, to envision together the outcome or outcomes the group hopes to achieve, and to build a sense of team enthusiasm and encouragement. Through "team-building" processes like this, groups can help their members make the team and its work a high priority and look forward to the process. As a member of the group, you can help to build commitment by taking time to converse with other members and by asking others what excites or intrigues them about the project.

6. A collaborative climate of open, honest, and direct communication. In effective teams, members cooperate with each other by speaking openly, honestly, and directly. Not only must they provide each other with feedback openly and honestly, as discussed earlier, but they also must communicate with each other about all aspects of the project. For groups to reap the benefits of having several minds thinking and working together, team members must be comfortable about sharing their ideas. The interpersonal communication skills of questioning, describing feelings and behaviors, asking for and giving criticism, assertiveness, and conflict management aid team members as they interact. With virtual teams, communication must be more direct and explicit so as to avoid faulty assumptions and conclusions that can occur when team members are not physically situated together (Brown, 2007).

7. Standards of excellence. Effective teams expect and receive excellence from each member; otherwise some members may become overwhelmed aiding others or the team process may collapse entirely. This expectation should be communicated at the outset and maintained by all members as they handle their individual work assignments. As a team member, to help maintain standards of excellence, gently but firmly confront team members who are not working up to standard and encourage them to begin to meet the agreed-upon standards. Do not simply take on their workload for them or expect other competent team members to do so.

8. Strong leadership. Effective teams have exceptionally good leaders who are focused on the overall goals and, at the same time, motivate members to perform at the highest levels they can. Leaders are the people who influence the group's procedures, task accomplishment, and relationships between members by stepping in and assuming a combination of roles needed by the group but not appropriately assumed by other members. To be effective, leaders must be adept at listening to the group and becoming attuned to what the group needs at a particular time. Based on what they have heard, leaders adapt their behaviors to various situations, provide what the group needs, and, in so doing, influence the group to attain its overall goal.

▷ Communication Roles of Team Members

As work teams meet regularly to plan their work, troubleshoot problems, and make other decisions, team members take on a variety of communication roles that go beyond their skill area roles. These communication roles fall into two general categories: task roles and maintenance roles. **Task roles** are communication behaviors that help a team focus on the issues under discussion. **Maintenance roles** are communication behaviors that improve interaction among team members.

Task roles include those of initiator, information or opinion giver, information or opinion seeker, analyzer, and orienter.

1. Initiator. You play the initiator role when your comment gets the discussion started or moves it in a new direction. A team member would be performing

Task roles—communication behaviors that help a team focus on issues under discussion.

Maintenance roles—communication behaviors that improve interaction among team members.

the initiator role by suggesting, "Let's begin by looking at the current problems in our inventory control system." Or, "Perhaps we should move on to a discussion of quality concerns we have related to our vendors and suppliers."

2. Information or opinion giver. You play the information or opinion giver role when you provide content for the discussion. People who perform this role well are those who have expertise or are well informed about the task at hand and share what they know with the team. A team member taking on the information or opinion giver role would make statements such as, "Well, in the meeting I attended last week with Human Resources, we were told that sales associates could not take vacations between Thanksgiving and New Year's. So I think we want to make sure that our department vacation policy reflects this." Or, "In my experience, telling customers that something is simply against company policy just makes them angrier, so I don't think that is what we want to say in this situation."

3. Information or opinion seeker. You play the information or opinion seeker role when you ask questions that probe others for their ideas and opinions. Typical comments by those performing the information or opinion seeker role include remarks such as, "Before going further, what information do we have about how raising dues is likely to affect membership?" Or, "How do members of the group feel about this idea?"

4. Analyzer. You play the analyzer role when you help the group to examine, scrutinize, question, explore, probe, or evaluate an idea or piece of information. To make good decisions, team members must critically examine ideas or suggestions provided by members as well as the facts and data gathered by the team. A team member would be performing the analyzer role by saying such things as, "I do think a change to our weekly schedule should be based on our customer needs as well as on our own personal preferences. So let's look at our hourly sales records to see if there is a pattern to when we are busy and when we are slow." Or, "The numbers we have here on annual enrollment in our program look very sound to me because they are consistent with monthly totals."

5. Orienter. You play the orienter role when you help the team to understand where it stands regarding a decision or discussion, when you let the team know when it is off track, or when you summarize points of agreement and disagreement so that the team understands what issues are unresolved. It's easy for a team to get so involved in a discussion that it loses track of the "big picture" or goes off on tangents and wastes time with irrelevant issues. Thus, it is important that someone on the team monitor the group process. A team member would be performing the role of orienter by making comments such as, "I think we've agreed that a good solution must be one that fits our budget, but are there other criteria that are important as well?" Or, "We had agreed that we would spend this meeting discussing ways to improve record keeping. It seems to me that we are off track right now in our discussion of human resource budgeting." Or, "It seems to me that we are basically in agreement that we need a new Web site with improved graphics and direct links to each of our product lines. Is that true? Does everyone agree?"

Maintenance roles include those of gatekeeper, encourager, and harmonizer.

1. Gatekeeper. You play the gatekeeper role when you ensure that everyone on the team has an opportunity to speak and be heard. In some group discussions, certain people may talk more than their fair share while others remain silent, contributing little or nothing. By performing the gatekeeping role, a team member helps to create more balanced participation among members so that the group can benefit from a variety of viewpoints and information sources. A team member would be taking on the role of gatekeeper when making statements such as, "Just a second, Lonnie, I think Dominique has something to say on this topic. Dominique, you have some experience with coaching employees for improved performance, don't you? What has been your experience?" Or, "Lonnie, your examples of how you have used peer orientation to help new employees are very interesting, and I think that we all now understand your process, so I'd like to hear from other folks about alternative ways we might consider handling new employee orientation."

2. Encourager. You play the encourager role when your messages provide support for the contributions of other team members. Participants in a group discussion need to have their ideas acknowledged and supported from time to time. Otherwise, they are unsure about whether they are being heard or if their ideas are being taken seriously. When taking on the encourager role, you might say, "That was a really good suggestion that Kent just made because it deals exactly with the problem we have in meeting client specifications." Or, "I think we should keep in mind Miranda's point about maintaining requirements until the next quarter. She made some good observations about the dangers of moving too quickly." Notice that in both cases the encourager was able to say something helpful as a result of having first listened closely to what had been said.

3. Harmonizer. Finally, you play the harmonizer role when you help the group to relieve tension and manage conflict. Team decision making inevitably becomes stressful at times, and conflicts may emerge. A team member who acts as a harmonizer may temporarily relieve the tension by saying something witty or may help the group effectively deal with an emerging conflict. When taking on the harmonizer role, you might make statements like, "The task of planning this product launch reminds me of dealing with Godzilla. Anyone see that movie?" Or, "We seem to be at odds around the issue of partnering with other schools. It seems that Elana and Nils strongly represent alternate perspectives. Before we get too polarized around these two options, maybe we should look at a range of possibilities."

▷ Communication Technologies for Teamwork

Communication technology provides numerous tools to enhance communication among team members, especially when those teams do not have the opportunity to meet face-to-face. Common tools such as e-mail, instant messaging, voice mail, faxing, and videoconferencing enhance communication for all members of work teams, whether members work in the same location or across the country from one another. Increasingly, additional communication technologies such as electronic newsletters, e-calendars, blogs, podcasts, e-surveys, and wikis provide easy and efficient communication among members of work teams. These communication technologies, used individually or in combinations, provide enormous capacity for team members to communicate easily, regularly, and at low cost as they seek to accomplish team goals. To ensure your success in the workplace, it is essential that you are capable of using these and other technological tools that are emerging to enhance productivity in the workplace. Let's examine the more recently developed communication tools listed here and the ways in which they aid teamwork.

1. **Electronic newsletters.** Electronic newsletters are regularly distributed online publications that share team information. They can be used to introduce team members to each other, recap past work, preview upcoming events, and set work expectations (Brown, 2007). Such publications can reduce the need for or the number of face-to-face or electronically facilitated meetings and handily provide written information needed by all team members.

2. **E-calendars.** E-calendars are online scheduling tools that can be viewed by all designated members. An e-calendar allows team members to have access to each other's schedules. In some cases, access is limited to viewing others' calendars to ascertain their availability for project meetings, conference calls, or videoconferencing. Such viewing access eliminates the time-consuming task of contacting all team members to check their availability for project meetings. In other cases, the team leader or all members may have the capability to actually schedule an event on everyone's calendar, thereby easing the process of scheduling meetings and tracking deadlines.

3. **Blogs.** We have already discussed what blogs are, but we have not yet considered them in the context of team communication. Naturally, by their collaborative nature, blogs can greatly facilitate communication among team members. Blogs allow team members to record their progress, thoughts, or questions about a shared project for all team members to view. In doing so, they mimic ongoing face-to-face conversations without the inconvenience of travel, replace compilations and distributions of reports, and provide a shared archive where everyone can read and reread the history of the team's communications.

4. **Podcasts.** Podcasts are digital media files distributed over the Internet for playback on computers or portable media players. This technology allows team members to listen to a lecture, conference presentation, or meeting after its occurrence from a remote location. Such technology may enable team members to learn information they need for a project, obtain information from a communication event they were unable to attend, or have a reviewable record of a communication event that they did attend.

5. **E-surveys.** E-surveys are electronic tools for creating and analyzing online surveys. Survey software, typically available from subscription services, provides

survey templates to aid in the design of surveys, links for the easy and anonymous completion of surveys, and tools for analyzing and summarizing survey results. This tool can aid teams when gathering and reporting information they need for team decision making.

6. Wikis. Finally, wikis are collaborative Web sites that allow users to add and edit content. Wiki software requires secure registration before a member can post to the Web site to prevent unauthorized users. Once team members are authorized to participate in a wiki, every change to the material posted on the wiki made by any member of the team is accepted and all previous versions of the material are stored. This powerful communication tool allows team members to collaboratively create a report at each team member's own convenient time and place.

INTER-ACT WITH ⊙ TECHNOLOGY

Interview a manager from any type of company or organization. Determine how much of that person's work-related communication occurs through technology. What forms of communication technology do they use the most? The least? How does the use of certain types of communication technologies such as e-mail, instant messaging, voice mail, blogs, fax, videoconferencing, and so on relate to the purpose or content of the messages sent through them?

▷ Guidelines for Running Team Meetings

In addition to performing task and maintenance roles during a team meeting, there are duties to be completed before the meeting begins. By performing these jobs before leading a meeting, you can make sure that meeting time is spent productively and little time is wasted. When running a meeting you should complete five tasks.

1. Define and communicate the specific meeting purpose. It can be frustrating to be expected to attend a physical or virtual meeting for which you do not know the purpose or don't know the purpose in sufficient detail. Participants can't prepare mentally beforehand if they don't know the specific purpose of the meeting, and they can't know which materials to bring to the meeting either. For example, if the upcoming meeting of teachers involves curriculum planning, the purpose should be defined even more clearly so that the participants can get their thoughts organized beforehand and bring what they may need to bring, such as materials from curriculum conferences they've attended and other related materials. The memo announcing the meeting might say, "We will examine our existing curriculum goals and course topics as they relate to state curriculum requirements in the area of science."

2. List specific outcomes that should be reached by the end of the meeting. Even with a clearly stated meeting goal, participants may not know what tasks should be accomplished or what decisions should be made by the conclusion of the meeting. Listing specific outcomes keeps the meeting focused on clear goals and serves to keep the group on track. For example, in our curriculum meeting example, the meeting leader might specify, "By the end of our curriculum planning meeting, we should have a written statement of eleventh and twelfth grade science goals that are consistent with state requirements, and we should have a list of state-mandated course topics that are not currently addressed by our eleventh and twelfth grade science courses."

3. Communicate and stick to starting and ending times for the meeting. To use the limited time allotted for a meeting efficiently and to be fair to those members who arrive on time, meetings should begin promptly. By waiting for latecomers, meeting leaders set a precedent that enables participants to arrive at meetings late in the future. Likewise, in the workplace, people have very busy schedules and need to know when a meeting will end. The meeting leader should closely monitor time as the meeting proceeds to make sure the meeting will end on time.

4. Send out a detailed agenda, which includes the date, time, and location of the meeting, as well as the topics to be discussed, with an approximate amount of time allocated to each agenda item. This schedule of topics and times will allow the discussion to proceed efficiently and will keep the group discussion focused on concrete items. An agenda like the one shown in Figure 14.4 is also useful for participants who cannot attend the entire meeting or guests who need not be present for the whole meeting. By knowing ahead of time which items will be discussed and when, those not concerned with the entire agenda can schedule their attendance accordingly.

5. Make physical or technical arrangements. Making arrangements may include reserving a meeting room with a particular seating format or setting up teleconferencing or streaming video capabilities. The physical space for a meeting can have a large impact on the productivity of a meeting. A space that is too crowded or impedes the ability of attendees to see each other or visual presentations can hinder team effectiveness. Likewise, poor technological arrangements for

---

March 1, 2009

To: Interns at Metrotek

From: Janelle Smith

Re: Agenda for discussion group meeting, March 8, 2009, 3:00–5:00 P.M., Conference
        Room A

Agenda for Group Discussion
Please come prepared to discuss questions 1 through 5. We will consider question 6 on the basis of our resolution of the other questions.

Meeting topic: What should be done to integrate interns into planning, decision making, and social functions at Metrotek?

1. What is the number of interns per department?	(3:00–3:10)
2. Why aren't interns involved in planning, decision making, and social activities?	(3:10–3:30)
3. What specific factors hinder their involvement?	(3:30–3:50)
BREAK	(3:50–4:00)
4. What criteria should be used to test possible solutions to the problem?	(4:00–4:15)
5. What are some of the possible solutions to the problem?	(4:15–4:45)
6. What one solution or combination of solutions will work best to solve the problem?	(4:45–5:00)

FIGURE 14.4 Agenda for discussion group meeting

a virtual meeting can impede communication and team functioning and reflect negatively on the credibility of the team leader and workplace organization.

▷ Member Responsibilities in Team Meetings

Although team members take on particular skill and expertise roles during team meetings, members of effective teams also need to take on overall responsibilities to make their meetings successful. Here are some guidelines to help team members prepare for, participate in, and follow up after a meeting to increase its effectiveness.

1. Preparing. Too often, people think of a team meeting as a "happening" that involves face-to-face or virtual participation but no particular preparation. People often attend meetings unprepared, even though they may be carrying packets of material that they received in advance of the meeting or have relevant information elsewhere in computer files that they have neglected to review. The reality is that meetings should not be treated as impromptu events but as carefully planned interactions that pool information from well-prepared individuals. Here are some important steps to take prior to attending a meeting.

- **Study the agenda.** Carefully consider the purpose of the meeting, and determine what you need to do to be prepared. The agenda is an outline on which to base your preparation.
- **Study the minutes of the previous meeting.** If this is one in a series of meetings, study the minutes and your own notes from the previous meetings. Since ongoing meetings on the same topic are not unrelated events, what happened at one meeting should provide the basis for preparing for the next meeting.
- **Be ready to contribute.** In addition to studying the agenda to anticipate what topics will be important and what materials to bring, consider the agenda in terms of how you plan to contribute to the conversation. Do your own research to become better informed about items on the agenda. Have available any materials that you have uncovered that will help the group accomplish its agenda. If appropriate, discuss the agenda with appropriate people who will not be participating in the meeting to solicit their ideas.
- **List questions.** Make a list of questions related to agenda items that you would like to have answered during the meeting.

2. Participating. Go into the meeting with the expectation that you will be a full participant. If there are five people in the group, all five should participate actively. Here are some tips on how to be an active participant:

- **Listen attentively.** Concentrate on what others are saying so that you can effectively complement, supplement, or counter what they have presented.
- **Stay focused.** In a group setting, it is easy to get the discussion going in nonproductive directions. Keep your comments focused on the specific agenda item under discussion. If others have gotten off the subject, do what you can to get them back on track.

- **Ask questions.** Asking questions helps to stimulate discussion and build ideas. Be sure to ask "honest" questions, that is, questions whose answers you do not already know, are directly relevant, are not designed to embarrass other team members, and are not presented simply to say something to appear involved.

- **Take notes.** Even if someone else is responsible for providing the official minutes of the meeting, you will need to take your own notes that help you follow the line of development. Also, these notes will help you remember what has been said after the meeting and not forget about any responsibilities you have agreed to take on.

- **Play devil's advocate.** When you think an idea has not been fully discussed or tested, be willing to voice disagreement or encourage further discussion.

- **Monitor your contributions.** People who are well prepared for meetings have a tendency to dominate discussions. Make sure that you neither dominate the discussion nor abdicate your responsibility to share insights and opinions with others.

3. Following up. When meetings end, too often people leave and forget about what took place altogether, or they expect others to catch them up in the next of a series of meetings. But letting what you learned or did in a meeting evaporate the minute the meeting is over both hinders your ability to remember important information learned and impedes your ability to be a more effective participant in the future. Several guidelines will help you follow up after a meeting.

- **Review and summarize your notes.** Try to do this shortly after you have left the meeting, while ideas are still fresh in your mind. This will not only help you organize and remember what you learned but will also prepare you for the next meeting, if there will be another meeting on the same or similar topic.

- **Review the minutes.** When they become available, also review the official meeting minutes. Compare the official minutes to your own notes, and report any significant discrepancies that you find to those who may need to know.

- **Evaluate your effectiveness.** Consider how effective you were in helping the group move toward achieving its goals so that you can be a better meeting participant in the next meeting you attend. Where were you strong? Where were you weak? What should you do next time that you did not do in this meeting?

- **Communicate with others.** Don't just let what you learned stay only with you if others may benefit from it. Inform others who may not have participated in the meeting but need to know about information conveyed and decisions made in the meeting.

- **Complete responsibilities.** Make sure you complete all of the assignments you received at the meeting or tasks you volunteered to take on.

⊙ Communicating in a Diverse Workplace

Today's workplace reflects the increasing diversity of our country as women and men and people of various races, ethnicities, ages, socioeconomic status, and political and religious perspectives come together to work side by side. The increasing diversity of today's workplace in the United States is a result of social changes and federal laws that have opened opportunities for those who in previous decades found it difficult to secure equal opportunity employment, particularly women and members of minority groups. It also stems from two more recent developments: increased immigration and an ever-expanding global market brought about in part by the ease of international communication facilitated by the Internet (Potoker, 2005). This means that for you to be successful in the workplace, it is increasingly important that you be able to understand and communicate with people who are different from you. You may face various challenges at work stemming from the increasing diversity of our workforce, including culture-based work style differences, intergenerational work value differences, sexual harassment problems, and organizational romance. Let's take a brief look at each of these.

▷ Culture-Based Work Styles

How we approach our work depends on our culture. Some cultures value work over relationships, while others value relationships over work. In addition, some cultures value a sequential approach to large tasks, while others favor a holistic approach. When we go to work we bring our cultural bias toward how to accomplish work with us. When we work with others from different cultures our culture-based work style differences can cause conflict (Varner & Beamer, 1995).

A **results-oriented culture**, like the dominant culture of the United States, prioritizes the results of work over building relationships at work, whereas a **relationship-oriented culture**, like those of Japan, Spain, and Mexico, prioritize building relationships at work over the results of work (Varner & Beamer, 1995). Employees who come from results-oriented cultures see little need for spending time establishing or maintaining relationships, preferring to get right down to business. They view time as precious, and their ultimate goal is to get the work done and reach goals. Getting to know customers or business associates on a personal level before doing business with them is not considered necessary. In fact, anything that deters from the business objective would be seen as annoying or counterproductive. On the other hand, employees who come from relationship-oriented cultures see the quality of their personal relationships with customers and business associates as the primary business concern. People from these cultures prefer not to conduct business until they have established or refreshed a personal relationship.

As you can imagine, business associates who come from such different cultural perspectives are likely to experience problems when they work together. For example, imagine that Geoffrey, a sales representative and a "typical results-

Results-oriented culture—culture that prioritizes the results of work over building relationships at work.

Relationship-oriented culture—culture that prioritizes building relationships at work over the results of work.

oriented American," is making his first sales call on Rosa, a purchasing manager for one of his company's largest clients and a "typical relationship-oriented Mexican." After being escorted into Rosa's office and quickly introducing himself, Geoffrey immediately begins his sales pitch by describing the new product line that he thinks Rosa's company will be interested in purchasing. Unless Rosa has worked with typical Americans before, she may think Geoffrey rude because he introduces business topics before they have had an opportunity to get to know each other. Rosa may find it odd that they haven't talked about each other's families or that they haven't dined together. For Rosa, getting to know Geoffrey personally is part of doing business. She needs to learn about his personality and his family background so she can decide whether to trust him as a business associate. Meanwhile, Geoffrey may find Rosa's questions about his family to be a violation of his privacy and unrelated to their business relationship. In fact, he may even misperceive Rosa's questions as flirtatious. Similar misunderstandings can occur between colleagues or teammates who come from different cultural backgrounds.

A second culturally based work style difference is the value placed on one of two approaches to completing work on large or complex tasks. A **sequential task completion culture** is a culture that believes that large or complex tasks should be broken down into separate parts and completed one part at a time, in order; that is, Step A is finished before step B is begun, and so on, until the task is completed. In contrast, a **holistic task completion culture** is a culture that believes in tackling large and complex tasks in their entirety. Rather than completing one part of the task before beginning work on another, holistic task completion cultures advocate simultaneously working on all parts of the task, that is, working on one part, then another, then back to the first, in an iterative fashion. As you can imagine, when teammates from sequential task completion cultures work with those from holistic cultures, problems arise. For example, suppose that department store assistant managers Greg (who is a "typical Canadian sequential task completer") and Chun-Hae (a "typical Korean holistic task completer") have been asked by their boss to work together to develop a plan for displaying the store's new fall merchandise. Chun-Hae would be inclined to look at the whole problem at once, talking for a few minutes about what to put where, then bouncing around her ideas about how to physically handle the moving process, then describing how possibly to involve the sales associates in the plan, and finally returning to discussing new ideas about what to put where. While another holistic task completer would be comfortable with this approach, Greg is likely to become confused and frustrated, wishing Chun-Hae would focus on one issue, work through it, make decisions, and then move on to the next topic. Likewise, if Greg initiates the discussion and tries to hold Chun-Hae to his step-by-step process, she is likely to become frustrated and bored.

Effective business communication depends on awareness of and sensitivity to cultural differences in work styles without assuming some approaches are better than others. It is also important to realize, too, that a person from a particular

Sequential task completion culture—culture whose members prefer to break larger tasks down into separate parts and complete one part at a time, in order.

Holistic task completion culture— culture in which members prefer to work on an entire task at once.

The Group: A Japanese Context

by Delores Cathcart and Robert Cathcart

Team roles and decision-making styles are greatly influenced by culture. In this excerpt, the authors describe how interdependence leads to a climate of agreement and decision making based on consensus in Japanese groups.

One of Japan's most prominent national characteristics is the individual's sense of the group. Loyalty to the group and a willingness to submit to its demands are key virtues in Japanese society. This dependency and the interdependency of all members of a group is reinforced by the concept of *on*. A Japanese is expected to feel indebtedness to those others in the group who provide security, care, and support. This indebtedness creates obligation and when combined with dependency is called *on*. *On* functions as a means of linking all persons in the group in an unending chain because obligation is never satisfied, but continues throughout life. *On* is fostered by a system known as the *oyabun–kobun* relationship. Traditionally the *oyabun* is a father, boss, or patron who protects and provides for a son, employee, or student in return for his or her service and loyalty. This is not a one-way dependency. Each boss or group leader recognizes his own dependency on those below. Without their undivided loyalty he or she could not function. *Oyabun* are also acutely aware of this double dimension because of having had to serve a long period of *kobun* on the way up the hierarchy to the position at the top. All had *oyabun* who protected and assisted them, much like a father, and now each must do the same for their *kobun*. *Oyabun* have one or more *kobun* whom they look after much as if they were children. The more loyal and devoted the "children," the more successful the "father."

This relationship is useful in modern life where large companies assume the role of superfamily and become involved in every aspect of their workers' lives. Bosses are *oyabun* and employees are *kobun*. . . .

This uniquely Japanese way of viewing relationships creates a distinctive style of decision-making known as *consensus decision*. The Japanese devotion to consensus building seems difficult for most Westerners to grasp but loses some of its mystery when looked at as a solution to representing every member of the group. In a system that operates on *oyabun–kobun* relationships nothing is decided without concern for how the outcome will affect all. Ideas and plans are circulated up and down the company hierarchy until everyone has had a chance to react. This reactive process is not to exert pressure but to make certain that all matters affecting the particular groups and the company are taken into consideration. Much time is spent assessing the mood of everyone involved and only after all the ramifications of how the decision will affect each group can there be a quiet assent. A group within the company may approve a decision that is not directly in its interest (or even causes it difficulties) because its members know they are not ignored, their feelings have been expressed and they can be assured that what is good for the company will ultimately be good for them. For this reason consensus decisions cannot be hurried along without chancing a slight or oversight that will cause future problems.

The process of consensus building in order to make decisions is a time-consuming one, not only because everyone must be considered, but also because the Japanese avoid verbalizing objections or doubts in order to preserve group harmony. The advice, often found in American group literature, that group communication should be characterized by open and candid statements expressing individual personal feelings, wishes, and dislikes, is the antithesis of the Japanese consensus process. No opposing speeches are made to argue alternate ideas; no conferences are held to debate issues. Instead, the process of assessing the feelings and mood of each work group proceeds slowly until there exists a climate of agreement. This process is possible because of the tight relationships that allow bosses and workers to know each other intimately and to know the group so well that needs and desires are easy to assess.

Excerpted from Cathcart, D., and Cathcart, R. (1997). The group: A Japanese context. In L. A. Samovar and R. E. Porter (Eds.), *Intercultural Communication: A Reader* (8th ed., pp. 329–339). Belmont, Calif.: Wadsworth. Reprinted by permission of the authors.

culture may or may not communicate in the style typical of that culture, so you should not assume that, for instance, all Americans are results-oriented and sequential or that all Koreans are relationship-oriented and holistic. A strategy for dealing with cultural differences is to acknowledge and communicate about respective cultural styles. Parties working across global lines may benefit from talking about preferred ways of doing business and negotiating an agreement between the business partners. Indeed, as workplaces become more culturally diverse, employees may need to be flexible in using various styles, including their natural work style and learned alternate styles.

For another example of how people from different cultures use different styles, see also this chapter's "Diverse Voices" box, in which Delores Cathcart and Robert Cathcart describe how Japanese workers work differently in groups than many of us in the United States do.

▷ Understanding Intergenerational Differences

Because there is no mandatory retirement age in the United States and other countries and because today's students are more likely to work at least part-time, there is more opportunity for age-based misunderstandings to occur. Scholars have identified five areas in which older and younger employees tend to differ: their views of authority, their approaches to rules, their priorities regarding work versus leisure, their technology competence, and their degree of company and career loyalty (Zemke, Raines, & Filipczak, 2000).

1. Views of authority. In general, people who are age sixty or older tend to have greater respect for authority. They grew up in a time when questioning authority figures such as parents, teachers, religious leaders, and bosses was considered unacceptable behavior. They demonstrate their respect by addressing people using formal terms of address (Mr., Ms., Dr., Sir, and so on). In contrast, people under the age of thirty tend to be more skeptical of authority and less formal when dealing with authority figures. They grew up in an era of more permissiveness, when questioning parents, teachers, and religious

How can you communicate effectively across generational differences at work?

leaders was tolerated, and, as a result, they are more likely to question their managers and to openly disagree with decisions made by those in positions of authority. Likewise, younger people are more likely to call authority figures and co-workers by their first names. This communication difference may lead to misunderstandings between and resentments among employees.

2. Approaches to rules. Similar to how they view authority differently, co-workers may display age-related differences regarding how they view company rules. Older individuals are more likely to strictly adhere to company rules and expect others to do so as well. They are likely to perceive that employers have the right to make rules and that employees have the responsibility to follow those rules as a condition of employment. They may also view company rules as comforting because they provide predictability. For many younger co-workers, however, rules may be seen as suggestions to be followed or not, depending on one's own analysis of a situation. Having been raised with situational ethics, younger people may believe that extenuating circumstances call for flexibility, thus allowing them to ignore or bend the rules. Such differences in perspective may cause us to judge one another, thereby impeding team cohesiveness at work.

3. Priorities regarding work versus leisure. For many older individuals, work always takes priority over family and leisure. In fact, a "strong work ethic" is considered to be one of the most respectable personality traits in the eyes of older Americans. Family responsibilities may have led many people over the age of sixty to sacrifice leisure to work hard to provide for their families. In contrast, many individuals under thirty have not yet experienced the challenges of providing for a family or may not consider raising a family to be a primary life goal as in generations past, so they may place a higher priority on leisure. In addition, some younger workers, having seen the toll that work has taken on their parents and other older workers, are more aware of the need to balance work and leisure. The presence of these generational tendencies at work may cause us to wrongly attribute motives of work professionalism and commitment to our colleagues or to become defensive with each other.

4. Technology competence. There is also often a generational difference regarding the use of and competence with technology. Today, those over sixty did not grow up with the vast amount of information, communication, and entertainment technology that exists today. For many older employees, learning to use technology is challenging and creates anxiety. As a result, technology may not be regarded as an asset but as a burden. For younger people, especially very young employees, however, ever-changing technology is a given part of life, and the need to adapt to evolving technology is natural and ever-present. Some older employees may be resentful of being expected to use technology for which they have no expertise and of having to constantly adapt themselves, while younger employees may resent the added burden of assisting older colleagues with technological tasks.

5. Degree of company loyalty. Older and younger employees also often disagree about loyalty to one's employer. Many older employees began working in the era when loyalty to an employer was expected and rewarded. In fact, they are likely to have begun their careers expecting to work for the same organization for their entire work lives. Staying with one company for a long time was in the past the means to advancement and a definition of success, and frequent job changes were viewed by employers and co-workers as problematic. With the massive layoffs that have been the hallmark of business during the last twenty-five years, however, younger employees have grown up without the expectation that they will be able to rely on one company to nurture and support their careers and ease them into retirement. Today, most younger employees understand that career success depends on personal expertise, regardless of how often one changes organizations. In fact, for many younger employees, frequent job change is seen as the means of career advancement. As a result, intergenerational conflicts may ensue, even though many older workers have also experienced a changing perspective on company loyalty. Unless we understand these varying perspectives about company loyalty, we may mistakenly hold others to our own standards.

These differences in values can conflict when older and younger employees work together. It is important to keep in mind that there is not one right set of values and one wrong set of values. But generational differences in values and behaviors can create enormous challenges with regard to workplace communication. The more we understand and are sensitive to age-related differences in workplace behavior, the more we can be flexible communicating across the age span at work. Communicating directly about one's values and behaviors can go a long way in managing generational differences. Using the interpersonal skills of assertiveness, questioning, perception checking, describing behavior, and owning feelings may also prove useful in preventing or managing intergenerational communication conflicts at work. For example, an older employee may say to a younger colleague, "Being quite a bit older than you, I was raised to see formal terms of address like Mr. and Mrs. as a sign of respect. I realize that you do not mean any disrespect when you call me by my first name, but I would prefer that you address me as Mrs. Sofranko rather than Edna. How would you like me to refer to you?" Or a younger colleague may say to an older counterpart, "I can understand that you have not had a great deal of experience with database management. But this project requires all of us to maintain and manipulate sales data. Would you consider taking the database management course that Human Resources offers? I understand that it is quite good, and employees with little technology experience have praised the instructors for their patience and thoroughness with all participants." Such open and direct communication can allow us to understand our colleagues better and to appreciate different workplace values and behaviors rather than harbor resentments that may lead to conflict episodes at work.

▷ Avoiding or Coping with Sexual Harassment

Sexual harassment is unwanted verbal or physical sexual behavior that interferes with work performance. More specifically, according to the Federal Equal Employment Opportunity Commission (EEOC), "sexual harassment is a form of

Sexual harassment—unwanted verbal or physical sexual behavior that interferes with work performance.

sex discrimination that violates Title VII of the Civil Rights Act of 1964," which includes "unwelcome sexual advances, requests for sexual favors, and other verbal or physical conduct of a sexual nature when this conduct explicitly or implicitly affects an individual's employment, unreasonably interferes with an individual's work performance, or creates an intimidating, hostile, or offensive work environment." The EEOC recognizes that sexual harassment can occur in a variety of circumstances, "including but not limited to the following:

- The victim as well as the harasser may be a woman or a man. The victim does not have to be of the opposite sex.
- The harasser can be the victim's supervisor, an agent of the employer, a supervisor in another area, a co-worker, or a non-employee.
- The victim does not have to be the person harassed but could be anyone affected by the offensive conduct.
- Unlawful sexual harassment may occur without economic injury to or discharge of the victim.
- The harasser's conduct must be unwelcome."

Prevention is the best way to eliminate sexual harassment in the workplace. Employers are encouraged to prevent sexual harassment from occurring in their workplaces by clearly communicating to employees that sexual harassment will not be tolerated. They can do so by disseminating a policy statement that defines and gives examples of sexual harassment, providing training to their employees to help them both identify and avoid sexual harassment, establishing an effective complaint or grievance process, and taking immediate and appropriate action when an employee complains.

If you perceive that you are the target of sexual harassment in the workplace, there are two main communication strategies to use. First, you should begin by informing the harasser directly that his or her conduct is unwelcome and must stop. At the first instance of harassment, you should privately create a written document of the incident and of your communication exchange, which you date, sign, and keep for possible future use. Second, you must decide whether to use the employer complaint mechanism or grievance system available to you. If you perceive the first instance of sexual harassment to be extremely offensive or serious, make a formal complaint. On the other hand, if you consider the first instance of harassment to be only mildly offensive, you may refrain from making a formal complaint, trusting that the behavior will not continue. If the offensive behavior does continue after you have communicated to the harasser that his or her conduct is unwelcome, you should inform the harasser of your intention to file a formal complaint and then follow through using the appropriate channels. Again, it is important to keep an objective written record of all communications with the harasser and with workplace authorities handling the complaint. This written record of communications will prove invaluable in the event of a formal investigation, which may take place long after the harassing episodes have occurred and memories of specific remarks have faded. Once a formal complaint has been made at work, it is the responsibility of the organization to investigate and provide appropriate remedies.

▷ Organizational Romance

Organizational romance is sexual or romantic involvement between people who work for the same organization. Since co-workers have much in common and are in frequent contact, it is no surprise that some become attracted to each other. In addition, employees who spend long hours at work may have little free time in which to meet partners elsewhere. The issue of organizational romance is a controversial one, however. Some people believe in separating workplace from personal relationships completely, while others see the workplace as a good source for developing social and romantic relationships. Most organizations allow co-workers to date but forbid romantic relationships between supervisors and their subordinates because of the inherent conflict of interest in such relationships (Berryman-Fink, 1997).

The factors to consider when deciding whether to date a work colleague include the company policies on romantic relationships, potential reactions from co-workers and managers, the effects interoffice dating may have on your career, and the possibility that the relationship could end badly, making it difficult for both former partners to work together. Of these factors, workplace employees who agree that they would like to be romantically involved should be the most careful about reviewing and following their workplace policy about organizational romance. If the policy allows co-workers to date, then the partners should agree upon standards for appropriate verbal and nonverbal communication with each other while they are at work and should continue to self-monitor their communications to make sure that they exhibit professional behavior in the workplace at all times.

◐ Summary

At work we use our interpersonal skills to get a job, to relate to managers and co-workers, to participate in and lead teams, and to interact with a diverse workforce.

Before you are interviewed for a job, you need to take the time to learn about the company and prepare an appropriate résumé and cover letter designed to motivate an employer to want to speak with you. When you get an interview, you should prepare for the interview by doing your homework, preparing a list of questions about the organization and the job, rehearsing for the interview, dressing appropriately, planning to arrive on time, and bringing supplies. During the interview, you need to use

Organizational romance—sexual or romantic involvement between people who work for the same organization.

OBSERVE AND ANALYZE ◗

Diverse Workplaces

Interview someone who has worked at an organization for at least one year. Ask him or her about diversity issues at his or her workplace, including culture-based work styles, intergenerational communication, sexual harassment, and organizational romance. Does the workplace tend to be results-oriented or relationship-oriented, sequential or holistic in its approach to task completion? How are people who differ from the norm treated? What types of intergenerational misunderstandings occur in the workplace? How are these misunderstandings handled? Does the workplace have strategies in place for preventing and reporting sexual harassment? What is the workplace policy on organizational romance?

active listening, think before answering, be enthusiastic, ask questions, and avoid discussing salary and benefits. After the interview, write a thank-you note, self-assess your performance, and contact the interviewer for feedback if you don't get the job.

The majority of work relationships occur between managers and employees and among co-workers. To establish effective manager-employee relationships, managers need to instruct employees, provide them with useful feedback, and influence them to accomplish their tasks. For their part, employees need to do more than is expected of them by assessing their skills and knowledge, volunteering to use their skills and knowledge on the job, and continuing to develop the relationship to the point of mutual trust. Co-worker relationships are also important and are enhanced by interpersonal communication skills like turn-taking, listening, collaboration, empathizing, and supporting.

To function well on a work team, you should know the characteristics of an effective work team (clear group goal, clear individual member roles, regular feedback about individual and group performance, combination of expertise and people skills in team members, commitment to the team and its success, collaborative climate, standards of excellence, and strong leadership). You also need to perform both task roles (initiator, information or opinion giver, information or opinion seeker, analyzer, and orienter) and maintenance roles (gatekeeper, encourager, harmonizer). In addition, you need to be competent utilizing workplace communication technologies, possess the skills needed for leading team meetings, and be an active meeting participant.

To communicate effectively in a diverse workplace, it is vital to understand the complex issues of culture-based work styles, intergenerational differences, sexual harassment, and organizational romance.

A QUESTION OF ETHICS ▽ What Would You Do?

After three years of working at Everyday Products as a clerk, Mark has decided to look for another job. As he thought about preparing his résumé the other day, Mark was struck by how little experience he had for the kind of job he wanted. When he talked with Ken about this, Ken said, "Exactly what have you been doing at Everyday?"

"Well, for the most part I've been helping others look for information—I've also done some editing of reports."

"Hmm," Ken thought for a while. "Why not re-title your job as editorial assistant? It's more descriptive."

"But my official title is clerk."

"Sure, but it doesn't really describe what you do. This way you show major editorial experience. Don't worry, everybody makes these kinds of changes—you're not really lying."

"Yeah, I see what you mean. Good idea!"

1. Is it interpersonally ethical for Mark to follow Ken's advice? Why?
2. How should we deal with statements like, "Everybody does it"?

◒ Chapter Resources

Communication Improvement Plan:
Workplace Communication ▼ Find more on the web @ www.oup.com/us/interact12

Would you like to improve your use of the following skills discussed in this chapter?

- Task roles in decision making
- Maintenance roles in decision making

Pick a skill, and write a communication improvement plan. You can find a communication improvement plan worksheet on our website at www.oup.com/us/interact12.

Key Words ▼

Résumé, *p. 392*

Cover letter, *p. 392*

Interview, *p. 396*

Team, *p. 403*

Task roles, *p. 406*

Maintenance roles, *p. 406*

Results-oriented culture, *p. 414*

Relationship-oriented culture, *p. 414*

Sequential task completion culture, *p. 415*

Holistic task completion culture, *p. 415*

Sexual harassment, *p. 419*

Organizational romance, *p. 421*

Skill Practice ▼ Find more on the web @ www.oup.com/us/interact12

Skill Practice exercises challenge you to master the material you have read in this chapter. For additional Skill Practice activities, visit our website at www.oup.com/us/interact12.

Preparing a Cover Letter and a Résumé

Prepare a cover letter and a résumé that reflect your current experience and expertise. What is missing on your résumé? Are there some experiences, skills, or accomplishments that would make you more competitive? Develop a plan to gain these experiences, skills, or accomplishments.

Inter-Act with Media ▼ Find more on the web @ www.oup.com/us/interact12

Television

Ace of Cakes (2008). Duff Goldman.

Brief Summary: According to the Charm City Cakes Web site, "We only have one rule at Charm City Cakes, and that is whatever we do, we must have fun! Charm City Cakes is a very relaxed, creative environment—and that spirit is reflected in every cake we bake." Viewers can watch baker Duff Goldman and his congenial staff in action on Food Network. Although Duff admits in the show's opener that he hired his talented friends, he maintains a well-organized, openly communicative, professional environment. Charm City Cakes creates any custom cake a client can imagine, including a model of Wrigley Field, Chinese takeout, a Candyland game board, and a Harley motorcycle. To navigate the immense number of orders, Duff and his team meet weekly to review the orders, decide who will work on what cakes based on individual talents, and examine deadlines. The team maintains open communication, asking for assistance if stuck on a particular cake's structure or design and rallying around each other to ensure completion of orders. Viewers identify a mutual respect among Duff and his colleagues. Duff offers consistent praise and even makes ice cream sundaes for his staff. In turn, his staff works tirelessly, often until all hours of the night, when necessary. *Ace of Cakes* exemplifies a work team that has clear group goals, consistent feedback, commitment, standards of excellence, and a collaborative climate of open communication.

IPC Concepts: Communicating in managerial and co-worker relationships, communicating on a work team, characteristics of effective work teams, communicating to make team decisions.

Cinema
Office Space (1999). Mike Judge (director). Ron Livingston, Stephen Root, Gary Cole, Jennifer Aniston.

Brief Summary: Bored Peter Gibbons (Livingston) works in cubicle-land at "Initech Corporation," which runs ineffectively with too many middle managers and inefficient paper trails. Meetings occur with employees standing around the cubicles and the boss, Bill Lumbergh (Cole), linearly communicating happenings or new procedures to them. No interactivity occurs around decision making, nor is communication invited. In one meeting, Lumbergh announces the hiring of an efficiency expert. The message about the consultant's role is vague, which incites nervousness about downsizing and firings from employees—all except for Peter, who has already checked out. When the consultants interview Peter about his job, his lack of commitment to his role is clear in both his verbal and nonverbal communication. Slouched in a chair and dressed in jeans, he tells the consultants he has eight bosses, feels unmotivated to perform, and is unrooted in his role in the company. Essentially, he works just enough to avoid being hassled. The management style and lack of collaborative environment at Initech inevitably cause stagnation, which undoubtedly aligns with dysfunctional communication practices and weak leadership.

IPC Concepts: Leading team meetings, clear group goals, clear member roles, effective work teams, communicating to make team decisions.

What's on the Web
Find links and additional material, including self-quizzes, on the companion website at www.oup.com/us/interact12.

Glossary

Accommodating—resolving a conflict by satisfying the other person's needs or accepting the other person's ideas while neglecting one's own needs or ideas.

Acoustic space—area over which one's voice or music can be heard.

Acquaintances—people we know by name and talk with when the opportunity arises, but with whom our interactions are limited.

Adaptors—gestures that are unconscious and respond to a physical need.

Advice-giving—presenting relevant suggestions and proposals that a person could use to satisfactorily resolve a situation.

Affection need—need to express and to receive love.

Aggressive behavior—behavior in which one states opinions or shares feelings too strongly, in a manner that shows little regard for the situation or for the feelings, needs, or rights of others.

Altruism—display of genuine and unselfish concern for the welfare of others.

Appreciative listening—listening that focuses on the enjoyment of what is said.

Appropriateness—being polite and following situational rules of conversation.

Artifacts—possessions we use to decorate our territory and communicate about our space.

Ascribing motives—behavior in which one assumes that one knows what another person is thinking or why that person is behaving in a certain way.

Assertiveness—act of sending messages that declare personal preferences and defend personal rights while at the same time respecting the preferences and rights of others.

Asynchronous communication—delayed communication that occurs through an electronically mediated system.

Attending—the process of willfully striving to perceive selected sounds that are being heard.

Authenticity—communicating information and feelings that are relevant and legitimate to the subject at hand directly, honestly, and straightforwardly.

Autonomy—the desire to act and make decisions independent of one's partner or one's relationship.

Back-channel cues—verbal and nonverbal signals demonstrating listener response to the speaker.

Badgering—light teasing, taunting, and mocking behavior.

Behavioral flexibility—the ability to analyze a communication situation and adapt your use of various communication skills to fit the situation.

Body language—nonverbal communication through body motions.

Body orientation—posture in relation to another person.

Casual social conversations—interactions between people whose purpose is to enhance or maintain a relationship through spontaneous exchanges about general topics.

Channels—the sensory routes by which messages travel.

Chronemics—study of the way the perception of time differs by individual and by culture.

Claims—simple statements of belief or opinion.

Clarifying question—response designed to get further information or to remove uncertainty from information already received.

Clarifying supportive intentions—openly stating that one's goal in a supportive interaction is to help the person in need of support.

Closedness—the desire to maintain privacy.

Close friends or intimates—those few people with whom we share a high degree of commitment, trust, interdependence, disclosure, and affection.

Co-cultures—groups of people living within a dominant culture who are clearly different from the dominant culture.

Codeswitching—the use of two languages or linguistic styles simultaneously or interchangeably.

Coercive power—potential to influence based on the ability to physically or psychologically hurt another.

Collaborating—resolving a conflict by using problem solving to arrive at a solution that meets the needs and interests of both parties in the conflict.

Collectivist culture—a culture that emphasizes community, collaboration, shared interests, harmony, the public good, and avoiding embarrassment.

Combined paraphrase—paraphrase that conveys one's understanding of both the denotative and emotional meaning behind a speaker's verbal message.

Commitment—choice to obligate oneself and one's resources to an intimate partner.

Communal relationships—relationships in which we allow the costs to exceed the rewards and yet still consider the relationships to be satisfactory.

Communication accommodation theory—theory explaining how people adjust their language patterns to accommodate their partners during communication.

Communication competence—the impression that communicative behavior is both effective and appropriate in a given relationship.

Communication privacy management (CPM) theory—theory that provides a framework for understanding the decision-making processes people use to manage disclosure and privacy.

Comparison level of alternatives—other choices a person perceives as being available that affect the decision of whether to continue in a relationship.

Competence—perception that the speaker is well qualified to provide accurate and reliable information.

Complementary exchange—communication that reflects differences in power between the people involved.

Compliance-gaining strategies—simple verbal arguments designed to get people to act in a way they are not naturally inclined to act, which draw heavily on one component of persuasion.

Comprehensive listening—listening that focuses on learning and remembering information.

Compromising—resolving a conflict by mutually agreeing with one's partner to partially satisfy each other's needs or interests.

Co-narration—two people finishing each other's sentences in a conversation because they know each other's style of conversation very well.

Concrete words—words that help clear up ambiguity by appealing to our senses.

Confirmation—expressing a warm affirmation of others as unique persons without necessarily approving of their behaviors or views.

Conformity orientation—degree to which families create a climate that stresses similarity of attitudes, values, and beliefs.

Connection—the desire to link one's actions and decisions with another person.

Connotation—the feelings or evaluations we personally associate with a word.

Constructive criticism—skill of diplomatically describing the specific negative behaviors or actions of another and the effects those behaviors/actions have on others.

Content paraphrase—paraphrase that conveys one's understanding of the denotative meaning of a verbal message.

Context—the setting in which a communication encounter occurs, including what precedes and follows what is said.

Control need—need to influence the events and people around us.

Convergence—adapting to the language style of our partner.

Conversation—an interactive, locally managed, sequentially organized, and extemporaneous interchange of thoughts and feelings between two or more people.

Conversational audience—intended or unintended participants in a conversation.

Conversational coherence—the extent to which the comments made by one person relate to those made previously by others earlier in a conversation.

Conversation orientation—degree to which families create a climate of open communication and exchange of ideas.

Cooperative principle—principle stating that contributions to a conversation should be cooperative—in line with the shared purpose of the conversation.

Coordinated management of meaning—theory explaining how people come to agree on the rules of meaning in an interaction.

Costs—outcomes that a person does not wish to occur.

Counterblaming—behavior in which one moves the focus of an argument away from oneself by blaming the other person.

Cover letter—short, well-written letter expressing your interest in a particular position.

Covert intimacy—delivering messages signaling closeness, trust, and equality by using mild insults, competition, or put-downs.

Credibility—extent to which the target believes in the speaker's expertise, trustworthiness, and likability.

Critical-evaluative listening— listening that focuses on being able to judge or evaluate the information heard.

Critically evaluating—process of interpreting what you have understood to determine how truthful, authentic, or believable you judge the meaning to be.

Cultural context—the set of beliefs, values, and attitudes that belong to a specific culture and are used by each participant in an interpersonal encounter.

Cultural identity—a sense of self that people form based on the cultural groups with which they most closely align themselves.

Culture—the system of beliefs, values, and attitudes shared by a particular segment of the population.

Culture shock—the psychological discomfort of adjusting to a new cultural situation.

Cyber stalking—use of information and communication technology, particularly the Internet, to harass others.

Dating information—information about time or time period used in communication to improve clarity.

Decoding—the process of interpreting messages that we receive from others.

Demand-withdrawal—pattern of behavior in which one partner consistently demands while the other consistently withdraws.

Denotation—the direct, explicit meaning of a word found in a dictionary.

Describing behavior—skill of accurately recounting the specific behaviors of others without drawing conclusions about those behaviors.

Describing feelings—skill of explaining emotions one feels in a precise and unemotional manner.

Direct-request strategy—using influence messages that seek compliance by simply asking the target to comply.

Disclosure—revealing confidential information.

Disclosure-privacy dialectic—tension between sharing personal information and keeping personal information confidential; also called the openness and closedness dialectic.

Discrimination—negative actions toward people based on the groups of which they are members.

Discriminative listening—listening that focuses on gaining an accurate understanding of the message.

Displaying feelings—skill of accurately showing emotions through facial expressions, body language, or paralanguage.

Dispositional attribution—attributing behavior to someone's internal disposition, or personality.

Distributive strategy—using influence messages that evoke negative emotions that can be neutralized by complying with the request.

Divergence—consciously speaking in a language style different from that of our partner.

Diversity—the variations between and among people.

Dominant culture—a culture within a society whose attitudes, values, beliefs, and customs hold the majority opinion.

Efficiency—being direct in the interest of achieving conversational goals in a short amount of time.

Egocentricity—selfish interest in one's own needs to the exclusion of everything else.

Ego conflict—conflict that results when both parties in a disagreement insist on being the "winner" of the argument.

Emblems—gestures that can substitute completely for words.

Emoticons—typed or graphic symbols that convey emotional aspects of online messages.

Emotional intelligence—the ability to monitor your own and others' emotions and to use this information to guide your communication.

Empathic listening—listening that focuses on understanding the feelings of others.

Empathic responsiveness— experiencing an emotional response parallel to another person's actual or anticipated display of emotion.

Empathizing—cognitive process of identifying with or vicariously experiencing the feelings, thoughts, or attitudes of others.

Empathy—the ethical principle of understanding the feelings of others; demonstrating an understanding of another person's point of view without giving up one's own position or sense of self.

Empathy-based strategy—using influence messages that seek compliance by causing the other to emotionally identify with your situation.

Encoding—the process of forming messages by putting our thoughts and feelings into words and nonverbal cues.

Equality—treating conversational partners as peers, regardless of the status differences that separate them from other participants.

Ethics—a set of moral principles that may be held by a society, a group, or an individual.

Ethnicity—classification of people based on shared national characteristics such as country of birth, geographic origin, language, religion, ancestral customs, and tradition.

Ethnocentrism—the belief that one's own culture is superior to others.

Exchange strategy—using influence messages that seek compliance by offering the target something he or she values if he or she complies with what is being requested.

Exchange theory—theory that proposes that relationships can be understood in terms of the exchange of rewards and costs that takes place during interactions.

Expectations—those things that we notice because we are habituated to noticing them.

Expert power—potential to influence others based on the real or perceived command of a subject area with which others are less familiar but have a need to know.

External noises—sights, sounds, and other stimuli that draw people's attention away from intended meaning.

Eye contact—how and how much we look at the people with whom we are communicating.

Face-maintenance strategy—using influence messages that seek compliance through indirection as a means of maintaining face for the influencer, the target, or both people.

Face-saving—helping others to preserve their self-image or self-respect.

Face-threatening act (FTA)—statement of support that a person in need may interpret as a threat to his or her public self-image.

Facial expression—arrangement of facial muscles to communicate emotional states or reactions to messages.

Fact conflict—conflict that is caused by a dispute over the truth or accuracy of a piece of information.

Facts—statements whose accuracy can be verified or proven.

Fairness—the ethical standard of achieving the right balance of interests without regard to one's own feelings and without showing favor to any side in a conflict.

Family—group of intimates who through their communication generates a sense of home and group identity, complete with strong ties of loyalty and emotion, and experiences a history and a future.

Faulty attributions—inaccurate reasons we give for our own and others' behavior.

Feedback—a receiver's response to a message that indicates to the sender whether his or her message was received effectively; providing verbal and physical responses to people and/or their messages.

Feelings paraphrase—paraphrase that conveys one's understanding of the emotional meaning behind a speaker's verbal message.

Feminine culture—a culture in which people regardless of sex are expected to assume a variety of roles based on the circumstances and their own choices.

Filtering messages—perceptional distortions of messages we receive that reinforce what we already think.

Flaming—hostile interactions between Internet users.

Forced consistency—the inaccurate attempt to make several of our perceptions of another person agree with each other.

Forcing—resolving a conflict by satisfying one's own needs or advancing one's own ideas with no concern for the needs or ideas of the other person or for the relationship.

Formality—degree to which a conversation must follow rules and procedures.

Framing information—providing support by offering information, observations, and opinions that enable the receiver to better understand or see his or her situation in a different light.

Friends—people with whom we have voluntarily negotiated more personal relationships.

Friendship competencies—the communication skills people use to make and keep friends.

Generic language—language that may apply only to one sex, race, or other group that is used in a way that assumes it represents everyone.

Gesture—movement of hands, arms, and fingers to describe or to emphasize.

Good relationship—one in which the interactions are satisfying to and healthy for those involved.

Gossip—message exchanges about other people who are not present in a conversation.

Grammar—the set of rules by which words are put together to structure messages.

Halo effect—inaccurately perceiving that a person has a whole set of related personality traits when only one trait has actually been observed.

High-context culture—culture in which messages are indirect, general, and ambiguous.

High power-distance culture—culture in which power is distributed unequally.

High uncertainty-avoidance culture—a culture characterized as having a low tolerance for and a high need to control unpredictable people, relationships, or events.

Historical context—the background provided by previous communication episodes between the participants that influences understandings in the current encounter.

Holistic task completion culture—culture in which members prefer to work on an entire task at once.

Impersonal relationship—a relationship in which a person relates to another person merely because the other fills a role or satisfies an immediate need.

Implicit personality theories—inaccurate perceptions of others based on the association of physical or other characteristics with personality traits.

Impression management—the process of consciously trying to influence what others are thinking about you during an interaction.

Inclusion need—need to be in the company of other people.

Incongruence—situation in which there is a gap between self-perception and reality.

Independent couples—couples who share an ideology whose values differ from traditional ones, are interdependent, and engage in conflict.

Indexing generalizations—the mental and verbal practice of acknowledging individual differences when voicing generalizations.

Individualism-collectivism—the extent to which people in a culture are integrated into groups.

Individualistic culture—a culture that emphasizes personal rights and responsibilities, privacy, voicing one's opinion, freedom, innovation, and self-expression.

Inferences—claims or assertions based on the fact presented.

Informal space—space around the place a person occupies at a given moment.

Information and idea exchanges—message exchanges that focus on sharing important facts, opinions, and beliefs in a conversation.

Information co-ownership—mutual protection of private information.

Integrity—the ethical standard that necessitates maintaining consistency in belief and action (keeping promises).

Intercultural communication—interactions that occur between people whose cultures are so different that the communication between them is altered.

Intercultural empathy—imaginatively placing yourself in another person's cultural world to attempt to experience what he or she is experiencing.

Interests—those things that prompt our curiosity but aren't essential to sustain us biologically or psychologically.

Internal noises—thoughts and feelings that interfere with meaning.

Interpersonal communication—the process through which people create and manage their relationships, exercising mutual responsibility in creating meaning.

Interpersonal conflict—disagreement between two interdependent people who perceive that they have incompatible goals.

Interpersonal influence—practice of preserving or changing the attitudes or behaviors of others.

Interpersonal needs theory—theory that proposes that whether a relationship is started, developed, or maintained depends on how well each person meets the interpersonal needs of the other.

Interpersonal relationship—a series of interactions between two individuals known to each other.

Interview—structured conversation with the goal of exchanging information needed for decision making.

Intimate relationship—close and caring personal relationship in which both partners have detailed knowledge of each other's history, personality, and aspirations as a result of observations and mutual disclosures that have occurred over an extended period of time.

Intonation—variety, melody, or inflection of a person's voice.

Jargon—technical terminology whose meaning is understood only by a select group based on their shared activities or interests.

Jealousy—intense feeling of suspicion that one's partner values, likes, or loves someone else more than oneself.

Johari window—a visual framework for understanding the extent of and connection between self-disclosure and feedback in a relationship.

Kinesics—the study of body language.

Language—a system of words, sounds, and gestures common to a group of people used to communicate messages.

Legitimate power—potential to influence granted to a person who occupies a legal position of authority.

Likability—perception that the speaker is congenial, friendly, and warm.

Linguistic sensitivity—choosing to use language that respects others and avoiding language that others perceive as offensive.

Listening—the process of receiving, constructing meaning from, and responding to spoken and/or nonverbal messages.

Low-context culture—culture in which messages are expected to be direct, specific, and detailed.

Low power-distance culture—culture in which power is distributed equally.

Low uncertainty-avoidance culture—a culture characterized as being accepting and having a low need to control unpredictable people, relationships, or events.

Maintenance roles—communication behaviors that improve interaction among team members.

Managing privacy—skill of making a conscious decision to withhold information or feelings from others.

Manner maxim—the requirement to cooperate by being specific and organized when communicating one's thoughts in a conversation.

Marking—the unnecessary addition of sex, race, age, or other designations in addition to a general description of someone.

Masculine culture—a culture in which people are expected to adhere to traditional sex roles.

Masculinity-femininity—the extent to which notions of "maleness" and "femaleness" are valued in a culture.

Maxims—rules of conduct that cooperative conversational partners follow.

Meaning—the significance of what is said and how what is said is interpreted.

Mediator—a neutral and impartial guide, structuring an interaction that enables the conflicting parties to find a mutually acceptable solution to their problems.

Messages—a person's verbal statements and nonverbal behaviors that transmit meaning during communication.

Metaconflict—conflict that is caused by disagreements about the process of communication itself during an argument.

Mnemonic device—any artificial technique used as a memory aid.

Monochronic—linear and sequential perception of time.

Moral dilemma—a situation in which none of the choices of action are satisfactory.

Morality maxim—the requirement to cooperate by meeting moral/ethical expectations in a conversation.

Needs—those things we consciously or unconsciously feel we require to sustain us biologically or psychologically.

Negative facework—providing messages that offer information, opinions, or advice to protect a person's freedom and privacy.

Netspeak—language in which the rules of style, grammar, spelling, and abbreviations are varied in technology-moderated communication.

Neutralization—the strategy of compromising between the desires of one person and the desires of the other.

Noise—any stimulus that interferes with shared meaning.

Nonparallel language—language in which unnecessary asides are added to a sentence to point out someone's sex, race, or other characteristics.

Nonverbal communication behavior—bodily actions, use of vocal qualities, and other behaviors that typically accompany a verbal message.

Novelty—the desire for originality, freshness, and uniqueness in a partner's behavior or in one's relationship.

Olfactory communication—nonverbal communication through smells and scents.

Openness—the desire to share intimate ideas and feelings with one's partner and in one's relationship.

Organizational romance—sexual or romantic involvement between people who work for the same organization.

Other-benefit strategy—using influence messages that seek compliance by identifying how complying will benefit the other person.

Other-centered messages—messages that focus on the needs of the person in need of support through active listening, expressions of compassion and understanding, and talk encouragement.

Owning feelings or opinions—skill of making "I" statements rather than generalizations to identify yourself as the source of a particular idea or feeling.

Paralanguage—communication through nonverbal sounds.

Paraphrase—attempt to verify one's understanding of a message by putting it in one's own words and sharing it with the speaker.

Participants—the people who communicate, assuming the roles of senders and receivers during the communication.

Passive-aggressive behavior—behavior in which one exhibits aggressive behavior, but in a passive manner.

Passive behavior—behavior in which one is reluctant or unable to state opinions or share feelings that are in one's interests to express.

Pattern recognition—the organization of stimuli into easily recognizable patterns, or systems of interrelated parts.

Perception—the process of selectively attending to information that we receive through our senses and assigning meaning to it.

Perception check—sharing your perception of another's behavior to see if your interpretation is accurate.

Personal feedback—disclosing information about others to them.

Personal relationship—a relationship in which people care about each other, share large amounts of information with each other, and meet each other's interpersonal needs.

Perspective taking—imagining yourself in the place of another person.

Persuasion—art of skillfully and ethically influencing the attitudes or behaviors of others through verbal arguments using reasoning, credibility, and emotional appeals.

Physical context—the place where the participants exchange messages.

Pitch—highness or lowness of a person's vocal tone.

Platonic relationship—intimate relationship in which the partners are not sexually attracted to each other or do not choose to act on their sexual attraction to each other.

Policy conflict—conflict that is caused by a disagreement over a plan or course of action.

Politeness—relating to others in ways that meet their need to be appreciated and protected.

Politeness maxim—the requirement to cooperate by showing respect and courtesy to others during a conversation.

Polychronic—nonlinear and flexible perception of time.

Positive facework—providing messages that affirm a person or a person's actions in a difficult situation to protect his or her respectability and approval.

Possessiveness—desire to control another person to ensure that he or she is one's exclusive partner.

Posture—position and movement of the whole body.

Power—potential that one person has to influence the attitudes, beliefs, and behaviors of others.

Power distance—the amount of difference in power between people, institutions, and organizations in a culture.

Praising—skill of sincerely describing the specific positive behaviors or accomplishments of another and the positive effects those behaviors/accomplishments have on others.

Precise words—words that narrow a larger category to a smaller group within that category.

Predictability—the desire for consistency, reliability, and dependability.

Prejudice—inaccurate perceptions of people based simply on the groups of which they are members.

Prejudicial language—language that blatantly denigrates, stigmatizes, or marginalizes others based on their race, sex, ethnicity, sexual orientation, religion, age, ability, or other factors.

Presentness—willingness to become fully involved with another person by taking time, avoiding distraction, being responsive, and risking attachment.

Primacy effect—tendency to remember information that we heard first over what we heard in the middle.

Privacy—withholding confidential or secret information to enhance autonomy and/or minimize vulnerability.

Probing questions—questions by which we search for more information or try to resolve perceived inconsistencies in a message.

Problem consideration conversations—interactions between people in which the purpose for at least one of the participants is to elicit cooperation in solving a problem or meeting a specific goal.

Proxemics—the study of informal space.

Pseudoconflict—conflict that is caused by perceptual difference between partners and is easily resolved.

Psychological context—the moods and feelings each person brings to an interpersonal encounter.

Quality—sound of a person's voice.

Quality maxim—the requirement to cooperate by providing information that is truthful in a conversation.

Quantity maxim—the requirement to cooperate by providing a sufficient or necessary amount of information to satisfy the informational needs of others in a conversation.

Racism, ethnocentrism, sexism, heterosexism, ageism, able-ism—various forms of prejudice, in which members of one group believe that the behaviors or characteristics of their group are inherently superior to those of another group.

Rate—speed at which a person speaks.

Reasons—statements that provide valid explanations or justifications for a belief or action.

Receiver—the participant in an interaction who assumes the role of listening, interpreting, and reacting to the messages of others.

Recency effect—tendency to remember information that we heard last over what we heard in the middle.

Reciprocity—mutual exchange of information.

Referent power—potential to influence based on having the respect and admiration of others.

Reframing—the strategy of changing perceptions about the level of dialectical tensions.

Relational dialectics—the conflicting pulls that exist in relationships as well as within each of the individuals in a relationship.

Relational uncertainty—feeling of doubt about the nature of a relationship.

Relationship—a set of expectations two people have for their behavior based on the pattern of interaction between them.

Relationship-oriented culture—culture that prioritizes building

relationships at work over the results of work.

Relationship transformation—continuing to interact and influence a partner through a different type of relationship after one type of relationship has ended.

Relevancy maxim—the requirement to cooperate by providing information that is related to the topic currently being discussed in a conversation.

Religion—a system of beliefs, rituals, and ethics shared by a group and based on a common perception of the sacred or holy.

Remembering—process of moving information from short-term memory to long-term memory.

Repetition—saying something two, three, or even four times.

Respect—the ethical standard of showing regard or consideration for a person, that person's point of view, and that person's rights.

Responding—process of reacting to what has been heard while listening and after listening.

Responsibility—the ethical standard of being accountable for one's actions.

Results-oriented culture—culture that prioritizes the results of work over building relationships at work.

Résumé—summary sheet outlining your work history, educational background, skills, and accomplishments.

Reward power—potential to influence based on the ability to provide monetary, physical, or psychological benefits that others desire.

Rewards—outcomes that are valued by a person.

Ritualized touch—touch that is scripted rather than spontaneous.

Role taking—the process of meeting the perceived demands of the communication situation by adopting a role comprised of an expected or appropriate set of behaviors.

Romantic relationship—intimate relationship in which the partners do act on their sexual attraction to each other.

Rules—unwritten prescriptions that indicate what behavior is required, preferred, or prohibited in certain contexts.

Sapir-Whorf hypothesis—a theory stating that language shapes how people think and perceive.

Scriptedness—the use of routine conversational phrases from past encounters applied appropriately to a new situation.

Selective perception—the tendency to inaccurately pay attention only to what we expect to see or hear and ignore what we don't expect.

Self-concept—our description of our competencies and personality traits.

Self-disclosure—sharing biographical data, personal ideas, and feelings with others.

Self-esteem—our evaluation of our competence and personal worthiness.

Self-fulfilling prophecies—events that happen as the result of being foretold, expected, or talked about.

Self-monitoring—the internal process of being aware of yourself and how you are coming across to others when you communicate with them.

Self-perception—the overall view people have of themselves, of which self-concept and self-esteem are parts.

Self-talk—communicating with yourself through your thoughts.

Semantic noises—distractions aroused by a speaker's symbols that interfere with meaning.

Sender—the participant in an interaction who assumes the role of forming messages and attempting to communicate them to others.

Separate couples—couples who share a traditional ideology but are independent and avoid conflict.

Sequential task completion culture—culture whose members prefer to break larger tasks down into separate parts and complete one part at a time, in order.

Sexual harassment—unwanted verbal or physical sexual behavior that interferes with work performance.

Simplification—the organization of stimuli into easily recognizable forms.

Situational attribution—attributing behavior to an external situation, outside of a person's control.

Skills—goal-oriented actions or action sequences we can master and repeat in appropriate situations.

Slang—informal vocabulary developed and used by particular groups in society.

Small talk—message exchanges on inconsequential topics that meet the social needs of participants with low amounts of risk.

Social class—level in the power hierarchy of a society whose membership is based on income, education, occupation, and social habits.

Social context—the type of relationship that may already exist between the participants.

Social penetration theory—theory holding that over time relationships move from lesser to greater intimacy based on the increasing number of topics that partners discuss and the degree of personal information disclosed on those topics.

Social perception—the set of processes by which people perceive themselves and others.

Spatial usage—nonverbal communication through the use of the space and objects around us.

Specific language—language in which concrete and precise words, as well as details and examples, are used to clear up ambiguity.

Speech community—a group of people who share a common language.

Spiraling negativity—pattern of behavior in which both partners in an argument trade increasingly negative and/or hostile remarks.

Spontaneous touch—touch that is automatic and subconscious.

Stereotyping—assigning attributions to people that ignore individual differences and assume everyone in a cultural group is the same.

Strategic ambiguity—being purposefully vague or offering a response that is not precisely on topic when communicating.

Stubbornness—behavior that is characterized by unyieldingness and inflexibility.

Supporting—helping people feel better about themselves and their behaviors.

Supporting-evidence strategy—using influence messages that seek compliance by offering good reasons.

Supporting response—statement whose goal is to validate, show

approval, encourage, soothe, console, cheer up, or bolster confidence.

Supportive interaction—conversation or series of conversations in which support is provided.

Supportiveness—encouraging the other participants in a conversation to communicate by praising their worthwhile efforts.

Symbolic interactionism—theory stating that the meaning of words results from social interaction.

Symbols—words, sounds, and actions that represent specific ideas and feelings and are used to convey meaning.

Symmetrical exchange—a communication that reflects similarity in power between the people involved.

Sympathetic responsiveness—feeling concern, compassion, or sorrow for another person because he or she is in a distressing situation.

Synchronous communication—real-time communication that occurs through an electronically mediated system.

Talk time—the share of time participants each have in a conversation.

Task-related touch—touch used to perform a certain unemotional function.

Task roles—communication behaviors that help a team focus on issues under discussion.

Team—formally established group with a clear purpose and appropriate structure in which members know each other's roles and work together to achieve goals.

Temporal selection—the strategy of choosing one side of a dialectical contradiction while ignoring the other for a period of time.

Territory—space over which we claim ownership.

Theory of muted groups—theory stating that whoever is dominant in a social hierarchy has the power to shape everyone's perceptions via language.

Time orientation—time period on which people focus their attention.

Time perception—how people view and structure their time.

Topical segmentation—the strategy of choosing certain areas in which to satisfy one desire while choosing other areas to satisfy the opposite desire.

Topic change—method by which people introduce new topics into a conversation.

Touch—formally known as haptics, or putting part of the body in contact with something.

Traditional couples—couples who maintain a traditional ideology about

their long-term relationships, are interdependent, and engage in conflict.

Trust—confidence that your partner will not intentionally harm you.

Trustworthiness—perception that the speaker is dependable, honest, and acting for the good of others.

Truthfulness and honesty—ethical standards that compel us to refrain from lying, misleading, or deceiving.

Turning point—any event or occurrence that leads to a major change in a relationship.

Turn-taking—alternating between speaking and listening in a conversation.

Uncertainty avoidance—the extent to which the people in a culture avoid unpredictability regarding people, relationships, and events.

Uncertainty reduction theory—a theory that explains the ways in which individuals monitor their social environments in order to know more about themselves and others.

Understanding—the process of accurately decoding a message so that you share its meaning with the speaker.

Unnecessary association—emphasizing a person's association with another person when the second person is not relevant to the discussion.

Value conflict—conflict that is caused by disagreements about deep-seated moral beliefs.

Vocal interferences—extraneous sounds or words that interrupt fluent speech.

Volume—loudness or softness of a person's vocal tone.

Withdrawing—resolving a conflict by physically or psychologically removing oneself from the conflict.

Words—arbitrarily chosen symbols used by a speech community to name things.

References

Chapter 1

Andersen, P. (2000). Cues of culture: The basis of intercultural differences in nonverbal communication. In L. A. Samovar & R. E. Porter (Eds.), *Intercultural Communication: A Reader* (9th ed., pp. 258–266). Belmont, Calif.: Wadsworth.

Berger, C. R. (2002). Goals and knowledge structure in social interaction. In M. L. Knapp & J. A. Daly (Eds.), *Handbook of Interpersonal Communication* (pp. 181–212). Thousand Oaks, Calif.: Sage.

Gilligan, C. (1982). *In a Different Voice: Psychological Theory and Women's Development.* Cambridge, Mass.: Harvard University Press.

Johannesen, R. L, Valde, K. S., & Whedbee, K. E., (2008). *Ethics in Human Communication* (6th ed.). Long Grove, Ill.: Waveland Press.

Madrid, A. (1994). Diversity and its discontents. In L. A. Samovar & R. E. Porter (Eds.), *Intercultural Communication: A Reader* (7th ed., pp. 127–131). Belmont, Calif: Wadsworth.

Population Reference Bureau. (2006). www.prb.org/articles/2006. Accessed on September 29, 2008.

Salovey, P., & Mayer, J. D. (1990). Emotional intelligence. *Imagination, Cognition, and Personality, 9,* 185–211.

Spitzberg, B. H. (2000). A model of intercultural communication competence. In L. A. Samovar & R. E. Porter (Eds.), *Intercultural Communication: A Reader* (9th ed., pp. 375–387). Belmont, Calif.: Wadsworth.

Spitzberg, B. H., & Duran, R. L. (1995). Toward the development and validation of a measure of cognitive communication competence. *Communication Quarterly, 43,* 259–274.

Terkel, S. N., & Duval, R. S. (Eds.). (1999). *Encyclopedia of Ethics.* New York: Facts on File.

U.S. Census Bureau State and Country Quickfacts. www.quickfacts.census .gov/qfd/states. Accessed November 8, 2008.

Watzlawick, P., Beavin, J. H., & Jackson, D. D. (1967). *Pragmatics of Human Communication.* New York: Norton.

Chapter 2

Aron, A., Mashek, D. J., & Aron, E. N. (2004). Closeness as including other in the self. In D. J. Mashek & A. Aron (Eds.), *Handbook of Closeness and Intimacy* (pp. 27–41). Mahwah, N.J.: Erlbaum.

Baron, R. A., & Byrne, D. (2003). *Social Psychology* (10th ed.). Boston: Allyn & Bacon.

Berger, C. R., & Bradac, J. J. (1982). *Language and Social Knowledge: Uncertainty in Interpersonal Relations.* London: Arnold.

Campbell, J. D. (1990). Self-esteem and clarity of the self-concept. *Journal of Personality and Social Psychology, 59,* 538.

Centi, P. J. (1981). *Up with the Positive: Out with the Negative.* Englewood Cliffs, N.J.: Prentice Hall.

Chen, G. M., & Starosta, W. J. (1998). *Foundations of Intercultural Communication.* Boston: Allyn & Bacon.

Demo, D. H. (1987). Family relations and the self-esteem of adolescents and their parents. *Journal of Marriage and the Family, 49,* 705–715.

Downey, G., Freitas, A. L., Michaelis, B., & Khouri, H. (2004). The self-fulfilling prophecy in close relationships: Rejection sensitivity and rejection by romantic partners. In H. T. Reis & C. E. Rusbult (Eds.), *Close Relationships* (pp. 435–455). New York: Psychology Press.

Engdahl, S. (Ed.). (2007). *Online Social Networking.* New York: Thomson Gale.

Guerrero, L. K., Andersen, P. A., & Afifi, W. A. (2007). *Close Encounters: Communication in Relationships* (2nd ed.). Thousand Oaks, Calif.: Sage.

Hattie, J. (1992). *Self-Concept.* Hillsdale, N.J.: Erlbaum.

Hazen, C., & Shaver, P. R. (2004). Attachment as an organizational framework for research on close relationships. In H. T. Reis & C. E. Rusbult (Eds.), *Close Relationships* (pp. 153–174). New York: Psychology Press.

Hollman, T. D. (1972). Employment interviewers' errors in processing positive and negative information. *Journal of Psychology, 56,* 130–134.

Jones, M. (2002). *Social Psychology of Prejudice.* Upper Saddle River, N.J.: Prentice Hall.

Leary, M. R. (2002). When selves collide: The nature of the self and the dynamics of interpersonal relationships. In A. Tesser, D. A. Stapel, & J. V. Wood (Eds.), *Self and Motivation: Emerging Psychological Perspectives* (pp. 119–145). Washington, D.C.: American Psychological Association.

Littlejohn, S. W., & Foss, K. A. (2005). *Theories of Human Communication* (8th ed.). Belmont, Calif.: Thomson Wadsworth.

Michener, H. A., & DeLamater, J. D. (2004). *Social Psychology* (5th ed.). Belmont, Calif.: Thomson Wadsworth.

Miller, G. R., & Steinberg, M. (1975). *Between People: A New Analysis of Interpersonal Communication.* Chicago: SRA.

Mruk, C. (2006). *Self-Esteem: Research, Theory, and Practice* (3nd ed.). New York: Springer.

Neuliep, J. W., & McCroskey, J. C. (1997). The development of a U.S. and generalized ethnocentrism scale. *Communication Research Reports, 14,* 385–398.

Rayner, S. G. (2001). Aspects of the self as learner: Perception, concept, and esteem. In R. J. Riding & S. G. Rayner (Eds.), *Self Perception: International Perspectives on Individual Differences* (Vol. 2, p. 42). Westport, Conn.: Ablex Publishing.

Sampson, E. E. (1999). *Dealing with Differences: An Introduction to the Social Psychology of Prejudice.* Fort Worth, Tex.: Harcourt Brace.

Shedletsky, L. J., & Aitken, J. E. (2004). *Human Communication on the Internet.* New York: Pearson Education.

Sunnafrank, M., & Ramirez, A. (2004). At first sight: Persistent relational effects of get-acquainted conversations. *Journal of Social and Personal Relationships, 21,* 361–379.

Thurlow, C., Lengel, L., & Tomic, A. (2004). *Computer Mediated Communication: Social Interaction and the Internet.* Thousand Oaks, Calif.: Sage.

Weiten, W. (2002). *Psychology: Themes and Variations* (5th ed.). Belmont, Calif.: Thomson Wadsworth.

Chapter 3

Allen, B. J. (2001). Sapphire and Sappho: Allies in authenticity. In A. Gonzalez, M. Houston, & V. Chen (Eds.), *Our Voices— Essays in Cultural Ethnicity and Communication* (3rd ed., pp. 179–183). Los Angeles: Roxbury.

Aron, A., Aron, E. N., Tudor, M., & Nelson, G. (2004). Close relationships as including other in the self. In H. T. Reis & C. E. Rusbult (Eds.), *Close Relationships* (pp. 365–379). New York: Psychology Press.

Baxter, L. (1982). Strategies for ending relationships: Two studies. *Western Journal of Speech Communication, 46,* 223–241.

Baxter, L. A., & Bullis, C. (1993). Turning points in developing romantic relationships. In S. Petronio, J. K. Alberts, M. L. Hecht, & J. Buley (Eds.), *Contemporary Perspectives on Interpersonal Communication* (pp. 358–374). Chicago: Brown and Benchmark.

Baxter, L. A., & Erbert, L. A. (1999). Perceptions of dialectical contradictions in turning points of development in heterosexual romantic relationships. *Journal of Social and Personal Relationships, 16,* 547–569.

Baxter, L. A., & Montgomery, B. M. (1996). *Relating: Dialogues & Dialectics.* New York: Guilford Press.

Baxter, L. A., & West, L. (2003). Couple perceptions of their similarities and differences: A dialectical perspective. *Journal of Social and Personal Relationships, 20,* 491–514.

Canary, J. C., & Dainton, M. (2002). Preface. In J. C. Canary & M. Dainton (Eds.), *Maintaining Relationships Through Communication: Relational, Contextual and Cultural Variations* (pp. xiii–xv). Mahwah, N.J.: Erlbaum.

Cupach, C. R., & Metts, S. (1986). Accounts of relational dissolution: A comparison of marital and nonmarital relationships. *Communication Monographs, 53,* 319–321.

Duck, S. (1987). How to lose friends without influencing people. In M. E. Roloff & G. R. Miller (Eds.), *Interpersonal Processes: New Directions in Communication Research* (pp. 278–298). Beverly Hills, Calif.: Sage.

Duck, S. (1994) *Meaningful Relationships: Talking, Sense and Relating,* Thousand Oaks: Sage.

Duck, S. (2007). *Human Relationships* (4th ed.). Thousand Oaks, Calif.: Sage.

Duck, S., & Gilmour, R. (Eds.). (1981). *Personal Relationships.* London: Academic Press.

Encarta(r) World English Dictionary [North American Edition] © & (P)2009 Microsoft Corporation.

Knapp, M. L., & Vangelisti, A. L. (2005). *Interpersonal Communication and Human Relationships* (5th ed.). Boston: Allyn & Bacon.

LaFollette, H. (1996). *Personal Relationships: Love, Identity, and Morality.* Cambridge, Mass.: Blackwell.

Littlejohn, S. W., & Foss, K. A. (2008). *Theories of Human Communication* (9th ed.) Belmont, Calif.: Thomson Wadsworth.

Luft, J. (1970). *Group Processes: An Introduction to Group Dynamics.* Palo Alto, Calif.: Mayfield.

McDowell, S. W. (2001). The Development of Online and Offline Romantic Relationships: A Turning Point Study. Unpublished Master's Thesis. University of Washington.

Moore, D. W. (2003, Jan. 3). Family, health most important aspects of life. *Gallup Poll Tuesday Briefing,* pp. 19–20.

Parks, M. R. (2007). *Personal Relationships and Personal Networks.* Mahwah, N.J.: Erlbaum.

Patterson, B. R., Bettini, L., & Nussbaum, J. F. (1993). The meaning of friendship across the life-span: Two studies. *Communication Quarterly, 41,* 145.

Rabby, M., & Walther, J. B. (2003). Computer mediated communication effects in relationship formation and maintenance. In D. J. Canary & M. Dainton (Eds.), *Maintaining Relationships through Communication* (pp. 141–162). Mahwah, N.J.: Erlbaum.

Rubin, R. B., Perse, E. M., & Barbato, C. A. (1988). Conceptualization and measurement of interpersonal communication motives. *Human Communication Research, 14,* 602–628.

Rusbult, C. E., Olsen, N., Davis, J. L., & Hannon, P. A. (2004). In H. T. Reis & C. E. Rusbult (Eds.), *Close Relationships* (pp. 287–304). New York: Psychology Press.

Samter, W. (2003). Friendship interaction skills across the lifespan. In J. O. Greene & B. R. Burleson (Eds.), *Handbook of Communication and Social Interaction Skills* (pp. 637–684). Mahwah, N.J.: Erlbaum.

Schutz, W. (1966). *The Interpersonal Underworld.* Palo Alto, Calif.: Science & Behavior Books.

Shedletsky, L. J., & Aitken, J. E. (2004). *Human Communication on the Internet.* New York: Pearson Education.

Taylor, D. A., & Altman, I. (1987). Communication in interpersonal relationships: Social penetration theory. In M. E. Roloff & G. R. Miller (Eds.), *Interpersonal Processes: New Directions in Communication Research* (pp. 257–277). Beverly Hills, Calif.: Sage.

Thibaut, J. W., & Kelley, H. H. (1986). *The Social Psychology of Groups* (2nd ed.). New Brunswick, N.J.: Transaction Books.

Trenholm, S. (1991). *Human Communication Theory* (2nd ed.). Englewood Cliffs, N.J.: Prentice Hall.

Ward, C. C., & Tracy, T. J. G. (2004). Relation of shyness with aspects of online relationship involvement. *Journal of Social and Personal Relationships, 21,* 611–623.

Walther, J. B. (1996). Computer mediated communication: Impersonal, interpersonal, and hyperpersonal interaction. *Western Journal of Communication, 57,* 381–398.

Wood, J. T. (2000). Dialectical theory. In K. M. Galvin & P. J. Cooper (Eds.), *Making Connections: Readings in Relational Communication* (pp. 132–138). Los Angeles: Roxbury.

Wood, J. T., & Inman, C. C. (1993). In a different mode: Masculine styles of communicating closeness. *Journal of Applied Communication Research, 21,* 279–295.

Chapter 4

Blumer, H. 1986. *Symbolic Interactionism: Perspective and Method.* Berkeley: University of California Press.

Brown, K. M. (2007). *Managing Virtual Teams.* Plano, Tex.: Wordware Publishing.

Burke, K. (1968). *Language as Symbolic Action.* Berkeley: University of California Press.

Chen, G. M., & Starosta, W. J. (1998). *Foundations of Intercultural Communication.* Boston: Allyn & Bacon.

The Columbia Encyclopedia, Sixth Edition. 2008. New York: Columbia University Press.

Giles, H., & Coupland, N. (1991). *Language: Contexts and Consequences.* Pacific Grove, Calif.: Wadsworth.

Gmelch, S. B. (1998). *Gender on Campus: Issues for College Women.* New Brunswick, N.J.: Rutgers University Press.

Griffin, E. A. (1997). Muted groups theory of Cheris Kramarae. In E. A. Griffin, *A First Look at Communication Theory* (pp. 459–473). New York: McGraw-Hill.

Holtgraves, T. (2002). *Language as Social Action: Social Psychology and Language Use.* Mahwah, N.J.: Erlbaum.

Horrigan, J. Mobile Access to Data and Information. Pew Internet and American Life Project. 3/5/08, www.pewinternet.org/PPF/r/244/report_display.asp

Jones, R. 2006. *The Internet Slang Dictionary.* Morrisville, N.C.: Lulu.com.

Larkey, L. K. (1996). Toward a theory of communicative interactions in culturally diverse work groups. *Academy of Management Review, 21,* 463–491.

Leeds-Hurwitz, W. (Ed.). (1995). *Social Approaches to Communication.* New York: Guilford Press.

Littlejohn, S., & Foss, K. A. (2005). *Theories of Human Communication* (8th ed.). Belmont, Calif.: Thomson Wadsworth.

Philipsen, G. (1995). The coordinated management of meaning theory of Pearce, Cronen and associates. In D. P. Cushman & B. Kovacic (Eds.), *Watershed Research Traditions in Human Communication Theory* (pp. 13–43). Albany: State University of New York Press.

Sillars, A. L. (1998). (Mis) Understanding. In B. H. Spitzberg & W. R. Cupach (Eds.), *The Dark Side of Close Relationships* (pp. 73–102). Mahwah, N.J.: Erlbaum.

Stewart, L. P., Cooper, P. J., Stewart, A. D., & Friedley, S. A. (2003). *Communication and Gender* (4th ed.). Boston: Allyn & Bacon.

Tanno, D. V. (2001). Names, narratives, and the evolution of ethnic identity. In A. Gonzalez, M. Houston, & V. Chen (Eds.), *Our Voices—Essays in Cultural Ethnicity and Communication* (3rd ed., pp. 25–28). Los Angeles, Calif.: Roxbury.

Thurlow, C., Lengel, L., & Tomic, A. (2004). *Computer-Mediated Communication: Social Interaction and the Internet.* Thousand Oaks, Calif.: Sage.

Woolard, K. (2004). Codeswitching. In A. Duranti (Ed.), *A Companion to Linguistic Anthropology* (pp. 79–94). Malden, Mass.: Blackwell.

Chapter 5

Axtell, R. E. (1998). *Gestures: The Do's and Taboos of Body Language around the World* (rev. ed.). New York: Wiley.

Burgoon, J. K. (1994). Nonverbal signals. In M. L. Knapp & G. R. Miller (Eds.), *Handbook of Interpersonal Communication* (2nd ed., pp. 229–285). Thousand Oaks, Calif.: Sage.

Burgoon, J. K., Buller, D. B., & Woodall, W. G. (1996). *Nonverbal Communication: The Unspoken Dialogue* (2nd ed.). New York: Harper & Row.

Cegala, D. J., & Sillars, A. L. (1989). Further examination of nonverbal manifestations of interaction involvement. *Communication Reports, 2,* 45.

Chen, G. M., & Starosta, W. J. (1998). *Foundations of Intercultural Communication.* Boston: Allyn & Bacon.

Furlow, F. B. (1996). The smell of love. *Psychology Today, 29* (Mar/Apr), 38–45.

Gudykunst, W. B., & Kim, Y. Y. (1997). *Communicating with Strangers: An Approach to Intercultural Communication* (3rd ed.). Boston: Allyn & Bacon.

Gudykunst, W. B., Ting-Toomey, S., Sudweeks, S., & Stewart, L. P. (1995). *Building Bridges: Interpersonal Skills for a Changing World.* Boston: Houghton Mifflin.

Hall, E. T. (1969). *The Hidden Dimension.* Garden City, N.Y.: Doubleday.

Henley, N. M. (1977). *Body Politics: Power, Sex and Nonverbal Communication.* Englewood Cliffs, N.J.: Prentice Hall.

Johnson, K. R. (2004). Black kinesics: Some non-verbal communication patterns in the black culture. In R. L. Jackson (Ed.), *African-American Communication and Identities* (pp. 39–46). Thousand Oaks, Calif.: Sage.

Kleinman, S. (2007). *Displacing Place: Mobile Communication in the Twenty-First Century.* New York: Peter Lang.

Knapp, M. L., & Hall, J. A. (2006). *Nonverbal Communication in Human Interaction* (6th ed.). Belmont, Calif.: Thomson Wadsworth.

Lozano, E. (2007). The cultural experience of space and body: A reading of Latin American and Anglo American comportment in public. In A. Gonzalez, M. Houston, & V. Chen (Eds.), *Our Voices: Essays in Culture, Ethnicity, and Communication: An Intercultural Anthology,* 4th edition (pp. 274–280). New York: Oxford University Press.

Martin, J. N., & Nakayama, T. K. (2006). *Intercultural Communication in Contexts* (4th ed.). New York: McGraw Hill.

Mehrabian, A. (1972). *Nonverbal Communication.* Chicago: Aldine.

Patterson, M. L. (1994). Strategic functions of nonverbal exchange. In J. A. Daly (Ed.), *Strategic Interpersonal Communication* (pp. 273–293). Hillsdale, N.J.: Erlbaum.

Pearson, J. C., West, R. L., & Turner, L. H. (1995). *Gender and Communication* (3rd ed.). Dubuque, Iowa: Brown & Benchmark.

Samovar, L. A., Porter, R. E., & McDaniel, E. R. (2007). *Communication between Cultures* (6th ed.). Belmont, Calif.: Thomson Wadsworth.

Walther, J. B., & Parks, M. R. (2002). Cues filtered out, cues filtered in: Computer-mediated communication and relationships. In M. C. Knapp & J. A. Daly (Eds.), *Handbook of Interpersonal Communication* (pp. 529–563). Thousand Oaks, Calif.: Sage.

Wood, J. T. (2007). *Gendered Lives: Communication, Gender, and Culture* (7th ed.). Belmont, Calif.: Wadsworth.

Chapter 6

Andersen, P. A., Hecht, M. L., Hoobler, G. D., & Smallwood, M. (2003). Nonverbal communication across cultures. In W. B. Gudykunst (Ed.), *Cross-Cultural and Intercultural Communication* (pp. 73–90). Thousand Oaks, Calif.: Sage.

Bright, W. (2000). The sociolinguistics of the "S-word:Squaw in American placenames. Retrieved September 27, 2006 from www.ncidc.org/bright/Squaw_revised.doc.

Bonvillain, N. (2003). *Language, Culture and Communication: The Meaning of Messages* (4th ed.). Upper Saddle River, N.J.: Prentice Hall.

Carlo-Casellas, J. R. (2002, Jan. 14). Marketing to US Hispanic population requires analysis of cultures, National Underwriter Life and Health. Farmington Hills, Mich.: The National Underwriter Company p. 9. www.highbeam.com/doc/1G1-81892605. Accessed November 17, 2008.

Chuang, R. (2004). An examination of Taoist and Buddhist perspectives on interpersonal conflict, emotions and adversities. In F. E. Jandt (Ed.), *Intercultural Communication: A Global Reader* (p. 38–50). Thousand Oaks, Calif.: Sage.

Ellis, D. G. (1999). *Crafting Society: Ethnicity, Class and Communication Theory.* Mahwah, N.J.: Erlbaum.

Haviland, W. A. (1993). *Cultural Anthropology.* Fort Worth, Tex.: Harcourt, Brace, Jovanovich.

Hofstede, G. (1980). *Culture's Consequences.* Beverly Hills, Calif.: Sage.

Hofstede, G. (1997). *Cultures and Organizations: Software of the Mind.* New York: McGraw Hill.

Hofstede, G. (1998). (Ed.). *Masculinity and Femininity: The Taboo Dimension of National Cultures.* Thousand Oaks, Calif.: Sage.

Hofstede, G. (2000). The cultural relativity of the quality of life concept. In G. R. Weaver (Ed.), *Cultural Communication and Conflict: Readings in Intercultural Relations.* Boston: Allyn & Bacon.

Hotz, R. L. (1995, Apr. 15). Official racial definitions have shifted sharply and often. *Los Angeles Times,* p. A14.

Jandt, F. E. (2001). *Intercultural Communication: An Introduction* (3rd ed.). Thousand Oaks, Calif.: Sage.

Klyukanov, I. E. (2005). *Principles of Intercultural Communication.* New York: Pearson.

Lorenzo, J. What Do You Say? *The Other Side,* March-April 1998, vol. 34, no. 2, p. 48.

Luckmann, J. (1999). *Transcultural Communication in Nursing.* New York: Delmar.

Neuliep, J. W. (2006). *Intercultural Communication: A Contextual Approach* (3rd ed.). Thousand Oaks, Calif.: Sage.

Samovar, L. A., Porter, R. E., & McDaniel, E. R. (2007). *Communication between Cultures* (6th ed.). Belmont, Calif.: Thomson Wadsworth.

Skeggs, B. (1997). *Formation of Class and Gender: Becoming Respectable.* Thousand Oaks, Calif.: Sage.

Ting-Toomey, S. (1999). *Communicating across Cultures.* New York: Guilford Press.

Ting-Toomey, S., Yee-Jung, K., Shapiro, R., Garcia, W., Wright, T., & Oetzel, J. G. (2000). Cultural/ethnic identity salience and conflict styles. *International Journal of Intercultural Relations, 23,* 47–81.

Wood, J. T. (2007). *Gendered Lives: Communication, Gender, and Culture* (7th ed.). Belmont, Calif.: Wadsworth.

Zemke, R., Raines, C., & Filipczak, B. (2000). *Generations at Work.* New York: AMACOM.

Chapter 7

Berger, C. R. (2002). Goals and knowledge structures in social interaction. In M. L. Knapp & J. A. Daly (Eds.), *Handbook of Interpersonal Communication* (pp. 181–212). Thousand Oaks, Calif.: Sage.

Brown, P., & Levinson, S. (1987). *Politeness: Some Universals in Language Usage.* Cambridge, England: Cambridge University Press.

Dickson, D., & Hargie, O. (2006). Questioning. In O. Hargie (Ed.), *The Handbook of Communication Skills* (3rd ed., pp. 121-146). New York: Routledge.

Duck, S. (2007). *Human Relationships* (4th ed.). Thousand Oaks, Calif.: Sage.

Engdahl, S. (Ed.). (2007). *Online Social Networking.* New York: Thomson Gale.

Ford, C. E., Fox, B. A., & Thompson, S. A. (2002). Introduction. In C. E. Ford, B. A. Fox, & S. A. Thomson (Eds.), *The Language of Turn and Sequence* (pp. 3–13). New York: Oxford University Press.

Fraley, B., & Aron, A. (2004). The effect of a shared humorous experience on closeness in initial encounters. *Personal Relationships, 11,* 61–78.

Grice, H. P. (1975). Logic and conversation. In P. Cole & J. L. Morgan (Eds.), *Syntax and Semantics* (Vol. 3, *Speech Acts,* pp. 41–58). New York: Academic Press.

Gudykunst, W. B., & Matsumoto, Y. (1996). Cross-cultural variability of communication in personal relationships. In W. B. Gudykunst, S. Ting-Toomey, & T. Nishida (Eds.), *Communication in Personal Relationships across Cultures* (pp. 19–56). Thousand Oaks, Calif.: Sage.

Hecht, M. L. (1978). Measures of communication satisfaction, *Human Communication Research, 4,* 350–368.

Holtgraves, T. (2002). *Language as Social Action: Social Psychology and Language Use.* Mahwah, N.J.: Erlbaum.

Johannesen, R. L., Valde, K. S., & Whedbee, K. E. (2008). *Ethics in Human Communication* (6th ed.). Long Grove, Ill.: Waveland Press.

Kellerman, K., & Park, H. S. (2001). Situational urgency and conversational retreat: When politeness and efficiency matter. *Communication Research, 28,* 3–47.

Kennedy, C. W., & Camden, C. T. (1983). A new look at interruptions. *Western Journal of Speech Communication, 47,* 55.

Littlejohn, S. W., & Foss, K. A. (2008). *Theories of Human Communication* (9th ed.). Belmont, Calif.: Thomson Wadsworth.

Lovink, G. (2008). *Zero Comments: Blogging and Critical Internet Culture.* New York: Routledge.

McLaughlin, M. L. (1984). *Conversation: How Talk Is Organized.* Newbury Park, Calif.: Sage. http://groups.sims.berkeley.edu/backchannel/downloads/backchannel.pdf

Sawyer, R. K. (2001). *Creating Conversations: Improvisation in Everyday Discourse.* Creskill, N.J.: Hampton Press.

Shedletsky, L. J., & Aitken, J. E. (2004). *Human Communication on the Internet.* New York: Pearson Education.

Shimanoff, S. B. (1980). *Communication Rules: Theory and Research.* Beverly Hills, Calif.: Sage.

Svennevig, J. (1999). *Getting Acquainted in Conversation: A Study of Initial Interactions.* Philadelphia: John Benjamins.

Chapter 8

Anderson, R. (1997). The new digital presence: Listening, access and computer-mediated life. In M. Purdy & D. Borisoff (Eds.), *Listening in Everyday Life: A Personal and Professional Approach* (2nd ed., pp. 139–161). New York: University Press of America.

Bostrom, R. N. (2006). The process of listening. In O. Hargie (Ed.), *Handbook of Communication Skills* (3rd ed., pp. 267–291). New York: Routledge.

Brownell, J. (2006). *Listening: Attitudes, Principles, and Skills* (3rd ed.). Boston: Allyn & Bacon.

Carbaugh, D. (1988). *Talking American: Cultural Discourses on Donahue.* New York: Ablex Publishing Corporation.

Ellinor, L., & Gerard, G. (1998). *Dialogue: Rediscover the Transforming Power of Conversation.* New York: Wiley.

Estes, W. K. (1989). Learning theory. In A. Lesgold & R. Glaser (Eds.), *Foundations for a Psychology of Education* (pp. 1–49). Hillsdale, N.J.: Erlbaum.

Halone, K. K., & Pecchioni, L. L. (2001). Relational listening: A grounded theoretical model. *Communication Reports, 14,* 59–72.

O'Shaughnessey, B. (2003). Active attending or a theory of mental action. *Consciousness and the World, 29,* 379–407.

Pew Internet and American Life Project. (2001). Teenage life online: The rise of the instant message generation and the Internet's impact on friendships and family relationships. www.pewinternet.org/reports/toc.asp?report;eq36

Purdy, M. (1996). What is listening? In M. Purdy & D. Borisoff (Eds.), *Listening in Everyday Life: A Personal and Professional Approach* (2nd ed., pp. 1–20). New York: University Press of America.

Steil, L. K., Barker, L. L., & Watson, K. W. (1983). *Effective Listening.* Reading, Mass.: Addison-Wesley.

Ward, C. C., & Tracey, T. J. G. (2004). Relation of shyness with aspects of online relational involvement. *Journal of Social and Personal Relationships, 21,* 611–623.

Wolvin, A., & Coakley, C. G. (1996). *Listening* (5th ed.). Dubuque, Iowa: Brown & Benchmark.

Chapter 9

Ahuja, N. (2007). *Hopelessness and Social Support as Predictors of Physical Status for Breast Cancer Patients Coping with Recurrence.* Columbus: Ohio State University Knowledge Bank.

Albrecht, T. L., & Goldsmith, D. J. (2003). Social support, social networks and health. In T. L. Thompson, A. M. Dorsey, K. I. Miller, & B. R. Parrott (Eds.), *Handbook of Health Communication* (pp. 263–284). Mahwah, N.J.: Erlbaum.

Bambina, A. (2007). *Online Social Support.* Youngstown, N.Y.: Cambria Press.

Barbee, A. P., & Cunningham, M. R. (1995). An experimental approach to social support communication: Interactive coping in close relationships. In B. R. Burleson (Ed.), *Communication Yearbook 18* (pp. 381–413). Thousand Oaks, Calif.: Sage.

Brown, P., & Levinson, S. (1987). *Politeness: Some Universals in Language Usage.* Cambridge, England: Cambridge University Press.

Burleson, B. R. (1994). Comforting messages: Significance, approaches, and effects. In B. R. Burleson, T. L. Albrecht, & I. G. Sarason (Eds.), *Communication of Social Support: Messages, Interactions, Relationships, and Community* (pp. 3–28). Thousand Oaks, Calif.: Sage.

Burleson, B. R. (2003). Emotional support skills. In J. O. Green & B. R. Burleson (Eds.), *Handbook of Communication and Social Interaction Skills* (pp. 551–594). Mahwah, N.J.: Erlbaum.

Burleson, B. R., & Goldsmith, D. J. (1998). How the comforting process works: Alleviating emotional distress through conversationally induced reappraisals. In P. A. Andersen & L. K. Guerrero (Eds.), *Handbook of Communication and Emotion: Research, Theory, Applications, and Contexts* (pp. 248–280). San Diego, Calif.: Academic Press.

Burleson, B. R., & Samter, W. (1990). Effects of cognitive complexity on the perceived importance of communication skills in friends. *Communication Research, 17,* 165–182.

Carpenter, K. (2006). *The Stress-Buffering Effect of Social Support in Gynecological Cancer Survivors.* Columbus: Ohio State University.

Cunningham, M. R., & Barbee, A. P. (2000). Social support. In C. Hendrick & S. S. Hendrick (Eds.), *Close Relationships: A Sourcebook* (pp. 272–285). Thousand Oaks, Calif.: Sage.

Eisenberg, N., & Fabes, R. A. (1990). Empathy: Conceptualization, measurement, and relation to prosocial behavior. *Motivation and Emotion, 14,* 131–149.

Goffman, E. (1959). *The Presentation of Self in Everyday Life.* Edinburgh: Edinburgh Social Science Research Center.

Goldsmith, D. J. (2000). Soliciting advice: The role of sequential placement in mitigating face threat. *Communication Monographs, 67,* 1–19.

Goldsmith, D. J. (2004). *Communicating Social Support.* Cambridge, England: Cambridge University Press.

Holtgraves, T. (2002). *Language as Social Action: Social Psychology and Language Use.* Mahwah, N.J.: Erlbaum.

Howard, L. Unless You're Mixed, You Don't Know What It's Like to Be Mixed. In S. Nieto. (2000), *Affirming Diversity: The Sociopolitical Context of Multicultural Education* (3rd ed., pp. 50–60). Boston: Allyn & Bacon.

Jerome, L. W., DeLeon, P. H., James, L. C., Folen, R., Earles, J., & Gedney, J. J. (2000). The coming age of telecommunications in psychological research and practice. *American Psychologist, 55,* 407–421.

Kunkel, A. W., & Burleson, B. R. (1999). Assessing explanations for sex differences in emotional support: A test of the different cultures and skill specialization accounts. *Human Communication Research, 25* (March), 307–340.

Leathers, D. G. (1997). *Successful Nonverbal Communication: Principles and Applications* (3rd ed.). Boston: Allyn & Bacon.

Omdahl, B. L. (1995). *Cognitive Appraisal, Emotion, and Empathy.* Mahwah, N.J.: Erlbaum.

Samter, W., Burleson, B. R., & Murphy, L. B. (1987). Comforting conversations: The effects of strategy type of evaluations on messages and message producers. *Southern Speech Communication Journal, 52,* 263–284.

Segrin, C. (1998). Disrupted interpersonal relationships and mental health problems. In B. H. Spitzberg & W. H. Cupach (Eds.), *The Dark Side of Close Relationships* (pp. 327–365). Mahwah, N.J.: Erlbaum.

Stiff, J. B., Dillard, J. P., Somera, L., Kim, H., & Sleight, C. (1988). Empathy, communication, and prosocial behavior. *Communication Monographs, 55,* 198–213.

Uchino, B. N., Cacioppo, J. T., & Kiecolt-Glaser, J. (1996). The relationship between social support and physiological processes: A review with emphasis on understanding mechanisms and implications for health. *Psychological Bulletin, 119,* 488–531.

Walther, J. B., & Parks, M. R. (2002). Cues filtered out, cues filtered in: Computer-mediated communication and close relationships. In M. L. Knapp & J. A. Daly (Eds.), *Handbook of Interpersonal Communication* (3rd ed., pp. 529–563). Thousand Oaks, Calif.: Sage.

Weaver, J. B. III, & Kirtley, M. B. (1995). Listening styles and empathy. *Southern Communication Journal, 60,* 131–140.

Zillmann, D., (1991). Empathy: Affect from bearing witness in the emotions of others. In J. Bryant & D. Zillmann (Eds.), *Responding to the Screen: Reception and Reaction Processes* (pp. 135–167). Hillsdale, N.J.: Erlbaum.

Chapter 10

Afifi, W. A., & Guerrero, L. K. (2000). Motivations underlying topic avoidance in close relationships. In S. Petronio (Ed.), *Balancing the Secrets of Private Disclosures* (pp. 165–179). Mahwah, N.J.: LEA.

Altman, I. (1993). Dialectics, physical environments, and personal relationships. *Communication Monographs, 60,* 26–34.

Altman, I., & Taylor, D. A. (1973). *Social Penetration: The Development of Interpersonal Relationships.* New York: Holt, Rinehart & Winston.

Bahrampour, T. (2007). What used to be private thoughts are now made public. In S. Engdahl (Ed.), *Online Social Networking* (pp. 185–189). Farmington Hills, Mich.: Thomson Gale.

Derlega, V. J., Metts, S., Petronio, S., & Margulis, S. T. (1993*). Self-Disclosure.* Newbury Park, Calif.: Sage.

Dindia, K. (1988). A comparison of several statistical tests of reciprocity of self-disclosure. *Communication Research, 15,* 726–752.

Dindia, K. (2000). Sex differences in self-disclosure, reciprocity of self-disclosure, and self-disclosure and liking: Three meta-analyses reviewed. In S. Petronio (Ed.), *Balancing the Secrets of Private Disclosures* (pp. 21–36). Mahwah, N.J.: LEA.

Hendrick, S. S. (1981). Self-disclosure and marital satisfaction. *Journal of Personality and Social Psychology, 40,* 1150–1159.

Jourard, S. M. (1971). *The Transparent Self.* New York: Van Nostrand Reinhold.

Kleinman, S. (2007). *Displacing Place: Mobile Communication in the Twenty-First Century.* New York: Peter Lang.

Knobloch, L. K., & Carpenter-Theune, K. E. (2004). Topic avoidance in developing romantic relationships: Association with intimacy and relational uncertainty. *Communication Research, 31,* 173–205.

Margulis, S. T. (1977). Concepts of privacy: Current status and next steps. *Journal of Social Issues, 33* (3), 5–21.

Pennebaker, J. W. (1995). Emotion, disclosure, and health: An overview. In J. W. Pennebaker (Ed.), *Emotion, Disclosure and Health* (pp. 3–10). Washington, D.C.: American Psychological Association.

Petronio, S. (2002). *Boundaries of Privacy: Dialectics of Disclosure.* Albany: State University of New York Press.

Roloff, M. E., & Ifert, D. E. (2000). Conflict management through avoidance: Withholding complaints, suppressing arguments and declaring topics taboo. In S. Petronio (Ed.), *Balancing the Secrets of Private Disclosures* (pp. 151–163). Mahwah, N.J.: LEA.

Samovar, L. A., & Porter, R. E. (2001). *Communication between Cultures* (4th ed.). Belmont, Calif.: Wadsworth.

Snell, W. E., Belk, S. S., & Hawkins, R. C. II (1986). The masculine and feminine self-disclosure scale: The politics of masculine and feminine self-presentation. *Sex Roles, 15,* 249–267.

Tardy, C. H. (2000). Self-disclosure and health: Revisiting Sidney Jourard's hypothesis. In S. Petronio (Ed.), *Balancing the Secrets of Private Disclosures* (pp. 111–122). Mahwah, N.J.: LEA.

Tracy, K., Dusen, D. V., & Robinson, S. (1987). "Good" and "bad" criticism. *Journal of Communication, 37,* 46–59.

Chapter 11

Alberti, R. E., & Emmons, M. L. (2001). *Your Perfect Right: Assertiveness and Equality in Your Life and Relationships* (8th ed.). San Atascadero, Calif.: Impact Publishers.

Dillard, J. P., & Marshall, L. J. (2003). Persuasion as a social skill. In J. O. Greene & B. R. Burleson (Eds.), *Handbook of Communication and Social Interaction Skills* (pp. 479–513). Mahwah, N.J.: Erlbaum.

Dillard, J. P., Anderson, J. W., & Knobloch, L. K. (2002). Interpersonal influence. In M. L. Knapp & J. A. Daly (Eds.), *Handbook of Interpersonal Communication* (3rd ed., pp. 425–474). Thousand Oaks, Calif.: Sage.

French, J. R. P. Jr., & Raven, B. (1968). The bases of social power. In D. Cartwright & A. Zander (Eds.), *Group Dynamics* (3rd ed., pp. 259–269). New York: Harper & Row.

Guerrero, L. K., Andersen, P. A., & Afifi, W. A. (2007). *Close Encounters: Communication in Relationships* (2nd ed.). Thousand Oaks, Calif.: Sage.

Guerrero, L. K., Andersen, P. A., Jorgensen, P. F., Spitzberg, B. H., & Eloy, S. V. (1995). Coping with the green-eyed monster: Conceptualizing and measuring communicative responses to jealousy. *Western Journal of Communication, 59,* 270–304.

Hample, D., & Dallinger, J. M. (1998). On the etiology of the rebuff phenomenon: Why are persuasive messages less polite after rebuffs?

Communication Studies, 49, 305–321.

Hample, D., & Dallinger, J. M. (2002). The effects of situation on the use or suppression of possible compliance-gaining appeals. In M. Allen, R. W. Preiss, B. M. Gayle, & N. Burrell (Eds.), *Interpersonal Communication Research: Advances through Meta-Analysis* (pp. 187–209). Mahwah, N.J.: Erlbaum.

Hinken, T. R., & Schriesheim, C. A. (1980). Development and application of new scales to measure the French and Raven (1959) Bases of Social Power. *Journal of Applied Psychology, 74,* 561–567.

Jandt, F. E. (2001). *Intercultural Communication: An Introduction* (3rd ed.). Thousand Oaks, Calif.: Sage.

Jorgensen, P. E. (1998). Affect, persuasion, and communication process. In P. A. Anderson & L. K. Guerrero (Eds.), *Handbook of Communication and Emotion: Research, Theory, Applications, and Contexts* (pp. 403–422). San Diego, Calif.: Academic Press.

Kellerman, K., & Cole, T. D. (1994). Classifying compliance gaining messages: Taxonomic disorder in strategic confusion. *Communication Theory, 4,* 3–60.

Kellerman, K., & Shea, B. C. (1996). Threats, suggestions, hints, and promises: Gaining compliance efficiently and politely. *Communication Quarterly, 44* (2), 145–165.

Kleinman, S. (2007). *Displacing Place: Mobile Communication in the Twenty-First Century.* New York: Peter Lang.

Knowles, E. R., Butler, S., & Linn, J. A. (2001). Increasing compliance by reducing resistance. In J. P. Forgas & K. D. Williams (Eds.), *Social Influence: Direct and Indirect Processes* (pp. 41–60). Philadelphia: Psychology Press.

Levine, T. R., & Boster, F. J. (2001). The effect of power and message

variables on compliance. *Communication Monographs, 68,* 28–48.

Martin, M. M., Anderson, C. M., & Horvath, C. L. (1996). Feelings about verbal aggression: Justifications for sending and hurt from receiving verbally aggressive messages. *Communication Research Reports, 13* (1), 19–26.

Mehmet, E. (2003). Self-reported assertiveness in Swedish and Turkish adolescents: A cross-cultural comparison. *Scandinavian Journal of Psychology, 44,* 7–12.

Miller, L. C., Cody, M. J., & McLaughlin, M. L. (1994). Situations and goals as fundamental constructs in interpersonal communication research. In M. L. Knapp & G. R. Miller (Eds.), *Handbook of Interpersonal Communication* (2nd ed., pp. 263–313). Beverly Hills, Calif.: Sage.

Niikura, R. (1999). The psychological process underlying Japanese assertive behavior: Comparison of Japanese with Americans, Malaysians, and Filipinos. *International Journal of Intercultural Relations, 23,* 47–76.

O'Hair, D., & Cody, M. J. (1987). Machiavellian beliefs and social influence. *Western Journal of Speech Communication, 51,* 286–287.

Parks, M. R. (2007). *Personal Relationships and Personal Networks.* Mahwah, N.J.: Erlbaum.

Petty, R. E., & Cacioppo, T. T. (1996). Attitudes and persuasion: Classic and contemporary approaches. Boulder, Colo.: Westview Press.

Petty, R. E., DeSteno, D., & Rucker, D. (2001). The role of affect in persuasion and attitude change. In J. Forgas (Ed.), *Handbook of Affect and Social Cognition* (pp. 212–233). Mahwah, N.J.: Erlbaum.

Petty, R. E., Wheeler, S. C., & Bitzer, G. Y. (2000). Attitude functions and persuasion: An elaboration likelihood approach to matched versus mismatched messages. In G. R. Maio & J. M. Olson (Eds.), *Why We Evaluate: Functions of Attitudes* (pp. 133–162). Mahwah, N.J.: Erlbaum.

Rathus, S. (1973). A 30-item schedule for assessing assertive behavior. *Behavior Therapy, 4*, p. 398.

Samovar, L. A., & Porter, R. E. (2001). *Communication between Cultures* (4th ed.). Belmont, Calif.: Wadsworth.

Trenholm, S. (1989). *Persuasion and Social Influence.* Englewood Cliffs, N.J.: Prentice Hall.

Chapter 12

Adler, R. B. (1977). *Confidence in Communication: A Guide to Assertive and Social Skills.* New York: Holt, Rinehart, & Winston.

Canary, D. J. (2003). *Maintaining Relationships through Communication: Relational, Contextual, and Cultural Variations.* Mahwah, N.J.: Erlbaum.

Canary, D. J., Cupach, W. R., & Messman, S. J. (1995). *Relationship Conflict: Conflict in Parent-Child, Friendship and Romantic Relationships..* Thousand Oaks, Calif.: Sage Publications.

Canary, D. J., & Lakey, S. G. (2006). Managing conflict in a competent manner: A mindful look at events that matter. In J. G. Oetzel & S. Ting-Toomey (Eds.), *The SAGE Handbook of Conflict Communication: Integrating Theory, Research, and Practice* (pp. 185–210). Thousand Oaks, Calif.: Sage.

Caughlin, J. P., & Golish, T. D. (2002). An analysis of the association between topic avoidance and dissatisfaction: Comparing perceptual and interpersonal explanations. *Communication Monographs, 69*, 275–295.

Caughlin, J. P., & Huston, T. L. (2006). Demand/withdraw patterns in marital relationships: An individual differences perspective. In R. M. Dailey & B. A. LePoire (Eds.), *Applied*

Interpersonal Communication Matters: Family, Health, & Community Relations (pp. 11–38). New York: Peter Lang.

Cupach, W. R., & Canary, D. J. (1997). *Competence in Interpersonal Conflict.* New York: McGraw-Hill.

Gordon, T. (1970). *Parent Effectiveness Training.* New York: Peter H. Wyden.

Gordon, T. (1971). *The Basic Modules of the Instructor Outline for Effectiveness Training Courses.* Pasadena, Calif.: Effectiveness Training Associates.

Guerrero, L. K., Andersen, P. A., & Afifi, W. A. (2007). *Close Encounters: Communication in Relationships* (2nd ed.). Thousand Oaks, Calif.: Sage.

Hashem, M. The power of wastah in Lebanese speech. In A. Gonzales, A. M. Houston, & V. Chen. (Eds.) (2004). *Our Voices: Essays in Culture, Ethnicity and Communication* (4th ed., pp.150–154). Los Angeles, Calif.: Roxbury.

Lulofs, R. S., & Cahn, D. D. (2000). *Conflict: From Theory to Action* (2nd ed.). Boston: Allyn & Bacon.

Putnam, L. L. (2006). Definitions and approaches to conflict and communication. In J. G. Oetzel & S. Ting-Toomey (Eds.), *The SAGE Handbook of Conflict Communication: Integrating Theory, Research, and Practice* (pp. 1–32). Thousand Oaks, Calif.: Sage.

Roloff, M. E., & Cloven, D. H. (1990). The chilling effect in interpersonal relationships: The reluctance to speak one's mind. In D. D. Cahn (Ed.), *Intimates in Conflict: A Communication Perspective* (pp. 49–76). Hillsdale, N.J.: Erlbaum.

Roloff, M. E., & Miller, C. W. (2006). Social cognition approaches to understanding interpersonal conflict and communication. In J. G. Oetzel & S. Ting-Toomey (Eds.), *The SAGE Handbook of Conflict Communication: Integrating Theory, Research, and Practice* (pp. 97–128). Thousand Oaks, Calif.: Sage.

Sagrestano, L. M., Heavey, C. L., & Christensen, A. (2006). Individual differences versus social structural approaches to explaining demand-withdraw and social influence behaviors. In K. Dindia & D. J. Canary (Eds.), *Sex Differences and Similarities in Communication* (2nd ed., pp. 379–395). Mahwah, N.J.: Erlbaum.

Sillars, A. L., & Weisberg, J. (1987). Conflict as a social skill. In M. E. Roloff & G. R. Miller (Eds.), *Interpersonal Processes: New Directions in Communication Research* (pp. 140–171). Beverly Hills, Calif.: Sage.

Thomas, K. W. & Kilman, R. H. (1974). *The Thomas-Kilman Conflict Mode Instrument.* Palo Alto: Calif.: Consulting Psychologists Press.

Ting-Toomey, S. (2006). Managing intercultural conflicts effectively. In L. A. Samovar & R. E. Porter (Eds.), *Intercultural Communication: A Reader* (11th ed., pp. 366–377). Belmont, Calif.: Wadsworth.

Whetten, D. A., & Cameron, K. S. (2007). *Developing Management Skills* (7th ed.). Upper Saddle River, N.J.: Prentice Hall.

Chapter 13

Bloch, J. D. (1980). *Friendship.* New York: Macmillan.

Boon, S. D. (1994). Dispelling doubt and uncertainty: Trust in romantic relationships. In S. Duck (Ed.), *Dynamics of Relationships* (pp. 86–111). Thousand Oaks, Calif.: Sage.

Demo, D. H. (1987). Family relations and the self-esteem of adolescents and their parents. *Journal of Marriage and the Family, 49*, 705–715.

Dickson, F. C. (1995). The best is yet to be: Research on long-lasting marriages. In J. T. Wood & S. Duck (Eds.), *Under-Studied Relationships: Off the Beaten Track* (pp. 22–50). Thousand Oaks, Calif.: Sage.

Family time: An interview with Bill Doherty. (2002). *The Early Show.* CBSWorldwide: New York. http://www.cbsnews.com/stories/2002/09/20/earlyshow/living/parenting/main522830.shtml

Fehr, B. (1996). *Friendship Processes.* Thousand Oaks, Calif.: Sage.

Fischer, J. L., & Narus, L. R. Jr. (1981). Sex roles and intimacy in same-sex and other-sex relationships. *Psychology of Women Quarterly, 5,* 444–455.

Fitzpatrick, M. A. (1988). *Between Husbands and Wives: Communication in Marriage.* Beverly Hills, Calif.: Sage.

Fitzpatrick, M. A. (2006). Epilogue: The future of family communication theory and research. In L. H. Turner & R. L. West (Eds.), *The Family Communication Sourcebook* (p. 491). Thousand Oaks, Calif.: Sage.

Fitzpatrick, M. A., & Badzinski, D. M. (1994). All in the family: Interpersonal communication in kin relationships. In M. L. Knapp & G. R. Miller (Eds.), *Handbook of Interpersonal Communication* (2nd ed., pp. 726–771). Thousand Oaks, Calif.: Sage.

Fitzpatrick, M. A., & Bochner, A. (1981). Perspectives on self and other: Male-female differences in perceptions of communication behavior. *Sex Roles, 7,* 523–535.

Fitzpatrick, M. A., & Caughlin, J. (2003). Interpersonal communication in family relationships. In M. Knapp & J. Daly (Eds.), *Handbook of Interpersonal Communication* (pp. 726–778). Thousand Oaks, Calif.: Sage.

Fitzpatrick, M. A., & Koerner, A. (2002). A theory of family communication. *Communication Theory, 12* (1), 70–91.

Fitzpatrick, M. A., & Ritchie, L. D. (1994). Communication schemata within the family: Multiple perspectives on family interaction. *Human Communication Research, 20,* 275–301.

Galvin, K., Byland, C., & Brommel, B. (2007). *Family Communication: Cohesion and Change, 7th Ed.* New York: Allyn and Bacon.

Gould, O. (2004). Telling stories and getting acquainted: How age matters. In M. W. Pratt & B. H. Fiese (Eds.), *Family Stories and the Lifecourse* (pp. 327–351). Mahwah, N.J.: Erlbaum.

Knobloch, L. K., & Solomon, D. H. (2002). Information seeking beyond initial interaction: Negotiating relational uncertainty within close relationships. *Human Communication Research, 28,* 243–257.

LaFollette, H. (1996). *Personal Relationships: Love, Identity, and Morality.* Cambridge, Mass.: Blackwell.

Marsh, P. (Ed.). (1988). *Eye to Eye: How People Interact.* Topsfield, Mass.: Salem House.

Mills, J., & Clark, M. S. (2001). Viewing close romantic relationships as communal relationships: Implications for maintenance and enhancement. In J. Harvey & A. Wenzel (Eds.), *Close Romantic Relationships: Maintenance and Enhancement* (pp. 13–25). Mahwah, N.J.: Erlbaum.

Peplau, L. A. (1993). Lesbian and gay relationships. In L. D. Garnets & D. C. Kimmel (Eds.), *Psychological Perspectives on Lesbian and Gay Male Experiences* (pp. 395–419). New York: Columbia University Press.

Reis, H. T. (1998). Gender differences in intimacy and related behaviors: Context and process. In D. J. Canary & K. Dindia (Eds.), *Sex Differences and Similarities in Communication: Critical Essays and Empirical Investigations of Sex and Gender in Interaction* (pp. 203–231). Mahwah, N.J.: Erlbaum.

Rusbult, C. E., Olsen, N., Davis, J. L., & Hannon, P. A. (2001). Commitment and relationship maintenance mechanisms. In

J. Harvey & A. Wenzel (Eds.), *Close Romantic Relationships: Maintenance and Enhancement* (pp. 87–113). Mahwah, N.J.: Erlbaum.

Ryan, E. B., Pearce, K. A., Anas, A. P., & Norris, J. E. (2004). Writing a connection: Intergenerational communication through stories. In M. W. Pratt & B. H. Fiese (Eds.), *Family Stories and the Lifecourse* (pp. 375–398). Mahwah, N.J.: Erlbaum.

Sabourin, T. C. (1996). The role of communication in verbal abuse between spouses. In D. D. Cahn & S. A. Lloyd (Eds.), *Family Violence from a Communication Perspective* (pp. 199–217). Thousand Oaks, Calif.: Sage.

Pelusi, N. (2006). "Jealousy: A voice of possessiveness past." *Psychology Today, 39,* 64-65.

Taylor, J. (2002). Performing commitment. In J. N. Martin, T. K. Nakayama, & L. A. Flores (Eds.), *Readings in Intercultural Communication* (pp. 310–318). New York: McGraw-Hill.

Turner, L. H., & West, R. L. (2006). *Perspectives on Family Communication* (3rd ed.). Boston: McGraw Hill.

Werner, C. M., Altman, I., Brown, B. B., & Ginat, J. (1993). Celebrations in personal relationships: A transactional/dialectical perspective. In S. Duck (Ed.), *Social Context and Relationships* (pp. 109–138). Newbury Park, Calif.: Sage.

Williams, A., & Nussbaum, J. F. (2001). *Intergenerational Communication across the Lifespan.* Mahwah, N.J.: Erlbaum.

Winstead, B. A., Derlega, V. J., & Rose, S. (1997). *Gender and Close Relationships.* Thousand Oaks, Calif.: Sage.

Wood, J. T. (2003). *Gendered Lives: Communication, Gender and Culture* (5th ed.). Belmont, Calif.: Wadsworth.

Wood, J. T., & Inman, C. C. (1993). In a different mode: Masculine styles of communicating closeness. *Journal of Applied Communication Research, 21,* 279–295.

Yerby, J., Buerkel-Rothfuss, N., & Bochner, A. P. (1995). *Understanding Family Communication* (2nd ed.). Scottsdale, Ariz.: Gorsuch Scarisbrick.

Chapter 14

Berryman-Fink, C. (1997). Gender issues, management style, mobility and harassment. In P. Y. Byers (Ed.), *Organizational Communication: Theory and Behavior* (pp. 259–283). Boston: Allyn & Bacon.

Brown, K. M. (2007). *Managing Virtual Teams.* Plano, Tex.: Wordware Publishing.

Cathcart, D., & Cathcart, R. (1997). The Group: A Japanese Context. In L. A. Samovar & R. E. Porter (Eds.) *Intercultural Communication: A Reader* (8th ed., pp. 329-339). Belmont, Calif: Wadsworth.

Conrad, C., & Poole, M. S. (2005). *Strategic Organizational Communication in a Global Economy.* Belmont, Calif.: Thomson Wadsworth.

Cram, C. M. (2007). *New Perspectives on Communication in Business Technology.* Boston: Thomson Course Technology.

Eisenberg, E. M., & Goodall, H. L. (2004). *Organizational Communication: Balancing Creativity and Constraint.* New York: Bedford St. Martin's.

Farr, M. J. (2008). *The Quick Resume and Cover Letter Book: Write and Use an Effective Resume in Only One Day.* Indianapolis: JISTWorks.

Graen, G. (1976). Role making processes within complex organizations. In M. D. Dunette (Ed.), *Handbook of Industrial and Organizational Psychology* (pp. 1201–1245). Chicago: Rand McNally.

Jablin, F. M., & Krone, K. J. (1994). Task/work relationships: A life-span perspective. In M. L. Knapp & G. R. Miller (Eds.), *Handbook of Interpersonal Communication* (2nd ed., pp. 621–675). Thousand Oaks, Calif.: Sage.

Kleinman, S. (2007). *Displacing Place: Mobile Communication in the Twenty-First Century.* New York: Peter Lang.

Larson, C. E., & LaFasto, F. M. J. (1989). *Team Work: What Must Go Right/What Can Go Wrong.* Newbury Park, Calif.: Sage.

Potoker, E. S. (2005). *Managing Diverse Working Styles: The Leadership Competitive Advantage.* Mason, Ohio: South-Western.

Varner, I., & Beamer, L. (1995). *Intercultural Communication in the Global Workplace.* Chicago: Irwin.

Whetten, D. A., & Cameron, K. S. (2005). *Developing Management Skills* (6th ed.). Upper Saddle River, N.J.: Prentice Hall.

Zemke, R., Raines, C., & Filipczak, B. (2000). *Generations at Work.* New York: AMACOM.

Photo Credits

Index